YOUTH HOSTELER'S GUIDE TO EUROPE

Revised Edition

YOUTH HOSTELS ASSOCIATION

COLLIER BOOKS
A Division of Macmillan Publishing Co., Inc.
New York

PHOTO CREDITS: Austrian Information Service, p. 29; Belgian National Tourist Office, facing p. 31, p. 43; Danish Tourist Board, p. 46, facing p. 66; British Tourist Authority, p. 81, facing p. 357; Finnish Tourist Board, facing p. 111; German National Tourist Office, p. 168, p. 177; Greek National Tourist Office, p. 211, facing p. 213, p. 222; Irish Tourist Board, p. 240, p. 242; Italian Government Tourist Office, p. 256, p. 265; Netherlands National Tourist Office, p. 292, p. 307; Norwegian National Tourist Office, facing p. 309, p. 333; Polish National Tourist Office, p. 339; Heyward Associates, Inc., facing p. 347; Spanish National Tourist Office, p. 382; Yugoslavia State Tourist Office, p. 459.

Macmillan Publishing Co., Inc.
866 Third Avenue
New York, N.Y. 10022
Collier Macmillan Canada, Ltd.

Library of Congress Catalog Card Number: 72–89051

First Collier Books Edition 1977

Fifth Printing 1979

Printed in the United States of America

CONTENTS

LIST OF MAPS AND PLANS

INTRODUCTION

It is exciting to share with you this introduction to the 1977 revision of *Youth Hosteler's Guide to Europe*. Since the Macmillan Publishing Co., Inc. first published this book in the early 1970s, thousands of American travelers have used it to help make their first hosteling trip to Europe a more memorable, lasting experience. With its complete listing of geographical, cultural and touring information about each country, *Youth Hosteler's Guide to Europe* is a perfect companion to the *International Youth Hostel Handbook*, Volume I (Europe and Mediterranean countries).

Hostelers are a unique breed of traveler. They go to places that tourists are looking for and seldom find, and they do it all inexpensively because they use their own "go power"—bicycles, canoes, hiking, etc. Hosteling means gaining, *with others,* a greater understanding of the world and its people "under your own steam." Hostelers travel through an area at a pace designed to absorb their environs, instead of whizzing by in fast cars, trains and planes. They hear, smell and feel a country, instead of just looking at it.

The worldwide organization that promotes youth hosteling is the International Youth Hostel Federation, which is based in London. Fifty countries comprise this federation and, collectively, they operate more than 4,500 hostels (simple, inexpensive, overnight places to stay) throughout the world. The name "youth hostels" is really a misnomer, because membership in the organization is open to everyone regardless of age, creed, color or political beliefs. One or two countries do give reservation preference to hostelers under 30 years of age, but even they welcome the "over-30 bunch" on a space-available basis.

You don't have to be a herculean athlete in order to hostel. It isn't necessary to bicycle 50 miles a day or to set a new world's walking record to use each country's hosteling facilities; but you *are* expected to forsake motorized transportation and see the area around each hostel on your own while visiting a facility.

I have already mentioned that the basic premise of hosteling is to create an environment in which *all* people, especially youth, can gain a greater understanding of each other through educational and recreational travel—inexpensively. While each country in the IYHF sets forth similar goals, each varies its emphasis slightly in order to cater to the particular needs

1

and traditions of its own people. For example, in England and Scotland, where a great deal of industry is packed into a small area, particular emphasis is placed on promoting easy access to the countryside. In Germany, preventive health measures are stressed, while the Belgian Association promotes the social, civic and cultural training of youth in its hosteling program. And, though these goals vary slightly, each of the 50 member countries mentions the establishment and operation of *youth hostels* as a means of attaining them.

The roots of the International Youth Hostel Federation began in Germany in 1901, when a gentleman named Carl Fischer—who was a senior pupil at a secondary school in Berlin—started a movement that was eventually destined to reach all parts of Europe. His movement was called *Wandervögel,* which translates into "birds of passage." This group involved students and other young people who took to the countryside in comradeship and free spirit in an effort to search out cultural origins. While the *Wandervögel* movement was relatively brief, it did initiate the idea— especially appealing to schoolteachers and other educators in Germany— of getting the students out of the industrialized cities and into the countryside to study nature firsthand.

It followed that schoolteachers were encouraged to take their students into the countryside during term time for as long as a day or a week. But a problem encountered by the teachers was a lack of places to stay, and they improvised quarters in barns and farmhouses as the *Wandervögel* group did. However, this was not very satisfactory for entire groups of schoolchildren and, of course, staying in any of the regular overnight guest houses and facilities was beyond their financial means.

One of the educators was a young man, Richard Schirrmann, who was teaching at an elementary school in Altena in the West German province of Westphalia. The area in which he taught was just outside the industrial area of Ruhr, and in order to get his students away from the pollution of industry, Schirrmann would take them on trips lasting as long as eight days, often *walking* as much as 180 miles. Of course Schirrmann and his group were plagued by the same problem that the other groups faced: finding suitable places to stay overnight while on these jaunts.

On August 26, 1909, during one of their trips, Shirrmann and his group passed an empty schoolhouse. The thought flashed into Schirrmann's mind that every town and village in Germany had a schoolhouse that probably wasn't being used during holidays and the times when school was out. As the idea germinated, Schirrmann visualized classrooms turned into separate boys' and girls' dormitories, with local schoolteachers to oversee the operation. As he pondered the idea, it grew even larger and Schirrmann envisioned a chain of schools or *hostels* dotting the countryside across Germany. He saw students paying a modest overnight fee to cover any unforeseen cost of operating these hostels and, to keep the fees low, the students would be required to do minor tasks, such as cleaning up after themselves and helping keep the school/hostel clean. To put his thoughts into actuality, Richard Schirrmann opened the world's first youth hostel in his own school in Altena. This was later replaced by the castle of Altena, which is still an operating youth hostel today.

In 1912, Schirrmann rekindled an acquaintance with a young industrialist, Wilhelm Münker, whom he had met six years previously. Together they formed a youth hostel subcommittee called the "Sauerland Mountain Club," with Schirrmann as chairman. For the next twenty years Herr Münker carried on the organizational work of the movement so that Schirrmann could travel the German countryside trying to set up hostels close enough to each other to provide an easy one-day walk for the students utilizing them.

It was in 1919, right after the First World War, that the duo formed the German Youth Hostel Association. Since there were tremendous war surpluses of beds, mattresses, and the like, large quantities could be purchased very inexpensively, thus helping the German Youth Hostel Association movement develop more rapidly. Financial support for the movement was first secured at local levels and finally, as the movement grew, from the German government itself.

It wasn't until 1925 that the idea of youth hosteling spilled over the German borders—the Swiss founded their youth hostel organization. The Polish government followed suit two years later in 1927, when they set up the Ministry of Religion and Public Education to assist the development of youth hostels in their country. By the end of the decade youth hostels were in existence in England and Wales, Scotland, Denmark, the Netherlands and finally in France and Norway at the beginning of 1930.

When war broke out in 1939, the youth hostel movement faltered; but interestingly enough, while Germany turned its youth hostels into hospitals and barracks, the youth hostel movement made giant strides in England. For many of the war workers in England, hosteling became their only chance for recreation and relaxation. Hence, the English government resisted hospital and army staffs that wanted to take over the hostels and turn them into facilities to house patients and troops. An example of this interesting rise in youth hosteling during the war is reflected by the fact that youth hosteling membership in England and Wales increased by 50,000 in the five years from 1939 to 1944. For the rest of the continent of Europe, the youth hosteling movement seemed nonexistent at the end of the war; but its recovery happened almost overnight. By 1947, more than 500 youth hostels had sprung up again all over Europe and more than 170,000 overnights by young foreign visitors were recorded.

In the next fifteen years, utilization of youth hostels throughout Europe increased by leaps and bounds. Overnights rose from 7 million in 1950 to more than twice that many in 1963. Just after 1951 the youth hostel movement left the boundaries of Europe and moved into Asia. Between 1951 and 1966 nine countries in the Middle East and Far East joined the Youth Hostel Federation—Israel, India, Pakistan, Japan, Malaya, Thailand, Syria, Ceylon and Lebanon.

Today, more than 4,500 hostels in 50 countries are in the International Youth Hostel Federation. Each is required to maintain separate dormitory-type accommodations for males and females, although a few offer accommodations for families. They are run by houseparents or, as they are called in Europe, wardens or supervisors. In addition, each hostel is required to have a common room where hostelers may congregate in the evening for relaxation and an exchange of ideas. Most hostels offer cooking facilities, so hostelers can prepare their own food if they wish. Overnight hostel fees vary from country to country, but the average range is somewhere between $1.50 and $3.50 a night, which in some European areas includes a hearty breakfast.

The International Youth Hostel Federation Secretariat in London encourages members of the IYHF to purchase their hostel passes in their own countries. These passes are then honored at hostels in all of the member nations.

As of this writing, 31 International Youth Hostel Federation Conferences have been held in various countries around the world. The last was in San Francisco in 1976, the very first conference ever held in the United States. Its opening ceremonies took place in the San Francisco War Memorial Auditorium where the United Nations' Charter was signed. In 1978, the IYHF's 32nd International Conference is scheduled to be held in France, with the 33rd set for Australia and New Zealand in 1980.

At the beginning of this introduction, I mentioned that the *Youth Hosteler's Guide to Europe* was a perfect companion to the *International Youth Hostel Handbook,* Volume I, which covers Europe and the Mediterranean areas. Printed yearly in two volumes (Volume II for Africa, America, Asia and Australasia), the handbook lists pertinent information about each hostel, including the facilities that are available, overnight charges, particular rules and regulations of each country, telephone numbers, addresses and whether or not meals are served. The *International Youth Hostel Handbook,* Volumes I and II, can be purchased from American Youth Hostel Headquarters at Delaplane, Virginia 22025.

American Youth Hostels, Inc., a nonprofit organization, was founded in 1934 by Monroe and Isabel Smith, two schoolteachers from Northfield, Massachusetts. The Smiths had traveled to Europe to meet Richard Schirrmann, and with the assistance of people such as President and Mrs. Franklin D. Roosevelt, who were honorary presidents of AYH, brought the hosteling movement to the United States. Today, American Youth Hostels has more than 200 hostel facilities throughout the United States, with the largest number located in the northeast, where AYH originated.

Our membership is approximately 60–70,000, with members ranging in age from 4 to 94. While many of the world's other youth hostel associations receive financial support from their governments, AYH receives none from the U.S. government, but relies largely on money earned from its membership fees and tax-deductible contributions from corporations, foundations and private individuals.

We hope, in your future travels, you will try hosteling, not only here in the United States, but in various parts of the world. When you do, be prepared for the "hosteling experience." Basically stated, it is a unique, exciting way of traveling, without any of the usual frills, and yet a way that offers you an opportunity to see other places and countries as they are; to speak and exchange customs with other people; to learn the whys and wherefores of the things other people do differently. On your visits to hostels, you will, unlike stays at hotels and motels, be utilizing only basic necessities, such as bunks for sleeping, a place to wash and clean up and a place to prepare your own meals. In this do-it-yourself society of ours, hosteling is *really* do-it-yourself, but the intrinsic rewards are far greater than any other form of travel known today.

That hosteling is not limited to just a few is evidenced by these figures supplied to us by the International Youth Hostel Federation for 1975: The IYHF had a total of 2,670,210 members in hostel associations around the world. These over-2½ million members logged 26,369,677 overnights at worldwide facilities and, of these, 5,924,239 were by hostelers who were traveling *outside* their own countries—indeed, the 1975 figures showed that American hostelers accounted for 556,251 overnights at foreign hostel facilities. You can readily see from these facts and figures that, for some, hosteling is a way of life.

I'd like to point out that hosteling is not for everyone. To those who like the comfort and enjoyment of traveling first class, may I suggest you continue to travel that way. But to those of you who are looking for a new experience and who want to return to the basics of natural enjoyment while traveling, I say the "hosteling experience" might be just the right thing for you. And to those of you who have that sense of adventure, I say try hosteling—GO where the average tourists DON'T—and SEE what they MISS!

Robert W. Yeates
Executive Director
American Youth Hostels, Inc.
Delaplane, Virginia 22025

Important Notes for Users

Arrangement Each chapter begins with a general description of the country, its people and its culture, followed by special information for the tourist. Then comes a detailed description of all the most important areas, arranged in the form of Routes (**R.1, R.2,** etc.), with side-routes to more "out of the way" places (**R.1 (i), R.1 (ii),** etc.), printed in smaller type.

Routes The routes are not intended to be followed slavishly; in many cases, in fact, they are too long to be covered in the course of a single holiday; they indicate lines of communication and provide a means of linking the various towns and other places which the traveller may wish to visit.

Places which are specially worth seeing or which are important centres of communication are printed in the text in bold type (e.g. **Bregenz**); all other place names are printed in italics. The index lists all place names except those which are mentioned only in passing—i.e. without any description or comment.

Maps The outline maps in the text must be supplemented by good cyclists' or walkers' maps, as mentioned under each country.

Plans Plans of many of the principal towns are included at their appropriate place in the text. They are diagrams only, to indicate the location of the main "sights".

Youth Hostels Youth hostels are indicated (**Y.H.**). In *all* cases their continued existence and location should be checked from an *annual* publication, i.e. the *International Youth Hostel Handbook* or the national youth hostel handbook of the country concerned.

Prices and Fares Rail fares quoted are second class. All prices and fares are liable to alteration. Up-to-date information on fares and other variable charges together with passport and currency regulations can be found in the *Y.H.A. Continental Travel Key*, an inexpensive annual publication.

Rail, Bus and Steamer Services Where these are stated to be seasonal (e.g. "summer only") care should be taken to check availability. The tourist season for some services (e.g. certain steamer routes in Norway) is short. In all cases departure times should be checked from current sources.

Language

You *can* tour the whole of Europe without knowing a word of any language except English; thousands of hostellers do it every year. But they suffer two grave disadvantages. Their holiday usually costs them more, because ignorance always costs money and, more important, they miss much of the value of contact with the inhabitants of the country and understanding of its traditions. Such travellers should consider, at least for their first trip abroad, one of the organised walking or cycling tours arranged by Y.H.A., with a competent leader who speaks the language.

For travelling on your own in France a slight knowledge of French is almost indispensable, the French being almost as bad linguists as the English and French will often come in useful in Belgium, Luxembourg and Switzerland; it will also help a little in Italy. Avoid shops and restaurants which advertise "English spoken"—they generally charge extra for the privilege.

A knowledge of German is extremely useful in Germany, Austria and Switzerland, but in all these countries you will meet more people, particularly young people, who can speak some English; this applies mainly to the towns, however, and not to country districts.

In Holland, Norway and Denmark, English is widely understood, but again in country districts you may run into difficulties. Nearly all post-office and railway clerks know some English, and most youth hostel wardens have learned enough to deal with their guests.

A small phrase-book, such as the "*International Conversation Book for Hostellers*", can be helpful and, of course, goodwill and a friendly smile are valuable aids to understanding. When talking to a foreigner in English try to talk slowly and clearly, but don't lapse into "pidgin-English".

Clothing

Hints for special clothing and equipment in each country are given in the various chapters, but the following information applies to all countries during the summer months.

For walking or cycling take the lightest possible clothes, but with some warm garments for the evening or for sudden changes of weather, particularly in the mountains. Keep your arms and neck protected from the sun for the first day or two at least, to avoid painful sunburn.

Women should avoid wearing shorts or slacks in some Catholic countries where they may give considerable offence.

For walking on mountain paths boots are essential, preferably fitted with the moulded and grooved rubber soles of 'Vibram' or 'Commando' type – or with hobnails.

7

Continental Measures

The metric system (based on multiples of 10) is used in all continental countries. Distances are measured in kilometres, length and heights in metres, weight in grams.

Kilometres to Miles

For approximate conversions, divide by 8 and multiply by 5.

Km.	Miles	Km.	Miles
1.0	5/8ths	100	62
1.6	1	200	124
8	5	300	186
10	6¼	400	249
16	10	500	311
50	31	1,000	621

Length

30 centimetres = 1 foot.
1 metre = 39.37 inches.

Weight

10 grams = 1 dekagram = ⅓ oz.
100 grams = 1 hektogram (or "10 dekas") = 3½ oz.
500 grams = ½ kilo = just over 1 pound. (lb.)
1,000 grams = 1 kilo = 2¼ lbs.

Volume

1 litre = 1¾ pints.

Metres to Feet

Height of mountains and passes is measured in metres. One metre is 39.37 inches, or 3.28 feet, but for rough calculations multiply the figure in metres by 3.3.

Metres	Feet	Metres	Feet
100	328	500	1,640
200	656	1,000	3,280
300	984	2,000	6,560
400	1,312	3,000	9,840

The 24-hour Clock

Time (for railway and other official purposes) is measured by the 24-hour clock in which the hours from 1 p.m. to midnight are called 13 to 24, e.g. 4 p.m. becomes 16.00. British Summer Times corresponds to normal time in all European countries included in this Guide except Finland, Greece, Italy and Poland, where the clock is one hour ahead of it, and Iceland, where it is one hour behind; but Greenwich Mean Time, used in Britain in winter, is one hour behind all European countries except Finland and Greece (2 hours behind their time) and one hour ahead of Iceland.

AUSTRIA

Geographical Outline

Land Three hundred and fifty miles long, and barely twenty-five miles broad at some points, Austria is scarcely a geographical unity. The western provinces (*Vorarlberg, Tirol* and *Salzburg*) consist entirely of high mountain ranges, and these ranges extend deep into the eastern provinces, leaving only a narrow plain along the Czech and Hungarian frontiers.

The main mountain chains run from west to east. There is a central line of very high peaks of ancient rocks (10-12,400 ft.) consisting largely of granite in the *Ötztaler, Stubaier* and *Zillertaler Alps,* the *High Tauern* and the *Lower Tauern.* To the north and south of this line lie chains of younger rock, principally limestone, with peaks ranging from 7,000 to 9,000 ft.; the southern chain, forming the border with Italy and Yugoslavia, but the northern chain (along the German frontier) extends through the *Lechtaler Alps,* the *North Tirol Limestone Alps,* the *Salzburg Limestone Alps* to the *Salzkammergut* and the *Vienna Forest.*

The main river is the Danube (*Donau*) which crosses the north-eastern part of the country from *Passau* to *Vienna.* Into it flow a number of Alpine rivers, including the *Inn* (originating in the Swiss *Engadine* and passing through *Innsbruck*), the *Salzach* (on which *Salzburg* lies) and the *Traun,* which drains part of the *Salzkammergut.*

There are two main groups of lakes: the beautiful *Salzkammergut* lakes and the *Carinthian* lakes which are notable for their warm temperature.

Climate The climate of most of Austria is Alpine. Snow generally covers the whole country during January, lasting until the end of March in the mountain areas and until the end of April on the higher slopes (6,000 ft. and above). The permanent snowline occurs at about 8,500 ft. With the melting of the snows, come spring flowers, followed usually by a hot summer. Rainfall is higher in the west (*Tirol* and *Salzburg*) than in the south and east (*Carinthia* and *Vienna*) and the latter areas also enjoy more sunshine.

The best months for a visit are from January to March or April for winter sports, May and June for spring flowers, and July to September for walking or climbing at high altitudes.

Plants and Animals The mountain slopes are frequently covered up to about 6,500 ft. with spruce and pine forests, whose dark green is broken by the emerald of alpine meadows. Amongst the many alpine flowers are several varieties of gentian and saxifrage and, close to the snow line, the edelweiss. Most of the rarer flowers are protected by law and ought not to be picked.

Animals likely to be seen include the chamois, wild goat, mountain hare and marmot.

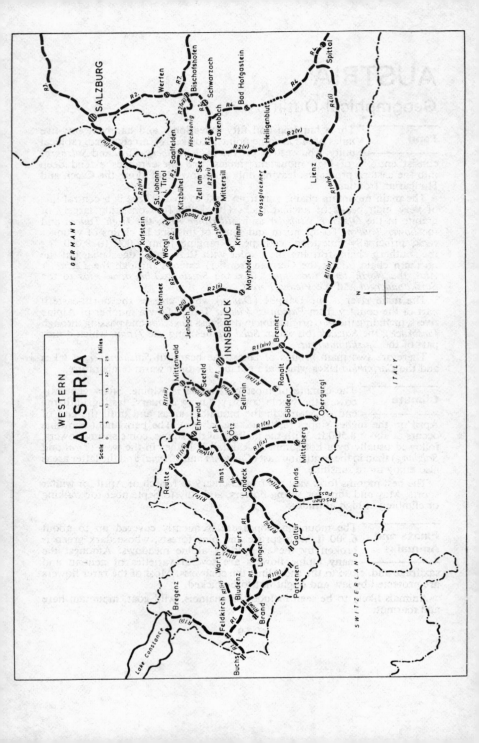

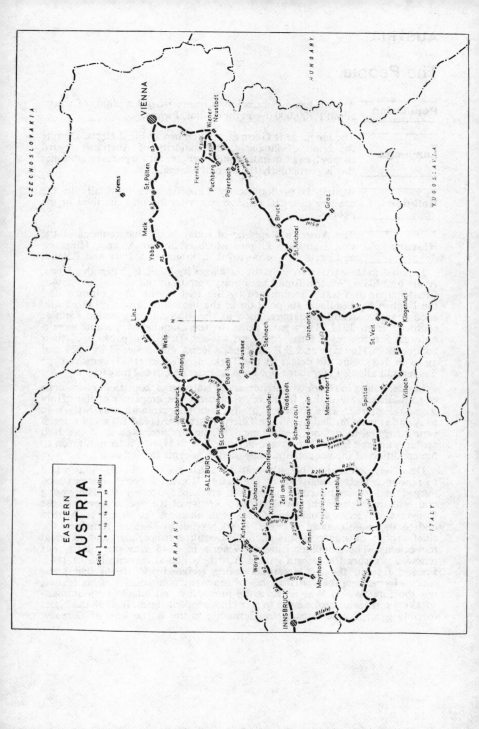

AUSTRIA

The People

Population

Austria has a population of more than 7 million, of whom about 1,700,000 live in the capital, *Vienna*.

Language

The language is German, spoken in varying dialects. Despite the bond of language, the majority of Austrians regard themselves as an independent people, with separate traditions; this is particularly the case in *Vienna*.

Religion

Austria is predominantly Catholic and, especially in the country districts, religion is a vital force in the lives of the people.

History

The Austrian Republic of today is all that remains of the vast Habsburg Empire which embraced Austria, Hungary, and parts of Czechoslovakia, Yugoslavia, Italy and Poland.

Exposed to the east, overrun in the dark ages by Vandals, Visigoths, Huns, Avars and Slavs, Austria found temporary respite in the 8th century under Charlemagne and was Christianized by the Irish monk St. Columba and the English St. Boniface. Its position in the heart of Europe required and encouraged a strong monarchy, such as the Habsburgs provided for five centuries from 1272. They gave peace to the Danube basin, and were a bulwark for the rest of the continent against Turkish expansion of their conquests in Hungary and S.E. Europe. Vienna was besieged in 1529 and again in 1683. But the defeat of the Turks at *Mohács* (1687) removed the danger and allowed Hapsburg power to be extended over Hungary.

Besides ruling in their own territories the Habsburgs, consistent champions of Catholicism, were also, for nearly four centuries, emperors of the "Holy Roman Empire". This dispersal of interests and strength was little help to Austria: it embroiled her in the Thirty Years War (1618-48) and in irrelevant struggles to defend remote parts of the Empire. Not until the 18th century, under Maria Theresa and her son Joseph II, was attention given to the condition of the people, and long-needed reforms carried out.

Decisively defeated by Napoleon at *Austerlitz* in 1806, the Habsburgs had to renounce their pretensions to the "Holy Roman Empire" but emerged purged and strengthened in their own re-shaped dominions. The young and brilliant Metternich, the supreme diplomat of the age, achieved in the Congress of Vienna a balance of European alliances favourable to Austria and to the maintenance of peace. Until his fall in 1848 he remained the chief arbiter of Europe's affairs, but insensitive to popular and national movements. The popular rising in Vienna in 1848 was put down, but renewed pressure for reform gained Austria a liberal constitution in 1867. Francis Joseph, the last great Habsburg, (reigned 1848-1916) had some success in meeting the varied wishes of the many nationalities of his realms, but the First World War finished the monarchy and all the non-German-speaking territories broke away to form independent states. In 1938 the Nazis forcibly incorporated Austria in Germany, giving it the title of *Ostmark*

("The Eastern Marches"), but at the end of the Second World War it resumed its existence as an independent state.

Government Austria is a democratic federal republic of nine provinces (*Länder*) including the Province of Vienna. The two-chamber government consists of a national diet of 165 members elected by direct vote and a federal diet elected according to the proportionate strength of parties in each of the *Länder*. The president is elected for six years. The *Länder* have a considerable measure of self-government.

Resources Austria is a poor country. A high proportion of its land is uncultivable mountain and there are few natural resources except oil and some iron. But the peasant population makes full use of every square foot of cultivable land, and crops of grass for fodder are grown on the most precipitous hillsides. Timber is a major product of the alpine areas and hydro-electric power is being developed. The major industrial areas are in the eastern part of the country, particularly in and around *Vienna*.

Customs The Austrians are a gay and carefree people; the Viennese, in particular, have a reputation for good-natured wit and gaiety.

Austrian manners are courteous; it is usual to shake hands on meeting and parting and, amongst city-dwellers, a man will often kiss a woman's hand in greeting. A frequent greeting, particularly in the countryside, is *Grüss Gott* (God Greet you).

In country districts, particularly in the *Tirol*, picturesque national costumes of various types are still worn, at least on Sundays and holidays. Short leather trousers are often worn by men of all ages as workaday attire, with green-lapelled jackets and green hats, sometimes with a tuft of chamois hair. National dances and yodelling are popular in many villages, and saints' days (of which there are many, in a predominantly Catholic country) provide the opportunity for all kinds of local celebrations.

Small shrines (or calvaries) often piously decked with fresh flowers, are a frequent feature on the roadside or on mountain paths.

Culture

Music Music is the typical art of Austria. *Vienna* was the home of the great classical musicians of the 18th and 19th century—Haydn, Mozart, Beethoven and Schubert—and of many masters of light music such as Johann Strauss (father and son) and Lehar; also, in the 20th century, of Schönberg, whose 12-tone system—a major break with tradition—makes him one of the great innovators among composers. The *Staatsoper* (National Opera), Vienna Philharmonic Orchestra, Vienna Symphonic Orchestra and the *Salzburg* Festival have won international fame. Festivals are also held at *Vienna* (May/June) and *Bregenz* (July/August).

AUSTRIA

Architecture Architecture has played a rôle second only to music in Austria's cultural history. Gothic style is represented in parts of the *Stefansdom* (St. Stephen's Cathedral) in Vienna, in the Church of *Maria am Gestade* (also in Vienna), and in the choir of the *Franziskaner* Church in *Salzburg*. Among the landmarks of the Renaissance style is the tomb of Kaiser Maximilian in the *Hofkirche* in *Innsbruck*. But it was in the 17th and 18th centuries that Austrian architecture reached its finest flower. *Salzburg* Cathedral (1630) is a notable example of early Baroque style, under strong Italian influence; early in the 18th century came a series of magnificent buildings in Vienna designed by Fischer von Erlach (father and son)—the National Library, the Winter Palace of Prince Eugene—and by Lukas von Hildebrandt—the Belvedere Castles, *Schönbrunn* (designed, but not built, by Hildebrandt).

Painting Modern Austrian painters, with the exception of Kokoschka, are little known outside their own country, because their work is in localized styles in isolation from the rest of Europe.

Literature The works of a number of 20th century authors have been translated into English, amongst them von Hoffmannsthal, Schnitzler, Kafka, and Zweig. The stories of Kafka, in particular, haunt the mind as disturbing modern parables.

Science In two fields—psychology and philosophy—Austrian (or, more strictly, Viennese) contributions have had a profound effect on the modern world. Freud (1856-1939) is the founder of psycho-analysis. Wittgenstein, the leading member of the "Vienna Circle" of philosophers, has been the most original thinker in the now dominant school of linguistic philosophy. In economics, also, an "Austrian School", leader Böhm-Bawerk, has influenced theory.

Touring Information

Touring Areas
Austria's fame as a tourist country rests on its mountains, and it is the mountain provinces of Western Austria which are most popular—*Vorarlberg, Tirol* and *Salzburg*. The southern province of *Carinthia* (*Kärnten*) has become popular in recent years because of its particularly dry and sunny climate and its warm lakes. *Upper Austria* is less mountainous, except at its south-eastern extremity, which contains the famous *Salzkammergut* lakes. *Styria* (*Steiermark*) contains many mountains of 7,000 ft. or more but is less well known; it is an admirable region for travellers who wish to get off "the beaten track". Finally, there is *Vienna*, which has its own attractions: architecture, music, modern social developments (kindergartens, well-planned municipal housing, etc.) alongside the carefree life of cafés and wine-taverns.

As in most countries, the famous tourist centres are generally more crowded and more expensive than the less-known areas. *Salzburg* (particularly during the Festival month of August), *Innsbruck, Kitzbühel, Zell-am-See, St. Anton-am-Arlberg, Pertisau, Velden, Seefeld, Pörtschach/Wörthersee*—are fashionable centres at which the youth hosteller with his modest purse will not find such a warm welcome. But elsewhere, particularly in small towns and villages, living is inexpensive; where there is no youth hostel or mountain hut a bed at a small inn or in a private house can often be had for 30 Austrian Schillings, with full pension for S.90. What is more, there is a tradition of economical touring in the mountains of Austria and the traveller who has little money to spend is nevertheless welcome.

Access
The main land approaches to Austria are (a) via Switzerland, arriving in *Vorarlberg;* (b) via Germany, arriving in *Salzburg* or *Innsbruck;* (c) via Italy, arriving in *Salzburg* or *Vienna.*

Transport
The railways provide the only satisfactory means of long-distance transport. Owing to the difficult terrain, trains cannot travel at high speeds although most of the lines are electrified. Second class carriages on expresses and some other services are quite comfortable, but a few local trains have wooden seats; they are often crowded, particularly in summer. Restaurant cars, operated by Wagons-Lits Cook and by Deutsche Schlafwagengesellschaft are expensive, but Wagons-Lits Cook also operate buffet cars and on many trains a private vendor of refreshments is allowed to travel, and his prices are usually reasonable; in addition, the long stops at main stations give time to purchase refreshments from the platform.

There are few long-distance motor-coaches in Austria, but for shorter distances, particularly in mountain districts, the motor-buses operated

AUSTRIA

by the Post Office (*Postkraftwagen*) offer the best and sometimes the only means of transport.

Many cable railways (*Seilschwebebahn*), chair-lifts (*Sessellift*) and ski-lifts connect the main tourist centres to peaks and viewpoints. Downward journeys are often 25% cheaper and many lifts allow further reductions for return fares.

Steamboats or motor-boats ply on most of the lakes and on the R. *Danube*, providing a pleasant, but usually more expensive, means of transport.

Money The Austrian coinage consists of the *Schilling* (abbreviated as ö.S. or simply S.) which is divided into 100 *Groschen*.

Clothing As in all mountain countries, the rule for summer attire is: as light as possible by day, particularly in the valleys and in towns, but with a reserve of warm clothing for the evenings and for high altitudes. A raincoat or cape is necessary, even in the height of summer, as sudden heavy rainstorms occur from time to time. For walking on mountain paths boots are essential, preferably fitted with the moulded and grooved rubber soles of 'Vibram' or 'Commando' type – or with hobnails.

Restaurants A good, but not elaborate, two course meal can be obtained at almost any restaurant or inn in Austria for about S.25 including either a meat or an egg dish. Green salad is frequently served with meat, but cooked vegetables are less frequent and potatoes are often replaced by macaroni unless the former are specially requested. Tea is unprocurable (or undrinkable) except in large towns, and coffee is very expensive, particularly if ordered with whipped cream—known as *Schlagobers*. Unfermented apple-juice (*Apfelsaft*) is an excellent drink obtainable everywhere. Soups are always excellent, particularly those containing small dumplings (*Nockerl* or *Knödel*). *Jause* is the local Austrian name for light refreshments, particularly in the afternoon.

The principal types of meat which you will find on a menu are *Rind* (beef), *Schwein* (pork), *Kalb* (veal), *Wurst* (sausage), *Schinken* (ham), *Speck* (bacon), Other useful words are: *Eier* (eggs), *Käse* (cheese), *Gemüse* (vegetables), *Kartoffel* (potatoes).

Maps Freytag & Berndt of Vienna publish a relief-shaded map of Austria on a scale of 1:600,000; this is the best of the general maps of the country. Cyclists wanting a larger scale will prefer Hölzel's four sheets at 1:200,000.

The most popular maps for walking tours are Freytag & Berndt's 1:100,000 series. Each of the 45 sheets covers an area of about 20 by 30 miles, and is accompanied by a text, in German, which is very useful in the planning of high-level tours. The best detail for climbers is in the magnificent maps of the most important massifs published by the Austrian Alpine Club on a scale of 1:25,000.

Walking and Climbing

Austria is an ideal country for walking and climbing. All the mountain ranges are traversed by paths, inconspicuously but adequately marked by occasional coloured signs on trees or rocks; these coloured markings are reproduced on all the large-scale maps, such maps also indicate the location of the many alpine huts, maintained by the Austrian Alpine Club and other organisations, which provide inexpensive accommodation for all walkers and climbers and supplement the Austrian youth hostel network. The huts are generally substantial stone or timber buildings, situated at altitudes of 3,000 to 9,000 ft., with a resident warden (at least during the summer months). The average charge for a mattress-bed is S.45 but half price for members of the Austrian Alpine Club. Meals, when provided, cost from about S.25 each. Cooking facilities are seldom available but boiling water for tea-making is provided at a nominal charge. Accommodation cannot be booked in advance but the huts are rarely full to capacity and visitors are never turned away; members of the Alpine Club do, however, receive priority in the allocation of sleeping accommodation.

The Austrian Alpine Club operates 270 mountain huts throughout the country. Membership for non-Austrians is 180 S. Rates for beds for non-members are 40 to 90 S; mattresses, 20 to 50 S. Members pay half price and have priority. For more information and a list of huts, write to Austrian Alpine Club, ÖAV, Wilhelm Greil Strasse 15, A-6010 Innsbruck, Austria.

For the serious rock and mountain climber Austria offers almost unlimited opportunities. There are superb rock-faces in the limestone mountains of northern *Tirol* (e.g., *Karwendel* and *Kaisergebirge*), whilst all types of glacier and snow work can be undertaken among the peaks of the central mountain chain (*Ötztaler Alps, Silvretta Group, High Tauern*). The *Wildspitze* (*Ötztaler Alps*) can be specially recommended. Guides can be hired in all the higher mountain villages to assist less experienced climbers.

Ski-ing

Austria is an ideal country for ski-ing, both for learners and experts. Snow conditions are usually at their best in January, February and March, but, above 5,000 ft. or so, good ski-ing can often be enjoyed at Christmas and Easter. The Western provinces (*Vorarlberg* and *Tirol*) are rather more fashionable—and hence more expensive—than *Salzburg, Upper Austria* and *Carinthia*. Skis and sticks can be hired, but the hiring of boots is not possible at all resorts.

Cycling

The main roads, metalled and well engineered, generally follow the river valleys. Secondary roads are often rough-surfaced, steep and sharply curved. Cyclists who enjoy riding rough will find plenty of opportunities to test their skill.

AUSTRIA

Touring Routes

R.1. Swiss Frontier (Buchs) to Brenner Pass, via Arlberg Pass and Innsbruck (134 miles)

This is the "classical" approach to Western Austria, following the route of the "Arlberg Orient Express", through the *Vorarlberg* province into *Tirol*. Fine mountain scenery on almost the entire journey.

Buchs (Swiss and Austrian Customs), 12 miles *Feldkirch* (Y.H.), 1,506 ft., a little fortified town with 15th century parish church.

R.1(i) From *Feldkirch* 24 miles to Bregenz, (Y.H.) capital of **Vorarlberg**, picturesque medieval town beautifully situated on *Lake Constance (Bodensee)*. Landesmuseum (Provincial Museum) containing medieval altars.

EXCURSIONS: (a) cable railway to *Pfänder* (3,350 ft.). (b) *Bregenzer Forest:* rail to *Bezau*, 22 miles, thence bus through magnificent wooded mountains to *Schröcken*, 19 miles, good centre for mountain tours. (c) Steamers on *Lake Constance* to Swiss and German resorts.

14 miles **Bludenz** (1,919 ft.), meeting of *Kloster* and *Montafon Valleys*.

R.1 (ii) *Bludenz* to *Partenen*, via attractive mountain valley of *Montafon*, leading to *Rhätikon* and *Silvretta* mountain groups on Swiss frontier. Picturesque houses, stone and wood, gabled front, half brown, half white; attractive local costumes ("Maidens' Crowns" worn by girls on Corpus Christi day—11 days after Whitsunday). Rail to *Schruns*, 8 miles (2,260 ft.) good mountain touring centre, chair lifts. On foot to *Sulzfluh* (9,300 ft.) via *Tilisuna Hut*. By bus further up *Montafon Valley* to *Partenen*, 11 miles (3,380 ft.) winter sports centre.

R.1(iii) Bus *Bludenz* to *Brandner Valley*, **Brand** (3,465 ft.); 8 miles; popular summer and winter resort at foot of *Schesaplana* (9,735 ft.). Cable railway to *Niggenkopf* (5,500 ft.).

EXCURSIONS: *Lünersee* (6,375 ft.) largest alpine lake in *Vorarlberg*, 3 hrs. to *Douglas Hut*. Thence in 3 hrs. to the *Schesaplana*.

R.1(iv) Bus *Bludenz* to beautiful **Walser Valley**: 12 miles to *Sonntag*, thence to *Fontanella* and *Faschinajoch Pass* (4,880 ft.). Fine views en route.

Continue up picturesque *Kloster Valley* 15 miles to *Langen* (3,995 ft.). Junction for route to *Lech Valley* and *Lech Stubenbach* (Y.H.).

R.1(v) Bus via *Flexen Pass* to *Zürs* (5,642 ft.) famous winter sports centre, along magnificently engineered road with superb views, to *Lech* (4,746 ft.) summer and winter resort, cable railway to *Oberlech*, (5,626 ft.). Continue to *Warth*, and down gently sloping *Lech Valley* to *Reutte* (Y.H.) (see R.1(viii)).

Main railway continues via *Arlberg* tunnel (6½ miles long) and road via *St. Christoph* and the **Arlberg Pass**, 5,911 ft., second highest in Austria. 7 miles to St. Anton (4,277 ft.) fashionable winter sports centre, just in the **Tirol**. Road and rail continue down *Stanzer Valley*, with *Lechtaler Alps* to North and *Ferwall Group* to South. 4 miles *Pettneu* (4,010 ft.) with easy climbs in 6 hrs. to *Hoher Riffler*, (10,400 ft.), 12 miles **Landeck** (2,676 ft.). Important centre of communications on River *Inn*; picturesque castle and parish church.

R.1(vi) Bus up upper *Inn Valley*, past series of mountain villages (*Pfunds, Hochfinstermünz* 31 miles to *Reschen Pass* (5,030 ft.) on Italian frontier. Connection to *Merano*.

R.1(vii) Bus up *Paznaun* Valley, 25 miles to *Galtür* (5,192 ft.), centre for tours in *Silvretta* mountains.

Main route continues down *Inn Valley*. 12 miles *Imst* (2,716 ft.), junction for principal road connection to *Reutte* and the *Zugspitze*.

R.1(viii) Bus *Imst-Reutte*, 34 miles via *Fern Pass* (3,993 ft.) *Lermoos* (3,264 ft.) tourist centre with fine views on to *Wetterstein* mountains. *Reutte* (Y.H.) is an old market town close to the German frontier, and a good centre for excursions by bus via *Füssen* to the castles of *Hochenshwangau* and *Neuschwanstein*.

EXCURSIONS: (a) on foot via *Stuiben* waterfalls to the *Plansee*, (b) via the tiny *Frauensee* to the *Otto Mayr Hut*, in the *Tannheim* mountain group.

R.1(ix) *Imst* is also junction for Pitz Valley, a beautiful unspoilt valley with fine glacier scenery. Bus from *Imst* to *Plangeross*, 24 miles; walk to *Mittelberg*, 2½ miles.

EXCURSIONS: Glaciers 1 hr., *Riffelsee* (lake and hut, 7,360 ft.) 2 hrs.

Continue 7 miles to *Ötztal*.

R.1(x) From *Ötztal* station up the *Ötz Valley*, one of the loveliest in Austria, 35 miles long (bus from *Ötztal* station to *Obergurgl*, nearly 3 hrs.). 3 miles *Schlatt*. 4 miles *Ötz* village; *Gasthof Stern*—gothic paintings; bathing at *Piburger Lake*, 40 mins. walk.

EXCURSIONS: (a) *Bielefelder Hut* on the *Acherkogel*, (7,111 ft.), 4 hrs. (b) bus to *Kühtai* with bus connection on to *Gries im Sellrain* (R.1(xi)). Or on foot *Ötz* to *Gries*, 9–10 hrs.

Continue up *Ötz Valley* to *Umhausen*, 5½ miles (see fine *Stuiben* waterfall, 500 ft., ¾ hr. walk. Not to be confused with *Stuiben* falls near *Reutte*). *Langenfeld*, 5½ miles, birthplace of Franz Senn, founder of German and Austrian Alpine Club.

EXCURSION: to *Winnebach Lake* and Hut, (7,827 ft.), via attractive village of *Gries im Sulztal*, 4½ hrs.

Sölden, 9¼ miles, (4,405 ft.), main tourist centre for valley. (On foot in 2 hrs., or by chair-lift in 16 mins., to *Hochsölden*, (6,790 ft.) good for late ski-ing.) At *Zwieselstein* (2½ miles) the valley forks, one branch leading to *Obergurgl*, 8 miles, highest parish in Europe, (6,321 ft.), the other to *Vent*, (6,270 ft.), at foot of the *Wildspitze* (12,309 ft.), highest peak in *Tirol*. Both *Obergurgl* and *Vent* are excellent centres for climbing to glaciers, mountain huts and peaks in *Ötztaler Alps;* from *Vent* the *Wildspitze* can be climbed in 6 hrs. (guide necessary).

From *Ötztal* continue 6 miles to *Stams*; Cistercian Monastery with fine carved altar and "Rose Railing" (1716), thence along broadening *Inn Valley* with *Mieminger Chain* to the North (charming mountains rising to 8,000 ft., best approach from *Telfs*) and *Stubaier Alps* to the South, 22 miles *Kematen*, important only as junction for **Sellrain Valley**.

R.1(xi) Bus to *Gries im Sellrain* (4,061 ft.), centre of attractive valley.

EXCURSIONS: on foot to *Kühtai*, small ski village with *Dortmunder Hut* at 6,487 ft., and by bus to *Praxmar* (5,579 ft.) for ascents to various mountain huts.

From *Kematen*, 7 miles to **Innsbruck**.

Innsbruck

Cultural and tourist capital of the *Tirol*, one of the most beautifully situated towns in Europe, lying in *Inn Valley*, with towering peaks, snow-capped until April–May, to N. and S. From railway station turn R. along *Südtiroler Platz*, L. via *Brixner Strasse*, *Bozner Platz* (for buses), *Meraner Strasse* into **Maria Theresien Str.**, main street of town with impressive mountain background and Baroque buildings. In centre of street, *Annasäule*, pillar commemorating liberation from Bavaria in 1703. Turn R. along *Maria Theresien Str.*, which leads into *Herzog Friedrich Str.*, centre of oldest part of town; where this street bears L., see **"Goldenes Dachl"** (Golden Roof), picturesque Gothic bay window, richly sculptured. Turn R. down

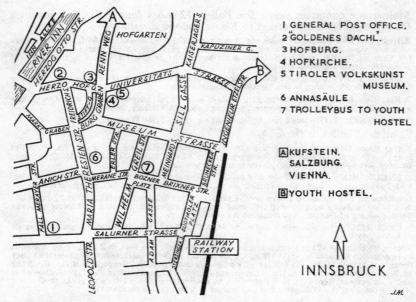

1 GENERAL POST OFFICE.
2 "GOLDENES DACHL".
3 HOFBURG.
4 HOFKIRCHE.
5 TIROLER VOLKSKUNST
MUSEUM.
6 ANNASÄULE
7 TROLLEYBUS TO YOUTH
HOSTEL

Ⓐ KUFSTEIN.
SALZBURG.
VIENNA.

Ⓑ YOUTH HOSTEL.

INNSBRUCK

Hofgasse (16th century houses) to *Hofburg*, former imperial palace (1496, renovated 18th century); conducted tours of palace including *Hofkirche*, built in 16th century to hold **Tomb of Emperor Maximilian.** Finest renaissance sculpture in Austria; two of statues designed by Albrecht Dürer. Next to church is *Tiroler Volkskunst Museum*, largest collection of peasant costumes and furniture in Austria or Germany. Behind *Hofburg* is *Hofgarten*, palace garden of shady lakes and great willows. **(Y.Hs)**.

Tram No. 3 or trolleybus 'B' from *Bozner Platz* to youth hostel in *Pradl*, *Reichenauerstrasse*, 18. Post Office in *Maximilian Strasse* (from railway station via *Salurnerstrasse* and across *Maria Theresienstrasse*).

EXCURSIONS: (a) Cable railway from *Mühlauer* Bridge, on N. side of city (terminus of tram route No. 1) to *Hungerburg* (2,860 ft.) fine view; further railways to *Hafelekar* (7,419 ft.) fine path along ridge. (b) Bus to *Ambras* (castle, with fine interior and view over city) and *Igls* (8 miles), smart resort. Thence cable railway ascends to *Patscherkofel* mountain (6,500 ft.) ¾ hr. walk to summit (7,450 ft.).

R.1(xii) Railway (narrow gauge) from *Innsbruck* up Stubaital to *Fulpmes* (11 miles), thence bus to *Neustift* (3,237 ft.), and *Ranalt* (4,150 ft.), both good centres for exploring *Stubaital Alps*.

R.1 (xiii) Mittenwald railway from *Innsbruck* to *Seefeld* (3,870 ft.), fashionable mountain resort, and *Scharnitz*, good centre for tours in *Karwendel Mountains*, in particular, magnificent 4-day walk up **Karwendel** *Valley* via *Karwendel, Falken* and *Lamsenjoch* huts to *Achensee. Maurach* (Y.H.) (R.2(i)). Train continues across German territory via *Mittenwald* and re-enters Austria at *Ehrwald* (3,267 ft.) resort at foot of Zugspitze (9,725 ft.) impressive mountain, with peak forming Austrian-German frontier. Cable railway from *Ehrwald* to summit.

R.1(xiv) Rail or road up the *Wipptal* to the **Brenner Pass** (23 miles) via *Steinach* (3,447 ft.) and *Gries am Brenner* (4,116 ft.), both popular small resorts. The *Brenner Pass* (4,494 ft.) is the lowest North-South crossing over the Alps, formerly a Roman road. Through train across Italian territory to *Lienz* (Y.H.) in *East Tirol* (see R.4(i)).

R.2. Innsbruck to Salzburg via Kitzbühel (160 miles)

This is a continuation of the Arlberg Express route. It follows the *Inn Valley* down to *Wörgl*, then climbs the watershed between *Kitzbühel* and *Zell* into the upper *Salzach Valley*. Scenery is superb all the way, but the journey is slow and takes 4 hours, even by express train.

Innsbruck to *Solbad Hall*, 6 miles, old town with fine parish church.

Further 11 miles to *Schwaz*, with many old houses, and a fine church (14th century) containing beautiful bell.

EXCURSION: on foot to *Kellerjoch* (7,700 ft.), easy ascent, wonderful view.

Continue 5 miles to **Jenbach** (Y.H.). *Tratzberg Castle,* containing frescoed *Habsburg* Family Tree (1507) and many notable paintings.

R.2(i) Rack railway *Jenbach-Achensee* (summer only) 4 miles. Achensee (3,045 ft.) is largest and loveliest lake in *Tirol*, 6 miles long. Steamer from rail terminus to *Pertisau*, fashionable lakeside resort. Y.H. at *Maurach* at S. end of lake.

R.2(ii) Narrow gauge railway from *Jenbach*, 20 miles up the beautiful Zillertal, *Stummerberg* (Y.H.), to *Mayrhofen* (2,066 ft.), starting point for tours into the *Zillertal Alps*.

EXCURSIONS: (a) *Ahornspitze* (9,900 ft.) 6½ hrs., (not difficult climb). (b) *Tuxer Valley*, leading to big glacier of *Gefrorene Wand* (Frozen Wall) and magnificent *Tuxer* waterfalls. (c) *Zemmtal Valley* to *Berliner Hut* (6,750 ft.). (d) *Zillergrund*, a full day's walk to *Plauener Hut* (7,700 ft.).

From *Jenbach*, 6 miles to *Brixlegg*, pleasant village with several castles nearby (*Matzen, Kropsberg.*) 1 mile further to *Rattenberg* an extremely picturesque town (Gothic *Hofer* Chapel).

EXCURSION: to lovely *Reintaler* lakes, 40 mins. walk, bathing.

Continue 9 miles to **Worgl**, junction for rail and road to *Kufstein* and *Munich*.

R.2(iii) Following *Inn Valley* 8 miles to *Kufstein*, (Y.H.) important summer and winter centre with good approach to *Kaiser Mountains*, wild and picturesque walking country, with huge rock walls, favourite ground for climbers. *Hintersteinersee*, a lake at W. end of range, and views from *Stripsenjoch* Hut.

Railway continues 6 miles to *Hopfgarten*.

EXCURSION: to the *Hohe Salve* (5,030 ft.), popular and fine viewpoint (3 hrs. on foot, or by ski-lift, longest in Europe).

6½ miles *Westendorf*, pleasant summer and winter resort, chairlift to *Alpenrosenhaus* (5,250 ft.) starting point for many mountain walks.

10½ miles further comes **Kitzbühel**, fashionable winter-sports and summer resort (2,503 ft.). Many suspension railways and ski-lifts to surrounding heights.

EXCURSIONS: (a) cable railway to *Hahnenkamm* (5,450 ft.), from here (1½hr.) to *Ehrenbachhöhe* (5,955 ft.) magnificent view. (b) cable railways, in 3 stages from *Kitzbühel* to *Kitzbüheler Horn*, exceptionally fine view from summit of *Horn*, ½ hr. walk; ascent on foot from *Kitzbühel* to *Horn* takes 3½ hrs. (c) bus or rail to *Schwarzsee*, warm-water lake, good bathing.

AUSTRIA

Railway and road continue, 5 miles, to *St. Johann-in-Tirol,* attractive small town at confluence of several valleys. Here main road to *Salzburg* leaves the railway line.

R.2(iv) Motor road St. Johann-Salzburg via *Lofer.* Across German territory via *Bad Reichenhall* or via *Berchtesgaden;* greatly shortens the normal route via *Zell-am-See* and *Bischofshofen.* Buses operate.

Railway continues via *Hochfilzen* and the *Griesenpass* (3,136 ft.) into the **Province of Salzburg,** descending to (23 miles) **Saalfelden** (2,240 ft.) a good centre for walking tours.

EXCURSIONS: (a) *Steinernes Meer*—Sea of Stone—a strange wilderness of boulders, lying along German frontier; access (with night's halt at the *Riemann* Hut) to beautiful *Königssee* in Bavaria. (b) via *Urschlaub* valley and *Hintertal* to climb the *Hochkönig* (9,690 ft.) not for inexperienced climbers; for an easier approach see under *Bischofshofen* (R.2(vii)).

In another 8 miles train reaches **Zell-am-See** (2,486 ft.), fashionable resort on *Zeller Lake,* centre for *Grossglockner* and *Pinzgau.* Y.H. by the lakeside.

EXCURSIONS: (a) by motorboat across lake to summer resort of *Thumersbach.* (b) on foot in 3 hrs, or by cable railway in 8 mins., to *Schmittenhöhe* (6,457 ft.), with magnificent views, including 31 peaks over 9,000 ft. high, and starting point of superb high-level footpath, the **Pinzgauer Path** stretching some 15 miles at 6,000 ft. above sea level, with fine views to the glacier-crowned mountains of the *High Tauern* across the valley. (c) to *Kaprun* (Y.H.) (6 miles), huge Tauern hydro-electric station.

R.2(v) Motor-coach from *Zell-am-See* to *Heiligenblut* (30 miles) via **Grossglockner mountain** road. A spectacular journey through wild alpine scenery, along one of highest roads in Europe, built 1930-35. Open June-October only. The road climbs, with many bends and tunnels, to nearly 9,000 ft. with a branch road (*Gletscherstrasse*) leading to *Franz Josefs Höhe* (7,900 ft.) looking out over the vast *Pasterze* glacier, with *Grossglockner* (12,457 ft., Austria's highest mountain) in background. From *Heiligenblut,* (Y.H.) there is a road to *Lienz* (Y.H.)and *Carinthia* (see R.4(i)). Bus from *Zell* to *Lienz* (6 hrs.); twice daily in Summer.

R.2(vi) From *Zell-am-See* by narrow gauge railway through Pinzgau (valley of the *Salzach*) 33 miles to *Krimml. Mittersill* (18 miles) is junction for main road via *Pass Thurn,* to *Kitzbühel* (fine views of *Tauern* mountains from road): also nearest point to noteworthy animals reserve in *Amer Valley* (80 sq. miles). *Neukirchen* (28 miles from *Zell*) is centre for climbers ascending the *Grossvenediger* (12,000 ft.). *Krimml* has famous waterfalls, largest in eastern Alps.

From *Zell-am-See* railway continues 10 miles to *Taxenbach,* station for *Rauris Valley* (bus to *Kolm-Saigurn,* lovely mountain centre at foot of *Hoher Sonnblick,* 10,200 ft. peak). Thence 11 miles to *Schwarzach St. Veit,* junction for *Tauern* Railway to *Carinthia* (see **R.4**). Continue 3 miles to *St. Johann im Pongau,* station for the *Leichtensteinklamm* (1 hr. on foot) an attractive gorge, with waterfall (admission charge). Train continues 5 miles to **Bischofshofen** (1,785 ft.), junction for railway to *Selzthal* and *Vienna* (see **R.7**).

R.2(vii) to the Hochkönig (9,600 ft.). *Bischofshofen* is an excellent starting point for visiting the *Salzburg Limestone Alps,* good walking country giving an impression of greater height than it actually possesses. *Bischofshofen—Mühlbach* (Y.H.)--*Arthurhaus* by bus (or direct on foot, choice of two paths, in 3 hrs.): on foot 1¾ hrs. to *Mitterbergalpe,* thence in 5 hrs. to the *Übergossene Alm* ("Iced Meadow"), a mountain-ridge 1 mile wide, permanent snow; in one further hour to summit of *Hochkönig* ("Tall King"), magnificent view, alpine hut.

Bischofshofen to *Werfen* (5 miles). Y.H. in castle, *Burg Hohenwerfen,* built in 11th century for Archbishop of *Salzburg.* Also *Werfen/Kalchau* **Y.H.**

EXCURSION: **Giant Ice Caves,** well worth a visit. Largest known caves in Europe, containing extraordinarily beautiful natural ice formations, electrically illuminated. Conducted tour takes 2 hrs. (Ascent from *Werfen* 3½ hrs. on foot.)

Train continues 11 miles to *Golling.*

EXCURSIONS: Waterfall at *Schwarzbachfall,* 1 hr., *Lueg Pass,* ¾ hr., *Hoher Göll* (8,310 ft.) 6¼ hrs. climb, so-called "Salzburg Dolomite Road", 20 miles long, via *Abtenau* to *Annaberg* skirting *Tennengebirge;* superb views; bus service.

6 miles to *Hallein* **(Y.H.),** *Dürrnberg* salt-mines, worked since Neolithic times, but now little more than electrically illuminated caves for tourists; 12 miles to **Salzburg.**

Salzburg

A town with many ecclesiastical, artistic and musical associations, beautifully situated on R. *Salzach* against a background of mountains and dominated by the citadel *(Hohensalzburg)*. Picturesque streets and many examples of noble architecture, palaces and spacious squares.

The old town lies on W. of river. Trolley bus from station to *Staatsbrücke* (view of river); follow trolleybus line beyond bridge as far as *Alter Markt,* then bear L. into large *Residenzplatz,* splendid 17th century fountain. On south side of square is the *Residenz,* built in 17th century formerly an archbishop's

1 CATHEDRAL
2 ABBEY OF ST. PETER
3 MOZART'S BIRTHPLACE
4 TOWN MUSEUM
5 MOZARTEUM

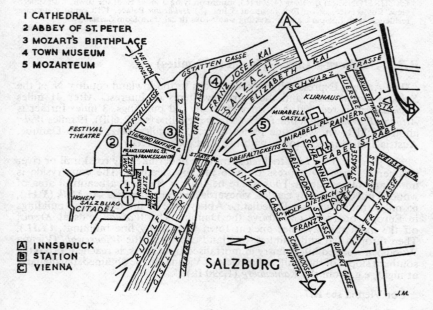

A INNSBRUCK
B STATION
C VIENNA

21

palace. Opposite is *Glockenspiel*, with fine set of 35 bells playing daily. Leading off the square is *Mozartplatz* with statue of *Mozart* (19th century). Cross *Residenzplatz* diagonally and pass via arcade into quiet *Domplatz* (Cathedral Square), where miracle play "*Jedermann*" ("Everyman") is performed during August. The **Cathedral**, fine early baroque building, dates from 1614-28 (painted ceilings and high altar). On opposite side of *Domplatz* is Franciscan church (romanesque nave and gothic choir), and to the left is the Benedictine **Abbey of St. Peter**, Austria's oldest monastery (7th century or earlier); *St. Peter's Church*, with 15th century Madonna and monument to Mozart's sister, and the *St. Peter-Stifskeller*, a popular restaurant in genuine medieval setting. Through the *St. Peters-Friedhof* (cemetery) to cable railway leading up to the citadel of **Hohensalzburg** (1,780 ft.), founded in the 11th century but present buildings date from early 16th century; formerly a home of the archbishops; excellent view from tower of *Reckturm*; mechanical organ ("*Stier*") built 1502, plays daily. Return to *Domplatz*, then via *Franziskaner Gasse* across *Max Reinhardt Platz* to *Hofstallgasse* and see on L. the *Festspielhaus* (**Festival Theatre** and concert hall). Continue via *Sigmundsplatz* (on L. is *Neutor*, a road tunnel built in 18th century) to *Gstättergasse*; at No. 13 is a lift on to the *Mönschsberg* (1,650 ft.) with café and fine view. Return along *Gstättergasse*, but bear L. down *Getreidegasse*. At No. 9 is **Mozart's birthplace**, with Museum. Return via *Rathausplatz* to *Staatsbrücke* (for trolleybus to station). **Y.Hs** in town and at *Walserfeld*, 3 miles S.W.

EXCURSIONS: (a) *Gaisberg* (4,200 ft.), mountain lying 3 miles E. of the town, with superb view. Bus service, or on foot in about 3 hrs. (b) *Hellbrunn* Palace, 17th century summer residence, with fine park and interesting water-toys (local train from *Salzburg*).

R.3. Salzburg—Linz—Vienna (199 miles)

The Arlberg Express railway route keeps to the lowland country N. of the *Salzkammergut* area, and there are few items of interest. After 41 miles *Vöcklabruck* is reached, a town with many old buildings. 3 miles further is *Attnang-Puchheim*, junction for *Salzkammergut* line (see **R.6(ii)**), 19 miles *Wels*, another old town, with fine parish church. 16 miles *Linz*, on the Danube, Austria's third largest town, with big steelworks. (**Y.H.**)

The journey from *Linz* to *Vienna* may be undertaken by road, rail or river steamer (2½ hrs. by express train, 6 hrs. by steamer). The countryside is unremarkable as far as *Ybbs* where begins the *Wachau*, a beautiful area of wooded hills with many castles, vineyards and fine churches. At *Melk* (**Y.H.**), 65 miles from *Linz*, is a Benedictine Abbey, one of finest baroque buildings in Europe, on rocky cliff above the Danube. The *Wachau* ends at *Krems*, off the main railway line; ancient town with many fine buildings, (**Y.H.**). Then through flat and uninteresting landscape until the *Wienerwald* (Vienna Woods), a wooded hill country immortalised by Strauss, is reached. From the southern slopes of these hills a fine view of Vienna can be obtained, particularly at night, e.g. from the *Kahlenberg* (1,590 ft.).

For Vienna see **R.7**

R.4. Innsbruck—Schwarzach—Klagenfurt, via Tauern Tunnel (209 miles)

For journey Innsbruck-Schwarzach, see R.2. At *Schwarzach St.* Veit the *Tauern* railway leaves the main line; it is a single track line and the only railway to cross the high Alps from N. to S. between the *Brenner Pass* and *Graz*. It climbs steeply and offers fine views, principally on the right-hand side.

13 miles *Bad Hofgastein* (2,800 ft.) fashionable resort and spa. 5 miles *Bad Gastein* (3,562 ft.) still larger and more fashionable (Y.H.); cable railway on to the *Stubnerkogel* (7,400 ft., magnificent views). 5 miles, *Böckstein* (3,700 ft.) a smaller and more modest resort, good centre for mountain tours.

EXCURSIONS: (a) on foot to *Nassfeld* (2 hrs., 5,240 ft.) a mountain and ski village in beautiful surroundings; electric underground railway to *Kolm-Saigurn* (see R.2, under *Taxenbach*). (b) ascent of the *Ankogel* (10,700 ft.).

The *Tauern Tunnel*, 5½ miles long, emerges in Carinthia at *Mallnitz* (3,887 ft.) a mountain resort enjoying increasing popularity. Fine situation and shares generally good weather of *Carinthia*.

EXCURSIONS: (a) via the *Hannoverhaus* (Alpine Club Hut) to the *Ankogel* (10,700 ft. or *Hochalmspitze* (11,000 ft.). (b) chair lift to *Hausleralm* (6,270 ft.).

The railway descends, offering further superb views, clinging to the side of the *Möll Valley*, through *Obervellach* (cable railway from station to village 1,155 ft. below). To **Spittal** (22 miles), (Y.H.), centre for *Millstätter Lake*. Buses to *Seeboden* and *Millstatt*, favourite summer resorts on beautiful warm lake.

R.4(i) From *Spittal* a branch line leads into East Tirol, an isolated, little known, but very attractive region, bordering on the Italian Dolomites. 21 miles *Greifenburg-Weissensee*, station for resorts on *Weissensee*, highest warm-water lake in Alps (3,050 ft., quiet and unsophisticated. 18 miles to *Lengberg*. 4 miles Lienz (2,200 ft.) (Y.H.) principal town of *E. Tirol*, pleasant, unspoilt and at junction of *Drau* and *Isel* valleys.

EXCURSIONS: (a) by bus to *Heiligenblut* (25 miles, 2 hrs.) (Y.H.) well-known mountain village at S. end of *Grossglockner Road* (continuation by bus over *Grossglockner* to *Zell-am-See*, see R.2(v)) with fine parish church, contains receptacle of the Holy Blood (whence the name *Heiligenblut*). (b) by bus to *Matrei-am-Venediger*, and *Hinterbichl* (4,300 ft.) highest point in *Virgental*, summer home of Vienna boys' choir, good centre for climbs in *S. Venediger Group*. (c) via *Huben* (13 miles) to the *Kalser* or *Defereggen Valleys* (bus services) offering fine views of *Glockner Group*. (d) up *Drau* valley 20 miles to *Sillian* (Y.H.) small climbing centre. (e) bathing at *Tristacher Lake* (2 miles).
From *Lienz*, railway continues via *San Candido* into Italy. Through trains run *Lienz-Brenner-Innsbruck*, across Italian territory (see R.1(xiv)).

Main railway continues from *Spittal*, 23 miles to **Villach** (1,670 ft.) (Y.H.) communications and trading centre, junction for railways to Yugoslavia and Italy.

EXCURSIONS: (a) *Villacher Alpe* (*Dobratsch*), 7,100 ft., 2½ hrs. walk, superb view. (b) by train or bus to the *Ossiacher See*, pleasant lake, 7 miles long, with numerous small resorts; less crowded and fashionable than *Wörther See*; cable railway from *Annenheim*, on *Ossiacher See* to *Kanzelhöhe* (4,900 ft.). (c) by rail up the *Gailtal* to *Hermagor* and *Koeschach*; isolated valley little known to foreign tourists. From *Hermagor*, ascent to the *Gartnerkofel* (7,200 ft.), the only place outside the Himalayas at which the blue flower,

Wulfenia, grows. (b) into the *Karawanken Mountains*, wild country skirting Yugoslav frontier; best centre is *Feistritz*, E. of *Rosenbach*. (e) by rail (8 miles, on line to *Rosenbach*) to *Faak* for delightful *Faaker See*, surrounded by forest.

From *Villach* 10 miles to *Velden*, expensive and fashionable resort on the warm *Wörthersee*. 5 miles *Pörtschach*, a similar resort, 9 miles *Klagenfurt* (Y.H.).

Klagenfurt, capital of *Carinthia*, attractive town but oppressive in summer. *Kartner Landesmuseum* (Carinthian Provincial Museum).

R.5. Klagenfurt—Semmering—Vienna (209 miles)

This is the southern, and longer, approach to *Vienna;* much fine mountain country en route, where few foreign tourists will be found. To left of railway lie the *Gurktaler Alps*, the *Lower Tauern*, and the *Styrian Limestone Alps*; to right are the *Seetaler Alps*, and the *Glein Alps*.

Klagenfurt to *St.-Veit-an-der-Glan* (11 miles), *Launsdorf* (5 miles).

EXCURSIONS: on foot in 1 hr. to *Hochosterwitz* Castle, magnificently situated on chalk spur, 2,400 ft. high; 16th century construction, contains weapons and armour.

10 miles *Treibach-Althofen*, junction for railway to *Gurk* (10 miles, fine 12th century cathedral). 9 miles to *Friesach*, 18 miles *Unzmarkt*, junction for railway to *Mauterndorf*.

R.5(i) From *Unzmarkt* to Mauterndorf by rail, 47 miles. This route follows the *Mur Valley* along S. slope of *Lower Tauern Mountains*. 17 miles, *Murau* (Y.H.), summer and winter resort. 14 miles *Preillitz* (bus to *Turracher Höhe*, 5,800 ft., steepest road in Austria, good winter sports centre) 10 miles, *Tamsweg* (3,349 ft.) good centre for the *Lurgau* (upper *Mur* valley). 7 miles, *Mauterndorf*, market town and resort. Railway ends here but road crosses *Radstädter Tauern Pass* (5,702 ft.) through *Obertauern* (5,400 ft., good ski centre) to *Radstadt* (see R.7).

12 miles *Judenburg*, 4 miles *Zeltweg*, junction for branch railway through *Lavant* valley (centre: *Wolfsberg*) to Yugoslav frontier. 20 miles *St. Michael*, junction for railway to *Selzthal* (see R.7) 4 miles *Leoben*, 13 miles *Bruck-an-der-Mur* (Y.H.); *Rathaus*, fine fountain (17th century) and Gothic *Kornmesserhaus* (early 16th century) with arcades. Junction for railway to *Graz*.

R.5(ii) *Bruck a.d. Mur* to Graz, 34 miles. Following the *Mur Valley* via Peggau (see the *Lurgrotte*, largest stalactite caves in Austria) to *Graz*, capital of *Styria*, second largest city in Austria; university, theatres, museums, etc. Although an industrial centre, it is attractively laid out, with plenty of open spaces. *Schlossberg* (Castle Mountain), 500 ft. high dominates city, fine view; on top is a 16th century clock-tower, with 7-ton bell (1587). Other sights: spiral staircase in castle (15th century), 13th century Madonna in *Leechkirche* (*Rittergasse*), altar piece in 15th century cathedral. (Y.H.).

From *Bruck*, main line, 18 miles *Krieglach*, 18 miles *Semmering* border between *Steiermark* (*Styria*) and *Lower Austria*. Tunnel, then train descends in spectacular curves, with many viaducts and tunnels to *Payerbach-Reichenau*, good approach to limestone alps to north, which are well worth a visit.

EXCURSIONS: (a) bus (6 km.) to *Hirschwang*, then by cable railway to edge of plateau (5,072 ft.), thence on foot to summit of Raxalpe, 6,029 ft., very fine views. (b) by bus to *Preiner Gscheid* (16 km.) then on foot in 3 hrs. to summit of *Raxalpe*.

Line continues over plain via *Neunkirchen* and *Wiener Neustadt* (Y.H.) to *Vienna*.

R.5(iii) *Wiener Neustadt* by branch line and cog railway (16 miles) to *Puchberg am Schneeberg* for Schneeberg (6,806 ft.) highest peak in *Lower Austria*; fine view; also rock walls *Hohe Wand* and *Dürre Wand*. On foot (13 miles) to *Pernitz* (Y.H.). Bus *Wiener Neustadt* or train *Vienna*.

R.6. The Salzkammergut

The *Salzkammergut* consists of two chains of lakes set among the lime-stone mountains N. of main line of the Alps. The eastern chain, along the River *Traun*, starts at S. end with two small and secluded lakes, the *Grundlsee* and the *Altausseer See* (both 2,300 ft.) and descends through the *Hallstätter See* (1,670 ft.) to the *Traun See* (or *Gmundner See*) (1,384 ft.).

The western chain consists of the *Wolfgang See* (1,770 ft.) which actually drains into the *Traun* via a tributary, the *Mond See* (1,580 ft.), and the *Atter* (or *Kammer*) *See* (1,530 ft.), both of which drain into the *Ager*.

The **Wolfgang See**, which has a beautiful setting, has acquired a world-wide reputation from the operetta "White Horse Inn" and is more crowded and expensive than the other lakes. Y.H. at *St. Gilgen*.

The **Hallstätter See**, less easy of access and quieter, is probably the most beautiful, being almost completely surrounded by lofty mountains which drop steeply nearly to the water's edge. Y.H. at *Hallstatt-Lahn*.

The **Atter See** is the largest mountain lake in Austria and the **Traun See** the second largest of the group, but the surroundings are less striking, although the *Traun See* reflects the peak of the *Traunstein* (5,580 ft.) on its eastern shore. Y.H.s at *Gmunden* and *Ebensee*.

The *Salzkammergut* has a somewhat higher rainfall than other parts of Austria but its great natural beauty outweighs this disadvantage.

There are three main mountain ranges in the area. The highest is the **Dachstein** group, to the S. of the *Hallstätter See*. The high *Dachstein* itself (9,800 ft.) can only be tackled by experienced climbers with a guide (9 hours from *Hallstatt*), but the **Dachstein caves** (4,400 ft.), huge chambers of bare rock, tunnels and ice caves, can be reached in 2½ hrs. by footpath from *Obertraun* (Y.H.) or by cable railway.

The second group is the **Totes Gebirge** ("Dead Mountains") to the N. of *Altaussee* and *Grundlsee*. Average heights 5-6,000 ft. forming a kind of high plateau, from the edges of which are very fine views. Vegetation is scanty, hence the name. Many mountain huts in this region and (Y.H.) at *Bad Aussee*, for approach by rail.

The third group is the **Höllengebirge** ("Mountains of Hell"), a small range between the *Atter See* and *Traun See*, approached from *Ebensee* (on the *Traun See*). Cable railway from *Ebensee* to the *Feuerkogel* (5,330 ft.).

Communications into the Salzkammergut are as follows:

R.6(i) By rail in 30 minutes from *Salzburg* to *Steindorf*, thence by bus through attractive scenery, to *Bad Ischl* (Y.H.) via *Mond See* (Y.H.) and *Wolfgang See*.

R.6(ii) Normal railway *Salzburg-Attnang-Bad Ischl* in 2½ hrs. via *Traun See*. This line continues via *Hallstätter See* to *Bad Aussee* (whence buses to *Altaussee* and *Grundlsee*). There are through trains *Salzburg-Bad Aussee*.

R.6(iii) Approach from the South by rail from *Stainach-Irdning* (on line *Bischofshofen-Selzthal*, see R.7) to *Bad Aussee*.

R.6(iv) Branch railways from *Vöcklabruck* or *Vöcklamarkt* (both on line *Salzburg-Attnang*) to stations on the *Atter See*

There are steamer and motor-boat services on all the lakes, and buses connect the majority of centres.

AUSTRIA

R.7. (Salzburg)—Bischofshofen—Selzthal—St. Michael—Vienna
(Bischofshofen—St. Michael 104 miles)

This is an alternative route to *Vienna*; although longer than the direct route via *Linz* (255 miles against 199) it passes through more attractive scenery. Diesel trains run from *Salzburg* to *St. Michael* and on via *Semmering* into *Vienna*.

From *Bischofshofen* (see **R.2**), the train climbs nearly 1,000 ft. in 15 miles to *Radstadt*, a village still surrounded by its wall, the junction for the road via the *Tauern Pass* into *Carinthia* (see **R.5(i)**).

12 miles, **Schladming** (2,427 ft.), excellent centre for mountain tours. **(Y.H.)**

EXCURSIONS: (a) *High Dachstein* (9,800 ft.) very rewarding, but only for good climbers, with guide. (b) *Ramsau*, a lovely mountain plateau, about 3,000 ft., 2 hrs. on foot. (c) *Hochgolling* (9,500 ft.), highest peak in *Lower Tauern*; very fine view; only with guide.

24 miles, *Stainach-Irdning*, (fine **Y.H.**, Schloss Trautenfels, in *Enns Valley*, 4 miles) junction for line to *Salzkammergut* (see **R.6(iii)**) 17 miles *Selzthal* (2,100 ft.), important railway junction, with connections to *Linz*, *Amstetten*, etc. Railway climbs to cross watershed between *Enns* and *Mur* valleys at *Schoben Pass* (2,790 ft.), with *Lower Tauern* range to S.W. and *Eisenerzen Alps* to N.E. It then descends to (39 miles) *St. Michael*, on main line *Klagenfurt-Vienna*. (For continuation of journey to *Vienna*, see **R.5**.)

Vienna

Vienna is quite different from the rest of Austria, a city with traditions of imperial grandeur, music, noble architecture and wealth. From 1945 to 1955 it was under four-power occupation but now the city has regained its poise and reputation as the capital of an independent Austria.

The old city is bounded on the N.E. by the *Danube Canal*, and surrounded on the remaining sides by the *Ring,* a vast boulevard, which changes its name from section to section (*Schubert Ring, Kärntner Ring, Opern Ring*, etc.); on either side of it are state buildings, theatres and museums, and beneath it is a fine shopping centre, nicknamed the *Jonas Grotto*. The modern industrial and shopping area, together with the railway terminals, lies further out, then the residential zone comes to the edge of the *Vienna Woods* on the N.W.

Central *Vienna* was badly damaged in the war, particularly along the *Danube Canal*, but its buildings and monuments have been meticulously restored and new amenities have been added.

The heart of the city is **St. Stephen's Cathedral** (*Stefansdom*) in *St. Stephen's Square*. It dates in part from the 13th century; the tower, which can be climbed to about 300 ft. (fine view) is early 14th century.

To the west, beyond *Graben* and *Kohlmarkt*, is the **Hofburg** (Imperial Palace); mixture of styles, dating from 1530 to the 19th century. The *Josefsplatz*, on the E. side, is particularly attractive.

AUSTRIA

Turn S.E. via *Stallburggasse* and *Plankengasse* into *Neuer Markt*, where there is a fine fountain, the *Donnerbrunnen* (early 18th century).

Cross *Kärntnerstrasse* into *Himmelpfortstrasse*; on right is former **Winter Palace of Prince Eugene**, magnificent baroque building begun by Fischer von Erlach the Elder in 1695.

Return to *Kärntnerstrasse*, turn left, walk to the **Ring**, turning right into the *Opern Ring*. The first building on the R. is the *State Opera*, repaired (1955) after severe war damage. Coming into *Burg Ring*, the *Hofburg* (W. front) is on right and the two museums of Natural History and Art History on left. Both have fine collections, particularly the Art Museum (16th and 17th century paintings, Egyptian, Greek and Roman antiquities). In the *Burg Ring*, Parliament House is on left, whilst in the *Karl Leuger Ring* the *Burg Theatre* is on right, with Town Hall (set back behind a park) and University on left. Most of these are of heavy 19th century design.

Other sights are (a) the **Belvedere**, a magnificent baroque palace (1700–23), with fine gardens, situated due S. of *Schubert Ring*. (b) former Imperial Palace of **Schönbrunn** (1694-1749) containing 1,400 rooms, with a superb park; on outskirts, S.W. from West Station. (c) the **Prater**, Vienna's "Hyde Park", with fun-fair attached, in S.E. of town near *Danube Canal*. (d) modern domestic architecture in various parts of town, e.g. large blocks of municipal flats on *Engels Platz* near *Malinowsky Bridge* (XXI district, N.E. of city), built 1930-33.

EXCURSIONS from Central Vienna: (a) **Grinzing**, the wine-growing village on the N. edge of the city; many taverns, known as *Heuriger*, where wine is drunk and music played by a *Schrammel* quartet (violins, guitar and accordion): when a tavern is selling *Heuriger* (i.e. new wine) a green wreath is hung over the door. (b) the *Kahlenberg* (1,590 ft.) and *Leopoldsberg* (1,390 ft.) two small peaks of the Vienna Woods, offering delightful views over the city and the Danube valley.

There are two Youth Hostels run by the municipality (a) former country house of *Pötzleinsdorf* (standing in a spacious park on N.W. outskirts of city); from *West Station* take tram No. 8 to *Währinger Strausse*, thence tram No. 41 to terminus at *Pötzleinsdorf*; from *South Station*, tram D (on Sundays tram 69) to *Schottenring*, then by tram 41 as above; (b) *"Hutteldorf-Hacking"*, *Schlossbergasse* 8 (*Hutteldorf Station* 1 km.).

The tram network is good and fares are cheap. Also a Metropolitan railway (semi-underground) forms a ring around city centre.

There are innumerable cafés and beer houses. A Viennese speciality is *Kaffee mit Schlag* (coffee with whipped cream). Beer is served in a *Seidel* (3/10 litre) or *Krügel* ($\frac{1}{2}$ litre).

27

AUSTRIA

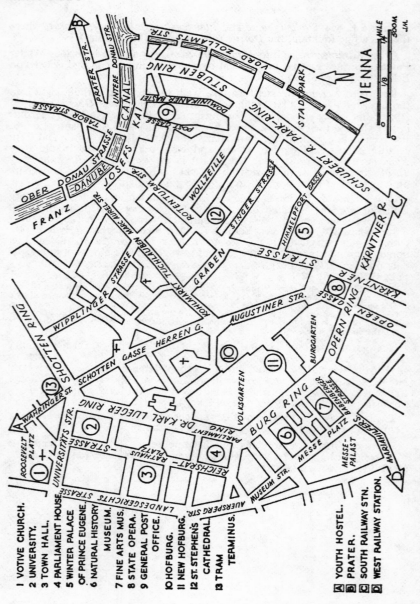

VIENNA

1 VOTIVE CHURCH.
2 UNIVERSITY.
3 TOWN HALL.
4 PARLIAMENT HOUSE.
5 WINTER PALACE
   OF PRINCE EUGENE.
6 NATURAL HISTORY
   MUSEUM.
7 FINE ARTS MUS.
8 STATE OPERA.
9 GENERAL POST
   OFFICE.
10 HOFBURG.
11 NEW HOFBURG.
12 ST. STEPHEN'S
   CATHEDRAL.
13 TRAM
   TERMINUS.

Ⓐ YOUTH HOSTEL.
Ⓑ PRATER.
Ⓒ SOUTH RAILWAY STN.
Ⓓ WEST RAILWAY STATION.

The monastery at Melk, in picturesque Lower Austria, is a short distance from Vienna.

BELGIUM

Geographical Outline

Land — Belgium is a compact country with an area of only 11,775 square miles. Its coastal provinces, *West* and *East Flanders*, comprise the fertile, historically tragic plain, fronted by a strip of reclaimed polder several miles wide which is protected from the sea by extensive sand dunes and dykes. The north-east extension of the plain, in the provinces of *Antwerp* and *Limbourg*, is known as the *Campine* and is an area largely consisting of heathland and bog. Southwards, between the rivers *Scheldt* and *Sambre*, and comprising the provinces of *Hainault* and *Brabant*, the land is a low plateau rising gently to about 600 ft. South again beyond the mineral-rich *Sambre-Meuse* region, lies the hilly, wooded country of the *Ardennes*, reaching over 2,000 ft. in the *Hautes Fagnes*.

Climate — The climate is similar to that of southern England, though a little colder in winter and warmer in summer. The average rainfall, rather less near the coast than in London, increases towards the south-east as the land rises. Fogs are frequent in the west.

Plants — About one-fifth of the country is wooded. Most of the woodland is mixed deciduous, except the pine woods in the *Campine* and spruce forests in the *Ardennes*. White poplar is common along the coast and hedgerows border fields and roads. Pig-wort, sea-lavender and juniper berry are found among the sand-dunes and the *Campine* is at its most attractive in late summer when the heather is in bloom.

The People

Population — With a population of nearly 10 million, the average density is 850 to the square mile, the second highest in Europe. This is not entirely attributable to the existence of many towns or to highly developed industry: some rural parts, particularly the plain of Flanders, are intensely cultivated and closely settled.

The people form two major groups of different ancestry. The Flemings of the north and west, slightly in the majority, are of the Salian Frankish (Germanic) stock which entered the country in the 4th and 5th centuries. The Walloons represent the older Celto-Roman peoples who were settled there before the Frankish invasions. Physical differences as between nordic and alpine types have been largely merged through centuries of mixing, but there remains a tendency for the Flemings to be taller and fairer.

Language — Language is today the chief distinction between the two groups. The Flemings speak Flemish (*Vlaamsch*, or, to give it the official name, *Nederlandsch*) which is nearly the same as Dutch. The Walloons speak French and their own three dialects of

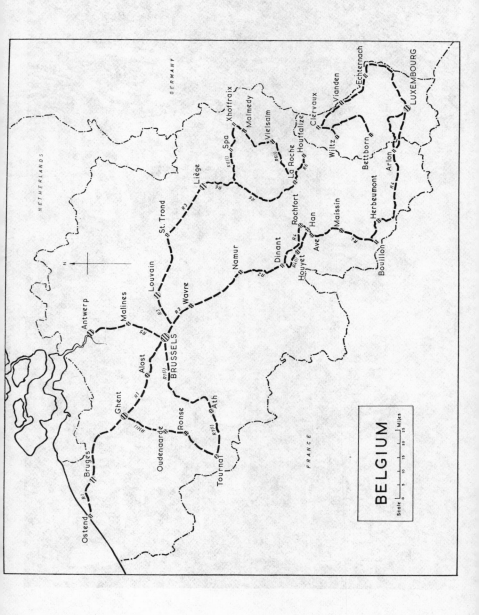

BELGIUM

Scale
0 5 10 15 20 25
Miles

Flower vendors at the famous Grand' Place in Brussels.

it. Both languages are official and of equal standing and such people as railway and post-office clerks, bank officials and tram-conductors are normally required to speak both. Many towns and villages, particularly in Flanders, have both a Flemish and a French version of their names. It is also quite common, near the border between Flanders and Wallonie, to see the street names in both languages.

A German-speaking minority of about 10,000 live in the *Eupen* and *Malmedy* area near the Eastern frontier.

Religion The overwhelming majority of the people belong to the Roman Catholic Church. Practising Catholics are more numerous among the Flemings and, generally, in rural areas rather than in the towns.

History The country enters history as the territory of the Belgae, the Celtic, Iron Age, tribes who gave Caesar so much trouble. After the collapse of Roman rule the Franks came in from the east and, a century later, their leader Clovis of *Tournai* led the further expansion which made them masters of what is now France. Under his dynasty and that of Charlemagne Belgium had no separate history but was a prosperous part of the Frankish kingdom. Flemish cloth was valued abroad until trade was brought to an end by the Viking raids. These, and the partitioning of the country at the death of Charlemagne, led to the rise of powerful local lords (e.g. the counts of Flanders) as each region sought security.

Trade and industry grew again from the 10th century, and with them a rich town life matched only in Italy. Two centuries of bustling individualism were marked by the rise of merchant classes, the winning of charter privileges by each town, and the growth of exclusive craft guilds. Rivalries and class war were intensely local.

Such vigorous independence contrasts sharply with what was to happen to these "southern Netherlands" during the next five centuries, during which authority was imposed from outside and they became caught up into the main stream of European affairs through dynastic marriages and alliances. Successively they became subject to the French crown (1226), to the dukes of Burgundy, and to the Spanish and Austrian Hapsburgs. Under the Burgundians, Philip the Bold and Philip the Good, in the 15th century, they were linked with the Dutch provinces to form a United Netherlands and in this form they passed by marriage into the fateful union with Spain. Being by far the best developed economically, the Belgian provinces benefited greatly from this association with a world empire: *Antwerp* in the 16th century, handling the products of the Spanish and Portuguese colonies, became the great centre of international trade, banking and exchange; and *Brussels* was the political capital of the emperor Charles V, who was a Belgian by birth.

In religious matters Charles' reign was less happy. The Reformation was put down only to revive in the reaction against his son, the unpopular Philip II of Armada fame. His bigotry, and the clumsiness of the governor, the duke of Alba, led to the famous revolt of the Netherlands, successful in the north but defeated in Belgium, by which the Dutch Republic became separated

BELGIUM

from modern Belgium in which Habsburg rule and the Catholic religion were re-established. The Dutch went forward to empire and prosperity. Belgium became, in the 17th and 18th centuries, a battleground of warring powers where Marlborough marched and Bourbons and Habsburgs contended.

A period of French rule, followed by a brief reunion with Holland (1815-30), led to a demand for independence. This was gained by the revolution of 1830 and the adoption of a liberal constitution and a guarantee of neutrality by the Powers. Belgium turned to the solution of internal problems—the "schools" question on religious instruction and the "language" question—and to development as a modern industrial state. But the two World wars again emphasised her strategic position and essentially international interests, as shown in her full participation in post-war economic and political regroupings in western Europe.

Government Belgium is governed by a parliamentary democracy under a limited monarchy. The Parliament has two houses—the Chamber of Representatives and the Senate. The people's representatives are elected every 4 years, both men and women of 21 years and over having the franchise.

Resources Belgium is very intensively cultivated, *Hainault, Brabant, Flanders* and the *Campine* being the main farming areas. Over 600,000 people are employed in agriculture. The soil—not naturally rich—is made to produce high yields per acre. For its size Belgium produces more grain than any other country in the world. Forestry is important in the *Ardennes*, but much timber is also imported.

Belgium's mineral supplies consist of coal, iron, copper, lead and zinc and the chief industry is mining. Heavy industry is concentrated around the coal mines, along the R. *Sambre*, and along the R. *Meuse* from *Namur* to *Liège*. *Charleroi* and *Liège* are particularly important for steel, iron and glass products and machinery of all kinds. *Liège* and nearby *Verviers* are centres of the woollen industry. Linen, cotton and silk goods are manufactured in *Antwerp* and *Ghent*. Other important products are lace (*Brussels, Malines, Bruges*), carpets (*Tournai*), beet-sugar (*Hainault*), and beer (*Louvain*). Fishing is relatively unimportant, the main fishing port being *Ostend*. In spite of an extensive international trade, Belgium has only a small merchant navy. The most important ports are *Antwerp* and *Ostend*. *Antwerp* is a world centre for the cutting of diamonds.

Customs Although the Belgians consist of two races, the Flemings and the Walloons, who each jealously guard their language and their customs, they are yet united as a nation and take great pride in their history and free institutions. The old costumes are no longer seen, but many festivals, parades and village fairs (*Kermesses*) are still kept up in all parts of the country. Of particular interest are: the Procession of the Penitents at *Furnes* (last Monday in July); its resemblance to Spanish ceremonies is a reminder of the Spanish rulers of the Low Countries; the colourful procession of the Holy Blood at *Bruges* (first Monday after May 2); the Carnival of *Binche*, three days of processions and festivities culminating with Shrove Tuesday; and the Trinity

Sunday celebrations at *Mons*, including a fight between St. George and the Dragon.

The playing of carillons originated in Belgium and hymn tunes are still commonly heard coming from the belfries of Belgian churches. Originally played on a keyboard, they are now often mechanically controlled.

Culture

Architecture At the beginning of the 11th century the first Romanesque architecture made its appearance in the church of *St. Jean* at *Liège;* this owes much to Rhenish influences; some of the original building is still in existence. This style, which is characterised by a large chancel, is found in many churches in *Limburg* and *Brabant.* The western part of the country, however, came under French influence during the Romanesque period. A wonderful example of this is *Tournai* cathedral, begun in 1110, which shows in the choir the transition from Romanesque to Gothic. The influence of this cathedral can be seen in buildings throughout *Flanders* and *Brabant.*

During the Gothic period, in the 13th century, there was little difference between the styles of the *Meuse* and the *Scheldt* regions. One of the best examples of this period is the church of *Notre Dame de Pamele* at *Oudenarde.* In *Brussels* a more florid style developed and examples of this can be found in churches in all parts of the country. Fine Gothic market halls and town halls are to be seen in many Belgian towns.

In the Gothic architecture of the 16th century, an Italian influence is apparent but in the following century a new trend began to appear and richer ornamentation was used. This was the Belgian Baroque period, examples of which may be seen not only in churches all over Belgium but in many town houses, particularly in *Antwerp, Ghent* and *Malines.* The *Grand Place* in *Brussels* consists, apart from the King's House and the Town Hall, entirely of Baroque buildings.

The 18th century produced a great deal of domestic architecture in the Louis XV and Louis XVI styles. In the 19th century styles were imitative and it was not until the end of the century that new life was infused into architecture with the appearance of the first buildings in modern style, designed by Victor Horta and Heinrik van de Velde. Much good work has been done since then and well-designed modern buildings of all kinds can be found in every Belgian town today.

Painting Painting is the characteristic art-form of Belgium, and of Flanders in particular. The first great name in Flemish art, Jan van Eyck, appeared in the early 15th century. His knowledge of perspective and capacity for precise and realistic details gave a lead to the Flemish School.

The early 16th century produced Pieter Breughel, a master of peasant portraiture, but his fame is outclassed by the great artist Pieter Paul Rubens (1577-1640) who showed in his work the influence both of his Flemish teacher and of the colour and beauty of the paintings of Italy, where he spent eight years of his life. Anthony van Dyck (1599-1641) came under the influence of Rubens, in whose studio he worked for several years; he is famous for his portraits, painted in mellow tones.

The two largest art collections in Belgium are in the museums of *Brussels* and *Antwerp*, where examples of the work of most of Belgium's painters may be seen.

Museums   The three principal museums of *Brussels* are the Museum of Antique Painting (for the study of the Flemish School), the Museum of Modern Painting, and the Royal Museums of Art and History. The most important museums of *Antwerp* are the Museum of Antiquities, Steen Maritime Museum, the Museum of Industrial and Decorative Arts, the Museum of Fine Arts and the Museum of Flemish Folklore.

Music   The Belgians are a musical nation; orchestral societies and choral societies flourish in all parts of the country. Musical education is provided in the Royal Conservatoires of *Brussels*, *Antwerp*, *Liège* and *Ghent*. Belgium has produced a great number of composers but the really outstanding one has been César Franck.

The principal opera houses are in *Brussels*, *Antwerp* and *Ghent*. In *Brussels* opera and ballet are produced at the *Théatre Royal de la Monnaie*, concerts and plays at the *Palais des Beaux Arts*, and plays at the *Théatre Royal du Parc*, and there are other theatres and concert halls. Foremost in *Antwerp* are the Royal Theatre (concerts) and the Flemish Opera House. There are theatres and concert halls in most of the larger towns.

Literature   Maeterlinck and Cammaerts and the historian Pirenne are writers best known in translation. Pirenne's works on the origins and sitings of towns will be of particular interest to historically-minded travellers.

Touring Information

Touring Areas   The most attractive scenery in Belgium, and the best walking country, is the hilly, wooded area of the *Ardennes*, where it is wild and practically untouched by industry or cultivation. There is some very pleasant, though flatter countryside, to the north-west of the *Ardennes*, and in the Flemish part of the country there is a wealth of architecturally interesting old towns. Along the sea coast the resorts are practically continuous; they have fine sandy beaches.

Access

The cheapest and best route to Belgium is by boat from Dover to *Ostend*, a 3½-hour crossing. In summer there are four services by day and one by night, with connecting boat trains from London and to *Brussels*. There are also special vehicle ferries, onto which cyclists can wheel their machines, which run from six to ten times daily in each direction. An air ferry, also for cyclists, is operated between Southend and *Ostend* by British Air Ferries, and British Airways provide direct flights between London and *Brussels*, with reduced fares for flights late in the evening or early in the morning. Fuller information about all means of travel to Belgium is given in the *Y.H.A. Continental Travel Key*.

Transport

Belgium is a small country with a dense railway network and an efficient service of trains, largely electrified. A season ticket for the whole network costs about 700 fr. for 5 days, 990 fr. for 10 days, 1,270 fr. for 15 days. Another season ticket for use on any 5 days in a 14 day period, valid from March to September, is also available. In addition to the state railways several tramways (*chemins de fer vicinaux*) link towns and villages (for example, *Ostend—Blankenberghe* and *Knokke*) and run the whole length of the coast. One class only, no return tickets, cheaper than rail for short journeys. There are also local trams in the large towns and a number of bus routes throughout the country.

A pleasure steamer operates between *Namur* and *Dinant* during the summer and there are boat trips from *Antwerp*.

Money

The unit of currency is the *franc*, divided into 100 centimes, but the smallest coin in general use is 20 *centimes*.

Food and Drink

The national beverages are coffee and beer. Breakfast usually consists of coffee, roll and butter, and jam. The main meal is at midday and supper is at about 7 in the evening. Coffee is often taken about 4 p.m. There is a high standard of cooking throughout the country and meals are ample. Cakes, pastries and coffee are served by many *patisseries*. There are no licensing hours but the sale of spirits is prohibited in restaurants and cafés. It is usual to give a 15% tip for meals or drinks, and a small tip of about 10% of the seat price should be given to the usherette in a cinema or theatre.

Holidays

Public holidays (on which Banks and most shops are closed) are: New Year's Day, Easter Monday, Ascension Day, Whit-Monday, National Festival (July 21), Assumption (Aug. 15), All Saints (November 1), Christmas Day. Banks are usually also closed between 12 noon and 2 p.m. on ordinary working days.

BELGIUM

Maps — The *Michelin* series of maps, scale 1:200,000 in two sheets, Nos. 2 and 4, are recommended for cyclists.
—————— A good general map is the *Geographia* map of Belgium and Luxembourg, scale 1:500,000.

Youth Hostels — There are two youth hostel associations in Belgium: the *Vlaamse Jeugdherbergcentrale* (V.J.H.C.) which operates in *Flanders*, and the *Centrale Wallonne* (C.W.A.J.) operating in the French-speaking area. The hostels of the former are large, highly organised and much frequented by schools and youth groups; the hostels of the C.W.A.J. are smaller and more informal, similar in some ways to those in France.

Touring Routes

R.1   Ostend—Brussels (75 miles)

Ostend, Belgium's main fishing port, popular holiday resort. Y.H. Take the road N.10 from the east side of the town, across a flat agricultural plain, dotted with houses and farms and intersected by canals and dykes.

About 15 miles from *Ostend*, medieval town of **Bruges** at junction of several canals. It has a great number of interesting buildings, notably the *Halles*, 13th century; the Town Hall (1376); the church of *Notre Dame* (*O.L. Vrouw Kerk*), mainly 13th and 14th century, containing Michelangelo's statue of "Virgin and Child" and some fine paintings; St. John's Hospital (founded 13th cent.); the Cathedral of *St. Sauveur* (*St. Salvator*), oldest brick church in Belgium partly 13th cent.; the famous *Belfry* with its fine view and the picturesque *Béguinage* (*Begynhof*) founded 13th cent. (Apart from two communities in Holland, the *Béguine* Sisters of Charity exist only in Belgium.) There are several museums containing fine works of art. Y.H. on *Baron Ruzette Laan*, *Assebroek* (S.E. suburb of *Bruges*).

Thirty miles from *Bruges*, where the *R. Lys* (*Leie*) flows into the *Scheldt*, stands the lovely town of **Ghent** on a number of islands formed by the arms of two rivers. Industrial and horticultural centre; second most important port with canal for ocean-going ships to *Scheldt* estuary; many 17th and 18th century houses in French style; many historic buildings; *St. Bavon's* Cathedral (Gothic, 12th century onwards); the Cloth Hall (*Halle aux Draps*) with fine 14th century belfry, 312 feet and affording wonderful view (lift); St. Nicholas Church (begun in 13th century); Town Hall, 16th century, part Gothic, part Renaissance; St. Michael's Church (begun 1440), the former Dominican Monastery; the Castle of the Counts of Flanders (*Château des Comtes*), parts of which date from 9th century; ruined Abbey of *St. Bavon*. Picturesque Y.H. in old Abbey of St. Peter (17th century) on *Sint Pietersplein*.

Alost, small town with large but unfinished 15th century Gothic church. *Hekelgem*, ruins of Abbey of *Affligem*; *Assche*, interesting Gothic Church. *Brussels* is entered from the north-west by the *Chaussée de Gand*.

Brussels

A city of modern buildings, wide avenues and many open spaces, though there are still numerous interesting old buildings. The main part of the city is a pentagon, bounded by wide boulevards; these are at their most attractive in May when the chestnut trees are in bloom.

South of the *Nord* railway station lies *Brussels'* "West End" (*Boulevard Adolphe Max, Place Brouckère* and *Rue Neuve*)—fashionable shops, cafés, restaurants. To the south-east of the *Bourse* and in the heart of the Old Town, with its narrow streets, lies the **Grand' Place**, a square bounded on one side by the Town Hall (*Hôtel de Ville*) and on the others by guild houses built in the Belgian Baroque style. The King's House (*Maison du Roi*) in late Gothic style, which has never in fact been occupied by the King and is now a museum, is also in this square. The **Town Hall,** dating from the 15th century, is one of the finest civic buildings in Gothic style in Belgium; certain rooms and the tower are open to visitors on week-days. A flower market is held in the *Grand' Place* once a week.

The *Rue de l'Etuve*, south of the Town Hall leads to the well-known fountain statuette of the *Manneken Pis*, a boy performing a natural function with no embarrassment. He has a selection of clothing to wear for festivals!

East of the *Grand' Place*, in the Upper Town, is the *Palais des Beaux Arts* (1928), with halls for concerts, art exhibitions and lectures. Nearby are the Museums of Modern Painting and of Antique Painting and Sculpture. At the far end of the *Rue de la Régence* is the *Palais de Justice* (Law Courts), a building larger than St. Peter's, Rome, built in Greco-Roman style towards the end of the last century.

The Royal Palace, rebuilt at the beginning of this century, stands at one end of the *Parc de Bruxelles*. At the other end, lies the *Palais de la Nation*, housing the Legislative Assembly. About 200 yards to the west is the *Cathedral of Sts. Michel and Gudule*, a lovely Gothic building, part of which dates from the 12th century; its façade has twin towers, a more common feature of French than of Belgian churches.

The King's Palace and Park of *Laeken* are closed to visitors; attractive public gardens adjoining. The favourite park of *Brussels* is the *Bois de la Cambre*, originally part of the Forest of *Soignes*, to the S.E. beyond the fashionable residential quarter of the *Avenue Louise*.

Brussels has two **Y.Hs.**—that of the C.W.A.J. in the *rue Verte* and of the V.J.H.C. in the *Poststraat* (both close to the North Station and the *rue Royale*).

BELGIUM

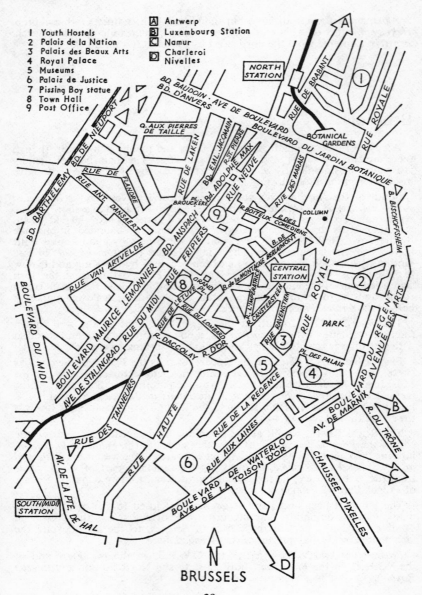

1 Youth Hostels
2 Palais de la Nation
3 Palais des Beaux Arts
4 Royal Palace
5 Museums
6 Palais de Justice
7 Pissing Boy statue
8 Town Hall
9 Post Office

Ⓐ Antwerp
Ⓑ Luxembourg Station
Ⓒ Namur
Ⓓ Charleroi
   Nivelles

NORTH STATION

BOTANICAL GARDENS

BD. BAUDOIN · AVE DE BOULEVARD
BD. D'ANVERS
BOULEVARD DU JARDIN BOTANIQUE
Q. AUX PIERRES DE TAILLE
RUE DE BRABANT
RUE ROYALE
B. BISCHOFSHEIM
BD. EML JACQMAIN
RUE DE LAKEN
R. ST. PIERRE
R. ADOLPHE MAX
RUE NEUVE
RUE DES MARAIS
PL. - Rd. DE BROUCKÈRE
RUE DE FLANDRE
BD. DE NIEUPORT
RUE DE
RUE ANT. DANSAERT
BD. BARTHELEMY
COLUMN
R. BOITEUX
R. DES COMEDIENS
R. DE L'IMPERATRICE
B. DE la MONTAGNE
R. CANSTERSTIEN
R. RAVENSTIEN
B. DE BERLAIMONT
CENTRAL STATION
RUE VAN ARTVELDE
BD. ANSPACH
FRIPIERS
GRAND PL.
R. DE l'ETUVE
RUE DU MIDI
RUE DU LOMBARD
R. D'OR
R. DACCOLAY
AVE DE STALINGRAD
BOULEVARD MAURICE LEMONNIER
BOULEVARD DU MIDI
PARK
RUE ROYALE
PL. DES PALAIS
RUE DE LA REGENCE
RUE AUX LAINES
RUE HAUTE
RUE DES TANNEURS
AV. DE LA PTE. DE HAL
SOUTH (MIDI) STATION
BOULEVARD DE WATERLOO
AVE. DE LA TOISON D'OR
CHAUSSEE D'IXELLES
AV. DE MARNIX
BOULEVARD DE MARNIX
AVENUE DES ARTS
AVENUE DU REGENT
R. DU TRÔNE

① ② ③ ④ ⑤ ⑥ ⑦ ⑧ ⑨

N

BRUSSELS

R.1(i) Detour from *Ghent* **via** *Tournai.* **Oudenarde,** 18 miles, splendid town hall (1535), flamboyant Gothic churches of *St. Walburga* and *Notre Dame,* 13th cent.; site of Marlborough's victory N. of town; *Ronse,* 7 miles (Y.H.) Roman crypt of *St. Hermes* church, walks on wooded hills of *Monts de Renaix:* Tournai. 15 miles, cathedral, romanesque and Gothic, finest church in Belgium; *Ath,* 17 miles, St. Julien's church, Gothic, town hall 17th cent.; *Geeraardsbergen,* 12 miles and *Ninove,* 8 miles industrial towns with character; *Brussels,* 15 miles.

R.2. Brussels to Namur (40 miles)

Highway N.4 leaves *Brussels* from south-east. Road passes through the Forest of *Soignes,* an area of woodland and lakes, 10,000 acres in extent. S.W. of forest, on road N.5, is site of battle of *Waterloo. Wavre* (15 miles), church of St. John the Baptist (15th century). Soon the gently undulating countryside gives way to a more hilly and picturesque landscape. *Gembloux,* remains of old ramparts; nearby fine *Corroy-le-Château.* Namur, in the valley, lies at the junction of the R. *Sambre* and R. *Meuse.* On a hill overlooking town stands the old citadel. Cathedral in classical style, begun 1751; cathedral of *Saint-Aubain*; museums; interesting houses and churches in older part of town. Y.H.

R.3. Brussels to Liège (62 miles)

Leave *Brussels* by *Avenue de Tervuren,* follow route N.3, through Forest of *Soignes,* along the valley of the *Voer.* Old church at *Bertem,* dating from 9th century, is an excellent example of Brabantine architecture.

Louvain on R. *Dyle,* former capital of *Brabant*; much damaged in both wars. Y.H. The magnificent 15th century Town Hall, flamboyant Gothic style, has scenes from the Old and New Testaments sculptured on the front. The *Halles,* lovely 14th and 15th century market-building, now houses the University and Library. The churches of *St. Quentin, St. Jacques* and *St. Pierre* are all historically interesting. *Abbey de Parc,* founded 1129, just south-east of the town, elaborate monastic buildings beautifully situated.

Tirlemont, small town, two churches dating from 13th century *Notre Dame du Lac* and *St. Germain.* Hakendover has been a centre for pilgrimages in January and on Easter Monday for more than 12 centuries. *St. Trond* is a district of cherry-orchards; *Béguinage* (frescoes and astronomical clock) and church of *St. Leonard.*

Liège important industrial town, at junction of R. *Ourthe* and R. *Meuse.* An excellent starting point for a tour of the *Ardennes,* following either the valley of the *Ourthe* or that of the R. *Amblève.* Cathedral of *St. Paul,* (begun 968); church of *St. Jacques,* outstanding example of flamboyant style; *Palais de Justice* (16th century and later): *Maison Curtius,* fine example of renaissance mansion, now Archaeological Museum.

Museum of Walloon Life; D' Assembourg Museum, rich 18th cent. interiors; *Museum of Fine Arts* (Belgian masters). Panorama of town and confluence of rivers from *Citadel.*

R.4. Namur to Luxembourg via Dinant (146 miles)

The most interesting route, well worth the extra miles, follows the *Meuse* as far as *Dinant.* The N.47 road on the eastern bank is more picturesque. Leave *Namur* by the suburb of *Jambes,* follow the narrow river valley past

BELGIUM

the little village of *Dave*, with its château. There are steep rocky sides to the valley and particularly striking are the *Frênes Rocks*, towering over the river at *Lustin* (grottoes).

Houx, ruins of *Château de Poilvache* (11th century). Just past *Houx* a ruined tower marks the site of former Abbey of the *Gérousarts*.

19 miles from *Namur*, at the foot of rocky heights, lies small holiday resort of **Dinant**; Church of *Notre Dame* and *St. Perpéte* (parts from 12th century). Good view from *Montfort* Tower, reconstruction of 14th century tower, on hill behind town; Grottoes of *Mont Fat* and *Rampeine*; town dominated by the *Citadel*, early 19th century.

Leave *Dinant* by N.47; about 1 mile branch left by N.48. About 15 miles from *Dinant*, fork left to little town of *Ciergnon*, on R. *Lesse* (royal château). At *Rochefort*, small grotto, right turn is taken to **Han (Y.H.)**, where the famed grotto should not be missed. It is 10,000 ft. long and, as the visit takes 3 hours in a fairly cool temperature, it is advisable to take some warmer clothing. Particularly wonderful is a huge cavern 500 by 465 ft., known as the *Salle du Dome*, on two levels; in the lower one is a small lake formed by the R. *Lesse*. The visit ends with a boat trip along the *Lesse*, flowing underground through lovely grottoes and labyrinths.

R.4(i). Footpath route Anseremme to Han. A recommended alternative route to Han for walkers is along a path of the *Touring Club de Belgique*, which follows the R. *Lesse* from *Anseremme* (southern outskirts of *Dinant*). Two miles along the path, the striking *Château de Walzin* is reached, a fortified manor-house perched on the edge of a rock which drops sheer to the river. A little farther on are the ruined tower of *Caverenne*, also built on a rock, and the 150 ft. high rock formation of *Chaleux*, known as "The Candle". The *Château de Vêve* is also passed and the tower of the *Château d'Ardenne*, standing in a large park, can be seen. About 10 miles from *Anseremme*, the pleasant little village of *Houyet* stands on the bank of the R. *Lesse* where it is joined by the R. *Hilan*. At *Houyet* the road to Han can be rejoined or the path can be followed for the remaining 15 miles.

From *Han*, via *Ave*, *Maissin* and *Paliseul* cross the *Ardennes* to the picturesque valley of the R. *Semois*. **Bouillon (Y.H.)** stands at the bend of the river, beneath rocky heights topped by an interesting ruined castle. The attractive twisting course of the river below *Bouillon* repays exploration, especially on foot.

Returning to *Sensenruth*, road to right should be taken, leading along *Semois* Valley to *Herbeumont* (Y.H.), at foot of wooded hill with ruined 12th century fortress. The river valley can be followed almost to *Florenville*, small market town, thence road N.50 to Abbey of *Orval*, where a new abbey has been built beside 12th and 13th century ruins of the original building. The road through *Etalle* leads to *Arlon* and *Luxembourg*.

R.5   Brussels—Antwerp—Dutch border (48 miles)

Leave *Brussels* by *Chaussée de Vilvoorde* following road N.1. *Vilvoorde*, church of *Notre Dame* (partly 14th century).

Halfway between *Brussels* and *Antwerp* lies the interesting old town of **Malines**, seat of the primate of Belgium. Cathedral of *St. Rombaut*, one of the finest examples of Gothic architecture in Flanders, has a 320 ft. tower, with a peal of 49 bells. Interesting buildings include: Town Hall (begun 1320); Baroque church of the *Grand Béguinage*, 15th century; church of *Sts. Jean-*

Baptiste et l'Evangéliste; *Notre Dame au delà de la Dyle* (Gothic); *Porte de Bruxelles* (medieval city gate); *Palais de Justice* (Gothic and Renaissance); the restored 16th century Hotel of the *Canon Busleyden* (now a museum) and many lovely old houses. **Y.H.** at *Hofstade*, 2½ miles S.E.

Antwerp

Main port and second largest town of Belgium; many interesting old buildings, the capital of Flemish culture and art. Although 55 miles from the sea, on R. *Scheldt*, it is one of the chief ports of the Continent. City Tourist Office at *6 Pelikaanstraat*, near Central Station.

A little farther on, in *Rubensstraat*, is the *House of Rubens*, a 17th century mansion, in which may be seen many of the master's original paintings. Reduced charge for hostellers. Returning to the *Meir*, the Royal Palace (Rococo, dating from 1745) is a few yards along on the left. Westward stands a 26 floor skyscraper, the highest dwelling-block in Europe, from the top of which is a fine view of the city. At the far end of the *Groenplaats*, a tree-planted square, is *Cathedral of Notre Dame*, one of the finest Gothic churches in Belgium, 14th-17th century, with Rubens paintings. Just beyond, in the *Grote Markt*, is 16th century *Town Hall*. *Plantin Museum*, workshop of 16th

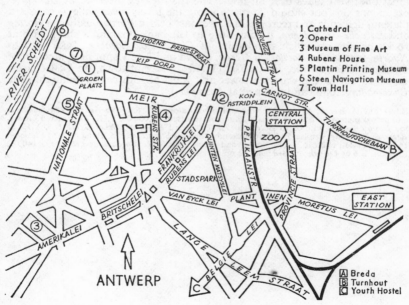

1 Cathedral
2 Opera
3 Museum of Fine Art
4 Rubens House
5 Plantin Printing Museum
6 Steen Navigation Museum
7 Town Hall

Ⓐ Breda
Ⓑ Turnhout
Ⓒ Youth Hostel

ANTWERP

century printer, and *Steen Maritime Museum,* in castle (most frequented museum in Belgium) are both nearby. **Y.H.**

Highway N.1 continues from the north side of *Antwerp,* reaching the Dutch frontier after 17 miles and continuing to *Breda.*

EXCURSIONS from *Antwerp:* (a) to *Lierre,* 9 miles S.E., quiet town on R. *Nèthe* with fine Gothic cathedral, *St. Gommaire.* Y.H. at *Nijlen,* 5 miles E. with woodland, heath and riverside walks. (b) to *St. Niklaas,* 13 miles, industrial and commercial centre of *Waas* district, the "garden of Belgium", fine market place; museum has unique Mercator collection including his original globe (his birthplace was *Rupelmonde,* 8 miles S.E. where there is his statue).

R.6   Liège to Houffalize (66 miles)

This route leads up the winding valley of the R. *Ourthe.* Leave *Liège* by highway N.31; just outside town N.34 branches off to the right across R. *Ourthe.* This road is taken, passing the industrial town of *Angleur* on right, soon after which the *Château de Colonstère* can be seen high up on right and, on the other bank of the river, the *Château de Sainval.* 7 miles from *Liège,* is *Tilff* (**Y.H.**), small village with interesting grotto. At *Poulseur* the old keep stands on a hill on one side of the river, with the ruined *Château de Montfort* opposite. Where the *Ambléve* flows into the *Ourthe* lie ruins of *Château d'Ambléve.* At *Comblain-au-Pont* are interesting grottoes in the limestone; visit takes over an hour. The road leaves the river at *Hamoir*—excursions on foot should be made along the lovely river valley—crosses a plateau, descends and recrosses the river just before *Durbuy.* Between *Hotton* and *Laroche-en-Ardenne,* it runs close to left bank, making a sharp turn at rocky heights on which stand ruins of *Château de Laroche.* Take road to *Nadrin,* for visit to *Rocher du Hérou,* a wild and lovely spot near junction of East and West *Ourthe. Houffalize,* (**Y.H.**) a pleasant town, on East *Ourthe,* damaged during the war; see tower and walls of 13th century church. (The *Luxembourg* road can be joined at *Bastogne.*)

R.6(i) The Ardennes. From *Comblain-au-Pont* E. along R. *Salm* to *Sougné-Remouchamps* and across plateau to *Spa,* 15 miles, fashionable resort, alt. 1,000 ft., Y.H.; *Xhoffraix,* 13 miles, for *Hautes Fagnes,* climbs to *Botrange* (2,277 ft.) and *Baraque Michel* (2,215 ft.), Y.H. at *Bévercé; Malmédy,* 9 miles, Folklore Museum; then via *Stavelot* and S. along river to *Vielsalm,* 15 miles, (Y.H., château, arboretum); road across hills S.W. (*Baraque de Fraiture,* 2,140 ft.) to rejoin R.6 at *Laroche-en-Ardenne,* 23 miles.

Antwerp, with the 14th-century gothic Cathedral of Our Lady in the foreground.

DENMARK

DENMARK
Geographical Outline

Land Denmark, with an area of 16,575 square miles, is just over half the size of Scotland. Its coast line is over 4,600 miles long and though the country is low-lying, nowhere higher than 570 feet, it is hardly flat. Scenery is mostly gentle, a green and homely landscape with many small lakes and fiords, no place far from the sea.

The peninsula of Jutland (*Jylland*), lying northwards from Germany, occupies about three-quarters of the total area. The remainder is made up of about 500 islands of which about 100 are inhabited. The most important are Zealand (*Sjælland*) on which stands Copenhagen (*København*), separated from South Sweden on the east by the narrow Sound, and Funen (*Fyn*) which lies between Jutland and Zealand, separated from these two by the Little Belt (*Lille Bælt*) and by the Big Belt (*Store Bælt*) respectively. Other larger islands to the south of Zealand are *Lolland* and *Falster*.

The Faeroe (*Færø*) Islands, lying between Scotland and Iceland, are a dependency of Denmark with home rule.

Bornholm in the Baltic Sea south-east of Sweden, and eight hours by steamer from *Copenhagen,* belongs to Denmark, but has scenery of granite, rugged cliffs and ravines, although the highest point is no more than 530 feet.

Difficulties of transport are considerable, but these have been overcome by an extensive system of state-owned and private ferries, as well as by the construction of bridges, masterpieces of engineering skill. The dispersed nature of the country allows of the continued existence of numbers of picturesque country and seaside villages where "time seems to stand still".

Climate The maritime climate is tempered by cold winters; January and February mean temperatures are at freezing point and the months between October and April are mostly dull and grey. The prevailing winds are westerly, and there is always a breeze. Annual rainfall averages 24 inches with least in spring and heaviest in late summer and autumn. The best holiday season is probably from May to September, with July the warmest month. Spring comes in mid April to early May with the beech trees breaking into leaf. Townspeople make excursions to the woods and bring home armfuls of the fresh green twigs for decoration in the home to symbolise the end of winter and the return of spring.

Plants and Animals Woodland occupies about a tenth of the land area, the most important trees being beech and Norway spruce. The beech forests are famous for their beauty and are the subject of many Danish poems and songs; the trees in the Deer Forest (*Dyrehaven*), north of *Copenhagen,* attain enormous size. Oak occurs in plenty but elm is comparatively rare. The largest forest is Rold near *Ålborg.*

45

There are about 90 youth hostels throughout Denmark. Above is the modern hostel at Copenhagen-Bronshoj.

Others occur near *Silkeborg* in Jutland, *Grib Skov* and *Dyrehaven* in North Zealand and *Almindingen* on *Bornholm*. Juniper flourishes on the chalky hillsides of the island of *Møn* off South Zealand.

In west Jutland there are extensive heather-clad hills and heaths and much of the country between *Esbjerg* and the frontier with Germany is marshland, drained by canals. The district of *Vendsyssel* north of the *Limfjord* in north Jutland is largely made up of sandhills. Much land has been reclaimed but there are considerable areas of drifting sand in which mare's-tail grass and gorse alone seem to flourish. The sand drifts over roads and paths, and at *Skagen* a church has been buried, leaving only the tower exposed.

The stork is the bird which most interests visitors, and it is held in the same esteem by the Danes as by the Dutch. The marshlands of Jutland are its especial haunt and cartwheel structures are placed on the tops of houses to encourage it to nest there. At *Ribe*, known as the town of the storks, nests may be seen within a stone's throw of the cathedral.

The People

Population   Denmark, with a population of nearly five million and average density of 40 to the square mile, is by far the most densely populated of the Scandinavian countries. Rather more than one and a quarter million people live in Copenhagen; more than half the population live in towns.

Language   The Danish language is related to Swedish, Norwegian and Icelandic, together with some affinities with English, Dutch and German. The Danes have three letters in their alphabet which are not found in English—å (sometimes written aa) pronounced like "or"; æ pronounced like "air"; and ø pronounced like "er"; these letters are placed at the end of alphabetical lists.

Religion   The Danish Lutheran Protestant Church is the State Church and the country is almost entirely Protestant.

History   Behind today's uneventfully democratic prosperity lies a long and complex story of national struggle. Strategically well placed but with few natural resources, the Danes from the 9th to the 12th century sought by conquest an outlet for their growing population. As Vikings ("sea-rovers") they, with the other Scandinavians, were feared from Russia to England and from northern France to Sicily. But, starting as mere raiders, they developed gifts as creators and rulers of states. They founded Normandy, and their descendants, in 1066, achieved the Norman conquest of England. Earlier, Canute's empire had comprised Denmark, England and Norway—the first of many unions in which Denmark was involved.

DENMARK

From the 12th century, when Absalon, the statesman-bishop of *Roskilde*, founded *Copenhagen* as one of several fortresses to defend the coast, the struggle for overlordship of the Baltic lands is a recurring theme in Danish history. Holding *Scania* (Skåne, now part of Sweden) Denmark commanded both sides of the Sound and all the channels at the outlet of the Baltic. The Sound dues which she was able to exact from shipping were a source of revenue but an irritation to other states and to the Hanseatic League, the great trading corporation of eighty towns.

The Union of *Kalmar* (1397), an alliance under one king of the crowns of Denmark, Norway and Sweden, in which Denmark was the dominant partner, was an attempt to counter the growth of German power. The link with Norway lasted for four centuries, but Sweden, more naturally a rival for power in the Baltic than an ally, seceded in 1448. Thereafter until 1720 the two countries were frequently at war, whilst other powers helped or hindered one side or the other to ensure that neither secured dominance in the Baltic. Denmark's strategic position made her at first the strongest of the Scandinavian states. But with the growth of powers with greater natural resources she was forced to give up her ambitions in the eastern Baltic and in Germany. Even Bornholm was lost, but was later recovered. *Skåne*, also, changed hands more than once and was finally lost in 1720.

Meanwhile, internal changes were marked by the acceptance of Luther's reformation in 1536 and by the constitutional revolution of 1660 in which the Kongelov (Royal Law), drawn up in secret, made the king for a century and a half the most absolute sovereign in Europe. Under this rule commerce expanded and the arts and sciences flourished, but the state of agriculture and of the peasantry pointed to the need for reform. This came in 1786 through a group of able ministers and liberal landowners, led by Bernstorff and Count Reventlow, who were determined to change the Danish countryside. In a few years the economic and social system based on feudalism was broken up; the serfs became freemen practising advanced farming; education became widespread. The pattern of modern Denmark was created.

The 19th century brought travail in foreign affairs but further progress at home. In 1807 England, seeking to forestall Napoleon, seized the Danish fleet by the bombardment of Copenhagen. Norway was lost in 1814. The long-unsettled question of Schleswig-Holstein led to wars in 1848 and 1864 and the loss of these territories to Prussia and Austria. Not until the plebiscite of 1920 was the northern (Danish speaking) half of Schleswig returned.

Denmark was overrun by the Germans in 1940 but the Danes maintained active resistance throughout the 5 years of occupation. Margrethe II, who, as Princess Margrethe, married a French commoner, became sovereign in 1972.

Government Since 1849 Denmark has been a parliamentary democracy under a limited monarchy.

The Parliament (*Folketinget*) consists of 179 members. The principal political parties are the Conservative, the Social Democratic, the Liberal (which looks after the farmers' interests) and the Radical (supported largely by the smallholders).

Women were given the vote in 1915 and all citizens over 20 are now enfranchised.

Resources

Denmark is primarily an agricultural country; 23 per cent of the population are engaged in farming. The only other group which exceeds or even approaches this is that of handicraft and industry, comprising 27 per cent of the people, but many of the industries, such as dairy machinery and canned goods, are dependent on the farming community. Other products are artistic porcelain, fine silverware, diesel engines, ships, and chemicals, some of which have a world-wide reputation.

Denmark has little mineral wealth. On *Bornholm*, clay for porcelain and earthenware manufacture is worked extensively and granite is quarried. Several of Copenhagen's most important buildings are of *Bornholm* granite. Brown coal is extensively dug for home consumption west of *Vejle* in east Jutland.

Prosperity in farming determines the well-being of the Danish state. The "Society for Reclaiming the Moors" was founded in 1866, following the loss of Schleswig-Holstein to Germany, and over the years has been the means of rendering fertile more than 2,000 square miles of moorland, sand and bog. Modern Danish agriculture dates from the 1870's, and now consists of over 200,000 farms, of which only a little over 2 per cent are greater than 150 acres, and about 65 per cent less than 13½ acres. More important than land reclamation have been the developments in scientific method and co-operative farming. In the 1870s as a result of United States competition, the Danish farmers, who had been primarily wheat growers, changed to the production of bacon and butter for export. The State in recent years has assisted by the compulsory parcelling out of the large estates and by loans to help in the establishment of smallholdings.

Co-operation and adult education have also helped tremendously in the success of Danish farming. Co-operative enterprises, started by the farmers themselves, cover every branch of farming—purchasing, breeding, production and marketing.

Folk High Schools

The People's High Schools, the idea of which was due to Grundtvig (1783-1872), have produced an educated rural population ready to appreciate the advantages of co-operation. They have played such an important part in the development of modern Denmark that brief mention of their aim and organisation is essential. Grundtvig held that people are not most receptive to education in their middle 'teens. The following years, when young people have begun seriously to face life's problems are, however, of the greatest importance for the whole of life. He had the idea of a school of young adults in which people from different parts and of different social status could meet together. The subjects taught should be civics, natural history, the history of Denmark, world history and other cultural matters. The idea was further developed by Christen Kold (1816-1870), a schoolmaster with a high sense of vocation. Scholars and teachers worked and lived together. Schools were held for young men from November to March when they could best be spared from the farm, and for young women from May to July. The general pattern has been maintained with about 10,000 students annually, representing about

DENMARK

one third of the age group concerned. The schools are generally privately owned, but supported by the state, both directly and by grants to students. Attendance is voluntary and there are no examinations. The young people trained in these schools form a valuable link in society, tending to acquire broader sympathies than others of their occupation or profession.

Customs

The whole-heartedness and seriousness with which the business of the day is conducted is impressive. Out of business the Dane plays hard and all the larger towns are well provided with sports centres (*Idrætsparker*) which include football pitches, tennis courts, running and cycling tracks and swimming baths. Yachting, rowing, swimming and all water sports are pursued with enthusiasm. Almost all organised sport in Denmark is amateur, even football, the most popular. At week-ends there is a large exodus from the towns to the shore, the woods and countryside. Many families have comfortable garden huts on allotments near the towns.

Visitors will be impressed by the flying of the national flag on every possible occasion; by the telephone habit; and by the crush of cycles on the streets. Danes are widely read, great readers of newspapers and well-informed in world affairs. Most of the young people from secondary schools have more than a working knowledge of four languages besides their own—English, German, French and Swedish.

Danish people are open minded and uninhibited; they have no censorship or licensing restrictions, their individual freedom is everywhere apparent, so is their high standard of living and their patriotism. Members of the Royal Family mingle unaccompanied with the people in the streets and there is not the cleavage between the classes of society which is met in some other lands. Denmark is said to be a land where few have too much and fewer have too little. The social services are world famous.

Danes are extremely polite; men raise their hats to each other and shake hands much more than in England and the use of titles in address is customary, a man being spoken of as "Hr. Stationmaster" or "Hr. Policeman".

Food and Drink

A choice of farm produce goes to make up the lavish menu in restaurants, but Danish families at home do not eat so extravagantly; prices are high and most foods are not subsidised.

The conventional breakfast, *morgen còmplet*, consists of egg, bread and butter and coffee. If you do not like the brown rye bread (*rugbrød*) which is thought by some to taste bitter, ask for sifted rye bread (*sigtebrød*) or white bread (*franskbrød*). *Morgen complet* costs about 7 kr. Lunch (*frokost*) consists usually of open sandwiches (*smørrebrød*) made of many varieties of fish, shrimp, chicken, ham, pork, egg, cheese, eel and sausage, and combinations of these. Four or five *smørrebrød* will make a substantial meal and with milk, coffee or a mineral water cost about 10 kr. The principal meal of the day is dinner (*middag*) in the early evening and consists of soup, fish or meat course and a light sweet resembling a cake, or a cornflour mould with fruit juice and cream (*rødgrød med fløde*) at a cost of about 12 kr.

Coffee (*kaffe*) is the Danish national drink but the quality is variable. Milk (*mælk*) is drunk extensively, and is cheap and good. The orangeade (*appelsinvand*), the non-alcoholic cider (*æblemost*) and the temperance beer (*dobbeltøl*) are delicious. The Danes themselves are great beer drinkers and favour lager of dark colour, such as Tuborg or Carlsberg. *Aqua vitae* is the Danish national drink, traditionally drunk at the beginning of a meal; a potent spirit, to be taken, if at all, with discretion.

Delightful features of *Copenhagen* restaurant life in summer are the little tables on the footpath under bright-coloured awnings, giving the city quite a southern Continental touch.

The Danes are most hospitable, and you may be invited home for coffee or even to dinner. A pleasant Danish custom is to toast one's host, hostess and fellow guests by raising one's glass, looking at the person to be toasted, who will do the same when one says "*skål*".

Culture

Architecture   Brick, tiles, lime and timber are the traditional building materials. In earlier times the surface clays, red from the atmospheric oxidation of the contained iron, were used to make bricks which fired to a pleasing red shade. Of recent years the deeper clays have had to be quarried and these, being less oxidised, fire to a less attractive pale yellow. The earliest houses were built of peat and clay and roofed with straw bound with seaweed or heather. They consisted of one long block—the same hipped roof covering both the farmer and his cattle. Such houses, now brick walled, may be found in western Jutland today. The conventional plan for the Danish farm of medieval times is, however, four-winged round a central yard or *gård*, the construction being half-timbered with a filling of brick. Similarly the churches were built of brick, with flints and granite incorporated in the outer walls. The interiors were often finished with plaster made from local lime, forming a suitable base for mural painting and design. The charm of the Danish country town or village today lies in its half-timbered houses, cobbled passages and flower-decked courtyards.

Copenhagen has suffered seriously from bombardment and fires, but the centre of the city still retains its high, steep-roofed half-timbered centuries-old houses and its narrow streets. In particular, Christian IV (1588-1648) has left some outstanding architectural gems—*Rosenborg Castle*, the Bourse and the Round Tower in *Copenhagen* and *Frederiksborg Castle* at *Hillerød* in north Zealand.

Outstanding examples of modern architecture in *Copenhagen* are Grundt-vig's Memorial Church, the Radio House, the Aquarium and the new Police Station; the Town Hall and the assembly hall of the new university at *Århus*

DENMARK

and the large dance hall and restaurant Kilden at *Ålborg*. Such examples of recent Danish architecture may make occasion for comment, but the work of Danish architects is internationally famous; their high standards may be explained by there being relatively more architects to inhabitants in Denmark than in any other country.

Most families in *Copenhagen* live in flats, heated by central heating or closed stoves. The individual flats have their own sun balconies, so built as to ensure privacy, and there are communal laundries, children's playgrounds and Kindergarten schools to serve the hundreds of families sometimes housed in one block.

Painting and Sculpture There were local craftsmen in Denmark in medieval times, as shown by the mural paintings and wrought ironwork in many churches, but the larger works of art of this period, such as the altar pieces in *St. Knud's* church at *Odense* and in *Roskilde* cathedral, are almost invariably the work of foreign artists. Denmark's best known artist is Thorvaldsen (1770-1844), the poor boy who became Europe's most famous sculptor. A whole museum is devoted to his works. Its painters have been largely inspired by the countryside—the peasant farms, the Jutland heathlands and, particularly of recent years, the sand dunes and the beaches at the Skaw.

Design Denmark is world famous for its industrial art; the Royal Copenhagen porcelain and the porcelain of Bing and Grøndahl, with the silverwork of Georg Jensen.

Museums The following museums are of special merit and peculiar to the country. *Rosenborg Castle* in *Copenhagen* (1608-17) was built by Christian IV in the Dutch Renaissance Style, in the *Kongens Have* (the Royal Gardens) off *Gothersgade*. It was used as a royal residence during the 17th and 18th centuries. It has been the custom of each king to add a portion of his treasures in furniture, jewellery, porcelain, etc., to the collection in the castle to illustrate the art of his period. The royal and crown jewels are also housed there.

The National Museum is housed in *Prinsens* Palace at the back of *Christiansborg* the Parliament House. The collections are rich, particularly those of the stone, bronze and iron ages, of Viking times, of coins and medals and of Eskimo ethnography. The collections at *Frederiksborg* Castle, *Hillerød*, and *Kronborg* Castle, *Elsinore*, are also part of the National Museum.

In *Charlottenlund*, about 3 miles north of the city centre by electric train, is the Danish Aquarium—one of the most modern and delightful aquaria in the world in which both salt and fresh water fish can be seen in huge tanks under conditions simulating their natural habitat.

The open-air museum at *Sorgenfri* (outskirts of *Copenhagen*) is a collection of farm and peasant houses from Denmark and South Sweden, furnished according to period and distributed over a considerable area. There is a similar museum in the town park at *Århus* (see under R.7).

Literature Denmark has an extensive and distinctive literature, but perhaps only two writers have attained world fame—and in strikingly dissimilar fields. Hans Andersen's fairy tales are loved by children and parents in many lands, and Denmark shows its pride in him in many ways. His contemporary, Kierkegaard (1813-55), was a profound thinker, originator among other things of the philosophy of existentialism. Among other writers whose works can be read in English the realist critic Brandes (1842-1927) has a more than national reputation.

Science The astronomer Tycho Brahe (1546-1601) enjoyed the patronage of Frederick II who built an observatory for him on an island in the Sound. His systematic work set a new standard of accuracy in observation and did much to confirm the Copernican theory of the universe. Another early scientist was Niels Stensen (1638-86), famous as an anatomist for his study of glands and of muscular contraction, and also as a geologist, being the first to appreciate the true origin of fossils.

Niels Bohr (1885-1962), the physicist, is known for his work on atomic structure and for his development of Planck's quantum theory. He was awarded a Nobel Prize in 1922.

Touring Information

Touring Areas Denmark can be conveniently divided into three parts for purposes of tourist travel.

The peninsula of **Jutland,** which consists of an extensive tract of marshland, heath and sand-dunes in the west, and of low hills and valleys in the east, with a coastline of picturesque fjords. The towns and places of interest are relatively widely separated and *Jutland* can well be regarded as a separate region. Excellent beaches occur on the west coast from *Blåvandshuk* to *Skagen* and on the islands of *Rømø* and *Fanø*.

Zealand and the islands constitute a convenient unit. Most of Denmark's tourist attractions are on *Zealand*, a country of pastoral beauty, of delightful beech woods and of large lakes and meres. *Copenhagen* and the other towns of *Zealand* teem with historical associations.

Bornholm lies in the Baltic, seven to eight hours sail from *Copenhagen*. All that is best in Denmark is to be found there in miniature and, at least, a long week-end should be spent there.

If only one holiday can be spent in Denmark and time is limited, a desirable circuit is across southern *Jutland*, through *Funen* to *Zealand* by the Little Belt Bridge and the Big Belt Ferry, and back either by ferry from *Kalundborg* in Zealand to *Århus* on *Jutland*, a 5-hour sail, or again over the Big Belt Ferry, well worth doing twice, through south *Funen* and over the ferry from *Fåborg* in *Funen* to *Mommark* and *Jutland*.

DENMARK

Access ———————— The best route from England is by ferry directly across the North Sea from Harwich to *Esbjerg* in 18 hours; from Newcastle to *Esbjerg* in summer only in 19 hours. Economy fare is £21·50 single. Another ferry route is from Harwich to *Hamburg* in 20 hours. Daily ferry and train services run via *Hook of Holland* or *Ostend* to *Copenhagen* in 25 hours from London; fare from £34·00 single.
Express boat-train connections from London, from *Esbjerg* to *Copenhagen*, via *Frederecia* and *Odense* and from *Hamburg* to *Copenhagen*.

Transport ———————— The principal railways are state-owned but certain local lines are owned privately or by the local communes. The fares on the State Railways are graded on a mileage basis, the price per kilometre being cheaper the longer the distance travelled. On many of the long distance trains seat reservations are compulsory. Refreshments are available on a few only of the long distance trains, but there are excellent restaurants on the Big Belt Ferry and Danish railway meals are always good.

Danish State Railways sell a ten day rover ticket for 450 kr., valid on all their rail network, buses and ferries, except those between Denmark and Sweden. For more information about railway travel write to the *Danish National Tourist Office, 75 Rockefeller Plaza, New York, N.Y. 10019.*

Motor-bus services connect most of the towns and there is a network of local buses, but such journeys can be tedious for stops are often frequent and sometimes lengthy.

There is a useful ferry between *Hundested* in north *Zealand* and *Grenå* in mid-*Jutland*; single fare 24 kr. Other ferries ply between *Frederikshavn* and *Oslo* and *Gothenburg*.

Night services between *Copenhagen* and *Rønne*, on the west coast of *Bornholm*, are operated by the 1866 Bornholm Steamship Company; single fare, 2nd class, no berth, 64 kr. There is a saloon, and a sleeping bag is a comfort on the night boat. Danish State Railways operate the ferry service from *Århus* to *Kalundborg*; single fare 31 kr.

Restaurants ———————— Danish food is excellent but, with the exception of certain restaurants mentioned below, prepared meals are expensive. Many work-a-day Danes take their own packets of open sandwiches and buy a cup of coffee at some place with the sign *"madkurve kan medbringes"*—"own food can be brought". Food in the country inns is good and the portions served are generous. Many Danish youth hostels are open at midday and serve *smørebrød* lunch at about 8 kr., as well as providing delicious packed lunches if ordered the evening in advance.

Cheap eating can be enjoyed in *Copenhagen* in some cafeterias on *Vesterbrogade*, at 'Vista' and temperance restaurants; price for lunch or dinner is about 10 kr.

DENMARK

Public Holidays 1st January, Maundy Thursday, Good Friday, Easter Sunday, Easter Monday, 25th April, Ascension Day, Whit Sunday, Whit Monday, Christmas Day and 26th December.

Information Most towns have a Tourist Association (*Turistforening*) to supply information and assist visitors in touring and sight-seeing; English is invariably spoken. Some museums, art galleries and other tourist attractions offer free entry, or reduced fee, to Y.H.A. members.

Maps 'Geographia' map of Denmark on a scale of 1:505,000 is the most useful general map of the country. The Danish Geodetic Institute publish more detailed maps on four sheets on a scale of 1:200,000.

Cycling Cycling is remarkably popular and during the 'rush-hours' in Copenhagen, thousands of cyclists occupy the main roads of the city and suburbs. Traffic keeps to the right and over-takes on the left. Priority belongs to vehicles coming from the right hand, except on numbered highways, which are clearly marked and permit traffic the right of priority. Some Danish motorists are rather reckless and may ignore any priority a cyclist may otherwise enjoy. Use of cycle-tracks, when provided, is compulsory. Pedestrian crossings are marked with a blue circle containing the words "*For gående*". The major roads are excellent outside of the towns; within town boundaries they are often surfaced with setts. They are straight and in the hilly parts go directly up and down hill with little attempt at levelling or at choosing the easiest contours.

In a country so cycle-minded as Denmark, there are numerous stockists and repair shops. Danish cycles are heavy machines and it is doubtful if spares for British sports models will be available; moreover, the screw threads are different. Cycles can be hired in *Copenhagen* from *Københavns Cyklebørs, Gothersgade 105* and the head office of the *Dansk Cyclist Forbund* is at *1, H.C. Andersen's Boulevard*.

Camping Denmark has more than 500 camping sites which are ap-proved and listed by the *Dansk Camping Union, 74 Gammel Kongevej, Copenhagen V.* A camping pass, at 5 kr. and valid one month, is issued by them, together with a handbook.

Canoeing The largest river is the *Gudenå* in *Jutland*, which forms a series of delightful lakes in the *Silkeborg* district. Canoes may be hired and at the end of the journey returned by rail at an inclusive price. This is one of many holiday facilities organised by the Danish YHA through their Travel Bureau, *Ungdommens Rejsebureau, Kultorvet 7, Copenhagen K.*

DENMARK

Copenhagen

The *Hovedbanegård* is the terminus for all main line trains; a particularly fine railway station, with the platforms below ground. Suburban electric or "S" trains also pass through it, linking it with local stations within the city.

Road approaches are from the west along No. 1 Highway from *Roskilde*, from the south along the coast from *Køge*, from the north along the delightful Danish Riviera—the coastway from *Elsinore*—and from the north-west by *Hillerød* (Frederiksborg Castle), *Birkerød* and *Lyngby*.

Buses and trams are the main means of transport in the city; all routes go through the city centre and fares are cheap. It is, however, easy to go sightseeing on foot; most of the places to visit are within a mile of the Town Hall.

The continuous stretch of narrow streets between *Rådhusplads* (Town Hall Square) and *Kongens Nytorv* (the King's New Market) is known as *Strøget* but the name will not be found on any map. Here are the most expensive shops and the pavements form a fashionable promenade; a cheaper shopping centre is along *Vesterbrogade* beyond the railway station.

The City Centre and East of the City

Start opposite Railway Station on *Vesterbrogade* and visit the *'Den Permanente'* showrooms of Danish handicrafts. In middle of road the *Pillar of Freedom* commemorates emancipation of Danish peasants from bondage. Turn east along *Vesterbrogade*; on right is entrance to *Tivoli*.

Copenhagen's *Tivoli* is unique yet typically Danish. A great pleasure garden, it has many cafés, lawns and flower beds, fountains, dance halls, concert halls, and side shows. You can have a wonderful evening very cheaply or spend a lot of money, according to your pocket. Amongst the things which are free after paying the modest admission charge to the Gardens is the famous Pantomime Theatre featuring mime and ballet. Take care where you eat; there are both cheap and expensive restaurants in *Tivoli*.

Rådhusplads (Town Hall Square) is the centre of modern Copenhagen. Note the novel barometer on the roof at the corner of *Vesterbrogade*, also three statues in the square: the statue of "the Little Bugler", the famous *Dragon fountain* designed by Joakim Skovgård and executed by Bindesbøll, and a tall pillar carrying figures blowing Denmark's ancient musical instrument, the *lure*. On south side is the Town Hall, built 1892-1902, worth visiting Statue of Bishop Absalon, founder of Copenhagen, over door. Contains also Jens Olsen's World Clock. Wonderful view from Town Hall Tower.

English books and papers may be purchased from *Politiken* and *B-T* bookshops in the square. The famous *Carlsberg Glyptotek* with its art treasures is in *H.C. Andersen's Boulevard* behind the *Tivoli*; fine collection of Greek and Roman statues.

Frederiksberggade, at eastern side of square, forms commencement of *Strøget*. Five minutes walk to *Gammel Torv* (the Old Market) on the left and *Ny Torv* (the New Market) on the right. Classical building in *Ny Torv* is *Law Courts*, connected by a 'bridge of sighs' with former prison. Little narrow streets in immediate neighbourhood contain many interesting antique shops and give good idea of old Copenhagen.

Note old fountain in *Gammel Torv*, where golden apples play in water on queen's birthday. Just off square is the cathedral, *Vor Fruekirke*, Church of Our Lady, built 1807; over entrance is a bas-relief of Christ preaching on the Mount, by Thorvaldsen. The only decorations inside are his famous and exquisite statues of Christ and the Twelve Apostles.

North of church lie old *University* buildings. Modern extensions are in north part of town beyond lakes. University, founded 1479, has 11,000 students. The *Zoological Museum*, notable for its collection of whales, is in the University Park.

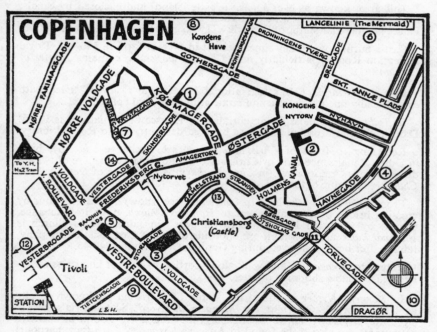

1. *Trinity Church.* 2. *Theatre.* 3. *Museum.* 4. *Ships to Malmo.* 5. *Town Hall.* 6. *Amalienborg.* 7. *University.* 8. *Rosenborg Castle.* 9. *Glyptotek.* 10. *Our Saviour's Church* (*Vor Frelsers Kirke*). 11. *Knippelsbro.* 12. *To Carlsberg Brewery.* 13. *Approach to Christiansborg Castle.* 14. *Gammel Torvet.*

DENMARK

Krystalgade leads to *Church of the Trinity* with Round Tower, 116 ft. high, built by Christian IV as an observatory. Tower may be ascended by broad spiral roadway up which Peter the Great of Russia is supposed to have driven a carriage and pair. Excellent view from the top. Nearby is Danish Youth Hostels Association Travel Bureau, in *Kultorvet* (the Coal Market). Return down *Købmagergade* rejoining *Støget* in section known as *Amagertorv*.

Note beautiful *Stork Fountain* in roadway. At No. 6 is shop of Royal Porcelain Factory and at No. 8 that of Bing and Grøndahl. Opposite is famous *Jordbærkælderen* (Strawberry Cellar) for fruit and cream and fancy cream cakes. Facing end of *Købmagergade* is *Højbroplads* with *Copenhagen's* open air flower market and fine statue of Bishop Absalon.

Gammelstrand is on immediate right; fishmarket, with some noted fish restaurants; also state pawnbrokers, for occasional bargains in jewellery. Cross canal to reach huge block of state buildings which cluster round *Christiansborg Palace* and *Thorvaldsen's* Museum.

This area, known as *Slotsholmen* (Castle Island) and enclosed by canals, marks marshy spot on which Absalon built his first fortress. In front of Palace is equestrian statue of Frederik VII who gave Denmårk its Constitution.

Castle burnt down many times, rebuilt in present form in 1907-22, Royal Reception Rooms particularly fine. *Christiansborg* also contains *Houses of Parliament*.

Pass over *Marble Bridge* to National Museum in *Prinsens Palace* with exceptionally fine prehistoric and arctic ethnographical collections.

In *Tøjhusgade*, almost facing entrance to Houses of Parliament is Royal Danish Arsenal Museum and close by is garden entrance to Royal Library.

Returning to front of *Christiansborg* we see Exchange close by, built in Dutch Renaissance style by Christian IV; note remarkable spire of twisted dragons' tails. Across river (in *Christianshavn*) is high spire of *Our Saviour's Church*, with figure of the saviour and external spiral staircase.

From *Knippelsbro* take boat to *Langelinie* (see below) or continue tour by crossing bridge over canal on left to *Holmens Church*, opposite Exchange, erected by Christian IV. Notice Royal pew. On same side as church is *National Bank*, and beyond it are imposing offices of East Asiatic Company, rebuilt after being destroyed during German Occupation 1940-45.

Return to *Amagertorv* and walk along portion of *Strøget* known as *Østergade*, fashionable shopping quarter.

In *Kongens Nytorv* is equestrian statue of Christian V, known locally as "The Horse". On right are *Magasin du Nord*, Scandinavia's largest store, *Royal Theatre*, and *Charlottenborg*, the art academy. Some inexpensive restaurants are also to be found in *Kongens Nytorv. Nyhayn* (new harbour) makes a pleasing picture with waterway extending up to the town and old houses flanking waterside; many are restaurants and cafes but this is a tough sailors' quarter, to be avoided at night. Hans Andersen lived at No. 67, 1846-65. Ferry from *Nyhavn* to *Christianshavn*.

Follow *Gothersgade* to *Kongens Have* (the King's Garden) on right hand containing well-known statues of Hans Andersen, "Boy with a Swan" and "Well with Dancing Girls". Cross park diagonally to *Rosenborg Castle* in *Østervoldgade* with wonderful art collection. On opposite side of *Østervoldgade*, and built on old ramparts, are *Botanical Gardens*, with Royal Observatory, *Botanical Laboratory* and Denmark's technical university.

Return to *Kongens Nytorv* and follow *Bredgade*, with superior shops, many in premises converted from town houses of the nobility. On left at end of *Frederiksgade* is the *Marble Church*, with dome over 200 ft. high and only few yards less in diameter than St. Peter's Rome; fine altar.

On opposite side of *Bredgade* lies *Amalienborg Palace*, actually four palaces, mid-18th century, rococo style; originally houses of noblemen but came to be occupied by Royal Family after fire at *Christiansborg* in 1794. Note fine Ionic colonnade which, owing to lack of funds, was constructed in wood. In centre of square is equestrian statue of Frederick V by Saly, considered most beautiful statue in Copenhagen. Observe picturesque uniforms of Life Guards and see Changing of the Guard at 12 noon, conducted with particular ceremonial on Sundays, attracting a large crowd.

Proceed long *Bredgade* to *Alexander Newsky Church*, Greek Catholic church, on left; built 1883, Byzantine style with three large gilt cupolas. At corner of *Bredgade* and *Toldbodvej* is "*Grønningen*", inexpensive restaurant. Continue along *Toldbodvej* past *Kastellet* to *English Church*, St. Albans, with graceful spire in typical English setting. By side of church is enormous statuary group and fountain by Bundgård which represents Gefion and her sons, whom she had converted into bulls, ploughing Zealand out of Sweden.

Continue northwards to famous promenade of *Langelinie*, with harbour and waters of *Sound* on right and beautifully planted shrubberies and flower-beds on left. Interesting sculptures, including, on rock on shore, famous statue by Eriksen of "*Little Mermaid*", one of Hans Andersen's characters, and fine statue, "*The Swimmer*", by Swedish sculptor, Børjeson. Northward along the *Linie* lies little pleasure boat harbour and extensive *Free Port*, 125 acres in extent, largest harbour in Baltic, with enormous international trade.

From *Langelinie* return to city centre by train or tram from *Østerport* station or by ferry.

A Tour West of the City

Take tram from *Vesterbrogade* to *Rahbeks Allé* for New Carlsberg Brewery, largest in world. Expert guide in attendance. You can taste the products, both alcoholic and non-alcoholic.

From Carlsberg proceed along *Pile Allé* and left into *Roskildevej* to Zoological Gardens. Near at hand is *Frederiksberg Palace* built by Frederik IV in early 18th century; Palace is not open to visitors but in adjoining park are fine avenues of enormous trees, with canals built for a king's pleasure.

Return to town by bus down *Frederiksberg Allé*.

DENMARK

Touring Routes

Each of these routes is limited to one main island, except **R.4** which crosses Denmark from east to west. Further tours can be made by combining parts of the various routes and linking them by the internal boat and ferry services.

R.1 Copenhagen-Elsinore-Copenhagen (65 miles)

Six miles north of *Copenhagen* lies *Klampenborg*, pleasure beach on shores of Sound. Crowded in summer; delightful setting.

Dyrehave (Deer Park) entered by Red Gate, near *Klampenborg* Station; over 2,000 acres in extent, enclosed by Christian V in 1670. Magnificent trees, principally beeches; large herd of deer. Near *Klampenborg* is funfair, *Dyrehavsbakken*. Numerous footpaths and cycle tracks. Favourite point is *Eremitagen* (Hermitage), built as Royal shooting-box in 1736, with wonderful view over Sound to Sweden. Y.H. at *Lyngby*.

Continue northwards along "**Danish Riviera**", lined continuously with gardens and villas. From *Nivå* see island of *Hveen* where famous Danish astronomer, Tycho Brahe, had his observatory. Fine new museum in *Humlebak*. Swedish coast and town of *Hälsingborg* now clearly in sight.

Twenty-eight miles from Copenhagen is **Elsinore** (*Helsingør*). (**Y.H.**). Principal feature is castle, *Kronborg*, commanding the Sound, here less than 3 miles wide, built on site of earlier fortress in 1574-85, fine Renaissance building surrounded by moats and ramparts. Shakespeare's "Hamlet" is sometimes acted in courtyard. Portion of castle now used as Maritime Museum. In dungeons is statue of *Holger Danske* sleeping but ready to respond to his country's call for help. Visit *St. Maria's Church* (medieval mural paintings) adjoining Carmelite Monastery, 15th century *St. Olaf's Church*, many beautiful old houses in *Strandgade* and *Stengade*, and 16th century *Marienlyst Palace*. Ferry across the Sound to *Hälsingborg* in Sweden, worth taking if only for view of *Kronborg* from the sea.

North from *Elsinore* are many holiday resorts with splendid sands for bathing; inland to *Fredensborg* (9 miles) for Fredensborg castle, one of the summer residences of Royal Family, built 1719-26, beautifully situated close to lake *Esrum Sø* in delightful park containing much sandstone and marble statuary.

South-west to **Hillerød** (6 miles) for *Frederiksborg* palace, built by Christian IV (1602–20) restored in 19th century and is finest Renaissance palace in Scandinavia; museum of national History housed here. Chapel, richly decorated, contains arms of the knights of Order of the Elephant, including those of our Queen Elizabeth, Duke of Edinburgh, and the Viscount Montgomery; famous organ (1612) with 1,001 pipes.

From *Hillerød* to *Copenhagen* is 23 miles via *Farum*, beautifully situated town by lakes and near nature park.

R.2 Copenhagen to Slagelse via Vordingborg and Møn (160 miles)

South Zealand is pleasantly pastoral but does not contain so much of interest as north Zealand. *Møn*, however, is said to be the most attractive of the Danish islands. *Køge* (23 miles) (**Y.H.**) has interesting church, tower of which was used as lighthouse. Medieval pirates hung from tower—hence term "*Køge chickens*". Many ancient houses.

Vordingborg (34 miles) has keep of castle, "Goose Tower", built by Valdemar III in 14th century. He placed a golden goose on the summit to annoy the Hanseatic towns which he called a flock of geese. Splendid view from top of tower over south Zealand and the famous *Storstrøm* bridge, leading to island of *Falster*: longest bridge in Europe, 3,500 yards.

Continue to *Kalvehave* (10 miles) by private railway, thence by bus to *Stege* (7 miles) over Queen Alexandrine's bridge to island of *Møn*. **Y.H.** at *Sømarke*, near *Borre*. **Møns Klint** (12 miles) is a magnificent stretch of chalk cliffs, approached by gradual climb terminating in beech forest (wild deer) perched 400 ft. above sea. Cliffs carved into numerous fanciful shapes—Queen's Throne, Greyback, Speaker, etc. Nearby is *Liselund*—pretty park with thatched mansion, Norwegian house, Swiss cottage and Chinese summer house. Many churches in neighbourhood richly ornamented with frescoes.

Return via *Vordingborg* to *Slagelse* (69 miles) (**Y.H.**) on main route to Jutland (see **R.4**).

R.3 Bornholm Island

An island of granite cliffs, beech woods and sandy beaches; runic stones and prehistoric remains abound. *Rønne* (**Y.H.**) at S.W. corner of island and *Bornholm's* port and chief town, picturesque setting and old houses expertly repaired after destruction caused by Russian bombing in 1945.

Round fortress-churches of *Bornholm* are famous and those at *Nylarskirke* and *Nykirke* are within easy reach of *Rønne*. *Olskirke* is close to *Tejn* and *Østerlarskirke* near to *Gudhjem* (**Y.H.**).

A week's tour of *Bornholm* could be had by making the bus journey of 25 miles from *Rønne* via *Neksø* to *Svaneke* (**Y.H.**), little harbour cut out of rock; curious smoke-houses where herrings were cured. Motor-boats to *Christiansø*, most easterly of Danish islands, and seal and bird sanctuary of *Græsholm*. Between *Neksø* and *Svaneke*, rock changes from sandstone to granite, and rugged coastline from here to extreme north of island becomes most picturesque. Take cliff and shore paths for 8 miles to *Gudhjem* (**Y.H.**) and on along cliffs for another 9 miles to *Sandvig* (**Y.H.**) nearest village to rocky northern corner, tracts of heather, birch and pine. Walk the 4 miles around promontary, said to be finest cliff walk in Denmark, to cliff-top *Hammershus* ruins of 13th century castle. From here a 6 mile cliff path connects with *Hasle* (**Y.H.**), thence by woodland foot-paths to *Rønne*.

DENMARK

R.4 Copenhagen to Esbjerg via Odense (170 miles)

This is principal route across the country, following main road; some interesting sightseeing alternating with rather monotonous stretches of countryside.

Roskilde (19 miles) (**Y.H.**) beautifully situated on fjord, famous for 12th century cathedral, with graceful spires added in 1635. Most Danish kings are buried here. Fine Renaissance reredos and 16th century clock with moving figures. In Christian I's chapel is pillar recording heights of many kings, including Peter the Great of Russia and Edward VIII.

Ringsted, 15 miles (**Y.H.**) in centre of Zealand, was capital in Viking times.

Sorø (13 miles) has Denmark's leading public school, the Academy (*c.* 1600). Church is part of old abbey established by Bishop Absalon, founder of Copenhagen. He is buried behind the altar.

Slagelse (9 miles) (**Y.H.**) rail junction for *Kalundborg* and *Århus* (**Y.H.**) ferry to north and for *Næstved* (**Y.H.**) and *Vordingborg* to south. An old-established town but little of antiquity remains, owing to many fires. *Korsør* (11 miles) (**Y.H.**) is Zealand terminus for Big Belt Ferry, a pleasing interlude in cross-country journey; restaurants on board. The express trains, which are carried on ferry, move off immediately on reaching harbour. *Nyborg* is terminus of ferry on *Funen* and junction for **Svendborg** (**Y.H.**) (see **R.5**).

Odense (**Y.H.**) (18 miles from *Nyborg*) is capital of *Funen* and Denmark's third largest town. Ancient town, somewhat industrialised, connected to fjord by canal and trading as a port. *St. Knud's* (Canute's) church, 13th century Gothic; in crypt are bones of holy King Canute, murdered by pagans in 1086. *Odense* is birthplace and early home of Hans Andersen. His childhood home is in *Munkemøllestræde* and there is a museum in *Hans Jensens Straede*. *Odense* has several beautiful parks. Opposite station is *Kongens Have* (King's Garden) with many fine fruit trees and lily-pond adjoining Royal Palace built in 1721.

Branch railway from *Odense* runs southwards to *Fåborg* (**Y.H.**) (see **R.5**).

At *Middelfart* (meaning middle-ferry), 29 miles, is Little Belt Bridge (1935) almost three-quarters of a mile long, 108 ft. high, which carries both railway and highway. See the Folk Museum and explore narrow streets around harbour.

Fredericia (6 miles) (**Y.H.**) railway junction, is a town built within ramparts. Church contains graves of Danish soldiers killed during the Prussian-Danish War of 1848-50, and memorial statue "The Brave Soldier" near the Prince's gate.

Kolding (14 miles) (**Y.H.**) is at intersection of east-west and north-south highways. Visit the *Koldinghus*, all that remains of medieval fortress, now museum of art and history. *Esbjerg* (**Y.H.**) (45 miles from *Kolding*) is modern port which has extensive trade with England.

Island of *Fanø* (ferry 20 mins. journey) famous for bathing beaches, peasant costumes and old houses at *Nordby* and *Sønderho*; well worth visiting.

R.5. Nyborg to Odense via South Funen (61 miles)

North Funen has little interest for tourists but southern and central parts of island are attractive. From *Nyborg* to *Svendborg* (21 miles) way goes through fruit-growing country. *Svendborg* (Y.H.) is situated on sound separating Funen from small island of *Taasinge*. Both commercial harbour and the pleasure harbours (yachting) are full of interest; numerous walks along the Sound and excursions by local ferry to *Taasinge*. State ferries connect with islands of *Langeland* (Y.H. at *Rudkøbing*), *Lolland* (Y.H.s at *Nakskov* and *Maribo*) and *Aerø* (many picturesque old houses) (Y.H. at *Marstal*).

Continue through undulating country, aptly named "Garden of Denmark", westwards to *Fåborg* (16 miles) (Y.H.) quaint town with numerous lanes and courtyards containing cottages with small gardens; known as artists' paradise. See the Bell Tower, only remaining part of medieval St. Nicholas Church, and the museum.

From *Fåborg* to *Odense* (Y.H.) over the *Funen* "Alps" (24 miles) or via *Kværndrup*, visiting lovely fortified manor house of *Egeskov* (16th century), built on piles in lake, with fine park and French garden (33 miles).

R.6. Esbjerg to Kolding via South Jutland (147 miles)

Ribe (Y.H.), 22 miles from *Esbjerg*, is a wonderful town in which to spend first night in Denmark—you step back centuries. Oldest town in Denmark (948) with one of oldest cathedrals in Scandinavia (1130). Large tower, built in part as defence, gives wonderful view from top. Note carvings at entrance. Custom of town-crier calling evening curfew. Storks and their nests, particularly round cathedral, are of great interest.

Road to *Tønder* (Y.H.) goes across marsh country, in places only a yard above the sea, with dykes to prevent flooding. Y.H. on *Rømø*, rough heathland and desolate sand dunes; connected by 5 mile causeway to mainland. Cyclists may wish to miss *Tønder* and travel across country to *Åbenrå* (Y.H.) or *Sønderborg* (Y.H.) but train travels via *Tønder* (29 miles) in region which was under German rule from 1864 to 1920.

Tønder, 2 miles from German border, is home of *Tønder* lace, cottage industry, recently revived. Old houses and quaint doorways are worth seeing. To take the train to *Sønderborg* you must change stations, and all that is worthwhile of *Tønder* can be seen in a walk between the two.

Continue via *Tinglev* (junction) to *Sønderborg* (43 miles) situated on *Als Sound* which separates island of *Als* from mainland. Fine situation, popular yachting centre. Castle, now used in part as museum, contains relics of Danish-Prussian wars and of German occupation.

Mommark (11 miles from *Sønderborg*) is connected by ferry to *Fåborg* in South Funen (*see* R.5). Our route is northwards to *Åbenrå*, either direct by road or rail via *Tinglev* and *Rødekro*.

DENMARK

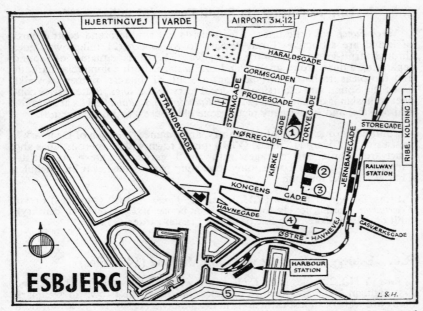

1. *Youth Hostel.* 2. *Bus Station.* 3. *Town Hall.* 4. *Water Tower.* 5. *Arrival Quay for steamers from England.*

Åbenra (21 miles by road from *Sønderborg*) pleasing town on pretty fjord, with some interesting old houses. From *Åbenrå*, continue through *Haderslev* (Y.H.), with newly restored cathedral, to *Kolding* (32 miles) (Y.H.).

R.7 Esbjerg to the Skaw via North Jutland (315 miles)

This area cannot easily be included in a circular tour. Almost all places of interest are on the more fertile eastern side of peninsula along main road from *Kolding* to the *Skaw* in extreme north. West coast is singularly uninteresting from *Esbjerg* northwards to *Struer*. Those with limited time should, on arrival at *Esbjerg*, make for *Silkeborg*, via *Grindsted*, explore the lakes, continue to *Århus*, and cross by boat to Zealand. In order to describe North Jutland, however, which has a charm of its own, we shall follow route to extreme north via east coast.

From *Esbjerg* via *Kolding* (Y.H.) and *Vejle* (Y.H.), prettily situated on a fjord, up attractive *Grejsdal* valley to *Jelling*, 68 miles by road from *Esbjerg*. In village are two mounds about 25 ft. high, burial mounds of Gorm and Thyra, the first known Danish king and queen and great grand-parents of King Canute. Two large runic stones in church yard, with remarkable carvings, one erected by Gorm to Thyra, the other by King Harald Bluetooth to his parents. Norman church contains interesting mural paintings. *Horsens* (Y.H.), 16 miles from *Vejle*.

Skanderborg (Y.H.), 14 miles from *Horsens*, is tourist centre, and approach to **Denmark's Lakeland**, of which principal town is *Silkeborg* (Y.H.), 20 miles from *Skanderborg*. Railway and road skirt lakes, backed by range of beautiful tree- and heather-covered hills. Good walking, canoeing and fishing in the neighbourhood but bathing restricted owing to much water-weed. Hill with tower on opposite side of lake to railway is *Himmelbjerget*, 482 ft. high and Denmark's second highest "mountain". Lakes served by pleasant little paddle-steamers. Diversion is to leave train from *Skanderborg* at *Laven*, cross by steamer to *Himmelbjerget*, climb hill, and complete journey to *Silkeborg* by steamer.

Return via *Skanderborg* to Århus (Y.H.) (26 miles from *Silkeborg*), second largest town and terminus of boat services to *Copenhagen* and *Kalundborg*. Make point of seeing Old Town (*Den Gamle By*). Situated in Botanical Gardens in *Vesterbrogade*, remarkable collection of old houses, grouped together on banks of stream to form village, complete with mayor's house, shops and windmill. Shops have old trade signs and are fitted out with all tools for crafts. Cathedral, 12th century Romanesque, partly rebuilt in Gothic style in 15th century, of red brick and is longest church in Denmark (320 ft.); spire (275 ft.) is modern. Note wrought iron doors, medieval reredos and frescoes. *Århus* is famous also for modern architecture, the Town Hall with 200 ft. tower, imposing exterior and still more impressive interior; several conducted tours every day.

From *Århus* continue north-west, leaving main line and highway on right, and come to *Viborg* (40 miles), (Y.H.) ancient town well situated on *Hald Lake*. Cathedral is principal attraction; Romanesque with twin towers; wonderful frescoes by Joakim Skovgård decorating whole cathedral. From *Viborg* turn north-eastwards through pretty lake country for 20 miles to *Hobro* (Y.H.), then 15 miles due north to *Rebild* (Y.H.) in national park of heather-clad hills.

Ålborg (15 miles), (Y.H.) on *Limfjord*, has many beautiful parks, modern domestic architecture and several examples of modernistic sculpture in streets and gardens. See *Jens Bang's* house in *Østerå*, 1624. A pleasant excursion from *Ålborg* is by bus to *Blokhus* (Y.H.) on west coast; some of finest sands in Europe.

Continue via *Sæby* (Y.H.) to *Frederikshavn* 39 miles, (Y.H.) (boat service to *Larvik*, *Oslo* and *Gothenburg*) and the *Skaw*, past island of *Læsø*. Beyond *Frederikshavn* the railway is a private line; country becomes increasingly sandy and barren. On left before *Skagen* is *Råbjerg Mile*, square mile of drifting sand, and on right is church of which only tower can be seen above sand. *Skagen*, 25 miles, (Y.H.) is pretty village with fishermen's cottages and gardens, home or summer residence of many writers or artists. Fine beach and rolling sandhills. Beyond lighthouse and German gun emplacements comes *Grenen*, extreme tip of Europe's only northwards-pointing peninsula, where ridge of shingle sticks hook-wise out into sea, always lashed in foam, between waters of *Skagerrak* and *Kattegat*.

DENMARK

erected by Gorm to Thyra, the other by King Harald Bluetooth to his parents. Norman church contains interesting mural paintings. *Horsens* (Y.H.), 16 miles from *Vejle.*

Skanderborg (Y.H.), 14 miles from *Horsens,* is tourist centre, and approach to **Denmark's Lakeland,** of which principal town is *Silkeborg* (Y.H.), 20 miles from *Skanderborg.* Railway and road skirt lakes, backed by range of beautiful tree- and heather-covered hills. Good walking, canoeing and fishing in the neighbourhood but bathing restricted owing to much water-weed. Hill with tower on opposite side of lake to railway is *Himmelbjerget,* 482 ft. high and Denmark's second highest "mountain". Lakes served by pleasant little paddle-steamers. Diversion is to leave train from *Skanderborg* at *Laven,* cross by steamer to *Himmelbjerget,* climb hill, and complete journey to *Silkeborg* by steamer.

Return via *Skanderborg* to **Århus (Y.H.)** (26 miles from *Silkeborg),* second largest town and terminus of boat services to *Copenhagen* and *Kalundborg.* Make point of seeing Old Town *(Den Gamle By).* Situated in Botanical Gardens in *Vesterbrogade,* remarkable collection of old houses, grouped together on banks of stream to form village, complete with mayor's house, shops and windmill. Shops have old trade signs and are fitted out with all tools for crafts. Cathedral, 12th century Romanesque, partly rebuilt in Gothic style in 15th century, of red brick and is longest church in Denmark (320 ft.); spire (275 ft.) is modern. Note wrought iron doors, medieval reredos and frescoes. *Århus* is famous also for modern architecture, the Town Hall with 200 ft. tower, imposing exterior and still more impressive interior; several conducted tours every day.

From *Århus* continue north-west, leaving main line and highway on right, and come to *Viborg* (40 miles), (Y.H.) ancient town well situated on *Hald Lake.* Cathedral is principal attraction; Romanesque with twin towers; wonderful frescoes by Joakim Skovgård decorating whole cathedral. From *Viborg* turn north-eastwards through pretty lake country for 20 miles to *Hobro* (Y.H.), then 15 miles due north to *Rebild* (Y.H.) in national park of heather-clad hills.

Ålborg (15 miles), (Y.H.) on *Limfjord,* has many beautiful parks, modern domestic architecture and several examples of modernistic sculpture in streets and gardens. See *Jens Bang's* house in *Österå,* 1624. A pleasant excursion from *Ålborg* is by bus to *Blokhus* (Y.H.) on west coast; some of finest sands in Europe.

Continue via *Sæby* (Y.H.) to *Frederikshavn* 39 miles, (Y.H.) (boat service to *Larvik, Oslo* and *Gothenburg)* and the *Skaw,* past island of *Læsø.* Beyond *Frederikshavn* the railway is a private line; country becomes increasingly sandy and barren. On left before *Skagen* is *Råbjerg Mile,* square mile of drifting sand, and on right is church of which only tower can be seen above sand. *Skagen,* 25 miles, (Y.H.) is pretty village with fishermen's cottages and gardens, home or summer residence of many writers or artists. Fine beach and rolling sandhills. Beyond lighthouse and German gun emplacements comes *Grenen,* extreme tip of Europe's only northwards-pointing peninsula, where ridge of shingle sticks hook-wise out into sea, always lashed in foam, between waters of *Skagerrak* and *Kattegat.*

Scandinavia is famous for its good food and many inns. Here, some youth hostelers stop to eat at Hvidsten Inn, Jutland, Denmark.

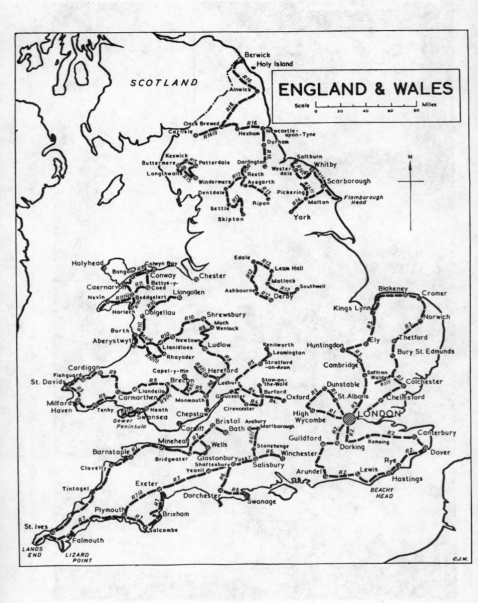

ENGLAND & WALES

Scale |___|___|___|___| Miles
0   20   40   60   80

ENGLAND AND WALES

Geographical Outline

The British Isles   Lying north-west of the European mainland, in the shallow seas of the "continental shelf", the British Isles include two principal islands, Great Britain and Ireland, together with numerous small islands either standing alone such as *Man* and *Arran*, or forming groups, such as the *Shetlands, Orkneys, Hebrides, Scilly Isles* and *Channel Islands*. Even considering only those which are inhabited, it is unlikely that anyone has ever visited them all.

This diversity is much enhanced by the complexity of their structure—the unexpected fact that in this small section of the earth's surface almost every part of the geological succession is present. The effect is seen not only in dramatic contrasts of scenery and ways of life, but also in subtle variations over small areas, within a single parish or even a single farm.

Diversity also comes from the many settlers and invaders who have contributed to the islands' story, whose subsequent history includes their transition from poor and remote outposts of the inhabited world to a strategic position in world communications and trade, vigorous centres of dispersal of men and ideas whose influence is still at work in every continent.

The present political division is an example of history over-riding geographical considerations. The largest political unit does not include the whole of the British Isles though it comprises more than the principal island. It is the *United Kingdom* (*U.K.*) *of Great Britain and Northern Ireland*, and includes, in effect, all the British Isles with the exception of the independent *Republic of Ireland*.

The southern and larger part of Great Britain comprises the two countries of *England* (50,874 sq. mls.) and *Wales* (7,466 sq. mls.).

Land   The basic division is between *Lowland Britain*, lying roughly south and east of a line from the mouth of the *Exe* to the mouth of the *Tees*, and *Highland Britain* to the north and west.

The lowland is rarely a plain but is a region of broad river valleys, low undulating hills, and a fairly regular succession of scarplands exposing comparatively young rocks. Its better soils, from light chalklands to heavy clays, permit good arable farming, but there are many areas of woodland and open heath. Lacking in extremes and genial to settlement, its villages and towns closely succeed one another. The River *Thames* spans it from west to east and communication between *London* and other parts is relatively easy.

Highland Britain provides a sharp contrast. It is built of older rocks, lower in succession than the Coal Measures. In many cases they are immensely ancient and there has been far more time than in the Lowlands for them to be affected by earth movements and weathering. They were high mountains before the great chains of Europe and Asia, the *Alps* and the *Himalayas*, were upfolded, and, as seen today, are only the worn-down stumps of the great ranges of early times. What remains is a dramatic, extremely varied upland region, mostly above a thousand feet, and rising higher in, for example, the granite mass of *Dartmoor*, the sandstones of the *Black Mountains*, the rugged igneous mountains of *Snowdonia* and the *Lake District*, and the Carboniferous rocks of the *Pennines*. On the fringe of the region, where the Coal Measures tend to occur, mining and heavy industry support dense populations. But as a whole it is sparsely peopled, settlement elsewhere being confined either to the coasts or to isolated hill farms, or villages in the narrow valleys between which, as in the region as a whole, communication is difficult. With its generally thin soils and higher rainfall, grassland and rough pasture predominate, supporting a pastoral, dairying and stock-rearing type of farming.

The first of many contrasts between *England* and *Wales* is that *Wales* is part of the highland zone, whilst *England* comprises the whole lowland zone together with parts of the highland zone—the *Pennines*, the *Lake District* and the peninsula of *Devon* and *Cornwall*.

Working outwards from *London*, the *London Basin* is bounded north and south by open chalk uplands, the *Chilterns* on the north, the *North Downs* on the south—a name which contrasts them with the *South Downs*, also of chalk, forming billowing rounded hills behind the coast of *Sussex*. It is this chalk, appearing again in Northern France, which was breached by the sea when it rose with the melt waters at the end of the Ice Age, separating Britain from the Continent. Similarly the *North Downs* extend eastwards through *Kent* to break on the coast in the white cliffs of *Dover*. The two lines of downs are the supporting sides of what was once a dome of chalk, the top of which has been eroded away to expose the clays and sands of the *Weald*, an intimately varied country crowned by *Leith Hill*.

The chalklands reach furthest north at *Flamborough Head* in *Yorkshire* but all converge on *Salisbury Plain*—a fact which made it the hub of the country in pre-historic times, as they were free from the oak forest with its dense and almost impassable undergrowth which then covered the heavier soils.

Moving across lowland England from south-east to north-west the cyclist especially will become aware of a succession of scarplands. After the gentle climb out of the *London Basin*, comes the *Chiltern* edge and the sharp drop to a clay vale. The process is repeated in a further gentle rise across the oolitic limestone which crosses the country from the *Dorset* coast to the moors of north-east *Yorkshire*, forming everywhere striking scenery, enriched by churches and villages of outstanding beauty built from the local stone. This is well seen in the *Cotswolds* from which there is an impressive drop over the western scarp into the *Vale of Severn*.

Such scarps may be thought of as providing a framework for the lowland country, within which are many other features such as the reclaimed levels of the *Fens*; the *Broads*, rivers and estuaries of *East Anglia*; the extensive sandy heaths of *Surrey* and *Hampshire*; the *Isle of Wight*; and, finally, the course of the *Thames* itself which, after a leisurely passage across the broad clays of

Oxfordshire, breaks through the *Chilterns* at *Goring* to enter the *London Basin*.

Nearly equal to the lowland of the scarps is the other lowland that lies between it and the highland zone, like an inverted triangle whose apex is the *Vale of Severn* and which broadens out to form the *Midlands* and the *Cheshire Plain*, with extensions northward on both sides of the *Pennines* in the *Lancashire Plain* and the *Vale of York*. Projecting through its clays and rich red sandstones are isolated inliers of the ancient rocks—*Charnwood Forest*, the *Malvern Hills* and the *Wrekin* of *Shropshire*. In *Herefordshire* and *Shropshire* the lowland laps against the border hills of *Wales*.

In the north country, beyond the *North York* moors already mentioned, a fine coast runs north from *Bridlington* to *Saltburn*, and again in *Northumberland* past the *Farne Islands* and *Holy Island* to *Berwick*.

Inland, the *Pennines*, running north for some 200 miles from the *Peak District* of *Derbyshire* to the *Cheviots* and the *Scottish Border*, are well called the "backbone of England". Their bleak gritstone and limestone tablelands, reaching 2,930 ft. in *Cross Fell*, form a barrier between the populous lowlands on either side. But their dales (a northern name for valleys) have much fine scenery, and the areas of carboniferous limestone are remarkable for their cliffs, caves, pot-holes and underground streams, particularly in the *Craven* area around *Ingleborough*.

The other chief hill mass of the north contains the famous *Lake District*, with many lake-filled dales radiating from a dome of mountains, of which *Scafell Pike* (3,210 ft.) is the highest point in England. The more rugged and precipitous central part, formed of volcanic rocks, is flanked on the north by older slates, and on the south by younger (but still ancient) slates, giving rise to smoother and softer scenery north of *Derwentwater* and around *Coniston* and *Windermere*.

Combinations of volcanics and slates are seen in *North Wales* in the *Berwyn Mountains* and more spectacularly in the mountain and coastal scenery of *Snowdonia* (*Snowdon* 3,560 ft.). The latter are composed in part of the yet older Cambrian series, while, across the *Menai Strait*, is *Anglesey* much of which is structurally the most ancient part of south Britain.

Mid-Wales is a comparatively smooth upland whose chief beauty is in its rivers and valleys. The *Severn*, *Wye* and many more flow out to the English lowland, whilst others, such as the *Rheidol* and *Dyfi* (*Dovey*), reach the sea direct.

South of the *Wye* the scarp face of the *Brecon Beacons*, cut in Old Red Sandstone, is a prelude to the varied and colourful landscape of *South Wales*. Away from the mining valleys (not uninteresting in themselves) the *Vales* of *Neath* and *Glamorgan*, the coasts of *Gower* and *Pembrokeshire*, the *Prescelly Hills* and the little-known hills of *Carmarthenshire*—from *Carmarthen Van* to those around the *River Cothi*—present a rich diversity of scene.

Moving back into England through the *Forest of Dean*, the same is true of the south-west peninsula. Out of its warm and mellow farmlands rise scenically varied hills: the *Mendips*, *Quantocks*, *Exmoor* and *Dartmoor*. And its famous

ENGLAND AND WALES

coasts from *Minehead* on the north, from *Portland Bill* on the south, converge south-west through *Devon* and *Cornwall* to meet at *Land's End*.

Climate — The prevalent south-westerly winds from the Atlantic account for the general mildness and humidity of the climate. Its variability is due partly to the alternating sunny and showery conditions produced by oceanic influences, partly to occasional winds from eastern Europe bringing more extreme conditions of cold in winter and heat in summer.

The wettest parts are the hill districts, especially in the west (over 60 inches), and rainfall decreases to under 30 inches in the east. The extreme cases are over 200 inches in the centre of the *Lake District* and under 20 inches in the *Thames* estuary.

Temperature decreases from west to east in winter and from south to north in summer. But nowhere is it ever very hot or ever very cold. Winters in the British Isles are warmer than in any other country in the same latitudes.

Spring and early autumn are delightful seasons for touring. Of the summer months, June and September tend to be more settled than July and August.

Plants and Animals — Only a few species of plants survived the Ice Age, during which most of the country north of the *Thames* was covered by ice sheets. At their retreat the country was re-colonized by vegetation from the Continent, but this was interrupted by the cutting of the Channel so that many plants common in Europe are absent. The Scots pine is the only native conifer.

The natural cover on heavy soils is oak forest, with alder along river banks, giving way to marsh and fen where subject to floods; on chalk and limestone it is birch, ash and beech; on sandy soils, Scots pine and heathland flora.

Little of the natural forest survives. From Anglo-Saxon times heavy soils were gradually put to the plough or converted to meadow; later the chalk downs and limestone uplands were turned to close-cropped pasture by the sheep rearing industry to supply the great export market in English wool. And further inroads were made by the demand for charcoal for iron smelting prior to the development of coal-mining. Much of this was necessary to secure improved land use, but in some of the wetter parts loss of the forest has produced a bog vegetation of little practical value.

Despite such changes the diversity of natural and semi-natural vegetation is considerable on account of the varied soils, the survival of uncultivated common lands and the great range of habitats on the 2,750 miles of coast. Finally, in the uplands, there are large areas of cotton grass and heather moors with, in the higher parts, a tundra vegetation of lichens, mosses and bilberry.

Introduced species, in a country whose plant collectors have explored the most remote parts of the world, are numerous.

Wild animals have suffered even more than plants from the claims of man. But red deer flourish in the combes of *Exmoor* and on the *Quantocks*, and other deer are increasing in the plantations of the Forestry Commission; semi-wild ponies are sure to be seen in *Central* and *South Wales* and the *New Forest*; the fox, badger, stoat, weasel, hare and rabbit occur everywhere; the red squirrel competes for territory with the introduced grey squirrel; the pine marten is being seen again in the *Lake District*; and the coypu, an introduction from South America, flourishes wild in the waterways of *East Anglia*. The grey seal and the common seal are frequently seen on the Atlantic coasts, and there is a large colony of grey seals on the *Farne Islands* off the coast of *Northumberland*. Only two snakes occur: the harmless grass snake and the poisonous viper, or adder, which is widely distributed, chiefly on pine and heath lands.

Bird life is remarkably rich. It includes game birds, such as grouse, pheasant and partridge; many species of hawk and owl; waders and wildfowl, especially on the many estuaries; the raven, starling, magpie, cuckoo, swallow, swift, and many smaller birds of field, wood, stream and hedgerow. The sea-cliffs and offshore islands are breeding places of large colonies of sea-birds, including the puffin, razorbill, gannet, guillemot, cormorant, shearwater and various species of tern and gull.

The People

Population Of the population of some 49 million, about 2,700,000 live in *Wales*. In both countries about four out of five live in towns or built-up areas, the main concentrations being *Greater London* (8,000,000) and the traditional industrial areas (often associated with coalfields)—including *Tyneside*, parts of *Lancashire* and the *West Riding of Yorkshire*, the *Birmingham* region and the *South Wales* coalfields. *Birmingham* (1,086,000), *Liverpool* (677,000), *Manchester* (594,000), *Leeds* (503,000) and *Sheffield* (530,000) are the other cities with half a million or more people. But these and others are regional centres for the clusters of smaller industrial towns in which the majority of the people live. *Greater London* and the *Birmingham* region are still growing and attracting industry and people from other areas.

This extreme concentration in a few areas, occupying only about 10% of the area of the country accounts for the preservation of so much good farm land and comparatively wild countryside which may surprise the visitor who knows that this is one of the most densely populated countries in the world.

Language It might be thought that English, the most widely used language in the world, would be spoken to a standard form by the people of its homeland. But, as a little experience in hostels will show, there are intriguing differences of vocabulary and intonation. The almost Scots lilt of *Northumberland* contrasts with the slow burr of the *West Country*; the suppressed consonants of the *London "Cockney"* and of rural *Hertfordshire* contrast with their careful over-emphasis in *Lancashire* and *Yorkshire*. Vowels undergo every possible change between light and heavy as one travels the English shires.

Such differences go far back in history, surviving the many changes in the language since the tribes of the English settlement brought the dialects of their

ENGLAND AND WALES

West Germanic tongue; and since the later Scandinavian and Norman invaders added much from Norse and French.

Welsh, spoken by nearly a million people in *Wales,* is one of the surviving Celtic languages, once widespread in *Western Europe* but now confined to a few parts of the Atlantic seaboard. The other living Celtic tongues are Irish, Gaelic (in parts of *Scotland*) and Breton (in *Brittany*). Others which have become extinct are Cornish and Manx. In Wales the native tongue is sustained by a rich and ancient literature and kept vigorous and receptive by the annual Eisteddfod—a competitive festival of poetry and song. But nearly all who speak it are bi-lingual and English is understood almost everywhere.

Religion   Protestantism in England and Wales has not stopped at one movement of reformation producing the break with Rome. Chapels of various sects, Wesleyan Methodist, Baptist, Congregationalist and many more are as familiar a sight in town and village as is the ancient church of the Established religion—the protestant Church of England—whose head is the Queen, with a hierarchy of archbishops, bishops and clergy. The historical reasons for these differences may appear remote today in a country where only a minority now adhere (other than nominally) to any religious organization. Yet such loyalties still greatly enrich the national life: *Wales* remembers how it was revitalised by its Methodist revival; the Society of Friends ("Quakers"), always small in numbers, is large in influence and example; two-thirds of those born in England are baptised in church; and it is still the case that much varied social life and social service is centred on churches, chapels and such bodies as the Salvation Army. Roman Catholics number more than 3 million. There is a considerable Jewish community.

History   Britain was for 400 years a province (Britannia) of the Roman Empire. The lowland zone was brought under control, with towns for the natives in each tribal area, villas and farms in the countryside, and advanced military bases at *York, Chester* and *Caerleon* for the conquest (only partially successful) of the highland zone. Here they built only forts, but their road-making was as persistent as in the lowlands. The emperor Hadrian's wall from the *Solway* to the *Tyne* was built in A.D. 122 and the decision in A.D. 211 to make it the northern frontier of the province marks the abandonment of the attempt to conquer the north of the island.

In 410 the Roman legions were withdrawn. Even earlier the province had been suffering raids from all quarters. Now it was defenceless. The attempt to keep out the Picts of the north by inviting over the Angles—a Germanic people from Schleswig—led only to a long and bloody struggle. Waves of invaders from across the *North Sea*—Angles, Jutes and Saxons—exterminated the people of south-east Britain, establishing their own tribal areas, still remembered in the names of districts and counties such as *East Anglia, Wessex, Essex* and *Sussex* (the kingdoms of the Angles and of the West, East, and South Saxons).

The highlands of the west were a refuge. Elsewhere, the Anglo-Saxons, settling in countless village communities and making clearings in the forest for beast and plough, laid down the basic pattern of what was to become

England. Dominion lay first with *Northumbria* (7th century), then with *Mercia*, a midland kingdom (8th century) and with *Wessex* (9th century). Christianity was re-introduced by the missions of St. Columba from Ireland and of St. Augustine from Rome. Despite the times there was progress in arts and learning. Bede of *Jarrow*, the first English historian, was one of the greatest Europeans of the dark ages. Alfred the Great, king of Wessex, was educator and law-giver as well as warrior against the Danes.

The fearful Danish raids introduced another element still noticeable in place-name and dialect in the north, and it was a Danish king, Canute, who first ruled unquestionably over all England.

The civilization which sprang from this tribalism was a matter of pride to the English. They were freemen living under their local laws. But all this was changed in the fatal year of 1066 when Harold, having defeated a Norwegian invasion in the north, marched south to heroic defeat against Duke William of Normandy and England came quickly under the iron hand of the Conqueror. The feudal system was imposed. Great castles dominated the land. Norman authority was made visible in Church and State and the Domesday survey provided knowledge of the wealth of each locality for effective central control.

Under Henry II the justice of the king's courts became accessible to all and gave protection against local tyranny. From these reforms stems the English legal system and its clear concept of the rule of law.

Trade expanded, with wool as the staple export. Craft guilds and merchant guilds were formed in the towns. It was the city of London as well as the baronage which extracted, from the autocratic John, the *Great Charter* (*Magna Carta*) which ensured rights and liberties (at least to the powerful). Out of the practice of the kings in calling knights and representatives of the towns to take part in council along with the baronage grew Parliament. And out of its insistence on redress of grievances before providing money for campaigns and other royal needs grew its capacity to submit bills for the making of new laws.

Persistent efforts to unify the islands brought success in Ireland under Henry II, in Wales under Edward I, but disaster at *Bannockburn* (1314) against the Scots. The large territories in southern and western France of which the kings were lords involved the country in constant war. The Hundred Years War with France fills the period with sound and fury, but signifies nothing unless it be, with the Wars of the Roses (entirely on home ground), the final spiritual bankruptcy and demise of medieval chivalry. Feudalism was, in any case, collapsing from another cause: its subsistence economy, with its labourers tied to the manor, was being dissolved by the money which flowed from trade and by wages offered in competition when labour became scarce after the Black Death (1349). The serf fled to the risks and freedom of wage-earning.

The new world of enterprise put the Welsh Tudors on the throne (1485). Everything was astir, and the Church, standing for old values, went down under the despotism of Henry VIII and the reign of terror of his minister Thomas Cromwell. Many of the best of Englishmen were beheaded and abbeys in England today are thought of most naturally as ruins.

ENGLAND AND WALES

Under Elizabeth I (1558-1603) religious strife died down, Protestantism was securely established, a threat from Catholic Spain receded after the Armada (1588), and the new learning and new lands filled the minds of the nation, above all of Shakespeare.

The Scottish Stuarts, ruling separately as kings of each country, found the English Parliament determined to be rid of absolutism. The Stuarts had other ideas and Charles I tried to rule without Parliament. The clash brought civil war, the execution of the king (1649) and Parliament's declaration of its own supremacy. This, though not at first secured, became the only practicably acceptable position for the future. The latter part of Oliver Cromwell's rule was a dictatorship; the last of the restored Stuarts forced his own ideas against the will of the nation, but had to flee when William of Orange was invited from the Continent to secure a free and legal Parliament (1689). A *Bill of Rights* defined the liberties of the subject and England entered the 18th century as a land of security for men of property in an age of increasing plenty.

At home, Scotland and England were united in a joint Parliament (1707); the beginning of party politics came with the grouping of opinion into Whig and Tory; Cabinet government, headed by a Prime Minister, emerged; scientific crop rotation and stock breeding worked a revolution on the land; and the famous Industrial Revolution brought a movement from cottage industry to factory and from countryside to town.

Abroad, England had developed two main interests. First, the colonies, the results of sea-power, exploration and trade. The *American Colonies* were lost by 1783, but great acts of nation-making were still to be done in new and almost empty lands and in the teeming sub-continent of *India*. Secondly, there was the need to ensure that no one power became too dominant on the Continent. This was the basis of the many wars from Marlborough's campaigns to the struggle against Napoleon culminating in *Trafalgar* and *Waterloo*.

The 19th century settled into the long Victorian prosperity with Britain the workshop of the world, centre of a wide empire, and a profound believer in free trade. The new industrial classes developed trade unionism; extensions of the franchise were won and were followed by much-needed reforms of labour and social conditions and of the harsh criminal code.

In the 20th century Britain has adapted itself to conditions in which many nations compete as industrial powers and in which sea-power is no longer an island's secure defence. Constitutionally it has evolved further towards effective democracy: at home, in the curtailing of the power of veto of the House of Lords and in the establishment of women's rights after a gallant campaign; abroad, in the emergence of self-governing Dominions, a change in fact and spirit from Empire to Commonwealth.

Government Britain is a parliamentary democracy under a limited monarchy. The sovereign is also head of the Commonwealth. Parliament, the legislative body, consists of two Houses, the House of Lords, composed of hereditary peers, life peers, archbishops and bishops, and the House of Commons made up of 630 members of Parliament, elected by direct universal suffrage to represent constituencies in Great Britain and Northern Ireland.

The executive is nominally the Crown, but in practice it is a Cabinet of Ministers headed and chosen by the Prime Minister who is himself dependent on the support of a majority in the House of Commons.

Resources

The industrial strength of the nation depends far more on research, inventiveness, a wide range of traditional but adaptable skills and heavy accumulation of capital equipment than on natural resources. But the country is fortunate in the distribution, quality and variety of its coal measures and the ample reserves which they contain. The coal industry employs about 300,000 workers producing about 140 million tons a year. Iron ore (chiefly low grade from opencast sites) is worked on a considerable scale in the *East Midlands* and the *Cleveland* district of *Yorkshire*, but a large import is also necessary. Recently discovered oil fields in the North Sea are now being drilled; they are likely to yield enough oil to meet as much as half the U.K. demand.

Success in foreign trading is a necessity for a country whose people depend on imports for a third of their food. Manufacturing industry is therefore concerned as much with exports as with home requirements though these with a rapidly rising standard of living present a vast market. Many industries remain localized on or near the coalfields where they grew at the time of the Industrial Revolution—cotton textiles in *Lancashire*, woollens in the *West Riding of Yorkshire*, cutlery in *Sheffield*, the "*Potteries*" around *Stoke-on-Trent*. But newer industries, using electric power, have tended to settle near markets or ports—the ancient university city of *Oxford*, conveniently near to *London*, has become a principal centre of the motor vehicle industry. And *London* itself, once largely administrative and commercial, is now also the most important centre for many light industries. Among heavy industries, the U.K. holds a high place in steel production and shipbuilding.

Agriculture employs about 300,000 workers and is highly mechanised in the arable areas in the east where farms average 100 acres. Permanent grass predominates in the midlands and the west. Wheat, barley, oats, potatoes and sugar beet are the chief crops. Regional specialities include hops, apples and pears in *Kent*, plums in the *Vale of Evesham*, bulbs in south *Lincolnshire*, cut flowers around *Penzance* and early potatoes on the *Pembrokeshire* coast.

British stock rearing is famous and its products have improved the herds of Commonwealth and other countries. There is a 200 years old tradition of scientific breeding and many types of cattle and sheep are to be seen. Among cattle the black and white *British Friesian* (the highest milk yielder) and the red and white *Shorthorn* (reared both for milk and beef) predominate. The *Ayrshire*, white with red markings, is a good yielder on poorer land. The sable-coloured *Jersey* and the light brown and white *Guernsey* are prized for the richness of their milk. The chief English beef breed is the handsome rugged *Hereford*. In *Wales* the *Welsh Black* is valued as a dual purpose animal.

Forestry employs comparatively few people but, under the direction of the Forestry Commission, is working great changes in the landscape, particularly on marginal land.

ENGLAND AND WALES

Fishing is of major importance and is carried out both from great trawling ports such as *Fleetwood, Hull, Grimsby* and *Yarmouth* and from countless villages around the coast.

Food and Drink
Breakfasts are substantial, usually of three courses: porridge or dry cereal with milk, a cooked course traditionally of bacon and eggs, followed by bread or toast with marmalade (an orange preserve), coffee or tea.

The midday meal is also substantial. It is called "dinner" when (as in many homes) it is the main meal of the day, or "lunch" by those who take their main meal ("dinner") in the evening. In either case it will generally be of three courses: soup, meat or fish with vegetables, followed by a sweet course or cheese or fruit and coffee.

Afternoon tea, at about 4 p.m., was an English invention and, despite its informality, almost a ritual. It survives in leisured homes and more widely at weekends. Though tea, ideally served from silver teapots, is its central feature it is also a light meal with buttered toast, honey, jams (preserves) and cakes. Workaday folk substitute a "high tea"—a quickly prepared cooked meal—for the family on return from work or school.

In comparison with the Continent English cooking tends to be plain and competent rather than imaginative. It is at its most reliable in standard dishes such as roast beef and Yorkshire pudding, or roast lamb and mint sauce which can be excellent because of the generally high quality of the meat available. Fish also—even the cheaper sorts such as cod and haddock—is of high quality; plaice is a popular fish delicacy. The smoked herrings, called kippers, are served as a cheap and nourishing dish except at main meals. Other good examples of plain cooking are fruit pies, such as apple, blackberry, bilberry and gooseberry, and steamed puddings served as a sweet.

Tea is the universal drink. Beer is the most popular alcoholic drink, except in the cider country of the south-west. Cider, made from fermented apples, is pleasant, refreshing and cheap, but unexpectedly potent. Wines and spirits, being heavily taxed, are expensive.

Alcoholic drinks of all kinds are only obtainable during certain hours and from licensed premises (which include railway buffets, inns, the majority of hotels and some restaurants).

Sport
Cricket, the traditional summer game, has endearing qualities even for those who do not pretend to understand its finer points. Not even the giant tussles of Commonwealth Test Matches have quite gone to its head and it is still played for its own sake in its original setting on village greens. Its team requirements are a solvent of class differences.

Cup Tie or International games in Association football or Rugby football are great popular occasions, as also are the *Oxford and Cambridge Boat Race* and some of the "classic" horse races—the *Derby, Oaks* and *St. Leger* in the flat season, and the *Grand National* which is raced over obstacles.

Field sports are still part of the life of the countryside and they include fox hunting (huntsmen mounted on horseback, but followed on foot in the

Lakeland mountains); stag hunting on *Exmoor*; hare hunting by harriers or beagles, and otter hunting. These are chiefly supported by regular country-dwelling followers, whereas grouse shooting lends itself to moorland excursions by well-to-do townsmen. At the other extreme, fishing claims a larger number of participants than any other sport.

The many creeks and estuaries provide good anchorages and a wide range of inshore sailing. *Cowes* on the *Isle of Wight* and *Burnham-on-Crouch* in *Essex* are the principal yachting resorts, but many others meet the less fashionable needs of week-end yachtsmen.

Culture

Architecture The few churches surviving from the Saxon period show Romanesque influence but have characteristic features in a narrow nave long and short stonework and a massive tower divided into stages by horizontal strips. Re-building of churches was taken up energetically by the Normans soon after the Conquest and within thirty years work had begun on most of the cathedrals. The style was the full Romanesque which is therefore in England called Norman. *Durham* cathedral is its finest achievement, but there are many other examples.

Cistercian monks, coming from France in 1129, introduced the pointed arch. Its use in lancet windows, with other features such as clusters of shafts instead of massive piers, distinguishes the *Early English* style—the first of the three styles of *English Gothic*. *Salisbury* cathedral shows it to perfection. The *Decorated* style (early 14th century) has wider windows, with flowing curves in the window tracery, as in the choir of *Ely* cathedral. It was soon followed by the even lighter and airier style known as *Perpendicular*—peculiar to Britain and representing a great technical advance, seen in the audacious slenderness of columns supporting the roof and the intricacy of the fan vaulting. Famous examples include *Henry VIIth's Chapel* in *Westminster Abbey* and *King's College Chapel, Cambridge*.

Renaissance influences were delayed by the Reformation. Instead, there was a *Tudor* style of domestic architecture, of native inspiration, seen in great houses, such as *Hardwick Hall*, created for the new aristocracy. Under the first two Stuarts Inigo Jones first looked to Italian and classic models and introduced the *Palladian* style in the *Banqueting House* of *Whitehall* and the *Queen's House* at *Greenwich*. After the Restoration (1660) classic models were universally favoured and the re-building of *St. Paul's* cathedral and other London churches by Sir Christopher Wren after the Great Fire (1666) showed that *Gothic* was dead. Wren's work was further developed by Hawksmoor and Vanbrugh (early 19th century). But such grandoise architecture as Vanbrugh's *Blenheim Palace* in *Oxfordshire* and *Castle Howard* in *Yorkshire* is professionally admired rather than liked, for the *Baroque* style never gained popularity in Britain. The dominant style of the century, called *Georgian*, at first followed Palladio and Inigo Jones. Its early exponent, William Kent, was also originator of English landscape gardening. The style entered a richer, more ornate, phase in the second half of the century through the work of the Scottish brothers Adam, particularly Robert, whose art is best seen in exquisite interiors, including *Ken Wood, Hampstead.*

Late *Georgian* included (from 1810) the flourish of the *Regency* period but was challenged by the *Gothic Revival*—a movement of taste which produced Barry's *Houses of Parliament* and *St. Pancras* station, scattered mock ruins over the countryside in pursuit of the cult of the picturesque, and fostered Victorian excesses to be seen in almost every town in the country. Its champion was Ruskin, but he lived to regret it. Gothic detail, such as the leaves of the chapter house at *Southwell,* was the product of the individual response and devout labour of craftsmen. Its easy repetition in the new machine age was devoid of feeling and meaning.

The functional architecture appropriate to such an age, and which had been developed on the Continent, was late in gaining acceptance and has only been widely adopted by British architects since the Second World War. Their most influential contribution to it in individual buildings appears to be in the design of schools. But the post-war decision to build several *new towns* has led to experiments in planning the whole social environment; those near London are *Harlow, Hemel Hempstead* and *Crawley.*

Art   Illuminated manuscripts and stone crosses were the chief expressions of Anglo-Saxon art. Later, popular craftsmanship was concentrated upon the Gothic churches and cathedrals. The Reformation of the 16th century, followed by Puritanism in the 17th century, cast a blight over much of the work of the past and prevented native participation in the great contemporary achievements in the visual arts on the Continent. The Court employed foreign artists: Holbein, Rubens and van Dyck.

Change came with the wealth and confidence of 18th century society. Hogarth captured the vitality of the age. Patronage at last produced a portrait painter of the first rank in Gainsborough. It also founded an Academy around the dominating figure of Reynolds. The annual exhibition of this Royal Academy remains a notable event of the London season. In the applied arts the demands of aristocratic society fostered exquisite craftsmanship, notably in silverware and in the furniture made by Chippendale and Sheraton.

Landscape painting, both in water colour (a peculiarly English medium) and oil, developed particularly in *East Anglia.* Chrome, Cotman, Girtin and Richard Wilson are minor masters. Constable and Turner break the bonds of English provincialism.

The so-called *Pre-Raphaelite* movement of the early Victorian age was an attempt led by D. G. Rossetti to recapture the simplicity of the Italian primitives. Its influence, though considerable, was wholly local. Its results excited both admiration and disfavour at the time, and traces of the controversy persist. Whistler, who had studied in *Paris*, livened the scene and founded a group in *Chelsea* on the misty bank of the Thames.

The 20th century has seen work of real power in the haunting sculptured forms of Henry Moore, Epstein's allegorical and religious figures (at *Coventry* and *Llandaff* cathedrals) and in his portrait bronzes. Among painters, Paul Nash, Ivon Hitchins, Graham Sutherland and John Piper are only a few among those whose style is unmistakably their own.

Music The country was certainly musical in the "merrie England" of Elizabethan times. Madrigal singing was its characteristic expression. A native tradition of composition led, despite Puritanism, to Purcell (1659-95) the greatest of English composers. But it is the German, Handel, (1685-1759), whose main works were written in England, who has reigned in popular affection. It may be partly this and partly the lack of a substantial native composer over the next 150 years that caused the English to submit with docility to the charge that they were not a musical nation.

Belatedly, towards the end of the 19th century, came Elgar, in the line of the great Central European composers and at this time the light operas of Gilbert and Sullivan created a new popular theatrical tradition.

English musical life gained new vigour from diverse sources in the 20th century. Holst turned to astrological and oriental mysticism, whereas Vaughan Williams and many lesser composers sought to illustrate the peculiar character of English folk song. Only Britten (b. 1913) of living composers yet seems likely to acquire a lasting international reputation, devoted as he is to accuracy of musical expression, especially in the setting of words.

Literature The beginnings of English poetry and prose are found in the native British epics of Arthur—oral stories originating, perhaps in the 6th century, in *South Wales* and *Cornwall* which later incorporated the Christian ideas of medieval chivalry and entered into literature all over Europe. The Angles, too, brought their own epic, Beowulf, from Scandinavia. English prose begins with the Anglo-Saxon Chronicle in which the terse style develops flexibility as the record unfolds but never loses the capacity to move the reader by economy of words and understatement.

With the foundations of romance and realism so well laid British writers have as frequently looked back to native sources as across the Channel to classic or other models. Wherever you go in England or Wales poets, novelists, historians or commentators have been there before you. Chaucer can still be a merry companion between *Southwark* and *Canterbury*; Shakespeare's accurate descriptions of nature are a perpetual delight and he haunts parts of *London* as Johnson, Lamb and Dickens haunt others. Matthew Arnold broods over the middle *Thames* as does Dyer over *Grongar Hill*. You can be with Crabbe in *East Anglia*, Hardy in *Dorset*, Wordsworth over every yard of the *Lake District* and Emily Brontë on *Wuthering Heights*. You can travel *Wales* with Giraldus, or Borrow, or be with Dylan Thomas "Under Milk Wood". Defoe, Celia Fiennes and J. B. Priestley are factual and tireless predecessors almost wherever you may go.

ENGLAND AND WALES

The strand of topographical comment is only one small part of the whole literature which has mirrored the life and feeling of each generation and perhaps ranged more widely than that of any other language.

Science   This is the land of Newton (1642-1727) who first brought comprehensive understanding of the physical forces governing the universe; of Darwin (1809-82) whose theory of natural selection brought similar comprehension of evolution to explain the marvellous abundance of living things; and of Keynes (1883-1946) who, working in the less predictable field of human affairs, brought an understanding of economic forces which has contributed to well-being wherever governments have accepted its teaching.

These men were not alone. Each had contemporaries almost equally eminent. The foundation of the Royal Society in 1662 had quickened interest in experimental science. Harvey's discovery of the circulation of the blood and Dalton's atomic theory were early successes. By the 19th century every science was progressing and men such as Faraday were contributing to several branches. Nowhere is the greatness of the Victorian era better seen than in its scientists, and the line of research has gone forward into the specialisms of the 20th century around such names as Fleming and Rutherford.

Art Galleries   Only *London* is comprehensive. But there are good collections in other cities, including *Birmingham, Leeds, Liverpool* and *Norwich*. A vast amount of artistic wealth is held privately in country houses, many open to the public for a fee at certain times. But, generally there is more satisfaction in visiting an historic house in the care of the *National Trust* or other public body.

Museums   Besides the great national collections in *London* there are numerous museums throughout the country. Outstanding are the *National Museum of Wales, Cardiff; Welsh Folk Museum, St. Fagan's; Fitzwilliam Museum, Cambridge; Ashmolean Museum, Oxford; Bowes Museum, Barnard Castle, County Durham; Castle* and *Railway Museums, York; Castle Museum, Colchester.* Two more recent collections are the *Museum of English Rural Life, Reading,* and the *Montague Motor Museum* (antique cars, bicycles, etc.) at *Beaulieu, Hampshire.*

Hiking at Borrowdale, Cumberland.

Touring Information

Travel in Britain

Rail: The rail network provides comfortable travel, particularly on expresses; trains usually run to time, but Sunday, when track maintenance is carried out, is sometimes an exception. Seats may be booked in advance (30p) on principal trains.

Reduced rates on (a) *Period Return tickets*, valid outwards only on day of travel, homewards 17 days (b) *Economy Return tickets*, valid outwards only on day of travel, homewards within 1 month, on Tuesdays, Wednesdays and Thursdays; must be purchased at least 21 days before date of travel; considerable saving over ordinary tickets, but £3 minimum fare. (c) *Weekend Return tickets*, valid for outward travel only on Fridays, Saturdays or Sundays for return on the Saturday, Sunday or Monday of the same weekend. (d) *Cheap Day tickets* and *Excursion tickets* at bargain fares to the seaside, walking areas, for sporting events and day tours by rail, road and river steamers. (e) *Road/Rail tickets;* bus return tickets between certain points can be used for return journey by train providing ticket is changed at rail ticket office for rail exchange ticket (supplementary fare usually payable).

Also two types of "season" tickets are available (a) *Holiday Runabout tickets* issued March–October allowing 7 days unlimited travel in a specified area (b) *Rail Rover tickets* affording unlimited travel on British Rail anywhere in Great Britain, issued March–October, 7 days £24·00, 14 days £37·00. Selected Regional Rovers also available.

Bus and Coach Services: cover most parts of Britain. Usually cheaper than rail, e.g. *London* to *Glasgow* or *Edinburgh* £3·50 single. Coach stations act as terminals for long-distance services and are connected with local bus services. Reduced rates are often available for day or period return and, on some services, for mid-week travel. "Coach Master" tickets for overseas visitors, valid 8 or 15 days for £8·00 or £15·00; for use throughout Great Britain. *Red Bus Rover tickets;* 50p, valid for one day on London buses.

Money
The unit of currency is the *Pound Sterling* (£.—symbol derived from the Latin *"libra"*). It is divided into 100 pence. Coins are issued for ½p, 1p, 2p, 5p, 10p and 50p. Bank of England notes are issued for £1, £5, £10 and £20.

Clothing
It is advisable to carry a sweater and waterproof at all times. Nowhere is there any objection to girls wearing shorts or jeans for cycling or walking.

Restaurants
Eating out, particularly at restaurants, is not cheap. In the countryside, the many small establishments, often in houses or cottages, displaying the sign of the *Cyclists' Touring Club* are open to all and understand the needs of wayfarers. Their prices are reasonable.

Public Holidays
1st January, Good Friday, Easter Monday, last Monday in May or first Monday in June, last Monday in August, Christmas Day and 26th December. Most shops are closed on public holidays and bus and railway services are restricted. Also every town has one early closing day (1 p.m.) weekly. Most shops close by 6 p.m.

Maps and Guide Books
The official *Ordnance Survey* maps, scale 1:50,000, are ideal for detailed exploration. *Bartholomew's* 1:100,000 series are particularly useful for cycling. Hostels often stock the local sheet in both series. The Ordnance Survey ¼ inch to a mile series are excellent maps for motorists. Y.H.A. map of England & Wales, showing hostels, roads and railways, scale 1:1,000,000, is a cheap and useful map for planning purposes.

There are many country and local guides which vary greatly in quality. Admirable publications of *Her Majesty's Stationery Office* (H.M.S.O.) for the *Countryside Commission* are the guides to the *Dartmoor, Exmoor, Northumberland, Lake District, Brecon Beacons, Snowdonia* and *Peak District National Parks*; also those published for the *Forestry Commission* on certain Forests and Forest Parks.

Accommodation There are about 260 youth hostels, chiefly in the countryside but also in cathedral cities and other interesting towns. Advance booking is essential during the winter months from November to February, advisable mid-July to first week of September, also Easter and Spring Bank Holiday and on Saturday nights throughout the year; essential at all times for school parties and other groups.

Other reasonably priced accommodation is listed in the handbooks issued to their members by the *Cyclists' Touring Club*, 69 Meadrow, Godalming, Surrey and the *Ramblers' Association*, 1 Crawford Mews, London W.1. These are usually small pleasant places of *pension* type where bed and breakfast will cost about £1·50 instead of more normal price of £2·00 upwards.

Camping Camping is permissible at certain hostels (see Y.H.A. handbook). Membership of the *Camping Club of Great Britain and Ireland*, 11 Lower Grosvenor Place, London, S.W.1 is advantageous. Permission of farmer or landowner should always first be obtained.

Walking Footpaths abound in every parish as the one-inch Ordnance Survey sheets will show, but they are not all rights of way. Each *National Park* provides extensive and varied walking, often over open country, but there are many other lovely areas, including the *Surrey* commons, the *Chilterns*, the *Downs of Kent, Sussex, Surrey, Berkshire* and *Wiltshire*, the *Isle of Wight, Dorset, Mendips, Quantocks, Wye Valley* and *Gower*.

Long-distance routes designated by the *Countryside Commission* are the *Pennine Way* (*Derbyshire to Scottish Border*), *Offa's Dyke* (along the *Welsh Border*), *South Downs Way, North Downs Way, Ridgeway Path* (from *Avebury* in *Wiltshire* to *Ivinghoe Beacon* in *Buckinghamshire*), *Cleveland Way* (around the *North York Moors*) *Pembrokeshire Coast* and around the *South-West Peninsula* (coast of *Somerset, Devon* and *Cornwall*).

National Parks There are ten: *Northumberland, Lake District, North York Moors, Yorkshire Dales, Peak District, Snowdonia, Pembrokeshire Coast, Brecon Beacons and Black Mountains, Exmoor, Dartmoor.*

The public has no additional rights in them, but they contain much open country as well as ordinary farmland and each could take up more than one holiday. There are also National Forest Parks where the Forestry Commission particularly encourages visits to its plantations.

Rock Climbing Details of climbing clubs can be obtained from the *Hon. Secretary, British Mountaineering Council, 26 Park Crescent, London W1N 4EE*. Courses are arranged by *Y.H.A., Trevelyan House, St. Stephen's Hill, St. Albans, Herts.*

Rock climbing areas are in *Snowdonia*, the *Lake District* and to a lesser extent in *Cornwall*. Gritstone outcrops in parts of the *Pennines* and a few sandstone outcrops in *Kent* and *Surrey* attract some climbers. Guide books are issued describing each climb in detail. In hill areas get local advice, remember that weather conditions can turn treacherous; leave word about your proposed route or climb.

Caving and Potholing
Only to be undertaken with an experienced party. Information can be obtained from the *Hon. Secretary, Cave Research Group of Great Britain*, 369 Stone Road, Trentham, Stoke-on-Trent.

Chief areas are the *Craven* district of *Yorkshire*, the *Mendips* near *Bristol*, *Derbyshire Peak District* and the limestone areas of *South Wales*.

Same cautions as above under rock climbing. Additional danger is underground flooding after rain which may come with unexpected suddenness. Guide books detailing underground routes and advice are published for many areas.

Cycling
England and Wales are ideal for cycle touring. The villages are close to one another, and accommodation is plentiful and moderate in price. All roads are tar-bound and are generally in good condition, but main roads are often too busy for cyclists. Except in Eastern England the country is hilly and a change speed gear is advisable. Nearly every town has its cycle agent where running repairs can be carried out.

The rule of the road is "Ride on the left and overtake on the right". Cycles are taken on all trains and the charge is calculated at half the second class adult fare subject to maximum charge of £3·40 single, £6·80 return.

If you are a member of your own national cycling organization, affiliated to the *Alliance Internationale de Tourisme,* you have the benefits of free reciprocal membership of the *Cyclists' Touring Club* during your stay here.

Canoeing and Boating
Craft can be hired by the hour, day or week on many rivers and on *Norfolk Broads, Windermere* and at coastal resorts.

Entrance Fees Historic Building
The *Department of the Environment* issues a *"Season Ticket to History"*, £1·00, giving admission to over 600 monuments and buildings in their care in England, Scotland & Wales, including the *Tower of London* and *Hampton Court.* Valid 12 months. Can be bought at *25 Savile Row, London W.1., Government Bookshops* and at principal monuments. Membership (£2·00) of the *National Trust, 23 Caxton Street, London, S.W.1* secures free admission to over 100 properties. Visitors from overseas can buy a composite ticket from the *British Tourist Authority, 64 St. James's Street, London S.W.1,* costing £2·50 and valid one month, which secures admission to both *Department of Environment* and *National Trust* properties.

Time
12 p.m.
The 24 hour clock as used in continental countries is not so widely used in Britain. Hours from midnight to noon are called 1 to 12 a.m. and hours from noon to midnight are called 1 to

London

Practical Hints. Even the visitor's London covers a large area, and careful planning is needed if you are to make the most of your time. Diagrams of the public transport system, bus and Underground, are issued free at information offices at *St. James's Park* and *Piccadilly Circus* stations.

Shopping centres are numerous. *Oxford Street* is a popular thoroughfare with several large department stores; parallel is *Piccadilly*, and linking them are *Bond Street*, with many luxury shops, and the handsome curve of *Regent Street*. Among *West End* centres are *Kensington* with several famous stores. Some streets specialise in particular goods, *Carnaby Street* for fancy garments for modish young persons; *Charing Cross Road* for bookshops.

Theatres, concerts and cinemas. Daily newspapers list brief advice of these. Details are given in "This Month in London", an official magazine for visitors, published monthly.

Galleries and Museums are not open on Sundays until 2 or 2.30 p.m.

Cafes and restaurants. There is a wide choice of many, but look at the list outside, or a meal may cost you the price of a week's hostelling. Best value in the popular ranges is not in the tempting and rather flashy new snack bars but in the many small unpretentious places in the side streets.

Youth Hostels: Holland House (King George VI Memorial Youth Hostel); Earls Court; Highgate.

Y.H.A. Services Ltd., for equipment, books, maps, railway, coach, air and steamship tickets and advice on travel problems, *29 John Adam Street, WC2N 6JE* (2 minutes from *Charing Cross*).

Modern London has grown around two cities. The first is old London, known as *"the City"*, dating from Roman times, centre of business, finance and trade, governed by its Lord Mayor and Corporation. Its narrow streets are dominated by *St. Paul's*, but towering offices challenge the steeples of its many ancient churches. It suffered the Great Fire of 1666 and bore the brunt of air raids 1939-45.

The second is the *City of Westminster*, a mile or so further up the *Thames*, which grew around its Abbey and Palace, the original royal residence, to become the centre of government of the country.

Remember these distinctions, which still hold good; they will help you to understand today's complex scene where much of interest, but subsidiary importance, lies outside these two.

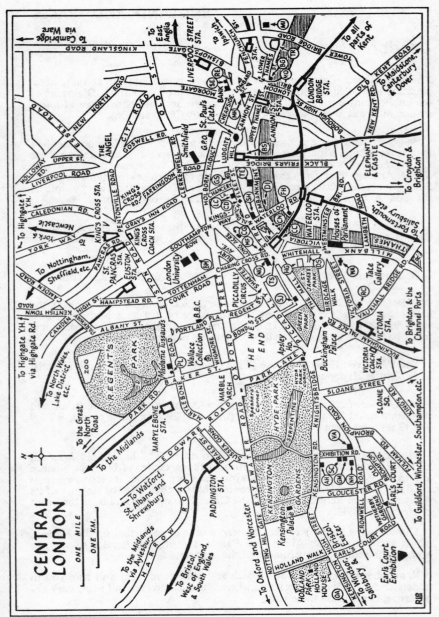

CENTRAL
LONDON

ONE MILE
ONE KM.

N

Key to plan of Central London

AH	Royal Albert Hall	MO	Monument
BG	Billingsgate Fish Market	NG	National Gallery
BM	British Museum	NH	Natural History Museum
BS	Blackfriars Railway Station	OA	Olympia
CC	Charing Cross Railway	PL	Planetarium
	Station	RC	Roman Catholic Cathedral,
CD	St. Clement Danes Church		Westminster
CG	Covent Garden Opera House	RE	Royal Exchange
CN	Cleopatra's Needle	S	Y.H.A. Services, Ltd.,
DI	The "Discovery"		29 John Adam Street
DS	No. 10 Downing Street (Prime	SC	Science Museum
	Minister's Residence)	SE	Stock Exchange
FH	Royal Festival Hall	SH	Somerset House
GM	Geological Museum	SJ	St. James' Palace
GS	Gough Square	TE	Temple
	(Dr. Johnson's House)	TR	Tower
HG	Horse Guards Parade	TS	Trafalgar Square
LC	Law Courts	VA	Victoria and Albert
MF	St. Martin-in-the-Fields		Museum
MH	Mansion House	WA	Westminster Abbey

1. The City

From *Charing Cross* walk E. along *Strand*. Second church is *St. Clement Danes* (finest restored interior after air raid destruction; R.A.F. memorial church). Enter *City* at *Temple Bar, Fleet Street* (newspaper world; *Royal Courts of Justice* on left); passages, right, to *Temple* and lawyers' chambers around *Pump Court* and other courts; associations with Johnson, Goldsmith, Lamb, Dickens; *Middle Temple Hall* (*Twelfth Night* performed here 1602). Return to *Fleet Street*. In *Chancery Lane* is *Record Office Museum* (Domesday Book, Shakespeare's signature, Gunpowder Plot letter, Log of Nelson's *Victory*).

Further along *Fleet Street*, left, through *Hind Court* to *Gough Square, No. 17, Johnson's House* (his famous Dictionary compiled here). *St. Bride's* (Wren church restored). *Ludgate Hill* to *St. Paul's Cathedral* (Wren's masterpiece; new *High Altar*, 1958; *American Memorial Chapel*, 1958; statue of John Donne from Old St. Paul's; Wren's grave in crypt; climb to famous *Whispering Gallery* and *Stone Gallery*, view over London, or 627 steps to the *Ball*.)

From N.E. end of *St. Paul's Churchyard*, along *Cheapside*, once the market place (note names of streets running off). *St. Mary-le-Bow* (of Bow Bells fame).

Left, up *King Street* to *Guildhall* (see *Great Hall* and *Library*). E. by *Lothbury* and *Throgmorton Street* to *Stock Exchange* (charming female guides explain all-male cult of dealings). W. along *Threadneedle Street* between *Bank of England* and *Royal Exchange* houses important relics of early London, including Mithras head). Ahead is *Mansion House*, Lord Mayor's residence.

S.E. by *King William Street* to **The Monument** (by Wren and Hooke, commemorates Great Fire 1666; good view of City from top). Around is *Billingsgate Market* (fish). *London Bridge* (until 1750 only crossing of river); scene of much history, including Viking battle; near S. bank, upstream, stood Shakespeare's *Globe Theatre*: downstream is *Pool of London* and *Tower Bridge*.

Across bridge is *Southwark*. **Cathedral** has fine memorial to Shakespeare, tombs of John Gower and Lancelot Andrewes, *Harvard Chapel* in N. transept; John Harvard baptised here, 1607; *Lady Chapel*; look also for amusing memorial to Lockyer, an 18th century pill maker; wooden effigy of knight, 1280; collection of roof bosses, W. end of nave.

Re-cross *London Bridge*; turn right along *Eastcheap* and *Great Tower Street*. Church of *All Hallows, Barking* (another phoenix risen from the ashes; connections with *Tower*, Toc H and shipping). To the **Tower** (dark memorial of despotism). Return (thankful for representative government) by boat from *Tower Pier* to *Westminster*. Before *Waterloo Bridge* note, by N. Bank, Captain Scott's ship, *Discovery*; beyond bridge, *Cleopatra's Needle*, and, S. bank, *Royal Festival Hall* and *National Theatre*.

2. Westminster to Trafalgar Square

Stand on *Westminster Bridge*, where Wordsworth wrote his famous sonnet; fine views along river in shadow of *"Big Ben"*. To *Parliament Square*, flanked by statues of statesmen. Enter by W. door **Westminster Abbey**. *Tomb of Unknown Warrior* and, all around, the nation's history in tomb and monument; *Statesmen's Corner* N. transept; *Poets' Corner* S. transept; behind *High Altar* is *Edward the Confessor's Chapel* with tombs of early kings and queens; *Coronation Chair*; steps lead to **Henry VII's Chapel**. From S. aisle through *Cloisters* is *Chapter House*, scene of early parliaments.

St. Margaret's Church, just N. of Abbey, 15th century Gothic; famous East window; memorials to Caxton and Raleigh; windows to Milton and to Raleigh and splendid new windows by Piper.

Houses of Parliament (still officially the *Palace of Westminster*). To attend debates you queue for a place in the Gallery. To see round you must go on Saturdays or Bank Holidays. Enter by *Victoria Tower* in *Old Palace Yard*; *Royal Gallery, Princes Chamber*, **House of Lords**, with Throne of Queen's Speech, and Woolsack; **House of Commons** (re-built 1948); *St. Stephen's Hall*, used by Commons for 300 years, statues of kings, queens, statesmen, historical scenes on panels; **Westminster Hall** (1097) with famous 14th century hammer-beam roof, scene of state trials including Sir Thomas More, Guy Fawkes, Charles I, Warren Hastings; *St. Stephen's Crypt*.

Walk along *Parliament Street* past government offices and *Cenotaph*; *Downing Street*, left, with *No. 10*. Further along, *Parliament Street* is called *Whitehall*, after *Whitehall Palace*, of which only Inigo Jones' *Banqueting House* remains; from an upper window Charles I stepped out to scaffold; continue along *Whitehall*: on left, *Horse Guards*. Pass statue (1635) of Charles I.

Trafalgar Square, with *Nelson's Column*, fountains; *St. Martin-in-the-Fields* (by Gibbs, 1721-26). **National Gallery**, superb collection chief schools of painting; each room needs separate visit.

In *St. Martin's Place*, by statue of Nurse Cavell, **National Portrait Gallery**, (the great and famous in all spheres over 500 years of history).

3. Buckingham Palace, Parks and Squares

Trafalgar Square. Through *Admiralty Arch* to *St. James's Park*, its lake, and *Mall* (processional way) to *Buckingham Palace*, London residence of the Queen; *Changing of the Guard* daily at 11.30 a.m. Along *Constitution Hill*, by *Green Park* to *Hyde Park Corner*. *Apsley House* (*Wellington Museum*, with Adam drawing-room and fine paintings).

Walk E. side of *Hyde Park*, or bus along *Park Lane* to *Marble Arch*; along *Oxford Street*, left up *Duke Street* to *Manchester Square* for **Wallace Collection** (treasury of paintings, furniture, arms, armour, objets d'art). Return down *Duke Street*, continue along it, crossing *Oxford Street*, to *Grosvenor Street* and turn right, into *New Bond Street and Old Bond Street* (luxury shops) to *Piccadilly*.

Some other major sights

(Best undertaken by special visits. Nearest underground station stated in brackets).

Westminster Cathedral: Roman Catholic, built 1895-1903 by Bentley in Byzantine style, splendid structure, interior still to be lined with marble and mosaics. (Victoria)

St. Bartholomew the Great: (1123), Norman Priory Church, finest church to survive the Great Fire. (Barbican)

London Museum, in *Kensington Palace*; history of London from Roman times. (High St. Kensington)

British Museum: immensely rich; treasures include Elgin marbles, Rosetta Stone, Codex Sinaiticus, Portland Vase, Sutton Hoo Ship-burial. Visit at least the *Edward VII Galleries*. (Tottenham Court Rd.)

Courtauld Institute Galleries, *Woburn Square*; recent and distinguished addition to London's art collections. (Tottenham Court Rd.)

South Kensington Museums: these include, in separate buildings, **Victoria and Albert Museums** (vast art collections, all countries; see especially the Raphael Cartoons); **Geological Museum, Natural History Museum, Science Museum.** (South Kensington)

ENGLAND AND WALES

Soane Museum, 13 *Lincoln's Inn Fields*; has Hogarth's "Rake's Progress" paintings, etc. in a pleasing house (closed Mondays and all August). (Holborn)

Tate Gallery, *Millbank*; chief collections of British paintings and sculpture, notably Hogarth, Blake, Constable, Turner; important also for modern foreign schools from French Impressionists onwards. (Westminster)

Regent's Park: pleasing in itself; contains also famous **Zoo** (cheaper on Mondays). Huge collection, feeding time 2 p.m. winter, 3 p.m. summer, and **Aquarium.** (Gt. Portland St.)

Madame Tussaud's: waxworks, of the famous and infamous. (Baker St.)

Planetarium: projection of the skies, popularly explained; frequent showings lasting about an hour. (Baker St.)

Hampstead Heath and **Ken Wood House.** House has fine Adam room, furniture and paintings (*Iveagh Bequest*). (Hampstead)

Excursions around London

Accessible quickly by Underground or train. River steamers (summer) are a pleasant alternative for outward or homeward journey.

Greenwich. Royal Naval College (by Wren; *Great Hall* painted in Baroque style by Thornhill); open afternoons only, closed Thursdays. **Queen's House** (by Inigo Jones, with *National Maritime Museum* and library). **Greenwich Park** with fine view of *London* and *Thames*.

Kew. Royal Botanic Gardens. Spacious, delightful for stroll or study; the world's flora in open air or hot house. May be combined with visit to *Richmond*.

Richmond. Immediately S. of *Kew*. From *Richmond Bridge* (18th century) walk up *Hill Rise* to the **Terrace**, famous view of *Thames* valley, and *Richmond Hill*. In *Richmond Park*, over 2,000 acres, deer roam freely.

Hampton Court. Wolsey's great house, enlarged by Henry VIII and Wren; largest royal palace. *Gatehouse, Tennis Court*, astronomical clock. *State Apartments, Galleries, Great Hall, Cellars, Kitchens*, fine formal gardens, *Maze*.

Windsor. (Y.H.) State rooms of **Castle** open when Court not in residence; great storehouse of art and craftsmanship. **St. George's Chapel**, perfect example of Perpendicular style. *Windsor Great Park*, deer and ancient oaks. *Eton College Chapel*.

Touring Routes
South-East England

This is the chalkland of England, first seen by visitors from the Continent in the white cliffs of *Dover*. Between its three ranges of low hills—the *North* and *South Downs* and the *Chilterns*—are wide lowlands containing rich farming country and the great metropolis of *London*. Despite growth of population it is still a land of tidy farms and quiet villages.

R.1. The Chilterns. London-Dunstable-St. Albans-London (95 miles)

The chalk hills of the *Chilterns*, with their fine beech woods, rise gently from the *London Basin* to fall suddenly in a steep escarpment to the plains beyond. Nearly every town and village has good examples of English domestic architecture.

Train from *Marylebone Station* to *Beaconsfield* to get clear of *London* environs. *Beaconsfield* (many Georgian houses). *Chalfont St. Giles* (cottage of John Milton open to public). 2 miles S. is *Jordans* (**Y.H.**) associated with William Penn and American State that bears his name; his grave is in burial ground of Quaker Meeting House. *High Wycombe* (centre of furniture trade). *West Wycombe* village, a double row of houses, is protected by *National Trust;* houses cover 15th-19th centuries, yet styles form harmonious picture. Church above has armchair pulpit. **Y.H.** at *Bradenham.*

All along line of *Chilterns* dry valleys run up from S.E. to scarp slope. Roads tend to follow them, but footpaths and tracks enable walker and cyclist to follow line of hills. Scarp runs in series of rounded headlands, some wooded, others covered with short springy turf. A beautiful peaceful landscape with fine views. Villages follow foot of scarp at point where spring water issues. At *Bledlow* and *Whiteleaf* are crosses cut into chalk hillside. *Fingest* in beautiful *Hambleden* valley has interesting Norman church.

Ivinghoe (**Y.H.**); centre for walks; *Ivinghoe Beacon* (view); *Duncombe Terrace; Ashridge.* Nearby is *Whipsnade Zoo* where animals roam in large outdoor pens. From *Dunstable* return via **St. Albans** (**Y.H.** summer); Roman Verulamium, remains of wall, tesselated pavement and theatre. Cathedral stand where St. Alban, Britain's first Christian martyr, died, A.D. 305 Earliest Norman tower in England, largely built from Roman materials. 11th century wall paintings. Town has 15th century clock tower and one of oldest inns in England—*The Fighting Cocks.* Train to *London.*

R.2. The North Downs, South Downs and Weald. London—Canterbury—Chichester—London (250 miles).

Train from *Victoria* or *Charing Cross Stations* to *Merstham* across south London suburbs. Downs run E. with *Pilgrims' Way* at their foot on edge of the *Weald*—a country of orchards and hop fields on clay soils, with much woodland including *Ashdown Forest.* Oast houses for drying hops are a feature. Many delightful villages.

ENGLAND AND WALES

Crockham Hill (**Y.H.**) overlooking *Weald. Kemsing* (**Y.H.**); *Doddington* (**Y.H.**); both on *Pilgrims' Way. Chilham*, perhaps prettiest village in *Kent*; houses grouped around church and castle.

Canterbury (**Y.H.**); historic cathedral; archbishop is Primate of England; *Shrine of Becket* a place of pilgrimage for centuries. City has other ancient churches; see also *West Gate, Christ Church Gate, St. Dunstan's Street* with *Falstaff Hotel, Butchery Lane*; town walls in *Broad Street*.

Dover (**Y.H.**); its white cliffs almost a symbol of England; Roman lighthouse, Saxon tower, Norman keep.

N. along coast; *Deal*, where Julius Caesar first landed; *Sandwich*, oldest of *Cinque Ports*, with old gatehouse. Flemish and Dutch weavers settled in this area in 14th century; traces of their brickwork and gables add slightly foreign touch to villages.

From *Dover* the *Vale of Kent* is reached via *Folkestone*. Its notable villages include *Tenterden* (birthplace of Caxton), *Smarden, High Halden, Biddenden* and *Goudhurst* (**Y.H.**). *Sissinghurst Castle*; gardens open in summer. *Bodiam*, impressive moated castle.

Coast road leads to *Rye* and *Winchelsea*, two more *Cinque Ports*, now silted, but with many relics of their former importance. *Hastings (Guestling* **Y.H.** 3 miles N.E.): seaside resort with interesting old fishing town. The famous battle was fought 7 miles inland where *Battle Abbey*, built by William the Conqueror, stands to commemorate his victory.

Beachy Head, 18 miles W. of *Hastings*, great chalk cliff where **South Downs** reach the sea. Their rounded whale-backed hills, cut by several small rivers, covered with short springy turf in east, wooded in west, provide good walking country, especially around *Alfriston* (**Y.H.**) and cycling country west of *Lewes* (town clustering below its Norman keep). **Y.H.** at *Patcham*. Many other pleasing towns and villages. *Steyning: Amberley* (castle); *Arundel* (**Y.H.**) (castle); *Bignor* (remains of Roman villa); *Petworth* (great mansion, *Petworth House*); *Midhurst* (*Cowdray Park*, entered from its High Street, is fine example of English parkland).

Chichester, dignified town; cathedral with beautiful precincts; Roman remains; stately houses.

N. from *Midhurst*, road climbs to heathlands around *Hindhead* (**Y.H.**) with natural amphitheatre of *Devil's Punch Bowl. Milford* (**Y.H.**). *Guildford* (notable modern cathedral; 17th century Abbot's Hospital; St. Mary's Church with pre-Norman tower; castle; Castle Arch House; much Georgian brickwork, tile-hung houses, pointed gables).

Between *Guildford* and *Reigate*, 15 miles E., *Box Hill* and other chalk slopes contrast with sandy country around *Leith Hill* (965 ft., highest point in S.E.). Both hills have extensive views. Pleasant villages about here include *Albury, Shere, Friday Street* and *Abinger* (**Y.H.** *Holmbury St. Mary*). From *Dorking* train to *London*.

East Anglia

The large, eastward-extending bulge of *Norfolk* and *Suffolk*, together with parts of adjacent counties, is termed *East Anglia*. It is the driest part of England and its countryside, almost untouched by modern industry, is a scene of placid and prosperous farmlands under a great dome of sky. It is rich in domestic architecture and fine churches.

R.3. London—Cambridge—Norwich—Colchester (228 miles)

Train (*Liverpool St.*) to *Audley End*; mansion, covering nearly 5 acres, one of greatest 16th century houses. *Saffron Walden*, delightful market town; wealth of Tudor buildings, including **Y.H. Cambridge**, one of the two ancient university towns; great historical and architectural interest. Colleges usually admit visitors to courts all day and to other parts at certain times. Oldest is *Peterhouse* (1284). *Trinity College*, *King's College*, with famous chapel, and *Queen's* are well known. *The Backs*, riverside lawns, give most characteristic view of main colleges **(Y.H.)**.

N.W. from *Cambridge* main road follows line of Roman road, *Via Devana*, to *Huntingdon* and delightful group of villages on *R. Ouse*. Oliver Cromwell and Samuel Pepys were educated here. Eastwards *Ouse* flows past *Houghton Mill* **(Y.H.)** through *Hemingford Abbots* and *Hemingford Gray* (with 12th century manor house) to *St. Ives*; stone bridge with ancient chantry chapel.

Country here (the *Fens*), flat and partly below sea level, extensively drained. Towns and villages stand where a slight rise gave drier setting. Cathedral at *Ely* on such a hill, dominates countryside for miles around; Norman and Early Gothic with unique octagonal lantern tower. **(Y.H.)** summer only. 8 Miles S. is *Wicken Fen*, one of few remaining pieces of natural fen, preserved by *National Trust* as ecological sanctuary. Reclaimed Fenland makes rich agricultural land, especially for wheat, sugar beet, fruit and flower production. *R. Ouse* reaches sea by way of *Downham Market*, (buildings of "gingerbread stone") and *King's Lynn* **(Y.H.)**, busy market town and seaport; Guildhall, 15th century, has characteristic East Anglian flint flushwork; Renaissance Customs House; medieval merchants' houses; churches of *St. Mary* (Early English chancel) and *St. Nicholas* (tiebeam roof; beautiful south porch). *Sandringham, Norfolk*, home of the Royal Family, 8 miles N.E. **(Y.H.)** at *Hunstanton*. Along coast are quiet villages, many once ports, now separated from sea by salt marshes. *Burnham Thorpe* (15 miles E. of *Hunstanton*) birthplace of Nelson. *Holkham Hall* nearby is masterpiece of 18th century architect Wm. Kent. **(Y.H.)** at *Walsingham*, famous shrine. *Blakeney Point*, shingle spit, bird sanctuary. *Sheringham* **(Y.H.)**, *Cromer* and *Overstrand* have fine sandy beaches. North-eastwards from *Norwich* are the *Broads*, shallow, partly tidal, waters, popular for yachting and study of natural history **(Y.H. at *Martham*)**. **Norwich (Y.H.)** chief market centre of East Anglia: market square, with numerous stalls beneath distinguished modern *City Hall* and fine medieval church of *St. Peter Mancroft*. Cathedral, 11th-16th century, cloisters, lofty spire; Norman castle has museum and art gallery; ancient *Maddermarket* with theatre; many other interesting buildings.

ENGLAND AND WALES

From *Norwich*, through *S. Norfolk, Suffolk* and *N. Essex* are many towns and villages, important centres of cloth trade in Tudor times with old houses, churches and guildhalls. *Wymondham*, S.W. of Norwich, has curious market cross (1616) standing on pillars. *Thetford*, 25 miles, ancient Guildhall. Due S. for 12 miles to *Bury St. Edmunds*, burial place of Edmund, last king of *East Anglia*, martyred by Danes in 870; Abbey Gateway (1347), Norman tower, *St. James' Church* and *St. Mary's Church* with tomb of the Mary Tudor who married Louis XII of France. *Lavenham*, 10 miles S., has streets of unspoilt Tudor architecture; great 15th century church, built when wool brought prosperity. *Long Melford*, 5 miles S.W., rivals it; famous for stained glass *Nedging Tye* (**Y.H.**) is 8 miles E. and *Castle Hedingham* (**Y.H.**) is 12 miles S.W.

R.3(i) *Castle Hedingham* to *Finchingfield* (8 miles W.) and W. 7 miles to *Thaxted*, perfect unspoilt village 15th century houses, Perpendicular church; 11 miles *Bishop's Stortford*, train to London.

Blaxhall (**Y.H.**) near upper reaches R. *Alde* and 8 miles from old seaside town of *Aldeburgh*, associated with Benjamin Britten's opera "*Peter Grimes*" and festival of music and arts held annually in June.

Colchester (**Y.H.**) (18 miles S. of *Long Melford* via *Sudbury*); many Roman remains, including town walls and Balkerne gateway; Saxon, Norman and later buildings. Good museum in castle. Near *East Bergholt*, 10 miles N.E. are *Willy Lott's cottage* and *Flatford Mill*, associated with John Constable, born at *Bergholt*. From *Colchester* return to London by train.

The Cotswolds, Vale of Severn and Stratford-on-Avon

The *Cotswold Hills*, lying N.E. from near *Bath* to the *Northamptonshire Uplands* form an upland area of farmland; small towns and villages of honey-coloured limestone famous for their mellow dignity. To W. and N. the stone escarpment falls to the clay lands around the rivers *Severn* and *Avon*—a fruit-growing district with villages of timber and thatch, and historic towns such as *Gloucester* and *Stratford-on-Avon*.

R.4. The Cotswolds. Oxford to Gloucester (61 miles)

Oxford (**Y.H.**) with its famous University, starting point for *Cotswold* tour but also a place to linger. Twenty-two colleges, many open to visitors on enquiry at lodges. *University* (oldest, 1249), *Merton* (library and chapel), *New* (almost unchanged since 1379; beautiful garden), *Magdalen* and *Christ Church* (whose chapel is also the cathedral). Also *Ashmolean* and *University* museums, *Bodleian Library*, *Radcliffe Camera* (view from dome) and *Sheldonian Theatre*.

Road to *Gloucester* joins valley of *Windrush*, a tributary of *Thames*. *Witney*, important for manufacture of blankets, seen hung on poles to dry. Ancient town hall and butter cross in High Street. 8 miles W. is *Burford* one of finest towns in *Cotswolds*. Steep main street lined with Tudor houses. See the *Tolsey* in main street, church which housed prisoners of war in the Civil War, and adjacent almshouses.

The *Cotswolds* are so rich in beautiful villages, that it is hardly necessary to do more than suggest those specially worth visiting. From *Burford* choice of routes (a) S. to *Lechlade* on *Thames*, and via *Fairford* to *Cirencester*, pleasant town, wide, curving main street; museum, excellent display of Roman remains. Between *Cirencester* and *Gloucester* is one of best stretches of *Cotswolds*; wooded valleys, innumerable tracks and lanes for walker and cyclist; ancient towns and villages of *Tetbury, Nailsworth, Minchinhampton, Bisley, Painswick*, the *Duntisbournes* (*Duntisbourne Abbotts* Y.H.) and *Birdlip* (fine view on *Cotswolds* edge). *Chedworth* (Roman Villa). (b) N. from *Burford* to *Stow-on-the-Wold* (**Y.H.**) ancient town; lovely villages of *Upper* and *Lower Slaughter, Upper* and *Lower Swell, Bourton-on-the-Water*. At *Bourton*, R. *Windrush* flows through village, spanned by series of bridges. Beyond *Stow* are other fine examples of local architecture in *Chipping Campden, Chipping Norton, Moreton-in-Marsh*. Near *Chipping Norton* are *Rollright Stones*, one of best ancient stone circles in Midlands, and *Great* and *Little Tew*, two of loveliest villages in *Oxfordshire*. W. from *Stow* ground rises steadily then drops in scarp slope to the *Severn* plain. Views N. and W. across hills of *Welsh Border* country. (c) W. from *Burford* to *Northleach*, which like so many Cotswold towns owed its original prosperity to now departed wool trade. *Cleeve Hill* (finely situated **Y.H.**); down escarpment to *Cheltenham* (fashionable residential town) and *Gloucester*.

Along foot of *Cotswold* escarpment is region of fruit and dairy farming, a peaceful land with stately towns and villages.

R. 5. Gloucester—Stratford-on-Avon—Warwick—Kenilworth (48 miles).

Gloucester: busy, historic city; magnificent cathedral of many periods, Norman nave, splendid Perpendicular choir. Lady chapel, cloisters, view from tower. *New Inn* (1455) has galleried courtyard. 12 miles N.E. is *Tewkesbury*, on R. *Severn*: abbey church (Norman) and much Tudor domestic architecture.

Evesham, 14 miles, centre of fruit farming area; few miles S.E. is *Broadway*, a show village of Cotswolds, 18 miles to **Stratford-on-Avon (Y.H.)** Shakespeare's birthplace, Guild House, Grammar School where he was educated, *Holy Trinity Church* with Shakespearian associations, *New Place Museum, Falcon Inn, Memorial Theatre, John Harvard's House, Anne Hathaway's Cottage* at *Shottery*.

Warwick Castle, overlooking R. *Avon*, is among best in Midlands. In the town, finest building is *Leycester Hospital*, by *West Gate*. *Mill Street* has many old houses. Two miles to *Leamington Spa*, pleasant town, good centre for exploring region. *The Parade* is most graceful street in Midlands.

Kenilworth: Castle, priory gatehouse, and much old red brick architecture.

Western England and the South West

The West of England is rich in prehistoric sites, and has, also, many old towns and cities. The peninsula of *Cornwall, Devon* and *North Somerset* has fine coastal scenery, quaint seaside villages and challenging open moorland country. Characteristic of *Devon* are the "cob" houses with thatched roofs and whitewashed plaster walls.

R.6. Winchester—Salisbury—Swanage (91 miles)

Western England can be said to begin with **Winchester (Y.H.)** first capital of England, where Alfred the Great had his court; now county town of *Hampshire.* Cathedral, impressive interior, longest nave in Europe, tomb of William of Wykeham, founder of famous college in the city and of *New College, Oxford.* Interesting misericords under seats in choir. In *Castle Hall* is legendary *King Arthur's Round Table.* Old West Gate adjoins castle. 15th century Butter Cross.

Salisbury (Y.H.), 20 miles W. Cathedral is noblest example of early English style, 404 ft. spire, tallest in England. Beautiful cathedral close has Renaissance *Mompesson House* and other pleasing houses.

R.6 (i) **Salisbury to Stonehenge, Marlborough and Avebury.** 2 miles N. *Old Sarum*, on conical hill, with remains of successive settlements by Celts, Romans and Normans, remains of Norman Abbey within Iron Age fort. Site abandoned when *Salisbury* cathedral was built. On chalk expanse of *Salisbury Plain* 8 miles N. is magnificent prehistoric group of Stonehenge. Carved into chalk hills of *Salisbury Plain* and *Berkshire Downs* are outlines of many white horses, some ancient. The horse at *Uffington*, on N. edge of *Berkshire Downs*, gives its name to *Vale of the White Horse. Marlborough* 20 miles N. of *Stonehenge*, 2 miles to Avebury, largest megalithic stone circle in Europe, outer ditch enclosing area of 28 acres; Britain's most important survival from early Bronze Age. Many related tumuli and stone avenues in vicinity; *Silbury Hill*, largest artificial mound in Europe.

S.W. from *Salisbury* on A.354: at *Coombe Bissett*, 4 miles, turn W. through *Broad Chalke* and along *Ridge Way* (fine views) N. of *Cranborne Chase. Shaftesbury*, 20 miles, old market town, steep twisting streets. 7 miles S.W. B.3092 to *Sturminster* and S. across *Dorset Downs* to *Milton Abbas*, 16 miles, beautifully situated village and abbey. At *Cerne Abbas*, 10 miles W. is giant prehistoric figure cut in chalk hillside.

The river *Piddle* flows through several delightful villages of which *Tolpuddle* is famous for the "martyrs" transported to Australia (1834) for forming a trade union.

Dorchester, county town of *Dorset,* country of Thomas Hardy's novels. Pleasing town, tree-lined avenues, links with Pilgrim Fathers; *Maumbury Rings,* at S. end is a Roman amphitheatre.

Maiden Castle, 2 miles S.W., huge prehistoric site, 45 acres. On a natural hill was built, about 2,000 B.C. a great fortified village, later abandoned, but used again in early Iron Age. Much later a Roman temple was built on the site. Traces of defensive ramparts, hut circles and other buildings.

E. of *Dorchester, South Dorset Downs* reach sea near *Swanage,* 30 miles **(Y.H.)** Hardy's "Knollsea" lying between two headlands; ruins of *Corfe Castle.* 16 miles W., beautiful landlocked *Lulworth Cove,* an almost circular bay.

ENGLAND AND WALES

R. 7. Salisbury—Exeter—Plymouth—Land's End—St. Ives—Minehead—Bristol—Bath (445 miles)

Many interesting towns and villages on road to *Exeter*. *Shaftesbury* (see **R.6**) *Stalbridge*, *Sherborne*, 18 miles: abbey with magnificent fan vaulting; ancient school, castle partly built by Sir Walter Raleigh. *Yeovil*, 15 miles, church of St. John the Baptist (1380); ancient inns; museum. Great house of *Montacute* (Tudor) 4 miles W. *Crewkerne*. *Chard* (ancient inns; fine houses). *Honiton*, 27 miles. *Ottery St. Mary* (birthplace of Coleridge).

Exeter, 20 miles **(Y.H.)** county town of *Devon*, Cathedral (Decorated style 14th century). Many old churches.

R.7(i) Dartmoor National Park. Between *Exeter* and *Plymouth* is *Dartmoor*, an area of granite, largely overlain by moorland, but exposed in highest parts in tors, among which *High Willhays* reaches 2,039 ft. Abounds in stone circles, stone avenues and other prehistoric remains. Into edge of moor several rivers have cut deep wooded valleys—e.g. the *Teign*, *Bovey* and *Dart*. *Postbridge* is site of ancient stone "clapper" bridge. At *Buckfast* under S.E. end of moor, is abbey almost entirely rebuilt during present century by its Benedictine monks. (*Tavistock* Y.H. and small hostels on moor).

Totnes and *Dartmouth*, interesting old towns. Between them R. *Dart* broadens into estuary to reach sea at *Start Bay* **(Y.H.)**. Between *Exeter* and *Dartmouth* are many coastal towns and villages, crowded in summer. *Brixham* is, perhaps, the most attractive. S.W. from *Dartmouth* is beautiful estuary of *Salcombe* **(Y.H.)** where stretch of cliffs between *Bolt Head* and *Bolt Tail* is gem of *S. Devon* coastline. Area S. and W. of *Dartmouth* is rolling farmland, a patchwork of fields in which red soil combines with greenness of crops to form a colourful landscape.

Plymouth, finely situated on Plymouth Sound; starting point of Elizabethan voyages of discovery; here Drake sailed to defeat Armada (1588) and *Mayflower* put out with Pilgrim Fathers (1620): severely bombed in war; now rebuilt **(Y.H.)**.

From *Plymouth* to *Land's End* chief attraction is wonderful coastline: many picturesque ports and fishing villages, *Looe*, *Polperro*, *Fowey*, **(Y.H.** at *Golant*) *Mevagissey* (*Boswinger* **Y.H.** 4 miles S.W.), *Falmouth* **(Y.H.**, in *Pendennis Castle*) *Helston*, *Marazion*, *Penzance* **(Y.H.)**, *Newlyn*, *Mousehole*. *Lizard Point* is most southerly point in England, as *Land's End* **(Y.H.)** is most westerly. Climate sub-tropical, almost every garden has its palm tree. *St. Michael's Mount*, reached by causeway at low tide from *Marazion*, is a conical hill crowned with battlemented castle on site of Benedictine monastery.

From *Land's End* return by N. coast; fine scenery, quaint villages: *St. Ives* **(Y.H.** at *Hayle*), *St. Agnes*, *Newquay*, *Tintagel*, *Boscastle* **(Y.H.)** and *Clovelly*. N. of *Newquay* are *Bedruthan Steps*, great detached masses of rock on beach below towering cliffs; **(Y.H.)** at *Treyarnon*. At *Tintagel* **(Y.H.)** is *King Arthur's Castle*, where Cornish chough, an uncommon bird may be seen.

Clovelly, perhaps most visited village in England, has cobbled main street that is a series of steps from harbour to village. Less crowded but no less worthwhile are great cliffs of *Hartland Point* (*Elmscott* **Y.H.**) with views over *Bristol Channel* to *Lundy Island*.

E. from *Clovelly* lie valleys of rivers *Torridge* and *Taw*, whose joint estuary reaches sea at *Appledore*; fishing village of Kingsley's *"Westward Ho!"*; *Bideford* (*Instow* **Y.H.**) on *Torridge* and *Barnstaple* on *Taw* retain a sense of past importance.

From *Barnstaple* roads lead to **Exmoor**, another National Park, astride *Devon-Somerset* border; wide expanse of rolling hills covered with coarse grass or heather and bracken, crossed by many minor roads and trackways. As on *Dartmoor*, rivers cut deeply, forming famous *Doone Valley* and wooded valleys of the *Barle*, *Exe*, and *Horner Water*. *Dunkery Beacon* (1,707 ft.) is highest point. Along N. Coast, on edge of moor, are fine cliffs and old towns and villages; **Y.H.** at *Lynton*. *Selworthy* W. of *Minehead* (**Y.H.**) has some of best cob and thatch cottages in S.W. England. *Dunster;* ancient Yarn Market and Butter Cross in main street.

Road E. from *Minehead* skirts northern end of *Quantock Hills*, (**Y.H.** at *Holford* and *Crowcombe*), delightful small range of heather-clad hills, well served by footpaths—and on to *Bridgwater*. Here one road runs direct to *Bristol* and another along line of *Polden Hills* to *Glastonbury* (**Y.H.** at *Street*, 3 miles S.). Here was *Isle of Avalon* of the Arthurian stories, reputed end of pilgrimage of Joseph of Arimathea, bringing the Holy Grail, supposed to be buried under *Glastonbury Tor*. On *Sedgemoor*, beyond *Polden Hills*, King Alfred hid and prepared to defeat the Danes, ending with signing of Treaty at *Wedmore* (878) near *Cheddar* (**Y.H.**). **Wells:** cathedral, masterpiece of Early English and Decorated styles; famous W. front has over 600 statues. Town gates; 14th century houses, old inns, museum. Town stands at foot of *Mendip Hills* a limestone tableland with spectacular gorges, the most famous being *Cheddar*, best approached from N.E. Several caves open to visitors both here and along line of hills.

Bristol; historic seaport, important trade with America. Brunel's famous *Clifton Suspension Bridge* spans Avon Gorge. There is a cathedral but the outstanding church is *St. Mary Redcliff*, one of finest in England (late Perpendicular).

Bath (**Y.H.**), a spa since Roman times: Roman bath finely preserved. Town, remodelled in 18th century by John Wood, was made most fashionable spa in country by Beau Nash. Good examples from this period are the *Pump Room*, *Royal Crescent* and *Pulteney Bridge*.

Wales and the Welsh Border

The contrasts with England are many. The country is wilder and, except in the S.E., less populous. The gentle rhythms of the English landscape are replaced by dramatic changes of scene. The streams are often mountain torrents, but many descend to fertile lovely valleys. The Welsh people have their own distinctive culture and ancient language and look back to different origins.

Between Welsh highlands and English lowlands, the Border zone shares some of the features of each, but—as so often on frontiers—has an exhilarating atmosphere of its own.

R.8. The Welsh Border. Chepstow to Shrewsbury (109 miles)

Approach direct from *Gloucester* or by *Severn Bridge*, 15 miles N. of *Bristol*, to *Chepstow* (Y.H.): fine castle above R. *Wye* which follows beautiful and extraordinary course between *Monmouth* and *Chepstow*; deep wooded banks, high limestone cliffs. *Tintern Abbey* (Cistercian) 5 miles N. magnificent ruins. At *Bigsweir*, 4 miles, cross river and up 2 miles to *St. Briavels Castle*, Norman castle now Y.H. overlooking *Forest of Dean*, once a royal hunting ground.

Monmouth, 8 miles, at confluence of *Monnow* and *Wye* has only remaining fortified bridge (*Monnow Bridge*) in England. 5 miles N.E. *Symonds Yat*, famous viewpoint, where *Wye* makes great loop. *Goodrich* village and castle; *Welsh Bicknor* (Y.H.); *Ross-on-Wye* is small town with fine stone market hall. Northwards are many examples of half-timbered architecture of black and white appearance; houses of timber frames with white plastering, best seen in *Ledbury* and *Hereford*. On for 7 miles to *Much Marcle* and to Y.H. at *Rushall*.

R.8(i) Hereford and Herefordshire villages *Rushall* to *Woolhope* and *Fownhope*, among low hills geologically famous. Hereford, 12 miles. County town, interesting houses and inns. Cathedral has unique map of world (*Mappa Mundi*, 1313) and over 1,400 chained books, including Caxtons. *Weobley*, superb half-timbered village is 8 miles N.W. of *Hereford*.

Main route continues 7 miles to *Ledbury* at S. end of **Malvern Hills,** (1,395 ft.) Many paths along grass-covered hills, wide views, remains of early British camp on *Hereford Beacon*.

Malvern Wells (Y.H.); beautiful priory church spared by Henry VIII at dissolution of monasteries. 5 miles N. to *Bransford* and N.W. along *Teme* valley- to *Tenbury Wells* and on to **Ludlow** (Y.H.), 23 miles, one of the most attractive towns in England; wealth of old buildings, *Feathers Hotel*, castle; *St. Lawrence's* is a noble guild church with beautiful glass. S.W. is lovely wooded country on *Radnorshire* border; many half-timbered villages.

7 miles N.W. is *Stokesay Castle*, fine example of 13th century moated fortified manor house; Tudor gatehouse; adjacent church has "horse box" pews. *Wenlock Edge*, limestone escarpment, runs 15 miles N.E. to *Much Wenlock*, with (12 miles) *Wilderhope Manor* (Y.H.), a Tudor house set in lovely farmland.

Church Stretton, 8 miles W., centre for walks on surrounding hills, including *Long Mynd*, with steep dry valleys, and *Caer Caradoc* which has traces of ancient British settlement. The *Port Way* which runs its switchback way along *Long Mynd* is excellent route for walkers and cyclists; small Y.H. at *Bridges* on W. side of hills. 4 miles N. of *Church Stretton* leave main road at *Leebotwood*. 5 miles N.E. *Acton Burnell* castle, in park, reputed meeting place of first Parliament (1265). Continue 6 miles E. to *Much Wenlock*, ancient market town. 3 miles N. by R. *Severn* is fine Norman abbey at *Buildwas*. *Coalbrookdale* is an early centre of Industrial Revolution; at *Ironbridge* is world's first iron bridge (1779); still in use. *Wroxeter* 6 miles, (remains of Roman town, *Uriconium*). **Shrewsbury**, 6 miles, (Y.H.), historic town in bend of *Severn*; fine churches, groups of timbered houses, narrow lanes and passageways; statue of Charles Darwin who was educated at its famous school.

ENGLAND AND WALES

R. 9. South Wales. Monmouth—Brecon—Carmarthen—Tenby— St. David's (145 miles)

From *Monmouth* (see **R.8**) to *Rockfield*, 2 miles, and N.W. by minor road through *St. Maughans Green* to *Skenfrith*, 5 miles, castle; W. 7 miles to *Llanvetherine* (fine 12th century *White Castle* 1 mile S.E.) 5 miles *Abergavenny* and on to *Crickhowell* (**Y.H.**) 6 miles N.W. Picturesque village with 13 arch stone bridge over *R. Usk* which here passes between hills of *Brecon Beacons* and *Black Mountains*. Excellent walking country.

EXCURSION: *Sugar Loaf* (1,995 ft.), isolated hill, 3 miles E., fine view.

R.9(i) *Crickhowell*, N.E. up *Grwyne Fawr* valley to *Llanbedr*, *Pont Newydd* and *Partrishow*. 5 miles, (tiny, lonely church in wild valley). Return 1 mile and take lane E. into famous Vale of *Ewyas*. *Llanthony*, 7 miles, 12th century Abbey (Transitional Norman). Continue 4 miles to *Capel-y-Ffin* (King George VI Memorial **Y.H.**) Walking and riding in *Black Mountains*— open breezy heights up to 2,600 ft. with huge and colourful views.

Main route continues up Usk valley; road and path on N. bank and climb to *Bwlch*, 6 miles, fine view. *Brecon*, 7 miles, (**Y.H.** *Ty'n-y-Cae*, 2½ miles E.) county town of *Brecknockshire*; cathedral built of red sandstone. *Pen-y-Crug* (1,088 ft.) 1½ miles N.W. good view over town and of *Brecon Beacons* (highest point, *Pen-y-Fan*, 2,907 ft.).

R.9 (ii) 2 day walk from *Brecon* over *Brecon Beacons* via *Cwm Cynwyn* and *Pen-y-Fan*, descend W. to *Storey Arms* (**Y.H.**), 10 miles S.W. over *Fan Fawr* (2,409 ft.) to *Ystradfellte*, 10 miles, (small **Y.H.**), centre for gorges and waterfalls of upper *Neath* and *Mellte* valleys. On hills W. is section of Roman road, *Sarn Helen*. 6 miles S. is *Pontneathvaughan* from which take bus through industrial area to *Neath* and *Swansea*, port and centre of tinplate industry; fine modern Guildhall with large pictures by Brangwyn.

R.9(iii) West of Swansea is famous *Gower Peninsula*. S. coast has limestone cliffs, caves, fine bays, many wild flowers: inland are sandstone hills with extensive views: castles and small distinctive churches: **Y.H.** at *Port Eynon*. Bus services from Swansea.

R.9(iv) Cardiff. Metropolis of Wales, handsome group of public buildings, including *National Museum of Wales* (illustrating all aspects of Wales and Welsh life; also art gallery and *National Portrait Collection*). Castle. *Llandaff Cathedral*, 2½ miles N. (12th century; unique feature is the statue of Christ, by Epstein, and arch bearing it). *St. Fagan's Castle*, 4 miles, has *Welsh National Folk Museum*.

Main route continues W. *Brecon* to *Senny Bridge*, 9 miles, then on to *Trecastle*, 3 miles, turn S. and W.S.W. on Mountain Road to *Llanddeusant* (**Y.H.**) 9 miles.

EXCURSION: Walk to source of *R. Usk* and *Carmarthen Van* (2,632 ft.), very extensive view.

Llangadock, 7 miles, picturesque small town in fertile *Towy* valley; on to *Llandilo*, 7 miles.

EXCURSION: *Caregr Cennen*, 4 miles S.E., dramatically sited 13th century castle.

At *Broadoak*, 4 miles, turn S. to *Llangathen* (lane W. from village leads to *Grongar Hill* (410 ft.) in centre of *Towy Valley*, subject of famous poem). Cross *Towy* to *Carmarthen*, 14 miles, counry and market town, St. Peter's church, Guild Hall, museum; coracles still in use on *Towy*.

EXCURSION: 10 miles S. to Kidwelly. Huge 11th century castle, well preserved. Beautiful estuaries of *Towy* and *Gwendraeth*.

From *Carmarthen* to *Llanstephen*, 12 miles, attractive village, castle. W. 2 miles to ferry across R. *Taf* to *Laugharne*, handsome small town with ancient charter (1307): associations with Dylan Thomas: harbour, castle. Continue W. on coast road to *Pendine* (5 miles) good sands; at *Amroth* enter *Pembrokeshire*. Y.H. at *Pentlepoir*, near *Saundersfoot*.

Tenby, small port and seaside resort of great charm, unspoilt; historic houses, narrow streets; centre for south part of splendid *Pembrokeshire* coast.

EXCURSIONS: (a) via *Lamphey* (ruins of bishop's palace) to *Stackpole* and St. Govan's Head (from this point to *Elegug Stacks*, 4 miles W. is good section of coast). (b) via *Manorbier Castle* and *King's Quoit* (dolmen) to *Lydstep Point* and *Giltar Head*. (c) *Carew* (castle, church and Celtic cross) and delightful scenery of inner creeks of *Milford Haven*, especially the *Cleddau*.

Pembroke, 3 miles, large castle; continue via *Neyland* ferry to *Haverfordwest*, 11 miles, county town. N.W. to *Solva*, picturesque village on creek, and, 16 miles, **St. David's**: ancient centre of Christianity, associated with patron saint of Wales. Cathedral, unique site in hollow to escape notice from sea (Viking raiders were active on this coast); superb Norman nave, many interesting details. Ruins of Bishop's Palace of great beauty. (Y.H.) 2 miles N.W. near *Whitesand Bay* (bathing). **St. David's Head**: many pre-historic remains; magnificent cliffs typical of whole *North Pembrokeshire coast*, which can only be seen by walkers. Good view from *Carn Llidi* (595 ft.).

Continue on minor road via *Llanrhian*, *Trevine* (**Y.H.**) large dolmen 1 mile N.E., *Abercastle* (hamlet on creek), *Abermawr* (storm beach) to *Pwll Deri* (**Y.H.**), 17 miles, finely sited on coast 2 miles S. of *Strumble Head*.

EXCURSION: *Garn Fawr*, Iron Age fort above Y.H. and E. through *Llanwnda* to *Careg Gwastad Point*, scene of last enemy landing on British soil (1797); return along cliffs via *Strumble Head* (lighthouse).

Fishguard, 5 miles, port for *Ireland*; *Dinas*, *Newport* (**Y.H.**) (prehistoric camps on *Carn Ingli*, 1½ miles S.); *Nevern*, picturesque village, church and Celtic cross; coast road via *Moylgrove* to *Cemaes Head*, 20 miles, (*Poppit Sands* **Y.H.**).

St. Dogmaels and *Cardigan*, both finely placed on R. *Teifi*; coracles used for salmon fishing. 2 miles S. turn E. to *Cilgerran*, Norman castle above gorge. Continue up beautiful *Teifi* valley to *Cenarth*; salmon leap and coracles, *Newcastle Emlyn* via *Henllan* to *Pentre Cwrt*, 21 miles. *Llandyssul*, picturesque market town, 2½ miles E.

From *Pentre Cwrt* return can be made S. to *Carmarthen*, 16 miles, or N. to central Wales (**R.10**) via *Tregaron*; Y.Hs at *Blaencaron* and *Tyncornel*.

R.10. Central Wales. Shrewsbury—Welshpool—Llanidloes— Devil's Bridge—Aberystwyth—Dolgellau—Llangollen (150 miles)

From *Shrewsbury* (**Y.H.**) take *Welshpool* road. At *Middletown*, 14 miles, climb to *Rodney Pillar* on *Breidden Hill* (1,195 ft.), fine viewpoint. *Welshpool*, 5 miles, market town, old houses, Powysland Museum, *Powis Castle* and *Park* with famous gardens.

ENGLAND AND WALES

Cross R. *Severn* and turn S. Near *Forden*, 5 miles, *Offa's Dyke*, ancient boundary between England and Wales, runs just E. of road. *Montgomery*, 3 miles, picturesque old borough, smallest in country. On to *Newtown*, 9 miles; memorial museum to Robert Owen, social reformer.

Continue up *Severn* valley to *Llanidloes*, 14 miles, small town with old market hall. At *Llangurig*, 5 miles, enter *Wye* valley; minor road S. on W. bank to *Nant-y-Dernol*, 5 miles, (small **Y.H.**).

R.10(i) Elan Valley. *Nant-y-Dernol* S. to *Rhayader*, 7 miles S.E. up *Elan* valley. Beyond *Elan* village, 4 miles, road continues past fine series of reservoirs for 9 miles to *Pont ar Elan*: then rough road W. on north side of river reaching, 5 miles, headwaters of R. *Ystwyth* and follow down valley 5 miles W. to join road N.W. to *Devil's Bridge* 4 miles. An adventurous route for cyclists.

Main route returns to *Llangurig*, 5 miles, and ascends upper *Wye* valley, *Eisteddfa Gurig*, 8 miles, is 2 miles S. of *Plynlimon* (2,468 ft.) source of *Severn*, *Wye* and *Rheidol*. Road descends to *Ponterwyd*, 4 miles. Turn S. for **Devil's Bridge**, 4 miles; famous river scenery. (Small **Y.H.** at *Ystumtuen*, 3 miles).

R.10(ii) *Ystumtuen* (**Y.H.**) to *Borth* (**Y.H.**). Route for walkers. N.W. from *Ponterwyd* on mountain road to *Elerch* and *Talybont*. Total distance 19 miles.

Main route follows road above *Rheidol* valley with fine views. *Aberystwyth*, 11 miles, university town and seaside resort. Welsh National Library. *Borth*, 7 miles, (**Y.H.**) Bathing. *Machynlleth*, 14 miles, in *Dovey* valley; up *Dulas* valley to *Corris* (**Y.H.**), slate quarrying village, and down to *Minffordd* in *Dysynni* valley, 9 miles, with views of **Cader Idris** (fine route to summit for walkers from *Minffordd* via *Llyn-y-Cau*, descending by *Foxe's Path* to *Kings* **Y.H.**). Road continues to *Dolgellau*, 7 miles, county town of *Merioneth*. Many walks around *Mawddach* estuary, on *Cader Idris* and in wild hills N. of estuary Railway viaduct across to *Barmouth* has track for cyclists and walkers. Sea bathing at *Barmouth* and *Fairbourne*.

Dolgellau up *Wnion* valley to Lake *Bala*, 22 miles, (*Plas Rhiwaedog* **Y.H.** 2 miles S.E.).

EXCURSIONS: (a) *Arenig Fawr* (2,800 ft.); (b) *Aran Benllyn* (2,901 ft.); (c) cylists 42 miles, circuit of rough hill roads crossing *Bwlch Rhiw Hirnant* to *Lake Vyrnwy* and *Llanfyllin*, returning via *Llangynog* and over *Milltir Cerig*.

From *Bala* down beautiful *Dee* valley. *Cynwyd* (**Y.H.**), 12 miles, (walks in *Berwyn Hills*). At *Corwen*, 2 miles, join main road and continue 10 miles to **Llangollen**; small town on *Dee*, famous for scenery and for International Eisteddfod (annually, July) (**Y.H.** 1½ miles E.).

EXCURSIONS: (a) *Eglwyseg valley* and *Valle Crucis Abbey*; (b) *Llantysilio Mountain*; (c) *Dee valley*; (d) *Ceiriog valley*.

R.11. North Wales. Colwyn Bay—Bettws-y-Coed—Snowdon—Caernarvon—Colwyn Bay (74 miles)

The eastern end of the North Wales coast is spoilt by caravan sites and industry and should be avoided by travelling direct by train or bus to *Colwyn Bay* (**Y.H.**); seaside resort.

ENGLAND AND WALES

EXCURSIONS: (a) *Llandudno, Little Orme's Head, Great Orme's Head*; (b) **sea trips** *Llandudno to Menai Bridge*; (c) steamer up R. *Conway, Deganwy to Trefriw.*

Conway, 6 miles, ancient walled town, 13th century castle; up *Conway valley* 5 miles to *Ro Wen* (Y.H.) and on to *Llanrwst*, 7 miles, 17th century bridge; *Oaklands* (Y.H.), 3 miles.

EXCURSIONS: (a) *Llyn Crafnant, Llyn Geirionydd* and *Llanrhychwyn*, old church; (b) *Bettws-y-Coed*, Roman road (*Sarn Helen*) to *Lledr valley* and *Dolwyddelan* (castle).

Bettws-y-Coed (*Swallow Falls* on R. *Llugwy*); *Capel Curig* (Y.H.), 7 miles, or *Idwal Cottage* (Y.H.), 13 miles.

EXCURSIONS: walks and climbs on **Tryfan,** *Glyder mountains, Carnedd Llewelyn* and *Carnedd Dafydd.*

Capel Curig, W. to *Pen-y-Gwryd*, 5 miles. Road continues over *Llanberis Pass*, but take S.W. road down beautiful **Nant Gwynant.** *Bryn Gwynant* (Y.H.), 4 miles.

EXCURSIONS: (a) *Watkin Path* route up **Snowdon** (3,560 ft., highest summit in Wales); (b) ridge walk, **Snowdon Horseshoe;** (c) *Llyn Dinas, Beddgelert, Aberglaslyn Pass,* returning by *Nanmor valley;* cyclists can extend round to include *Portmadoc* and *Borth-y-Gest* (sea bathing).

Beddgelert, 4 miles, N.W. to *Snowdon Ranger* (Y.H.) beside *Llyn Cwellyn*, 5 miles.

EXCURSIONS: (a) routes up *Snowdon*; (b) *Moel Hebog* and *Pennant valley*; (c) *Nantlle valley* and fine ridge walk, *Craig Cwm Silin* to *Rhyd-ddu.*

R.11(i) Beddgelert to Harlech. *Beddgelert, Aberglaslyn,* **Harlech,** 19 miles, (Y.H.); finely situated and well preserved 13th century castle; beach.

EXCURSIONS: (a) *Moel Senigh* (1,019 ft.), 1 mile E., view of *Snowdon* and all *Cardigan Bay;* (b) *Llanbedr* and circuit of *Rhinog Fawr* via *Cwm Bychan, Roman Steps* and *Bwlch Drws Ardudwy*, a fine 20 mile walk. (See also R.10).

R.11(ii) Lleyn. Remote and quiet peninsula; mostly Welsh-speaking. Cyclists can make a circuit from either *Snowdon Ranger* Y.H. or *Harlech* Y.H. Bus service along S. coast to *Aberdaron* and up to *Nevin.* Railway to *Pwllheli.* Chief features of interest are *Criccieth* (old town, associations with British Prime Minister, Lloyd George); *Abersoch* (small resort, *Penkilan Head,* sea trips to *St. Tudwal's Islands,* with cliffs, caves and seabird colonies); *Aberdaron* (picturesque fishing village, cliff walk to *Braich-y-Pwll,* boat to *Bardsey Island*); *Nevin*; the three hills of Yr Eifl (1,849 ft.) with fine views and Iron Age village, Tre'r Ceiri. *Lleyn* has several interesting churches; *Llanengan, Llangwnadl, Llanaelhaiarn* and *Clynnogfawr.*

From *Snowdon Ranger* (Y.H.) an easy track for walkers crosses hills to *Llanberis.* Main route follows road to **Caernarvon,** 8 miles, on *Menai* Strait. Historic walled town with splendid 13th-14th century castle. *Llanberis,* 7 miles, (Y.H. at foot of *Llanberis Pass* and start of *Snowdon Mountain Railway*).

EXCURSIONS: (a) *Llanberis Pass* and one of routes up *Snowdon* from *Pen-y-Pass* (Y.H.); (b) *Cwm Glas*; (c) across *Glyder* mountains from *Nant Peris* to *Idwal Cottage* Y.H. via *Devil's Kitchen.*

From *Llanberis*, route returns to coast. *Bangor*, 13 miles, (Y.H.), busy small town with cathedral and university college, good centre.

EXCURSIONS: Anglesey. (a) by ferry to *Beaumaris,* attractive resort, castle, views o Snowdonia; (b) Telford's suspension bridge (1826) across *Menai Strait*; 4 miles S.W. in parish of *Llandaniel Fab* the great circular barrow at Bryn-celli-ddu; then by southern route to *Holyhead* (bus) via *Newborough* (nature reserve), *Aberffraw* and *Rhosneigr.* At *Holyhead* (boat service to *Dublin*) see fine coast scenery of *Holyhead Mountain* (719 ft.) with ancient contorted strata.

103

ENGLAND AND WALES

Byrn Hall 7 miles S.E. is base for numerous walks in *Carnedd* mountains.

From *Bangor*, coast road to *Aber*, 6 miles, (glen, waterfall), *Penmaenmawr*, *Conway* and *Colwyn Bay* (Y.H.), 15 miles.

Chester (Y.H.) should be seen on entering or leaving Wales. City walls, almost intact, make interesting 2-mile walk. Main streets follow Roman plan, meeting at the Cross. The medieval *Rows*—covered walks with shops at first floor level—are unique. Also many medieval houses in *Watergate Street* and *Lower Bridge Street*, making finest assemblage in Britain. *Bishop Lloyd's House* and *Stanley Palace* are open. Cathedral of red sandstone; fine choir (Decorated), 14th century stalls with misericords. Lady Chapel, chapter house and refectory are Early English. *Grosvenor Museum* has notable Roman collection.

The Peak District

At their southern end the *Pennine* hills of the north country impinge on the *Midland* plain in a mass of moorland whose dark sandstone (Millstone Grit) edges face inwards upon a landscape of striking contrast—the pastel greens and creams of Carboniferous Limestone country.

The two landscapes make up the so-called *Peak District* which, though it lacks peaks, has much good hill country containing river valleys of extraordinary interest and beauty.

The following route (which, between *Ilam* and *Matlock*, can form the basis of a walking tour) follows the *River Dove* upwards and strikes north across the limestone to the *Peak* before bearing south again down the *Derwent* to *Matlock*. The quartet of great houses visited is without a rival in any district in England of similar size.

R.12 Derby—Dovedale—Edale—Matlock—Southwell (110 miles)

Derby; industrial city, home of first silk mill (1717), fine porcelain (Crown Derby), Rolls Royce engines, etc. 4½ miles N.W. **Kedleston Hall** (1760), a masterpiece of Robert Adam, work by Chippendale etc. (open Easter-Sep.).

Ashbourne, market town, fine 13th century church. Up *Dove* valley to *Ilam Hall* (Y.H.), centre for walks in *Dove* and *Manifold* valleys (the *Izaak Walton* country). Riverside path through *Dovedale*, *Wolfscote Dale* and *Beresford Dale* to *Hartington* (Y.H.).

Continue up dale to *Longnor*. E. to *Monyash* and *Bakewell* (Y.H.), walkers can go via *Lathkill Dale* and *Over Haddon*. *Bakewell* church has important family monuments; Saxon cross. **Haddon Hall**, 2 miles S.E., Elizabethan and Jacobean great house, shows evolution of styles through five centuries (open Easter-Sep.).

Monsal Dale; Cressbrook (early Industrial Revolution mill); *Millersdale* (*Ravenstor* Y.H.).

104

Tideswell, small market centre; finest church in district; *Little Hucklow; Castleton* (Y.H.); caving centre, *Blue John Mine, Treak Cliff Cavern* (stalactites), *Speedwell Mine* with underground stream explored by boat.

Edale, (Y.H.) under *Kinder Scout* (the *"Peak"*), south end of *Pennine Way* (Long-Distance Route); village has National Park information centre. Routes up gritstone water-courses (*Crowden, Grinds Brook*, etc) lead to desolate *Kinder Scout* plateau.

Walk over *Win Hill* (view) to *Bamford* and down *Derwent* to *Hathersage; Leam Hall* (Y.H.); *Wet Withens* (Bronze Age stone circle); *Eyam*, famous plague village (Y.H.); *Baslow*. **Chatsworth**, superb 17th century Palladian home of Duke of Devonshire; famous state rooms; huge art collection, pictures, drawings, tapestries, etc.; large formal gardens (open Apr.-Sep., closed Mon. and Tues.). *Rowsley* (16th century *Peacock Inn*); *Matlock Bath* (Y.H.). *Cromford*, 2 miles S. pleasing early Industrial Revolution village with Arkwright's mill (1771).

Hardwick Hall, 12 miles E. of *Matlock*, great Elizabethan house built by Bess of Hardwick; fine furniture, tapestries, pictures, gardens (open Apr. to Oct. afternoons; closed Mon., Tues., Fri.).

Southwell, 20 miles S.E. of *Hardwick*, quiet cathedral town almost by-passed by modernity; splendid minster, chiefly Norman, with chapter-house (Decorated style) one of marvels of 13th century craftsmanship.

The Yorkshire Dales

The rivers flowing off from the *Pennine* "backbone" are famous for their individual beauty. Here, as in the *Lake District*, hill, valley and waterfall become fell, dale and force—the *fjell, dal* and *foss* of the Scandinavian settlers, who found this sweeping landscape well suited to their activities as herdsmen. So, at a later date, did the monks, especially the Cistercians, whose large-scale sheep ranching destroyed the woodlands to create the open fell-sides seen today. The wealth it brought them accounts for the number and magnificence of Yorkshire abbeys. When the monasteries were dissolved the wool trade survived. Textiles in Yorkshire mean woollen goods, and *Bradford* is still a world centre for wool-clip sales.

The unspoilt dales country (*Yorkshire Dales National Park*) is splendid for walking and cycling. The *Craven* district is the principal centre for caving and pot-holing.

R. 13. Walking Tour: Skipton—Ingleton—Aysgarth—Ripon (130 miles)

Skipton, readily accessible by rail. Name means "sheep town"; market centre for dales; castle 13th-17th century (open daily). Bus to *Linton* (Y.H.) from which walking tour begins.

EXCURSION: Riverside path down *Wharfedale* by *Burnsall, Barden Bridge*, the *Strid* (where river narrows to 4 ft. but fatally dangerous to attempt jumping across), *Bolton Abbey*.

Grassington, picturesque village; path from top end of village through *Grass Wood* to *Conistone; Kilnsey Crag; Kettlewell* (Y.H.).

ENGLAND AND WALES

EXCURSIONS: (a) *Upper Wharfedale* and *Langstrothdale Chase*; (b) *Arncliffe* and *Littondale*.

Kettlewell, Kilnsey; *Mastiles Lane* (old drove road across fells) to **Gordale Scar** (chasm in limestone), *Malham* (**Y.H.**) near precipitous *Malham Cove*.

Kirkby Malham; *Settle*, small town with picturesque market square; potholing and caving museum of *British Speleological Association*; *Stainforth* (**Y.H.**).

EXCURSION: *Penyghent*, 3 hours climb (2,273 ft.).

Stainforth Force (R. *Ribble*); *Feizor*; *Austwick*; *Clapham*; *Ingleton* (**Y.H.**). Chief pot-holing and caving centre.

EXCURSIONS: (a) *Ingleborough* (2,373 ft.), *Gaping Gill, Trow Gill, Clapham*: (b) Falls and glens of R. *Greta*; *White Scar Caves* (open to public).

Weathercote (cave): *Dentdale* (**Y.H.**)

EXCURSION: *Dentdale, Dent* (picturesque village) and *Deepdale.*

Fell lane past *Dent Station* to *Garsdale Head* (**Y.H.**)

Hawes, (**Y.H.**) small market town in *Wensleydale* (see below); *Hardrow Force*; *Buttertubs Pass* (1,726 ft.) to *Thwaite* and *Keld* (**Y.H.**) in *Swaledale,* centre for fell-walking and fine river scenery of upper dale.

Muker, Reeth, Grinton (church), *Grinton Lodge* (**Y.H.**)

EXCURSION: *Lower Swaledale* and Richmond, historic, finely situated town, castle (1071) with massive keep; circular cobbled market place with church in centre; *Greyfriars Tower*; handsome Georgian houses; steep narrow "wynds" down to river; riverside path to *Easby Abbey* (1152); *Easby Church* has medieval wall paintings.

R.13(i) Teesdale. *Grinton Lodge* (**Y.H.**), *Arkengarthdale Moor, Brignall, Greta Bridge,* and *Rokeby* (famous river scenery; *Tees* is boundary between *Yorkshire* and *Durham*): *Barnard Castle* (**Y.H.**), old gated town and castle (1132). Town has Bowes Museum (modelled on the *Tuileries* and containing art collection).

EXCURSIONS: (a) *Middleton-in-Teesdale,* High Force (waterfall), Caldron Snout; (b) *Raby Castle,* seat of the Nevilles, a great north country family, until 1569.

By moorland road to *Wensleydale,* most spacious of the dales, home of famous cheese, many beautiful villages.

Bolton Castle; Redmire, Aysgarth (waterfalls on R. *Ure*) (**Y.H.**).

EXCURSIONS: (a) *Askrigg, Bainbridge, Semerwater*; (b) *Thoralby, Bishopdale, Buckden Pike* (2,302 ft.), *Waldendale*; (c) *Middleham High Moor* to *Middleham* (castle), *East Witton, Jervaulx Abbey, Ellingstring* (small **Y.H.**).

Bus via *Masham* to **Ripon** (cathedral, market square, old houses). **Fountains Abbey,** 4 miles Cistercian (1132) very extensive remains of abbey church and domestic buildings.

North York Moors and Coast

East of the *Vale of York* are the *North York Moors* (a *National Park*), the *Vale of Pickering* and the *Wolds*, a continuation via *Lincolnshire* of the chalklands of the south, which reach the coast at *Flamborough Head.*

R. 14. York—Scarborough—Whitby (65 miles)

York (**Y.H.**): Roman *Eboracum,* where Constantine was proclaimed emperor. Medieval walls and gates ("Bars"; *Bootham, Micklegate, Monk* and

Walmgate). "Minster" is the largest ancient cathedral in England; Early English to Perpendicular; famous stained glass 14th, 15th century: beautiful chapter-house. *St. William's College; Treasurer's House; Merchant Adventurers' Hall*: 18th century *Mansion House;* Castle *Museum (Kirk Collection* notable for reconstructed streets and shops.) *Railway Museum.* Walk on town walls and in ancient streets, *Shambles, Stonegate, etc.*

Malton, 19 miles (Y.H.). Market centre in *Vale of Pickering.*

EXCURSIONS: (a) *Kirkham Abbey* on R. *Derwent; Howardian Hills:* **Castle Howard,** Vanbrugh's great Baroque masterpiece (Easter-Sep. afternoons; closed Mon. and Fri.); (b) *Helmsley* (Y.H.) (castle); **Rievaulx Abbey;** *Byland Abbey; Coxwold* (where Sterne, author of *"Tristam Shandy",* was vicar).

R.14(i) *Pickering,* small market town, castle; church has 15th century wall paintings: *Lastingham,* church has famous early crypt; *Hutton-le-Hole; Farndale* one of many beautiful dales leading into moors.

Scarborough, 23 miles (Y.H.); large, popular seaside resort on two bays with *Castle Hill* between. A fine coast runs. S. to *Flamborough Head* and N., 30 miles, to *Runswick Bay* and *Staithes* (picturesque fishing villages) via *Robin Hood's Bay (Boggle Hole* Y.H. and **Whitby** (Y.H.): old seaport town with clustered red-tiled roofs; church steps (199) lead up to Abbey, important in early English church history: the home-town of Captain Cook.

R.14(ii) **Eskdale, the Moors and Cleveland Hills.** Good walking country. *Whitby, Little Beck, Goathland, Wheeldale* (Y.H.); *Glaisdale, Castleton, Westerdale* (Y.H.); *Roseberry Topping* (view) *Guisborough, Saltburn-by-the-Sea* (Y.H.).

The Lake District

Despite its small scale the English *Lake District* has the features of a mountain region. Its fame rests on the infinitely subtle variations on a repeated theme of mountain, dale and lake to be found in a single day's walk. The form of the district, with valleys radiating from a hub, makes it possible to pass from one to another in quick succession and yet have a sense of being in scenery of noble proportions. It is unsurpassed in England as a walking area, and the many youth hostels facilitate a great variety of tours. Chief access points by rail are *Windermere, Penrith, Kendal* and *Ravenglass.*

R. 15. Walking tour: Windermere to Windermere via Patterdale, Keswick and Buttermere (80 Miles)

Bowness-on-Windermere; steamer to *Waterhead, Ambleside* (Y.H.). Footpath E. of *Loughrigg Fell* and S. side of *Rydal Water; Loughrigg Terrace* (Y.H. *High Close);* **Grasmere** (Y.Hs.); Wordsworth's home, Dove Cottage, open to public.

Grisedale Pass to *Patterdale.* From top of pass more strenuous route over *Dollywaggon Pike* leads to *Helvellyn* (3,118 ft.) and ridge walk over *Striding Edge* and down to *Patterdale* (Y.H.).

EXCURSIONS: (a) Steamer on *Ullswater* to *Howtown* and *Pooley Bridge;* (b) *Aira Force* (waterfall), *Dockwray, Glenridding.*

Patterdale via *Glenridding, Greenside* (Y.H.) and *Sticks Pass* to N. end of *Thirlmere* (Y.H.) or over *Helvellyn,* descending to *Thirlspot Inn.* Bus to **Keswick** (Y.H.).

ENGLAND AND WALES

EXCURSIONS: (a) *Latrigg* (1,203 ft.) best general viewpoint of *Derwentwater* and mountains; (b) *Stone Circle, Castlerigg; Wallow Crag, Falcon Crag, Lodore*, boat to *Keswick*; (c) ferry to *Nicol End*, lakeside walk through *Brandelhow Park*, boat to *Keswick* from *High Brandelhow*; (d) boat *High Brandelhow*, walk *Grange-in-Borrowdale*; over *Grange Fell* to *Watendlath; Ashness Bridge*; lakeside road and path by *Stable Hills* and *Friar's Crag* to *Keswick*; (e) *Skiddaw* (3,053 ft.); (f) *Saddleback* (2,847 ft.) from *Threlkeld* via *Scales Tarn* (care required over *Sharp Edge*).

Keswick, ferry to *Nicol End*, path S. over *Cat Bells, Maiden Moor, Eel Crag* and W. over *Dale Head* (2,473 ft.), *Hindscarth* and *Robinson. Buttermere* (Y.H.).

Buttermere, Scale Force (waterfall), *Ling Comb, Red Pike, High Stile, Scarth Gap, Haystacks, Fleetwith, Longthwaite* (Y.H.).

Brandreth, Green Gable, Great Gable (2,949 ft.) classic rock climbs on S. face, view; *Styhead, Stockley Bridge, Seathwaite* (rainiest inhabited place in England); *Longthwaite* (Y.H.).

Stockley Bridge, Grains Gill, Esk Hause, S.W. to **Scafell Pike** (3,210 ft., highest point in England); return to *Esk Hause; Angle Tarn, Rossett Gill* to head of *Langdale*; bus down dale; *Elterwater* (Y.H.) *Windermere* (Y.H.).

R.15 (i) **The South-Western valleys.** *Elterwater* (Y.H.), *Little Langdale, Tilberthwaite Glen, Hawkshead* (picturesque place; Wordsworth was educated at its grammar school; Y.H. by *Esthwaite Water*). Coniston (Y.H.s); by *Walna Scar* road or *Coniston Old Man* (2,635 ft.) to *Seathwaite-in-Dunnerdale*, dale of Wordsworth's "*Duddon Sonnets*" *Duddon* (Y.H.); *Hardknott Pass* (Roman camp); *Eskdale* (Y.H.).

EXCURSION: By *Burnmoor* to *Wasdale Head* and *Wastwater*. For strong walkers a fine return route, requiring local advice or guidance, is via *Lingmell Gill, Mickledore, Lord's Rake*, Sca Fell and *Slight Side*. Alternatively, return via *Wastwater Screes* and *Mitredale*.

Eskdale Y.H.; along *Upper Eskdale* (one of the finest valleys in *Lake District*); climb out E. to *Three Tarns*; descend the *Band* to *Langdale*.

The North

Even though disfigured by coal mining *County Durham* is worth exploring. It is the county of Bede, of the most glorious of Norman cathedrals, of the Washington family and of the invention of the locomotive steam engine. In the west the Pennine moors and dales are as lonely and lovely as those of Yorkshire.

Northumberland is one of the most sparsely inhabited of English counties. Memories of the times of Border strife are written into the landscape in its scarcity of villages, many castles and *Hadrian's Wall*. The coast is of outstanding beauty. The fell country from the Wall to the *Cheviots* is a National Park.

R.16. Darlington to Berwick-on-Tweed (140 miles)

Darlington Station: Stephenson's "Rocket", Locomotive No. 1, on platform, still carefully polished and oiled.

Durham: on typical medieval town site in sharp bend of R. *Wear*. Splendid grouping of cathedral, monastery and castle. Cathedral begun 1093, shrine of St. Cuthbert; great Norman nave, stone vaulting, incised pillars; Bede's tomb in 12th century Galilee Lady Chapel. Monastic buildings include refectory, now cathedral library. Castle has crypt chapel (1072), dining hall, kitchen and buttery, fine carving of 17th century *Black Staircase*. Riverside walks. Boating.

Washington Old Hall, 12 miles N., home of Washington family for four centuries to 1613.

Newcastle-on-Tyne, 7 miles, metropolis of the north; many bridges, quays, impressive streets and buildings; cathedral; castle with Henry II keep and museum of Roman antiquities.

Hexham, 20 miles, small market town; priory church (Early English with Saxon apse, crypt and bishop's chair). Town has moot hall and other interesting buildings (Y.H. *Acomb,* 2 miles N.).

From *Acomb,* 3 miles, reach **Hadrian's Wall** at *Chesters* (*Cilurnum;* military station; excavated forum, gateways). *Housesteads,* 8 miles (*Borcovicium;* military station; excavations, museum. *Once Brewed* (Y.H.) 3 miles.

R.16(i) Once Brewed to Carlisle (26 miles). *Hadrian's Wall* can be followed W. past more military stations at *Great Chesters (Aesica), Carvoran (Magnae), Birdoswald (Camboglanna);* those at *Castlesteads* (Fort XIII) and *Stanwix* (Fort XIV) have been destroyed. 4 miles S.W. of *Birdoswald* are *Lanercost Priory* (Augustinian), built of stone taken from Wall and, across fine 18th century bridge, *Naworth Castle,* home of Earl of Carlisle. *Brampton,* picturesque town with stocks and bullring. *Carlisle,* county town of *Cumberland:* castle, early Norman keep, dungeons; cathedral, great east window with medieval glass, fine wood carving, nave destroyed in Civil War; *Tullie House,* museum and art gallery; *Redness Hall,* 14th century. (Y.H.).

Main route continues N. 16 miles to *Bellingham* **(Y.H.)** in *Tynedale, Otterburn* in *Redesdale* and *Rothbury* 23 miles, in *Coquetdale;* good centre for walks; gardens of *Cragside* open daily.

EXCURSIONS: (a) *Upper Coquetdale,* for walks in *Cheviots;* (b) *Simonside Hills;* (c) *Brinkburn Priory,* 12th century; (d) *Warkworth,* near mouth of *Coquet,* magnificent ruined castle above interesting little town.

Alnwick, 11 miles: castle, home of Duke of Northumberland, finest of the Border fortresses, many art treasures. See also *Hulne Park* with ruins of *Hulne Priory* and *Alnwick Abbey. Rock Hall* **(Y.H.)** 5 miles.

EXCURSIONS: (a) the coast, with castles of *Dunstanburgh* and *Bamburgh* (open Easter-Sept.); (b) *Farne Islands,* spectacular sea-bird colonies, many species; also grey seals; (boat from *Seahouses*); (c) Holy Island (Lindisfarne), by walk at low tide across causeway or sands; monastery founded here by St. Aidan (635); present ruins are 11th century; picturesque small castle.

Wooler **(Y.H.)** 17 miles, pleasant small town.

EXCURSIONS: (a) The *Cheviot* (2,676 ft.), *Hedgehope* (2,348 ft.) and *Harthope* valley; (b) *Yeavering Bell* (Hill Fort) and *College* valley; (c) *Chillingham Park* with herd of wild white cattle.

At *Crookham,* 8 miles N.W. take secondary road to *Branxton,* 1½ miles; near church is *Flodden Field Monument* on the site of battle (1513). 9 miles N. by R. *Tweed,* is *Norham Castle* (of Scott's *Marmion*) fine keep (1160). **Berwick-on-Tweed,** 7 miles, historic Border town, impressive ramparts (1565) and bridges.

FINLAND

Geographical Outline

Land   Finland (Finnish: *Suomi*, "the land of fens and lakes",) is situated between the 60th and 70th degrees of latitude; bordered on the west by Sweden, on the east by Russia, and on the north by Norway. In the south it is a peninsula, between the Gulfs of Bothnia and Finland. Nearly 10 per cent of its area of 130,085 sq. miles is taken up with lakes and rivers.

The land is largely composed of rocks representing an immensely remote period of the earth's history; so ancient that there has been time for parts to be twice uplifted and twice eroded to produce the comparatively level landscape seen today. The solid base is mostly overlaid by sands and gravels left by glaciers of the Ice Age; when these occur as moraines—as in the *Salpausselkä* ridge—they form a major elevated feature running far across the country.

From a coastal plain with hundreds of off-shore islands the land rises to a central plateau of some 300 ft. altitude on which most of the lakes (said to number 60,000) are situated. Many, such as *Saimaa* and *Päijänne*, are of great extent. Their smooth surfaces are in strong contrast with the many rivers linking them one with another which are often broken by rocks and rapids. In the far north the land rises again, forming an upland region whose highest point is *Haltiatunturi* (4,440 ft.).

Climate   The climate is considerably warmer than might be expected, and the temperature is about 12°F. higher than at other places of a similar latitude outside Europe. The coldest month is February. In winter the rivers, lakes and the sea are frozen but the ports are kept open by icebreakers and the Stockholm/Turku ferry route is open all year. The warmest month is July, when the temperature in Helsinki is higher than that of London. The summer is warm, bright and exhilarating, the "midnight sun" is visible at the 70th degree of latitude from the middle of May to the end of July. The winter is cold but dry; it rarely rains for long periods, the annual rainfall being only about 21 inches although there are heavy falls of snow.

The main touring season begins in June and continues until the middle of September; July is the most popular month. In the winter there is ski-ing on gentle slopes in the south from January to March, and in Lapland from March to the end of April.

Plants and Animals   The greater part of the country is forest, predominantly spruce and pine, but birch, alder and ash are also evident. Oak occurs only in the south. In Lapland, the forest gives way to a tundra vegetation with lichen and moss.

Reindeer and bear are protected by law; a few wolves and lynx live in the forests. There are many species of birds, especially waterfowl. In Lapland a form of blue capercailzie prized as a game bird is sometimes found. The salmon is common in the rivers.

One of the many "holiday villages," this site is at Husö in Åland, Finland.

The People

Population
Of the population of nearly 4½ million, only a quarter live in towns. The largest cities are *Helsinki* (500,000), *Turku* (*Åbo*) (136,000) and *Tampere* (142,000).

The eastern Finns, who make up the majority of the nation, tend to be fair, broad-headed and of medium stature, and have been classed racially as neo-Danubian. The Swedish Finns of the south and west tend to show the Scandinavian characteristics of long-headedness and greater height. The few thousand Samian Lapps, on the tundra, are sallow complexioned with dark hair and dark eyes, very broad-headed and short in stature.

Language
The country is bilingual—92 per cent. of the people speak Finnish, and the rest Swedish. Finnish is a distinctive language. Together with Estonian it is the chief European representative of the Finno-Ugrian group of languages. It is difficult to learn, as the grammar is particularly complicated. Most educated Finns speak Swedish; and, in the cities, many speak English or German.

Religion
Some 93 per cent of the people belong to the Evangelical Lutheran Church. The chief minority group (1.8 per cent.) consists of members of the Greek Orthodox Church. Both are national churches.

History
The Finns probably came from the Volga basin (east Russia) and crossed to Finland from Estonia. In 1157 Eric IX of Sweden led a crusade into Finland, introducing Christianity. This union with Sweden, in which Finland had some measure of independence, lasted until 1809. In the 17th century a Diet was inaugurated; formed of representatives of the nobles, burghers, clergy and peasants, it lasted until 1906. In 1809 Finland was incorporated in the Russian Empire as a Grand Duchy. She proclaimed her independence on December 6th, 1917, and it was finally achieved by General Mannerheim in 1918.

Finland's decision to remain neutral (1935) in the coming struggle in Europe was unwelcome to Russia who, seeking security for Leningrad, took territory in the south-east at an early stage of the Second World War. It included the Karelian isthmus and the shores of Lake Ladoga. Later the country was used by Germany as a base for operations against north Russia. The Finns themselves, after temporarily regaining the lost territory, had to cede it again to Russia with certain bases at the armistice of 1944; the bases were later returned but the Finns find it necessary to adopt a cautious policy towards their powerful eastern neighbour, and they do not belong to any western political alliances.

FINLAND

Government Finland is a democratic republic, the government consisting of the President and the House of Representatives (Diet). The President nominates the Cabinet, which has to have the support of the House of Representatives. There are three main political parties. Finland was the first country in Europe to give women the franchise; everyone over 21 has the right to vote. Municipal government is carried out by the burgomaster and aldermen.

Resources Being the most heavily wooded country in Europe, forests are the main resource. Coal is absent but hydro-electric schemes are well developed. Though less than 10 per cent of the land is suitable for cultivation agriculture is the foremost occupation, 28 per cent are thus employed, with 35 per cent in industry. Three-quarters of the agricultural workers are independent farmers. The main exports are timber and paper, but there are rapidly growing textile, clothing and metal industries. Other exports are copper from the *Outokumpu* mine in *Northern Karelia* and glass and pottery of modern design.

Sauna The main institution is the sauna steam-bath, every house in country districts having its own bath-house. An oven of stones is heated to about 140°F, and then sprayed with water; the bathers sit on a high wooden platform in the steam produced and whisk themselves with birch branches to open the pores. This is followed in towns by a cold shower and in the country by a swim.

Costumes and Customs Local costumes are worn for festivals and sometimes at weekends, especially by the girls. The Lapps have their own distinctive dark-blue dress, which they wear at all times.
The main holiday of the summer is the Midsummer Festival, which is of pagan origin. Large bonfires are lit on lake shores and the people gather to sing and dance in the half-light, and let off fireworks.

Food and Drink Finnish meals conform to the Scandinavian pattern: coffee and rolls for breakfast, lunch between 11 a.m. and 1 p.m., and the main meal of the day between 5 p.m. and 7 p.m. Meals ordered outside these times are usually more expensive. Finns eat a great deal of porridge, *puuro*, made not only of oats but of rye, semolina or rice. Potatoes, butter, all kinds of bread from black rye bread, various kinds of brown to pure white, and crispbread are popular foods. A main meal will often begin with a variety of sausage, cheese and salt herring, and continue with a hot dish, probably of pork or veal.

Sport Ski-ing, which is still a mode of transport in remote country districts, is the favourite winter sport of the entire population. School children are given a week's ski-ing holiday in February and many people go up to the Lapland fells to ski. In summer, they swim in the sea and lakes. In relation to their population, they have led the world in the Olympic Games. The main sport is athletics, in which they excel; there are many stadiums and gymnasiums. The Finns are a nation of sportsmen, not spectators.

Culture

Architecture The architecture of Finland can be divided into three main groups. Firstly the medieval architecture of the 13th to 15th centuries—a simple, almost primitive form in grey stone. Examples of this period are the Cathedral and Castle of *Turku*, and *Olavinlinna* Castle (1475). There was then a considerable period of rather poor architecture until the latter half of the 18th century, during which time the undecorated grey stone castles continued to be built, with little change from the medieval style.

The new architecture of the 18th century was a version of the Swedish rococo. Perhaps the best example is the Fortress of *Suomenlinna* (1748), the King's Gate of this castle being particularly fine. The wooden manor houses of this period, with their mansard roofs, are to be found in delightful settings. The more modest wooden churches have baroque tendencies and, with the manor houses, show the Finnish feeling for atmosphere. Examples of these are *Petäjävesi* Church (1764) and *Keuruu* Church (1758).

Carl Ludvig Engel, a German who died in 1840, is perhaps the outstanding name of the 19th century. His neo-classical style is noble and artistic and he designed many of the public buildings of *Helsinki*, notably the Great Square.

The final period of Finnish architecture is probably the greatest and is likely to be of most interest to the visitor. The essentially functional style of these modern buildings commenced in the 1920's, and was influenced by the work of Le Corbusier and Frank Lloyd Wright outside Finland. Excellent examples are the *Helsinki* Railway Station (Eliel Saarinen), *Paimio* Sanatorium (Alvar Aalto), *Sampo* Insurance Company building (Erik Bryggman) and the *Helsinki* Stadium (Yrjö Lindgren and T. Jäntti), to mention one by each of the foremost architects. *Helsinki*, in fact, and the garden suburb of *Tapiola*, contain many recently designed buildings by Aalto and other well-known contemporary architects—the Sirens, Rewell, Ervi and Blomstedt. They have also done work for other rapidly expanding towns.

Literature Finland's greatest literary work is her national epic—the *Kalevala*—compiled by Elias Lönnrot (1802-84) from the native ballads. It is an outstanding story, relating the beginnings of the country and its subsequent history, interwoven with love stories and fables. It has been the basis of much of her later art in music, painting and literature.

Translations have been made into many languages and it inspired Longfellow's *Hiawatha*. Novels translated into English are Linnankoski's *"Song of the blood-red flower"*, Sillanpää's *"Fallen asleep when young"* and Linna's *"Unknown Soldier"*.

FINLAND

Painting and Sculpture

Great strength and deep feeling characterize the work of Gallen-Kallela (1865-1931) in his portraits, landscapes and, above all, his frescoes as at the Athenaeum, *Helsinki*, illustrating scenes from the *Kalevala*, and those in the Mausoleum at *Pori*. The same can be said of the sculptor Aaltonen (born 1894); his bronze of the runner Nurmi in the Athenaeum, *Helsinki*, and his massive granite figure for the war memorial at *Savonlinna*.

Music

The wonderfully original orchestration of Sibelius (1865-1957) evokes more widely than anything else the beauty and drama of the north—its story and legend and untamed spaciousness. It may be that his great innovation in symphonic form—the breaking out from the mould of conventionally accepted movements, appropriate to a world where man is dominant—was a necessity for one inspired more by nature at work on the grandest scale.

Folk-song and dance

There has been a revival of Finnish folk-dancing in recent years; it is similar to English, mostly being danced in sets of eight. The *Kantele*, a type of Finnish zither which is mentioned in the *Kalevala* is found only in *Karelia*.

The art of the runo-singer is gradually being lost. Two peasants would sit opposite each other, hands clasped and, swaying to the rhythm, could chant folk stories in turn. From these old folk songs Lönnrot wrote the *Kalevala*.

Design

Finnish designers enjoy world-wide fame for the beauty and simplicity of their glassware, plain or of exquisite colour (Tapio Wirkkala, Timo Sarpaneva, Nanny Still), ceramics both artistic and practical (Kyllikki Salmenhaara, Kaj Franck), textiles and modern versions of the "ryijy" rug (Eva Brummer) as well as cutlery, furniture and light fittings.

Touring Information

Access

Finland may be reached from England by several routes, e.g. direct by sea, London-*Helsinki* ($3\frac{1}{2}$ days, minimum single fare £33·00); by sea and rail via *Hook of Holland*, Denmark and Sweden (minimum single through fare £46·25).

Transport

Finnish railways have a network of rather over 3,000 miles, covering most of the country except the far north. Locomotives vary from steam engines to fast diesels and long distance fares are cheap; a journey of 600 miles, for instance (from *Helsinki* to *Rovaniemi*, capital of *Lapland*) costs about 50 *marks*. Seat reservation is obligatory on express trains. The standard bus fare is 2 *marks* for 20 miles.

Timetable

A comprehensive timetable *Suomen Kulkuneuvot*, costing 6·00 *marks*, includes all rail, bus and steamer services, with a useful general map.

Money

The unit of currency is the mark (*Markka*), which is divided into 100 pennies (*Pennia*).

Clothing

During the summer season ordinary summer clothing is suitable, but some warmer clothing should be taken, as evenings are sometimes cool. In winter warm clothing, especially underwear, is essential; fur hats are normally worn, and fur-lined or fur coats.

Restaurants

Meals cost about 7 *marks* at the smaller restaurants and. coffee bars, e.g. *Elanto, Colombia*. Some youth hostels provide meals and many have cooking facilities.

Tourist Information

Information and leaflets can be had from the *Finland National Tourist Office, 75 Rockefeller Plaza, New York, N.Y. 10019.*

Maps

The *Geographia* map of Finland, 1:1,500,00, is a good general map showing roads and railways. For cycling or canoeing there is the *Suomen Tiekartta*, scale 1:200,000, 13 sheets, 8 *marks* each, or the *Autoilijan Tiekartta* on a scale of 1:750,000, 2 sheets 8 *marks* each. Seven areas of Lapland, including the *Pallas-Ounastunturi National Park* and *Kilpisjarvi* areas are shown on excursion maps at 1:50,000, published by the National Board of Survey.

FINLAND

Accommodation There are over 100 youth hostels in Finland, mostly small and many of them in school buildings which are available only for the three months of June to August. The Helsinki Youth Hostel is at Stadionin the Maja, in Sports Park at the end of *Mannerheimintie*.

Camping There are more than 300 camp sites distributed throughout the country; most of them open from early June to late August.

Walking The scale of the country is not in general suited to walking tours, but there are splendid exceptions such as the *Kainuu* district around *Kajaani* in central Finland and the *Kuusamo* district in the east. There are a number of mapped trails in *Lapland*, and a booklet about them (with maps) is available in Finnish; but details of four trails (the *Pallas-Hetta*, the *Saariselkä*, the *Five Fells* and the *Haltia*) are also issued in English.

Cycling The roads are good, except the smaller ones which are likely to be stony and dusty. Cycling is not popular with the Finns.

Canoeing and Boating Finland, with its myriad winding waterways, and large calm lakes, is an ideal country for canoeing. Detailed information can be obtained from *Suomen Kanoottiliitto Retkeilyosasto, Hämeenlinna, Finland*.

Helsinki

The city was founded in 1550 by Gustav Vasa of Sweden to draw some of the trade of the Hanseatic League. In 1812 it succeeded *Turku* as capital of Finland.

There is only one railway station; travel within the city is by tram, bus or trolley-bus. A tourist tram ticket, costing 3·50 *marks*, can be bought at the *City Tourist Office, Pohjoinen Esplanaadikatu* 17 (near South Harbour); it entitles visitors to unlimited journeys for 24 hours on all buses and trams in central Helsinki.

On the right of the south harbour is the President's House; market place, City Hall; west by fine *Esplanaadi* to *Mannerheimintie*, bus terminus, Head Post Office, impressive Parliament Building (Diet), National Museum (Stone Age to modern times). East of Post Office is *Rautatientori* (Railway Square), containing most beautiful railway station in Europe; built 1919 designed by Eliel Saarinen, murals by Järnefelt. In same square, Athenaeum Art Gallery and Finnish National Theatre. Continuing by *Hallituskatu*, *Senaatintori* (Senate Square) in which are held all parades and celebrations, especially the welcoming of the New Year. The Cathedral (*Suurkirkko*) which dominates the city, built 1830, altar piece by Russian artist, Neff, is approached by 45 steps. On west side of square is University (1820), University Library (fine example of modern style); on east side, Government Offices. Central statue of Alexander II.

FINLAND

Other interesting churches: Johannes Church in *Korkeavuorenkatu*, Gothic style (1893) has 3 naves and 2 spires; *Vanha Kirkko*, oldest church in city (1826) in Lönnrotinkatu; *Kallion Kirkko*, on north of city beyond *Töölönlahti*, fine view from tower.

The Opera House and the Museum of European Art are in the *Bulevardi* and there is an open-air Museum of Finnish buildings at *Sewiasaari*, an island north-west of the city.

In Sports Park at end of *Mannerheimintie* is magnificent stadium used for Olympic Games of 1952.

There are several beaches for bathing and sun-bathing.

EXCURSIONS: 1. Open air island zoo, *Korkeasaari*, from North Harbour by ferry. 2. *Suomenlinna* from S. Harbour: old island fortress. 3. *Porvoo*, about 30 miles eastwards along the coast, many beautiful 18th century buildings, a picturesque waterfront of old wooden warehouses. Home of poet Runeberg, now a museum. 4. *Gallén-Kallela Museum*, about 3 km. north of suburb of *Tapiola*; a delightful exhibition of this artist's work displayed in his former studio and home. By tram to end of No. 4 route, then 1 mile walk.

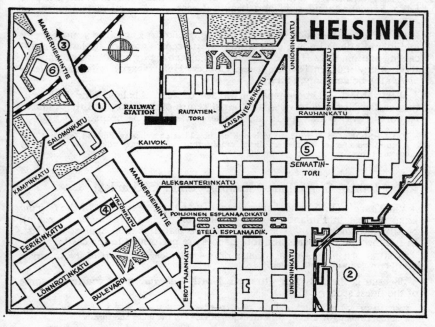

1. *Post Office.* 2. *South Harbour.* 3. *Route to the Stadiums.* 4. *Finnish Y.H.A. Office.* 5. *Cathedral (Suurkirkko).* 6. *Parliament House.*

FINLAND

Touring Routes

R.1. The Cities of Finland—round trip of 600 miles

Turku (*Åbo*), old capital, important port. The Swedish crusaders landed here in 1157. Finland's first monastery and school were founded in *Turku*. Most of the old buildings were burnt down in 1827; the present city is modern with wide boulevards and stone bridges. Cathedral, 1229; 13th century castle. Two Universities (Swedish and Finnish), Museums, including Handicrafts museum in old part of town saved from fire, Observatory.

EXCURSION: *Naantali*, about 10 miles north-west, small attractive coastal town.

Tampere (*Tammerfors*), industrial centre a fine city in a beautiful position between two lakes. It was founded as an industrial centre by Scottish settlers and many of the Finns still have Scots names. Cathedral, very fine frescoes; *Näsilinna* (provincial museum). View from *Pyynikki*, a ridge 240 ft. high overlooking the city, has open-air theatre with revolving auditorium. The *Tammerkoski* Falls pass right through the town.

Jyväskylä, cultural centre, buildings by Aalto, lying at the northern end of Lake *Päijänne*, amid wild and beautiful scenery. Annual Arts Festival in July.

Down the eastern side of the 75 mile long lake to **Lahti**, the youngest city in Finland (1905) known as a winter sports centre and for its large broadcasting station. City Hall (designed by Saarinen) is in brick and of unusual style; many modern buildings, e.g. Concert Hall. Nearby is famous *Vierumäki* athletic academy. (Y.H.)

Westwards to **Hämeenlinna**, birthplace of Jean Sibelius. Fine 13th century castle. Near the town is the tourist centre of *Aulanko*, and the *Aulanko* National Park. Water-bus route, *Tampere—Aulanko*, 5½ hours.

EXCURSION: To *Hattula*, to visit one of the oldest churches in Finland (about 1250). A good example of Finnish medieval architecture, with typical pillars and beautifully coloured frescoes.

R.2. Lahti—Savonlinna—Kuopio—Lahti (525 miles)

Via *Kouvola* (Y.H.) and *Lappeenranta* (Y.H.), along the east of the *Saimaa* Lake (largest in Finland), to **Savonlinna** (or by boat from *Lappeenranta*). Nearby is *Olavinlinna* Castle (1475), built as a fortification against the East. In summer, plays, operas and folk dances are performed in the castle.

EXCURSION: to *Punkaharju*, winding ridge 4 miles long. This part of the country is well-provided with youth hostels.

Joensuu is the only large town in North *Kareilia*: good centre for some of the finest scenery. (Y.H.)

EXCURSION : to *Koli*, on Lake *Pielisjärvi*, for *Koli* Peaks, highest land in southern Finland, rising to over 1,000 ft., with excellent views of the lakes and forests.

Kuopio on Lake *Kallavesi*, centre for lake steamers. Return to *Lahti* direct via *Mikkeli* or by boat via *Savonlinna* and *Lappeenranta*.

R.3. Lapland

Rovaniemi on the Arctic Circle, capital of Finnish Lapland. **(Y.H.)** 18 hours by rail from *Helsinki*. Almost entirely rebuilt since 1944 in uncompromising up-to-date style. Bus terminus for all Lapland routes.

Lapland is a sparsely populated area, but there are tourist inns and motor buses serve the main centres. The Lapps, whose characteristic blue smock is common to the race in all the Scandinavian countries, keep many of their old customs but are no longer nomadic and have settled in permanent houses. Their chief occupations are the breeding of reindeer and fishing. Of the total of about 30,000 Lapps only some 2,000 live in Finland, and Finns are in the majority, even in Finnish Lapland.

Pallastunturi (120 miles, 5 hours by bus from *Rovaniemi*) is in a National Park, in a district of rounded fells. Camping site here and tourist hotel run by Tourist Association.

Kilpisjärvi (270 miles, 10 hours by bus from *Rovaniemi*) is situated among the highest fells of Finland where its frontier meets Sweden and Norway in the N.W. Nature reserve, *Pikku Malla,* can be visited by rowing boat. Bus connections with Norway.

Ivalo (209 miles, 8 hours by bus from *Rovaniemi* or 1 hour by plane) is a good departure point for journeys farther north: e.g. to *Inari* (24 miles, 1¼ hours by bus) on lake and *Utsjoki* (78 miles, 3 hours by bus) on a river on northern frontier with Norway with which there are bus connections **(Y.H.)**.

FRANCE

Geographical Outline

Land
France (212,895 sq. miles), is over three times as large as England and Wales, and shows probably the greatest landscape variety of any country in Europe.

Its basic structure consists of the ancient, uplifted blocks of the *Central Massif, Brittany, Ardennes* and *Vosges,* the more recent fold mountains of the *Pyrenees, Alps* and *Jura,* and the two great lowlands of the *Paris* basin and *Aquitaine.*

Aquitaine is watered by the *Garonne* and its tributaries, some flowing from the *Pyrenees,* others from the *Central Massif.* The *Paris* basin contains the *Seine* and its many tributaries. Largely composed of chalk and limestone, it is bounded north by the *Channel* and the hills of *Artois,* east and south-east by the characteristic chalk and clay scarplands of *Champagne,* by the *Langres* plateau and the heights of the *Côte d'Or.* The valleys of the other chief rivers complete the broad pattern of the landscape. The *Loire,* rising deep in the *Massif,* links several regions, following a long course through the *Paris* basin, from *Nevers* to *Tours,* and finally across the plain of *Anjou* to *Nantes.* The *Saône* flows in a corridor, between the *Côte d'Or* and the *Jura,* which is continued below *Lyons,* where the *Saône* joins the *Rhône,* coming from the *Lake of Geneva.* After a narrow passage between the *Massif* and the *Alps of Dauphiné,* the hills recede south-west and the *Rhône* flows through *Provence* to its delta, the *Camargue.* France has a frontier on the *Rhine,* in its rift valley section between the *Vosges* and the Black Forest, and contains also the headwaters of the *Moselle* and the *Meuse.*

Aquitaine is connected with the *Paris* basin by the "gate of *Poitou*" and with the plain of *Languedoc* and the *Rhône* valley by the vital gap of *Carcassonne.* Otherwise, the great upland area running south-west to north-east is readily crossed only through the *Belfort* gap south of the *Vosges* and the *Saverne* gap to the north.

Within this structure, fringed by its mountain frontiers and its *Mediterranean, Biscayan* and *Channel* coasts, France has an almost infinite variety of regional and local characteristics, partly the result of history but strongly influenced by natural diversity. Regionally, the key to them is to be found in the old provincial divisions, such as *Brittany, Burgundy, Auvergne, Guyenne* rather than in the artificial boundaries of the modern *départements.* Locally the many "*pays*"—the traditional name applied by its inhabitants to a locality—offer a fascinating study of distinctions often based on land use and types of soil. This is especially true of the *Paris* basin: e.g. *Pays de Beauce,* with rich arable farms working the fertile covering of loam ("*limon*") over limestone; *Pays de Bray,* a clay region of meadows, woods and streams. *Pays* names occur also in the *Alps:* e.g. the distinction between the upper valley of the *Isère,* known as *Maurienne* and the middle valley, *Grésivaudan.*

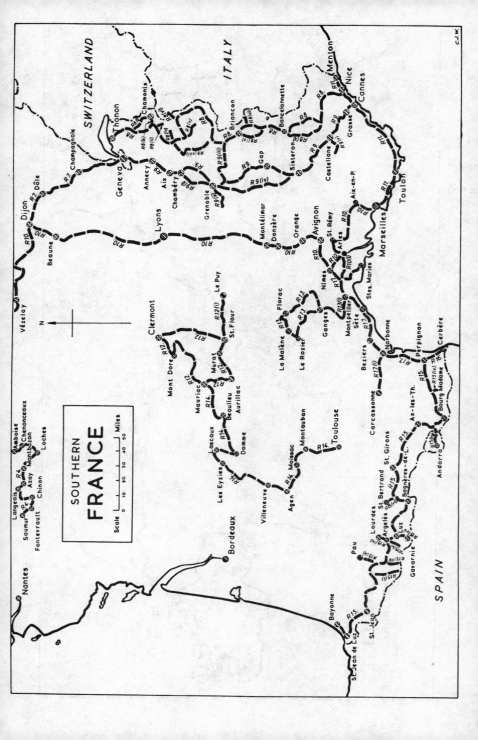

SOUTHERN
FRANCE

Scale
0   10   20   30   40   50 Miles

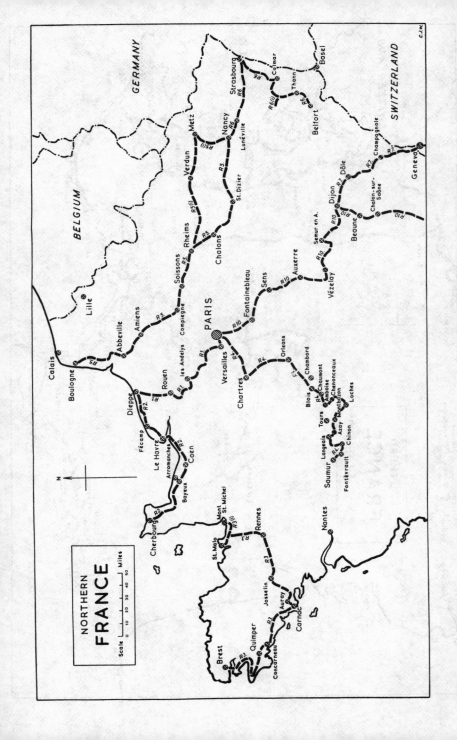

Further details of the main regions are given at the head of each section of the touring routes.

Climate

The climate of the north is rather warmer and drier than that of southern England. But there is a change from oceanic conditions in the west to those of central Europe in the east, felt in the greater range of temperature in *Lorraine* and the change in rainfall from a winter to a summer maximum. In the south, Atlantic conditions prevail over *Aquitaine* in contrast to the warm wet winters and hot dry summers of Mediterranean *Provence*. The main touring season for most regions is summer, though many people prefer to visit the south in late spring or early autumn to avoid the great heat of July and August. The ski-ing season is from the end of December to the end of March or April in the *Alps, Jura* and *Vosges*, slightly earlier in the *Pyrenees*.

Plants and
Animals

Some 30 million acres, or about 20 per cent. of the surface, is covered by forest. Deciduous woodland is the natural cover of much of the north and west, and the remaining forests of this type include those of *Fontainebleau* and *Compiègne*. Dense conifers clothe the *Ardennes* and the *Low Vosges* and have been extensively planted on the sands of the *Landes*.

Provence is distinct from the rest of the country in its Mediterranean flora. Here the natural forest is of evergreen oak and maritime pine. But, through uncontrolled felling and over-grazing, it has been succeeded over large areas either by a tangled scrub (*maquis*), including wild olive, myrtle, laurel and holm-oak, or by the almost naked *garrigue*, with stunted evergreens and aromatic plants such as lavender and thyme. Along the Provençal coast and the Riviera the orange, lemon, almond, Barbary fig and cacti flourish. In the *Cévennes*, chestnuts have replaced the beech because of their importance for food.

Animals native to France include the following—the bear, occasionally found in the *Pyrenees;* the wolf still found in the *Cévennes* and the *Vosges* but rapidly disappearing; the fox, marten, badger and weasel in most regions; the marmot in the *Alps*; the chamois and wild goat in the *Alps* and *Pyrenees*. In many of the forests, the red deer and roe deer are preserved whilst the wild boar is hunted. Hares, rabbits and squirrels are common.

Insects include the praying mantis and the cigale, or cicada, whose whirring song is so typical of the south.

The People

Population

France has a population of 51 million, of whom some 8 million live in *Greater Paris*, i.e. within 15 miles of its centre. The ascendancy of the capital is emphasized by the fact that only four other cities exceed 300,000: *Marseilles* 900,000, *Lyons* 560,000, *Toulouse* 380,000 and *Nice* 320,000. But settlement is dense in the mining and industrial areas of the *Nord* and the *Pas de Calais*.

Racially, the people chiefly stem from the three main types of early settlers, Alpine, Mediterranean and Nordic. There has been considerable inter-

FRANCE

mixing, but the stocky, broad-headed Alpine type predominates, particularly in a wide zone from *Lorraine*, through the *Savoy Alps* and the *Central Massif* to the *Pyrenees*. In contrast, in *Provence*, the predominant type is slender, with a long head and narrow features and a tendency to be darker than the Alpines. Waves of Nordic immigrants have reached the north at various periods, the most significant being the Salian Franks (5th cent.) who gave their name to the country, and the Norsemen (9th cent.) who created the duchy of *Normandy*.

The *Basques* of *Béarn* are probably a survival of much earlier stock, as may also be some of the people of the *Dordogne*. The *Bretons* were emigrants from Britain in the 5th and 6th centuries.

Language The language derives from the Latin introduced into Gaul by the Romans. With the decline of the Empire, unity of speech was lost. The change into Romance forms produced the Provençal tongue of the intensely romanized south, still spoken there, and possessing its own distinctive literature. Change went further in the north, to produce various forms of French, of which that spoken in the *Ile de France* became the standard, and the basis of the modern language.

Minority groups speaking other languages occur at the extremes of the country and have been incorporated, chiefly by extension of the frontier, at various times. These languages are Breton, Basque, the Catalan of *Roussillon*, the Italian of *Nice* and the German of *Alsace*.

Religion The majority of the church-going population is Roman Catholic, but there are about 1¼ million Protestants and ½ million Jews. There is also a very strong anti-clerical (*laïque*) element and the question of religious influence in state schools is still a burning issue in French life.

The dates of the many Roman Catholic ceremonies of interest to visitors can be found in the Calendars of Events issued by the French National Tourist Office. Amongst the better known are the *Pardons* in Brittany, the Blessing of the Sea at *Stes.-Maries-de-la-Mer* in *Provence*, and Pilgrimages to *Lourdes* and *Lisieux*.

History After the fall of the Roman Empire, some continuity of civilized life was maintained in the towns of the south. This made it possible for the distinction between north and south to survive the unification of the country under the Frankish king, Clovis (481), and his Merovingian successors.

Needing the help of Christian *Provence* to rid *Aquitaine* of the Visigoths, Clovis was himself converted to Christianity—the beginning of a process in which the barbarians adopted the superior culture, including the language, of the people they had conquered. Later, under Charlemagne (771–814), they were to become its active champions, a movement culminating in Charles' coronation (800) as Emperor, with dominion over the whole of western Christendom.

At Charles' death the great Frankish Empire fell apart. Not even its partition (843) among his three grandsons could prevent further disintegration. France, now part of *Carolingia* (named after its king, Charles the

Bald), was suffering Viking invasions up its estuaries, even including the *Garonne*; Paris was sacked four times; *Aquitaine* and *Brittany* were in revolt. People looked to local lords for such protection as they could give; effective authority extended no further than duchies, as in *Gascony*, or was even limited to counties, as in those of the counts of *Blois* and *Anjou*. The Norsemen were granted lands on the lower *Seine*, but, in creating *Normandy* (which became a duchy), they discovered a skill in government and administration which did not stop at the *Channel*.

The recovery of central authority, and with it the rise of *Paris* and of the idea of French nationhood, stems from the election (987) of Hugh Capet, duke of *Francia*, as king of France. At the outset, only first among equals, the Capet dynasty gradually increased its power and wealth. Under Philip Augustus (1180-1223), *Paris* was established as the capital. The *Louvre* was built, the university of the *Sorbonne* founded. *Notre Dame* was one of 16 cathedrals started in his reign in the new Gothic style of the north.

The kings gained prestige through the superior justice of their courts. Their nominal feudal authority was gradually turned into direct sovereignty throughout the land. In the south this followed the horror of the Albigensian war (1209-29), which ended the virtually independent rule of the counts of *Toulouse* and brought the royal power to the Mediterranean. *Dauphiné* was acquired in 1349 and *Provence* (except for *Avignon* and *Orange*) in 1481.

In the north and west, the result of the Hundred Years' War was that the English crown surrendered its long overlordship of the Angevin dominions. It also discredited the feudal system whose nobility was killing itself off in senseless and greedy warfare. The true heroes of these times are found outside the orders of chivalry in the simple figure of Joan of Arc and in the meek dignity of the burghers of *Calais*.

The fortunate accession of Henry IV of *Navarre* (1589), himself a Calvinist, moderated the terrible civil strife between Catholics and Huguenots. His *Edict of Nantes* (1598) gave the Huguenots liberty of conscience and full civil rights. His encouragement of agriculture, trade and industry laid the foundations for the Age of Louis XIV. The statesmen-cardinals, Richelieu and Mazarin, further improved the efficiency of the government and the stage was set for Louis himself "to rule as well as reign".

During his long reign, (1643-1715), the brilliance of the court and of French intellectual achievements dazzled the rest of Europe, but Louis' aggressions in his attempts to dominate the continent led to a succession of wars which nearly exhausted the country, and his ill-judged revocation of the *Edict of Nantes* led large numbers of Huguenots to immigrate with their skills to more tolerant lands.

A further 80 years of wars and colonial rivalries, whilst the luxury of the court and of the nobility went unreformed, led to the Revolution of 1789-93, the "*Declaration of the Rights of Man*" and the violent sweeping away of the *ancien régime*.

Yet the heir of the Revolution turned out to be not democracy but a totalitarian regime. It seemed that only a strong man could save the new Republic from itself and from its enemies abroad, and in Napoleon was displayed perhaps the most brilliant combination of political and military genius that the world has seen. As First Consul (1799) and later as Emperor

FRANCE

(1804), his campaigns made him master of Europe, maker and unmaker of kings and states. The balance of power having gone, Britain was alarmed and alert. She became the ultimate enemy whose defeat was necessary if Napoleon's *"continental system"* was to survive. Great schemes—the campaign in Egypt, the attempt to close the Baltic, the assembly of invasion transports at *Boulogne*, even the march to Moscow when Russia went over to the enemy—were designed to that end. But the Channel, Britain's mastery of the seas, and the navy's tenacious years-long vigil off the French ports, proved that, in that age, sea power could be decisive. The march of Allied armies on *Paris* (1814) forced the Emperor's abdication. His return, after a year on *Elba*, lasted only a hundred days and ended with *Waterloo*.

Napoleon, in exile, professed that his aims had been liberal and that this would have become more apparent had he been allowed peace. His true glory, he said, lay not in having won forty battles but in his code of civil law. And this *Code Napoléon*, selecting the best out of the ancient laws and, for the first time, making all men equal before them, has (with the criminal and commercial codes of the same period) been almost universally admired and become a pattern for the codes of many other states.

Napoleon was also modern in his attitude to science and technology—ahead of his time in a country whose industrial revolution came only in the 1850s.

There is space only to list the numerous, and possibly confusing, regimes successively established during France's search for stability after the Revolutionary upheavals—a search which still continues.

1789-1804	1st Republic	(Including the Consulate from 1798).
1804-1814	1st Empire	Napoleon I.
1814-1830	Bourbon Restoration	Louis XVIII (1814-24). Charles X (1824-30) His attempted return to *ancien régime* led to revolution. (1830).
1830-1848	Monarchy "by will of the people".	Louis Philippe I His similar attempt also led to revolution (1848).
1848-1852	2nd Republic	Louis Napoleon (nephew of Napoleon I) elected President.
1852-1870	2nd Empire	Louis Napoleon declared Emperor, after a *coup d'état*, ruling as Napoleon III, with absolute power. An era of progress for France, and of brilliance for *Paris* (in which Haussmann's town planning created the present pattern of boulevards). Ended by France's speedy defeat at *Sedan* in the Franco-Prussian war.
1870-1940	3rd Republic	Two-chamber legislature. The Republic began with the Germans in occupation of *Paris*, (1870) survived the aggressions of World War I, and ended with the German occupation of most of France in 1940.

FRANCE

1940–1944	Vichy Government	Unoccupied France, (about one-third of the country) under Pétain as Head of State, with supreme power, but increasingly under German instructions. In London de Gaulle formed a provisional government of the 4th Republic.
1944–1958	4th Republic	On the liberation of *Paris* (1944) de Gaulle's government recognized by Allies as government of France, and new constitution drawn up (1946). Instability of system shown by fall of 26 cabinets, 1946-58.
1958–	5th Republic	de Gaulle recalled. Present constitution drawn up. de Gaulle elected first President of 5th Republic. Pompidou as President, 1969-73. Giscard d'Estaing elected President, 1973.

Government Under the Constitution (1958) of the 5th Republic the position of the President (who is elected for 7 years) has been greatly strengthened, both as executive head of the Republic and as President of the French Community i.e. metropolitan France with the territories overseas. The *Executive Council* consists of the Prime Minister, the heads of government of each member state and of the ministers responsible to the Community for common affairs. On joining the Council ministers relinquish their parliamentary seats. Parliament consists of two chambers, the *National Assembly*, elected by universal adult suffrage, with proportional representation, and the *Senate* consisting of delegates of the Assembly and of those of other member states. Of its 284 members, 186 represent the French Republic.

For the purposes of administration, France is divided into 90 *Départements* usually named after natural features, such as rivers. They are sub-divided into *arrondissements*, each of which is an electoral unit returning one representative to the *Assemblée Nationale*.

The *Arrondissement* is divided into *Cantons* and *Communes*. A *Canton* is a judicial unit and sends one representative to the *Conseil Général* of the *Département*. The *Commune* corresponds to a parish and is presided over by a *Maire*. In large towns the *Maire* is a dignitary of some importance, but in villages he often follows a humble calling. Paris is divided into 20 *arrondissements*, each with its *Maire*.

Resources France is famous for its quality products—fine wines, perfumes and clothing; but in the last fifty years or so large-scale industry has developed rapidly and France is now an important producer of coal, steel, textiles, chemicals and aluminium. Coal imports are also necessary, but there is a large export of iron ore for which she is one of the world's chief sources.

Careful and intensive use of land is encouraged by the predominance of family holdings of less than 25 acres, and the country is largely self-sufficient in food. Agriculture employs about a quarter of the working population. Arable preponderates north from *Bordeaux* and from the *Central Massif*, wheat being the chief cereal, especially where *limon* covers the chalk and limestone. Wheat is also grown in the south, as in *Languedoc* and the valleys of

FRANCE

the middle *Rhône* and *Garonne*. Barley and oats are grown in the north, rye in the *Central Massif*, rice in the *Camargue*. Other main crops are potatoes (especially in *Brittany*) and beet.

Many varieties of fruit are grown; cider apples in the west and north-west; plums, currant and raspberries in the east; cherries in the *Rhône* valley and *Lorraine;* peaches in the neighbourhood of *Lyons*, and apricots, almonds, figs, oranges and olives in the south.

Cattle are raised to supply the increasing urban population with meat and milk, and to serve the milk product industries, especially for the cheeses, which are world famous. In the mountainous areas the cattle, together with the cowherds and the cheesemakers, spend the summer months on the high pastures (*alps*) at 6,000 ft. or more. The Provençal shepherds migrate to the *Dauphiné alps* with their sheep from June to October each year, contributing to beautiful pastoral scenes of chalet villages with cattle grazing, and the mellow sound of cow and goat bells.

Forestry is important, concentrated chiefly in the *Ardennes* and the forests of *Compiègne, Fontainebleau* and *Orléans.*

Sea fishing is practised on all the three great coasts of France, chiefly from the North Sea, Channel and Atlantic ports. The main fishing industry is centred in Brittany. Oysters are cultivated in the Bay of *Cancale*. Sardines are caught in the warmer southern waters and tunny is fished in the Atlantic.

Wines and Vineyards

France is the world's leading producer of fine wines and her vineyards are the most important section of her agriculture. It is interesting in touring France to notice the names of famous vineyards such as *Châteauneuf-du-Pape*, near *Avignon*, and to notice the effect of climate on the vintage; a wet season increases the juice but reduces the sugar content, so that often the quality is in inverse proportion to the quantity.

The principal wine growing areas are *Burgundy, Bordeaux, Champagne*, the *Loire* valley, *Alsace, Lorraine*, the *Rhône* valley and *Languedoc.*

Customs

The custom of hand shaking is practised much more in France than in English-speaking countries. It is usual to shake hands always on greeting and parting from friends or acquaintances; in the same way guests in a French home shake hands with their host and hostess when retiring at night and at breakfast next morning. Visiting cards are used for informal invitations and acceptances and for exchanging wishes on New Year's day, in preference to sending cards at Christmas time. A pleasant custom is that of taking a gift or flowers or a gâteau to one's hostess when invited to dinner.

It is considered discourteous to address a person without using his or her title. In asking the way or shopping, people should always be addressed as Madame, Mademoiselle or Monsieur as the case may be.

Food

The French give a proper consideration to the art of eating and drinking; in this all classes and all income groups are connoisseurs. There is no hurried eating of snacks; the midday lunch break is from 12 to 2 p.m.

In the south, the cooking is very different from the north as olive oil is used in place of butter and margarine. The finest *cuisine* is said to be in *Touraine,* but every region has its special local dishes which are well worth trying and give an added interest to touring.

Sport The younger generation is keen on sport and the open-air. Football enjoys a considerable popularity. In addition, ski-ing has a large following, as has hunting (usually of hares or rabbits, on foot) in country districts, whilst the most popular sport of all is bicycle racing, culminating in the great *Tour de France* race in July, in which international competitors race all round France, through streets lined with cheering crowds.

Culture

France has a long tradition of excellence in the Arts stretching from Roman times to the present day, and French influence has made itself felt in music, painting, literature and drama, architecture and, more recently, the cinema.

Architecture Some of the finest examples of Roman architecture are to be found in Provence. The magnificent theatre at *Orange,* whose façade is still almost complete, gives some idea of what the other theatres in *Paris, Lyons, Vienne* and *Arles* were like. The *Maison Carrée* at *Nîmes* and the similar temple at *Vienne,* the Arenas at *Nîmes* and *Arles* and the beautiful *Pont du Gard* aqueduct all influenced the development locally of the Romanesque style of church architecture. This style came late in France (11th and 12th cent.) but produced important regional variations as in *Auvergne* (the *chevet*), *Burgundy* (the pointed arch) and *Normandy* (ribbed vaulting).

From such elements sprang the supreme building achievement of the middle ages—the Gothic style, originating in the *Ile de France* and becoming in the 13th century the model for church architecture throughout Christendom. The cathedrals of *Chartres, Amiens* and *Rheims* are among its finest examples.

The Renaissance movement, spreading from Italy, was taken up with enthusiasm and there emerged the French style of classical architecture so familiar today in public buildings all over France. An early example is the *Francis I* wing (1515-25) of the *château* at *Blois,* a later example the *F. Mansart* wing (1635-38) of the same *château,* and still later the *Louvre* front in *Paris.*

France again became the arbiter of taste with the secularized baroque of Louis XIV's *Versailles* (architects Le Vau and J. H. Mansart) and with the succeeding style of Louis XV, the rococo, which appealed so greatly to the princely courts of Germany. In the 19th century, the classical tradition was continued in the great town planning schemes, such as Haussmann's for *Paris.*

Modern French architecture may be seen in all the larger towns. In *Paris,* examples are the *Palais de Chaillot,* the *Beaujon Hospital* and the *Maison Suisse* of the *Cité Universitaire* by the well-known architect le Corbusier. Just outside *Marseilles,* le Corbusier has designed a vast block of flats in an uncompromisingly modern style.

FRANCE

Dams, such as that at *Génissiat*, and beautiful, reinforced concrete bridges, show how successful contemporary French architects have been in combining function and appearance. Perhaps the most distinguished was André Coyne (1891-1960), designer of over 100 remarkable dams including the great *Kariba* on the *Zambesi*.

Painting and Sculpture   For the pre-historic cave art of *Lascaux* and the south-west see R.14.

Decorative sculpture was greatly developed in the Romanesque period. Its finest examples are included in the routes: *Moissac, Souillac, Beaulieu-sur-Dordogne, Vézelay, Issoire, Clermont-Ferrand (Notre Dame du Port)* and *Toulouse (St. Sernin)*. Sculpture was again the characteristic art form of the Gothic period, when a new naturalism finds expression, seen in the west fronts of the cathedrals of *Chartres, Amiens* and *Rheims. Chartres* is also the richest treasury of stained glass of the 12th and 13th centuries.

With the coming of Renaissance, religious themes (and patrons) are no longer the sole inspiration, and painting becomes the chief means of artistic expression. The two great French artists of the 17th century are Poussin and Claude—the one classic, the other romantic: two contrasted modes of feeling which have since constantly recurred in French art. Claude's naturalism and atmospheric effects were developed further in the 18th century by Watteau, whose brilliant technique and careful observation prepared the way for the achievements of the 19th century.

Nowhere has the search for a satisfying idea of art been pursued with such relentless and uncompromising vigour as in France during the last 150 years. All the great movements have originated there, either through French artists or those attracted to the country to take part in this intellectual ferment.

Beginning with the classic Ingres and the romantic colourist Delacroix, the line continues through the out-of-doors realism of Courbet, the painters of the Barbizon school and the Impressionists, with their revolutionary vision, to culminate in Cézanne, Gauguin and van Gogh. Inspiration, even then, did not flag. Seurat allied classic forms to a *"pointilliste"* technique, and the 20th century opened with Bonnard and Vuillard as self-styled prophets. But the shock troops of a new and disturbing artistic vision soon appeared; first, in the group called the "Fauves", led by Matisse and Rouault and, a little later, in the first Cubist works of Picasso and Braque. Throughout the subsequent movements in 20th century art these men, especially Picasso and Matisse, have retained their leadership.

Rodin (1840-1917) stands first among French sculptors in achievement and influence.

Music   Despite the importance of Couperin, Berlioz, Bizet and César Franck, the essentially French contribution to music was made by those who broke with the tradition of the great German composers. In particular, Debussy (1862-1918), opened up a new impressionist world of sound and feeling; Ravel (1875-1937) was equally in revolt against romantic over-statement.

Literature French literature, remarkable in range of thought and in versatility of expression, has faithfully reflected all aspects and periods of French civilization. Its writers have had a powerful influence on Western culture in general, particularly during times of transition. Its prestige throughout Europe in the "Age of Enlightenment" in the 18th century was due to its long humanist tradition of confidence in man's powers of reasoning and observing, stemming respectively from Descartes and Montaigne. The tradition was inherited by Voltaire, Montesquieu, Condorcet and other providers of the philosophy of revolution and progress.

In contrast, but serving at first the same end, was the revolt against these intellectual concepts, seen in Rousseau's impassioned emphasis on feeling and the importance of individual freedom. Such ideas, taken up by Madame de Staël, led to the production of many works of romantic imagination by poets and novelists of the early 19th century, such as Hugo, Dumas and Stendhal.

A return to close observation of character and of the world around them is seen in the works of Balzac, Zola and Maupassant. In the same period Baudelaire and the "Symbolist" poets worked a revolution in the use of words comparable in influence to the work of the Impressionists in painting. They are the originators of modern poetry.

Among the many remarkable French writers of the 20th century perhaps the most influential have been Proust, on account of the depth and range of his 15-volume novel *"Remembrance of things past"*, and Sartre as the chief exponent of "Existentialism".

Theatres The best-known theatre in France is the *Comédie-Française* which has two buildings in Paris, the *Salle Richelieu* and the *Salle Luxembourg*. In the provinces most of the large cities have a theatre or opera-house, usually with a weekly change of programme. Perhaps the most interesting are the Roman theatres, such as those at *Vienne* and *Orange*, where performances of plays and music are given during the summer.

Science French scientists include some with a special claim to fame: Buffon (1707-88) the naturalist; Lamarck (1744-1829) the biologist and first person to state a theory of evolution; Lavoisier (1743-94) the founder of modern chemistry; Pasteur (1822-95) founder of bacteriology and of the techniques of immunization which make him rank as one of the greatest benefactors of mankind; A. H. Becquerel (1852-1908) discoverer of radio-activity; Pierre and Marie Curie, who followed up Becquerel's discovery and themselves discovered radium.

The work of Comte (1798-1857) the founder of positivism (which aims to bring all knowledge within the sphere of scientific investigation) has been particularly significant for the social sciences. It was Comte who coined the word "sociology".

FRANCE

Touring Information

Touring Areas

The following are the areas described in this chapter. (Route Nos. 1-18). Where, as in most cases, the best approach by train from Britain is via *Paris* (usually involving a change of stations) the station of departure is given in brackets.

Area	Means of Access
Normandy (R.1 and 2)	*Newhaven—Dieppe* or *Southampton—Le Havre*
Brittany (R.3)	*Southampton—Cherbourg* or *Plymouth—Roscoff*
Châteaux of the Loire (R.4)	*Paris (Austerlitz)* to *Orléans* or *Tours*
Picardy and Champagne (R.5)	*Folkestone—Boulogne* or *Folkestone/Dover—Calais*
Ile de France and Burgundy (R.10)	*Paris (Lyon)—Dijon*
Alsace and Lorraine (R.6)	*Dover—Dunkerque—Nancy* or *Folkestone/Dover—Calais—Strasbourg*
The Jura (R.7)	*Paris (Lyon)—Dijon*
The Alps (R.8 and 9); Savoy	*Paris (Lyon)* to *Chamonix, Annecy* or *Chambéry*
Dauphiné	,, ,, to *Grenoble* or *Briançon*
Maritime	,, ,, *—Nice*
Provence (R10)	,, ,, *—Avignon*
Côte d'Azur (R.11)	,, ,, *—Marseilles*
Auvergne (R.12)	,, ,, or *(Austerlitz)—Clermont-Ferrand*
Tarn Gorges and Cévennes (R.13)	*Clermont-Ferrand* to *Florac* or *Alès*
The Dordogne (R.14) and other valleys of the south-west (R.14)	*Paris (Austerlitz)* to *Brive, Cahors* or *Toulouse*
The Pyrenees (R.15):	
Western	*Paris (Austerlitz)* to *Bayonne* or *Lourdes*
Central	,, ,, *—Bagnères-de-Bigorre*
or	,, ,, *—Toulouse—Luchon*
Eastern	,, ,, *—Perpignan*
Languedoc (R.16 and 17)	,, ,, — ,,
or	,, *(Lyon)* *—Avignon*
Corsica (R.18)	*Marseilles* to *Bastia* or *Ajaccio. Nice* to *Bastia Calvi* or *Ajaccio.*

Railways The French Railways are very efficient and the system covers most of the country; basic fare is about 15 *centimes* per km. Reduction of 30 per cent for parties of 10, 40 per cent. for parties of 25, and 50 per cent. for parties of 10 people aged under 21. For individual travellers "Tourist" tickets, giving a reduction of 20 per cent. for 1,500 km return or circular journey are available. Accompanied bicycles, carried for about 5 *francs* any distance over 99 km., must be labelled with owner's name, address and destination and registered at departure station about ½-hour before the time of departure of train.

Bus Services Most of these are run by SNCF (French Railways) and they often terminate at a railway station; only a few long distance routes but local bus services exist everywhere. Bicycles are usually carried on the roof. Bus fares are similar to those on the railways but alpine bus fares may be higher and a charge made for luggage.

Clothing Visitors from countries which enjoy a more subdued climate should note that extremes of temperature can be experienced in the same season and that in the south, or in the mountains, it can be very hot by day and yet cold by night. Particularly when cycling in the mountains, sufficient woollen and windproof clothing should be carried to be donned at the top of the pass before descending again. Failure to do this all too often results in a severe chill. Always take extra clothing when walking in the mountains.

Restaurants Every town in France is amply provided with restaurants almost always providing a good, freshly cooked meal at any hour of the day. Menus are displayed outside, and it usually pays to have the set meal (*menu à prix fixe*) or the *menu touristique*. However, with *à la carte* service you can have as many or as few courses as you wish, and the *plat du jour* (today's special dish) will often make a meal on its own. Particularly economical are cafés advertising *casse-croûte à toute heure* (the nearest equivalent to a snack) and, in the cities, any establishment calling itself a *brasserie*.

It is always very much cheaper to buy fruit outside rather than to have it as a dessert in a restaurant.

Look at the bill after the meal to see if the service charge has been included; if not, the tip should be 12 to 15 per cent. of the price shown. There is no service charge for coffee, etc., taken at a buffet counter, but you should add about 10 per cent. for lemonade or beer served at a table.

If, instead of asking for one of the expensive bottled wines on the list in the restaurant, you order *un quart de vin blanc* (or *vin rouge*) it will not cost more than a *franc* or two for the quarter litre. Mineral waters such as Perrier, Evian, and Vichy are cheap and pleasant. Beer is also obtainable and there are many other alcoholic drinks; the *apéritif* drunk before a meal, and the *liqueur* taken as a *digestif* afterwards.

FRANCE

Tea is not much drunk, and is seldom drinkable. It is preferable to drink coffee, which is always served black unless *café crème* or *café au lait* is specially ordered.

Drinking Water and Milk
Many visitors remain doubtful of the safety of tap water in France although, in general, water supplies are regularly supervised and tap water is safe to drink.

Pasteurised milk in bottles is generally available in every town, but unpasteurised milk should always be boiled.

Holidays and Closing Days
There is no "early closing day" for shops in France and no formal closing on Sundays, still less on Saturdays. Some shops in some areas close on Mondays (either for the morning only or for the whole day) whilst others close on Sundays. Banks are always closed on Sundays and either on Saturdays or on Mondays. Most shops, banks, museums, etc., are closed daily between 12 noon and 2 p.m., but they normally remain open until 6 p.m. or later.

Particular attention should be paid to public holidays (*jours de fête*) on which everything closes, almost without exception. In addition to New Year's day, Easter Monday, Whit Monday and Christmas day the following public holidays are observed: Labour Day (1st May), Ascension (variable date in May), Bastille Day (14th July), Assumption (15th August), All Saints' Day (1st November) and Armistice Day (11th November).

Local Information
Information about local places of interest, train and bus times, pamphlets and maps, can be obtained, usually free of charge, from the office of the *Syndicat d'Initiative* to be found in all tourist resorts and most towns of any size.

Maps
Bartholomew's contoured map in two sheets and the *Michelin* road map, both on scale 1 : 1,000,000, are good general maps. For cycling the best maps are the *Michelin* series, scale 1 : 200,000, whilst walkers should obtain the French Official Survey maps on a scale of 1 : 50,000.

Accommodation
In addition to listing youth hostels, the handbook of the French Youth Hostels Association, (*Federation Unie des Auberges de Jeunesse*), gives details of *maisons amies* and other hostel-type accommodation.

Camping Possession of a *carte de campeur*, or *international camping carnet*, is not compulsory for camping in France but such a document is needed when using official camp sites. International camping carnets are issued by the *Camping Club de France, 218 boulevard Saint-Germain, Paris 7;* or the *Touring Club de France*, whose London agency is at *178 Piccadilly, London W1V 0BA.* Camping on what may appear to be common land is always unwise, and discourteous, without first making enquiry and obtaining permission from the offices of the local *Maire.* Camping in state forests is permitted only on official sites.

Walking The *Vosges* and the *Jura* provide splendid hill walking, as also do many parts of the *Pyrenees* and the *Alps*, for example the country between *Chamonix* and the *Lake of Geneva.* The *Maritime Alps*, which are of little interest to climbers, await discovery by the walker.

In the *Central Massif: Auvergne*, the *Monts du Forez*, and the *Cévennes* offer many possibilities.

River valleys, from the *Meuse* in the north-east to the *Dordogne* and its tributaries, the *Corrèze* and the *Vezère*, in the south-west will repay leisurely and detailed exploration.

Way-marked routes cover more than 4,000 miles; details may be had from *Comité National des Sentiers de Grande Randonnée, 65 Avenue de la Grande Armée, Paris 16*, or from the local *Syndicat d'Initiative.*

Climbing The best mountaineering country is found in three regions: the *Savoy Alps* (centre *Chamonix*), chiefly comprising the *Mont Blanc* range; the *Dauphiné Alps—Meije, Ecrins, Bans* and *Pelvoux* group—centred round the small village of *La Bérarde;* and the *Pyrenees* (the *Vignemale, Mont Perdu, Balaïtous*, etc.). *Cauterets* is a good centre.

The *Pyrenees* are a good starting place for guideless climbers of some experience in the British hills. Although the scale is alpine there are only a few small glaciers and the ice-work as practised in *Dauphiné* or *Savoy* is seldom necessary here. While severe climbing may be found, the principal summits may be reached by reasonably easy routes. The *Ledormeur* Guide is excellent for the normal routes.

It cannot be too strongly emphasized that successful mountaineering in the higher ranges of the *Dauphiné* and *Savoy* is a serious undertaking, demanding considerable technical skill and physical fitness.

The *Club Alpin Français, 7 rue la Boétie, Paris 8*, has huts well situated for most of the important climbs—overnight fee about 10 fr. (3.50 fr. for unwardened huts). Membership is expensive but it secures generous reductions in hut fees. Where there is a warden, soup, coffee, etc., is available. The *Touring Club de France* also owns some mountain chalets where dormitory accommodation costs about 3 francs a night; other charges as in hotels. You may bring your own food; no cooking facilities.

FRANCE

Ski-ing There is good ski-ing in all the mountain regions of France. Class instruction is available at the main centres and there are often cable-railways or ski-hoists. The season in the *Alps* and *Pyrenees* is approximately end of December to April and in the *Vosges* and *Auvergne*, January to March. The best centres for ski-ing are usually those which are less popular in summer and beginners should avoid resorts which are also mountaineering centres, since the slopes are usually steep and difficult, e.g. *Chamonix*.

The U.C.P.A. (*Union des Centres de Plein Air*), *45 rue Raffet, Paris 16*, organises ski-ing courses for young people in youth hostel type accommodation; also climbing courses in the summer.

Cycling Roads shown in red or yellow on the Michelin maps are tarred and well kept-up but those shown in white often have a surface of loose stone or earth; cobbled stone surfaces, making cycling unpleasant, remain in some towns.

If a cycle tour in the mountains is planned, it is well to remember that many passes are closed by snow between the end of September and the end of May or June. For cycling in mountainous districts it would save much uphill walking to emulate the French and fit a double chain wheel, giving 10 speeds (2×5 "double-plateau" derailleur gear). Hub-type 3-speeds are unknown in France and English-type saddlebags and cycle-lamp batteries are unobtainable.

Canoeing Canoeing and boating may be practised in most parts of France, and it is possible to cross the country from the Channel to the Mediterranean by river and canal. There is good sailing on the lakes of *Savoy* and around the coasts. Maps showing the possibilities of the rivers and streams are given in some of the folders of General Information on various districts issued by the *Commissariat Général au Tourisme, 8 avenue de l'Opera, Paris* and by the *French Government Tourist Office, 610 5th Avenue, New York, N.Y. 10019*.

Key to Plan of Paris

1. *Arc de Triomphe*
2. *Palais de Chaillot*
3. *Eiffel Tower*
4. *La Madeleine*
5. *Opéra*
6. *Place de la Concorde*
7. *Louvre*
8. *Invalides*
9. *Palais de Justice*
10. *Hôtel de Ville*
11. *Notre Dame*
12. *Palais du Luxembourg*
13. *Panthéon*
14. *The Sorbonne*
15. *Tuileries Gardens*
16. *Bastille*
17. *Chamber of Deputies*
18. *Pont Neuf*
19. *Air Terminal (Aérogare des Invalides)*

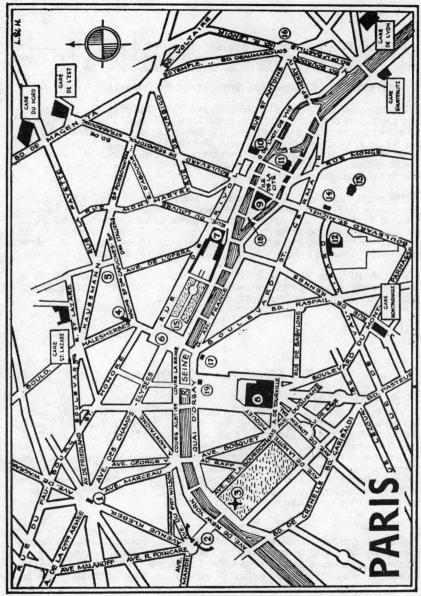

PARIS

FRANCE

Paris

Practical Hints. By train from England one arrives at either the *St. Lazare* or *Nord* stations; by road from *Dieppe* by N.15, from *Calais* and *Boulogne* by N.1, or from *le Havre* by N.14; by air at the *Aérogare des Invalides*.

Youth Hostels at *Choisy-le-Roi, Suresnes* and *Châtenay-Malabry*.

Public transport: *Métro* (Underground) 1.30 fr. 2nd class, for single journey any distance: buses 1·30 fr. per ticket for a journey of 2 stages. For a stay of more than one day, or for a party, it is cheaper to buy a *carnet* of 10 tickets for 8 *francs*, valid on *Metro* and buses. Bus stops are marked by yellow discs on post which bears route number and list of principal stopping places. Where traffic is heavy, there is a box containing numbered tickets (take one, no charge) to indicate position in queue.

The most "Parisian" shopping centres are the *rue de Rivoli* and the area around the *Opéra*—shops such as *Printemps, Galeries Lafayette, Bon Marché*. Central Paris shops are open all day Saturday, closed Sunday and Monday, except for food shops, which open either on Sunday morning or on Monday and dept. stores, which open on Monday afternoons. Some surburban shops open Mondays, notably *boulevard de Clichy* near *Montmartre*.

A copy of "The Week in Paris" (in English and French) obtainable at any bookstall is very useful for seeing what is on. Entrance to art galleries, etc., on Sundays is usually either free or half price.

The City—Quarter by Quarter

Ile de la Cité

The cradle of Paris, inhabited in pre-Roman times. *Pont Neuf,* oldest bridge has statue of Henri IV. *Quai-des-Orfèvres,* France's "Scotland Yard"; *Palais de Justice* (Law Courts) old clock on corner, 1370; (closed Sundays). *Sainte-Chapelle*, 1248, late Gothic, magnificent windows, carved door to upper chapel. Flower and cage-bird market near *Cité* Metro station. *Conciergerie*, Marie Antoinette imprisoned here. Cathedral of *Notre Dame*, mostly 13th century; sculptured west door, fine nave, rose windows; scene of national celebrations—Napoleon crowned here. Outside—flying buttresses, gargoyles. Fine view from north tower.

Latin Quarter

Student quarter; *boulevard St. Michel* main thoroughfare. *Sorbonne,* University of Paris, on left going up, between *rue des Ecoles* and *rue St. Jacques. Panthéon*, at end of *rue Soufflot*, formerly a church, built 1754-1780, closed Tuesdays. Contains tombs of great men, e.g. Rousseau, Voltaire;

wall paintings depict history of France and include Ste. Geneviève, patron saint of Paris. Church of *St. Etienne-du-Mont*, N.E. of *Panthéon*, 16th century; wonderful carved screen, shrine of *Ste. Geneviève*. *Arènes de Lutéce*, remains of Roman amphitheatre, near *Jardin des Plantes* (zoo). *Luxembourg Gardens*, across *boulevard St. Michel. St. Germain-des-Prés*, (1163) oldest church in Paris. Romanesque tower (1014). Cheap accommodation can be found in this district.

Louvre and Tuileries

The *Louvre* was originally a royal palace, now an art gallery. Treasures include the Victory of Samothrace, Venus de Milo, Mona Lisa (closed Tuesdays). Outside are gardens with *Arc de Triomphe du Carrousel*. View under arch through *Tuileries* Gardens, across *place de la Concorde*, up *Champs Elysees* to *Arc de Triomphe*—nearly 2 miles. *Tuileries*—formal gardens. *Salle-du-Jeu-de-Paume*, Impressionist paintings (closed Tuesdays). *Rue de Rivoli*, besides *Tuileries*—fashionable shops under arches. *Comédie-Française*—French National Theatre.

Hôtel de Ville (City Hall) and District

Where Paris receives official guests. Built and furnished on the grand scale. *Ile St.-Louis*, quiet provincial atmosphere. Old houses. *Place de la Bastille*, site of prison destroyed in French Revolution (1789); part of site is marked by stones in pavement between *boulevard Henri IV* and *rue St. Antoine*. Column commemorates revolutions of 1830 and 1848. To the N.W., *place des Vosges*, attractive secluded square, *Victor Hugo* museum. *Musée Carnavalet, rue des Francs-Bourgeois*, N.W. of *place des Vosges*; house of *Mme. de Sévigné*, museum of old Paris (closed Tuesdays).

Opera and Madeleine

Opéra (1875), prices moderate, interior splendid. *Place de l'Opéra*, one of busiest squares in Paris, centre of luxury shopping area. *Madeleine*, 19th century neo-Classic church; *rue Royale*, expensive shops; *place Vendôme*, designed by Mansart, fine architectural unity; Napoleon's victory column.

Place de la Concorde, Champs Elysées

Place de la Concorde, site of the guillotine during French Revolution, obelisk sent from Egypt to King Louis-Philippe. Across the bridge, *Palais Bourbon* (Chamber of Deputies). *Champs-Elysées*, wide avenue leading to *Arc de Triomphe* in *place Charles de Gaulle*, from which 12 avenues radiate. Arch planned by Napoleon completed 1836. Sculpture by Rude *Le Départ* on right pillar. Tomb of Unknown Warrior beneath archway. View from top of arch—(closed Tuesdays). *Avenue Foch* leads through smart residential district to *Bois de Boulogne*, large park, trees, ornamental gardens.

Eiffel Tower and Invalides

Eiffel Tower erected 1887-89 for Paris World Fair, 984 ft. high. Extensive views. *Palais de Chaillot*, built 1937, for Paris Exhibition, containing *Musée de*

FRANCE

l'Homme (fine anthropological collection) and *Musée National des Monuments Français et de la Fresque* (copies of frescoes from churches all over France). *Champ-de-Mars*, scene of Roman victory; military pageants under Napoleon. *Ecole Militaire, Hôtel des Invalides*, built by Henri IV for his old soldiers (*invalides*); enlarged by Louis XIV. Tombs of Napoleon and other great military leaders, e.g. Marshal Foch, General Leclerc (closed Tuesdays).

Montmartre

Artists' quarter on right bank of river; old streets, cheap shops, very expensive restaurants and night clubs. *Sacré Coeur*, 20th century neo-Byzantine church; a superb view over Paris. *Place du Tertre* is nearby; almost entire square occupied by restaurant tables. Church of *St. Pierre*, 12th century.

Other Sights

Time should be found to walk along the *quais* by the river, with their second-hand bookstalls; or along the old tow-path, haunt of amateur fishermen.

The modern *Cité Universitaire* is near the *Porte d'Orléans*. Separate buildings house students of each nationality.

The Flea Market (*Marché aux Puces*) near *Porte de Clignancourt* and *Porte de Saint-Ouen* (18th *Arrondissement*) has over 1,000 stalls selling all kinds of antiques, curios and junk (open on Saturdays, Sundays and Mondays).

Excursions from Paris

St. Denis, 6 miles north; bus from *Métro* station *Porte-de-la-Chapelle*. Abbey where many French kings are buried.

Versailles 12½ miles south-west. Leave from *Gare Montparnasse*. Palace begun by Louis XIII, mostly built by Louis XIV, statue is in courtyard. Vast rooms, tapestries, paintings. *Galerie-des-Glaces* (Hall of Mirrors) court ballroom; Treaty of Versailles signed here (1919). Gardens laid out by Le Nôtre under Louis XIV, superb example of formal garden. *Grand Trianon* (Louis XIV) and *Petit Trianon* (Louis XV) built to provide means of escape from court ceremonial. *Hameau* (hamlet) of Marie Antoinette, where she and ladies of her court played at leading a simple country life. *Musée-de-Voitures*, museums of state coaches, open weekday afternoons. Palace closed on Tuesdays.

Fontainebleau, 37 miles; magnificent forest. Former Royal Palace, second only to *Versailles*—various periods, but mainly 16th and 17th century.

Rueil-Malmaison, 9 miles (train from *St. Lazare* station or bus 158 from *Pont de Neuilly*). Empress Josephine's palace of *Malmaison* (closed Tuesdays). Rose gardens.

St. Germain-en-Laye, 13 miles—see R.1.

Touring Routes

Normandy

The Normans are partly descended from the Northmen (Scandinavians) who invaded the area in the 8th and 9th centuries. From 1066, when Duke William became King of England, until 1204 Normandy was ruled by English kings.

A pastoral countryside, with rolling hills, farms and orchards, some woodland, and cliffs along large sections of the coast. The first D-Day landings of the Allied invasion (1944) took place between *Arromanches* and *Courseulles* and many towns and villages suffered extensive war damage, now almost entirely repaired and rebuilt.

Local specialities include cider, perry (a similar drink made from pears), and *calvados*, a potent spirit distilled from cider; many varieties of cheese (*Brie, Camembert, Pont l'Evêque, Petit Suisse*); meat dishes based on pork; apple dishes and *pain chocolat*.

R.1. Dieppe to Paris via Rouen and Seine Valley (130 miles)

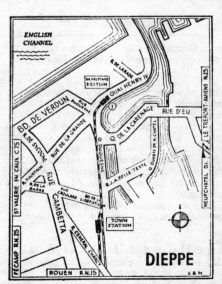

Dieppe (disembarkation from Newhaven steamer, marked (1) on plan), fishing port; old castle; church of *St. Jacques*, 13th and 14th centuries. (Y.H.).

Route from *Dieppe* to *Rouen* not particularly interesting, can well be covered by train (40 miles, 60 mins.). If proceeding by cycle, leave main road N.27 at *Sauqueville*, 5 miles, and follow minor road D.3 along the valley of the *Scie* to *Longueville* (ruined castle), *Auffay* (old church) and *Clères* (zoological garden in grounds of chateau); thence by D.155 by the valley of the *Clérette* to *Malaunay*, rejoining main road N.27 for *Rouen*.

Rouen industrial town (cotton goods, metals, chemicals), important river-port, on the *Seine*, old capital of *Normandy*. In the Old Market Place Joan of Arc was burned at the stake. Cathedral (13th-16th century), *St. Ouen* Church (14th-15th century), Law Courts (old Parliament, 16th century), *Grosse Horloge* (clock made in 1447 over an archway), *rue Eau-de-Robec* (old houses lining bridged stream). Excellent view over city from *Bonsecours* hill on N.14 (S.E. of *Rouen*). **(Y.H.).**

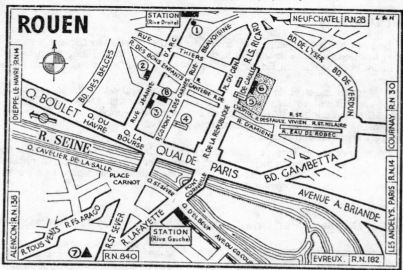

1. *Tour Jeanne d'Arc.* 2. *Post Office* 3. *Grosse Horloge.* 4. *Cathedral.* 5. *St Ouen Church.* 6. *Hôtel de Ville.* 7. *Youth Hostel (rue Diderot).* 8. *Law Courts (Palais de Justice).*

From *Rouen* to *Paris* by the *Seine* is a pleasant journey through undulating country, often wooded, with chalk bluffs above the river and a succession of attractive small towns and villages. Follow N.840 through the forest of *Rouvray* to *Elbeuf* (cloth industry 600 years old), then by side roads on the N. and E. side of the river through *Les Andelys* (ruins of *Château Gaillard*; fine view of the *Seine*), forests of *Andelys* and *Vernon* to *Giverny*; follow the River *Epte* to *Gasny*, returning to the *Seine* at *la Roche-Guyon* (old castle); *Haute Isle*, on N.313, has a church cut in the rock and some cave-dwellings; follow N.313 to *Meulan* (old town) and *Saint Germain-en-Laye* (Renaissance palace, with museum of national antiquities). From here to *Paris* either via N.13, visiting Napoleon's country house at *Malmaison* (see **Paris 10**) or by N.184 to *Versailles* (see **Paris 10**). The two trunk roads by-passing *St. Germain* and *Versailles* are closed to cyclists.

R.2. Dieppe to Cherbourg via Le Havre and Bayeux (175 miles)

Dieppe (see **R.1**). Direct by N.25, or by picturesque but rough, hilly, coast road, D.75, to *Saint-Valéry-en-Caux*, small port **(Y.H.)**. Over *Caux* plateau to *Cany-Barville*, Renaissance church; 17th century castle 1½ miles south. *Fécamp*, (small **Y.H.**) cod-fishing port; 12th century Trinity Church; Benedictine Museum, including distillery, where liqueur-making may be seen.

Another **Y.H.** at *Yport* (5 miles). *Etretat*, fine cliffs with the *Aiguille* rock rising 220 ft. out of the sea, 12th century church of Notre Dame.

61 miles, **Le Havre**, third most important French port. Frequent ferry service from Southampton. **(Y.H.).**

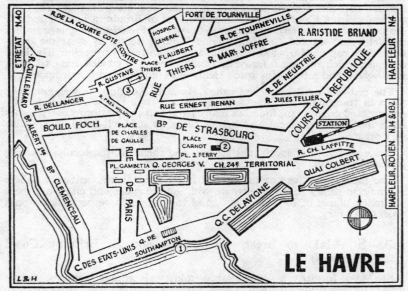

1. Southampton ferries dock here. 2. Post Office. 3. Cathedral.

Cross R. *Seine* by *Pont de Tancarville* to *Honfleur*, picturesque port and old town; 15th century church of *Ste. Catherine* built of wood, with separate bell-tower; museum (Norman) costumes. *Trouville, Deauville*, seaside resorts. Small **Y.H.** at *Pennedepie*.

Caen, residence of William the Conqueror before he became King of England. He built the Castle and the *Abbaye-aux-Hommes* (St. Stephen's Church) while his wife, Matilda, built the *Abbaye-aux-Dames* (Trinity Church). Church of *St. Pierre* (13th-16th century). **(Y.H.).**

EXCURSION: 18 miles S.W. of *Caen* lies the *Bocage*, a region of miniature hills and gorges traversed by the river *Orne*; orchards and meadows alternate with woodlands.

Bayeux, 13th century Cathedral; Museum of Queen Matilda, containing the famous "Bayeux Tapestry", 72 scenes of the Norman Conquest sewn on linen 231 ft. long, shortly after Conquest. **(Y.H.).**

EXCURSION: to *Arromanches* (7 miles) one of main British landing points in 1944 invasion; remains of "Mulberry" artificial harbour.

Through important dairy-farming area via *Isigny-sur-Mer* **(small Y.H.)** to *Carentan*, old houses, old church; **Cherbourg**, Atlantic port. **(small Y.H.).**

EXCURSION: West of *Cherbourg* lies peninsula of *La Hague*; wild rocky coast; fine high-level road from *Cap de la Hague* to *Nez de Jobourg*—cliffs over 400 ft. high.

FRANCE

Brittany

Brittany, the last French province to come under the crown (1492), did so only on condition that it should keep its customs and liberties, and the Bretons still retain some feeling of isolation and independence. They are descended from Celtic migrants from the west of Britain in the 5th and 6th centuries A.D., and many speak Breton (as well as French), a language similar to Welsh and the old Cornish tongue. Women frequently wear the traditional lace cap (*coiffe*) which varies in style from region to region. The local costume, which appears at festivals, usually consists of a black dress, trimmed with velvet, and a beautiful apron richly embroidered and lace-trimmed.

The festivals of Brittany are called *Pardons*. Religious processions take place in traditional costume, followed by a village fair. *Calvaires*, heavily ornamented crosses, are found in many parts and the platforms carry scenes from the New Testament and figures of saints. Church interiors are also very ornate.

Amongst the local specialities are fish and shell-fish, (especially lobsters), pancakes and cider.

The most attractive coastal scenery is on the Atlantic seaboard, where magnificent sandy beaches alternate with granite rocks and cliffs, but there are many places of interest inland, and the suggested route includes both types of country.

R.3. St. Malo to Brest, via Rennes and S. Brittany Coast (331 miles)

St. Malo, formerly a pirates' stronghold; walk round ramparts, almost intact, though medieval town carefully rebuilt after destruction by German army in 1944. (Y.H.)

R.3 (i) to Mont St. Michel. By coast road (33 miles). A rocky island, linked to the mainland (except at very high tide) by a causeway. A picturesque old village flanks the south east of the island and on the summit is a 13th century abbey, with a church whose gallery is 400 ft. above sea level, From the ramparts superb views over the bay. One of the most interesting sights in France, but very crowded in summer.

By train or bus to *Rennes*, (Y.H.) capital of the old province of Brittany; *Museum of Breton History*; *Fine Arts Museum* with paintings by French school and Jordaens, Rubens; *Botanical Garden*. West by N.24 to *Ploermel* (38 miles) and *Josselin*—very fine château on bank of River *Oust*. (Bus from *Rennes* Station to *Ploermel* and *Josselin*). Cross the *Landes* (moors) to Ste.-Anne-d'Auray, most famous place of pilgrimage in Brittany; *Pardon* July 25 and 26.

12 miles S.W., Carnac, seaside village surrounded by world's greatest concentration of neolithic and early bronze age monuments. Tumulus of *Saint Michel* (to N.E.) has underground tombs, and at *Ménec* (to N.W.) are over 1,000 menhirs (standing stones) in long lines. Many isolated standing stones and dolmens (old tombs), including two on *Auray-Plouharnel* road. partly excavated. Church of *Carnac* dedicated to *St. Cornély*, patron saint of horned animals; blessing of local cattle on second Sunday in September.

Carnac-Plage—sea-bathing; view of *Quiberon* peninsula. **Y.H.** at *Quiberon*; *Pardon* last Sunday in September. From *Belz* across bridge to *Port Lorois* and *Hennebont*. Remains of old fortifications at *Lorient*. **(Y.H.).** *Pont-Scorff*—picturesque village with pretty river valley to north. *Quimperlé*—high town and low town. In latter church of *Ste. Croix*; Romanesque style, built on plan of Church of Holy Sepulchre, Jerusalem. Carved screen. The Forest of *Carnoët* lies a few miles south. *Pont-Aven*; Gauguin lived here."Gorse Bloom Festival"; 1st Sunday in August. *Concarneau*—main tunny-fishing port, resort; **(Y.H.)** *Ville Close* (old walled town) on island. "Blessing of the Nets" last Sunday but one in August. Follow picturesque road along coast to *La Forêt* (*Château-de-Kériolet*, 3 miles, museum of tapestry and Breton costumes).

Quimper **(Y.H.).** Fine cathedral, 13-15th century. Spires 17th century, 15th century windows. Chancel out of line. Folk festival on fourth Sunday in July. Breton museum, furniture, costumes, etc. Town hall has rich art gallery.

Audierne—lobster fishing. *Pardon* last Sunday in August. Beyond *Audierne* the country becomes wilder and the cliffs culminate in the *Pointe du Raz*, most westerly headland of France. Along the north coast the cliffs are continuous as far as *Douarnenez*. Return to *Audierne* and continue to *Pont Croix*, old town; *Douarnenez*, fishing port. "Blessing of the Sea" 3rd Sunday in July. *Morgat*—small seaside resort. Visit caves: *Grandes Grottes* by boat, *Petites Grottes* accessible from shore at low tide. Excursions to magnificent rocky coast all round peninsula of *Crozon*. From *Le Fret*, ferry to *Brest*. Alternative by road: *Douarnenez—Brest* 50 miles, via *Locronan* (15th century church of *Pénity*), *Chateaulin* (salmon fishing), *Plougastel-Daoulas* (excursions can be made to fruit-growing peninsula of *Plougastel*—old traditional way of life). **Brest,** important port and naval station, badly damaged during siege in 1944, and now expertly reconstructed, retaining its traditional character. **(Y.H.).** Small beaches westwards towards *St. Mathieu*, headland facing Atlantic; *Ushant* in view from lighthouse.

The Loire Valley

This is pastoral country, soft and pleasant, with views of fields, woods and vineyards in every direction. The *châteaux*, for which this part of France is so well known, are mainly situated about the broad, slow-flowing *Loire* or its tributaries; there are more than a hundred of them between *Gien* and *Angers*.

In summer there are coach tours from *Blois*, *Tours* and *Saumur*, which enable several *châteaux* to be visited during one day; at other times of the year the local buses and trains are so infrequent as to make "one day—one *château*" the rule unless a bicycle is used. Possibly the three finest *châteaux* are *Blois*, *Chambord*, and *Chenonceaux*, although the selection is largely a matter of taste. The majority of the *châteaux* are open from 9 to 12 and 2 to 6 or 7 p.m. in the summer months; admission charges are small. School parties and youth groups can obtain reduced admission charges to the State-owned *châteaux* (*Chambord*, *Chaumont*, *Azay*) and *Fontévrault* abbey by previous application to *Service du driot d'entrée, Monuments Historiques, 3, Rue de Valois, Paris 1*.

From June to October the castles of *Azay, Chambord, Chenonceaux, Loches*, and *Villandry* are floodlit after sundown. But apart from this the *Loire* is best visited out of season when coaches and crowds are absent.

R.4. Paris—Saumur (210 miles)

The most direct route from *Paris* to the *Loire* is via *Etampes*, but the extra 30 miles spent on the detour via *Chartres* are well worth while.

Chartres (55 miles), 1 hour from *Gare Montparnasse*, is one of the most beautiful cathedrals in Europe, early Gothic. Dissimilar spires—north 12th century, south 16th century. Three magnificent entrances; the west is called a "Bible in stone". Beautiful stained glass, mostly 13th century. Carved choir screen, scenes from the life of Virgin Mary. The statues on the exterior of the building are the most important. **(Y.H.)**.

Orleans (45 miles) cathedral re-built, 17th-19th century in Gothic style. Famous as the town from which Joan of Arc drove the English in 1429. Important centre for road traffic.

35 miles, **Blois**, pleasant town, mostly rebuilt. Important *château* with wings in different styles. Church of *St. Nicholas*, most beautiful; cathedral of

St. Louis, 17th century. 11th century crypt. (**Y.H.**).

Chambord (10 miles E. of *Blois*) is the largest of the *châteaux*, built 1523, the royal palace of *François I*, standing in a vast park. **Y.H.** at *Beaugency Beauregard* (5 miles S. of *Blois*, near *Cellettes*) is a later building with a fine portrait-gallery. *Cheverny* (8 miles S.E. of *Blois*) dates from 1634, but is still lived in; fine interior furnishings of 17th century. Small **Y.H.** at *Montlivault*.

Chaumont, standing above the river, 12 miles S.W. of *Blois*, dates from 1475 and is more grimly medieval. *Amboise* castle (1495) dominates the small town and gives fine views up and down the river.

Leave the *Loire* by D.31 via *Bléré* to *Chenonceaux*, a *château* whose beauty is greatly enhanced by its unusual situation—it is built like a bridge across the river *Cher*. 15 miles S.E. lies the *château* of *Montrésor* (11th century, restored 19th century) with a fine collection of jewellery. Turn westward to *Loches* (11 miles) a charming little fortified town on the *Indre*, within which stands a *château*, once the home of Anne of Brittany, who married two French kings in succession; one ticket gives entry to the *Donjon*, *Logis Royaux*, *Tour Ronde* and *Martelet*.

Follow the river *Indre* westward (**Y.H.** at *Tours*, less interesting than most of the *Loire* towns) to *Montbazon* (ruined fortress); D.17 to *Azay-le-Rideau*, a 16th century *château* of great beauty built partly over the river *Indre*.

Turn north to *Villandry*, on the *Loire*, a *château* remarkable for its magnificent ornamental gardens. Continue down the *Loire* to *Langeais*, a fortified 15th century castle with a well-furnished interior. Near the junction of *Indre* and *Loire* is the *château* of *Ussé*, a turreted building of fairy-tale quality (16th century).

Chinon, on the river *Vienne*, is a picturesque little town whose *château* is famous for the first meeting between Joan of Arc and the *Dauphin* (Charles VII).

Near the junction of *Vienne* and *Loire* is the Abbey of *Fontévrault*, which provides a change of scene from the *châteaux* and is well worth a visit. The abbey, which formerly housed a community of thousands, is a masterpiece of Romanesque architecture, and the church contains the death-masks of several English sovereigns, once buried there.

Saumur, (**Y.H.**), marks almost the end of the *château* country and from the summit of its own *château* there is a fine view over the town and river.

The North and North-East

Flanders, *Artois* and *Picardy* will usually be visited *en route* from one of the Channel ports to the *Vosges* or central Europe. The low hills of *Artois* form the outer northern rim of the *Paris basin* dividing it from the intensely settled and industrialised *Plain of Flanders*, a small but important part of which is

FRANCE

French territory. To the south-west of *Artois* lies the chalk upland of *Picardy* cut into separate blocks by the rivers *Somme, Authie* and *Canche*, and to a large extent covered with the fine loam (*limon*) which permits intense cultivation. Absence of this loam in the chalklands of *Champagne* explains the contrast found here in the vast bare landscape. But the wealth of *Champagne* comes chiefly from its valley slopes with their famous vineyards.

R.5. Picardy and Champagne to Lorraine (200 miles)

Boulogne (Y.H.) N.1 to *Montreuil* (23 miles) (Y.H.). Continue on N.1. until 2½ miles S. of *Vron*; take N.338 through *Forest of Crécy*; panorama table N.E. of village of *Crécy* (22 miles) on site of battle (1346); D.10 to *St. Riquier* (9 miles) abbey church, flamboyant Gothic; *Abbeville* (6 miles). D.218 W. side of *Somme* valley to (28 miles) **Amiens** (Y.H.); cathedral late Gothic, largest in France, famed for its perfect form and for statuary on door-arches; *Musée de Picardie*, archaeology etc., and excellent collection of pictures from 15th century to Matisse; water-market on boats sells produce from reclaimed meanders of *Somme*.

N.35 to (20 miles) *Montdidier*; cemeteries and memorials of 1918 battles; on to *Compiégne* (23 miles) Louis XV château, 16th century town hall. (Y.H.). N.373 through *Forest of Compiègne* (35,000 acres); *Pierrefonds* castle (restored); return by N.335 to N.31; *Soissons* (19 miles) market centre of *Soissonnais*; cathedral Gothic, with beautiful 12th century transept. N.31 to *Fismes* (18 miles) (Y.H. *Chéry-Chartreuve*, 3¾ miles along N.367); *Rheims* (17 miles).

Rheims, principal city of *Champagne* (Y.H.). Magnificent cathedral (13th to 15th centuries, restored after 1914-18 war; west front particularly fine); room in technical college where armistice signed at end of Second World War; visits to *Pommery's* and other wine cellars can be arranged.

EXCURSION: to Laon, 30 mls. Finely situated town with wide views over *Picardy*; cathedral (1160-1220) one of earliest Gothic buildings; walk on city walls (13th cent.).

Soon after leaving *Rheims* the *Champagne* vineyards are reached; at *Epernay* the wine cellars of *Moët et Chandon* company can be visited. *Châlons-sur-Marne*, (Y.H.) cathedral has interesting exterior and 16th century stained glass. Y.H. at *St. Dizier. Bar-le-Duc*, old quarter of town has many houses of 15th-17th century. *Ligny-en-Barrois*, fascinating small town of 18th century buildings.

R5. (i) Alternative route (25 miles extra) from *Rheims* to *Nancy* via *Verdun*, scene of the worst battles of the 1914-18 war—a bleak part of France. *Metz*, cathedral, exterior more interesting than interior, good stained glass; 18th century *Hôtel de Ville* and several churches of interest.

Nancy, spacious and beautiful old capital of *Lorraine*; magnificently uniform *Place Stanislas* must be seen for its ensemble and the beautiful wrought-iron work; *Hôtel de Ville* and other buildings in the *Place* are worthy of attention; *Lorraine* museum in Duke's Palace; *Cordeliers'* church. Birthplace of Joan of Arc at *Domrémy*, just south-west of town.

Alsace and Lorraine

The provinces of *Alsace* and *Lorraine* record a chequered history, having been fought over and occupied by French and German troops in many wars. Since 1918 they have been French (with the exception of the period 1940-44). The local dialect (principally in *Alsace*) is basically German, but with a strong admixture of French.

The main attraction of this region for the tourist lies in the **Vosges** mountains, a fine range running from north to south for some 60 miles, from *Strasbourg* to *Belfort*. The highest peaks (3,500-4,500 ft.) lie in the granite portion of the *Vosges*, south of *Strasbourg* and the river *Bruche*; to the north are lower mountains of red sandstone. The mountains are well wooded, principally with conifers and beech trees, and the whole region is similar to the Black Forest of south-west Germany. The word *Ballon*, which appears in a number of place names, derives from the rounded shape of the hill tops. There is a good network of youth hostels and it is one of the finest pieces of country for walkers in the whole of France.

R.6. Nancy to Belfort via Strasbourg (262 miles)

Nancy to *Lunéville*, 18th century *château*; N.59 to *Raon-l'Etape* and N.392A through attractive forest-covered hills of northern *Vosges* to *Col du Donon*, old frontier between *Lorraine* and *Alsace*; climb to top of *Le Donon* 3,300 ft., good view—*Vosges*, plain of *Alsace*, Black Forest. *Grandfontaine* (Y.H.). *Schirmeck*, small resort; down valley of river *Bruche* via *Molsheim*; Renaissance town hall.

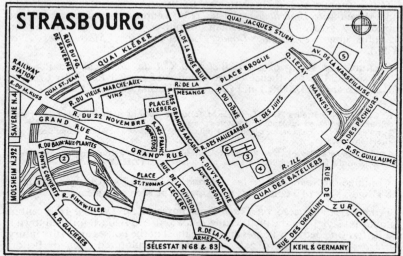

1. *Ponts Couverts.* 2. *La Petite France.* 3. *Cathedral.* 4. *Château de Rohan.* 5. *Post Office.* 6. *Maison Kammerzell.*

147

FRANCE

Strasbourg. (Y.H.), capital of *Alsace*; one of the most attractive cities in France; cathedral fine Gothic style, built 1015-1439; very fine west front; spire 469 ft. high; astronomical clock—mechanical figures with procession of apostles at noon. Old part of town called *La Petite France*—well-preserved old houses bordering canal; *Rue du Bain-aux-Plantes*—narrow street with fine timbered houses; *Ponts Couverts*—bridges guarded by 14th century towers; *Château de Rohan*—18th century palace, famous for connection with story of Queen's necklace (*Marie-Antoinette*), containing fine museum of archaeology, ceramics and paintings; *Maison Kammerzell*, handsome 15th century house.

Between *Strasbourg* and *Colmar* bus goes by circuitous route through interesting villages. *Obernai*, picturesque market place, 16th century buildings, ramparts. Vineyards, then forest, *Mont Ste. Odile*, crowned by convent from whose terrace is the wonderful view of plain of *Alsace*. Pilgrimages at Easter, Whitsun, 15th August. Nearby is *Mur Paien*, ancient wall, 6 miles long, perhaps Celtic fortifications. *Hohwald*, small resort in high valley surrounded by forests, *Sélestat*, picturesque old town; two interesting churches; ramparts and gateways. A few miles north of *Sélestat* the storks of *Alsace* usually assemble in second half of August for homeward flight to Africa. *Haut Koenigsbourg*—castle reconstructed in its original form; gives a superb panorama over surrounding country.

On to *Ribeauvillé* and then through important wine-growing region (*Riesling, Traminer* and other wines) to *Riquewihr*, charming little town with many quaint houses and corners.

Colmar, purely Alsatian in character, storks' nests perched on every height. Fine Museum *de Unterlinden*, cloister (13th century), paintings of religious subjects by great masters, German Primitives. In medieval quarter are beautiful houses – *Ancienne Douane, Maison Pfister, Maison des Têtes*. (Y.H.).

Continue up valley of river *Weiss* to *Col du Bonhomme*, along road giving splendid views; thence by mountain road named *Route des Crêtes* to *Col du Luschpach* (3,200 ft.) and *Col de la Schlucht* (3,700 ft.) Y.H. at *Lautenbach*.

EXCURSIONS: 3 miles N. of *La Schlucht*, footpath leads in 10 mins. to *Lac Vert;* green colour due to lichens suspended in water.
2½ miles S. of *La Schlucht*, cart track in 1 mile to the *Hohneck* (4,500 ft.) magnificent view; direction indicator.

R.6.(i) Via upper valley of river *Vologne* (picturesque lakes), to Gérardmer, good centre for excursions in the forest and hills. Fine lake over a mile long. (Y.H. *Xonrupt*).

Continue on *Route des Crêtes* to *Grand Ballon* (4,700 ft.) highest point of the *Vosges*. View of 3 countries; the Alps can be seen on a clear day.

From *Cernay* proceed via *Thann* (fine church of *St. Thiébaut* 16th century flamboyant style), via the picturesque *Route Joffre* to **Belfort**, fortified town in the *Belfort Gap* between *Vosges* and *Jura*; most of the houses are 17th century; *Porte de Brisach*, fortified gateway; immense sculptured Lion of Belfort, commemorating defence of town in 1870. (Y.H.).

EXCURSION: Via *Giromagny* to *Col du Ballon*, 17 miles, fine view (Y.H.)(½ hour to summit of *Ballon d'Alsace*, 4,000 ft.).

The Jura

South of *Belfort* the long ridges of the *Jura* mountains run north-east to south-west along the Swiss frontier. There are comparatively few tourists, and no grand hotels, but narrow river valleys, gorges, forests, waterfalls and no less than 70 small lakes make an attractive and unspoiled region. The main industry of the mountain farms is the manufacture of Gruyère-type cheese in small co-operatives known as *fruitières*, and during the long rather severe winter a home-craft industry of wooden toy making.

R.7. Dijon to Geneva (120 miles)

From *Dijon* (see **R.10**) main road N.5, rising on to the foothills at *Dôle*, birthplace of Pasteur. From *Les Rousses* (**Y.H.**), passing through an interesting area of forests, caves and subterranean streams to *Champagnole* and crossing main ridge of the *Jura* at *Col de la Faucille* (4,070 ft.) with fine views on descent to *Lake of Geneva*. From the col, the *Dôle* (5,653 ft.) can be climbed in 2 hrs. for possibly the finest view of the lake and the distant *Alps*; it can also be reached direct from *Les Rousses*.

The Alps

The zone of mountainous country, often 60 to 80 miles wide, which extends for some 250 miles from the Mediterranean to the Lake of Geneva is mostly in French territory, and the French Alps, reaching 15,782 ft. in *Mont Blanc*, contain some of the finest mountain scenery in Europe. The outer ranges are of limestone, often exposed in sheer cliffs, usually with a "back-stairs" of grassy slopes, woods, and fertile valleys. The central mass, including the highest peaks, is of granite or other hard rock, forming a landscape on the grandest scale, with extensive snowfields and glaciers, sharp pinnacles, and deep river valleys, forest clad on their lower slopes. South of *Briançon* owing to lower rainfall and brilliant sunshine, the country grows more arid, glaciers fewer, and alpine vegetation is replaced at lower levels by tough plants such as thyme, lavender, Aaron's rod. The chalet houses of Savoy (stone ground-floor, wooden upper storey) give way to square stone farmhouses. Further south are the parched, scrub-covered, Maritime Alps, with small villages clinging to their slopes.

Several routes pass through the Alps to the Mediterranean the *Route des Grandes Alpes*, through *Briançon*; the *Route Napoléon*, through *Grenoble* and *Gap*; the railway from *Grenoble* via *Sisteron* or *Digne*. Motor coach services connect most of the main areas, and in summer there are many coach excursions. Buses serve a great many of the villages, though there may be only one bus each day.

R.8. Thonon (Lake Geneva) to Nice, via the Route des Grandes Alpes (450 miles)

One of the finest mountain road routes in Europe. Many very steep passes (6,000 ft. or more), but practicable for good cyclists with low-geared machines. Highest passes open only July-September, being snowed-up during rest of year, but detour, via valleys, can be taken.

FRANCE

Tourist motor coaches in three stages, each daily in high summer as follows: *Evian* (via *Thonon*) to *Chamonix*, 3 hrs. *Chamonix* to *Briançon*, via *Galibier* and *Lautaret* passes, 12 hours. *Briançon* to *Nice* via *Izoard* and *Cayolle* passes, 11 hours.

Thonon-les-Bains, Lake of Geneva. Small resort, old town; bathing, sailing; lake steamers to *Geneva*, *Lausanne* and *Montreux*. Excursions into Alps. Take N.202 up the valley of the *Dranse* (gorges), peaks rising to 6,000 ft., *Pont-des-Plagnettes* (2 miles to *Lake of Montriond*), *Morzine*. (Y.H.) small mountain and ski resort, *Col des Gets* (3,845 ft., view) through pine forests, *Gorge de Foron*, *Taninges*.

EXCURSION: by valley of the *Giffre* to *Cirque dur Fer à Cheval* (15 miles by road to *Sixt*; thence 4 miles). Here more than 20 waterfalls cascade down a half-circle of cliffs (best seen in June).

R.8 (i) by bus to *Sixt* (10 miles) then on foot for fine two-day trip via *Col d'Anterne* (7,425 ft.), night at *Chalet de Moëde*, continue via *Col du Brévent* (6,975 ft., fine view of Mt. Blanc) and descend by cable railway or on foot to *Chamonix*. Passes on this route should not be attempted in bad weather or when snow still lying.

Continue via *Col du Châtillon*, descent into *Arve* valley, *Cluses* (watch-making school, museum); road, rail and river continue between crags. Valley widens, view of *Mont Blanc*, *Aigulle de Varens* (8,163 ft.), *Saint-Gervais-les-Bains*, resort, spa.

R.8 (ii) Up valley to *Montjoie* to *les Contamines* (5 miles south). From slopes of *Mont Joly* fine endways view of *Mont Blanc* range (*Aiguille de Trélatête*, *Dôme de Miage*, *Aiguille de Bionnassay*, glaciers).

R.8 (iii) To *Chamonix* (13 miles east) by valley of the *Arve*. Gorges of the *Arve*, *Servoz* (Gorges of the *Diosaz*—entrance fee); narrow rocky defile; *Les Houches*—to the right *Dôme du Goûter*, *Mont Blanc*, *Aiguille du Midi*; *Les Bossons*, just below magnificent *Bossons* glacier. On left of road, practice-rocks of *les Gaillands*. *Chamonix*, popular but expensive centre; many walks and graded climbs. Cable railways to *Brévent* (8,284 ft.), for extensive views of *Mont Blanc* range, also to *Aiguille du Midi* (12,608 ft.) in two stages, 16 minutes' journey. East of *Chamonix* many sharp rocky peaks, *Charmoz*, *Grépon*, *Dru*, etc. Excellent and often very difficult climbs. *Mer-de-Glace*, lower portion of immense *Géant Glacier Argentières* centre for climbing peaks near Swiss frontier and the easier *Aiguilles Rouges* to west. Into *Switzerland*—on foot, *Col de Balme*; by road, *Col des Montets*, both good view points. Owing to the steep valley sides, ski-ing use *Chamonix* is not recommended for beginners. Y.H. at *Les Pèlerins*.

Chamonix is a suitable starting point for the classic **Tour du Mont Blanc**, a 5-6 days' walking circuit of the range by low passes: *Col de Balme*, *Trient*, *Bovine*, *Champex*, *Ferret*, *Entrèves*, *Col de la Seigne*, *Col du Bonhomme*, *Les Contamines*, *Col de Tricot* and *Les Houches*. A road tunnel connects *Chamonix* with *Courmayeur* on the Italian side.

Mégève, well-known but expensive ski-resort, two teleferics. Along river *Arly* to *Albertville*; old town of *Conflans*, on hillside, picturesquely medieval.

R.8 (iv) To the north-east is the pleasant, unspoilt region of the **Beaufortin**, local costume frequently worn on Sundays, e.g., at *Hauteluce*.

The road now enters the valley of the *Isère*, which becomes a long narrow trough, known as the *Tarentaise*. *Moutiers*, chief town of region, is good centre for excursions.

EXCURSION: *Mont Jovet* (8,400 ft.); N.E. of *Moutiers*; 6-7 hours' easy climb; chalet hotel; magnificent view).

R.8 (v) to *Pralognan* (18 miles, 4,600 ft.) best centre for *Vanoise* group of mountains; pine forests; fine scenery; good ski-ing.

Continue up *Isère* river; valley widens; 19 miles *Bourg-St. Maurice*.

R.8 (vi) to the Little St. Bernard Pass (18 miles, 7,200 ft.). Excellent approach to Italian valley of *Aosta* (largely French-speaking). Through bus to *Aosta* connects with train arriving at *Bourg* in early morning. *Little St. Bernard* said to be pass crossed by Hannibal with his elephants.

The road starts to climb the upper valley of the *Isère* (average gradient 1 in 17). Village of *Sainte-Foy*, perched 500 ft. above the river. On the right *Mont Pourri* (12,428 ft.) and its glaciers. Barrage-lake of *Tignes*. The country becomes wilder, bends and narrow defiles, *Val d'Isère*, climbing and ski-ing centre. The *Col de l'Iséran* (9,085 ft., highest road in Europe) is finally reached by many hair-pin bends; fine views. *Tarentaise* group to north, *Maurienne* to south, and peaks along Italian frontier. Down the valley of the *Lenta* (average gradient 1 in 13) and into the *Maurienne* (valley of the river *Arc*); upper valley (above *Modane*) is pleasant; lower part industrialised and oppressively hot in summer. *Lanslebourg* (Y.H.)—junction for road via *Mont Cenis* into Italy; *Modane*—start of *Mont Cenis* railway tunnel.

At *Saint-Michel-de-Maurienne* leave N.6 for N.202 (this road number reappears at intervals on *Route des Grandes Alpes*) ascending steeply through woods, fine views, to *Valloire*, small ski and mountain resort, 17th century church, local costume still worn on Sundays. The valley becomes wilder, gradient up to 1 in 12, *Col du Galibier*, 8,386 ft. (road through tunnel open only from July to September). Path to top of pass, 8,721 ft. View north includes three *Aiguilles d'Arves*, southward fine view of *Oisans* group, *La Meije* (13,065 ft.) surrounded by glaciers. Descent to *Col du Lautaret* (6,752 ft.) views, *Le Monetier*, small spa; *Chantemerle* (cable railway to *Serre Chevalier*, 8,150 ft.) (Y.H. *Le Bez*).

Briançon, fortified old town on hill where four roads meet, picturesque streets, excellent walks in mountains all round town, which is 4,000 ft. above sea level. Road into Italy via *Montgenèvre* Pass.

Gorges of the *Cerveyrette*, forest, *Col d'Izoard* (7,835 ft.) fine view. *Casse Déserte*, extraordinary wilderness of sand and red rocks, into the valley of the *Guil*.

R.8 (vii) To the east is *Château Queyras*, picturesque fortress, still garrisoned; high isolated *Queyras Valley*, refuge of the *Waldensian* Protestants, *St Véran* (6,693 ft.).

Gorges de la Guil, approx. 7 miles long, road and river pass between marble cliffs then into open country at *Guillestre*. View of *Oisans* mountains to north, forests. *Sainte-Marie-de-Vars*, scree and pasture, *Col de Vars* (6,939 ft.), the boundary between *Dauphiné* and *Provence*. Descent through pastures and farms, *Saint-Paul-sur-Ubaye*, valley often wild and rugged; *Barcelonnette*, mountain and ski-ing resort.

Chestnuts and acacias give way to pines and larches, *Bachelard* gorges, waterfalls, *Col de la Cayolle* (7,717 ft.) fine view of *Var* valley and *Maritime Alps*. From here cyclists have an almost unbroken downhill run of over 80 miles to *Nice*, following the valley of the river *Var*. *Gorges de Daluis* cut by the *Var* through wild reddish rocks, across limestone country to *Pont de Gueydan*.

At *Entrevaux*, an 18th century fortress town, road joins light railway which runs down to *Nice* and follows it to *Pont-de-Cians* (for *Gorges du Cians* about 14 miles long, lower gorges in limestone, upper through red rocks wild and picturesque), *Touët-sur-Var*, vineyards and olive groves, *Gorges du Ciaudan*, cliffs rising to 2,000 ft. Road continues down the valley of the *Var*, several perched villages. *Nice* (see R.11, sec. 4). There are several unguarded level-crossings between *Entrevaux* and *Nice*.

R.8 (viii) to by-pass the *Col d'Iséran*. From *Albertville* follow N.90 to *Saint-Pierre-d'Albigny*, then N.6 up valley of river *Arc*, narrow and wild, forming the district of *Maurienne*. *Saint-Jean-de-Maurienne*, ancient capital of district, cathedral (12th-15th century). Y.H. at *La Toussuire*. Saturday market at *Saint-Michel-de-Maurienne*.

R.8 (ix) to by-pass the *Col d'Izoard*. From *Briançon* by N.94 follows the valley of the *Durance*, *L'Argentière* (for *Vallouise*, *Ailefroide*, excursions and climbs in *Oisans* group), *Mont-Dauphin*, fortress, *Guillestre*.

R.8 (x) to by-pass the *Col de la Cayolle*. At *Uvernet* (south of *Barcelonnette*) take N.208 via gorges of the *Malune* to *Col d'Allos* (7,382 ft., fine view during ascent) Y.H. at *La Foux*, 4 mls. S. of col; then 6 mls. to *Allos* village, small summer and winter resort (about 3 hours on foot to charming lake of *Allos*). *Colmars*, old walled town; *La Colle St. Michel* (4,940 ft.); unbroken downhill cycle run from here to *Nice*; beyond *Annot* (picturesque little town) rejoin main route, N.202. Alternatively, 12 mls. S. of *La Colle St. Michel*, join R.9 at *Castellane*.

R.9. Geneva to Cannes by the Route Napoléon (290 miles)

This route, sometimes called the *Route des Alpes*, as distinct from the *Route des Grandes Alpes* (**R.8**) is lower than the latter; it does not exceed 5,000 ft. in altitude, and the passes are free of snow for a much longer period. South of *Grenoble* is the *Route Napoléon* proper, the route taken by the Emperor on his return from *Elba* in 1815. Note the milestones topped with the imperial eagle. Tourist motor coaches from *Geneva* (*Place Dorcière*) to *Grenoble* in 4 hours, from *Grenoble* (Railway Station) to *Cannes* in 9½ hours.

From *Geneva* to *Annecy* direct route is via *St. Julien*, by Swiss road No. 1 and French road N.201 (15 miles) but the route via *Mont Salève* is strongly recommended (38 miles). Cyclists enter France at *Annemasse*, then follow winding G.C.41 along crest of *Salève*, 4,000 ft. up, with magnificent views over Alps and Lake of *Geneva*. Walkers take tram from *Geneva* (*Rive*) to *Veyrier*, then cable railway to *Salève* and follow footpath and road along crest and down to *Cruseilles* (4-5 hours).

Annecy, picturesque old town with arcaded streets, canals, medieval castle, in beautiful setting on lakeside; bathing, sailing, lake steamers in summer. (Y.H.).

EXCURSION: to *Génissiat* dam, 25 miles N.W. Bus to *Frangy* (1 hour) thence about 8 miles. Dam 328 ft. high across upper *Rhône*, with artificial lake 12 miles long.

Aix-les-Bains, fashionable spa, about a mile from *Lac du Bourget*, France's largest lake, bathing, sailing. **Chambéry**, former capital of *Savoy*, tourits centre, but too far from mountains for excursions on foot; *Château*, former home of Dukes of Savoy, and *Les Charmettes* (1¼ miles S.) home of Rousseau and Mme. de Warens. From *Chambéry* follow *Grésivaudan* valley (River *Isère*), richly cultivated with maize, vines and fruit.

Grenoble, capital city of *Dauphiné*; *Palais de Justice* (16th century), Museum (good art collection), *Bastille* Fort on N. side of River (cable railway; good view from summit 900 ft. above river). (Y.H.).

EXCURSIONS: (a) to *St. Nizier* from which the **Moucherotte** (6,253 ft.) can be climbed in 2¼ hrs; fine view of *Grenoble, Dauphiné Alps* and *Mont Blanc*. (b) to *Chamrousse* **(Y.H.)**, centre for climbing and ski-ing in *Belledonne* range.

R.9 (i) alternative route from *Chambéry* to *Grenoble* via the **Grande Chartreuse** range; wooded slopes and sheer rock. N.512 from *Chambéry*. *St. Pierre-de-Chartreuse*, excellent centre for excursions, finely situated.

EXCURSIONS: (a) to the famous monastery of the *Grande Chartreuse* (3 miles N.W.) founded 1084, now mostly ruined, but partly inhabited by monks. Remains of big distillery, where *Chartreuse* liqueur made until 1935, are at *Fourvoirie*, 5 miles further west. (b) easy climbs to *Grand Som, Chamechaude, Charmant Som*, all about 6,000 ft., or to *Dent de Crolles*, with number of deep potholes.

Continue via *Col de Porte* (4,440 ft.) to *Grenoble*.

R.9 (ii) South-west of *Grenoble* is the **Vercors** range, famous for the "Resistance" particularly during 1944. Many forests, rock faces and gorges. Best circuit from *Grenoble* via *Villard-de-Lans*, gorges of the *Bourne, Pont-en-Royans, Petits Goulets, Grands Goulets* (gorges). *Corrençon*; climbing, caving, ski-ing.

R.9 (iii) to join the *Route des Grandes Alpes* **(R.8)** at **Col du Lautaret**; tourist bus from *Grenoble* in 3¼ hours. Stiff cycling, but most rewarding scenery. From *Vizille* follow N.91 up valley of *Romanche* (lower part somewhat industrialised), dominated to the north by the *Belledonne* and *Sept Laux* ranges. Good rock-climbing. *Bourg d'Oisans*, small centre for *Oisan* region; excursions to *La Bérarde*, wild valley surrounded by highest peaks of the district. *Alpe d'Huez*, ski-ing centre. Gorges of the *Infernet, Chambon Dam* (artificial lake), *La Grave*, large village, climbing and walking centre, fine view of *Meije* and other 13,000 ft. peaks. 55 miles *Lautaret* pass, 6,752 ft. (see **R.8**).

R.9 (iv) From *Grenoble* to *Sisteron* the most direct route is by N.75 (89 miles) or by the railway, both crossing the *Col de la Croix Haute* (3,860 ft.) and giving a view (on right, between *Monestier* and *Clelles*) of the *Mont Aiguille*, a striking isolated rocky peak, 6,800 ft. high, first climbed in 1492 by soldiers of Charles VIII (said to be the first recorded mountaineering exploit in history).

The *Route Napoléon* proper, follows N.85 from *Vizille*, passing *Laffrey* (4 lakes, fine views, statue of Napoleon, commemorating Royalist troops who went over to his support) and *la Mure*, centre for *Valjouffrey* and other attractive valleys leading up to *Massif du Pelvoux* (mountaineering area, nature reserve) which can also be approached by the delightful *Valgaudemar* valley from *St. Firmin*. Upper valley of R. *Drac* can be explored from *Orcières* **(Y.H.)**, reached by turning off N.85 at *St. Bonnet* and taking N.545 out of village, then either D.34 or N.544 up valley beyond *Chabottes*. *Col Bayard* (4,088 ft.) descent through increasingly Mediterranean vegetation to *Gap* (large town) and valley of *Durance*. 39 miles further south, *Sisteron*, old town in narrow defile, war-damaged, fine view from Citadel. Beyond *Digne* are the *Alpes de Provence*, bare sunbaked mountains where torrents have cut gorges known as *clues*. *Col des Lèques* (3,765 ft.), hairpin-bend descent to *Castellane*, small town at foot of 600 ft. rock.

R.9 (v) To magnificent canyons of the river *Verdon*, 13 miles long in places nearly 2,300 ft. deep in limestone rock. Excellent views from road south of gorge ("*Corniche Sublime*"), particularly at *Balcons de la Mescla*. Walkers can follow the *Martel* footpath from *La Palud* via *la Mescla* to *Point Sublime* (about 8 hours; recommended, but stiff). Bus service *Castellane-Moustiers* passes *La Palud*. **(Y.H.)**.

Castellane to *Grasse*, fine road, crossing 4 passes including the *Col de Valferrière* (3,830 ft. but open all year) with magnificent views to Mediterranean coast.

Grasse, a picturesque town built on the hillside above a flower-growing plain, is the centre of the French perfume industry. It has a 12th century church and a museum devoted to the painter Fragonard. From *Grasse* the road winds steeply down to *Cannes* (see **R.11, sec. 3**).

FRANCE

Ile de France, Burgundy, Saône and Rhône Valleys

R.10. Paris to Marseilles (500 miles)

This is the "classic" tourist route from *Paris* to the *Riviera* by road N.6 to *Lyons*, thence by N.7. From the river valleys of the *Ile de France*, the route enters the wine producing regions of *Bourgogne* (Burgundy) and *Côte d'Or*, continues between the *Maconnais* hills and the poultry-farming region of *Bresse*, with distant views of the *Jura*, to *Lyons*, and down the *Rhône* valley into the sun-baked countryside of *Provence*. *Paris*, Y.H. at *Choisy-le-Roi*, *Fontainebleau*. *Sens*, cathedral (1130-60) earliest transitional building in France; treasury has vestments of Thomas à Becket. *Auxerre*, fine Gothic cathedral; church of *St. Germain*, 5th and 10th century. 9th century frescoes in crypt. 25 mls. S. of *Auxerre* at *Sermizelles* take N.151 to *Vézelay*, 9 mls. finely situated little town, magnificent Romanesque basilica, associations with Becket and Crusades (Y.H.). N.457 to *Avallon*. 9 mls. N.6 to *Rouvray* (11 mls.), N.70 to *Précy* (11 mls.) and N.80 to *Semur* (8 mls.), a delightful little town off the tourist routes; fortress, walks on ramparts and on low road from *Pont Joly*; 11th century church of *Notre Dame*; fine view of town and R. *Armancon* from *Tour de l'Orle d'Or* which contains museum of *Auxois* history. Train to *Dijon* (50 miles).

Dijon, old capital of Burgundy, 196 miles from Paris, Palace of Dukes of Burgundy—Louis XIV style (museum and art gallery); Archaeological Museum, *Magnin* Museum (paintings), *Musée Perrin de Puycousin* (folklore); cathedral of *St. Bénigne*, Burgundian Gothic, 13th century; also churches of *Notre Dame* and *St. Michel*. Many fine 17th century houses. *Dijon* is famous for its good food and Burgundy wines. (Y.H.)

N.74 to *Beaune* (24 miles) famous wine centre; *Hôtel-Dieu* (Hospital), built 1450; nurses wear ancient costume; annual wine sale in November. *Chalon-sur-Saône* (21 miles) (Y.H.) N.6 to *Tournus* (17 miles) *Abbey of l'An Mille; Burgundian Museum*. *Mâcon* (19 miles) famous boating centre.

EXCURSION: *Solutré*, open-air encampment, late Old Stone Age, remarkable for fine workmanship of flints (small museum).

Lyons (42 miles)—319 miles from Paris, third city of France, famous for its restaurants and silks. Very interesting museum of fabrics; rich *Fine Arts Museum* (*Place St. Pierre*). Cathedral of *St. Jean-Baptiste* (12th-15th century), magnificent 13th century windows, 14th century astronomical clock. Good view from tower of basilica of *Notre Dame de Fourvière*. Picturesque streets; quays of *Rhône* and *Saône*. Y.H. at *Vénissieux*, 4 miles S.

Vienne, 17 miles. Roman remains; Temple of Augustus and Livia; Roman theatre; 12th-15th century church of *St. Maurice*. Route follows *Rhône*, between *Vivarais* mountains (W) and *Vercors* mountains (E) *Valence*, 45 miles, (Y.H.); cathedral. *Mirmande* (Y.H.), 18 miles. *Montélimar*, 9 miles, home-town of nougat. Canal connects *Donzére* and *Mondragon* and here is most powerful electricity plant in Europe. *Pont-St.-Esprit*, famous bridge over the *Rhône*, largely 13th century, 25 arches. At *Orange*, 34 miles, route enters *Provence*—Roman triumphal arch, nicely preserved Roman theatre; seats 7,000; plays performed in early August. Birthplace of Dutch royal house of Oranje.

EXCURSION: to *Vaison-la-Romaine* (17 miles N.E. of *Orange*); fine excavated remains of Roman city; medieval upper town with Castle of the Counts.

Avignon, 17 miles, famous as the home of the Popes (in rivalry with Rome) from 1309 to 1403, as the residence of the Italian poet Petrarch, and the burial place of John Stuart Mill. Fine city walls and gates. The Palace of the Popes; open to visitors and conducted tours lasting an hour are given a few times a day; 12th century cathedral; *Promenade du Rocher des Doms*, good view; *Pont-Saint-Bénézet*, the bridge of the song, said to have been built by the shepherd boy saint *Bénézet* and his disciples in the 12th century; only four arches remain.

Across the river is *Villeneuve-lès-Avignon*, former town of the Cardinals. Fine view from Tower of Philip le Bel and *Fort St. André*. *Chartreuse du Val de Bénédiction* (old Carthusian monastery).

EXCURSION: from *Avignon* by bus, 18 miles eastwards via *l'Isle-sur-la-Sorgue* to *Fontaine de Vaucluse* (Y.H.), beautiful still pool at foot of cliff, source of river *Sorgue*; immortalised by Petrarch.

From *Avignon*, N.100 west across hills to *Remoulins* (14 miles); 2 miles N.W. to *Pont-du-Gard*, magnificent Roman aqueduct, in 3 tiers, nearly 900 ft. long, constructed 19 B.C., to carry water from *Uzès* to *Nîmes*. Through wine-growing country to **Nîmes,** 12 miles, many important Roman buildings, *Maison Carrée*, well-preserved temple, finest piece of Roman architecture in France; arenas; Roman amphitheatre, still used for bull-fighting; *Temple of Diana* (ruins); *Tour Magne*, near *Jardin-de-la-Fontaine*, gives wide views. (Y.H. 2 miles N.W.).

Arles, immense Roman amphitheatre (seated over 20,000), Roman theatre (*Théâtre Antique*)—musical and dramatic performances each year in early July—*Palais Constantin* (largest Roman baths in Provence); 11th-15th century church and cloister of *St. Trophime* (porch and cloister are masterpieces). (Y.H.).

R.10 (i) The *Camargue.* South of *Arles* stretches the vast wild plain of the Camargue, partly cultivated, partly marsh. Nature reserve of the *Etang de Vaccarès*, with ibis, flamingoes and other birds. Cattle-breeding, wine and rice-growing. Herds of bulls and small white horses. Beware mosquitoes by night. *Aigues-Mortes*, city of the Middle Ages, entirely enclosed by walls and towers. At one time on the coast, it is now high and dry on account of the silt brought down by the *Rhône*. Tower of Constance is open to visitors. *Les-Saintes-Maries-de-la-Mer*, according to tradition the place where Mary Magdalene and her companions landed when fleeing from persecution. Pilgrimage by the gipsies on May 24 and 25 and by local inhabitants on October 21 or first succeeding weekend in honour of their patron, Sarah, maid-servant to the refugees. Processions, local costumes, bull-fights. Picturesque village with fortified church.

Tarascon (15th century castle) was immortalised by Alphonse Daudet in "*Tartarin de Tarascon*". (Y.H.). Strike eastward to *St. Rémy* and 1 mile S. (on D.5) to site of Greek and Roman city of *Glanum*; Roman mausoleum and

FRANCE

triumphal arch still standing. Across the limestone hills of the *Alpilles* to *Les Baux*, curious ruined city built on a rock, with good views over the surrounding country; has given its name to bauxite (aluminium ore). Provençal custom of the shepherds bringing their lambs to Midnight Mass on Christmas Eve survives here.

Continue eastward, up the *Touloubre* valley (gorges) across the plateau and down to *Aix-en-Provence,* claimed to be the most beautiful town in France. Music festival in July; 15th-16th century cathedral and cloister; many fine 17th and 18th century houses; many fountains. **(Y.H.)**.

Marseilles (Y.H.), second city and chief port of France. Basilica of *Notre-Dame-de-la-Garde* (19th century) superb viewpoint. *La Canebière* is the main street, centre of life and activity. The Old Port, a picturesque but vicious area to N. of the old harbour, was blown up by the Germans in 1943. The *Cité Radieuse,* an ultra-modern block of flats on the S.E. outskirts of the city designed by Le Corbusier can be reached by tram No. 22 from the Prefecture. Built 1952, 17 storeys, 1,600 residents.

EXCURSION: boat from *Quai des Belges* (at head of Old Port) to *Château d'If,* a fortress and former prison made famous by Dumas's *"Count of Monte Cristo"* (about 2 hours' round voyage).

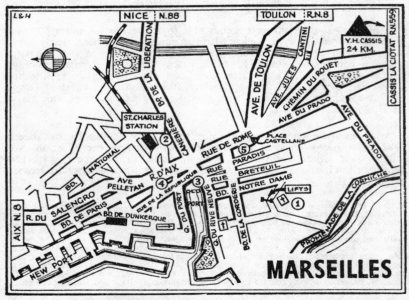

1. *Notre Dame-de-la-Garde* (*church*). 2. *Coaches for Cassis* (*Y.H.*) *start here —* *N. side of Canebière.* 3. *Quai des Belges—boats for Château d'If.* 4. *Post Office.* (*Rue Colbert*). 5. *Préfecture.*

156

The Côte d'Azur

Between *Marseilles* and *Menton*, on the Italian frontier, lies the *Côte d'Azur*, the legendary Mediterranean coast which is frequently, but incorrectly, called the *French Riviera*; the *Riviera* proper is the easternmost of the five natural regions into which the coast is geographically divided.

The *Côte d'Azur* owes its fame largely to its climate, which is unique in Europe; the temperature of the sea, which remains constant at about 55°F., summer and winter alike, has a strong influence on the climate, giving an extraordinarily mild winter and a relatively fresh summer. This temperature refers to the open sea, not to the shallower coastal waters which are much warmer in the summer. The tide rises only a few inches, and the sea, under the almost incessant sunshine is brilliantly blue. In consequence of its international popularity the *Côte d'Azur* suffers from an excess of tourists and motor cars.

Daily coach service along coast road from *Marseilles* (St. Charles Station) to *Toulon* (2¼ hours), *Cannes* (9 hours), and *Nice* (10 hours).

The most famous local speciality is *bouillabaisse*, a kind of fish stew. Others are fish soup, shellfish, and dishes prepared from tomatoes and aubergines, many of them flavoured with garlic.

R.11. Marseilles—Menton (190 miles)

Côte des Calanques, The *calanques* are miniature fjords between steep limestone cliffs; small sheltered harbours. From *Marseilles* over *Col de Carpiagne* (1,070 ft. fine view) to *Cassis* (**Y.H.**), picturesque *calanques* to S.W. Good coast walk from here to *La Ciotat* (6 miles). Road continues via *Bandol* and *Sanary*, quiet and attractive little resorts with fishing ports (**Y.H.** at *Six-Fours*) to *Toulon*—large naval port; charming old town.

Côtes des Maures, wide bays between granite headlands; a few miles inland the wild, wooded hills of the *Maures* rising to 2,000 ft. (pine, cork-oak and chestnut forests). The railway leaves the coast at *Toulon* and bypasses the *Maures* region, making this part of the coast less crowded than other parts. Taking the coast road from *Toulon*, proceed to *Hyères*, picturesque old Provençal town. About 5 miles to *Giens* for boat to island of *Porquerolles*, ideal for camping, or from *Salins d'Hyères* for boat to island of *Port Cros*. From *Le Lavandou* the road follows the coast for 15 miles of splendid views, then turns inland through plantations of cork trees to *La Foux*; 3 miles along coast to fashionable *St. Tropez*, 5 miles inland to *Grimaud*, good example of *village perché*, old Provençal village built high on hillside for safety; 8 miles N. is **Y.H.** at *La Garde-Freinet*. Quiet sandy coast, with pine plantations, ideal for camping (where not forbidden) to *Fréjus*, town founded by Julius Caesar, Roman ruins, amphitheatre and theatre; 5th century baptistry, 13th century cloister and cathedral. At *Fréjus* the railway rejoins the coast road. (**Y.H.**).

157

FRANCE

The Esterel. Splendid coast road, often cut out of the rock; small bays between red cliffs (porphyry) with red rocks and islets. The hills are not high but are wild, with many ravines and gorges; very few villages and inns in the interior; heather and other flowering shrubs grow beneath the pines and cork-oaks. **Y.H.** on coast at *Le Trayas*. **Cannes**, accidentally come across in 1834 by Lord Brougham, a British Lord Chancellor, on his way to Nice. Aristocratic winter resort, now all-year round haunt of film stars and millionaires. Annual film festival in April. *Boulevard de la Croisette*, fashionable promenade where battles of flowers take place.

EXCURSION: to the beautiful pine-covered *Lérins* (islands) by boat from the harbour near the Municipal Casino. On *Ile Ste. Marguerite* is fort which housed the "Man in the Iron Mask" from 1687-98.

Côte d'Antibes. A flatter coastline, with large bays. From *Cannes* to *Antibes* the coast is almost completely urbanised and unattractive. *Antibes* is the centre of the flower-growing industry. *Cagnes*, old town, picturesque walls, gates, castle.

Nice, popular, relatively inexpensive resort with Italian atmosphere (it was ceded to France, by the House of Savoy, in 1860). *Promenade des Anglais*, pretty old town and flower market. Port and departure point for *Corsica*; see **R.18**. Carnival (early February) for 12 days—processions, fireworks, battle of flowers and confetti. **(Y.H.)**

EXCURSIONS: Numerous excursions into Maritime Alps, such as to *Gorges du Loup* (picturesque winding road, 30 miles, via *Gattières* and *Vence*) 6 mile long gorge with many waterfalls.

Riviera. Here the *Maritime Alps* rise from the Mediterranean, reaching 3,000-4,000 ft. a few miles inland, and the three *Corniche* roads, with splendid views, lead to *Menton*.

The *Corniche Inférieure* follows the coast to *Villefranche*, for *Cap Ferrat* and the Principality of *Monaco*—no customs barrier, but own postage stamps. *Monaco*, Prince's Palace in Italian Renaissance style. Aquarium is one of best in Europe. **Monte Carlo**, Casino and Opera House, good view from terrace. Art Gallery.

The *Moyenne Corniche* is a road some 1,200 ft. above the sea. *Eze*, one of the "perched villages", built on a rocky height for protection, now almost uninhabited, has picturesque steps and narrow streets, with fine views of coast. The *Grande Corniche* was constructed by Napoleon on an old Roman road, rising to nearly 1,700 ft. At *La Turbie* is *Trophée d'Auguste*, ruined but impressive Roman monument. Best view of coast from the *Rondo Roquebrune*, 10th century fortified village and castle.

Menton, small **Y.H.**, good climate all the year round. Harbour, interesting old quarter built on the hillside. Lemon-gathering *fêtes*, second half of February. Carnivals begin in August and continue into September.

The Central Massif

The *Central Massif,* occupying one sixth of the country, has great diversity of scenery reflecting its complex geological structure. Uplifted crystalline rocks form the *Limousin* plateau on the west and north-west and again predominate in the forest and meadow covered *Monts du Forez* between *Vichy* and *Le Puy;* later sediments occur as coal measures and as the bare limestone plateaux of the *Causses* in the south. The heart of the region is characterized by past volcanic activity, seen in the lava plateau of *Aubrac* and the spectacular volcanic cones (*puys*) of *Auvergne.* In the south-east, the *Massif* ends abruptly in the torrent riven granite and slate scarps of the *Cévennes,* a region of chestnut woods and oak scrub, whose isolated villages were strongholds of the Huguenots and where Protestantism remains stronger than elsewhere in France.

Architecturally the main interest is in the Romanesque churches of *Auvergne,* often built as the place of rest of a treasured statue of the Virgin and the object of pilgrimages from afar. Particularly renowned for their beauty are the exteriors of the eastern ends of these churches; the *chevets* (radiating chapels) were a local feature which later influenced the rise of Gothic in the *Ile de France.*

R.12. Circuit of Auvergne from Clermont (260 miles)

Clermont-Ferrand. (Y.H.). Main communications centre for S. Central France, lying at the foot of the *Puy de Dôme* and on the edge of a rich plain. Cathedral, 13th century Gothic, some good glass. More interesting is the fine church of *Notre Dame du Port* (11th and 12th century Romanesque), fine east end, capitals of pillars of ambulatory carved with figures. Old part of town interesting—see courtyard of No. 3 *Rue des Chausettiers,* 13th century. Petrifying springs at *La Fontaine du Pont Naturel* and *Les Grottes du Peron.* Several museums. Excursion to *Royat,* spa, fortified church of *St. Leger.*

Leave *Clermont* by N.141A to **Puy de Dôme** (4,800 ft.), or by footpath from *Col de Ceyssat.* Fine panorama of the *Dôme* group, nearly 60 extinct volcanoes between 3,000 and 4,000 ft. high, some with rounded summits, others containing craters. Summits easily accessible; two of the most interesting are the *Puy de Pariou* (crater 300 ft. deep) and the *Puy de la Vache,* near *Randanne,* where lava stream nearly 4 miles long has blocked valley to form lake of *Aydat.*

Continue by secondary road via *St. Bonnet* to *Orcival,* fine Romanesque church; behind the high altar, 12th century, statue of Virgin. Return to main road near *Col de Guéry* (4,147 ft.) fine views of *Roche Tuilière* and *Roche Tanadoire;* lake of *Guéry.* The road enters the *Mont Dore* mountain group. *Banne d'Ordanche* (4,900 ft.) good view; gliding club aerodrome nearby.

Mont Dore, resort and spa; winter sports. **(Y.H.)** *Puy de Sancy* (6,188 ft.) highest point of Central France. Ascent by cable railway then 20 mins. walk. Superb view as far as *Dauphiné* Alps on a clear day. 5 miles to *La Bourboule,* pleasant resort; excursion to gorges of the *Avèze.*

FRANCE

By N.496 over *Col de la Croix Morland* to *Chambon* (Y.H.)—attractive lake, boating, swimming, *Murol*, picturesque (2,500 ft.), medieval castle.

At *Grandeyrolles* take N.678 to south. Near *Le Cheix* are the *Grottes de Jonas*—caves inhabited in prehistoric times (entrance fee). From *Le Cheix* a detour may be made via *Saurier* and the fine gorges of the *Courgoul*. *Besse-en-Chandesse*, old fortified town, picturesque houses built of lava. Lake *Pavin*—beautiful lake containing large trout. Easy walk to summit of *Puy de Montchal* (4,600 ft.). To the west the plateau of *Artense*, several lakes and marshes, to the east the pasturelands of the *Cézallier* mountains. *Condat*, barrage-lake of *Essarts*; fine wooded gorges of the *Rhue*.

Take N.679 to *Bort-les-Orgues*, on river *Dordogne*, pleasant little town named after the basalt "organ pipes" which rise above it; good view from summit. Large hydro-electric scheme has transformed the upper valley of the *Dordogne* into a series of lakes. Dams at *Barrage de Marèges*, and *La Triozoune*. For lower *Dordogne* see **R.14**.

Mauriac, agreeable town in pleasant situation; basilica of *Notre Dame des Miracles* is possibly the finest Romanesque church in the *Auvergne*. Continue either via the beautiful valley of *Falgoux* and the gorge of *St. Vincent* via N.122 and N.680 through *Salers*, picturesque fortified town with fine old mansions; *Grande Place* should be seen; church 16th century. *Col de Néronne* to the *Cirque de Falgoux* below the *Puy Mary* (5,860 ft. fine view of the *Cantal Mountains*).

Continue by the *Pas de Peyrol* (5,210 ft.) and the valley of *Mandailles* to *Aurillac*, new town built around picturesque old quarter; 14th and 15th century churches, old mansions; view of old quarter from *Pont Rouge*. Follow N.126 along fine wide valley of the *Cère* (altitude 2,000 ft.), *Vic-sur-Cère*—small spa; House of the Princes of Monaco (15th century); Romanesque church. The road climbs up by the *Pas de la Cère*, a rocky ravine, and the waterfall of *La Roucole*, to *St.-Jacques-des-Blats* on the heights of the *Cantal*. Several peaks can be climbed from the head of the valley, such as *Puy Griou* (5,600 ft.), *Puy de la Poche* (4,900 ft.) and the *Plomb du Cantal* (6,090 ft.) highest peak of the *Cantal* group. Through the tunnel of *Lioran* into the narrow valley of the *Alagnon*.

Murat, town dominated by statue of the Virgin on a rocky height. Continue on N.126 to *St. Flour* (3,000 ft.) picturesque, fortified; cathedral, severe 15th century Gothic, 17th century Town Hall.

R.12 (i) From *St. Flour*, long but worthwhile detour to town of *Le Puy* (Y.H.) N.590 over the forest plateau of *Margeride*, crossing the *Allier* at *Langeac*. Le-Puy-en-Velay—fantastic sight from the distance; town built round three volcanic cones. Fine Romanesque cathedral on steep rock shows Moslem influence; notice vaults of the nave, west front, cloisters; interesting relics, Bible of time of Charlemagne; many other churches.

Return from *Le Puy* to *Clermont* (80 miles) via *Brioude*, joining N.9 at *Lempdes*, (excursion to gorges of the *Alagnon*).

The direct route from *St. Flour* to *Clermont* follows N.9 over *Col de la Fagéole* (3,373 ft.) on to the plateau of the *Margeride*; valley of the *Allier*, particularly attractive between *Issoire* (which has famous Auvergne-Romanesque church) and *Coudes*. Pass beautiful hilly plateau of *Gergovie*, scene of victory of Vercingetorix over Julius Caesar (monument), and enter *Clermont*.

FRANCE

R.13. The Tarn Gorges and the Cévennes—Circuit from Florac (185 miles)

To the west is the region of the *Causses*, originally covered with forests, but now stony plateaux with just enough vegetation for sheep grazing, cut by fantastic gorges and narrow river valleys. To the east is the wild, arid *Cévennes*.

The best starting point is *Florac*, a pleasant little town on local railway from *Ste-Cécile-d'Andorge* on the *Clermont-Ferrand—Nîmes* line. The original footpath through the Gorges has been made into a tarred road and, whilst this is convenient for the cyclist, the walker has also to keep to it.

From *Florac* follow road N.107b northwards to *Ispagnac*, small town at entrance to canyon (12th century Romanesque church), *Quézac* (17th century bridge and earlier church). *Castelbouc*, curious village worth the small detour involved, *Ste-Enimie*, picturesque village below cliffs of gorge. *St. Chély* and *Cirque de St. Chély*—pretty village and natural amphitheatre of cliffs, *Château de la Caze*, 15th century castle in fine setting at river's edge, *La Malêne*, village from which it is suggested that a boat should be taken through the narrowest part of the gorge to the *Cirque des Baumes*. On this stretch the cliffs rise to some 1,200 ft. *Les Vignes*—make the excursion to *Point Sublime*, magnificent view of the gorges from above.

Gorges continue to *Le Rozier* and *Peyreleau*, picturesque village. Excursion to *Montpellier-le-Vieux*—a curious desert of natural rock formation which resembles a ruined city. A circular trip can be made down the *Tarn* to *Millau* famous for its glove-making industry, in a fertile valley among almond and peach trees, returning to *Peyreleau* by the valley of the *Dourbie*, including excursion to *Montpellier-le-Vieux*.

From *Le Rozier* follow N.596 through the gorges of the *Jonte*. Less grandiose than those of the *Tarn* they are however equally impressive because of their narrowness. It is preferable to follow the river upstream but the most convenient approach is from *Le Rozier*, after descending the gorges of the *Tarn*. *Belvédère des Terrasses*, fine view over the gorge, *Meyrueis*, pleasant town at entrance to the gorges, situated at 2,200 ft.

EXCURSIONS: (a) *Aven Armand*—large underground grotto (120 x 300 ft.) filled with stalactites and stalagmites of remarkable forms.
(b) Grotto of *Dargilan*—the most remarkable of the caverns in the district; several impressive chambers, (one 150 yards long) containing a variety of stalactite formations.
(c) *La Couvertoirade*, fortified centre of Templiers of 15th century, 20 miles south of *Le Rozier*, via *Montpellier-le-Vieux* and *Gorges de la Dourbie*.

From *Meyrueis* via *Col de Montjardin* and *Bramabiou* where underground stream reappears as waterfall, *Col de la Séreyède* for excursion to *Mont Aigoual* (5,139 ft.) highest point of *Cévennes*—fine view, down picturesque valley of river *Hérault* to *Valleraugue* and *Ganges*. From *Ganges* work north-eastwards to *St. Jean du Gard*, (small **Y.H.**) typical old town of the *Cévennes*, and by the *Corniche* of the *Cévennes*, road on ridge (D.9), good views, to *Florac*.

R.13 (i) Alternatively, continue south to *St. Bauzille de Putois* and make excursion to *Grottes des Demoiselles*, several large caverns with stalactite formations. *Causse de la Selle*, Gorges of the *Hérault*. *St. Guilhem le Desert*, 11th century abbey church, *Pont au Diable*, thence to *Montpellier* and the Mediterranean. (*Ganges—Montpellier* 45 miles).

161

FRANCE

Périgord, Quercy and Toulouse

The middle reaches of the rivers of the *Garonne* system, rising either in the *Central Massif* or the *Pyrenees*, provide some of the most beautiful valley scenery in France. The *Dordogne* and *Lot* and their tributaries have cut deeply into the high limestone country and there is a striking contrast between their fertile banks and the arid *causses* above. The region was much fought over during the Hundred Years' War with England and the *bastides*, towns constructed as fortresses, are reminders of the time when *Aquitaine* was under the English crown.

R.14. Mauriac, Lascaux, Toulouse (290 miles)

The route is planned to link with R.12 but can be joined direct from *Brive* (Y.H.) 5 hrs. by train from *Paris* on main *Toulouse* line. *Brive* can be used as base for walks in the *Corrèze* valley before following the *Vézère* via *Terrasson* to *Lascaux*.

From *Mauriac* (R.12) N.678 to *Spontour*, 11 miles. (Y.H.) 25 miles *Argentat*, picturesque town on *Dordogne*; road follows river to *Beaulieu*, 10 miles. (Y.H.), Romanesque church of Benedictine abbey, fine 11th century porch; Penitents' church, 12th century. N.140 to *Castelnau*.

EXCURSION: *Gouffre de Padirac*, deep underground river and lakes; *Rocamadour*, centre of medieval pilgrimages, village built on cliff below sanctuary.

Souillac, 25 miles, fine Romanesque church. At *Montfort*, 16 miles, cross river to *Domme*, *bastide* town on cliff, 13th century, commanding view over *Dordogne*. Re-cross river and 5 miles N. to *Sarlat* (Y.H.), small town of winding streets, medieval and renaissance buildings. 16 miles to *Montignac* on the *Vézère*, pleasant town. Above are the caves of Lascaux, world famous for wall engravings and paintings by Upper Palaeolithic hunters of perhaps 20,000 years ago. Other classic sites down valley are the caves at *Le Moustier* and the rock shelter of *La Madeleine*. River follows beautiful course between cliffs. 15 miles Les Eyzies, *Museum of Pre-historic Art* in castle; engravings and paintings in cave of *La Mouthe* above village, and in those of *Font-de-Gaume* and *Les Combarelles* up side valley of the *Beaune*. Trémolat 10 miles where *Vézère* joins *Dordogne*, fine river scenery. S. to *Beaumont-du-Périgord* and *Montpazier*, 25 miles, both English *bastides*. To *Biron*, 4 miles, splendid château. *Villeneuve-sur-Lot* (Y.H.), 20 miles, *bastide* town, two gateways and bridge.

EXCURSION: Up valley of the *Lot*, N.111 and D.158 to *Bonaguil*, 37 mls., interesting late medieval castle, built when artillery was coming into use.

N.21 to *Agen* (Y.H.), 17 miles, centre of *Agenais*, rich agricultural and fruit growing district, Roman remains, cathedral, 11th-15th century, old bridges over *Garonne*. Up valley by N.113 to *Moissac*, Romanesque abbey-church with fine carvings on porch and in cloisters; south to *Castelsarrasin* (Y.H.) 32 miles. N.658 to *Montauban*, 13 miles (Y.H.) attractive town, birthplace of Ingres; collection of his paintings and drawings in former bishop's palace.

EXCURSION: By road N.20 or rail to Cahors, 25 mls. medieval town, capital of *Quercy* Romanesque cathedral, superb *Pont Valentré*, finest medieval fortified bridge in Europe.

Toulouse, 32 miles, (Y.H.) old capital of *Languedoc*, cultural, market and route centre of S.E. *Aquitaine*. Church of *St. Sernin*, supreme among Romanesque basilicas of France; octagonal belfry, rich treasury. University founded 1230. Fine mansions, 16th-18th century; bridge, 300 yards long. Among several museums: *Musée des Augustus* (Romanesque sculpture; paintings, Rubens to Vuillard); *Musée St. Raymond* (*Place St. Sernin*) (applied arts and antique sculpture); *Musée Paul Dupuy* (*13 rue de la Pleau*) (ceramics; history of *Languedoc*).

The Pyrenees

The *Pyrenees*, a 250 miles long mountain chain forming a natural barrier between France and Spain. The western and central districts have a fairly high rainfall; maize, wheat, and fruit are grown at lower levels, and the summer heat in the mountains is tempered by cool air from the Atlantic. In the East (*Roussillon*) the climate and vegetation become more and more Mediterranean—olives, vines, and figs are cultivated. In the central section the peaks often exceed 10,000 ft. and reach 11,168 ft. in the *Pic de Néthou*.

In the western *Pyrenees*, on both sides of the frontier, is the country of the *Basques*, a people racially and culturally distinct and whose language is related to no other European tongue (but French is also spoken). They number about 600,000, of whom a fifth live in France. The local sport is *pelota*, in which a ball is played against a wall with the hand or a special bat. It is a fast and strenuous game. Local songs, and dances such as the *fandango*, still form part of the life of the country.

R.15.   Bayonne to Perpignan by the Route des Pyrénées (540 miles)

This is a fine high-level route, including a number of passes over 5,000 ft. There is no public transport over these, except for a regular coach tour in summer in four stages, *Biarritz–Lourdes, Lourdes–Luchon, Luchon–Font Romeu, Font Romeu–Carcassonne*, which can be booked separately. Cyclists will find themselves having to tackle some of the most strenuous ascents of the Tour de France route.

Y.H. at *Anglet* near *Biarritz*. *Route des Pyrénées*, numbered N.618 most of way leaves main road to Spain (N.10) at *St. Jean de Luz*, pleasant old town and modern resort on Atlantic coast, less expensive than *Biarritz*. Beyond *Ascain* (where the writer Pierre Loti lived) is *St. Ignace*.

EXCURSION: on foot (3 hours) or by rack railway (July-September, 30 mins.) to summit of *La Rhune*, 2,950 ft., fine views.

Continue by D.4 and D.20 through the Basque villages of *Aïnhoa, Cambos Itxassou* to rejoin N.618 for *St. Jean-Pied-de-Port*; picturesque, two lines of ramparts, beautiful 16th and 17th century houses in *Rue de la Citadelle*. It stands at foot of pass of *Roncesvalles* (site of epic story of Roland), but the pass itself is 11 miles beyond Spanish frontier.

N.618 continues via *Col d'Osquich* (1,280 ft.) to *Asasp*, where it crosses N.134.

FRANCE

R.15 (i) *Asasp-Col de Somport* (30 miles), following the *Gave* (stream) *d'Aspe*, up pleasant narrow valley; beyond *Accous* scenery becomes wilder. Near *Eygun*, branch road to *Lescun* for ascent of *Pic d'Anie* (8,200 ft., 4 to 5 hours) and several other summits about 7,000 ft. *Col de Somport* (5,380 ft., Spanish frontier, is one of few passes through Pyrenees).

Continue by N.618 to *Louvie-Juzon*.

R.15 (ii) *Louvie* to *Pau* (15 miles). Pau, resort once frequented by English visitors in winter; castle (various periods) with fine tapestries; from the *Boul. des Pyrénées*, famous view to the mountains; direction indicator.

Laruns, small town where fine local costumes may be seen at festivals, especially on August 15th.

R.15 (iii) *Laruns* to *Col du Pourtalet* (18 miles) by wild, forested valley; near *Gabas* bears are still seen. *Gabas* is good mountaineering centre (*Pic du Midi d'Ossau*, 9,460 ft., not an easy climb); cable railway to *Pic de la Sagette* (6,740 ft.) whence miniature railway to beautiful *Lac d'Artouste*. Spanish frontier at *Col du Pourtalet*, 5,880 ft., fine view.

Route des Pyrénées continues via *Eaux-Bonnes* (fashionable spa) and *Gourette*, winter-sports resort, over *Col d'Aubisque* (5,594 ft.), descending to *Argelès-Gazost*.

R.15 (iv) *Argelès* to *Lourdes* (8 miles). Beyond *Agos*, cable railway to *Pic de Pibeste* (4,538 ft., 8 mins.). Lourdes, pop. 12,400 is of absorbing interest to Catholic visitors; very crowded in summer; miraculous spring in grotto where Saint Bernadette had vision of Virgin Mary.

R.15 (v) *Argelès* to Cauterets (11 miles), good summer and winter centre. Many climbs of varying difficulty: *Pic de Vignemale* is highest point of district (10,821 ft., two-day ascent, guide essential). Experienced walkers can reach *Gavarnie* (see R.15 (vi)) via *Hourquette d'Ossoue* in about 10 hours.

Follow N.21 up impressive gorges to *Luz*; notable fortified church of 12th and 14th centuries.

R.15 (vi) *Luz* to *Gavarnie* (12½ miles; bus, 1 hour). Cirque de Gavarnie is magnificent natural rocky amphitheatre with cliffs rising nearly a mile high (summit 9,000 ft. above sea-level). Popular excursion in summer. Tremendous waterfalls (at their best before high summer). Climb *Pimené* (9,197 ft., 4 hours) for best view.

Eastward from *Luz* is the highest and probably finest section of the route. At *Barèges* (bus from *Luz* in 35 mins.) is a mountain railway climbing to 6,500 ft. on slope of *Pic d'Ayré*. From *Barèges* ascent on foot to *Pic du Midi de Bigorre* in 4-5 hours; 9,400 ft. peak with superb view; can also be approached by toll road from *Col du Tourmalet* to within ¼ hour of summit. Cable railway is only for use of observatory, situated just below summit. West of peak (2 hours) is beautiful *Lac Bleu* (6,400 ft.) on route down to *Bagnères*.

Col du Tourmalet (6,933 ft., normally open July-September only) is the highest point on the route; splendid view. *Ste.-Marie-de-Campan*, junction with N.135 for *Bagnères*.

EXCURSION: to caves of *Médous*, 5 miles down road to *Bagnères*; very fine stalactite caverns, discovered 1948, traversed by boat on underground river. Open in summer.

Col d'Aspin (4,912 ft.) offers fine view.

EXCURSION: on foot from the *Col* via the *Hourquette d'Arreau* to *Arreau* village; about 3 hours.

Continue via *Port de Peyresourde* (5,424 ft.) and the delightfully-named village of *Oô* (rivalled only by *Bun*, 4 miles S.W. of *Argelès*) to *Bagnères de Luchon*, fashionable health resort (2,070 ft.) with *Superbagnères*, still more fashionable (5,906 ft.).

EXCURSIONS: *Luchon* is a good base for climbs, e.g., *Pic de Cécire*, 7,875 ft., 2 hours from *Superbagnères*. The *Aneto* (or *Pic de Néthou*), 11,168 ft., highest peak of the Pyrenees is over the Spanish frontier and demands a two-day ascent, with guides; it lies in the barren *Maladetta* ("accursed") mountain group. Road over *Col du Portillon* to *Bosost* in *Valle de Aran*.

Down the attractive *Luchon* valley (N.125) to *Cierp*.

R.15 (vii) From *Cierp* bridge to *St. Bertrand-de-Comminges* (10 miles), decayed old town with finest cathedral in Pyrenees (Romanesque-Gothic.)

Turn E. to *St. Béat* and then N. to rejoin N.618, crossing *Col du Portet d'Aspet* (3,509 ft.) to *St. Girons* (**Y.H.**) and *Col de Port* (4,198 ft.) to *Tarascon-sur-Ariège*. Thence by road N.20, via *Ax-les Thermes*, good excursion centre, *Signal de Chioula* (4,900 ft.) for view. *Route des Corniches* (between *Bompas* and *Ax*) about 1,000 ft. above valley of *Ariège*. Road and railway continue up wild and interesting valley (**Y.H.** at *Mérens-les-Vals*) to *l'Hospitalet*, road junction for *Andorra*.

R.15 (viii) To *Pas de la Casa* (frontier) and over highest pass in Pyrenees, the *Port d'Envalira* (7,900 ft.) into the small independent state of **Andorra**. The country consists of two main valleys and comprises several villages and the capital *Andorra la Viella*. Visit the Parliament House (*Casa de la Vall*) 16th century, and church. There is only one main road and the country is entirely mountainous. The *Pic de Casamanya* (9,100 ft.) gives a view of all the country. French and Spanish are equally understood, but the native tongue is a form of Catalan.

Continue on N.20 from *l'Hospitalet* via *Col de Puymorens* (6,200 ft.) into the *Cerdagne*, south of the main watershed. Divided in the 17th century between France and Spain, the French portion is widest valley in the Pyrenees. The Spanish village of *Llivia* remains isolated in French territory. *Bourg-Madame*, on Spanish frontier.

Through the granite wilderness of *Targassonne* to *Font-Romeu;* pilgrimages to miraculous spring, near to chapel of *Notre Dame*, on 3rd Sunday after Whitsun and on August 15 and September 8. *Mont-Louis*, fortified town; junction with N.118 to *Carcassonne* (**Y.H.**) (see **R.17 (i)**).

Follow N.116 down the valley of the *Têt*. *Thuès-entre-Valls*, at entrance to *Gorges de la Carança* and on to *Villefranche*.

R.15 (ix) *Villefranche* to *Vernet* and the *Canigou*. *Vernet-les-Bains*, pleasant spa and old village, at foot of *Canigou*, most conspicuous peak of Eastern Pyrenees. Delightful shady, winding track (*Escala de l'Ours*) through forest of *Balatg* to *Chalet-Hôtel des Cortalets* (12½ miles from *Vernet*—overnight); thence in 2 hours, by boulder-strewn slope (perfectly safe) to summit of *Canigou* (9,137 ft.); magnificent view over whole of Eastern Pyrenees; direction indicator.

Prades, town with church decorated in Moorish style, in a fertile area of orchards and vineyards, olives and cypresses, typical of *Roussillon*, the old name for the country between *Cerdagne* and the Mediterranean, which was Spanish until 1659. Population is Catalan, and a French-Catalan dialect is spoken.

At *Bouleternère* the *Route des Pyrénées* (N.618) climbs southwards to reach valley of *Tech* but trip may well be shortened by 30 miles by continuing down N.116 to **Perpignan**, delightful town with Spanish atmosphere; 14th century brick fortress called the *Castillet*; *Loge de Mer*, former Exchange, 14th and 16th century; cathedral of *St. Jean*, Gothic, begun in 14th century; Palace of the Kings of Majorca, Gothic style. (**Y.H.**)

FRANCE

Coast of Languedoc

This falls into two contrasted regions, the 20 miles stretch of the *Côte Vermeille* where the *Pyrenees* fall abruptly to form a rocky coastline of alternating cliffs and bays; and the long dune belt, with lagoons behind it, lying northwards for about 90 miles, from *Collioure* to the *Rhône* delta.

R.16. Perpignan to Cerbère (32 miles)

The *Côte Vermeille*, unlike the *Côte d'Azur*, is unspoilt and unsophisticated. *Collioure*, picturesque little harbour, favourite subject of Matisse, Dufy and other artists. *Banyuls*, the most southerly seaside resort in France; produces wine similar to sherry. *Cerbère*, fishing port on the Spanish frontier.

R.17. Perpignan to Avignon (160 miles)

A little known part of the Mediterranean coast. Flat, sandy beaches, good bathing. N.9 *Perpignan* to **Narbonne**, pleasant town, cathedral of St. Just, Gothic, only choir completed. Town was important Roman settlement. In the distance inland are the *Cévennes* mountains.

R.17 (i) *Narbonne* to *Carcassonne*, 56 miles. Carcassonne is the showplace of the Middle Ages. The old town or *cité* is completely walled, built on a hill-top and crowned with many conical roofs. The lower town is more modern and has little of interest. (Y.H.)

Béziers, old part of town interesting; cathedral of *St. Nazaire* (12th-14th century) local Gothic. *Sète* (**Y.H.**) second largest Mediterranean port of France, small shadeless beach; passages on cargo vessels to *Oran* and *Mostaganem* in North Africa at low rate. **Montpellier**, capital of *Hérault*; one of most interesting towns of *Languedoc*; university founded 1289; cathedral; *Musée Fabre*, excellent art collection. (For route to *Gorges du Tarn* see **R.13** (i)). Continue via *Nîmes* to *Avignon*, on main route *Paris—Riviera* (see **R.10**).

R.18. The Island of Corsica

For a combination of rich Mediterranean vegetation, sunshine, blue sea, wild mountains and freedom from congestion, Corsica is ideal. Those in search of important works of architecture, museums, and art galleries should look elsewhere. The best time for a visit is May and June; earlier the mountain passes are likely to be snowbound, whilst the summer heat may be found excessive, at least on the east coast.

The language resembles Italian (Corsica having been Italian until the 18th century) but most people are bilingual, speaking French also. The only towns of any size on the island are *Bastia* and *Ajaccio*, the usual arrival ports from *Nice* or *Marseilles*. Night crossing about 11 hours from *Nice*, 15 hours from *Marseilles*. Minimum fare, from *Marseilles* about 60 francs, from *Nice* about 50 francs. Daily sailings in summer.

Cyclists should note that although the road surfaces are generally good the likelihood of obtaining spare parts is remote. Gears and brakes should be suitable for the twisting hills of all the most interesting routes. However, a bicycle is a good way of seeing the island. There are no youth hostels, but much of the island is ideal for camping; although it should be noted that fires may not be lit in forests.

The topography of Corsica does not lend itself to a description in terms of a continuous road circuit, and in preparing one's own itinerary due consideration must be given to the slow rate of progress on tortuous roads. Bus routes radiate from *Ajaccio* and *Bastia*, but elsewhere services are infrequent and erratic.

Except for a dull stretch southward from Bastia, the **coast** is entirely rocky and much indented, the only beaches being at the heads of some of the bays. Roads cannot generally hug the shore, but offer splendid plunging or distant views of the sea. Foremost of the island's coastal scenery: *Cap Corse*, the northern promontory, which makes a beautiful circuit of 77 miles from *Bastia*; the *Calanche* near *Piana*, a wilderness of red granite; the savage *Iles Sanguinaires*, visited by boat from *Ajaccio* (birthplace of Napoleon) and the sea-caves in the white limestone cliffs of the extreme south, visited by boat from *Bonifacio*.

A tour of the **interior** will leave an impression of continuously exciting views from mountain passes and in narrow valleys, with no one site obviously more memorable than the rest. *Corte*, once the island's capital, is a convenient base for the long *Gorges de la Restonica*, the *Gorges du Tavignano* (on foot only), the *Scala* (defile) *di Santa Regina* and the *Forest of Vizzavona*. The *Col de Bavella* farther south should also not be missed.

The high **mountains** are best climbed in two days, taking sleeping-bags and provisions, and spending the night close to the summit in the huts of shepherds who are traditionally willing to oblige in this way. The vast views, best appreciated at sunrise, from *Monte Cinto* (8,891 ft.), *Monte Rotondo* (8,612 ft.) and *Incudine* (7,008 ft.) will amply compensate for the rigours of the ascent.

Southern Germany boasts some of Europe's most beautiful mountains and forests.

GERMANY
Geographical Outline

Germany is a big, compact country, some four times as large as England and set squarely in Central Europe. Since 1945 it has been artificially divided into two parts, under Russian and Western influence respectively, with completely different political and social systems. The eastern part, which calls itself the *German Democratic Republic* (D.D.R.) lies behind the "Iron Curtain" and intending visitors should write directly to the *Komitee für Touristik und Wandern der DDR, Unter den Linden 36/38, Berlin,* who are the authority for youth hostelling in the *D.D.R.* For touring purposes this chapter describes the western part, known as the *German Federal Republic,* and the city of Berlin.

Land Owing to its central position in Europe, Germany is made up physically of parts of three major belts of country running across the continent from west to east: the Northern Lowland, the Central Uplands and the Alps. None of them lies entirely within Germany. The Lowland, for example, which is called the *North German Plain,* is continued westwards in the *Plain of Flanders,* and eastwards through Poland into Russia. This lack of a natural frontier on its eastern and western sides goes far to explain the historic tendency of Germany to fluctuate in size.

The Plain is farming country but with many marshes and heaths, including the famous *Lüneburg Heath* between the rivers *Weser* and *Elbe,* a huge area of rolling moorland, intensely interesting to the hosteller. In the extreme south-west of the plain lies the *Ruhr* district where the close mingling of vast industry and farming is typical of the area.

South of the Plain lie the Central Uplands, a richly varied region of hills and low mountains, forests and farmland, intersected by numerous rivers. Each range of hills has its own name, from the *Eifel, Taunus* and *Black Forest* in the west to the *Harz* and *Rhön* in the east, and each has its own attraction for the hosteller. They contain every type of rock, from limestone to granite, and the geological picture often changes every few yards, the soil varying from iron red to violet, black, yellow and ruddy brown. Here is the geologist's happy hunting ground. The soil is much less fertile than in the Northern Plain, but there is considerable mineral wealth and a wide variety of industry. It is also the region which best conforms to the picture of the German countryside of story and legend.

Only a narrow strip of the third belt, the *Alps,* lies within Germany. But between them and the Central Uplands is the interesting region known as the Alpine Foreland. It is a high plain, sloping gently from the *Alps* to the *Danube* and bounded on the west by *Lake Constance,* the largest lake in Germany.

Flowing into and out of *Lake Constance,* and linking all these regions, is the river *Rhine,* the principal waterway of Western and Central Europe. From the lake to *Basel* it forms the German-Swiss border, and from *Basel* to beyond

GERMANY

Strasbourg the German-French border. In this section it flows through a broad sheltered valley, rich in crops including wine and tobacco, but lacking the spectacular appeal of the gorge which the river enters after flowing westwards from *Mainz* to *Bingen*. The *Rhine* Gorge is probably the most celebrated stretch of river scenery in the world. The mountain-slopes, terraced for vines, fall steeply to the river, scarcely leaving room for a road and a railway on either side. Charming medieval towns and ancient villages line its banks and grim castles crown the towering crags. From *Bonn* the valley broadens again, and, churned by many tugs and no longer beautiful, the river flows, past *Cologne* and the great inland port of *Duisburg*, through *Holland* to the sea.

Climate Germany's climate is temperate, but frequent changes of weather occur; cold in winter and hot in summer. The Northern *Rhine* Valley has a more moderate climate but, with local exceptions, the extremes of heat and cold increase as you travel east and south.

Spring is a good season to visit the fruit-growing areas of the *Rhine*, *Pfalz* (Palatinate) and *Neckar*, where the blossom provides a wonderful sight.

Summer is an excellent touring time, provided one tackles the walking or cycling before noon or in the evening; in the afternoon the heat can be oppressive, except in the mountain areas.

For those whose interests include wine and its manufacture a trek through the *Rhine* or *Mosel* valleys in September or October can be recommended, whilst winter of course, is the time for the winter-sports enthusiast, who will make for the *Harz* Mountains, the *Black Forest* or *Bavarian Alps*.

Plants and Animals More of the natural forest cover has survived than in other densely settled parts of Europe. Forests cover about a quarter of the country, but the oak and beech forest of the north-west has been largely replaced by heath. Conifers, especially Scots pine, are the chief trees further east. Beech predominates in the Central Uplands, except where conditions favour the spruce, as in the *Fichtelgebirge*. Spruce is also the characteristic tree of the *Bavarian Alps*.

Plants of the Alpine pastures, northern heathlands, and coastal dunes and salt marshes are, in general, similar to those found in such areas in neighbouring countries.

Many woodland areas abound with animal life, stag and roe, fox, badger and even wild boar, and the huntsman has been a traditional figure in German life.

The People

Population The population of the *German Federal Republic* is about 58 million. A further 2,200,000 people live in *West Berlin*. (The *German Democratic Republic* has about 19 million, including the people of *East Berlin*.)

The largest cities of Western Germany are *Hamburg* (1,850,000), and *Munich* (1,250,000). Eight others exceed the half million: *Cologne, Essen, Düs-*

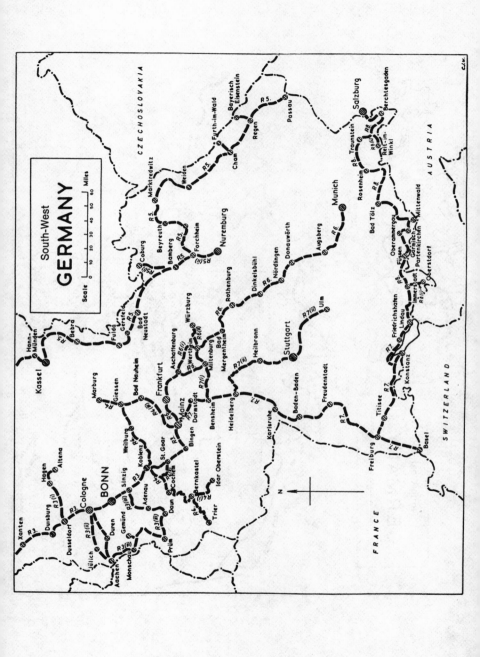

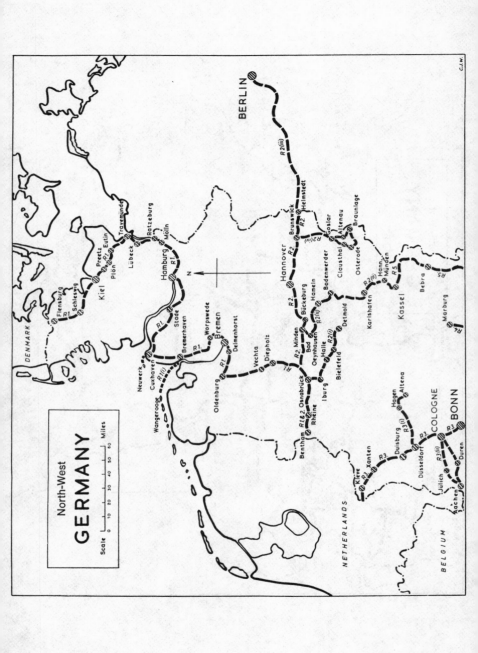

North-West
GERMANY

Scale
0 10 20 30 40 50 60 Miles

N

BERLIN

DENMARK

Flensburg
Schleswig
R1

Kiel
Preetz
Plön
Eutin
R2

Lübeck
Travemünde
Ratzeburg
Mölln

Hamburg
R1

Neuwerk
Cuxhaven
R1(i)
Wangerooge

Stade
R1

Worpswede
Bremerhaven
R1

Bremen
R1

Delmenhorst

Oldenburg
R1

Vechta
Diepholz

Bentheim
R1&2
Rhine
Osnabrück
Iburg

Minden
R2
Bad
Oeynhausen
Halle
R2(ii)

Bielefeld
Detmold

Hannover
R2

Bückeburg
Hameln
Bodenwerder

Brunswick
R2
Helmstedt

Goslar
R2(iv)
Clausthal
Altenau
Osterode
Braunlage

R2(iii)

Karlshafen

Hann.
Münden
R2(ii)

Kassel
R3

Bebra

Marburg
R4

Hagen
Altena
R3(i)

Duisburg
Xanten
R3
Düsseldorf

Kleve

COLOGNE
BONN
R3

Jülich
R3(ii)
Düren
Aachen

NETHERLANDS

BELGIUM

C.J.W.

seldorf, Frankfurt, Dortmund, Stuttgart, Hanover and *Bremen.* Two belts of dense settlement, along the northern edge of the Central Uplands and along the *Rhine* valley, converge in the industrial area of the *Ruhr* which has a population of more than 5 million. Distribution of population in the rest of the country is very uneven and many parts are sparsely settled.

Racially, Nordic physical characteristics tend to predominate in the north-west; elsewhere the German people are predominantly of the dark, thick set, broad headed Alpine type.

Language German dialects vary at least as widely as in England. *Hochdeutsch,* the standard German as taught in schools, is spoken at its best in the *Hanover* area, but adequately throughout Northern Germany and Central Germany. Only among peasants of the north who speak mostly *Plattdeutsch,* a dialect with many resemblances to English, and in the south are you unlikely to meet people who do not at least understand *Hochdeutsch,* even if they cannot speak it. Southern speech is soft, and consonants are less strongly articulated, so that Bavarian, Austrian and Swiss dialects are almost different languages. Even North Germans find them difficult to understand.

English is taught in many town schools and most people, especially of the younger generation, will be only too eager to help travellers out of difficulties, but a knowledge of German increases the enjoyment of your visit.

Religion As the home of the Lutheran Reformation north Germany became and has remained strongly Protestant. Areas of Protestantism extend also through *Hesse* to *Württemburg* in the south-west. On the other hand, *Bavaria* and much of the *Rhineland* are Catholic.

History Germany's tendency to resist unification makes the history of this great Central European territory almost impossible to summarise. But certain facts are worth bearing in mind.

It was never fully romanized. The Roman Empire at its most powerful was only able to hold the south and west, i.e. the *Rhineland* and the areas south of the *Danube,* together with *Rhaetia*—a wedge of territory behind an artificial frontier (the *"limes"*) running from *Regensburg* on the *Danube* to *Koblenz* on the *Rhine.* The destruction of three Roman legions by the Germanic tribes under Arminius (A.D. 9) settled the issue in one of the world's decisive battles: the lands around the *Elbe* and the *Vistula* were never to become Roman. For the future of the Empire this was a fatal circumstance. From the *North German Plain* came first the tribal penetrations of the Alemanni and the Franks and later the onslaughts of the Goths and Vandals which broke up the civilization of the Empire in the West (476).

Among the new groupings of restless migrating tribes which had destroyed this pattern of European life were peoples who were to create other patterns of civilization. Some, such as the Bavarians, Swabians and Thuringians, were to develop some of the distinctive regions of modern Germany. Others, such as the Saxons and Franks, were to play a large part in the building of the English and French nations.

The Franks, in fact, pacified and Christianized the other German tribes. In this work the greatest missionary was the Englishman, St. Boniface, the

GERMANY

"Apostle of Germany", who died in 754. For a time, under Charlemagne, the Frankish kingdom succeeded where Rome had failed. His great Christian empire, reaching from the *Pyrenees* to the *Elbe*, included a Germany now for the first time united. Its eastern frontier separated Christians from heathens, and Germans from Slavs.

It was in Germany also that, after the period of confusion following the partition of Charlemagne's dominions, the idea of the Empire was revived under Otto I (king 936-73, crowned emperor by the Pope in 962). This new Germanic version of the Holy Roman Empire survived, at least in name, until swept away by Napoleon in 1806, long after it had become an anachronism. But what should have been a partnership of Empire and Papacy became a struggle between them for supremacy, and German resources were wasted in Italian campaigns.

Internally, two systems of succession gave Germany the worst of both worlds. The Emperor was *elected* by seven princes, whose interest was generally to elect a weak man. On the other hand, the feudal princedoms were sub-divided by *inheritance* until Germany became a patchwork of hundreds of tiny states, picturesque but ramshackle and parasitic upon the peasantry. In these ways there came a decline from the early achievement of nationhood at a time when, elsewhere in western Europe and especially in France and England, the opposite tendency was at work creating powerful states.

While the princes fought each other the achievements of the people were local rather than national. The eastern frontier was advanced from the *Elbe* to beyond the *Oder* by penetration of German peasants into the Slav lands, partly by conquest under the Margraves (Marcher lords) and the Teutonic Knights, partly by invitation. It was their descendants, forming islands of German-speaking people within Slav territory, who made up the tragic streams of refugees from the east after the Second World War. The remarkable growth of towns was chiefly due to the enterprise of merchants, bankers and industrialists. In the north, the famous Hanseatic League, headed by *Lübeck*, operated as a trading empire independent of prince or emperor. In the south, towns such as *Augsburg* and *Ulm*, commanding routes across the *Alps* or bridges over the *Danube*, grew wealthy because of their central position on the trade routes between northern countries and those of the *Mediterranean* and the East.

The end of medieval times was marked by two movements. First, the strengthening of some of the princes such as the Hapsburgs and Hohenzollerns. Secondly, Luther's call (1517) for Papal reform, made widely known by the recent German invention of the printing press, produced the Reformation and the division of Western Christendom into Catholic and Protestant. After the *Peace of Augsburg* (1555) the German states, newly independent of both pope and emperor, enjoyed half a century of prosperity and a cultural activity which produced a northern renaissance.

The Thirty Years War (1618-48), in which Germany suffered both civil war and the invasion of foreign armies, was a struggle partly religious, partly against Hapsburg control. It ended with French power advanced to the *Rhine* and with other losses of German territory. The religious division of the country was confirmed: in broad terms, a Catholic south, a Protestant north and east, and a mixed pattern in the *Rhineland*.

GERMANY

The hundreds of sovereign states remained, making Germany a paradise for princes in the succeeding age of absolutism. Each was concerned primarily with his own magnificence, imitating as far as possible *Versailles* and the court of Louis XIV. The Baroque style mirrored these ambitions. To the prince the glory: to peasant and townsman the cost. On the other hand, it was in such courts that the genius of Bach was able to flourish; and, after about 1760, there was a brief "Age of Enlightenment" in some of the smaller states, producing such men as Beethoven, Goethe, Kant and Schiller—the greatest cultural period in German history.

Meanwhile, one state, *Brandenburg*, on the eastern frontier and far from the centre of gravity of the old Germany, was following a policy of war and expansion. This was to make its Hohenzollern rulers kings of *Prussia*; its capital, *Berlin*, the capital of Germany; and to produce a habit of unscrupulousness and ruthlessness among German leaders for which Germany and the world have paid bitterly. Prussia was faithless even to other German states. She failed them against Napoleon, whose policies reduced the number of states from over 400 to under 40, and whose armies brought the liberal revolutionary ideas which the country so greatly needed. But the delayed revolution (1848) was abortive. Later in the century Bismarck, whilst granting the franchise, ensured that the *Reichstag* then created should have no real power.

By 1871 the whole country had become a federation of states led by *Prussia* under the paternalistic rule of Bismarck, the "Iron Chancellor". As a result of his diplomacy Germany was at last united in a Hohenzollern Empire and was transformed, within a generation, into one of the greatest industrial powers.

The lack of real democracy and of training in political experience among the people inevitably produced tragic results when control of a nation so powerful passed to leaders less wise than Bismarck. It led, through the actions of Kaiser William II, to the First World War. It was an important factor (together with the ill-judged reparations policy of the victorious Allies) in the failure of the liberal Weimar Republic (1918-33), Germany's first experience of responsible representative government. Finally, it let in the regime (1933-45) of National Socialism (Nazism) under Hitler with its fantastic and abhorrent doctrines and its deliberate slaughter of millions of innocent victims. From this new dark age which descended on Europe the continent only escaped by the perilous way of a second World War.

Today Germany is again divided. The territory beyond the *Oder*, including *East Prussia* and *Pomerania*, has been incorporated into Poland. Between the *Oder* and the *Elbe* is the *German Democratic Republic* under Russian domination. The frontier of an independent Germany, the *German Federal Republic*, comprising the old west and south German lands, stands again on the *Elbe*.

Government The *German Federal Republic* sprang from the three western zones of Allied occupation. It acquired a constitution in 1949 and regained full sovereignty in 1955. The President is elected for 5 years and the Government is headed by the Chancellor. Parliament consists of two Houses, both elected for 4 years: the lower by

GERMANY

direct suffrage, the upper by delegates of the eleven Länder (regions) which comprise the Federation.

In East Germany the *German Democratic Republic* comprises the zone dominated by Russia. It has a Parliament of one House, the *Volkskammer*, elected by the Diets of the fourteen regions (now called *Bezirke* instead of *Länder*). Changes made in 1960 abolished the office of President, replacing it by a Council of State consisting of a chairman, 6 deputy chairmen and 16 other members. The Chairman, rather than the Prime Minister, is the effective head of the Government. His wide powers include the right to introduce personal decrees having the effect of law.

Resources   Mining and manufacture employ more than half of the working population. Coal and lignite ("brown coal") are by far the most important natural resources and form the basis of Germany's great manufacturing industry. Coal is mined chiefly in the *Ruhr*, with *Saarland* a poor second. Lignite, which occurs more widely, is a much inferior fuel but is economical as a source of electric power. There is great concentration of heavy industry in the Ruhr but other industrial activity is widespread. German precision engineering, as in the making of cameras, lenses and scientific instruments is world famous.

About a quarter of the working population are engaged in agriculture or forestry, and farming remains the largest single industry. Most of the farms are of under 25 acres and are worked by their owners. Rye and oats are the main cereal crops, wheat and barley being confined to the limited regions of good soils. Other major crops are potatoes and sugar beet. Dairying and stock rearing are based on permanent pasture only in the north-west and in the Alpine zone. Elsewhere, particularly on the northern plain, arable crops are grown for feeding to animals as in Denmark.

The valleys of the *Rhine* and the *Moselle* are famous for their vineyards which occur wherever the slope and situation are favourable.

There is a long tradition of good forest management and more than half the forests are publicly owned. Conifer plantations of spruce and pine have taken the place of much of the natural deciduous woodland and are the basis of important pulp, paper and synthetic fibre industries. Wood carving and toy making are old-established in *Bavaria* and the *Black Forest*. An interesting transition in the *Black Forest* has produced the modern clock and watch making industry, based on skills earlier acquired in making the famous wooden cuckoo clocks.

Food and Drink   Based on widespread agriculture, home-produced food is both plentiful and distinctive. It covers a wide gamut from the plain cheap meal, say, of the Youth Hostel (often noodle soup, bread and sausage) to the most sumptuous dishes of the more expensive price ranges.

The Germans excel in bread-making. Try rye bread, Westphalian *Pumpernickel*, *Schwarzbrot* (the fallacy that only poor people eat this black bread should be at once removed: it is delicious and certainly not cheap), *Vollkornbrot* (bread made of whole unground grains of wheat), to mention a few.

Sausage is inevitable with the bread and the variety is astounding. *Leberwurst* (liver sausage), *Rinderwurst* (beef sausage), *Bratwurst* (grilled type of pork sausage), *Blutwurst* (blood sausage) are common throughout Germany and there are many local varieties, all on display. Many appear unattractive but taste far better than they look. Bread and sliced sausage with a glass of beer can be had in any restaurant or *Würstlerei* at a moment's notice.

The variety and quality of cakes, pastry and real fruit tarts and ice-cream far exceed that generally found in the United States. Coffee is served strong with a little cream and is always well made; tea is weak.

Beer is brewed everywhere in Germany. It is usually much lighter than English beer and it is much cheaper. *Dortmund* and *Munich* beers have a reputation for high quality.

Wine, if bought in shops by the bottle, is comparatively cheap and tremendously varied. There are countless named wines and a correspondingly large number of flavours. The wines from the *Mainz-Bingen* area are said to be the best, especially the famous *Johannisberger*.

One of the most refreshing drinks is *Apfelsaft* (unfermented apple juice) which is obtainable at grocer's shops, restaurants and in most youth hostels.

The regional variety of food is not as great as one might imagine, for local dishes have been widely adopted in other areas.

Culture

Architecture Germany has not until recent times been an originator of architectural styles. But the Romanesque, Gothic and Baroque were taken up eagerly from abroad and adapted to express German ideas. Romanesque is seen in the cathedrals at *Aachen, Bamburg, Mainz, Osnabruck, Speyer* and *Worms* and in *Maria Laach* abbey. The finest examples of Gothic are the cathedrals of *Cologne, Marburg* and *Ulm*. The Baroque, imported from Italy and France during the Counter-Reformation, became even more exuberant than in its homelands and many wonderful examples occur in the churches of the south.

The Gothic spirit was not limited to church architecture but is expressed also in the houses, streets and market places of the medieval walled towns. Similarly, the Baroque imbues many of the palaces and princely towns of the period as at *Karlsruhe* and *Würzburg*.

Castles particularly abound along the *Rhine* and its tributaries; the majority are now in ruins but some have been adapted to make magnificent youth hostels as at *Freusburg* and *Altena*.

The modern movement in architecture owes a great deal to German architects, particularly in the design of factories, and in the use of glass and concrete as main materials. The pioneer was Peter Behrens (1868-1940). His pupil Walter Gropius founded the famous Bauhaus, the ideas and methods of which have had much influence on building and industrial design.

The rebuilding of bombed cities since the war has given great scope to architects, and imaginative new buildings can be found in most of the towns; many new youth hostels have also been constructed.

GERMANY

Painting

The greatest German artists worked during the brief period between the spread of Renaissance ideas north of the Alps and the onset of the Reformation. Dürer (1471-1528), the master of drawing, engraving and the woodcut, was eagerly receptive to the New Learning whilst remaining Gothic and German in spirit. His great contemporary, Grünewald, of whom almost nothing is known, preferred to work entirely in the medieval tradition but brought its expression to the highest pitch of intensity. Cranach (1472-1553) is famous for a portrait of Luther but his most significant work, done as a young man, leads the way to a romantic interest in scenery which was developed further by Altdorfer (1480-1538).

The Reformation brought artistic activity to a low ebb in almost every Protestant country. Holbein (1497-1543) was already a master artist when it forced him to leave the continent to seek a living in England, with the result that English portraiture was enriched by the work of one of the greatest of German artists.

In the field of modern art the movement called "Expressionism" was centred in Germany with Barlach (1870-1938) as its best known German exponent.

Music

Music is indisputably the art in which Germany has had the greatest cultural influence on the western world. Bach, Beethoven, Brahms, Wagner, Richard Strauss, to name a few, are all of great importance in the development of music. Almost every German city has its own symphony orchestra and concert hall, whilst many have municipally aided opera houses. But more important than these performances is the care devoted to musical training in German homes and schools. An ability to play a musical instrument—be it the piano, violin, recorder or guitar—is nothing like so rare as in the U. S., whilst singing (in two part or more elaborate harmony) is widespread.

German folk-songs are unique in their variety and tunefulness. In addition to the genuine anonymous folk-songs collected by Herder and others there are hundreds of well-known songs in folk-song style by authors and composers ranging from Goethe and Schubert to the twentieth-century poet Löns. Older Germans lament the passing of the *Wandervogel*, the rambler who travelled with his guitar or lute, but singing still plays a large part in the life of German youth hostels.

Literature

In literature, the name of Goethe overtops those of all other writers; his many-sided genius has enriched Germany and the world, particularly in the fields of drama and poetry; every German knows Goethe's "Faust" and is usually prepared to quote from it. Other famous names are Schiller (18th century dramatist), Heine and Mörike (19th century poets), Gerhart Hauptmann (late 19th century dramatist) and Thomas Mann (20th century novelist).

Since the time of Leibniz in the 17th century Germany has produced many thinkers of world renown, notably the philosophers of the idealist school—Kant, Fichte, Schelling and Hegel—and others belonging to no group, such as Schopenhauer and Nietzsche.

Markets can usually be found in the main squares of most German towns, as here in Freiburg. Good places for those on a budget to shop.

GERMANY

Science
Germany has an impressive record of major contributions in every field of science and technology, as the following brief li st will show. Gutenberg (1400-68), movable type and book production; Kepler (1571-1630), laws of planetary motion; Leibniz (1646-1716), infinitesimal calculus; Humboldt (1769-1859), naturalist, geographer and explorer; Gauss (1777-1855), mathematics and magnetism; Bunsen (1811-99), spectrum analysis and the "Bunsen" burner; Kekulé (1829-96), founder of organic chemistry; Koch (1843-1910), bacteriology; Röntgen (1845-1923), X-rays; Ehrlich (1854-1915), medical science; Diesel (1858-1913), internal combustion engine; Planck (1858-1947), quantum theory; Einstein (1879-1955) relativity; Koffka (1886-1941), gestalt psychology.

Touring Information

Access
The cheapest approach to Germany from England is via *Dover/Ostend* to *Aachen*; return fare from London £22·60 by rail in 9½ hrs. The cycling distance from *Ostend* harbour to *Aachen* is nearly 150 miles, some of it over cobbled Belgian road. From *Aachen* to *Cologne* is a further 45 miles; return fare from London via *Ostend* £25·20 in 10 hrs.

For northern Germany (*Bremen, Hanover*) best route is through Holland, crossing frontier at *Bentheim*. Night boat *Harwich* to *Hook of Holland* is recommended; 6-7 hours of sleep in a comfortable berth, and after leaving London at 8 p.m. you can be at *Bentheim* by 10.00 next morning or at *Bremen* by lunch time. This route is very popular, however, and in the holiday season early reservation is advised. *London-Bentheim* return £28·30, *London-Bremen* return £35·50. There is also a service every other day from *Harwich* to *Bremerhaven* (16 hrs.; return fare £28·00 without berth).

For travellers from the north of England boat services from *Hull* are advantageous; there is a service every day to *Rotterdam* (14 hrs. overnight; return fare from £25·20, including berth and meals on board). *Rotterdam* is actually nearer to *Cologne* than is *Ostend*.

GERMANY

Other approaches are via *Calais* and *Strasbourg* (for S. Germany) or via *Ostend* and *Luxembourg* to *Trier*—a very picturesque route to the *Mosel* and *Rhine*.

Means of Transport
Rail travel in Germany is efficient, the express trains being rapid and punctual. 2nd class basic fares are 12 *Pf.* per kilometre, decreasing to about 10 *Pf.* on longer journeys; return tickets offer a reduction of about 10% for journeys over 200 kms. Tickets are valid for unlimited breaks of journey. For parties of 10 adults travelling together there is a reduction of 30%. For parties of 25 adults, school parties and youth groups the reduction is 50%.

The local train (*Personenzug*) can be very slow indeed, and the wooden seats very hard, but it will bring you into touch with the ordinary folk of Germany, particularly in country districts.

Bus services are run by the Federal Railways (*Bahnbus*) to connect with the trains, and by the Post Office (*Postkraftwagen*) on routes not provided with rail services. The latter are yellow vehicles which penetrate to the remotest mountain villages; they also provide long-distance services in certain tourist areas. Fares are similar to 2nd class rail.

On the *Rhine*, *Mosel* and *Bodensee* (*Lake Constance*) there are regular steamer services in summer; rail tickets (for the parallel rail route) may be used on payment of a supplement of a few pfennigs per kilometre. Note that on the *Rhine* the *Schnelldampfer* (fast steamer) is much more expensive than the ordinary service.

On the *Rhine*, *Mosel* and other rivers there are ferries (*Fähren*—marked "F" on maps) which convey passengers (and bicycles) at a reasonable charge.

Money
The *Deutsche Mark* (abbreviated *DM.*) is divided into 100 *Pfennigs* (abbreviated *Pf.*) Coins are issued for 1, 2, 5, 10 and 50 *Pf.*, and for 1, 2 and 5 *DM.*, with notes for higher values. Beware of confusing the 1 and 2 *DM.* pieces, which are similar in size but not in design.

Clothing
For the mountains (particularly the *Bavarian Alps*) carry a sweater, windproof jacket, scarf and thick stockings or woollen trousers or slacks, with boots or heavy shoes; even in summer there can be sudden cold spells. Women are advised to wear skirts (not shorts) in Catholic areas (*Rhineland* and *Bavaria*).

179

GERMANY

Restaurants and Meals Meals at German Youth Hostels are usually substantial and economical; members' kitchens are few. There is not usually a set two- or three-course supper as in England; you make your own choice from the limited selection at the serving hatch and pay accordingly.

Hostel meals can be varied by an occasional restaurant meal without too much expense. There are restaurants in all but the smallest villages and a simple but good meal can almost always be had for about *DM.* 4 The principal types of meat found on the menu are: *Rind* (beef), *Schwein* (pork) *Kalb* (veal), *Wurst* (sausage), *Schinken* (ham), *Speck* (bacon). Pork and veal predominate over beef. Other useful words are: *Eier* (eggs), *Käse* (cheese), *Gemüse* (vegetables), *Kartoffeln* (potatoes). A 10% service charge is almost always included in the bill, replacing a tip.

Public Holidays Whit Monday; June 17; November 16 (Repentance Day); Christmas Day; December 26; January 1; Good Friday; Easter Monday; May 1; Ascension Day.

Information Services The *German National Tourist Office, 630 5th Avenue, New York, N.Y. 10019* supplies illustrated leaflets and brochures.

Maps Good large-scale walkers' maps of particular tourist areas (*Black Forest, Eifel*) are published by private firms (e.g., Stollfuss and Reise-und Verkehrsverlag); tourist paths and youth hostels are generally marked. (*See* maps in section entitled *Footpath Routes.*)

A good road map is *Michelin* No. 987 on a scale of 1:1,000,000 depicting Germany and Benelux. There are many series of motorists' or cyclists' maps including *Michelin*, 1:200,000, and *D.G.K.*, (same scale; hostels and footpaths marked).

Accommodation Germany is the home of the youth hostel movement, founded in 1909 by Richard Schirrmann, and there is an excellent network of about 800 hostels covering the greater part of Western Germany. Hostels in the popular touring areas (*Rhineland, Black Forest*) are crowded during the holidays and the average age of hostellers is much lower than in England (schoolchildren form a high proportion of them) so that strict organisation is necessary, particularly in the larger hostels. In smaller hostels off the beaten track the atmosphere is often more homely and informal. Hostels are usually open all day and mid-day meals can be provided if ordered beforehand. Lights are put out at 10 p.m. and many German hostellers make an early start in the morning.

Note that in *Bavaria* (routes **R.8** and parts of **R.5** and **R.6**) youth hostels are not open to visitors aged over 27 years. Youth hostels can be supplemented by other inexpensive quarters. The smaller country inn (*Gasthaus* or *Gasthof*) will often provide a bed for about *DM. 8.* The mountain huts of the *Deutscher Alpenverein (5 Praterinsel, Munich 22)* are open to nonmembers and provide a mattress bed for about *DM. 4*; they are situated principally in the *Bavarian Alps*.

Camping   There are well-equipped camping sites in many parts of the country; a list can be obtained from the *German National Tourist Office, 630 5th Avenue, New York, N.Y. 10019*. Before camping at places other than the recognised sites the permission of the owner must be sought and, in your own interest, the permission of the local police.

Walking   Many people consider Germany the finest walking country in Europe. It lacks the mountain splendours of Austria and Switzerland, the glaciers and fjords of Norway, the limitless sunshine of the Mediterranean, but it has a whole series of hill regions (2,000 to 4,000 ft.) where forest alternates with meadow and moor, where peaks provide unexpectedly wide views and every valley has its stream and neat villages. Footpaths, unobtrusively marked by an occasional coloured sign on a tree or boulder, follow the finest slopes and ridges, often leading the walker away from every trace of civilisation for hours on end except for an occasional—and very welcome—wayside inn.

The most famous of these districts is the *Black Forest*; less well known, and less visited by foreign tourists, are the *Eifel*, the *Odenwald*, the *Spessart* and the *Sauerland*. There are footpaths on the heights above the *Rhine*, the *Mosel* and other rivers, infinitely preferable to the crowded, noisy roads in the valley below. Because of the importance of these paths to the walker a special footpath section outlining the main networks, with sketch maps, is given below.

Cycling   This is an excellent way to see the country; a touring model, rather than a lightweight machine, is preferable and a multi-speed gear is almost essential except on the northern plain. Cycling on the *Autobahnen* is forbidden and cyclists are not officially allowed to cycle two abreast on any road; this is a wise precaution, as German roads have the highest death rate in Europe.

GERMANY

Touring Routes

In the sketch maps showing footpaths in Footpath Routes, youth hostels are marked, but this information must be checked from the current edition of the German Youth Hostels Handbook or the *International Youth Hostel Handbook*.

R.1. Dutch to Danish Frontier via Hamburg (470 miles)

This route leads through flat agricultural country, but it can be recommended to hostellers who like to get off the beaten tourist track and who are interested in architecture, the sea and the life of the people. The direct journey by rail—the route of the *Holland-Scandinavia Express*—is only 300 miles, and can be accomplished in 7 hours, but this suggested route for the cyclist follows a more winding course. There are youth hostels in the majority of the towns and at many points on the coast.

From *Bentheim* (Y.H.) (Dutch/German frontier) follow B.65, crossing the River *Ems* at *Rheine* (Y.H.) and enter **Osnabrück**, important rail and road junction set between two parallel hill ridges—the *Teutoburg Forest* and the *Wiehengebirge*. (See R.2(i)). Imposing 1,000 year-old cathedral and Gothic town hall with the Hall of Peace of Westphalia, where end of the Thirty-Years' War was negotiated in 1648. (Y.H.).

Turn N.E. by B.51. After 15 miles the *Dümmer* appears on the left, a lake some four miles wide with facilities for swimming and sailing. Smoked eel is a delicacy of this area. Across the marshes fork left at *Diepholz* (Y.H.) on B.69 to *Vechta*, in the midst of woods, meadows, and marshes. Just before the junction with B.213 on the right is the *Ahlhorner Heide*, an area of Stone Age funeral monuments called *Hünengräber*. On to *Oldenburg*—castle with gardens, several museums,(Y.H.). Halfway to *Bremen* on B.75 is *Delmenhorst*, magnificent town hall, in middle of wooded *Delmenhorster* marshes.

Bremen, the second port of Germany, with interesting dockyards, has all its tourist goals concentrated in one area on the north bank. St. Peter's cathedral has lead crypt; famous colourful town hall with beautiful Renaissance façade; *Liebfrauenkirche* is one of the finest churches; historical market place with *Roland Monument*; the *Schütting* guildhouse is one of finest buildings; botanical gardens; several museums; tourist information on main railway station. (Y.H.).

From *Bremen* take the secondary road north-eastwards through *Horn* turning left to *Worpswede* (Y.H.), artist colony with various exhibitions, in heart of flat marshy country where typical black-sailed boats can be seen. Cut across country to B.6 for *Bremerhaven*; largest fisherman's harbour in the world, a lively night life, fisheries, and the North Sea Aquarium. (Y.H.).

R.1(i) Bremerhaven to Wangerooge (Frisian Islands). Boat service, takes 4 hours, July to mid-Sept.; (can also be reached from *Wilhelmshaven*). *Wangerooge* is most easterly of the seven *Frisian* Islands, pleasant, sandy, good bathing;Y.H. on each island. Other islands can only be reached from the small ports of *Friesland* (*Harle*, *Norddeich*). Most attractive is *Spiekeroog* (the Green Island), a nature reserve.

From *Bremerhaven* take coast road northwards to *Cuxhaven*, **(Y.H.)**, important fishing town whose symbol is a huge ball-buoy mounted on the end of a jetty. A sail by smack to the island of *Neuwerk* is great fun. Turn east on B.73 through *Wingst* **(Y.H.)** and *Stade* **(Y.H.)** with its intact medieval buildings, countryside with farmhouses and steep thatched roofs, and on to *Hamburg*. **Hamburg**, largest port and second largest city after *Berlin*. Situated at confluence of rivers *Alster* and *Elbe*. Suffered tremendous destruction in War, but now rebuilt with many ultra-modern buildings. Was principal port of Hanseatic League (13th-17th centuries), later a Free City. Built on marshy soil, frequently on piles. Boat trips to harbour from *St. Pauli* wharf; *Elbe* tunnel (500 yds. long), from *St. Pauli* wharf; *Reeperbahn*, famous street of night-life and sailors' entertainments; renaissance Town Hall (*Rathaus*)— half-hourly conducted tours; "*Planten un Blomen*" park—magnificent flower gardens adjoining *Tiergartenstrasse*: boat trip on the *Alster*, leaving from *Alster* Pavilion; Art Gallery (*Kunsthalle*), near main station—number of old masters; area of old canals (called *Fleete*) between *Elbe* and Inner *Alster*, with interesting old streets round *St. Michael's* church. **Y.H.** on the *Stintfang*, an eminence overlooking the *St. Pauli* wharf.

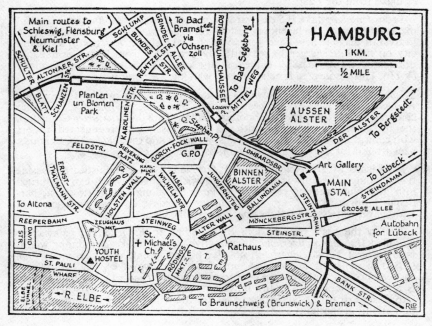

GERMANY

The Lüneburg Heath

R.1 (ii) Hamburg to the Lüneburg Heath. Due south of *Hamburg*—and S.W. of *Lüneburg* town stretches the *Lüneburg* Heath (*Lüneburger Heide*). Formerly a vast tract of heather and moorland, much has now been reclaimed for cultivation, and parts disfigured by British army manoeuvres, but round the *Wilseder Berg* (550 ft.) there is a nature reserve, with fine walking country; Y.H. at *Bispingen* and *Undeloh* give best access. Birch, juniper and pine trees among heather; shepherds and bee-keepers. Romantic associations for many Germans, due largely to writings of Hermann Löns (killed in action 1914), including much-loved song: "*Auf der Lüneberger Heide.*" Other good parts of the Heath are the *Arloh* (N. of *Celle*) and the lonely area east of *Müden* (Y.H.), said to be most beautiful town of Heath, with typical farm settlements protected by huge oaks. At *Walsrode* (on B.209) is a Heath Museum in 350-year-old group of farm buildings. *Lüneburg* itself (Y.H.) is picturesque old town with gothic brickwork and half-timbered buildings; old town hall has magnificent carvings and wall-paintings. At *Fallingbostel* (Y.H.) (S.W. of *Soltau*, on B.209) are prehistoric stone chambers known as the Seven Stone Houses; many archaeological finds have been made on the heath. For footpath routes see page 207.

From *Hamburg* to the Danish frontier follow the North Sea coast, a windswept solitude of dunes and dykes with many **Y.Hs**; or the Baltic coast, which is peaceful and wooded with many lakes. Rail route crosses the centre of the province, via *Neumünster*.

Schleswig-Holstein. Germany's most northerly province, was the starting point of the Anglo-Saxon invasion of England 1,500 years ago. It is now an agricultural area, thickly populated owing to the post-war influx of German refugees from the East.

From *Hamburg* take B.5 eastwards, and then B.207 to *Mölln*, the delightful medieval town of the legendary jester (*Till Eulenspiegel*) in whose memory a festival of plays is held each year. Y.H. on lake shore. *Ratzeburg*, an island city on the *Ratzeburger* Lake, and only two miles from East Germany, is dominated by its massive cathedral, the oldest brick church in Germany (Y.H.). This whole area is delightful for walking, swimming and yachting.

Lübeck, the first large town, is famous for its brickwork; the striking *Rathaus* (town hall) is the best example, retaining the black glazed tiles characteristic of the area. Other points of interest are the *St. Marien* Cathedral, the fortified *Holstein* Gate with its two massive interconnected towers with conical black roofs, the city walls, museum and the *Buddenbrooks* house, background for Thomas Mann's famous novel. (Y.H.).

B.75 leads to *Travemünde*, (Y.H.), Germany's most sophisticated seaside resort; unusual feature is the enormous wicker chairs which can be turned into individual bathing cabins. Further north along the Baltic coast, particularly north of *Kiel*, are many quieter seaside places, all with excellent bathing on wide sandy beaches backed by pine trees.

Follow the coast road to join B.76 leading to *Eutin* (Y.H.) gateway to so-called *Holstein Switzerland*, an attractive region of lakes set among woodland; several **Y.Hs.** *Bungsburg*, 450 ft., highest point, with fine view. *Plön* (Y.H.) in the heart of this area, surrounded by five lakes, has magnificent castle. Through the beautiful countryside around *Preetz* (Y.H.) where there is an ancient convent, to the university town of *Kiel* (Y.H.) where canal affords an exit to the North Sea; *Kiel* Regatta (end of June) is internationally famous; food speciality is *Kieler Sprotten* (sprats).

Continue to *Schleswig*, an ancient Viking city. **Y.H.** The cathedral contains the *Bordesholm* altar, one of the most famous works of art in Germany, a remarkable 16th-century wood-carving of 392 figures. The *Gottorp* castle on an island in the *Schlei* estuary is the largest in *Schleswig-Holstein*; houses Prehistoric Museum and *Nydam* boat, an Anglo-Saxon craft of the 4th century, and many other remains found in the marsh country.

From *Schleswig* B.76 to Germany's northernmost city, *Flensburg*—picturesque streets and houses, the *Nordertor* (a 16th century gate containing a house), a good museum, a 13th century church (the *Marienkirche*); an opera, theatre, and symphony orchestra make it a centre of music; excellent church choirs. **Y.H.** Two food specialities are *Flensburg* rum and smoked eel. Visit *Glücksburg* castle, majestically situated on beech-covered heights, 4 miles N.E. Continue to North Sea coast or to Denmark.

R.2. Dutch Frontier to East German Border via Hanover (190 miles)

This route follows the northern edge of the central German uplands, giving access to a number of pleasant holiday areas. By rail (via the *Hook*) you can reach *Minden*—on the *Weser*—in 16 hours after leaving *London* £33·50 return, *Hanover* in a further hour £35·90 return, and *Goslar*—for the *Harz* Mountains (see **R.2(iv)**) in 20 hours £39·90 return.

Follow **R.1** as far as *Osnabrück*.

The Teutoburg Forest

R.2(i) Osnabrück to Detmold, 50 miles. The *Teutoburger Wald*, a long narrow range of wooded hills rising to about 1,000 ft., provides good walking country and is well provided with **Y.H.s,** particularly round the *Dörenberg* (1,070 ft.) a fine viewpoint 9 miles S. of *Osnabrück*. The best road for cyclists (B.68) skirts the southern foot of the hills through *Iburg*—a picturesque little town with a 900-year-old castle (the *Sachsenburg*) and a Benedictine Abbey from the 11th century—*Halle* with its steep-roofed half-timbered houses, to *Bielefeld*, a beautifully situated manufacturing town symbolised by the pipe-smoking figures of the linen-weavers' monument. Thence by B.66 and 239 into *Detmold*, formerly chief town of *Lippe-Detmold*, one of the innumerable small principalities of Germany; pleasant little town, with H.Q. of German **Y.H.A.**, a fine castle and a museum (in the *Palais*) containing many relics from prehistoric times found in the area. 3 miles south on *Grotenberg* (1,250 ft.) is 180-ft. statue known as *Hermannsdenkmal*, commemorating victory of Germanic leader *Hermann* (Arminius) over the Romans, A.D. 9. **Y.H.** on hill to S.W. of *Detmold*.

From *Osnabrück* follow B.65 and keep to north of *Wiehengebirge*, one of the pleasant spurs of the *Weser* hills. **Y.H.** at *Bad Essen*. *Lübbecke* has some fine old buildings. *Minden*, a former *Hansa* city, has a noble cathedral recently rebuilt and remarkable aqueduct carrying *Mittelland* canal over River *Weser*. **Y.H.** at *Meissen*.

The Weser Hill Country

R.2(ii) The River Weser from Minden to Hannoversch-Münden. The *Weser*, a slow-flowing winding river, runs for over 100 miles through the charming *Weserbergland* (Weser Hill Country), an unspoiled region of deciduous forest (mostly beech or oak) interspersed with fertile farmland. The hills rise to an average of 1,000 ft. and a maximum of 1,716 ft. Good walking country (see walking routes, page 214) first-class for canoeing, wth **Y.H.** at riverside points every 15 miles or so. Leisurely steamer service *Hann.-Münden-Hameln* in 11 hrs., reverse direction in 2 days; May-Sept. only.

GERMANY

From *Minden* by B.61 south through the Westphalian Gap (*Porta Westfalica*) a geological curiosity, where the *Weser* in prehistoric times cut through the ridge of hills; Y.H. at *Hausberge* above gap. Fine view from terrace of Kaiser Wilhelm Monument. *Bad Oeynhausen*, small spa. By-roads (crossing *Autobahn*) to *Rinteln* (Y.H.) for steamer. *Hameln* (of "Pied-Piper" fame) has a picturesque "Rat-catcher's house", and sugar-rats can be bought in shops. Many fine old timbered houses, often with inscriptions and carvings. Y.H.

EXCURSION: 12 miles S.W. is *Bad Pyrmont*, one of most attractive small spas in Europe; fine gardens, lawns and shady walks.

Next town, *Bodenwerder* (Y.H.) was legendary home of Baron *Münchhausen*, teller of travellers' tales; Y.Hs at Polle and Holzminden. *Höxter* (Y.H.) is a good point for visiting *Corvey* Abbey (close to river) parts of which have been untouched since 850 A.D. and *Köterberg* (10 miles N.W.), the second highest point in hills west of river, 1,300 ft.,—excellent view. To east of river is *Solling* forest, densely wooded, rich in game; with highest peak on east bank, the *Grosse Blösse*, near *Silberborn*, 1,716 ft. Beyond *Karlshafen* (Y.H.) comes *Reinhardswald*, densely wooded hills where Grimm brothers collected many of their fairy tales (Y.H.); nature-reserve round *Sababurg*. *Hannoversch-Münden* is junction of Rivers *Fulda* and *Werra*, which form river *Weser*; attractive town, Y.H. For continuation S.E. see R.5.

6 miles beyond *Minden* is *Bückeburg*, picturesque old town; in surrounding districts women often wear traditional dress. *Stadthagen* has many well-preserved buildings. Hill country to south is worth visiting.

Hanover is former seat of Hanoverian kings; now an important industrial city, mostly rebuilt, with famous trade fair. *Herrenhausen* gardens (W. side of city), 17th century baroque style. (Y.H.)

R.2(iii) Hanover to Berlin. *Hanover* is convenient point of departure for *Berlin*; transit visa required to cross East German territory by rail or road, issued on train or at Frontier Control Point by stamping passport on payment of fee. Visa is valid for return journey. Bus recommended as frontier formalities usually cleared more quickly. **Berlin**, former capital of Germany, is now an "island" in East Germany. Free movement in Western and part of city, but not outside city boundaries. Most heavily-bombed city in Europe; new luxury buildings in western sectors, show-piece workers' flats in eastern sector, only point in Europe at which Communist worlds impinge, along the line of the "wall", *Charlottenburg* Castle. Famous Zoo, Aquarium and Botanical Gardens. Congress Hall (interesting modern design) in Tiergarten. Autobahn clover-leaf pattern on Potsdamer Chaussee, Dahlem Museum (fine collection of paintings; bust of Nefertiti). Pergamon Museum in East Berlin. Waldbühne (Forest Arena) huge open air cinema, concerts and sports shows. Pleasant woods (*Grunewald*) and lakes (*Havel*, good bathing) to S.W. of city. Several Y.Hs.

From *Hanover* to *Brunswick* route is dull. Oil discovered here, and industry developing. **Brunswick** a city dating from 9th century, was former capital of Lower Saxony, mostly rebuilt, but still many places of interest. Bronze lion in *Burgplatz* (1166) recalls Henry the Lion, who built the romanesque cathedral. (Y.H.)

EXCURSION: 12 miles N.E. of *Brunswick* is *Wolfsburg*, site of vast state-owned motor-car factories producing the *Volkswagen*.

The Harz

R.2(iv) Brunswick to the Harz Mountains. Some 30 miles S. of *Brunswick* are the *Harz* Mountains. These conifer-covered hills, rising to about 3,000 ft. are better known to German than English hostellers, being linked with many legends, above all the witches' Walpurgisnight in Goethe's *"Faust"*. There is good ski-ing on the higher slopes, excellent walking (with nearly a score of Y.H.), a number of caves, and several well-known spas. The eastern half of the range, including the famous *Brocken* (2,700 ft.) lies in East German territory, but the frontier is clearly marked and there is no danger of straying.

Goslar, at N. end of *Harz*, is rare and rewarding old town, containing street after street of domestic architecture of every period from 15th century; magnificent 15th century guild-houses, solid fortifications, narrow streets, Y.H. From *Goslar* road B.241 rises at times steeply into the *Oberharz* (Upper *Harz*) with lakes and hills, of which *Bocksberg* (2,350 ft.) rising above *Hahnenklee* is highest and gives fine view as far as distant *Brocken*. Strike N.W. by side-road through wonderfully wooded area of *Lautental* (Y.H. at *Bockswiese*) to *Wildemann*. To

GERMANY

W. is *Iberg*, 1,800 ft., with big stalactite caves. South of *Clausthal-Zellerfeld* (Y.H.), road B. 241 leads through idyllic 2-mile long *Lerbach* valley with heavy black forest on one side and open meadow on the other, to *Osterode*, a town with fine 16th and 17th century buildings (Y.H.). Follow B.243 to *Herzberg*, with lofty 900-year-old castle, caves and some fine views. Beyond *Scharzfeld* (Y.H.) take winding hilly road over the *Grosse Knollen* (1,970 ft.) to *Sieber* and up the *Sieber* valley to *St. Andreasberg*. This is highest of seven well-known *Harz* towns, in strange, barren but fascinating countryside. Strike down to B.27 for ski centre of *Braunlage* (Y.H.) only two miles from border of Russian Zone. Thence by B.4 over bleak mountain swamps at 3,000 ft. to *Torfhaus* (Y.H.) which faces the *Brocken*. Follow by-road to *Altenau* (Y.H.) past a large reservoir and into wild and romantic *Oker* valley; at *Romkerhall* the narrow defile lays bare many layers of the earth's crust. Return from *Oker* to *Goslar*.

The above circuit is approx. 140 miles from *Brunswick* to *Brunswick* or 80 miles from *Goslar* back to *Goslar*.

Eastward from *Brunswick* road B.1 skirts wooded hills known as the *Elm* and joins autobahn at *Helmstedt* (Y.H.), frontier town.

R.3. The Rhine from the Dutch Frontier to Mainz (228 miles)

The River *Rhine* is not merely the largest river in Western Europe, it is also a main artery of transport; huge barges ply from the industrial *Ruhr* to Holland and the North Sea. Passenger steamers do not run on this section, and because of the flatness of the country the Lower *Rhine* is not often visited by tourists. But the cyclist entering Germany from Holland should cross the frontier near *Nijmegen* to the picturesque little town of *Kleve* (Y.H.) on the edge of the *Reichswald* Forest. *Kalkar* and *Xanten* are also historical small towns.

Duisburg, on the east bank, is the second-largest inland port in the world, handling the coal, steel and other products of the *Ruhr*. Further south lies **Düsseldorf** a spaciously laid-out city outside the main industrial region, but the administrative centre for the province of *Rhineland-Westphalia*. Here are parks, tree-lined streets, elegant shops; the *Königsallee*, a mile long and nearly 200 yards wide, is a noble street. (Y.H.)

The Sauerland

R.3(i) **Düsseldorf to the Sauerland Hills.** A recommended trip for hostellers who wish to get right away from fellow tourists, to visit the "cradle" of the youth hostel movement and some of the finest modern Y.Hs. in Germany.

By road (not recommended for cyclists) 50 miles, by rail in 2 hrs. (change at *Hagen*) to Altena, in valley of *Lenne*. Here world's first permanent youth hostel opened in 1909 by Richard Schirrmann, young school-teacher, in castle above town. South of *Altena* stretches wooded hill country of *Sauerland*, some 60 miles from E. to W., which, with the contiguous *Bergisch Land* hills to the W., forms popular place of recreation from nearby *Ruhr* industrial area. Footpaths marked by *Sauerland* Mountain Association, close network of Y.H., including several fine post-war buildings, e.g. *Plettenberg* and *Dabringhausen*, and several converted castles. Thinly populated. Hills rise to maximum of 2,733 ft. (*Kahle Asten*, S.E. of *Meschede*), but cut by deep river valleys giving impression of greater height; many reservoirs, including that formed by the *Möhne* dam of war-time fame.

25 miles south of *Düsseldorf* and 87 miles from the Dutch frontier: **Cologne.** Founded by Romans in 38 B.C.; Latin *Colonia*; many Roman remains, especially *Dionysos* mosaic. Cultural and commercial capital of Rhineland; magnificent Gothic cathedral (begun 1248, finished in 19th century) is one of most beautiful in world; escaped serious war-time damage. Golden reliquary (Adoration of the Magi) and the painting by Stefan Lochner of *Cologne*,

both on the altar; fine view from tower—note semi-circular arrangement of streets, following former fortifications, and roads converging on city from all directions. The 15th century *Gürzenich*, built as a place for dancing and celebration, is still so used, especially during the Cologne Carnival on Shrove Tuesday and days immediately preceding it.

Y.H. converted by voluntary international work parties from a huge concrete air-raid shelter 20 mins. walk north from main railway station, near zoo; also large new **Y.H.** in right-bank suburb of *Deutz*. City information office in *Domkloster* 3, behind cathedral.

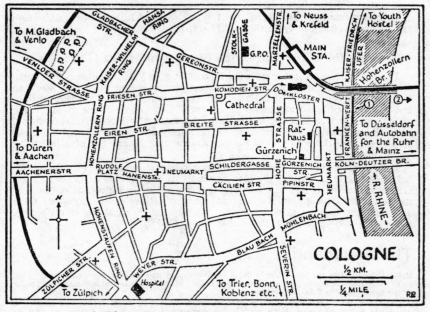

1. *Rhine steamers land here.* 2. *To Y.H. Deutz.*

R.3(ii) Cologne to Aachen, 45 miles. Not an interesting journey, but important as most direct access from England via *Ostend*. By fast train in about 1 hr. Choice of roads via *Jülich* or *Düren*. For *Aachen* itself see R.3(iii).

The Rhine Valley

South of *Cologne* the *Rhine* valley is about 25 miles wide and not at all spectacular. However, the river steamers ply from *Cologne*, and travellers with time to spare can go to *Mainz* by fast steamer in fourteen hours. Travellers with less time to spare should take cheaper slow steamer from *Koblenz* to *Rüdesheim* in six hours. Road and railway on each side of river, with

numerous ferries. Road B.9 follows the west (left) bank of the river, and
B.42 the east; packed with motor traffic in summer. Use steamer or make for
quiet hill country on either side. (*See* Footpath Routes.)

Leaving *Cologne*, take road B.9 to **Bonn**. Beethoven's birthplace; ancient
university town; celebrated museum—the *Rheinisches Landesmuseum*;
Poppelsdorfer Castle; seat of the Government of the West German Federal
Republic; the *Bundehaus* (Parliament) is an attractive modern building, by
riverside. **(Y.H.)**.

Bad Godesberg is the first of many tourist resorts on the route. **(Y.H.)**.

EXCURSION: Ferry to *Königswinter*, thence on foot into the Siebengebirge. (Seven
Mountains) miniature range of former volcanic peaks in area barely 4 miles by 3. Highest
peak is *Ölberg* (1,498 ft.) but wider view from *Drachenfels* (Dragon Rock—named after
Siegfried legend, based on this area) which rises immediately above river and has ruined
castle. Rack railway up from *Königswinter* in 10 mins. *Siebengebirge* have well-marked
footpaths, good walking, but becoming popular.

South of *Godesberg* the valley narrows and wine-growing area begins;
Y.H. at *Bad Honnef*; *Linz*, charming old walled town, many half-timbered
houses.

R.3(iii) Sinzig to Aachen via Ahr Valley and Eifel, 156 miles. A pleasant journey by relatively
quiet by-roads. No rail connection. Road surfaces sometimes rough, but strongly recommended for cyclists. Follow graceful *Ahr* valley (Germany's largest red-wine area) past
sophisticated spa of *Bad Neuenahr* to small towns of *Ahrweiler* and *Altenahr* (both with **Y.H.**),
entering *Eifel* mountains.

The Eifel

One of the wildest and most unspoiled regions of Western Germany. Extinct volcanic craters,
many now filled by small lakes (*Maare*) particularly near *Daun*, in sombre forest surroundings;
numerous hot springs confirm volcanic nature of area. Average height of region 1,500 to
2,000 ft. For footpath routes see map on page 190 and notes on page 206.

South from *Altenahr* on B.257 by *Adenau* (Y.H.) to famous motor-racing circuit of *Nürburg
Ring* (17 miles, 170 curves) crowded when racing in progress. Track dominated by *Hohe Acht*
(2,430 ft.), highest peak in *Eifel*. Continue by B.257 to *Daun* (Y.H.) centre of crater-lakes.
North and west by *Gerolstein* (small spa) to *Prüm* (Y.H.) with 1,200 year-old Benedictine
Abbey, one of many abbeys which helped to open up *Eifel* for settlement in Middle Ages.
West of *Prüm* is *Schnee-Eifel*, high and desolate range. N.E. by B.51 to *Blankenheim* (fine **Y.H.**
in castle), near source of R. *Ahr*. Proceed N.W. to *Gemünd* (Y.H.) for vast artificial reservoir
of *Urfttal*, supplying water and electric power to Rhineland towns. West by B.258 to *Monschau*,
frontier town, many half-timbered houses, tourist centre (Y.H. in castle). Road 258 now
crosses tongue of Belgian territory (*Hautes Fagnes*), traverses *Rötgen* forest, and enters *Aachen*.

Aachen (Aix-la-Chapelle) is historic town, capital of Charlemagne's Empire (9th Century);
cathedral partly build by Charlemagne; German kings were crowned here for 7 centuries.
Warm springs (hottest in Central Europe). Main approach for rail traffic from England via
Ostend. Fine Y.H. in *Maria-Theresia-Allee*, S. side of *Aachen*.

From *Sinzig*, 7 miles upstream to *Brohl*.

EXCURSION: 6 miles by road to *Laacher See*, largest of crater lakes in *Eifel* Mountains
with 9th Century *Maria Laach* abbey and fine abbey church.

Continue on left bank via *Andernach*, town established in pre-Roman times,
to **Koblenz**, Latin *Confluentes*, confluence of *Mosel* and *Rhine*, important
wine trade; *Deutsches Eck*, point at which the *Mosel* enters the *Rhine* and
their different-coloured waters mingle. Cross to *Ehrenbreitstein* (climb for
magnificent view) (Y.H.) in old fortifications. (For *Mosel* and *Lahn* Valley
routes from *Koblenz* see R.4.)

GERMANY

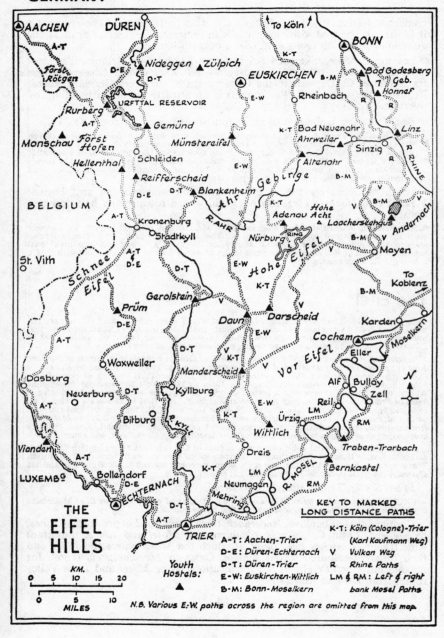

THE EIFEL HILLS

AACHEN
DÜREN
A-T
Forst. Rötgen
D-E Nideggen Zülpich
D-T
URFTTAL RESERVOIR
Rurberg
A-T Gemünd
Monschau Forst Hofen
Münstereifel
Hellenthal
Schleiden
Reifferscheid
BELGIUM
D-E D-T Blankenheim
A-T Kronenburg
Stadtkyll
St. Vith
Schnee Eifel
A-T
D-E
D-T
Gerolstein
Prüm
D-E
A-T
Waxweiler
Dasburg
Neuerburg D-T
Bitburg
Vianden
A-T
LUXEMBᴳ
Bollendorf
D-E
ECHTERNACH
D-T
A-T
TRIER

To Köln
K-T
BONN
EUSKIRCHEN B-M Bad Godesberg 7 Geb.
Rheinbach Honnef
R
E-W R
Bad Neuenahr Linz
K-T Ahrweiler Sinzig
Altenahr R RHINE
Ahr Gebirge B-M
K-T Hohe Acht
Adenau Loachersee haus V B-M
Nürburg RING Andernach
E-W Hohe Eifel V
Mayen
B-M To Koblenz
V V
Daun Darscheid
E-W Karden
V Cochem Moselkern
V K-T Eller
Manderscheid V Alf Bulloy
D-T Vor Eifel Reil Zell
Kyllburg LM
Ürzig RM
E-W
K-T Wittlich
Dreis Traben-Trarbach
LM MOSEL Bernkastel
K-T Neumagen RM
Mehring

N

KEY TO MARKED LONG DISTANCE PATHS

A-T: Aachen-Trier
D-E: Düren-Echternach
D-T: Düren-Trier
E-W: Euskirchen-Wittlich
B-M: Bonn-Moselkern

K-T: Köln (Cologne)-Trier (Karl Kaufmann Weg)
V   Vulkan Weg
R   Rhine Paths
LM & RM: Left & right bank Mosel Paths

Youth Hostels: ▲

KM.
0 5 10 15 20

0 5 10
MILES

N.B. Various E-W. paths across the region are omitted from this map.

The Rhine Gorge

From *Koblenz* to *Bingen* (40 miles) stretches the *Rhine* Gorge, where the river winds its way between steep hillsides, often covered with vineyards which produce most of Germany's wine, and dotted with ruined castles. Follow road B.42 to *Niederlahnstein* and *Oberlahnstein*—ancient town; picturesque houses and streets; Castle *Lahneck* worth visiting. Fine views of *Stolzenfels* Castle on opposite bank of *Rhine* (13th century restored in early 19th century). *Braubach*, ancient battlements; *Marksburg*, 700 ft. above river, a completely preserved medieval castle with fine collection of weapons. Continue up road B.42 and ferry to *Boppard*, charming picturesque old town; excellent starting point for day's walk in surrounding regions; **Y.H.** in former home of composer Humperdinck.

Ferry back to east bank, and continue through *Kamp* to *Bornhofen*. Above the village stand two ruined castles known as the *Feindlichen Brüder* (the enemy brothers). Legend has it that the lords of the two castles, who were brothers, killed each other in battle in *Bornhofen* church. *Wellmich*, five miles farther on, has a castle (restored) known as *Burg Maus* (Mouse Castle). The name was given in contempt by the owners of *Burg Katz* (Cat Castle) a mile farther upstream, who rejoiced in the name of Counts of *Katzenellenbogen* (Cats' Elbows).

Now comes the most romantic point of the *Rhine* Gorge. Here the river is barely 200 yards wide, but over 70 ft. deep and fast-flowing. On the west bank is *St. Goar*, a pleasant town said to have been founded by an Irish missionary of the same name **(Y.H.)**. Above is the ruined castle of *Rheinfels*, one of the largest on the *Rhine*. On opposite bank is *St. Goarshausen*, with the famous cliff known as the **Loreley** (Fairy's Rock) rising steeply out of the river. Here a beautiful maiden is supposed to have sat, combing her golden hair, and luring the boatmen to their death on the rocks below. River narrows dangerously and deep whirlpools appear. On top of cliff is an open-air theatre and a fine view.

Beyond *Urbar* (west bank) comes the Seven Maidens, a group of seven rocks in the water, visible only when the river is low (The Seven Maidens are said to have been turned into stone because of their hard-heartedness.) *Oberwesel* (west bank) is a picturesque old town, surrounded by a 13th century wall with 14 watchtowers. To the south of the town is the ruined castle of *Schönburg*, on a lofty cliff.

On a small island in the *Rhine* near *Kaub* stands the picturesque many-turreted *Pfalz*, built as a toll-house in the 14th century. Above *Kaub* is the magnificent castle of *Gutenfels* (well-preserved).

Bacharach, another walled town of great charm, is dominated by the castle of *Stahleck* (Hall of Knights, and a superb view from battlements). **(Y.H.)**.

Beyond *Lorch* **(Y.H.)** comes a series of castles on the west bank (*Heimburg*, *Sooneck*, *Rheinstein*). The river then bends eastwards, entering the *Binger Loch* (formerly rapids which could not be navigated) **Y.H.** at *Bingen*. On a small island stands the *Mäuseturm* (Mouse Tower); according to the legend, Bishop Hatto (10th century) who had burned some starving peasants, was chased into the tower by mice and eaten by them.

Opposite *Bingen*, on the north bank, stands the *Niederwalddenkmal*, a monumentally ugly statue of Germania, 120 ft. high, erected in 1877 to commemorate the creation of German unity by Bismarck; from its foot there is a fine view.

Rüdesheim, famous for wines, full of picturesque wine-cellars and restaurants and crowded with tourists. Y.H. on hillside 25 mins. above town. *Rüdesheim* to *Mainz* landscape is quite flat and richly agricultural; *Rheingau* vineyards for finest Rheinish wines. *Geisenheim* for *Schönborn* castle, *Heidesheim* for Y.H. and *Eltville*, celebrated wine town; *Schlangenbad*, thermal open-air swimming pool; *Wiesbaden* (Y.H.), celebrated spa, attractively planned town.

Mainz was an illustrious city in Roman times; retains traces of former glory and now capital of *Rhine Palatinate*. Birthplace of Gutenberg, inventor (1450) of movable type. Cathedral. Gutenberg statue and museums; art exhibitions. Y.H. on south edge of town.

R.4   Trier to Marburg, by Mosel and Lahn Valleys (186 miles)

An unusual approach to Germany for tourists, but a most rewarding route; less over-run than the *Rhine* Valley, which it crosses, and considered by some to be preferable. *Trier* can be reached via *Ostend* and *Luxembourg* and this *Mosel* valley journey can well be combined with a tour in *Luxembourg*.

Trier is oldest city in Germany; well established by Roman times, capital of all N.W. Europe under Constantine, focal point of church for many centuries. Now resembles gigantic open-air museum. *Porta Nigra*, massive gateway, northern entry to Roman empire; Roman baths, basilica and amphitheatre; numerous mosaics and statues; happy hunting ground for archaeological student. Y.H.

The Mosel

At *Trier* enter German section of *Mosel* valley. Delightful river, winding in huge leisurely curves, cutting way between *Eifel* Mountains to N. and *Hunsrück* to S. From *Trier* to *Koblenz* in direct line is about 60 miles, but river covers double this distance. Wine production is principal occupation, and river banks are terraced with vineyards. Many quaint old wine taverns in the sleepy red-roofed villages and towns. Some castles but few of the grim ruins characterising the *Rhine*. River has no rapids and is ideal for canoeing, although riverside hostels are sparse. By road, take B.53 to *Bullay*, then B.49 to *Koblenz*. Walkers can take all or part of the *Moselhöhenwege*, fine marked paths following the heights above the river. (*See* Footpath Routes.)

First place of note is *Neumagen*; here a Roman stone model of a wine-ship with tippling crew was discovered; original now in *Trier* museum, but copy in front of *Peterskapelle* in *Neumagen*. *Bernkastel-Kues*, one of many wine towns; picturesque market square in *Bernkastel* (timbered buildings from 16th century); Y.H. Town dominated by ruined *Landshut* Castle. Notable wine festival on first Saturday and Sunday in September.

The Hunsrück

R.4(i) Bernkastel to Idar Oberstein, 25 miles. South of the *Mosel* lies heavily wooded hill country known as *Hunsrück*. **Y.H.** at *Morbach* and follow B.269 southwards to foot of *Erbeskopf* (2,600 ft.) highest peak in *Rhineland* area, then take by-road E. to *Idar-Oberstein* **(Y.H.)** well known for precious-stone cutting industry; workshops can be visited. *Hunsrück* range continue W. past *Birkenfeld* **(Y.H.)** into *Saarland.* Not all of this territory is industrialised, and it has good **Y.H.** network. For footpath routes see page 206.

Continue along *Mosel* Valley pass *Urzig*, which has fine old timbered buildings. *Traben-Trarbach* **(Y.H.)** modern town dominated by ruined castle of *Grevenburg.* Between *Reil* and *Alf* (left bank) is particularly fine section of *Mosel* path, with good views; picturesque *Marienburg* ruin, S. of *Alf.* Here the ridge separating two loops of river is barely 500 yards wide; one of the finest views in *Mosel* area.

At *Eller* railway enters Germany's longest tunnel (2½ miles) while road follows river valley to *Beilstein* with picturesque market square partly cut out of rock.

Cochem **(Y.H.)**, originally pre-Roman, has remains of walls and gateways; castle above town (*Reichsburg*) rebuilt in 19th century to original plans— Start of marked *Eifel* footpath to *Prüm.*

Series of attractive small towns and villages both sides of river. *Moselkern,* confluence of River *Eltz,* beautiful valley with several castles.

EXCURSION: on foot in 1 hr. by *Eifel* path (cyclists can approach by-road) to Burg Eltz, best preserved of all *Mosel* castles. Vast building with many towers; parts date from 12th century. Castle can be visited (guide available). To north lies ruin of castle *Trutz-Eltz,* built by Bishop Balduin of *Trier* in 14th century to control insubordinate knights of *Eltz.*

Brodenbach **(Y.H.)** on right bank, small tourist centre, marks end of most attractive part of R. *Mosel*; following short-cuts to *Rhine* recommended.

R.4(ii) Brodenbach to the Rhine. Cyclists follow rough by-road over heights via *Gondershausen* to *St. Goar* (25 miles) **(Y.H.)** on *Rhine.* For walkers, choice of several fine footpaths in 4–5 hours to *Boppard* **(Y.H.)**, also on *Rhine.*

To L. of *Mosel* is fruit-growing area of *Maifeld*, to R. is spur of *Hunsrück* hills. *Winningen* has largest continuous area of vineyards on river.

Koblenz (see R.3) for *Rhine* Valley. Follow E. bank of *Rhine* southwards to *Niederlahnstein*, for confluence of R. *Lahn.*

The Lahn

A graceful river, flowing in smaller loops than the *Mosel*, between *Taunus* hills to S. and *Westerwald* to N. Narrow valley near mouth, meadow and hill country nearer source. Many interesting small towns. Some wine-growing. Railway follows river whole way; *Koblenz-Marburg* 91 miles, fast train via *Giessen* in about 2 hrs.; main roads leave valley, but side roads are recommended, following river most of way—total distance about 90 miles.

B. 260 to *Bad Ems* **(Y.H.)** celebrated spa, known in Roman times and given more modern fame by Bismarck's "Ems Telegram" of 1870; continue to *Nassau* (which gives its name to the Dutch royal family—*Orange-Nassau*), 16th century castles and half-timbered houses. Here main road turns south but route follows winding secondary road 20 miles via *Diez* **(Y.H.)** to

GERMANY

Limburg (*St. Georgs-Dom,* 13th century cathedral with seven towers), a picturesque medieval town. (Y.H.) Good starting point for expeditions into *Westerwald* and *Taunus,* and a communications centre for rail and road.

Runkel, 5 miles beyond *Limburg,* has fine castle and old bridge over *Lahn.* Y.H. at *Odersbach* near *Weilburg; Wetzlar* (Y.H.) is junction for one of rambling railways through *Taunus* to *Frankfurt,* has associations with Goethe, a very fine cathedral, an unusual number of steep streets and steps, and the *Leitz* factory where the famous Leica camera is produced. *Giessen* (Y.H.) is rail junction and centre of scientific research. On to **Marburg** (Y.H.), a town from the Middle Ages, set on the hills; *St. Elisabeth* church, first gothic cathedral built in Germany; Gothic town hall with noteworthy old clock; university (founded 1527) was first protestant university. 20 miles N. is town of *Battenberg*—from which English family of Mountbatten, and marzipan-covered cake, take their names.

The Taunus

One of many ranges making up Germany's central uplands. To the N., bordering R. *Lahn,* its woodlands are interspersed with pleasant farming country. To the S. the land rises to an average of 1,500 ft., thickly wooded and with many footpaths. For footpath routes see page 214. Highest point is *Feldberg* (2,860 ft.—not to be confused with *Feldberg* in *Black Forest*). A western spur of *Taunus* forms *Rheingau* hills, sheltering famous wine-growing region of that name (see R.3). *Königstein* is railhead for ascent of *Feldberg.*

R.4(iii) Giessen to Mainz via Homburg, 45 miles. An alternative return route to *Rhine,* skirting E. and S. edge of *Taunus* hills. B.3 to *Bad Nauheim* (fashionable spa), then B.455 to *Bad Homburg,* another spa, which gave name to Homburg hat; castle with fine garden; Y.H. Follow choice of footpaths via Y.Hs. at *Oberreifenberg* and *Wiesbaden* to *Mainz.*

R.5. Kassel to Passau by the Eastern Mountains (350 miles)

A route leading into some of the remotest and most unspoiled country in Germany. Too long for any but the most leisured (or toughest) cyclist, hilly all the way. Closely follows border of East Germany and of Czechoslovakia. No through rail connection, but parts of journey may well be taken by rail.

Kassel may be reached by extending R.2(ii) from *Hannoversch-Münden* (14 miles) or R.4 from *Marburg* (43 miles) or by rail from England via *Hook of Holland.*

The city (Y.H.) was three-quarters destroyed in war, but has been rebuilt as important industrial town. Fine art gallery, with many old masters; museum of tapestry and wall-papers in *Willhelmshöhe* Castle.

25 miles E. lies *Hoher Meissner,* hill plateau (2,437 ft.) on which German youth movement (*Freideutsche Jugend*) was founded in 1913; earlier claim to fame as scenes of Grimms' fairy tale of *Frau Holle;* now overlooks East German border. Y.H. at *Ludwigstein;* south through *Bebra,* a rail junction with many old half-timbered houses and Y.H. at *Rotenburg;* along R. *Fulda,* via Y.Hs. at *Bad Hersfeld* and *Schlitz* to *Fulda* (Y.H.), important religious centre (tomb of St. Boniface, English monk 8th century); many fine baroque buildings. Continue S.E. to the *Rhön.*

The Rhön

A thinly wooded hill region of volcanic origin, with interesting flora. Famous as German gliding centre and winter ski resort. Good walking country also. (*See* Footpath Routes.) Highest point is *Wasserkuppe* (3,037 ft.) with very fine view.

Follow B.279 through *Gersfeld* (**Y.H.**), centre for *Rhön*. Here enter *Franconia*.

Franconia

Franconia is a historical rather than geographical entity; it was one of the duchies of medieval Germany. It covers the whole of northern and eastern *Bavaria*, centred on *Nuremberg*, and includes some of the finest medieval cities of Germany (see also under **R.6**) and some pleasant hill country (*Fränkische Alb, Frankenwald*). It is the land of the *Meistersinger*.

B.279 leads through *Bischofsheim* (**Y.H.**) into *Neustadt*—pleasantly situated spa on R. *Saale*—over the steep-wooded ridges of the *Hassberge*, via *Sambachshof* (**Y.H.**) and *Königshofen* (fine market-place, many timbered buildings) to **Bamberg** near confluence of Rivers *Main* and *Regnitz*, beautiful cathedral city, famous equestrian statue of *Knight of Bamberg*; many fine old houses in area between cathedral and town hall (*Rathaus*); former Bishop's residences, now museums. **Y.H.**

R.5(i) Bamberg to Coburg, 28 miles. *Coburg,* home of Albert of *Saxe-Coburg-Gotha,* Queen Victoria's consort, to whom there is a statue in market place. City with many buildings in Gothic and Renaissance styles, dominated by massive *Veste,* one of largest and finest fortresses in Germany, which has many connections with Luther and the Reformation, now museum with huge collection of engravings. (**Y.H.**)

R.5(ii) Bamberg to Nuremberg, 38 miles. South by narrow valley of R. *Regnitz* through *Erlangen,* part of which (the New Town) was built to a plan, in baroque style, to house Huguenot refugees in 17th century. Nuremberg was formerly one of show cities of Germany, but heavily damaged in war. Many places of interest, either original or carefully rebuilt in original style: house of 16th century artist Albrecht Dürer (in *Bergstrasse*), city wall and castle (**Y.H.** in part of castle); many lovely gothic churches including the *Frauenkirche* (on the market square) which has clock with famous set of mechanical figures (the *Männleinlaufen*) showing seven electors paying homage to Emperor Charles IV; clock constructed 1509, plays at 12 noon daily; many associations with troubadours and *Meistersinger;* large Germanic National Museum, including interesting collection of toys and dolls. *Nuremberg* is centre of German toy industry and *Lebkuchen* (gingerbreads) are a special *Nuremberg* delicacy.

From *Bamberg* follow **R.5(ii)** to *Forchheim* (**Y.H.**) and turn into valley of R. *Wiesent*, entry to *Fränkische Schweiz*, one of many so-called "little Switzerlands", characterised by steep-walled valleys, jagged rock formations, summits rising to about 2,000 ft., caves, picturesque villages. **Y.Hs.** at *Gössweinstein, Streitberg* and *Pottenstein*, in heart of wild rocky country.

Through *Pegnitz* N. to **Bayreuth,** much baroque and rococo architecture, Festival Opera House, goal of Wagnerian devotees for annual festival July-August (**Y.H.**).

E. from *Bayreuth* into *Fichtelgebirge*.

The Fichtelgebirge

The *Fichtelgebirge* (Spruce Mountains) are horse-shoe shaped range, extensively covered with spruce forests; granite peaks rise to 3,000 ft.

GERMANY

These mountains are noteworthy as being watershed of tributaries of three main rivers of Germany—*Elbe, Danube* and *Rhine*. Excellent walking and ski-ing country. (*See* Footpath Routes.)

Main highway through mountains is **B.303**, *Ostmarkstrasse,* but cyclists will find secondary road preferable, branching from **B.2** near crossing of *autobahn*. Ascend *Steinach* valley to *Oberwarmensteinach* (**Y.H.**) at foot of *Ochsenkopf* (3,360 ft.) one of two main peaks of central part of range; wintersports centre. Beyond *Fichtelberg* join **B.303** for *Wunsiedel,* pleasant small resort (**Y.H.**); on *Luisenburg* (to S. of road) is extraordinary maze of rock used as background for open-air theatre performances in summer.

From *Marktredwitz* follow *Ostmarkstrasse* through the *Oberpfälzerwald,* with many **Y.Hs**, to *Cham,* northern gateway to the *Bavarian Forest.*

The Bavarian Forest

The frontier between Germany and Czechoslovakia is formed by a mountain barrier, heavily forested, completely unspoilt and little visited even by German tourists. Northern spur of forest is *Oberpfälzerwald,* while Czech side is known as Bohemian Forest. Forest extends unbroken into the Bavarian Forest (*Bayerischer Wald*) skirting *Danube* for some 90 miles. 70 years ago travellers were advised to take a pistol for defence against wild animals. Region is still sparsely populated, with hardy foresters and peasants. Many local festival plays, linked with ancient folk-lore. Many **Y.Hs**, often day's walk between them.

Cyclists can follow **B.85** for whole length of forest to *Passau,* and walkers can make use of road-rail bus service (*Cham-Passau,* 88 miles, 5 hrs., through-service daily). *Furth im Wald* (12 miles N.E. *Cham*) where picturesque killing of realistic dragon takes place on second Sunday in August (the *Drachenstich*) (**Y.H.**). Highest peak, *Grosser Arber* (4,780 ft.) with beautiful *Arbersee* below, can be climbed from *Bayer. Eisenstein* (**Y.H.**) or *Bodenmais*. Further S. peak of *Grosser Rachel* (4,765 ft.) accessible from **Y.H.** at *Waldhäuser;* nearer to the same hostel is the bare, rock-strewn summit of the *Lusen* (4,452 ft.) with one of most extensive views in Forest. For footpath routes see page 209.

Finally, *Passau,* southern approach to forest, is small town of character, standing at junction of *Inn* and *Danube;* cathedral has huge church organ (17,000 pipes); daily recitals in summer. (**Y.H.**) Good rail connections, also *Danube* steamers to Austria (*Passau* to *Linz* in 4 hrs., to *Vienna* in 13 hrs.).

R.6. Mainz to Munich by the "Romantic Road" (225 miles)

Named *die Romantische Strasse* by the tourist industry, it describes the route from *Würzburg* on R. *Main* to *Füssen* in Alps by road through series of picturesque places and areas in *Franconia* (see **R.5**) and *Upper Bavaria*. Cyclists will find main road busy with tourist traffic and should follow side-road links where possible.

From *Mainz* follow R. *Main* (dull stretch) to **Frankfurt,** formerly prosperous merchant city, home of German liberalism and of wealthy Jewish

196

families such as Rothschilds. Nazi rule and war brought ruin and devastation, but city has regained old commercial importance. Many associations with poet Goethe. Goethe House, No. 23, *am Grossen Hirschgraben*. Y.H. in modern riverside building.

Through *Offenbach* (famous for leather goods) and *Aschaffenburg*; (Y.H.) main valley narrows and acquires great charm, winding its way in huge bends past delightful old market towns like *Miltenberg* (Y.H.) and *Wertheim* (Y.H.), crowded with timbered houses.

The Spessart

R.6(i) Aschaffenburg to Wertheim by the Spessart, 32 miles. An alternative to the *Main* valley route. Trunk road B.8 is attractive though busy, crossing highest part of Spessart, but cyclists and walkers will wish to leave it to explore the side-roads and paths.

This is a triangle of forested hill country, some 1,000 ft. high, enclosed by huge bend of R. *Main*. Oak and beech trees, including some of oldest trees in Germany around *Rohrbrunn*, alternate with pines. Southern portion, centred on village of *Rohrbrunn* (on B.8) is most attractive. Highest point is *Geiersberg* (1,900 ft.) above *Rohrbrunn*. Nature reserve round *Rohrberg*. Most visited place is 15th century castle of *Mespelbrunn* on by-road from B.8, 10 miles S.E. of *Aschaffenburg*; castle stands on island in lake among woods; magnificent Hall of Knights. Y.H. at *Krausenbach*, 3 miles S.W. of *Mespelbrunn*. For footpath routes see page 209.

R.6(ii) Wertheim to Würzburg, 25 miles. Würzburg, old university town, seat of bishop, many masterpieces of baroque architecture; *Residenz*—Palace of the Prince-Bishops, but town damaged by war-time bombing. Y.H. *Würzburg* is official starting point of "Romantic Road" (see heading of R.6.).

At *Wertheim* route leaves *Main* to follow its tributary, the *Tauber*, an equally charming river. At *Bad Mergentheim* (Y.H.)., old town and spa on the plateau, proceed via *Weikersheim* (castle, worth visiting) and *Creglingen* (Y.H.), precious wood-carved altarpiece of the Virgin. To **Rothenburg ob der Tauber** (Y.H.) one of most extraordinary towns in Europe, almost unchanged from the Middle Ages; it is surrounded by a massive city wall, with numerous towers which give a fine view over the red gabled roofs and narrow valleys.

Southwards to *Feuchtwangen* (Y.H.), and on to *Dinkelsbühl*, (Y.H.), another medieval town, as is *Nördlingen*, (Y.H.) though neither equals *Rothenburg*. At *Dinkelsbühl* a historical festival, the *Kinderzeche*, is held in mid-July to commemorate saving of town from destruction in Thirty-Years' War.

At *Donauwörth* (Y.H.), on the R. *Danube (Donau)*, route enters Bavarian district of **Swabia** *(Schwaben,)* one of the historical but imprecisely defined regions like *Franconia*. The *Swabians* have a reputation, even among Germans, for their hard work.

Augsburg is large medieval city, famous in its day for wealthy merchant families; painter Holbein born here. Dürer, Titian and others worked here. Modern industries (Diesel engines and aeroplanes). Y.H. near cathedral. Good view of city from *Perlach* tower, adjacent to town hall. *Fuggerei*, a complex of alms-houses built in 1519 by Jakob Fugger, merchant prince and financier to the Habsburgs.

At *Augsburg* leave "Romantic Road" turning S.E. to *Munich*.

197

GERMANY

Munich, capital of *Bavaria*, third largest city of Germany, intellectual, artistic, industrial centre; many historical buildings destroyed or damaged in war, now rebuilt. Brick-built *Frauenkirche* with famous twin dome-capped towers, symbol of the city, has remarkable mechanical clock with enamelled copper figures which daily perform knights' tournament and shepherds' dance; *St. Nepomuk* church (fine rococo); *Deutsches Museum* one of finest science museums in world, fine art collection in *Pinakothek* galleries; *Hofbräuhaus*, world's most famous beer-drinking establishment. Imposing broad streets; *Prinzregentenstrasse*, one of main shopping streets, *Maximilianstrasse*, *Ludwigstrasse*. On clear days a view of the distant Alps may be had from the tower of the ruined *St. Peter's Church* and a white disc is displayed when visibility is good. On outskirts of city is *Nymphenburg Palace*, fine baroque building in lovely park with pavilions and lakes; *Amalienburg*, hunting lodge in the park, decorated in sumptuous rococo. Y.H. and youth guest house in city.

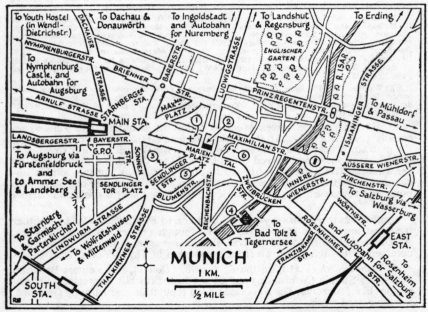

1. *Frauenkirche.* 2. *Town Hall.* 3. *St. Nepomuk Church* 4. *German Museum.* 5. *St. Peter's Church.* 6. *Hofbräuhaus.*

South-West Germany

The state of *Baden-Württemberg* occupies the south-west of Germany in the angle of the *Rhine* and Lake *Constance*. It is an area of great variety and charm—orchards, wooded uplands, winding rivers, old towns, villages and castles and, above all, from the youth hosteller's point of view, the *Black Forest*. The eastern portion of *Württemberg* is often called *Swabia* (*Schwaben*), an area which overlaps into *Bavaria* (see R.6).

R.7. Mainz to Lake Constance via the Black Forest (about 240 miles)

A fine route, keeping to the hill and mountain country above the *Rhine* valley. Rail from *Mainz* to *Freiburg* (*Black Forest*) by fast train in 3 hrs. Rail journey from *London* to *Freiburg* via *Ostend/Cologne* in 18-20 hrs., return fare £42·90. Post bus in summer from *Freiburg* to *Schaffhausen*, rail connection to *Constance*.

From *Mainz* to *Darmstadt*, across flat *Rhine* valley, journey by rail advisable. Leave *Darmstadt* (industrial town, Y.H.) by B.3., the *Bergstrasse* which skirts *Odenwald* Hills; particularly mild climate here—spring comes earlier than elsewhere in Germany and fruit blossom is fine sight. Succession of charming villages; vineyards; wine festival at *Bensheim* in autumn. Several Y.Hs.

The Odenwald

R.7(i) Bensheim to Miltenberg via the Odenwald, 46 miles. Road B.47, named the *Nibelungenstrasse*, is supposed to mark route to the *Nibelungen* (from Wagner's "Death of Siegfried"). It crosses (from W. to E.) the *Odenwald* forest, a compact woodland area between Rivers *Main* and *Neckar*. Western portion (above *Bergstrasse*) has deciduous trees, fruit and vineyards, and is substantially populated. Eastern portion is coniferous forest, wilder and less frequented.

Ascend from *Bensheim*; to N. is peak of *Melibocus* (1,690 ft.) good view, much visited; *Lindenfels*, health resort. Southwards to pleasant area around *Waldmichelbach*—Y.H.—and the 1,900 ft. *Tromm*. *Michelstadt*, *Erbach* (Y.H.) and *Amorbach* (Y.H.) are all very picturesque towns, 1,100 years old or more. At *Miltenberg* reach R. *Main* (see R.6).

Heidelberg, Germany's oldest (1386) and most famous university, charmingly situated on R. *Neckar*, with many quaint corners and buildings, particularly in and around the *Hauptstrasse* at foot of ruined castle, magnificently illuminated in summer; concerts and festivals held in courtyard. Y.H. Funicular railway to *Königstuhl* (1,846 ft., fine view). Famous promenade—the Philosophers' Path—on slope above N. bank of river.

R.7(ii) Heidelberg to Ulm via Neckar and Schwabische Alb, 136 miles. By rail (via *Heilbronn* and *Stuttgart*) in about 4½ hrs. By coach as far as *Heilbronn* in 2 hrs.

R. *Neckar*, flowing through gorge between *Odenwald* and hill country to S. is most attractive; vineyards, old castles; picturesque old towns and villages: *Dilsberg* (Y.H.) for *Neckarsteinach* where four castles dominate the river. *Eberbach* (Y.H.) probably most beautiful point on river; rail and road into *Odenwald*. *Mosbach* (fine Y.H.) has light railway into *Odenwald*. Near *Bad Wimpfen* R. *Neckar* joined by two tributaries: *Jagst* and *Kocher*, flowing through rolling wooded limestone plateau of *Hohenlohe*. *Heilbronn* (Y.H.), former free city.

S. and E. of *Heilbronn* stretches Swabian Forest, little known country similar to *Black Forest* but less lofty (rising to less than 2,000 ft.); small streams, sleepy villages, charcoal burners can still be encountered; central points: *Backnang* and *Murrhardt* (Y.H.).

Stuttgart, capital of *Baden-Württemberg*, economic and cultural centre of S.W. Germany. Noted for lovely setting between hills and vineyards. Fine modern architecture. Y.H. on heights to E. of town. Famous engineering works: *Mercedes-Benz, Bosch*.

GERMANY

The Schwäbische Alb

Road B.10 from *Stuttgart* to *Ulm* crosses the *Schwäbische Alb*, a plateau over 100 miles long, with white rocks, deep valleys, heights rising to over 3,000 ft. Forms continuation of *Swiss Jura*, hence sometimes called *Swabian Jura*, with similar rock formations—much limestone, many gorges and caves. Northern slope falls steeply to R. *Neckar*, with fortresses on rocky summits; southern slope falls gently to R. *Danube*. Many beech forests. As fine a walking country as *Black Forest*, but less well known; some Y.H. and huts of *Schwäbischer Albverein* and *Naturfreunde*.

Highest levels at S.W. end, known as *Heuberg*; above *Balingen* (Y.H.) several points above 3,000 ft.; good ski-ing. Castle of *Hohenzollern* family, rebuilt 19th century, 5 m. N.W., *Balingen*. Y.H. at *Tübingen* and *Sigmaringen*. N. and S. approaches to *Alb*. Central portion known as *Rauhe Alb* between *Reutlingen* (Y.H.) and *Geislingen*; some Y.Hs in between. Many well-marked footpaths; see page 209.

Ulm, ancient imperial city and modern industrial, commercial and route centre on *Danube*; fine Gothic cathedral, with highest spire in world (528 ft.), beautiful porch; other medieval buildings; well-planned museum, re-built post-war; riverside promenade, new bridges. *New Ulm*, across *Danube* in Bavaria, has interesting modern buildings, including Catholic church of striking design. (Y.H.).

South from *Heidelberg* through unexciting country to *Karlsruhe* (Y.H.), former princely city now busy with lawyers and technologists. 18th-century, fan-shaped town plan.

The Black Forest

From *Pforzheim* (S.E. of *Karlsruhe*) almost to the Swiss frontier, some 100 miles away, stretches the *Black Forest* (*Schwarzwald*) one of finest walking districts in Europe. The forest is no more "black" than any other pine forest, but its extent is larger. The summits above about 4,000 ft. are largely grass-covered, and from them—as from many intervening ridges—there are wide views over the forest, with its patches of meadowland, mountain streams and nestling villages. The northern part is the more richly wooded, with *Hornisgrinde* (3,820 ft.) as the highest point; the southern area, more open in appearance, has several greater heights, including *Belchen* (4,637 ft.) and the *Feldberg* (4,900 ft.) highest of all.

Villages are fascinating, with shingled cottages, steeply-pitched thatched farmhouses, centuries old. Sundays and holidays bring forth many types of authentic if somewhat local costumes.

Whole area is well provided with accommodation either in Y.H. or *Naturfreunde* huts, most of which are open to hostel members.

Walkers will, of course, follow the admirably marked footpaths, of which there are three running from N. to S. with connecting links, as mentioned below. For cyclists there is the *Schwarzwald-Hochstrasse* through northern section from *Baden-Baden* to *Freudenstadt*, scenically very fine, but busy.

Main tourist centres, from N. to S. are *Baden-Baden*, (Y.H.) fashionable spa elegant early 19th-century casino and *Kurhaus*; *Sohlberghaus*, an isolated Y.H. in magnificent situation high above *Ottenhöfen* near *Hornisgrinde* peak and *Freudenstadt* (Y.H.) a hill-top town with arcaded square. *Alpirsbach* (Y.H.) and on to *Triberg*, (Y.H.) at junction of three valleys, noted for cuckoo-clocks; nearby *Gutach* waterfall, 500 ft. cascade.

Freiburg (*Freiburg-im-Breisgau*) is chief town of *Black Forest*, many fine old buildings, carefully restored Gothic cathedral, with open lace-work spire; the *Kaufhaus*, 16th century merchants' hall; the *Schwabentor*, an old city gate. (Y.H.).

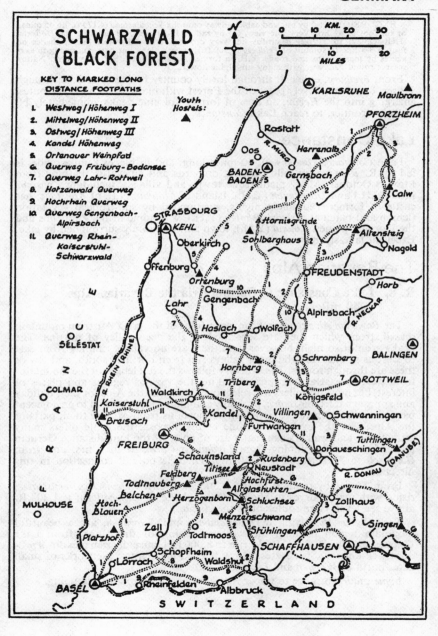

SCHWARZWALD
(BLACK FOREST)

KEY TO MARKED LONG
DISTANCE FOOTPATHS

1. Westweg/Höhenweg I
2. Mittelweg/Höhenweg II
3. Ostweg/Höhenweg III
4. Kandel Höhenweg
5. Ortenauer Weinpfad
6. Querweg Freiburg-Bodensee
7. Querweg Lahr-Rottweil
8. Hotzenwald Querweg
9. Hochrhein Querweg
10. Querweg Gengenbach-
    Alpirsbach
11. Querweg Rhein-
    Kaiserstuhl-
    Schwarzwald

GERMANY

EXCURSIONS: (a) by bus and cable railway onto the *Schauinsland* (4,173 ft.)in 45 mins., or on foot in 4½ hrs. Very fine view. (b) by rail in 35-50 mins. 18 miles up the *Höllental* (Hell Valley) to *Titisee*, beautiful but very crowded lake-side resort (Y.H.) thence on foot in 3-4 hrs. to summit of *Feldberg* (4,900 ft.); superb views but over-run owing to easy access by many paths and roads. Y.H. in former *Hebelhof* hotel, S.E. of summit. Nature reserve round *Feldberg*, with many sub-alpine flowers.

From *Freiburg*, either S. through lovely country to *Basel*, or S.E. through *Titisee*, by equally lovely parts of the Forest with many Y.Hs on both routes, emerging into the *Hegau*, an area of former volcanic peaks, immediately N. of Swiss frontier, to reach Lake *Constance*.

Lake Constance

Lake *Constance* (*Bodensee*), 40 miles long, and in places 8 miles wide, is fed by R. *Rhine*; very mild climate; orchards and vineyards; bathing from May to October. Many picturesque towns and villages, including *Konstanz* itself (Y.H.) and *Uberlingen* (Y.H.). Island of *Mainau*, N.E. of *Konstanz*, has castle of former Teutonic Knights, surrounded by sub-tropical vegetation (lemon and banana). *Friedrichshafen* (Y.H.), was home of the Zeppelins and the Dornier 'planes. *Lindau* (Y.H.), town almost entirely surrounded by lake. Excellent lake-steamer service.

The Bavarian Alps

R. 8. Lake Constance to Salzburg via the Bavarian Alps (240 miles)

The *Bavarian Alps* represent the outer folds of the great Austrian mountain massif, from which they are separated by the deep valley of the *Inn*. The peaks are not so high, however, and there are no valleys running from east to west as in Austria. The main valleys run from north to south, and few of these are through routes. The itinerary follows the full length of the mountains from west to east as a means of linking the various regions and places of interest, but most hostellers will select one portion of the Alps for their holiday and approach it from *Munich*, probably combining it with a visit to an adjacent part of Austria. There are good rail connections from *Munich* to all parts of the Alps. For the cyclist with time at his disposal the route offers many attractions, and walkers can make use of parts of the long-distance German postal bus service running from *Lindau* to *Garmisch* in 6 hrs. and from *Garmisch* to *Berchtesgaden* in 10 hrs. There is no rail connection in this direction.

From *Lindau* by roads B.18 and B.308, start of the *Deutsche Alpenstrasse*, rising with many curves to about 3,000 ft. Lake *Constance* itself is 1,300 ft. above sea level. Here route enters the *Allgäu*.

The *Allgäu Alps*, lying in *Württemberg* and *Schwaben*, are a beautiful mountain region forming the western section of the range, from Lake *Constance* to the R. *Lech*. Peaks rise to 8,000 ft. Unusually rich meadows produce well-known soft cheeses. Many fine ski-ing centres. Networks of small lakes north of *Wangen* and *Füssen*. (Y.H.)

Immenstadt, entrance to upper *Allgäu* on R. *Iller*; good ski-jumping.

R.8(i) Immenstadt to Oberstdorf, 13 miles. Road B.19. *Sonthofen, Oberstdorf,* alt. 2,700 ft. mountain centre giving access to seven valleys, including *Klein-Walser-Tal* (across Austrian frontier but uses German money, as no road communication with rest of Austria through *Bregenzer* Forest). Two Y.H.: at *Spielmannsau,* 5 miles S. of *Oberstdorf* and at *Kornau,* W. of *Oberstdorf.*

EXCURSIONS: Cable railways to *Nebelhorn* (6,279 ft.) cable railway followed by chairlift, and to *Kanzelwand* (6,800 ft., 16 mins. journey, valley station at *Riezlern*). *Nebelhorn* can be climbed on foot in 4 hrs. Circular trip on foot round slopes of *Hofat,* via *Oytal* and *Dietersbach,* 8 hrs.

From *Immenstadt* by B.310 to *Füssen* (**Y.H.**) charmingly situated town on R. *Lech*; fine castle, parts of town walls preserved. Follow side road into *Ammergebirge,* foothills of the Austrian *Wetterstein* mountains, for two castles of *Neuschwanstein* and *Hohenschwangau,* former residences of Bavarian royal house. **Neuschwanstein** is one of most romantic sights in Europe, fantastic turrets and towers, perched on rock; building begun in 1869 for King Ludwig II, patron of Wagner.

From *Hohenschwangau* bridle-path (3½ hrs. on foot—cycling difficult) to *Ammerwald* Hotel, just inside Austrian frontier, then small metalled road back into Germany and through unspoiled nature reserve of *Ammer* valley, 2½ hrs. on foot, to *Linderhof,* another of Ludwig II's castles, this time in style of 18th century France with fountains, terraces and statues. Reach main road (B.23) near **Oberammergau,** famous village of the Passion Play; play first performed 1634 in thanksgiving for end of plague, then every ten years; requires over 1,200 performers, all village people; sincerity of religious presentation maintained; next performance 1980. 10 miles N.W. is the *Wies* Church (1745–54), splendid example of the Bavarian rococo. (**Y.H.**).

Garmisch-Partenkirchen, (Y.H.) twin villages at head of *Loisach* valley, famous winter-sports centre; huge ski and skating stadiums. *Garmisch* (W. side of valley) is fashionable and expensive; *Partenkirchen* quieter and cheaper. Brightly-painted timber houses, peasant costumes.

EXCURSIONS: (a) by *Zugspitz* rack railway to *Schneefernerhaus,* 1¼ hrs., then by cable railway in 4 mins. to summit of **Zugspitze** (9,720 ft.) Germany's highest mountain. (b) by cable railway in 10 mins. to summit of *Wank* (5,677 ft.), (c) by cable railway in 8 mins. to the *Kreuzeck* (5,630 ft.), (N.B. Both *Wank* and *Kreuzeck* can be ascended on foot, each in about 3½ hrs.). Ascent of *Zugspitze* (via *Raintal*) for experienced climbers only, 10-11 hrs.

From *Garmisch* to *Mittenwald* by B.2, 11 miles, or by footpath via *Ferchen* valley and *Elmau,* 5½ hrs. *Mittenwald* lies in *Isar* valley, dividing *Wetterstein* from *Karwendel* mountains; in Middle Ages a key transit point for goods from Venice and Orient to S. German cities; in 17th century Italian-trained violin maker founded now famous violin industry; violinmakers' school and museum. Many gaily frescoed houses. (**Y.H.**).

EXCURSIONS: (a) by chair-lift and cable railway to the *Hoher-Kranzberg* (4,565 ft.); on foot in 2-2½ hrs. (b) rail to *Scharnitz,* then on foot up lovely *Karwendel* valley (4-day trip).

B.11 to **Walchensee,** large lake with steep, forest-clothed banks, dark green waters, background of alpine peaks. Y.H. at *Urfeld* (N. shore).

EXCURSIONS: (a) Hydro-electric works (water tunnel from lake to *Kochel See*). (b) tour of lake on foot–6 to 7 hrs. (c) on foot in three hrs., or by chair-lift in 11 mins, on to *Herzogstand* (5,680 ft.) with magnificent views; thence by narrow, precipitous ridge path in 1½ hrs. to neighbouring peak of *Heimgarten* (5,875 ft.), with footpath link to *Ohlstadt* in *Loisach* valley (3 hrs.).

From *Urfeld,* pleasant by-road through *Jachenau* valley with ancient peasant culture; farmhouses often in possession of same families for centuries. *Lenggries,* small resort on R. *Isar*; where timber rafts are floated downstream; **Y.H.** (6 hrs. on foot from *Urfeld*).

From *Lenggries* to *Scharling* (**Y.H.**) on the *Tegernsee* lake is 25 miles by road, via *Bad Tölz*, picturesque old town and spa, but choice of pleasant footpaths in 5 to 6 hrs. *Tegernsee* is sophisticated, with many small villas, and not so attractive as smaller neighbour *Schliersee*. Again, choice of footpaths to **Y.H.** at *Josefstal* above *Schliersee*, about 4 hrs. Mountain road, rough in places, via *Bayrischzell;* mountain resort, excellent ski-ing, down to B.15, or footpath via *Birkenstein* onto summit of *Wendelstein* (6,028 ft.—3 hrs. climb from *Birkenstein*) and thence by rack railway (55 mins.) or on foot (3 hrs.) down to *Brannenburg*, in upper *Inn* Valley; same river which forms Swiss *Engadine*, but now a powerful stream. Valley bottom lightly wooded, sides rise in terraces with fine views. Continue through *Rosenheim*; textile industry, rail junction; to *Sims See*, good bathing, and **Chiemsee**, largest of Bavarian Lakes; low-lying, marshy area, lacks grandeur of mountain-girt lakes, but notable for magnificent castle of *Herrenchiemsee*, on island of that name, built by same King Ludwig II of Bavaria who was responsible for *Neuschwanstein*, *Linderhof* and other fantastic buildings. *Herrenchiemsee* is modelled on *Versailles* (Hall of Mirrors, with 2,600 candlesticks); open to public daily, but best seen on Saturday nights when castle illuminated with candles. Steamers from *Stock* (near *Prien*) in 15 mins. **Y.H.** at *Prien*.

Skirt N. shore of lake, via **Y.H.** at *Hemhof*, pass *Traunstein* (**Y.H.**) spa and rail junction and southwards to small resort of *Ruhpolding*.

R.8(ii) Ruhpolding to Reit im Winkl, 15 miles. On the German Alpine Road, leading into one of less well-known parts of Bavarian Alps. *Reit im Winkl* has good ski-ing (very heavy snowfalls, excellent learners' slopes). *Nattersberg-Alm* 3,300 ft., is approached from *Seegatterl*, on Alpine Road, by steep path.

EXCURSION: from *Nattersberg-Alm:* ascent of *Fellhorn* (5,800 ft., 3 hrs.) with fine view over Alps.

From *Ruhpolding* via German Alpine Road (B.305) into grandiose mountain scenery of the *Berchtesgadener Land*, corner of German territory projecting into Austria. **Berchtesgaden** is picturesque town, famous for woodcarving, ski-ing and as one-time home of Hitler, whose mountain eyrie on the *Obersalzberg* was dynamited after the war. Dominated by the *Watzmann* (8,704 ft., can be climbed from *Ramsau-Wimbachbrücke* via *Münchener* Hut in 6-7 hrs.). 3 miles S. of *Berchtesgaden* lies **Königssee**, one of most beautiful alpine lakes, with clear green water 580 ft. deep surrounded by almost vertical cliffs rising to nearly 6,000 ft. **Y.H.** in *Strub*, S.E. of town.

EXCURSIONS: (a) circular tour on lake by motor-boat, 1 hr. 50 mins. (b) by cable railway from N. end of *Königssee* on to the *Jenner* (6,149 ft.) 22 mins. (c) by cable railway on to the *Obersalzberg* (3,345 ft.), 10 mins.; or on foot from *Berchtesgaden* in 1 hr. (d) by lake boat to *St. Bartholomä* on *Königssee* thence on foot (2-3 days) via *Funtensee* Hut, *Steinernes Meer* (an extraordinary wilderness of boulders) and *Reimann* Hut to *Saalfelden* in Austria.

From *Berchtesgaden* to *Bad Reichenhall*, spa; concentrated saline springs gave rise to important salt trade in Middle Ages. Interesting old monastery of *St. Zeno*. Cross frontier into Austria for *Salzburg*.

Footpath Routes

In this section fuller information is given about the principal networks of waymarked paths. The waymarking is not always complete, and a large scale, detailed, map is indispensable. The guidebooks mentioned are all printed in German, but some knowledge of the language is in any case desirable on a walking trip using these paths, as they pass through areas out of range of tourist traffic.

ALLGÄU
Path-marking by *Deutscher Alpenverein.*
Maps: Zumteins *Allgäuer Alpen,* scale 1:50,000; *Freytag & Berndt* 1:100,000, sheet 35.
Routes: Magnificent high-level path along E. side of *Allgäu* basin, from *Hindelang* via *Willersalpe* Hut, *Prinz Luitpold* Hut, *Kempter* Hut, *Rappensee* Hut to *Lechleiten* in *Lech* Valley (Austria). Route crosses and re-crosses frontier. 5 to 7 days' strenuous walking; only for experienced mountain walkers. Described in detail in Grieben's *"Allgäu".*

BAVARIAN FOREST
Path-marking by *Bayerischer-Wald-Verein, Straubing.*
Maps: *Fritsch Bayerischer Wald,* 1:100,000.

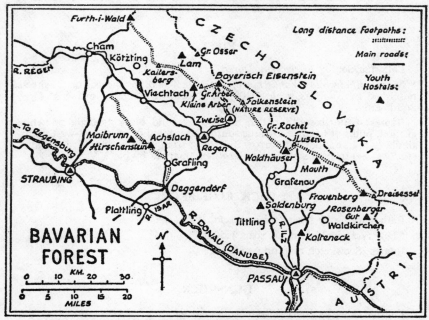

Routes: Principal marked path is the *östlicher Hauptwanderweg* (see sketchmap above), marked by green triangle. It follows highest ridges of mountains from *Furth* in the N. to *Obernzell* on *Danube* E. of *Passau.* Can be covered in 10-14 days, but some accommodation in inns must be used.

GERMANY

BLACK FOREST

Path-marking by *Schwarzwaldverein, Freiburg i.Breisgau.*

Maps: *Schwarzwaldverein,* scale 1:50,000, in 10 sheets but, in view of excellent waymarking, *Reise und Verkehrsverlag,* scale 1:75,000, in 3 sheets, are adequate.

Routes: 4 main north-south paths (see sketch-map on page 205) waymarked as follows

Eastern path (*Ostweg*)	..	Horizontal diamond, half red, half black.
Middle path (*Mittelweg*)	..	Red horizontal diamond with white vertical strip.
Western path (*Westweg*)	..	Red horizontal diamond.

Kandel path (*Kandelhöhenweg*) Red horizontal diamond with white K.

The many transverse and subsidiary paths are marked by various forms of horizontal diamond with blue or yellow in the design.

EIFEL

Path-marking by *Eifelverein, Düren.*

Maps: *Eifelverein Wanderkarte,* scale 1:50,000, 6 sheets, or 3 sheets published by *Stollfuss,* scale 1:100,000; North-west *Eifel,* North-east *Eifel,* South *Eifel.*

Routes: 6 north-south paths, marked by solid black triangle on white ground, point of triangle towards southern terminal point. 6 east-west paths, similarly marked, but with arrow instead of triangle. Also the "Crater Path" (*Vulkanweg*) from *Andernach* to *Gerolstein,* marked by black V.

FICHTELGEBIRGE

Path-marking by *Fichtelgebirgsverein, Wunsiedel.*

Map: *Fichtelgebirgsverein,* scale 1:50,000.

Routes: See sketch map on page 212.

HUNSRÜCK

Path-marking by *Hunsrückverein, Bernkastel.*

Map: *Hunsrück,* scale 1:100,000, published by *Stollfuss.*

Route: Main path runs W. to E. from *Merzig (Saar)* to *Bacharach (Rhein)* following highest ridges. Marked by white X. Stages are as follows:—
Merzig-Weiskirchen (**Y.H.**) 6½ hrs. *Weiskirchen-Hermeskeil* (**Y.H.**) 4¼ hrs.

Hermeskeil via *Erbeskopf* (highest point of *Hunsrück*, 2,600 ft.) to *Allenbach* 7½ hrs. (5 miles N.W. of *Allenbach* is Y.H. *Morbach*). *Allenbach* via *Katzeloch* to *Kempfeld*, 3½ hrs. (*Kempfeld* to *Idar-Oberstein* (**Y.H.**) 9 miles, buses). *Kempfeld* via *Idarkopf* (fine view) to *Rhaunen*, *Schneppenbach* and *Gemünden*, 10 hrs. *Gemünden* via *Alteburg*, forestry house *Thiergarten*, *Hochsteinchen* (view) and *Rheinböllen* to *Bacharach* (**Y.H.**) 9 hrs.

LÜNEBURG HEATH

Path-marking by *Lüneburg Heath Tourist Association.*

Map: *Niedersächsische Landesvermessungsamt*, scale 1:100,000, sheet "*Zentralheide*" shows major part of area.

Routes: Best route is *Niedersachsenweg*, running N.-S. from *Harburg* (South of *Hamburg*) via *Jesteburg*, *Undeloh* (**Y.H.**), *Wilseder Berg* (in nature reserve), *Soltau* (**Y.H.**), *Müden* (**Y.H.**), *Celle* (**Y.H.**). Total distance 87 miles. Marking interrupted between *Haverbeck* (S. of *Wilseder Berg*) and *Soltau*. Fuller description of this and 5 other main routes in Grieben's "*Lüneburger Heide*".

MOSEL

Path-marking by *Hunsrückverein, Bernkastel.*

Map: *Das Moseltal*, scale 1:100,000, published by *Stollfuss.*

Routes: There are two *Moselhöhenwege* (high-level paths) following course of river (often at considerable distance from it), both marked by white M. On right (S.E.) bank path marked completely from *Brodenbach* (half-an-hour by train from *Koblenz* to *Löf*, then ferry) to *Trier*, total walking time about 31 hrs.; breaks can be made at Y.Hs at *Brodenbach and Bernkastel*, then no Y.H. until *Trier*. On left (N.W. bank) path marked from *Güls* (outskirts of *Koblenz*) to *Karden* (8½ hrs.) and *Cochem* (**Y.H.**) to *Mehring* (18 hrs.). From *Mehring* to *Trier* follow right bank (3 hrs.) Y.Hs do not provide suitable stages for left bank, but a link to *Bernkastel* on other side is easily made. See *Eifel* footpath map on page 194.

ODENWALD

Path-marking by *Odenwaldklub, Darmstadt.*

Map: *Reise und Verkehrsverlag* No. 14, scale 1:100,000, includes a text.

Routes: 27 main paths.

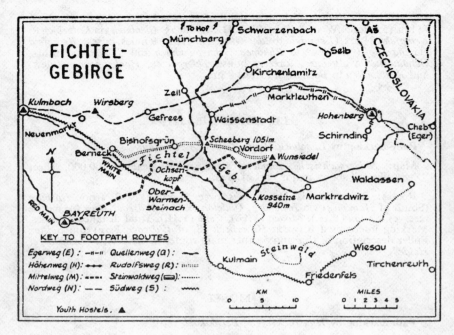

FICHTEL-
GEBIRGE

KEY TO FOOTPATH ROUTES

Egerweg (E) : –"–"   Quellenweg (Q) : ⌐⌐⌐
Höhenweg (H): ♦♦♦   Rudolfsweg (R) : ▒▒▒▒
Mittelweg (M): ▬▬▬▬   Steinwaldweg (▭): ∙∙∙∙∙∙
Nordweg (N) : ▬ ▬   Südweg (S) : ∿∿∿∿

Youth Hostels. ▲

RHINE

Path-marking by various local clubs through whose territory the paths pass.

Map: *Hunsrück*, scale 1:100,000, published by *Stolfuss*.

Routes: There are two *Rheinhöhenwege* (high-level paths) following course of river, often at considerable distance from it but giving fine views from hills above. Both paths marked by white R.

The path on the right (East) bank is complete from *Beuel* (opposite *Bonn*) to *Wiesbaden*; it can be covered in 12 days, as follows:—*Beuel-Honnef* (**Y.H.**) 6 hrs, *Honnef-Linz* 5½ hrs. *Linz-Altwied* 6 hrs. *Altwied-Sayn* 5 hrs. *Sayn-Ehrenbreitstein* (opposite *Koblenz*), 7 hrs. *Ehrenbreitstein-Niederlahnstein* 2¾ hrs. *Niederlahnstein-Bornhofen* 7½ hrs. *Bornhofen-St. Goarshausen* (**Y.H.** at *St. Goar*) 5 hrs. *St. Goarshausen-Lorch* (**Y.H.**) 6½ hrs. *Lorch-Rüdesheim* (**Y.H.**) 5¼ hrs. *Rüdesheim-Schlangenbad* 7 hrs. *Schlangenbad-Wiesbaden* (**Y.H.**) 6 hrs.

The path on the left (West) bank runs from *Bonn* to *Andernach* and from *Koblenz* to *Mainz*; it can be covered in 10 days as follows:

Bonn (Popplesdorf)-Godesberg (**Y.H.**) 3 hrs. *Godesberg-Remagen* across river at *Linz*, by ferry from *Kripp*, 6 hrs. *Remagen-Andernach* 11 hrs. Rail to *Koblenz* (**Y.H.** at *Ehrenbreitstein*). *Koblenz-Boppard* (**Y.H.**) 6 hrs. *Boppard-St. Goar* (**Y.H.**) 6 hrs. *St. Goar-Bacharach* (**Y.H.**) 6 hrs. *Bacharach-Niederheimbach* (**Y.H.** at *Lorch*, across ferry) 6 hrs. *Niederheimbach-Bingerbrück* (**Y.H.**) 6 hrs. *Bingerbrück-Heidesheim* (**Y.H.**) 6½ hrs. *Heidesheim-Mainz* (**Y.H.**) 3½ hrs.

Most travellers will wish to cover only part of route by footpath, combining this with steamer trip up or down river.

RHÖN

Path-marking by *Rhönklub, Fulda.*
Map: *Rhön*, scale 1:100,000, official map of *Rhönklub.*

Routes: (1) main N.-S. route *Tann* to *Gemünden.* (2) *Rhönhöhenweg*, N.E. to S.W., from Soviet Zone frontier near *Fladungen* to *Gemünden.* (3) Series of 7 routes running W. to E. All these routes marked by red triangle, partially duplicated by blue X of through footpath *Saar-Silesia* which runs concurrently with certain routes across area.

SAUERLAND

Path-marking throughout *Sauerland* and adjoining hill areas by *Sauerländischer Gebirgsverein, Iserlohn.*

Maps: *Wanderkarten*, scale 1:50,000, 16 sheets published by *Sauerländischer Gebirgsverein.*

Routes: More than 30 marked paths, indicated by white X. Described in detail in the *"Führer durch das Hauptwegenetz"*, published by *Sauerländischer Gebirgsverein.*

SCHWÄBISCHE ALB

Path-marking throughout *Schwäbische Alb* and several adjoining areas by *Schwäbischer Albverein.*

Maps: *Reise und Verkehrsverlag*, scale 1:100,000, 2 sheets, footpaths marked.

Routes: Two main routes, following northern and southern edges of the *Alb*, from *Donauwörth* (N.E. of *Ulm*) to *Tuttlingen* (where *Danube* and *Neckar* almost meet). Marked by red triangles with point towards *Tuttlingen.* Approach paths to main routes marked with yellow triangle (in area between two main routes) or blue triangle (in areas outside two main routes), pointing towards main route.

SPESSART

Path-marking by *Spessartbund, Aschaffenburg.*
Map: *Spessart*, scale 1:100,000, published by *Ravenstein.*

GERMANY

Routes: Complete network of marked paths. Four main high-level paths (*Höhenwege*), based on disused medieval trade roads; these are marked by initial letters in black on white ground. There are many shorter paths, marked with various symbols.

TAUNUS

Path-marking by *Taunusbund* (southern area) and *Rhein-Taunus Club* (western area).

Maps: official maps of above clubs: *Maintaunus* and *Rheintaunus*, scale 1:50,000. *Taunus*, scale 1:100,000, published by *Stolfuss*.

Routes: (1) *Eltville* (W. of *Wiesbaden*) to *Arnstein* (E. of *Nassau*) on the *Lahn;* 31 miles. Mark: horizontal diamond. (2) *Geisenheim* (E. of *Rüdesheim*) along full length of S. *Taunus* heights to *Bad Nauheim*. 69 miles. Mark: letter U resting on right side. (3) *Butzbach* (between *Bad Nauheim* and *Wetzlar*) to *Schlangenbad* (on road B.260, W. of *Wiesbaden*) via the *Feldberg*. 42 miles. Mark: letter T. From *Schlagenbad* the *Rhine* high-level path (right bank) leads to *Rüdesheim*, etc.; see under *Rhine* on page 212. (4) From *Friedrichsdorf* (N. of *Bad Homburg*) via *Usingen* to *Balduinstein* on R. *Lahn*, S.W. of *Limburg*. 56 miles. Mark: triangle.

These routes and many others described in Grieben's *"Taunus"*.

WESER HILL COUNTRY AND TEUTOBURGER FOREST

Path-marking by *Weserbergland Tourist Association* and *Teutoburger Wald Tourist Association*.

Maps: *Weserbergland*, scale 1:100,000, and *Teutoburger Wald*, scale 1:100,000.

Routes: Large number of paths marked uniformly with white X, size 6 in. x 6 in. Described in Grieben's *"Weserbergland"* and *"Teutoburger Wald"*.

GREECE

Geographical Outline

Land
The mainland of Greece is the southern extension of the *Balkan* peninsula into the *Mediterranean*, together with the coastlands of *Thrace* separating Bulgaria from the *Aegean Sea*.

The *Aegean* lies between the Greek mainland and Turkey and all its many islands, except two nearest the mouth of the *Dardanelles*, are part of Greece. South-east of the mainland lies the wide curve of islands comprising *Crete* and the *Dodecanese* and close to the west coast lie the *Ionian* islands.

Greece is a mountainous country and even the islands are, with a few volcanic exceptions, drowned extensions of the mainland ranges. The central spine is the *Pindus* range running north-north-west to south-south-east from the Albanian frontier towards the *Gulf of Corinth*. From this spine run south-eastwards a series of ranges which form the promontories of the east coast and which can be traced, partly drowned, in lines of islands in the *Aegean*. In the *Peloponnesus* the ranges follow the same general direction, but curve eastwards and then northwards in their extension in *Crete* and *Rhodes*. With some important exceptions limestone is the dominant rock.

Many peaks exceed 7,000 feet in height in *Central Greece*, the *Peloponnesus*, and in *Crete*, and several exceed 8,000 feet. *Mt. Olympus* in *Thessaly* is 9,550 feet.

Much of the scenery is moulded by the close juxtaposition of white limestone mountain ranges, tiny plains and valleys—sometimes dusty with sparse vegetation, sometimes green with olives and other trees—and deep inlets of the blue sea. It is a scenery with remarkable variety over small distances.

There are few important rivers and many are dry, or nearly so, in the summer months. In the north the lower reaches of the *Vardar* and *Struma* rivers are in Greek territory, but these rise deep in the *Balkan* peninsula.

Climate
Greece has the typical Mediterranean climate of hot dry summers with little or no rain, and mild winters. Only in the higher mountains of the north is any appreciable rain likely to fall in summer.

Average winter rainfall is heavy on the west coast and in the mountains of *Central* and *Northern Greece*, but on the east coast it is quite light. Rain in Greece tends to come in downpours interspersed with long periods of clear sunny weather. Winters are mild, particularly in the coastal regions, although the coastlands around *Salonica*, in the north, are subject to cold spells coming down from the interior of the *Balkans*.

Many visitors who do not take kindly to the summer heat, even though

211

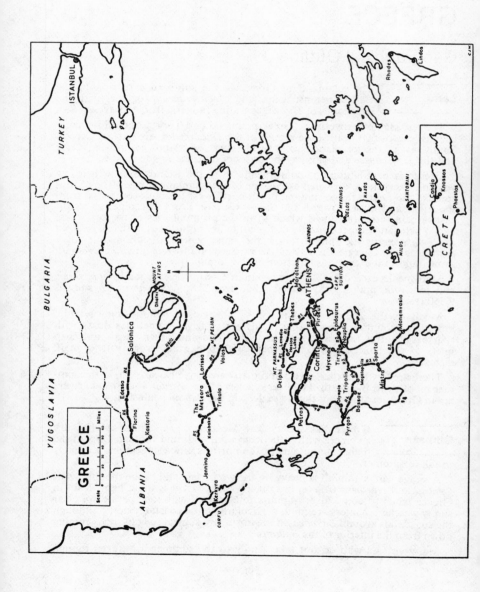

The Parthenon—one of the great monuments of Western civilization—dates from the fifth century B.C.

The Temple of Hera at Olympia, Greece.

this is tempered with afternoon sea breezes in the coastal areas, find the climate more acceptable from mid-March to the end of May, when temperatures are more like those of mid-summer in England, except that the sunshine is more reliable.

Plants and Animals Only a quarter of the land is suitable for cultivation, 15% is forest or woodland—mainly in the mountains—and no less than 60% of the country is barren or rocky.

The vegetation is very much determined by the dryness of the climate and the porous nature of the limestone soils.

Whole areas have been denuded of forest e.g. in *Attica*, by human action, and goats in particular have prevented it from returning. Forests have tended to persist in the mountains formed of crystalline rocks. Oaks and beeches, chestnuts and planes, pines and firs are found here, the latter mainly on the higher ground.

Sparse scrubland, mainly of the Mediterranean type, e.g. the maquis of the *Peloponnesus*, covers much of the uncultivated country. The Mediterranean vegetation on the lower ground is of trees, evergreen shrubs, and herbaceous plants. In *Attica* a more thorny scrubland is common.

A feature of the stony ground in the south and in the islands, in Spring, is the brilliant growth of flowers: crocus, tulip, iris, narcissus, anemone, poppy and others.

Among the fauna are porcupines, wolves, wild goats and jackals. Rarities in the remoter mountain areas include the European brown bear and the chamois. There is a great variety of birds, including eagles and vultures. Reptiles are common, especially in the *Peloponnesus* and the *Cyclades*, but only two kinds of snake are poisonous.

The People

Population Of the 9 million people nearly half live in the rural areas. *Athens*, the capital, with its port, *Piraeus*, has 1,800,000. *Salonica* (*Thessaloniki*), with 400,000, is the second city. All other towns are much smaller; the next largest is *Patras* (80,000).

It is generally supposed that the Greeks of classical times were a tall people, fair in colouring, of the Nordic racial type. Sculptures suggest as much, but how far these were a true likeness or how far they represented an ideal will probably never be known.

In the intervening centuries many non-Greek peoples have mixed with the indigenous population, e.g. Syrians, Slavs, Franks, Turks, Albanians. The Greeks of today are generally short of stature and dark in colouring.

Language Greek is spoken by all but a tiny fraction. In *Thrace* there are small pockets of Turkish speaking people and in *Macedonia* there are Slavonic speaking minorities.

Modern Greek is a direct descendant of the language of classical times, more closely related to it than, for example, is modern Italian to Latin. Its divergence is greater in pronunciation than in its written form.

GREECE

To speak of "Modern Greek" is in fact to speak of two languages—
Demotic (common) and *Katharevoussa* (pure). *Demotic* is the living spoken
language and the language of songs and ballads. *Katharevoussa* is a conscious
and artificial return to Ancient Greek. It is the official language and is taught
in schools and generally used in newspapers. What particularly distinguishes
it from *Demotic* is its refusal to use the many foreign words which have crept
into the spoken tongue. The common language is, however, gaining on the
purist form.

The written language uses, of course, the Greek alphabet. The visitor should
at least acquaint himself with the symbols corresponding to the Roman
alphabet so as to be able to read place names, menus, etc., which might
otherwise be unintelligible.

English is fairly widely understood, particularly in places frequented by
tourists.

Religion The vast majority of Greeks are of the Greek Orthodox faith,
which is the established religion under the Constitution.
There are small Moslem minorities in the north of the country.

History By 2,500 B.C., possibly earlier, a civilization flourished in
Greece—centred on *Crete*—known to us as the "Minoan".
Clear evidence of its existence was first revealed by the
excavations of Sir Arthur Evans at the *Palace of Knossos*. Who the peoples
were who evolved it and from where they came is still not known.

Some time after 2,000 B.C. the centre of civilization began to shift to the
mainland, particularly the *Peloponnesus*. This had developed by about
1,600 B.C. into what has come to be called the *"Mycenean culture"* after
one of its principal cities—*Mycenae*.

In its later stages this civilization was probably Greek speaking but it
differed in many important respects from the later "Classical" Greek
civilization, and the transition from the destruction of *Mycenae* and its
culture to the classical Greek period is obscure. Homer's story of the Trojan
War, once regarded as myth, almost certainly relates to this *Mycenean* age,
although he lived many centuries after the events related.

"Classical" Greece begins to emerge in the 8th century and by 600 B.C.
it had spread, through colonization, as far afield as *Marseilles* and the *Crimea*.

Although the Greeks were conscious and proud of their common "Hellenic" history and culture and regarded themselves as set apart from the rest
of mankind—a view which their achievements do much to support—they
were never a single "nation". They were a large number of fiercely independent city states sharing a common culture, but seldom sharing much else. By
the 5th century B.C. most of these city states had developed democratic
government, by various paths, from early monarchies through aristocratic
oligarchies. Supreme among these was *Athens*, and the prime exception to this
evolution was *Sparta*.

The golden age of Greece was the 5th century B.C., when a civilization
flourished which has never been equalled—unless civilizations are judged
merely by their material well-being. This age was ushered in by two wars
with the Persian Empire in which Greece fought for survival. The first, in

GREECE

490 B.C., was fought alone by *Athens* and was decided and won at *Marathon*. The second, ten years later, was the grand test and, for once, the Greek world united against the common enemy—except the ever treacherous *Thebes*. The Persians were defeated at sea in the battle of *Salamis*, and on land at *Plataea*. The victory left *Athens* supreme as a maritime power and on this she built what was virtually an Empire of city-states, known as the *Delian League*. In the next half-century Athens was at the height of her power, and it was during this period that Greece's greatest achievements in architecture, literature, philosophy and many other fields were witnessed. The power of *Athens*, however, was rivalled by that of *Sparta* and inevitably the two states clashed. The Peloponnesian war began in 437 B.C. and dragged on until 404 B.C. *Athens* was defeated and Greece did not recover from the devastating effect.

The hegemony of *Sparta* lasted until 371 B.C. when Thebes triumphed at the battle of *Leuctra*, but the Golden Age had ended. A weakened Greece fell prey to a new semi-Greek power in the north—*Macedonia*—under its king Philip. When Philip was assassinated (336 B.C.) his son, Alexander, succeeded him and began a new chapter in the history of Greece. In the remaining 13 years of his life he led Greek armies to conquer the Persian Empire and penetrated as far as Afghanistan and India. His Empire collapsed shortly after his death but the spread of Greek ideas into Asia had an incalculable influence on history.

Macedonia eventually came into conflict with the growing power of *Rome*. The issue was finally decided in 168 B.C. Greece passed to the Romans and for 500 years the country was in their hands. But the influence of Greece on the Roman Empire in the field of thought was profound.

When the Roman Empire split between east and west, at the beginning of the 4th century A.D., Greece came under the Eastern Empire based on *Constantinople*.

The Eastern (later, Byzantine) Empire was, however, often unable to defend its Greek territories and between the 4th and 8th centuries Greece was overrun with great destruction by Goths, Visigoths and Vandals, Huns and Slavs in turn. In 1204 a Crusade intended for the Holy Land was diverted to attack *Constantinople* and, as a result, Greece fell into the hands of the Franks.

There followed an age of strife, and, although the Byzantines returned for a short while, the country fell an easy victim to the Ottoman Turks in the 15th century. Ottoman rule lasted until the 19th century, although Greece was often a battleground between the Turks and the Venetians, and the latter held many footholds on Greek territory, particularly the islands.

The modern state of Greece was set up in 1832 after the people had risen against the Turks in the War of Independence—a long drawn out and bitter struggle. The new state consisted initially of little more than the *Peloponnesus*. Its growth was far from easy, hindered both by internal dissensions and by rivalries of the Great Powers over their interests in the *Balkans*. Little by little Greece added more to her territories—the *Ionian Islands* (from Britain) in 1864, *Thessaly* in 1881, and most of the north of the country and the *Aegean* islands in the Balkan War of 1912 (against Turkey). After the 1st World War the Greeks endeavoured to occupy the Turkish side of the *Aegean* but were driven out by Kemal Atatürk with disastrous results.

GREECE

There, but for the acquisition of the *Dodecanese* from Italy in 1947, the expansion of Greece has ended—although her interest in Cyprus is still considerable.

When Greece was freed from German occupation in 1944, civil war broke out, after a Communist attempt to gain power, and dragged on until 1949 seriously hindering the country's recovery.

Government

Since 1832 Greece has been a kingdom most of the time. The fortunes and popularity of the Monarchy have however fluctuated, and of her six kings since Independence four have been deposed and one assassinated. Between 1924 and 1935 the country was a Republic.

Since the Constitution of 1844, and more particularly since that of 1864 Greece has been a democracy. Like the Monarchy, however, the strength and popularity of the democratic institutions have fluctuated and on a number of occasions near-dictators have held power.

Resources

Greece is a poor country by West European standards. It lacks the raw materials to create the industries that have brought wealth to Western Europe and its agricultural land is under severe pressure from over-population. It is essentially an agricultural country, more than half the population being directly engaged on the land, although only a quarter is suitable for cultivation. Despite the compulsory break-up of large estates there is serious overcrowding and the average peasant farmer's holding is very small.

Tobacco, wheat, olives, maize, barley and grapes are the principal agricultural products. Grapes are grown for wine, for dessert fruit, and for drying as currants and sultanas. Citrus fruits are also important.

Tobacco, grown mainly in the north, is by far the most important export. Currants and sultanas are also important, *Patras* being the centre of this industry. The cultivation of the vine is mainly concentrated in the *Peloponnesus*. Much of the wine produced is for local consumption although some, like the sweet *Mavrodaphni* and *Samos* wines, are exported. Wheat is grown mainly in *Thessaly* and the north but much has to be imported.

A wide variety of minerals is mined—notably non-ferrous metals at *Laurion* and on *Euboea*.

Such industries as there are—mainly textiles—are concentrated around *Athens*.

Fishing is an important occupation and Greece also has a large Merchant Navy although a high proportion of the ships are registered under foreign flags.

Customs

The Greeks are a kindly, hospitable, emotional people with an uninhibited curiosity about strangers.

Like their classical forebears they take a passionate interest in politics, and feelings can run high on controversial issues.

A great deal of their time is spent in social life and in the "tavernas" talking politics, listening to national music and watching dancing. The dances are a mixture of Turkish influence and the traditions of classical Greece. The music will often sound strange to Western ears, having a distinctly Eastern character.

There are many festivals, ranging from picturesque local ones connected with saints' days to the performance of classical plays in the ancient open air theatres of *Epidaurus, Delphi,* and *Athens.* Easter is the time of great religious ritual and festivity, but its date is often different from Easter in western countries.

Food and Drink
Greek wines include *"Demestica"* (white), *Castel Danielis, Naoussa* (red), *Mavrodaphni, Kampa,* and *Samos* (very sweet). Wine impregnated with resin, called *retsina,* is very popular but it is an acquired taste. To obtain a wine without resin, ask for *aretsina,* or you may think you have swallowed a bottle of turpentine.

Ouzo—a spirit rather like *Pernod*—is widely drunk. Another spirit is *Mastica,* which is made from the gum-plant of that name.

Much of the traditional food is of Turkish origin and the specialities mentioned here are worth trying.

Dolmas, a richly seasoned rice wrapped in vine leaves and cooked in oil (as are many other foods); *Pilaff,* stuffed tomatoes, paprikas, and aubergines; *Kopanisti,* roe with sharp cheese.

Kataife—noodles with nut fillings are very very sweet. *Loukoumi* (Turkish Delight) is eaten all over Greece, and other sweet delicacies like crystallized fruits are common.

Turkish coffee, usually served in tiny cups, is practically a national drink. Varieties are: *sketo* (without sugar), *gleeko* (very sweet and strong) and *metrio* (medium sweet and strong).

Many fish dishes, such as red mullet, shell fish and octopus are excellent.

A visitor having difficulty with the menu may well be invited to the kitchen to select his food there.

Dress
National costume is largely of Turkish or Albanian origin— although in the *Ionian islands* there is Venetian influence. Western dress is widespread, particularly in the cities, although it is often mixed with the traditional. National costume has not entirely disappeared for Turkish costume is still to be seen – notably in Crete, the Islands and in the North of the country. Perhaps the most traditional Greek costume is that worn by the *Evzone*—the ceremonial Greek soldiers— with the short pleated skirt, white wool leg bindings and leather slippers. This is of Albanian origin.

Sport
Swimming, fishing, sailing and underwater swimming are the favourite sports during the summer. In winter there is ski-ing on *Mt. Parnes.*

Concerts and Festivals
The *State Symphony Orchestra* has a high reputation. Festivals include *Athens Music Festival,* Aug./Sept., *Epidaurus Drama Festival,* June/July. Various places stage national dances, e.g. *Megara,* 25 miles from *Athens,* Easter Tuesday.

217

GREECE

Culture

Greece is a country rich in architecture, particularly from the classical and Hellenistic periods, and from the Byzantine age.

The earliest remains of great architecture in Greece are those of the Minoan civilization in *Crete*, the most famous being the ruins of the palace of *Knossos* (near *Candia*) excavated by Sir Arthur Evans at the turn of the century. There had been continuous occupation here since before 2500 B.C. but most of the remains still to be seen date from the centuries just before 1400 B.C. The throne room and the royal apartments give a breath-taking glimpse of the architecture of this time. *Knossos* is by no means the only Minoan site to be seen; others include the palaces at *Phaestos* and *Hagia Triada* near the south coast of *Crete*.

With the Mycenean age the centre of power shifted to the mainland—particularly to the *Peloponnesus*—where many remains of this period are to be found. Foremost is *Mycenae* (south of *Corinth*) the great deserted citadel of Agamemnon dominating the plain of *Argos*. The town reached the height of its power some time after 1400 B.C. but was later abandoned. Notable here are the *Lion Gate*, the Cyclopean walls, the shaft graves, and the beehive tombs by the road to the palace. Other Mycenean sites of interest are the palace of *Tiryns* (near *Nauplia*), and the more recently excavated palace of *Pylos* near *Navarino* on the west coast.

Most of the surviving architecture of the "classical" Greek period consists of temples, monuments, and secular public buildings—notably theatres. Temples and other buildings are generally classified into three styles—Doric, Ionic, and Corinthian. All three styles developed and existed alongside each other, although the Corinthian is a later style more popular among the Romans than the Greeks. In mainland Greece the older buildings tend to be Doric in style e.g. the 6th century *temple of Apollo* at *Corinth*. The greatest achievement of the Doric style is the *Parthenon,* on the *Acropolis* at *Athens* (started in 447 B.C.). Another, almost complete, example is the *Theseum*, below the *Acropolis*. Other notable Doric buildings are the *Treasury of the Athenians* at *Delphi*, the remains of the *temple of Zeus* at *Olympia*, the *temple of Aphaea* on *Aegina*, and the *Propylaea* at *Athens*. Foremost among Ionic buildings are the *Erechtheum* and the *temple of Athene Nike*, both on the *Acropolis* at *Athens*, built a little after the *Parthenon*. Greek Corinthian buildings are rare; the earliest known example is that of the *monument of Lysicrates* in *Athens* (334 B.C.).

Among the finest examples of "classical" secular architecture are the theatres at *Epidaurus*, and of *Dionysus* in *Athens*, and the *stadium* for the Pythian games at *Delphi*.

Apart from the beauty of the buildings themselves the outstanding feature of the classical period is the marrying of the architecture with its physical surroundings. The great classical centres like *Athens*, *Delphi*, *Epidaurus*, *Delos*, and *Olympia* all bear witness to this, even if to-day often only ruins remain.

GREECE

Much of the architecture of the period when Greece was part of the Roman Empire carries on the classical styles and traditions. Examples are the Corinthian *temple of Olympian Zeus* (finished by Hadrian), the *theatre of Herodes Atticus* in *Athens*, and the *"House of Cleopatra"* at *Delos*. Town building, however, was more characteristically Roman in style, as can be seen in the ruins of *Roman Corinth*.

Byzantine architecture is in marked contrast to that of classical Greece, and Greece has many splendid examples—ranging from the 5th century church of *St. George* at *Salonica*, through the monasteries on the peninsula of *Mt. Athos* (10th-16th century) to the church at *Daphni* (near *Athens*) and the town of *Mistra* in the *Peloponnesus*. The latter is a deserted Byzantine town, surmounted by a Frankish fortress, dating from just before the Turkish conquest in the 15th century.

The island of *Rhodes* has an almost unique feature in the architecture of the knights of St. John (14th-16th century) with the distinctive fortress, streets, villas, and palaces of the city.

The Turks and their rivals, the Venetians, have left many examples of their architecture in Greece—although little that can be described as great. Venetian fortresses occur in many places in the *Aegean islands*, the *Ionian islands*, and in the *Peloponnesus*, and here and there are houses and churches of Venetian influence. Turkish town architecture, particularly the overhanging houses of slightly Tudor appearance, occurs in many areas—notably in the north of the country, in *Epirus*, *Macedonia*, and *Thrace* and in the *Aegean islands*. A number of mosques also survive e.g. the *Aslan Aga Mosque* in *Janina*.

Art Most of the surviving art of classical Greece, and before, is to be found in the museums of Greece—notably those in *Athens* and *Delphi*—and further afield, in those of Europe.

At *Knossos*, frescoes of the Minoan period are still to be seen *in situ* and give the impression of a rather gay civilization. Pottery and jewellery and other art of the period can be seen in the museum at *Candia*.

Many of the artistic finds from *Mycenae* are in the *National museum* at *Athens;* the metal-work in particular, is of a very high standard.

Archaic Greek statues (7th and 6th century B.C.) are very stiff and wooden, although often beautiful in execution. By the 5th century B.C. the statuary showed vivid movement and remarkable observation of the human form. Many of the greatest artists e.g. Phidias, Praxiteles, and Polycleitus are known to us from written descriptions and from later Greek and Roman copies of their works, but one statue is for certain an original, the Hermes of Praxiteles at *Olympia*. The museums of *Delphi, Athens and Olympia* contain fascinating examples of the sculpture of the period.

Sculpture was the most perfect form of artistic expression in classical Greece. In addition to free-standing statues, sculpture work was applied in great variety to adorning temples with friezes, pediments, etc., often depicting scenes from mythology. Perhaps the most famous of all friezes is that from the *Parthenon* (the *Elgin Marbles*) depicting the procession of the Panathenaic Festival—much of this is in the *British Museum*.

GREECE

Burial steles are another form of sculpture, interesting for depicting scenes in the lives of ordinary people of the classical cities. The *Ceramicus* in *Athens* has yielded many examples, a number of which have been removed to the museums.

Of classical Greek painting little or nothing survives, but in painted pottery there are rich remains. These are of three basic forms in their application— black figures on a red background, red figures on a black background, and coloured figures on a white ground (used mainly for burial purposes). This art reached its highest expression in *Athens* in the 5th century B.C. The subjects are usually scenes either from mythology or from everyday life.

The art of Greece, in the Hellenistic and Roman periods derives from the classical period but lacks its restraint and simplicity. The *Winged Victory of Samothrace* (now in the *Louvre*) is a splendid example.

Byzantine art contrasts sharply with that of classical Greece. It is the expression of the beliefs of the Orthodox Christian church, reaching its greatest achievements in the interior decoration of religious buildings. Classical Greek art gave beauty to the exterior: in Byzantine art the interior is all important and wall mosaics and paintings are its dominant media. The great bust of the *Pantocrator* at *Daphni* (A.D. 1100) is one of the finest examples of this art. In *Salonica* important mosaics of the 5th century survive (churches of *St. George* and *Hosios David*) and also of the 14th century— in the church of the *Holy Apostles*. Splendid examples of New Testament scenes of the early 11th century are to be found in the *Monastery of Hosios Lukas*, near *Delphi*. The monasteries on *Mount Athos* have many examples of later wall painting and mosaic work. The deserted town of *Mistra*, in the *Peloponnesus* is particularly rich in Byzantine wall paintings of the 14th century.

Literature With the shadowy figure of Homer the literature of Greece, and of the whole Western world, begins. He lived in *Ionia* (the modern coastland of Western Turkey), probably about 950 B.C. He produced two epics—the *Iliad* and the *Odyssey*—of unsurpassed genius, and they formed the backbone of Greek education throughout the classical period.

Only a few works survive from the five centuries between Homer and the great period of *Athens*—notably the love poems of Sappho, a few fragments of the satirist Archilochus, the shrewd and factual works of instruction on farming and sailing (in verse) of Hesiod, and some lyric poems of Pindar.

5th Century Greece, and notably *Athens*, produced a wealth of literature breath-taking in its scope and genius. From this period dates the birth of drama (tragedy and comedy), of history, philosophy, and scientific thought. Herodotus was the first historian, with a fascinating blend of absorbing stories and scientific fact. Thucydides, the Athenian, wrote a dramatic but objective account of the Peloponnesian War, through which he lived, which marks him as one of the world's greatest historians. Xenophon followed on from Thucydides but is less masterful, although his *Anabasis* (the retreat of the 10,000 from Persia) is a fascinating and human account of Greek discipline and heroism.

From the "golden age" of Athens three tragic dramatists stand above all others: Aeschylus, Sophocles, and Euripides. Nineteen of the latter's plays survive, seven of Aeschylus, and eight of Sophocles. Fragments of many others are known. Even after 2,500 years the works of these three are among the greatest. Living in the later years of Sophocles and Euripides was the great writer of comedy, Aristophanes. He did not hesitate to take a dig at the writings of his tragic contemporaries and although much of his humour is based on contemporary events his plays are still enjoyed.

Plato's contribution to philosophy is enormous and the dialogue form in which he generally wrote has often great literary merit.

In the 4th century B.C., although the power of Greece had declined, literature still flourished. Among the great names are Aristotle the philosopher, Menander the father of modern comedy, and Demosthenes the orator. After this, classical Greek literature dies and the writers of the centuries that follow, although they often owe much to the classical literature and wrote in Greek, drew their roots from other civilizations, notably the Roman and the Hebrew. Among these are Plutarch the historian, and Lucian, and the authors of the New Testament.

The literature of the long Byzantine age is mainly theology and history. It is not strictly speaking the literature of Greece. Its authors were drawn from all over the Byzantine world and relatively few came from what is now modern Greece. The language used was a "fossilized" form of classical Greek and faced an ever widening gulf from the living changing Greek language of the day.

Modern Greek literature has to some extent been a struggle between this "classical language" of the Byzantine period and the living language (*demotic*) of the people, from which the latter has emerged victorious. Notable writings in the living language date from Cretan literature of the 16th and 17th centuries and the so-called *Klephtic Ballads* of the period of Turkish occupation. The War of Independence brought in its train a revival of Greek literature, particularly in the form of poetry and the novel.

Science The Greeks, from the 6th century B.C. onwards, were the first people to make a systematic attempt to understand the natural world. Their achievements in most branches of science during the next 350 years make them the "most remarkable people who ever yet existed".

Abstract reasoning was their greatest strength: mathematics and astronomy therefore best demonstrate their genius. Even today our geometry is largely theirs—developed by Greek thinkers from Thales to Euclid, Archimedes and Apollonius. Heracleides discovered the rotation of the earth; Eratosthenes calculated its circumference; and Aristarchus anticipated Copernicus in suggesting that the sun was the centre of the planetary system. Hipparchus, their greatest astronomer, calculated the lunar month to within half a second and greatly developed trigonometry.

Aristotle was not only a philosopher but took the whole field of knowledge for his subject. He was the first to make biology a science, his achievements in marine biology and in the study of bees and other insects being especially remarkable. His pupil Theophrastus excelled in botany.

Hippocrates, the father of medicine, also belongs to the classical period. His ideal of conduct, embodied in the Hippocratic oath, still serves as a

GREECE

model for medical men, and much of the practice of his school is still accepted as sound. Much later, near the beginning of the Christian era, the work of Celsus shows a further advance in medical knowledge.

Early in the Christian era two names are outstanding: Galen, the physician, and Dioscorides, the botanist and pharmacologist. The works of these two, with those of Aristotle, became the basis of scientific knowledge in the Arab world and in Christendom up to the Renaissance.

Concerts and Festivals

The *State Symphony Orchestra* has a high reputation. Festivals include *Athens Music Festival*, Aug./Sept., *Epidaurus Drama Festival*, June/July. Various places stage national dances, e.g. *Megara*, 25 miles from *Athens*, Easter Tuesday.

Lindos Beach on the Island of Rhodes.

Touring Information

Access

London to *Athens*; (i) by air; night tourist return £87·20, valid 1 month; (ii) by rail daily via *Ostend* and through Yugoslavia, 3 days, £49·20 single, £98·40 return; (iii) by rail daily via *Calais/Milan—Brindisi* 36 hours, thence by sea. *London–Brindisi* £28·65 single £54·85 return. Service from *Brindisi* is to *Corfu*, *Igoumenitsa* and *Patras* nightly in summer, less frequent in winter; single fares from 962 dr to *Corfu* or *Igoumenitsa*, from 1258 dr to *Patras*, whence a motor coach connection (222 dr) continues the journey to *Athens*. Other less frequent service is to *Piraeus* from *Venice*, tourist class single fare 2220 dr. Cheaper fares for students are offered by most Greek steamship companies.

	Long distance motor coaches are cheaper and more comfort-
Transport	able than rail which is apt to be crowded on long distance
	trains. Local diesel electric trains are more comfortable.

No reduction for return fares on railways except at weekends and on public holidays. The *Athens-Piraeus-Peloponnesus Railways* give reduction for students, Apr. 1st-Oct. 31st. Trams and buses in *Athens* are very cheap. Do not leave it until the last minute to purchase a ticket for a train as often the ticket office opens only an hour before departure when immediately a long queue forms. Bus or steamer tickets should be booked the day before.

	The unit of currency is the *drachma*, which is divided into
Money	100 *lepta*.

	For a summer visit go prepared for very hot and dry weather
Clothing	from early July to early September, when shade temperatures
	are often in the nineties, and insects can be troublesome.

	Simple meals cost about 30 *drachma*. There are numerous
Restaurants	small cafés and restaurants which, however dilapidated they
	look, are likely to prove good and reasonable. The *tavernas*,

or restaurants with a local character, are among the cheapest eating places, although you may occasionally come across one which is on the smarter side and therefore more expensive.

	A useful general map is published by *Hallwag* on a scale of
Map	1:1,000,000, showing the mainland and all the islands on one
	sheet.

	The *Greek Youth Hostels Association* has about thirty
Accom-modation	hostels; ten of them on the islands.

There are about 80 *village guest houses*, where visitors stay with families at about 40 *drachma* per night. Visitors are accommodated in many of the *monasteries* either for a small charge or gratis.

A room in a cheap boarding house or *pension* costs about 60 *drachma* per night and in a better class hotel about 80 *drachma*. Hotels and boarding houses rarely offer inclusive terms: you eat in the hotel restaurant (if there is one) and pay as you go, or eat out.

In the countryside if you ask at a café or inquire of the *"proedros"* or village headman you can usually be accommodated very cheaply. For a stay of less than three nights at a *pension* or hotel a 10% supplementary charge is added to the bill. Most hotels and *pensions* give a reduction for students.

GREECE

Camping
There are practically no restrictions on camping anywhere in Greece, but it is always advisable to ask permission to camp on any farm or similar land. Weather is normally warm enough to camp without a tent, using a down sleeping bag.

Walking
Good areas for a walking holiday would be within a radius of *Athens* or in the *Peloponnesus*, an area of fertile plains, rich coastal strips and mountains, with many small towns and villages. *Mount Parnes* (20 miles from *Athens*) is popular with both climbers and walkers. There are mountain huts on *Olympus, Parnassus* and *Parnes;* they are used as youth hostels.

Cycling
Minor roads are poor and the summer heat is great, but apart from this cycling would be an excellent way of touring a part of Greece.

Canoeing
There is good canoeing to be had all along the *Saronic Gulf.*

Weights and Measures
While the metric system is in common use, there is also the *Oka,* a unit of weight equivalent to 2.83 lbs., and subdivided into smaller units. Among other measures is the *Peke,* equivalent to 25 inches.

Practical Hints
Banks open 9-12. Shops open daily except Sundays.

Two inexpensive general stores in *Athens* are *Chrysikopoulos'* and *Lambropoulos'.*

Free passes to museums etc., are often available to students and teachers.

Be advised to learn the Greek alphabet before you go: it will save a deal of difficulty later.

Take sunglasses, swimsuit, suntan ointment, insect repellent; also pills or medicine to counteract any adverse effect that cooking in oil may have on stomachs unused to it.

It is cheaper to take soap, toothpaste, toilet requisites and films as these are expensive in Greece due to the import duty.

In *Athens* and usually elsewhere it is safe to drink tap water. If in doubt stick to mineral waters such as *Nigzita* or *Souroty.*

Athens

The modern city dates from the 19th century, after the War of Independence. It is not very spectacular, but is pleasant and spacious, dominated by the *Acropolis* and *Mt. Lycabettus* and surrounded at a distance by the mountains of *Attica.* (**Y.H.** in city).

The **Acropolis** and immediate surroundings are the great centre of attraction. The buildings on it date mainly from the age of Pericles, and, even in their ruined state, are some of the most famous and beautiful in the world. They are the *Parthenon, Erechtheum,* and the *Temple of Athene Nike,* with the great entrance way, the *Propylaea.* The *Acropolis* is open until midnight when there is a full moon, and a visit then is particularly recommended.

GREECE

To the south of the *Acropolis* lie the *Theatres of Dionysus* (4th century B.C.) and of *Herodes Atticus* (built 2nd century A.D. by a rich noble). In the original *Theatre of Dionysus* many plays of the great Athenian dramatists were first performed.

South-west of the *Acropolis* is the hill of the *Pnyx* where assemblies of Athenian citizens once met, and nearby is the hill of the *Areopagus*. To the west is the site of the ancient *Agora*, which has two buildings of great interest : the extremely well-preserved temple called the *Theseum* (5th century B.C.). and the recent reconstruction of the *Stoa of Attalus* built to house the vast quantity of antiquities found on the *Agora*.

Other interesting remains are the *Tower of the Winds* (1st century B.C.). the *Arch of Hadrian* and the *temple of Olympian Zeus,* in the Roman quarter, and the *Ceramicus* and other cemeteries situated near the *Dipylon* and the *Sacred Gate.*

A visit to the *National Archaeological Museum* is highly recommended; it has some of the most splendid examples of Greek work uncovered by excavation.

Three Byzantine churches of note—all close to *Constitution Square*—are those of *Kapnikarea,* the *Small Metropolis* and *Sts. Theodores.*

EXCURSIONS: (a) *Piraeus*, 2 miles S., the port of *Athens*; little remains of the famous ancient port, but the modern one is busy, thriving and colourful (Y.H.); *Phaleron,* near *Piraeus,* bathing resort for the Athenians. (b) **Cape Sunion,** southernmost tip of *Attica,* 36 miles S., bus from *Aigypta Square*; has impressive remains of **temple of Poseidon** on lofty cliffs and magnificent views out to sea. (c) **Marathon,** 18 miles E., beyond *Mt. Hymettus,* on bay of same name; site of victory of Athenians over Persians, 490 B.C. Burial mound of Athenians killed in the battle can still be seen, 5 miles S. of village. Approach either on foot (9 miles) from *Pendelis monastery* (reached by bus from *Kaningos Square*) via summit of Mt. **Pentelikon** (3,635 ft., fine view) returning by bus, or on foot (8 miles) by road and path from *Ekali* (bus from *Kaningos Square*), or all way by bus from *Aigyptou Square.* (d) **Daphni,** 4 miles; on *Corinth* road, 11th century Byzantine church, one of finest examples extant. Particularly fine mosaic head of Christ in the dome. (e) **Aegina,** island in *Saronic Gulf;* early morning steamer, 1½ hours, from *Piraeus.* Quiet beaches; picturesque villages; Ruins of **temple of Aphaia,** with commanding view (bus, 7 miles, from harbour).

Touring Routes

G indicates village guest house; M—monastery receiving guests.

R.1. Athens to Delphi and Hosios Lukas (138 miles)

Leave *Athens* by *Corinth* road, turning N.W. off it just beyond *Eleusis* (Y.H. and slight remains of *Hall of Eleusinian Mysteries; museum*). At *Mandra* road climbs into wooded *Cithaeron* hills; at entrance to *Kaza* gorge by-road branches left to *Villia* (G). Main road enters plain of *Boeotia* descending to *Thebes,* city of Oedipus. Road continues past mountain of classic Sphinx to *Levadia,* 73 miles. Take left fork by direct mountain road to *Delphi,* 28 miles, (Y.H.).

Delphi, high on slopes of Mt. **Parnassus,** looking over N. shore of *Gulf of Corinth,* was main religious centre of ancient Greece, famous for its Oracle which issued advice and predictions—often shrewd though cryptic—to those who consulted it.

The classical ruins are imposing, set in beautiful spectacular surroundings. The *Temple of Apollo* was the focal point (foundations and several columns remain). Nearby, on *Sacred Way,* is *Treasury of the Athenians* (almost completely restored). Other remains, contributions of other city states, line the *Way.* Above the *Temple* is well-preserved *Theatre,* and higher still the *Stadium of the Pythian Games.* Further towards valley is another group of ruins, including the *Gymnasium,* the *Sanctuary* and *Temple of Athena Pronaea,* and the *Tholos.* The museum nearby, contains many interesting and beautiful works of art found on the site.

20 miles E., along road back to *Levadia,* take the *Stiris* road on right to reach, 17 miles, *monastery of Hosios Lukas* (*St. Luke*) (M). Its church contains very fine examples of Byzantine mosaic work, particularly the Pantocrator (Christ) in the dome, and scenes from the *New Testament.*

The Peloponnesus

R.2.   Athens—Corinth—Mycenae—Nauplia—Epidaurus (106 miles)

From *Eleusis* (R.1) road follows splendid mountainous coast with views to island of *Salamis;* ferry from *Megalo Pefko.* Continue through *Megara* to 4 miles wide *Isthmus of Corinth.* Road crosses Canal to *Corinth,* 53 miles. Modern town, rebuilt since earthquake in 1928, not very interesting. 5 miles S.W. is site of ancient *Corinth,* under shadow of fortified mountain, the **Acrocorinthos,** which has impressive remains and famous view. Most of the classical Greek city was destroyed by Romans in 146 B.C., but a few Doric columns of *Temple of Apollo* (6th century B.C.) still stand. Nearby are the more numerous remains of the Roman city, notably *Fountains of Peirene, Senate House, Agora, Odeon* and *Amphitheatre.*

Road through *Dervenakia Gorge* to plain of *Argos,* dominated by lonely rocky hill bearing remains of **Mycenae,** 24 miles, centre of civilization to which it gives its name. Approach is along by-road 2 miles from main road through *Charvati.* Entrance to the citadel with its gigantic walls is by the famous *Lion Gate.* Inside are shaft graves of *Royal Cemetery* (splendid finds from here are in *National Museum* in *Athens*), remains of *Royal Palace* and fascinating subterranean staircase leading to a water supply outside the walls. On road up to citadel are the curious Beehive Tombs, of which the two best known are the so-called *Tombs of Agamemnon* (*Treasury of Atreus*) and of *Clytemnestra.*

Continue S. through *Charvati* on by-road past *Heraion,* site of *temple of Hera,* to *Chonika* and *Tiryns* 9 miles: Mycenaean fortified palace, considerable remains.

Nauplion (Y.H.) 2 miles, picturesque port of *Gulf of Argolis,* dominated by *Acronauplia* (ancient Acropolis) and the *Palamedes* fortress, with their Venetian and Turkish fortifications. For a short time *Nauplion* was capital of modern Greece until *Athens* was captured from the Turks.

Epidaurus, 18 miles E., has what is probably the most perfect example of a classical theatre in Greece, lying almost complete in natural armchair in the hills; extraordinarily good acoustics. Drama festival June/July. Nearby are ruins of *Sanctuary of Asclepius,* a sort of religious health resort in classical times. *Ligourio* (G) 4 miles.

R.3. Nauplion—Sparta—Monemvasia (160 miles)

From *Nauplion* (**R.2**) through *Argos* and then magnificent mountain scenery descending to valley of *Arcadia* in which town of *Tripolis,* 48 miles, is route centre for much of *Peloponnesus.*

Sparta, 40 miles. Remains of ancient city, some 2 miles from modern town at foot of *Taegetus* mountains, are not very extensive: mainly walls on the *Acropolis,* small theatre, and foundations of *Temple of Artemis.*

Mistra, 4 miles W., clinging to slopes of *Taegetus* mountains, is deserted Byzantine town, mainly 14th century, crowned by earlier Frankish fortress constructed by William de Villehardouin. It was for a time capital of the *Peloponnesus* and an important cultural and religious centre. Below the fortress is the upper town with impressive ruins of *Palace of the Palaeologi* and then the lower town. Many Byzantine churches and monasteries in various states of preservation—notably *Peribleptos* monastery, church of *St. Demetrius,* church of *St. Theodore, Brontocheion* monastery (well preserved), church of *St. Sophia* (also well preserved) and convent of *Pantanassa* (still occupied). This town with its curiously haunted air, is one of most remarkable historic remains in Greece.

Monemvasia, 63 miles S.E. of Sparta, picturesque and historic port on high rocky promontory jutting into sea; occupied in turn by Franks, Byzantines, Turks, and Venetians, it contains examples of architecture of each.

R.4. Tripolis—Bassae—Patras—Athens (307 miles)

From *Tripolis* (**R.3**) road through mountains to *Megalopolis,* 22 miles; *Karitaina,* 11 miles, attractive village below 13th century Frankish castle; *Andritsaina,* 18 miles, attractive small town.

EXCURSION: New road up to **Temple of Bassae (Apollo Epicureius)** remote in hills at 3,776 ft. Doric temple in fine state of preservation; built by Iktinos, one of architects of *Parthenon,* 5th century B.C. Often considered most beautiful in Greece after *Parthenon;* splendid setting, with great views.

From *Andritsaina* bus to *Pyrgos,* 31 miles, from which bus or train to **Olympia (Y.H.)** 15 miles, in pleasant wooded valley of *R. Alpheus,* where *Olympic Games* were held throughout classical Greek and Roman times. It was never a town, but a religious and athletic centre. Remains extensive, but not particularly well preserved: destruction by man and nature (earthquakes and changing courses of rivers) have taken their toll. Notable are the stadium, with entrance way and starting and finishing lines preserved, *Temple of Zeus* (the centre of the sanctuary) and ancient *Temple of Hera* (7th century B.C.) The museum contains a great quantity of the finds of excavation on the site, in particular the statue of Hermes by Praxiteles.

From *Olympia* by road or rail through *Patras* (**Y.H.**), largest town of *Peloponnesus,* to *Athens* (215 miles).

GREECE

The Northern Provinces

Places of outstanding interest are: in *Thessaly*, the *Tempe Valley*, *Mt. Olympus*, *Mt. Pelion* and *Meteora*; in *Epirus*, *Jannina*, its chief town; in *Greek Macedonia*, *Salonica*, *Kastoria* and the peninsula of *Chalcidice* with its monasteries of *Mt. Athos*.

R.5. Volos—(Mt. Pelion)—Meteora—Jannina (172 miles)

Volos, 241 miles from *Athens* by rail-car via *Stavros*, or by weekly steamer in 12 hours.

EXCURSIONS: (a) Mt. Pelion (5,252 ft.) (Y.H.) 4 hr. walk to summit from *Portaria*, very fine view; (b) to charming villages along *Pelion Range*, such as *Makrinitsa*, 11 miles, *Zagora*, 31 miles, (G), *Tsangarada*, 36 miles (G) and *Ayios Jannis* (*Ionannis*) (G), which contain many splendid Turkish houses.

Larissa, 38 miles.

EXCURSIONS: (a) Tempe Valley. To *Tembi*, 22 miles, (rail) whence 4 hr. walk through valley between *Olympus* and *Ossa* to *Stomion*, small coastal resort. (b) Mt. Ossa (2 days). Guide necessary. *Ayia*, 20 miles (bus), *Anatoli* 3 hrs. and a further 3½ hrs. to summit (6,490 ft.).

Trikkala, 38 miles, on classic *R. Lethe*. *Kalabaka*, 14 miles, rail terminus, at foot of *Meteora*, famous monasteries built on great and almost inaccessible rocks in 14th century; originally 24, each on its own pinnacle; 4 still occupied. (M).

Continue by road, 82 miles through *Pindus Mts.* over *Metsovon Pass* (5,594 ft.) into *Epirus*, to **Jannina** (*Ioannia*) (Y.H.). its chief town; important in Turkish times and retains much architecture of the period, particularly in the old town within the walls, with its narrow streets and Turkish houses. The *Kastro* is a well preserved Turkish fortress; *Aslan Aga Mosque* is a landmark built on a cliff above the lake. On an island in *Lake Jannina* are several interesting monasteries (11th-13th century).

Daily coach service between *Jannina* and *Athens* (343 miles).

R.6. Salonica—(Mount Athos)—Kastoria (139 miles)

Salonica (*Thessaloniki*) chief port of north, 321 miles by rail from *Athens*. Modern city is on seafront; picturesque old Turkish quarters lie on hills behind. Much of old city walls remains. The architectural riches are the Byzantine churches covering 1,000 years of Byzantine art. Outstanding are 5th century church of *St. George*, *St. Sophia* (with splendid mosaics), *St. Demetrius* (7th century or earlier, almost destroyed by fire in 1917, but some old work survives), the lovely 14th century *Church of the 12 Apostles*, and the little church of *Hosies David* in the old town, with superb mosaic of the Pantocrator. (Y.H.).

R.6 (i) Mt. Athos Peninsula. Easternmost extension of *Chalcidice*, 31 miles long, rising to 6,670 ft. Cut at isthmus by Xerxes' canal (482 B.C.). Here lives a unique community of 5,000 monks, either in monasteries or as anchorites or hermits—an autonomous republic, *Ayion Oros*, under Greek sovereignty. No women allowed to enter peninsula; men must obtain permission from Ministry of Foreign Affairs in Athens, through own Embassy.

Approach by sea from *Salonica* (Fri. evening) arrive *Dhafni* next morning. (Return service leaves *Dhafni* Mon. evening). Visits to monasteries (there are 20) either on foot or by mule or boat.

GREECE

Pella (village) 24 miles, site of capital of Alexander the Great. *Edessa,* 31 miles, finely situated town. *Lake Vegorritis,* 11 miles. *Florina* 30 miles, market town (2,230 ft.). *Pisodherion Pass* (5,183 ft.), 18 miles.

Kastoria, 25 miles, town like *Jannina,* built beside a lake. Near Albanian frontier. Its history goes back to classical times, but little remains of this period. Chief attractions, apart from its lovely setting, are interesting Byzantine churches (e.g. *Taxiarch, St. George, St. Alipios*) and old Turkish quarters and bazaar.

The Islands

From *Piraeus* boats can be taken to almost all the islands of Greece. Sailings are regular and cheap, and the choice of which to visit is a difficult one. None will be disappointing and most are enchanting. The brief descriptions below cover only some of the highlights.

Crete

By far the largest of the islands; 140 miles long and mountainous along its entire length. Cradle of European civilization. In addition to its important archaeological sites *Crete* offers splendid scenery, quiet and colourful villages, and many customs and links with the past.

Heraklion (Y.H.) the chief town. Fortified by the Venetians. Much Turkish architecture. *Archaeological Museum* particularly interesting containing many of the finds of *Knossos.*

Knossos, 3 miles, Minoan palace earlier than 1400 B.C. Highly complicated site, excavated and restored with much imagination. Layout and artistic work quite different from classical Greek buildings. Courtyards, throne rooms, store rooms, stairways, frescoes, and even bathrooms and toilet are of great interest.

Phaestos, 40 miles from *Heraklion* (bus; accommodation at Tourist Pavilion). Another Minoan palace near south coast, reached by splendid journey over central mountains. Remarkable physical setting overlooked by *Mt. Ida (Psiloriti)* (8,193 ft.). Palace similar in many ways to *Knossos.*

Rhodes

Largest of the 12 islands of the *Dodecanese.* Claims most favoured climate in Greece. A beautiful island, noted for its flowers and gardens, medieval towns and villages.

The city of Rhodes is particularly noted for its palaces and houses built by Knights of St. John in varying forms of the Gothic style. Turkish mosques and houses are also much in evidence and there are several interesting Byzantine churches. All lie in old town enclosed completely by its medieval walls. Unusual feature of harbour is *Quay of the Windmills.* Behind city is the *Acropolis,* with ruins of *Temples of Apollo* and *Zeus* and well restored theatre.

As interesting and picturesque as city of *Rhodes* is town of Lindos, 35 miles, on S.E. coast, dominated by fortress built by Knights of Rhodes, and containing fascinating mixture of classical ruins, Byzantine churches (particularly *St. Demetrius*) and medieval houses.

The Cyclades

Mykonos. (Y.H.) The attraction of this island is centred in the little port of *Mykonos* itself, with its brilliant white houses, narrow streets, numerous churches, and the canvas-sailed windmills which dominate the town. It is the archetype of picture postcard scenes of the *Aegean.*

Delos. Small and uninhabited island approached by motor-boat from *Mykonos.* Once great religious and commercial centre; virtually open-air museum of whole period from classical Greeks to Romans, in a spectacular setting. Remains are extensive and complex.

Remaining islands of *Aegean* are visited not so much for their historic monuments, although there are many to be found and admired, but for their character and atmosphere springing from a harmony of architecture and natural surroundings, enhanced by the sunshine of a favoured climate. Three such islands—in the *Cyclades*—outstanding in their charm are Naxos, Paros and Santorin (Y.H.).

The Ionian Islands

Of this group, lying off the west coast of Greece, the most popular is Corfu (*Kerkyra*) (Y.H.), much more verdant than the others, covered with forests of pine, and orchards, cypresses and olives. Fine sandy beaches and pleasant towns where influence of Venetians is strong.

ICELAND

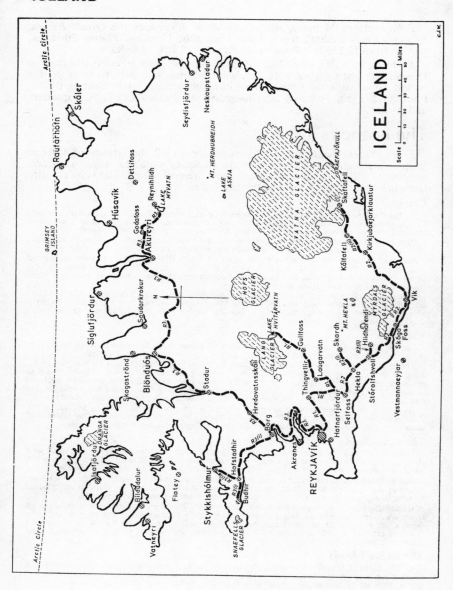

ICELAND

Geographical Outline

Land   Iceland lies in the North Atlantic some 500 miles north-west of Scotland. Measuring 300 miles from west to east and 190 miles from north to south, it is just under 40,000 sq. miles in area—about one-fifth larger than Ireland. Its coastline, except on the south, is heavily indented with fjords and extends to some 3,700 miles with numerous off-shore islands.

The name is deceptive. The mainland barely touches the Arctic Circle. Only one-eighth is covered with ice. It is much more a land of fire: signs of volcanic activity, past and present, are to be seen everywhere. Its rocks are all of igneous origin and are added to periodically by eruptions of lava and volcanic ash so that the processes of the country's formation can be seen at work. About 25 volcanoes have been active in historic times, some of them many times, notably *Hekla*, 23 times, the last in 1947. They occur along a crescent from *Eldeyjar* (S.W.) through *Hekla* and *Laki* to *Leirhafnarskördh* (N.E.). Acid hot springs follow the same line, but alkaline hot springs occur in all parts.

Vatnajökull (3,140 sq. miles) is the largest ice mass in Europe. *Hvannadals-hnukur* (6,954 ft.) in *Öræfajökull* is the highest summit. Other extensive glaciers are *Langjökull*, *Hofsjökull* and *Myrdalsjökull*. Lakes are innumerable, and rivers are powerful with many waterfalls. But apart from the ice caps the interior largely consists of a wilderness of rock, boulders and lava fields forming a tableland 2,300-3,300 ft. above sea level.

Climate   Winters are relatively mild, summers cool, with generally high humidity due to the prevailing south-west winds. Regional differences are caused by the set of ocean currents (Polar or Gulf Stream) and by the barrier effect of the high mountains of the south. Rainfall is heaviest along the south and south-west coasts. In the interior snow can fall at all seasons. Brilliant sunshine is frequent, but fog often occurs. The sun is above the horizon for 20 or more hours daily during May, June and July; best season for touring is mid-June to early September.

Plants and Animals   Plant cover is continuous in only a small part. Species are about one-sixth as numerous as in the British Isles, but are of great interest in illustrating early post-glacial conditions. The lowlands have arctic and southern plants, with grasses and dwarf willow dominant; in summer their higher exposed places are covered with yellowish mosses, whilst sheltered patches show up a vivid green. Woodlands of birch and mountain ash were once extensive, but now occur only in a few places.

The fox is the only native land mammal. The abundant bird life, especially sea birds and water fowl, is a great attraction to naturalists.

231

ICELAND

The People

Population   Most of the 170,000 people live on the coast in small towns or villages, but there are a few thousand farmsteads in pastoral valleys or on the better parts of the lowlands of the south-west. After *Reykjavík*, the capital (70,000), the next largest town is *Akureyri* (8,500).

The people are descended from the original Norse and Celtic colonists.

Language   Icelandic is the purest of the Germanic languages, having changed little from the Scandinavian of western Norway spoken by the first settlers. It includes also a few Gaelic names introduced by those Vikings who came from settlements in western Britain.

Religion   The Evangelical Lutheran Church is the state church.

History   Iceland was the last European country to be inhabited. Irish monks and hermits reached it late in the 8th century. Then came Scandinavian explorers, one of whom Floki Vilgerdharson, after a hard winter, called it *Island* (Iceland). In 874 came the first Norse settlers: Ingólfur Arnarson, founder of *Reykjavík*, and his foster-brother, who was soon murdered by his Irish slaves. The Irish fled to some islands, but were pursued and killed by Ingólfur, the islands ever since being known as the *Vestmannaeyjar* ("islands of the men from the west").

By 930 the settlement was complete, there being about 400 chief settlers, some, with their dependants, seeking freedom from the overlordship of King Harold Fairhair in Norway, others, including some who had become Christians, coming from the Hebrides and other Viking settlements in western Britain. But Christianity soon died out.

In 930, also, Iceland became a nation, forming a General Assembly, the *Althing*, and adopting a code of law recited annually to the *Althing* from the Rock of Law at *Thingvellir* where it met annually until 1798.

During the existence of the independent Republic (then unique in the world) Greenland was colonised (985), some Icelanders including Leif Ericsson reached North America (1000) and Christianity was accepted following a mission sent by the king of Norway. But dissension brought the Republic to an end in 1262 when the sovereignty of the Norwegian king was acknowledged.

After the *Union of Kalmar* (see Denmark) Danish influence gradually became dominant. The Reformation was enforced on Iceland under duress. Danish monopoly of trade brought economic decline, hastened in the 18th century by natural disasters—eruptions, plague and famine.

Recovery began in the 1830s. A cultural and political movement, parallel to what was happening in Norway and elsewhere, awakened a new national consciousness, fostered by scholars and leaders, above all by Jón Sigurdhsson (1811-79,) the founder of modern Iceland. The *Althing* was revived (1843), the right of free trade won (1854) and a constitution within the Danish kingdom obtained (1874).

In 1918 Iceland became a sovereign independent state united with Denmark under a common king. In 1944 it became, as it had been at first, an independent republic.

Government
The President and Parliament (*Althing*) are elected for 4 years. The modern *Althing* has 60 members, one-third in an Upper House, the remainder in the Lower House. There is proportional representation and adult suffrage.

Resources
The yield of the fishing banks is much greater than of the land and a fifth of the working population is employed in fishing and its associated industries. Cod-fishing is centred particularly on *Reykjavík, Isafjördhur* in the north-west peninsula, and the *Vestmannaeyjar*. Herring fishing is concentrated on the north and east coasts, notably on *Siglufjördhur*, which has large processing plants, and *Raufarhöfn*. *Hvalfjördhur* is the chief centre for local whaling.

Agriculture occupies almost a quarter of the working population, though only 0·5% of the land is cultivated. Hay and potatoes are the only main crops, but some turnips, oats and barley are grown. Hot-house cultivation, using hot springs, yields tomatoes, green vegetables and even grapes and bananas. Dairying and rearing of sheep, horses and poultry are important. Modern methods are increasingly used.

Collecting of sea-birds' eggs for food is specially important in the *Vestmannaeyjar* and the north-west peninsula and eider down from the nests of breeding birds is collected at many places on the north and east coasts, particularly *Flatey* in *Breidhifjördhur*.

The use of hydro-electric power is well developed and water from hot springs is used for heating houses.

Food and Drink
The diet is rich in protein, but fresh fruit and vegetables are scarce. Typical dishes are *skyr*, a creamy substance, not unlike curdled milk, served as dessert with sugar and cream; *hangikjot*, well smoked mutton, usually eaten with boiled potatoes or peas; *hardfiskur* or *ryklingur*, smoked dried fish, generally served with butter. Wafers or small pancakes with whipped cream are often served with tea or coffee.

Sport
Glima is a form of wrestling peculiar to Iceland. Skating, ski-ing, swimming, football and athletics are also popular.

Culture

Literature
The 12th and 13th centuries were periods of intense literary activity, producing the *Eddaic* poems, dealing with the gods and heroes of Europe, especially of Scandinavia; the *Landnámabók*, a unique prose record of the settlement; and the *Sagas*, also in prose, a northern equivalent of the Homeric poems. The sagas include the *Heimskringla*, a history of the kings of Norway, and many others such as the *Saga of Burnt Njál*, giving a vivid picture of Icelandic life or of historic events. There are many English translations.

ICELAND

The 19th century cultural revival brought renewed interest in the sagas and a new phase of literary activity which still continues. The realist novels of Icelandic life by Halldór Kiljan Laxnes (Nobel Prizewinner, 1955) are available in translation.

Music The native folk songs have been recovered by collectors but, Icelanders have also been much influenced by the musical traditions of the Continent. Choral singing is popular. *Reykjavík* has a symphony orchestra.

Sculpture The *Einar Jónsson Museum* in *Reykjavík* houses the works of Iceland's first and greatest sculptor.

Applied Arts Wood carving and tapestry working were practised from early times. Examples can be seen in the *National Museum, Reykjavík.*

Touring Information

Touring Areas These are, in the south-west, the neighbourhood of *Reykjavík* and *Thingvellir,* combining scenic, natural history and historic interest; routes E. or N.E. from *Selfoss* towards ice caps or to the central uninhabited areas; in the north, *Akureyri* and *Mývatn.*

Transport There are no railways, but buses and boats starting from *Reykjavík* and *Akureyri* cover nearly every habitable part. Cycles usually accepted free on them. Regular internal plane services at fares such as kr. 1,400 from *Reykjavík* to *Akureyri.*

Money The unit of currency is the *krona,* divided into 100 *aurar.*

Clothing Ordinary touring kit suffices for routine excursions. For longer inland journeys sweater, anorak, cape and boots are essential. Take bathing costume (opportunities for swimming in water from hot springs). Down bags recommended for hostel use.

Restaurants and Meals

Usual lunch hour 12-1. Dinner generally served between 6.0 and 8.30 p.m. Food plentiful, but, except in large hotels and best restaurants, menu is simple. Food, except milk, is expensive; the cost of chocolates and sweets is prohibitive.

Maps and Guide Books

Danish Geodetic Institute: (a) general map, 1:750,000 and 1:1,000,000, one sheet; (b) 1:250,000, 9 sheets; (c) 1:100,000, 87 sheets. "Shell" Road Map, 1:600,000, showing useful detail; from garages in Iceland. Various leaflets available from *Icelandic National Tourist Office, 75 Rockefeller Plaza, New York, N.Y. 10019.*

Place Names

Many natural and other features can be recognised on the map with the aid of a slight knowledge of the meaning of Icelandic place forms, such as the following:

Akvegur	road	*Kirkja*	church
Bær	farm	*Kjarr*	copse
Brú	bridge	*Laug*	hot spring
Eldjia	volcanic fissure	*Reykja*	steam, smoke
Eydibær	deserted farm	*Sandur*	sand
Foss	waterfall	*Sjóporp*	fishing village
Gígur	crater	*Skogur*	wood
Hraun	lava field	*Sogustadhur*	historical place
Hver	hot spring	*Sýslumot*	county boundary
Kaupstadhur	town	*Vatn*	water, lake
Kauptun med kirkju market town with church		*Vegur, gata*	bridle path
Kauptun an kirkju market town without church		*Verzlunarstadhur*	trading station
		Viti	lighthouse

Accommodation

(a) The *youth hostels* are open early June to end September. Some provide no pots and pans; a canteen set should be brought by those cooking their own meals. Petrol stove (rather than paraffin stove) also useful. (b) *Tourist Huts.* Usually of a good standard, with heating equipment, fuel and cooking utensils, but food must be brought. Permission to use them must be obtained from the tourist organization, *Ferdhafélag Islands.* (c) *Other huts; farms.* There are other more primitive huts or shelters, primarily for farmers when gathering sheep. The farmers are hospitable, generally willing to allow members to sleep in their barns; or accommodation may be offered indoors for about 500 kr. per night, provided members have their own down sleeping bag. (d) *Rooms.* In *Reykjavik* and *Akureyri* rooms available in private houses: minimum cost per day 900 kr. In the country cost is from 700 kr.

Camping

The Icelandic Y.H.A. recommends members to bring a tent as a means of extending the range of touring.

Walking

Best undertaken from centres rather than as a place to place tour, unless a fully planned trek into the interior, with ponies in support to carry food and equipment, is arranged.

Mountaineering

Only for experienced parties, and requires expedition technique. Movement on the larger ice caps, in particular, requires something more than alpine methods. On *Vatnajökull* polar equipment is essential; frequent 5-day blizzards must be prepared for.

ICELAND

<table>
<tr><td>Ski-ing</td><td>There are over 30 chalets for skiers and several ski-jumps.</td></tr>
</table>

Cycling

Motoring is on the left, overtaking on the right. Speed limit 60 km. (37·5 miles) per hour. There are 5,600 miles of road, generally of unscreened gravel, liable to be very dusty and hardly suitable for cycle touring. Roads off chief routes are very rough in parts, sometimes merely tracks worn in sand. Local advice should be taken before attempting any cross-country route.

Health

First aid kit should include burn ointment, as springs and geysers can burn even through climbing boots. Be cautious where you walk in areas of thermal activity. An insect repellant should also be taken as midges abound.

Touring Routes

Reykjavík, the capital, beautifully situated on north shore of *Seltjanarnes*. Chief sights are: (a) in main town near harbour: *Parliament building* and *Cathedral* in *Kirkjustræti*; *statue of Ingólfur Arnarson*, founder of *Reykjavík*, near N. end of *Ingólfs Str.*; *National Library* and *National Theatre* nearby; (b) beyond *Tjörnin* (lake): *National Museum* and *Art Gallery* near University; (c) ½ mile S.E. of harbour via *Skolavördu Str.*, *statue of Leif Ericsson*, discoverer of America, and nearby *Einar Jónsson Museum.* Y.H.

Reykjavík is best centre for organised tours in S.W. or further afield. Consult *Iceland Tourist Bureau* in *Laekjargata* and *Ferdafélag Islands*.

EXCURSIONS: (a) *Hafnarfjördhur*, 7 miles, cod-fishing port, built on lava. S. across lava fields to *Krísuvík*, 18 miles, boiling mud pools and sulphur pools; (b) **Heimaev, Westman Islands** (¼ hr. by air), fishing centre, famous breeding place of sea birds, including large gannet colony; (c) *Heidarból*, 10 miles E. on edge of large lava field (Y.H. No warden; key in *Reykjavík*).

R.1.   Reykjavík—Thingvellir—Selfoss—Hvítárvatn (135 miles)

Thingvellir, 35 miles, meeting place of Althing for over 850 years; lava plain between mountains and *Thingvallavatn*, largest lake; birds include whooper swan, whimbrel, ptarmigan, redwing. Continue E. side of lake and down valley of R. *Sog* to *Sogsbrú* and *Selfoss*, 30 miles. Area is chief farming region of Iceland.

EXCURSION: *Hveragerdhi*, 7 miles, village with hot springs used for hot-house cultivation.

Laugarvatn, 23 miles, beautifully situated on lake (warm water); **Stóri Geysir**, 14 miles, most famous geyser in world, all others named from it, jet 160 ft., many others in locality; **Gullfoss**, 3 miles, magnificent falls on R. *Hvítá*.

Hvítárvatn, 30 miles, in central stone desert under *Langjökull*, from which glaciers descend to lake.

R.2   Selfoss—Skóga Foss—Vík—Kirkjubæjarklaustur (116 miles)

Selfoss (R.1) to *Thjórsárbrú*, 10 miles, bridge over R. *Thjórsá*.

R.2(i) Hekla. 6 miles beyond bridge, road N.E. to *Skardh*, 18 miles, for ascent of Hekla (4,748 ft.) and treks to *Landmannahellir* and *Landmannalaugar* with fine scenery in desert area N. of mountain.

Ægisidha, 12 miles, ancient artificial underground caves. *Stórolfshvoll*, 10 miles. Y.H. at *Fljotsdalur*.

R.2(ii) Stórolfshvoll to Hlidharendi, 11 miles, farm mentioned in *Njáls Saga*.

Stóridalur, 12 miles. *Surtsey Island*—the outcome of the submarine volcanic eruption in November 1963—is 10 miles S.W. of here. Road passes S. of ice mass of *Myrdalsjökull*. Skóga Foss 200 ft. fall, 15 miles. *Vik*, 24 miles, small fishing settlement. *Kirkjubæjarklaustur* 43 miles, terminus of summer bus service.

R.2(iii) Towards Vatnajökull. *Kálfafell*, 20 miles, beyond which route across sand desert is difficult; many swift streams from glaciers of ice cap, unbridged and with changing courses (local guide required). But *Skaftafell*, 23 miles, and other settlements under Öræfajökull have splendid scenery.

R.3.   Reykjavík—Hredavatnsskáli—Akureyri—Lake Mývatn (350 miles)

Road follows coast, skirting *Hvalfjördhur* (whaling centre) to head of *Borgarfjördhur*, 70 miles.

R.3(i) Snæfellsnes Peninsula. From *Borg* on *Borgarfjördhur* road across plain of *Mýrar* with many lakes. *Budhir*, 55 miles.

EXCURSIONS: (a) spectacular basalt sea cliffs below *Snæfellsjökull* with caves and stacks; (b) lava fields and glacier of *Snæfellsjökull* (4,745 ft., extinct volcano).

From *Budhir* return 18 miles E. to near *Hofstadhir* where road crosses peninsula to *Stykkishólmur*, 18 miles, port (boats may be hired for visits to *Flatey* and other islands in Breidhifjördhur).

Hredavatnsskáli, 15 miles, beautiful volcanic scenery. Road reaches N. coast at *Stadhur*, 45 miles, on *Hrútafjördhur*. *Blönduós*, 60 miles.

Akureyri (Y.H.), 95 miles (bus and air connections with *Reykjavík*) second town of Iceland, sheltered situation. *Eyjafjördhur*, verdant country.

Godhafoss, waterfall, 30 miles; **Lake Mývatn**, 30 miles. Lake famous for variety of its volcanic landscape (craters, fissures, ashes, lavas) and as chief breeding place of many species of duck and other wildfowl.

EXCURSIONS: (a) *Dettifoss*, huge waterfall, 20 miles; (b) longer expeditions, requiring planning, can be made into desert area to south, notably to *Askja* (great eruption depression) and *Herdhubreidh*, a climbers' mountain.

IRELAND

Geographical and Historical Outline

Land   Ireland, the second largest of the British Isles, has an area of 31,840 sq. miles of which some 26,000 are in the independent *Republic of Ireland*, the remainder, i.e. six of the nine counties of the old province of *Ulster*, comprising *Northern Ireland*, which remains a part of the *United Kingdom*.

Structurally Ireland is a western continuation of Britain. The main mountain districts lie around the coasts whilst the centre is a limestone plateau. A striking feature is the large number of rivers and lakes, including the two largest lakes in the *British Isles—Lough Neagh* in *Northern Ireland* and *Lough Corrib* in the *Republic*. The basalt of the north-east gives rise to spectacular coastal features including the famous *Giant's Causeway*. The western seaboard is characterized by many islands, drowned valleys and deep bays.

Climate   The climate is like that of England, with very variable weather, though rather wetter, especially in the West, and with less snow and ice in winter. The prevailing wind is South-West. May and June are usually dry and pleasantly warm; July and August rather more changeable.

Plants and Animals   Though in many parts of the country the underlying rock is limestone, most of the mountain areas have a peaty soil, with great stretches of heathery moorland, similar to the highlands of *Scotland*. The peat of the central bogland is of great interest to ecologists and botanists. Ireland became a separate land mass early in the Ice ages, and many species which have since spread across Britain are unknown there. In compensation there are special rarities known also only in Portugal and N.W. Spain, or even in North America. The *Burren* of *County Clare* supports an astonishing mixture of arctic-alpine and mediterranean species, which makes it most worth visiting in early summer.

The country has suffered greatly from deforestation during the past three centuries, but efforts are now being made to re-afforest numerous mountain areas, largely with foreign conifers.

The fauna also shows the effects of isolation; the Irish hare and Irish stoat are examples. Snakes are famous for their absence. There is a wealth of bird life.

History   Ireland was never part of the Roman Empire—a circumstance which brought it two great if temporary advantages: the Celts, who had overrun the island about the beginning of the Christian era, were able to develop a native culture comparatively free of

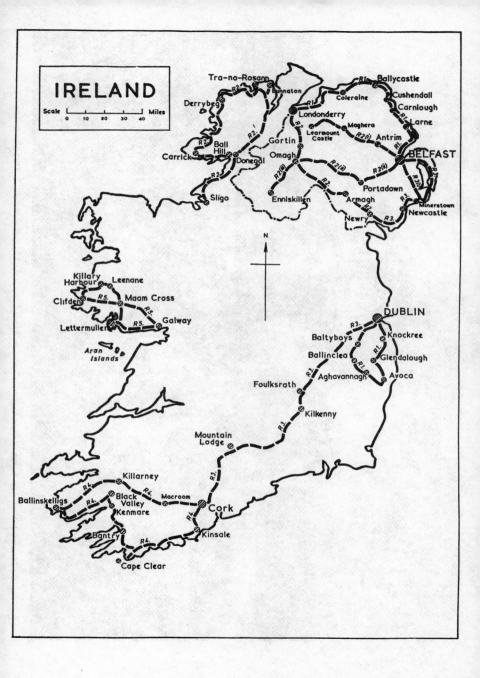

Gaily painted, five-berth "Gypsy wagons" can be hired for about $75 per week, including the horse.

outside influences until the Christianizing mission of St. Patrick in the 5th century; and the country avoided the general ruin which engulfed most of Europe when the Empire collapsed in the face of the barbarian invasions. Ireland in fact became in the Dark Ages a beacon of culture and peaceful progress which gave it a name in Europe as "the island of saints and scholars".

For centuries it remained divided into a number of separate kingdoms represented by the provinces of *Leinster, Munster, Connaught* and *Ulster*, the title of "high king", to whom the others owed allegiance, being held most of the time by the O'Neills of *Ulster* but subsequently, in the 11th and 12th centuries, by the O'Briens of *Munster* and the O'Connors of *Connaught*.

Viking invasions in the 9th and 10th centuries led to the founding of Norse settlements at *Dublin, Wexford, Waterford, Cork* and *Limerick*.

Two centuries of Anglo-Norman overlordship began in 1167 with the intervention of Henry II in Irish affairs. The country became divided into the Anglo-Irish territories within a boundary called the "Pale" and independent Celtic Ireland "beyond the Pale".

The subsequent history of relations between England and Ireland is not a happy one. The English land proprietors became for a time free of allegiance to the English crown. When the Tudors and Stuarts regained authority England had become Protestant and the old Catholic proprietors were expelled to be replaced by Protestants. Catholicism itself was repressed, the process being carried furthest by Oliver Cromwell.

Much of *Ulster* had been settled by Protestant immigrants from England and Scotland. Their support of William of Orange against James II in the famous siege of *Londonderry* (1689) and the battle of the *Boyne* (1690) was important in establishing the success of the English Revolution and the effective end of Jacobite hopes.

The English Parliament now virtually controlled Irish affairs, but it was not until the *Act of Union* (1800) that Irish representatives became entitled to seats at *Westminster*. The chief benefit was the gaining of Catholic emancipation (1829) largely due to the tenacious and valiant campaigns of Daniel O'Connell. But in economic affairs Parliament's belief in free trade operated to the disadvantage of Ireland. Except for linen and shipbuilding in the north-east the poorer country was unable to establish industries. The potato famine of 1845-49 was a major disaster for its dense population (over 8 million in 1841) and led to great decline by deaths and emigration.

Home rule for Ireland became a burning question, associated on the Irish side particularly with the name of Parnell and on the English side with Gladstone. By 1913 it had become a demand for a republic. Both were opposed by Protestant *Ulster*. Eventually, in 1921 an *Irish Free State* with dominion status was established, except for the six counties of *Northern Ireland* which elected to remain within the Union as a federal province. In 1937 the Free State became the sovereign independent democratic state of *Eire* (*Ireland*), and in 1949 it became a *Republic* formally separated from the *Commonwealth*.

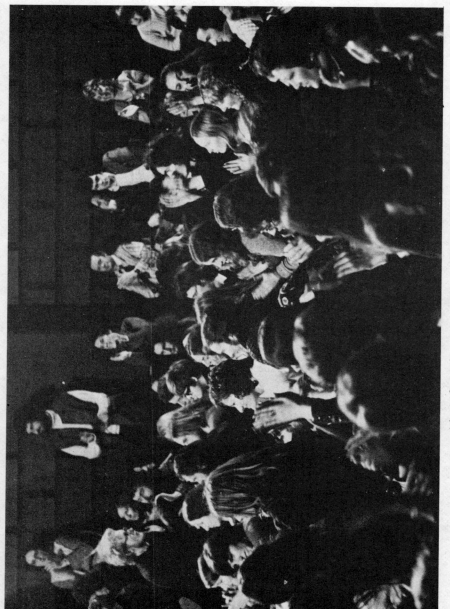

A festival of Celtic music at Trinity College, Dublin.

THE REPUBLIC OF IRELAND

The People

Population   Of the population of about 2,900,000 some 600,000 live in *Dublin*. *Cork* (75,000) is the second city, and about 270,000 more live in towns of over 10,000 inhabitants. Settlement is therefore predominantly rural. In many counties (such as *Donegal, Kerry, Clare* and *Meath*) and in the whole province of *Connaught* the density is under 75 per sq. mile.

There is probably some survival of pre-Celtic stock. The Celtic type as known to antiquity, tall and blond and often red-haired, is to be found most often in *Co. Donegal*, while the black-haired blue-eyed types of the south and west are also regarded as typically Celtic. Many Normans, Flemings, Welsh and English settled in the country following the Norman invasion and there has been a gradual influx of English and Scottish blood over the centuries especially in the towns. Germans from the *Rhine-Mosel* region who settled mainly in *Co. Limerick*, and French Huguenot refugees, have also left their mark.

Language   Irish, the ancient language of the country, is closely related to Scots Gaelic. It is spoken as a mother tongue in certain remote areas of the south and west and in *Co. Donegal*, but English remains the language of common use in the country as a whole.

Religion   The population is overwhelmingly Roman Catholic.

Government   The head of the state is the Uachtaran (President) and the executive head of government is the Taoiseach (Prime Minister) acting with an Executive Council or Cabinet. Parliament consists of the Dail, with 147 members, elected by citizens of 21 years and over, and a Senate or upper house, chosen partly by indirect election on a mainly vocational basis and partly by the Taoiseach's nomination.

Resources and Occupations   The main source of income is agriculture, particularly the raising of beef cattle, which are exported mainly to England. The soil, except in the mountain areas, is well suited to dairying and horticulture, though high summer rainfall makes cereal crops other than oats somewhat hazardous. The excellent bone-forming properties of the limestone soil make the rearing of thoroughbred horses an important national enterprise.

The want of minerals has in the past restricted industrial development, but an intensive programme of electrical development, using both water-power and peat fuel from the bogs, has done much to fill the gap, so that now more than half the employed population is engaged in industry. Manufactured foodstuffs of various kinds, beer, stout and whiskey are exported, together with handwoven tweeds and carpets.

IRELAND

Culture

Architecture
The Romanesque style of the pre-Norman period may best be seen in *Cormac's Chapel* on the *Rock of Cashel*, the doorway of *Clonfert* cathedral in S.E. *Co. Galway*, and various ruined churches, especially *Clonmacnoise*. For the Gothic period the most important buildings still in use are the two cathedrals in *Dublin*, *St. Patrick's* and *Christ Church*, and *St. Canice's* cathedral in *Kilkenny*. Of the many imposing monastic buildings of the Middle Ages, most are now in ruins; especially noteworthy are those of *Mellifont Abbey*, beside the *Mellifont* hostel, and *Jerpoint Abbey* in *Co. Kilkenny*. *Dublin* has many examples of Regency and Georgian architecture. Contemporary architecture is not much in evidence, though *Dublin's* fine airport is a notable exception, and many recently built churches show a pleasing blend of tradition and modernity. Much good modern stained glass is produced in Ireland: fine examples are to be found in *Donegal* town and in *Loughrea, Co. Galway*.

Music and Dances
There is an astonishingly rich background of folk music, modal in type, with many melodies of intense and haunting beauty. Singing in the traditional style may often be heard at local *"feiseanna"*—festivals in Irish music, dancing and story-telling somewhat on the lines of the Welsh eisteddfod. Irish traditional dancing is very like the Scottish; many tunes and dances are in fact identical, though differently named.

Drama
The Irish excel in the art of the theatre, having a talent for acting which makes for a high standard both professional and amateur. The *Abbey Theatre* in *Dublin*, the centre of the Irish dramatic movement of the beginning of the 20th century, is world famous. It specializes in plays with an Irish setting, while the *Gate Theatre* productions have usually a more cosmopolitan flavour. The *Damer Hall* in *St. Stephen's Green* is often used by Irish-speaking amateur companies both from *Dublin* and the provinces. Dramatic societies are numerous in provincial towns and even in some of the remote country districts, particularly in Irish-speaking areas.

Literature
Among the Gaelic languages Irish was for long the only literary form. Its classic stories, probably first written down in the 9th century, include heroic tales built around the lives of Cuchulain and Deirdre (the Gaelic equivalents of Achilles and Helen of Troy) or around the doings of Fingal and Ossian. The creation of Irish-Gaelic literature has been stimulated in the 20th century by the revival of interest in the spoken language.

Of wider significance has been the famous revival of Irish literature in the English language which developed as an expression of national consciousness at the same time as the growth of republican sentiments. Its chief glory was the dramatic movement based principally on the works of W. B. Yeats and J. M. Synge and whose later playwrights have included Lord Dunsany, St. John Ervine and Sean O'Casey. Yeats was also chief among the poets of the revival, whilst in prose there appeared the figure of James Joyce besides many excellent storytellers of more local achievement.

IRELAND

Apart from such writers in the Irish tradition, authors of Irish origin have made major contributions to the general body of English literature. They include Congreve, Swift, Goldsmith, Sheridan and Burke, and, more recently, Wilde and Shaw.

Touring Information

Information Services
Touring information and free copies of the booklets *Land of Youth* and *Land of Learning* can be obtained from any Irish Tourist Board office. They are located at 590 5th Avenue, New York, N.Y. 10036; 224 North Michigan Avenue, Chicago, Ill. 60601; and 681 Market Street, San Francisco, Calif. 94105.

Touring Areas
The scenic areas which attract the most visitors are the *Wicklow Mountains*, south of Dublin; the mountains of *Cork* and *Kerry* in the south-west, with Ireland's highest mountain, *Carrantuohill*, (3,414 ft.); the mountain and moorland region of *Connaught*, lying between *Galway Bay* and *Sligo Bay* in the west; the hills of *Donegal* in the extreme north-west. Less known mountain areas of greaty beauty are the *Galtee* and *Comeragh Mountains* of *Counties Tipperary* and *Waterford* in the south, and the *Carlingford Peninsula*, on the east coast, north of *Dundalk*.

Access
(a) **By sea from Great Britain.** (i) *Liverpool-Dublin*; (B and I Line), day and night services, both directions, 7–8¼ hours. (ii) *Holyhead-Dun Laoghaire*, with short train connection to *Dublin* is the quickest surface route from *London*; (British Rail), day and night services, both directions, 3¼ hours. (iii) *Fishguard-Rosslare*; (British Rail), daily service, except Sundays, and night services in mid-summer, 3¼ hours. (iv) *Swansea-Cork*; (B and I Line), daily services, 9 hours. Sailing tickets required at peak periods on all these services.

(b) **By air.** Aer Lingus, in conjunction with British Airways, operate services between *Dublin* and *London* and many other U.K. airports; also *London* to *Shannon Airport* near *Limerick*. Reductions for young persons under 22 years, 1 month excursion trips, mid-week travel, and (in case of *London*) for night and early morning flights.

Transport
The railway network links the towns, but does not extend into all the scenic areas.
The bus service covers most of the country; services infrequent except in neighbourhood of *Dublin* where weekday and Sunday buses serve points within walking distance of several *Co. Wicklow* youth hostels.
Coras Iompair Eireann issue 15-day Rail Rambler tickets and composite Rail and Bus tickets for 15 days.

IRELAND

Money
British money is current in Ireland, but Irish money is not acceptable in Britain. Irish banks will change Irish money into British without charge. Banking hours in small towns vary widely; they may be open only on a few days a week.

Bank Holidays
St. Patrick's Day (17th March), Good Friday, Easter Monday, Whit. Monday, First Monday in August, New Year's Day.

Restaurants
Restaurants serving cheap and simple meals are rare, except in towns. Meat courses are generally good and generously served.

Maps
The Ordnance Survey publishes maps, scale 1 inch to 1 mile for the *Dublin*, *Wicklow*, *Cork* and *Killarney* tourist areas; also a series at ½ inch to 1 mile in 25 sheets covering all the country. Bartholomew's maps, scale ¼ inch to 1 mile cover the country in 5 sheets.

Accommodation
The Irish Y.H.A., *An Oige*, has about 40 hostels, most of them comparatively small. Booking in advance is essential at weekends, particularly for hostels within reach of *Dublin*, and at all times for parties of any size. Cooked meals are not provided, but there is cooking equipment and crockery. The *Wicklow Mountains* and the south-west of *Donegal* are the areas best covered, but the other main scenic areas are also accessible and a circular cycling tour of Ireland can be made from hostel to hostel without runs over 100 miles.

Walking
Admirable walking country in most of the mountain areas served by hostels; in *Co. Wicklow* it is possible to plan a complete cross-country walking tour from hostel to hostel.

Cycling
Main roads are good; rough conditions may be met on minor roads and routes should be planned accordingly. The frequency of strong S.W. winds should also be allowed for.

Dublin

Dublin (Y.Hs.). Centre of city is formed by *O'Connell Street* and its intersection with *River Liffey*. Main shopping streets (a) S. of river: *Grafton Street*, where most fashionable shops are situated, and *Great George's Street*, parallel with it, nearer the river; (b) N. of river: *Henry Street* and *Talbot Street*, parallel to the river and crossing *O'Connell Street*.

18th century classicism is predominant architectural influence, seen in many streets and squares, especially in neighbourhood of *Merrion Square*. See also the *Custom House* (1791), on N. quayside E. of *O'Connell Bridge*, the *Law Courts* (1796) known as the Four Courts on N. quays W. of *O'Connell Bridge*, the *Bank of Ireland* (formerly Parliament House) (1729), *Trinity College*, of which the West front buildings were completed in 1759, the house of the Provost of *Trinity*, King's Inns in *Henrietta Street*, King's Hospital School, and the former Newcomen's bank, now corporation buildings, beyond top of *Dame Street*. *Dublin Castle*, off *Dame Street*, consists of a series of quadrangles (now government offices) of varying date, from medieval *Record Tower* to the early 19th century *Chapel Royal.*

The squares and playing fields of *Trinity College* form a green and peaceful oasis in middle of city; its library has some of greatest treasures of Celtic art, especially the **Book of Kells,** an early 9th century copy of the Gospels with illuminations of extraordinary complexity and beauty.

National Museum, Kildare Street, has superb examples of Celtic art; celebrated *Tara brooch* and *Ardagh* chalice. *National Gallery, Merrion Square,* has a particularly fine El Greco; Tiepolo and a Correggio Nativity. *Municipal Gallery, Parnell Square,* mainly 19th and 20th century artists.

There are two medieval cathedrals, *Christ Church* and *St. Patrick's,* the latter containing burial place of Jonathan Swift. *St. Michan's* church on N. side of river has fine 18th century interior and vaults where those with a taste for the gruesome may see a collection of naturally mummified bodies. The *University Church,* on *St. Stephen's Green,* is a fine example of modern building in the Byzantine style.

Touring Routes

R.1 Dublin to Aghavannagh through the Wicklow Mountains

Dublin Y.H.—*Knockree* Y.H.—*Glendaloch* Y.H.—*Aghavannagh* Y.H.—*Ballinclea* Y.H.—*Baltyboys* Y.H.—*Dublin,* gives a total distance of 122 miles. The area is of great scenic beauty, with heather-clad mountains rising to 3,039 ft. at their highest point. *Lugnaquilla,* easily climbed either from *Glenmalure, Ballinclea* or *Aghavannagh* hostels. The valley of *Glendaloch* is a celebrated beauty spot; ruins of pre-Norman monastic settlement (*St. Kevin's*) with round tower and other buildings, 6th-12th century. *Avoca* valley and *Glenmalure* (Y.H.) are also particularly beautiful. *Wicklow* is a county to linger in rather than pass through; several hostels are excellent centres for hill walking. Rock climbing in *Glendaloch* and at some points on flanks of *Lugnaquilla.*

R.2. Tir Chonaill (County Donegal)

Sligo—Ball Hill Y.H.—*Carrick* Y.H.—*Dunlewy* Y.H.—*Tra-na-Rosann* Y.H. *Bunnaton* Y.H. and back by *Ball Hill* to *Sligo* (301 miles).

Donegal is wild and rocky, and contains some of Ireland's most spectacular scenery, especially *Slieve League,* near *Carrick,* where a mountain of 1,972 ft. falls in a sheer cliff to the Atlantic, impressive cliffs of *Bloody Foreland,* near *Derrybeg,* and *Horn Head,* near *Tra-na-Rosann.* Highest mountains are *Errigal* (2,466 ft. accessible from *Tra-na-Rosann* by bicycle) and *Muckish* (2,197 ft. 8 miles from *Tra-na-Rosann*). *Dunlewy* Y.H. is in heart of Irish speaking area. County has little industry, but *Donegal* tweeds, hand-spun and hand-woven, are world famous; *Carrigart* is a main local centre for their sale.

R.3. Dublin to Cork, via County Kilkenny and the Galtee Mountains

Dublin—Foulksrath Y.H. 66 miles—*Mountain Lodge* Y.H. 57 miles—*Cork* Y.H. 53 miles.

IRELAND

This route makes accessible the *Barrow* valley and *County Kilkenny* and the mountain area of *County Tipperary*. *Foulksrath* can be the base for a visit to *Kilkenny*: important in Irish history, fine 13th century cathedral and other medieval churches. The *Galtee Mountains*, between *Mountain Lodge* Y.H. and *Ballydavid Wood* Y.H. are worth exploring; magnificent panorama from highest point, *Galteemore* (3,018 ft.). The *Rock of Cashel*, with cathedral ruins, chapel of *Cormac*, and an Irish high cross, is within reach for cyclists, and should not be missed. Near *Mountain Lodge* are *Mitchelstown* caves, a chain of limestone caverns.

R.4. Cork and the South-West

Cork, second city of Republic; partly built on island in river *Lee*, many bridges, fine quays. Protestant and Roman Catholic cathedrals; *St. Anne Shandon's* church, unusual sandstone and limestone spire. University has 16th century cloisters, charmingly laid out grounds, and *Honan* chapel— a tiny but exquisite gem of mosaic and stained glass. *Turner's Cross* church, one of few uncompromisingly modern churches in the country. Riverside walks and wooded heights give city a picturesque and tranquil charm, in contrast to the well-known energy of its inhabitants. **(Y.H.)**.

Within easy reach by bus is *Blarney Castle*, in park-like grounds, where those who wish to acquire the gift of eloquence the easy way can do it—or so they say—by kissing the *Blarney Stone*. Numerous seaside resorts around shores of *Cork Harbour*; swimming, boating, sea fishing. *Cobh*, on island in harbour, is port of call for trans-Atlantic liners. *Cork's* most important cultural event is annual film festival, which has an international reputation.

The mountain area of *Counties Cork and Kerry* contain Ireland's highest mountain, *Carrantuohill* (3,414 ft.) and most famous beauty spot, *Killarney*, Like *Wicklow*, it is a region to be lingered in; splendid opportunities for hill walking and scrambling, with **Y.H.** at *Black Valley* and *Killarney* well situated for the purpose. On west coast is *Ballinskelligs* **Y.H.**, sea-fishing, swimming, boating; it may also be possible to make the 9-mile sea trip to *Skellig Rocks* (on largest, *Skellig Michael*, are buildings of an early hermit settlement). **Y.H.** *Cape Clear Island*, reached from *Baltimore* harbour by ferry.

Cork **(Y.H.)** to *Kinsale* **(Y.H.)**, 18 miles; small fishing port, place of James II's landing (1689) in attempt to recover English crown. *Cape Clear* **(Y.H.)** (40 miles). Then via *Bantry* and *Bantry Bay*, one of many fine examples of drowned valleys of this coast, and through beautiful *Glengariff* valley noted for mild climate and Mediterranean vegetation to *Kenmare* (**Y.H.** at *Bonane*) and *Black Valley* **(Y.H.)** (80 miles) mountainous going, not possible in one day except for the tough. *Ballinskelligs* **(Y.H.)** (56 miles); then to **Killarney (Y.H.)** (48 miles). The famous lakes are sheltered by two sandstone ranges: *MacGillicuddy's Reeks*, which include *Carrantuohill*, and that which runs from *Cahirbarragh* (2,239 ft.) to *Mangerton* (2,756 ft.). Lower lake has many wooded islands; *Muckross*, on Middle lake, is site of ancient abbey; semi-tropical plants abound; many fine walks. Return to *Cork*, via *Macroom* (59 miles).

Districts of great beauty, not yet within easy reach of hostels, are (i) the *Beare Peninsula* running west from *Glengariff*; (ii) the *Dingle Peninsula*, chief Irish-speaking district of the southwest; (iii) *Gouganebarra*, in the heart of the mountains between *Bantry* and *Macroom*.

248

R.5   Galway, Connemara and the Joyce Country

Galway (train from *Dublin*, 3¼ hours), capital of the West; picturesquely situated on estuary of *Corrib* river; was formerly second city of Ireland, though of its medieval grandeur not much remains save imposing church of *St. Nicholas* and 16th century house in main street known as *Lynch's Castle*. Now flourishing seaside resort, and has many factories. Fine university buildings. Boating on river *Corrib*, and on lake from which it flows, is a favourite local pursuit. *Galway* races, last week of July, are sporting event of national importance.

Galway's western hinterland is a lonely but beautiful district of bare mountains and desolate boglands; countless lakes, from the great *Lough Corrib* to tiny moorland pools barely large enough to hold a trout, make it an angler's paradise. *Connemara*, properly so called, is the southern coastal region which remains largely Irish-speaking. The more mountainous northern section, the *Joyce Country*, is accessible from *Killary Harbour*. (Y.H.).

The *Connemara* coast is ideal for a holiday of boating, fishing and swimming; many good beaches, mostly empty, except at weekends.

Aran Islands: at head of *Galway Bay*; fishing boats make frequent crossings from *Lettermullen*. Those interested in antiquities should certainly make this trip and see *Dun Aengus*, prehistoric circular stone fortress on *Inishmore*, the largest island; also early Christian chapels, shrines and beehive huts. The islands are formed of limestone; their sparse soil is mixed with seaweed for the growing of barley and potatoes.

Killary Harbour (Y.H.); among some of finest scenery in the West; on southern shore of long sea inlet, opposite *Mweelrea* (2,688 ft.) highest mountain in county. Rock climbing on it and on mountain groups of *Beanna Beola* (*The Twelve Bens*) and *Maumturk* range south of hostel.

Circular tour from *Galway*, along coast road to *Lettermullen* (36 miles); thence N. to *Maam Cross* and W. to *Clifden*, capital of *Connemara*, near which first trans-Atlantic fliers, Alcock and Brown, made their landing (1919); then N. and E. circling mountains via *Letterfrack* and *Kylemore*, to *Killary Harbour* (Y.H.). (53 miles). Then by *Leenane*, through *Joyce Country* to *Maam Cross* and *Oughterard* (fishing centre on *Lough Corrib*) and back to *Galway*. (45 miles).

If time can be spared, coast road can be followed all the way from *Lettermullen* to *Clifden*, via charming small fishing town of *Roundstone* and, a little beyond it, *Dog's Bay*, finest bathing beach in *Connemara*.

R.5 (i) From *Leenane*, N. via *Westport* and round N. shore of *Clew Bay* to *Currane* (Y.H.) on *Achill Sound*, for a visit to *Achill Island* (linked to mainland by bridge); spectacular scenery, especially cliffs of *Croaghan* (2,192 ft.) plunging to Atlantic, and beautiful cone of *Slievemore* (2,204 ft.); fine bathing beaches. (*Leenane* to *Currane*, 45 miles).

NORTHERN IRELAND

The People

Population
Of the population of about 1,550,000 more than 50% are town dwellers, including some 360,000 in *Belfast* the capital.

The people are of varied ancestry: Irish, Scots, English and a few French. This diversity arises from the history of the province—the "Plantations" of the 17th century, for example, when Scots and English settlers were brought in. This explains the term "Scots-Irish" and "Ulster Scot" by which the Ulsterman not obviously of Irish origin is often known abroad. It also explains the political abyss between "Orange" (Protestant mainly and in favour of continued union with Great Britain) and "Green" (Roman Catholic mainly and in favour of union with the Republic).

Language
English is spoken everywhere, and in a variety of local accents, in some places closer to Elizabethan than to modern English, and sometimes influenced by the idioms of Gaelic. Almost all place names are of Gaelic origin.

Religion
The various Protestant denominations (Church of Ireland, Presbyterian, Methodist, etc.) account for 65% of the population, the remainder being Roman Catholics. The term "Church of Ireland" does not signify a state church. In spite of the strong religious affiliations of almost all its people, Northern Ireland is legally a secular state, no denomination receiving state support.

Government
Northern Ireland has, since 1800, been part of the United Kingdom; but it has a considerable measure of self-government with a separate legislative body, the Northern Ireland Assembly, dealing with domestic matters. It also sends twelve members to the United Kingdom Parliament at *Westminster* which is responsible for such matters as taxation, foreign affairs, defence and law and order.

The Northern Ireland Assembly, sitting at *Stormont*, on the outskirts of *Belfast*, consists of 78 members elected by proportional representation.

Resources
Farming is the chief occupation in a land of small farms which under a system of Government loans, are becoming the property of those who farm them. The standard is constantly being raised by application of scientific methods and mechanisation.

The other main occupations are in the world-renowned Irish linen industry; ship-building in *Belfast*; and the manufacture of aircraft.

Mineral resources are few. Coal occurs, but cannot be mined easily. This and the lack of raw materials has led to a policy of manufacturing goods of high specific value: for example, electronic computers and radio and electrical goods. Many of these industries are in the smaller towns, but *Belfast* itself has a great diversity.

As in the rest of Ireland there is a marked lack of woodlands. Fishing is carried on from a number of small ports, particularly in *Co. Down.* There is a considerable tourist trade.

National Character-istics The characteristic of the Ulsterman most likely to be noticed by the visitor is his interest in the stranger and his desire to help him—in particular in seeing those parts of the country which should not be missed, and to which he will be directed with obvious pride. A "bit of a crack" (a chat) is always appreciated and often worth the time spent on it.

In country districts a greeting may be expected from all passers-by—usually a comment on the weather, accompanied by a peculiar slow sideways tilt of the head.

Food and Drink The pattern is very like that in Scotland, particularly in the variety of bread and scones, including "soda" bread and "potato" bread, both usually in the form of *farls* baked on a griddle.

Sport Most town dwellers are keenly interested in sport, principally Association, Gaelic, or Rugby football, golf, cricket and hockey (or its Gaelic counterparts, hurley and camogie). In Gaelic football (a cross between the other two codes) a player can take three steps with the ball in his hands.

Culture

Folklore Ireland as a whole has been described as a "treasure house of old ways unrivalled in Western Europe" and *Ulster* as its most representative region.

While Northern Ireland is rich in folklore, systematic attempts at recording it have only been made in recent times. In some country districts vestiges remain of the old "*ceilidhe*" system of entertainment, by which people gathered in the home of a neighbour for conversation, song and dance, story telling, or even card playing, according to age. Superstitions abound, largely based on legends of the "wee people" (fairies) and even a hard-headed farmer will leave a "fairy thorn" tree standing in a ploughed field. In some parts, wishing wells are common, often with a nearby tree bearing pins or strips of cloth taken from the clothing, to transfer ailments from the person to the tree. Charms against the evil eye are still used, and the treatment of human ailments by charms is widespread. St. Brigid's Crosses are made of rushes cut on the eve of St. Brigid's Day. These charms are really of pagan origin and design. These are merely samples of the many ancient practices still to be found in the *Ulster* countryside.

Music Music is more for the participator than the listener, though there are worthwhile orchestral and choral concerts mainly during the winter. Bands abound: brass, bagpipe, flute and accordion. Choirs are numerous. There are well-supported musical festivals in *Belfast* and other places.

Touring Information

Touring Areas
The *Antrim* coast and basalt plateau of the north-east; the *Mourne Mountains*; the *Sperrin Mountains*; the lake district of *Co. Fermanagh*.

Access
(a) **By sea from Great Britain.** (i) *Stranraer (Scotland)—Larne*: (British Rail), day and night services, 2½ hours. Shortest sea route. Y.H. at *Minnigaff*, 20 miles from *Stranraer*, Y.H. at *Ballygally*, 4 miles N. of *Larne* at start of *Antrim* coast chain. (ii) *Liverpool—Belfast*: (Belfast Steamship Co. Ltd.), nightly except Sun., 9¾ hours. (iii) *Heysham—Belfast*: (British Rail), nightly except Sun., 7¼ hours. (iv) *Ardrossan—Belfast*: (Burns & Laird Lines Ltd.). Daily 4½ hours. Sailing tickets required at peak periods on all these services.
(b) **By air.** Services between *Belfast* and *London, Birmingham, Leeds, Manchester, Newcastle upon Tyne, Edinburgh* and *Glasgow*.
(c) **From the Republic.** A good train service, *Dublin-Belfast*, serves also intermediate stations such as *Newry* (for the *Mourne Mountains*). Elsewhere, access is mainly by local bus. Travelling from the Republic to Northern Ireland involves a customs examination.

Transport
There are two main railway systems, and an intricate network of bus services, all under the control of the *Ulster Transport Authority*.

Money
British money is used. (So, quite unofficially, is that of the Republic of Ireland.)

Public Holidays
The chief general holiday is 12th July, the day of the parades of Orangemen; in *Belfast* 20,000 men with bands and banners take part. The week in which this day falls is the traditional holiday week. Bank holidays are the same as in England, with the addition of 17th March (St. Patrick's Day) and 12th July.

Restaurants
Outside *Belfast*, not abundant; but in all towns it is possible to get a meal either in a restaurant or a hotel. The usual charge for a 3-course midday meal in a small hotel is about £1·00 and in a restaurant about 75p.

Maps
For the walker, the Ordnance Survey maps, scale 1 inch to 1 mile, covering the country in 9 sheets, are excellent. Bartholomew's maps, scale ¼ inch to 1 mile, on two sheets, are adequate for cyclists.

Accom-   The chain of youth hostels is closely spaced from *Larne*
modation   northwards along the *Antrim* coast, then south through *Derry*
           and *Tyrone*. Between *Omagh* and the *Mourne Mountain* chain
the gap can be bridged by train, *Omagh-Portadown* and *Portadown-Newry-
Warrenpoint*. Apart from this a circuit can be made in which the greatest
distance between hostels is about 30 miles, or much less by using buses. All
the hostels are small and meals are not provided, but members' kitchens are
everywhere well equipped, though cutlery is not provided.

*All reservations to be made through Y.H.A.N.I. Office, 93 Dublin Road,
Belfast.* A tour form can be obtained and a complete tour thus booked by
one application. Advance booking advised for Easter, July and August.

Walking   The best walking is in open country, often without road, path
           or track, in the upland areas mentioned above—first-class
           country in which hostels are within walking distance of each
other.

Rock climbing is practised in some parts of the *Mourne Mountains*, but for
ordinary hill walking no special skill is needed beyond the common sense
always called for in such country.

Touring Routes

R.1. Belfast to Londonderry via Antrim Coast Road (120 miles)

Belfast, lively industrial city and seaport. Around City Hall (Classical
Renaissance style) is excellent shopping centre and busy commercial area.
Much of city given over to factories and terraces of workers' houses, product
of rapid expansion in 19th century, but there are pleasant suburbs and
public parks, and surrounding hills provide a beautiful setting. Panoramic
views from Bellevue and Hazelwood Parks, of city, port area (massive cranes
and gantries of shipyards) and surrounding countryside. Buses for tour of
city from City Hall (*Donegal Square East*). *Belfast Museum* at *Stranmillis*
is worth a visit. **(Y.H.)**

Parliament House at *Stormont* (city transport direct) pleasantly situated on
low hill; extensive views.

Leave *Belfast* by *York Street, York Road* and *Shore Road*, passing shopping
centre and factory area (linen and tobacco). *Carrickfergus*; massive Norman
castle (1200) and ancient church of *St. Nicholas*. Along shores of *Larne Lough*,
noted for sea birds and wild fowl, to *Larne*, or train to *Larne* from *York
Road Station*. Those who have crossed on the *Stranraer-Larne* Ferry could
make this their starting point.

At *Larne* the famous **Antrim Coast Road,** one of most attractive roads in
Europe, begins. Below lies the sea; behind lie extensive moors and beautiful
Antrim Glens—all worth exploring by taking an extra day or two at any
County Antrim hostel.

Ballygally (**Y.H.**), attractive village, 4 miles north of *Larne*. Continue by road, either to *Carncastle* (and hence by moors), or to *Glenarm* and *Carnlough*, each with small harbour. Route continues north between cliff and sea round *Garron Point* (walkers can cross moors above *Carnlough* to *Parkmore* at head of *Glenariff*, and so avoid the dangerous *Glenariff* cliffs) and to *Red Bay* (good and quiet beach) and *Cushendall* (**Y.H.** *Moneyvart*), from which three of *Glens of Antrim* radiate. Here main road swings inland, but by-roads lead to *Cushendun*, quiet village, popular among artists.

To *Ballyvoy* and *Ballycastle*, choice of routes: main road; or *Torr Head* road by coast, with steep hills and very sharp bends; or, for walkers, by open moors east or west of main road. *Murlough Bay* and wild, open country around *Fair Head* are worth a detour, or a separate day's walking.

Ballycastle (**Y.H.**) quiet seaside resort, except on last Tuesday in August when famous Lammas Fair is held. *Rathlin Island* can be reached by motor boat.

Continue on road nearest coast, passing *Carrick-a-Rede Island* (linked to mainland by rope bridge), to beautiful strand of *Whitepark Bay* (**Y.H.**), chalk cliffs, sandhills, views over Atlantic to islands of *Scotland*.

4 miles west is **Giant's Causeway**, largest and most perfect example of columnar formation of basaltic lavas. Regular hexagonal columns, formed by rapid cooling of molten lava. From the causeway, either by footpath to *Portballintrae* and road to *Dunluce Castle* (ruin), *Portrush* and *Coleraine*; or by road via *Bushmills* to *Coleraine*; then by *Murder Hole Road* to *Stradreagh* (**Y.H.**), or if cycling, by either main (mountain) or coast road, via *Downhill* to *Limavady* and *Londonderry*.

Londonderry "Derry" means an oak grove; the prefix "London" commemorates colonization of city by the Companies of the City of London during reign of James I. On the site of modern Derry (the term almost always used in Ireland) Columba established a religious community before he went to *Iona* (6th century).

In 1689 Derry endured a siege of 105 days. It is the only city in the British Isles which preserves its city walls complete; they have a circuit of about a mile and are pierced by seven gates. Many of the old guns are still in position, and relics of siege can be seen in *St. Columba's Cathedral*.

R.2. Londonberry to Newry via Sperrin Mountains (93 miles)

Leave *Londonderry* by main *Belfast* road. Where huge *Altnagelvin* Hospital dominates landscape is a striking example of modern art—the bronze figure of Princess Macha. At village of *Claudy*, take road on right towards *Park*. Ridges of *Sperrin Mountains* are now visible. Just west of village of *Park* is *Learmount Castle* (**Y.H.**).

From the hostel, walkers can take interesting route on rough roads crossing the *Sperrin* ridges, by *Park*, the *Dart Pass*, *Cranagh* (a tiny village, notable in local story for having wearied of politicians and attempted to set up its own republic) and the *Barnes Gap* to *Gortin*. Cyclists can reach *Gortin* via *Plumbridge*. From *Gortin* the *Omagh* road lies in gorge of a former glacial channel. Just beyond top point of road, in a Ministry of Agriculture forest, is *Gortin Gap* **Y.H.** 6 miles south is *Omagh*, small market town, beautifully situated on *River Strule*.

Continue via *Aughnacloy, Caledon* and *Killylea* to orchard country of *Armagh*. County town, *Armagh*, is small ancient city with two cathedrals, observatory and some fine Georgian architecture; was site of St. Patrick's metropolitan church in 5th century, and is seat of two Archbishops, the Roman Catholic and Protestant Primates of all Ireland.

R.2(i) *Learmount Castle* (Y.H.) *Park, Ballydonegan* (see "sweat houses", ancient forerunners of Turkish baths) *Dungiven* (ancient Augustinian Priory) and *Glenshane Pass* to *Magher, Antrim* and *Belfast* (60 miles).

R.2(ii) *Omagh, Portadown, Belfast* (70 miles).

R.2(iii) *Omagh, Enniskillen* (lake district) and routes to *Sligo* and west coast of *Republic of Ireland.*

R.3. Newry to Belfast via Mourne Mountains (100 miles)

Newry, at head of *Carlingford Lough*, between *Mourne Mountains* and *Slieve Gullion*, contains pleasant Georgian buildings and is surrounded by very attractive country.

To *Warrenpoint* and *Rostrevor*. Then by hill routes or roads to any combination of youth hostels which, at short distances from each other, encircle the Mourne Mountains—*Kinnahalla* (Y.H., *King George VI Memorial Hostel*), *Slievenaman* Y.H., and *Newcastle* Y.H.

A suggested route for walkers is from *Knockbarragh* Y.H. by road and rough hill tracks and lanes to *Kinnahalla* Y.H. then by *Spelga Pass* or by open mountain to *Silent Valley* and by road to *Dunnywater Bridge*; then by track round flank of *Spence's Mountain* to *Bloody Bridge*. On by mountain track (the *Brandy Pad*) to beautifully situated small Y.H. at *Slievenaman* and by pleasant route through *Tollymore Forest Park* to *Newcastle* Y.H.

For cyclists: From *Restrevor*; by *Kilbroney* river valley to *Hilltown* and *Kinnahalla* Y.H., or by *Glen* river valley to *Kinnahalla* Y.H. (follow signposts marked "*Spelga Dam*" until hostel is reached). Then by *Spelga Pass* to *Silent Valley* and via *Kilkeel* and *Annalong*, two attractive small fishing ports, to *Newcastle* Y.H.

Newcastle is popular seaside resort at the foot of the mountains.

Route continues with fine views of mountains via *Dundrum* (impressive ruins of Norman castle) to *Minerstown* Y.H. near *St. John's Point*, with lighthouse and old church.

From *Minerstown* take road to *Strangford* and cross strait by ferry (cycles are taken) to *Portaferry*. Route now runs north alongside *Strangford Lough* to *Newtownards* and *Belfast*.

R.3(i) *Minerstown, Downpatrick* (ancient town, with reputed grave of St. Patrick, who began his ministry at *Saul*, 2 miles distant), *Saintfield, Belfast*. (28 miles).

Rome's Spanish Steps are a favorite meeting place of young Americans.

ITALY

Geographical Outline

Land Italy (116,300 sq. miles) has four main physical divisions: (i) the peninsula, centrally situated in the *Mediterranean* and whose core is the mountain range of the *Apennines*; (ii) the northern plain, watered by the river *Po* and its tributaries, and by the *Adige* and other Alpine rivers reaching the *Adriatic* direct; (iii) the *Alps*, continuous with the *Apennines* in the west, and forming a crescent-shaped barrier on Italy's frontier with France, Switzerland, Austria and Yugoslavia; (iv) the large islands of *Sicily* and *Sardinia*, and a number of small islands of which the best known are *Elba* and *Capri*. Within these divisions there is great regional diversity.

Italy shares with France the highest mountain in the *Alps*, *Mont Blanc* (*Monte Bianco*, 15,782 ft.), with Switzerland *Monte Rosa* (15,217 ft.) and the *Matterhorn* (*Cervino*, 14,782 ft.). The *Gran Paradiso* (13,324 ft.), in the *Graian Alps*, is the highest peak entirely within the country. The *Apennines* reach 9,560 ft. in the *Gran Sasso*.

Grouped around the southern end of the *Tyrrhenian* sea are several areas of continuing volcanic activity: *Vesuvius* (3,880 ft.) and the *Phlegraean Fields* near *Naples; Etna* (10,742 ft.) in *Sicily;* the *Lipari* islands, including *Stromboli.*

Climate Italy is a land of sunshine and, for the most part, of low humidity, with clear crisp air. Summer temperatures are high and particularly trying from *Rome* southwards in July and August. The hottest parts are *Sicily* and the *Gulf of Taranto.*

Winter shows greater ranges of climate over comparatively short distances, seen in the contrast between the mildness of the *Riviera* and the severe cold of the lowlands of *Piedmont*, and again in the warmth of the lake region (*Como, Garda*, etc.) below the *High Alps* where the coldest winters occur.

Rainfall is only typically Mediterranean, occurring in winter with summer drought, south of *Naples*. Elsewhere in the peninsula and on the northern plain it is greatest in spring and autumn, whilst in the *High Alps* precipitation occurs chiefly in summer and winter.

Plants and Animals The vegetation of the Alps and of the northern plain is Central European in type: that of the peninsula is Mediterranean.

Both types include coniferous forests. The broad-leaved trees and brushwoods of the north yield in the peninsula to evergreen trees and to a *maquis* type of brushwood. But in the mountains beech forests extend as far as *Sicily*. A further contrast is between the meadows and pastures of the north, which remain green in summer, and their different composition in the south where they have to survive in parched conditions.

257

ITALY

The natural vegetation has been replaced over large areas: the vine and groves of olive, lemon and orange are important features in the landscape.

Among wild animals lizards abound, somewhat making up in interest for the comparative lack of birds. The wild pig, wolf, bear, deer, chamois and moufflon occur. Also the ibex, in the *Gran Paradiso National Park*. Dangerous smaller animals include scorpions, certain centipedes and spiders, and vipers. In some country districts precautions may need to be taken against mosquitos.

The People

Population
The population of 53 million is highly urbanised; the majority living in the considerable number of small towns of fewer than 20,000 people. The six cities of over half-a-million inhabitants are: *Rome* (2,500,000), *Milan* (1,672,000), *Naples* (1,235,000), *Turin* (1,106,000), *Genoa* (848,000), and *Palermo* (633,000).

Language
Italian developed in the 13th century out of the Florentine dialect, one of the many local vernaculars based on Latin which gradually replaced the classical language after the break-up of the Empire. With the growth of trade there was again a need for a national language and Dante's writings provided a model to which others were glad to conform in writing and, to a lesser extent, in speech.

Italian is a finely resonant, smoothly flowing tongue, lending itself naturally to song.

French is the language of some of the alpine districts such as the *Val d'Aosta* and *Val Pelline*. Parts of the *Trentino* are German-speaking.

Religion
Italy is almost entirely Roman Catholic. Church influence, exercised through large numbers of clergy, is strong.

The position of the *Vatican City* as a sovereign state independent of Italy emphasises its world-wide responsibilities in spiritual matters. But the Pope is also Bishop of Rome and Primate of Italy, and Italian cardinals predominate numerically in the sacred college.

Saints' days are numerous and widely observed. Visits to shrines are an important feature of life. A great shrine such as that of St. Anthony of *Padua* draws people from great distances.

Protestants are the most numerous non-Catholic community. They include the Waldensians of the alpine valleys west of *Turin* whose history of persecution endured is as heroic and tragic as that of the Huguenots.

History
It was in Italy that Greek and Christian ideas found a powerful advocate in the practical genius of Rome and so acquired their profound influence on the whole of Western culture. The story of Italy abounds in local episodes glorious and sordid, but its great themes—the Empire, the Church, the Renaissance—occupy the world stage and command recognition in any assessment of man's limitations and possibilities. Italy has, too, its own noble if more local theme of the search, during 1400 years, for unity after collapse of the Empire in the West.

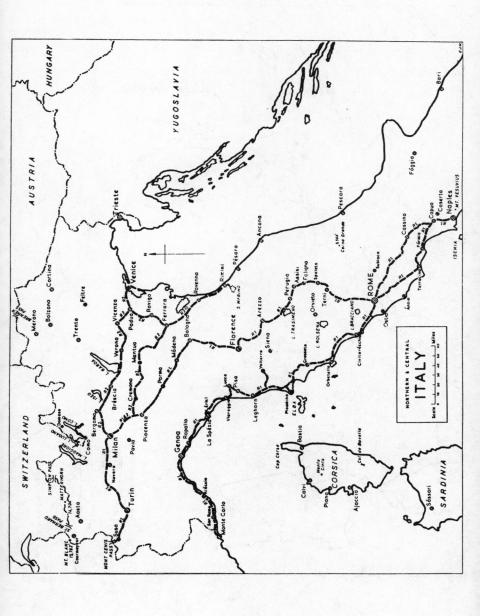

NORTHERN & CENTRAL
ITALY

Scale
0 10 20 30 40 50 60 70 80 Miles

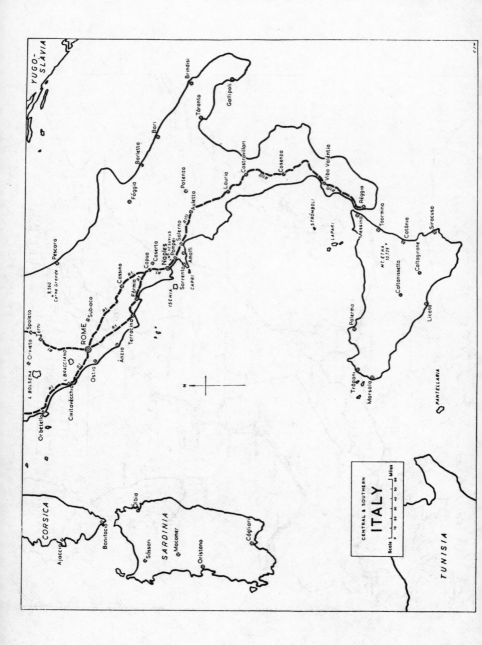

YUGO-
SLAVIA

Pescara

Corno Grande
8,560

Spoleto
Terni
Orvieto
L. BOLSENA
Orbetello
Civitavecchia
L. BRACCIANO
ROME
Subiaco
Cassino
Fórmia
Capua
Caserta
Ostia
Ánzio
Terracina
Naples
ISCHIA
Sorrento
CAPRI
Amalfi
Pompeii
VESUVIUS
Salerno

Fóggia
Barletta
Bari

Brindisi
Táranto
Gallipoli

Potenza
Auletta
Lauria

Castrovillari
Sila
Cosenza
Vibo Valentia
Sila
Réggio
Taormina

STRÓMBOLI
LIPARI
Messina
Catánia
Siracusa
MT. ETNA
10,739
Caltanissetta
Palermo
Tràpani
Marsala
Caltagirone
Licata

PANTELLARIA

TUNISIA

CORSICA
Ajaccio
Bonifacio
Óbia
Sássari
Mácomer
SARDINIA
Oristano
Cágliari

CENTRAL & SOUTHERN
ITALY
Scale
Miles
0 10 20 30 40 50 60

From the 8th century B.C. there were Greek colonies in *Sicily* and southern Italy (*Magna Graecia*), whilst north of the *Tiber*, another people, the Etruscans, were extending their power widely in the peninsula.

Rome itself emerged as a historical fact about 600 B.C. from a union of communities of Latin and Sabine stock. Ruled first by kings, including the Etruscan Tarquins, it later became a republic (509) and grew rapidly in organisation and power. First *Latium* was conquered; then the whole of Italy. By war and diplomacy in the East, in Africa, and Spain all the countries of the Mediterranean became Roman provinces.

After 400 years of republican rule civil strife brought dictatorship. Julius Caesar conquered Gaul but his seizing of power for life was misjudgment which brought his assassination (44 B.C.). Yet when Octavian, his adopted son, acquired full power he did so as Augustus Caesar and his long reign as emperor (30 B.C.—A.D. 14), bringing peace and prosperity, confirmed the transition from Republic to Empire.

The Empire, surviving until A.D. 476, became synonymous with civilisation in the West. Wherever the Roman peace was accepted cities were founded, communications were improved and men had before them the example of Roman power and love of order which found particular expression in architecture, town life and Roman law.

Christianity, at first persecuted, forced underground to the catacombs and made a spectacle of martyrdom by Nero, was later recognised by Constantine and adopted as the official religion of the Empire. In a sense it succeeded the Empire in the West. With the founding of Constantinople (330), and with the barbarian invasions, the civil power of Rome declined, but the city found a new role as centre of the Christian church. The barbarians overran it, but the Papacy survived.

Italy experienced the Visigoths under Alaric, who sacked Rome (410); then, more happily, the Ostrogoths under the wise rule (493-526) of Theodoric the Great. Imperial initiative was again secured under Justinian (famous for his code of law and his splendid *Byzantine* churches at *Ravenna*), only to be lost to the unruly Lombard invaders (568).

Henceforward, political unity was lost. Charlemagne took *Lombardy* (775). The Arabs, after a 50-year struggle, conquered *Sicily* (878) and disputed southern Italy with the Byzantine Empire. Elsewhere, power was in the hands of local lords until Otto I revived the Western Empire and the royal power. His coronation as Emperor of the Holy Roman Empire (962) united Germany and Italy (except the south). The next major event was the Norman conquest of *Sicily* (1061-91) and the south, both being united in the feudal Kingdom of Sicily.

The famous medieval struggle between popes and emperors on the question of supremacy was partly due to a difference of views on the relationship of spiritual to temporal power, later echoed in other countries. But popes were also temporal rulers (in the Papal States) and were opposed to imperial attempts to unify Italy. These seemed likely to succeed when the crowns of the Sicilian Kingdom and of the Empire came to be held by one man—the Hohenstaufen prince, Frederick II. But the popes proposed instead to unify Italy themselves by a federation of states with the Pope at its head. From this there arose the notorious party factions of Guelfs and Ghibellines, supporters respectively of papal and imperial supremacy.

Neither was successful. When the emperors ceased to interfere in Italy the newly risen and prosperous city states (*Florence, Milan*, etc.) refused to submit to papal authority. The Papacy fell. The Pope fled to exile in *Avignon* (1303-77). Nor was an attempt by Rienzi to revive the Roman republic more successful. Instead, each city went its own way either as a republic (such as *Venice*) or as an autocracy (such as *Milan* under the Visconti and *Florence* under the Medici).

These cities, with the returned Papacy and new power in the south—the Kingdom of Naples, under Aragonese rule—were the principal states at the beginning of the Renaissance in the 15th century. With the many other lesser but still brilliant states they provided unexampled patronage and stimulation to artists and scholars imbued with the new humanism. Yet politically they were a danger to each other, despite some success in co-operation. Their disunity encouraged outside intervention. First France (1494), then Spain (1503), then the Emperor Charles V (1521) invaded. Except for *Venice* and *Savoy* Italy was dominated by Spain (1559-1700) and by Austria (1713-96 and again 1815-70).

It was Napoleon's conquest of Italy (1796-99), and the liberal ideas then brought in, which opened the way to the *risorgimento*, as the movement for unification was now called. But it was not achieved without a further 60 years of struggle. Success was due finally to four leading patriots: Mazzini, its prophet, and founder of the "Young Italy" movement; Cavour, its statesman and political genius; Garibaldi, its popular hero and man of action; Victor Emmanuel II (of the House of Savoy), its focus of loyalty, as constitutional head, when a united independent Kingdom of Italy was proclaimed (1861).

In the century since unification the salient facts have been the economic expansion of northern Italy; the problem of the impoverished south (e.g., Danilo Dolci's work in *Sicily*); colonial expansion in Africa; the *Irredentist* movement to secure the *Trentino, Trieste*, etc.; the loss of political liberty under fascism; the creation of a sovereign *Vatican State* (1929); the Abyssinian War; alliances alternating between western and central Europe (including the fatal Rome-Berlin axis); Allied invasion and occupation; proclamation (1946) of a republic, and a return to progress and prosperity under representative government.

Government Parliament consists of two houses; a Chamber of Deputies whose 596 members are elected for five years by universal adult suffrage; and a Senate of 246 members elected for six years on a regional basis. Executive power rests with the Cabinet presided over by the Prime Minister. The President holds office for seven years.

Italy is divided into 19 *regioni* most of which are further divided into provinces. Four of the *regioni* are autonomous, having their own parliaments and governments: *Sicily, Sardinia, Aosta* (French speaking) and *Trentino-South Tirol* (whose two parts are respectively Italian and German-speaking).

Resources There are over 8 million workers in agriculture, a feature being the large numbers who live in towns but who go to work in the countryside. Holdings are generally small. Wheat, grown chiefly in the northern plain and in *Apulia* and *Sicily*, is by far the most important crop. Other cereals are maize and rice, grown chiefly in parts of the northern plain. Potatoes and sugar beet are widely grown. Olives and the vine are cultivated in every *regione*; citrus fruits, almonds and walnuts, in *Sicily* and the south. Other crops include tobacco, hemp and cotton.

Many coastal villages depend on fishing, particularly for sardines and tunny.

Minerals are generally inadequate for the country's needs. But Italy is a major exporter of sulphur and mercury and has important reserves of bauxite, zinc and lead. The comparative deficiency of coal is partly compensated for by abundant hydro-electricity resources, chiefly in the Alps.

The northern cities are the chief industrial centres. More than a million people are employed in clothing and textiles. Next comes engineering, including well-known motor vehicle, typewriter and electrical concerns. Pasta-making and the processing of other food and wine and tobacco employs over 400,000.

Among luxury products Venetian glass and Tuscan *majolica* represent a centuries-old tradition.

Food and Drink The main meal is taken in the evening. Animal fats are used in cooking in the north; olive oil takes their place further south. The staple item is *pasta* (processed wheat) in various forms— *spaghetti, ravioli, macaroni*, etc.,—the latter predominating in the south.

The variety of regional and local dishes adds to the pleasures of travel. Specialities include: fish soups—*brodetto* (Adriatic coast), *cacciucco* (Tuscan coast); other soups—*minestrone al pesto* (*Liguria*), *busecca* (*Milan*); meat dishes—*abbacchio* (*Rome*), sausages (*Emilia* and the *Marches*); fish dishes— *baccalà alla veneziana* (cod with milk and onions) (*Venice*), *triglie* (red mullet) (*Leghorn*); cheese dishes—*fondau* and *bagna cauda* (*Piedmont*), *mozzarella in carrozza* and *pizza Napolitana* (*Naples*); other savouries:—*fettuccine* and *gnocchi alla romana* (*Rome*), *cappelletti* and *tagliatelle alla bolognese* (*Emilia*).

Ice cream is an Italian and particularly a Sicilian speciality and is excellent in all its many varieties. Italy is, of course, the home of *caffè espresso*.

Wine is the main drink and is inexpensive, Italy being the world's second greatest producer, mostly for home consumption. It is worth while to ask about the local wines and in this way discover, in *Verona*, for example, the sparkling *Valpolicella*.

Culture

Italy is a treasure house of all the arts, the country of origin of the great movement of ideas of the Renaissance, of major styles in the Romanesque and the Baroque, and of a host of other components of Western culture.

Architecture Among Greek temples in *Sicily* and the south, those of Neptune at *Paestum* and of Concord at *Agrigento* are among the best preserved in Europe. There is a fine Greek theatre at *Syracuse*.

261

ITALY

The Romans, looking beyond Greek models, took the arch, the dome and the Etruscan vault and used them with a new grandeur to reach the technical achievements of the *Pantheon*, the *Colosseum* and the *Baths of Caracalla*. Specially interesting for their influence on the form of early Christian churches are the Roman basilicas, or courts of justice, now best seen in the *Basilica Aemilia* in the *Forum* and the *Underground Basilica* near the *Porta Maggiore*.

The least altered Christian basilicas in *Rome* are *S. Clemente* (A.D. 392) and *S. Sabina* (425). Two fine early churches at *Ravenna*—*S. Apollinare Nuoyo* (525) and *S. Apollinare in Classe* (549)—are also basilican in form.

Byzantine architecture is represented by the other great church of *Ravenna*, *S. Vitale* (526), and, above all, by *St. Mark's, Venice*. In the 12th century churches of *Palermo* it is combined with Arab and Norman features.

Romanesque is well seen in the fine group at *Pisa*: *Baptistry, Cathedral* and *Leaning Tower:* and in *S. Ambrogio, Milan; S. Zeno Maggiore, Verona; S. Miniato, Florence; S. Maria in Cosmedin, Rome;* and *Monreale Cathedral.*

Gothic came late to Italy and was accepted only partly and in modified form. Its chief examples are *Milan Cathedral; Florence Cathedral* and *Campanile; S. Francesco, Assisi.* In *Venice* the *Doge's Palace* and several other *palazzi* are local variants of the style.

Renaissance architecture, a return to classical forms, began in *Florence* with Brunelleschi (it is significant of humanism that architects' names now appear in contrast to the earlier impersonal tradition) and reached its height in *Rome* with Bramante, who began the rebuilding of *St. Peter's* (1506), and in *Venice* with Sansovino and Sanmichele. Its later freer development by Michelangelo in *Rome* and *Florence* led to the so-called Mannerist style. Its chief architect, Palladio, worked chiefly in his native *Vicenza* where his designs for villas became the models for other countries, especially England. Two well-known churches in *Venice*—*S. Giorgio Maggiore* and the *Redentore*—are also his.

The exuberance of Baroque architecture is seen particularly in the work of Borromini and Bernini in *Rome*, and in Longhena's *S. Maria della Salute* in *Venice.*

Adventurous experiments in contemporary building can be seen in *Milan.*

Mosaic, Painting and Sculpture

Mosaic floors, portrait busts and reliefs on triumphal arches were the chief artistic forms of the Roman period, but some paintings survive in *Pompeii* and *Rome*.

There are early Christian paintings in the catacombs. Then, for a thousand years, the art of wall mosaic was dominant—at first Roman, later Byzantine in style, as in the great groups at *Ravenna, Cefalù* and *Monreale.*

The transition from mosaic to fresco came in the 13th century with Cavallini, Cimabue, Duccio and the great new vision of Giotto. In sculpture Nicola Pisano's famous pulpit (1260) in the Baptistry at *Pisa* began a new tradition of naturalism in modelling the human form which was developed by his son Giovanni. The long dominance of medieval ideas was coming to an end. Simone Martinni (c. 1284-1344) was the first artist since classical times to paint a non-religious subject. Men were not only looking back to those times but were beginning to look about them with wonder and delight. These two sources of inspiration produced the Renaissance—a re-birth of thought and feeling.

Ghiberti (1378-1455) in bronze, Masaccio (1401-28), Uccello (1397-1475) and Piero della Francesca (1418-92) in painting, progressively solved the problems of light, shade, movement and perspective presented by the new interest in naturalistic representation. Pisanello (1397-1455), Antonio Pollaiuolo (1432-98) and Signorelli (c. 1440-1523) learnt to model with scientific realism. Botticelli (1444-1510) gave elegant form to pagan myths. But he and most artists of the time could also combine the new freedom with traditional piety.

Donatello (1386-1466) was the supreme sculptor of the early Renaissance and had perhaps the greatest influence on the future. He had great pupils in Pollaiuolo and Verrocchio (1435-88) and a follower in the painter Mantegna.

The masters of the High Renaissance, heirs of all this achievement, built on it each according to his own noble vision: the calm insight of Leonardo da Vinci (1452-1519), the grace and harmony of Raphael (1483-1520), the turbulent restless idealism of Michelangelo (1475-1564).

Mantegna (1431-1506), bringing to painting a sculptural quality, influenced the schools of *Padua, Ferrara, Milan* and *Venice*. The Venetians Giorgione (1478-1510) and Titian (1477-1576) now created a new worldly art of gorgeous colour and sensuous form, and Veronese (1528-88) added an imaginary classical background to scenes of Venetian pageantry. But Tintoretto (1518-94), no less grandiose, turned this richness to religious themes in numerous and enormous paintings. Religion also found a sophisticated interpreter in Correggio (1489-1534), working in *Parma*.

In *Rome*, reactions against Mannerism—the ineffectual attempts to imitate Michelangelo—came with Caravaggio's (1573-1610) return to realism and with Annibale Carracci's (1560-1609) refined classicism. In *Rome* also, a little later, the French masters Poussin and Claude were at work and Bernini (1598-1680) was making fluent sculpture an integral part of his Baroque architectural schemes. Salvator Rosa's (1615-73) wild landscapes started a fashion which influenced particularly the English cult of the picturesque.

The most attractive works of the 18th century are those by a group of artists in *Venice:* Piazzetta, Guardi, Canaletto, Tiepolo and Longhi. Painting then declined but Canova (1757-1822) produced finely carved if frigid sculpture in a further revival which looked back to classical Greece.

The most famous Italian contributors to modern art are Modigliani (1884-1920) and the surrealist painter Chirico (b. 1888).

Art Galleries The greatest galleries are the *Uffizi* and the *Pitti* in *Florence*, the *Vatican Museums* in *Rome*, *Accademia di Belle Arti* in *Venice*, *Brera* in *Milan* and *Capodimonte* in *Naples*.
Many of the finest works are in churches and palaces; the churches of *Rome* and *Florence* in particular are rich in outstanding paintings and sculptures.

Museums Very important are the *Vatican Galleries* (see notes on *Rome*), the *Capitoline Museum* (also in *Rome*) and the *National Museum* in *Naples*. There are many more, including museums dealing with weapons and armour, Christian and Roman excavated relics, etc. Public buildings and museums are often closed on Sunday afternoons, Mondays and public holidays. Churches are frequently shut between noon and 3 p.m. and after 5 p.m.

ITALY

Music
Italians of the 11th century invented our system of musical notation and also the tonic sol-fa. Most of the indications of expression—*andante, adagio*, etc.—are Italian as also are the names of many musical instruments including the pianoforte. The violin and its relations were first produced in *Brescia*, reaching perfection in *Cremona*, where Antonio Stradivarius (1644-1736) was only the greatest of a succession of famous makers.

Corelli (1653-1713) and Vivaldi (1675-1741) were among early developers of the violin concerto. Domenico Scarlatti (1685-1757) was the first great composer for the harpsichord.

The Renaissance had seen the culmination of Italian religious music in the unaccompanied masses of Palestrina (1525-94) and the beginning of the operatic tradition in the works of Monteverdi (1567-1643) who was also the first to use an orchestra. Classical opera was continued by Alessandro Scarlatti (1659-1725).

The popular fame of Italian opera today rests on the great series of works by 19th century composers writing in a romantic idiom: Rossini (1792-1868), Donizetti (1797-1848), and Verdi (1813-1901) and continued into the 20th century by Puccini (1858-1924).

The opera house was an Italian creation and is found in many towns. The main centres are *La Scala, Milan; San Carlo, Naples;* the *Teatro dell' Opera* and *Teatro Adriano, Rome.* A visit to an open-air performance in the *Baths of Caracalla, Rome,* or the *Arena, Verona* provides a memorable experience.

Itinerant musicians, playing popular music, are a feature of *Naples,* though one comes across them all over the country.

Theatres
Summer visitors will probably be most interested in the open-air performance of plays in, for example, the Greek theatre at *Syracuse* and the Roman theatre (not to be confused with the *Arena*) at *Verona.*

Cinema
Italy was one of the first countries to discover the excellent cinema material provided by scenes of ordinary life if presented in a simple straightforward way and backed by good technique. Italian films maintain their international reputation in this respect and can often be seen outside Italy.

Costumes and Dances
The chief areas for "local colour" of this kind are *Sardinia, Abruzzi, Umbria, Tuscany,* and the Alpine districts of the north. They are particularly to be sought, away from the main centres, in out of the way villages and towns. In some places local costume is only worn for dancing during a *fiesta.* But in others, such as *Gressoney,* it is worn on Sundays.

Literature
Dante (1265-1321) represents the medieval world at a time when the first signs of change were appearing. His immediate successors, Petrarch (1304-74) and Boccaccio (1313-75) are the first humanists.

The poets of the Renaissance have little appeal today, but its vigorous prose writers capture the spirit of the period and are wonderfully readable:

e.g. Cellini's (1500-71) uninhibited account of his life and times; Vasari's (1511-74) *Lives of the Painters, Sculptors and Architects* and Machiavelli's (1469-1527) politically realistic writings inspired by his vision of a united Italy.

Among novels available in translation is Manzoni's (1785-1873) great work *The Betrothed*. Those of Alberto Moravia (b. 1907) are widely read. Giuseppe Lampedusa's *The Leopard*, translated 1959, has become a classic.

Science   Leonardo da Vinci (1452-1519), the all-round man of the Renaissance, was as much scientist as artist and contributed to nearly every branch of the science of his time. Galileo Galilei (1564-1642), almost as versatile, devoted his life to observation and experiment to become both the founder of modern scientific method and the champion of its results against ideas surviving from the medieval period. His trial by the Inquisition was one of the turning points of history.

Reti (1621-97) and Spallanzani (1729-99), naturalists and micro-biologists, were rigorous experimenters, as unready as Galileo to take anything on trust. They disproved the various theories of spontaneous generation which were popular in their times.

Avogadro (1776-1856) was the first to distinguish between atoms and molecules. Dorati (1826-73) was the founder of spectroscopic astronomy. Another astronomer, Schiaparelli (1835-1910) is particularly associated with the study of Mars.

To Marconi (1874-1937) are due the first effective developments in radio-telegraphy.

Camping in Canazei, Trento, Italy.

ITALY

Touring Information

**Touring
Areas**

In no other land are there so many cities of major artistic and architectural significance. The countryside, also, ranges in beauty from the grandeur and romantic wildness of the *Alps* and the *Abruzzi* to the classic calm of *Umbria* and *Tuscany*. Each of the following areas would fully occupy a holiday visit.

1. *Piedmont* and *Aosta: Turin* and the mountains bordering France and Switzerland.
2. *Genoa* and the *Western Riviera*.
3. The lakes of *Como, Garda* and *Maggiore*.
4. The cities of *Lombardy*.
5. The *Venice* region and the *Dolomites*.
6. *Emilia* and *Romagna: Piacenza* to *Ravenna* and *Rimini*.
7. *Florence, Pisa, Siena:* a fine-art region in the lovely countryside of *Tuscany*.
8. *Perugia* and *Assisi:* Franciscan Italy, old and unchanged towns in the soft, pleasant countryside of *Umbria*.
9. *Rome:* a magnificent city rich in noble buildings and requiring a visit of at least a week.
10. The *Abruzzi* and the *Marches:* a wilder, more primitive Italy.
11. *Naples, Pompeii, Vesuvius, Salerno* and the south: different in physical conditions, history and culture, and with a climate somewhat akin to that of North Africa. Picturesque and often primitive.
12. *Sicily*.
13. *Sardinia*.

Access

For *Turin, Genoa* and the *Western Riviera* best and cheapest rail route is via *Paris* and *Modane,* changing stations at *Paris,* fare London-*Genoa*, using Newhaven-*Dieppe* crossing, $80 for one way, 2nd class.

For all other areas it is advisable to use the through boat train from *Calais* or *Boulogne* via Switzerland to *Milan*.

Transport

Rail is the cheapest means of travel. Sample 2nd class fares from *Milan*: to *Florence* (316 km.) $8.30; to *Rome* (632 km.) $16.60. On certain fast diesel or electric trains (known as *Rapido*) a supplement of about 30% is charged.

Reductions for (*a*) families (minimum four persons) 40% adults, 70% children; (*b*) parties (minimum 10 persons), 20%; (*c*) 15-day travel-at-will tickets $44.35 (valid on 2nd class *Rapido* without supplement); (*d*) circular tickets, frontier to same or different frontier, for itinerary of not less than 1,000 km. Valid 60 days if purchased outside Italy, valid 30 days if purchased in Italy.

There are a number of long-distance coach services, principally for the use of tourists.

Money

The unit of currency is the *lira* (plural *lire*). Coins are issued for 5, 10, 50, 100, and 500 *lire*; notes for 500, 1,000, 5,000 and 10,000 *lire*.

Clothing

Lightweight clothing most suitable in summer, but pull-overs will be useful for occasional chilly nights, or for expeditions in mountain areas. Shorts are widely worn in the country during the summer. It is well to avoid being conspicuous, and every effort should be made to wear clean and tidy clothing, especially when visiting galleries and churches.

In churches and *Vatican* museums women are required to have their shoulders covered; sleeves not less than half length should be worn, or a shawl over the shoulders.

Avoid wearing mountain boots or heavy shoes in southern cities; but sandals should have thick soles—pavements become uncomfortably hot.

Restaurants

Trattorie, restaurants with a local character, are among the cheapest and most interesting eating places. Cafés are more specifically for coffee, fruit drinks and ices, but sell also small cakes. In *Bottiglierie*, provided wine is ordered, you may eat your own food and make use of plate and cutlery.

One must get used to food cooked in olive oil, particularly as one travels further south. The various forms of *pasta* provide a substantial and nourishing dish.

Buying own Food

It is quite easy to buy bread, cheese and fruit, even in villages. Shops marked *Panetteria*, *Pane e Pasta* or *Fornaio* sell pasta, also bread and dry groceries. Shops marked *Pasticceria* sell sweets and biscuits. Salt (a state monopoly) is sold along with stamps, cigarettes and matches, in Government-run *Sale e Tabacchi* shops and in some cafes and bars displaying the state coat of arms, or a big "T"

Public Holidays

January 1st and 6th, March 19th, Easter Sunday, Easter Monday, April 25th, May 1st., Ascension Day, June 2nd, Whit Sunday, Corpus Christi, June 29th, August 15th (Assumption), November 1st (All Saints), November 4th, December 8th, Christmas Day, December 26th.

Maps and Guide Books

Michelin No. 988 is an adequate road map, scale 1:1,000,000. *Italian Touring Club* maps on a scale of 1:200,000 are published in 30 sheets. For some of the popular Alpine areas the *Italian Touring Club* publishes fine maps on a scale of 1:50,000 suitable for walkers and climbers.

Wonders of Italy series (*Rome*, *Florence*, etc.), published in English by *Fattorusso* of *Florence*, are excellent picture guides with accurate text, forming useful handbooks and souvenirs of the chief cities.

The *Guide Books to the Museums and Monuments in Italy* (in English) published by the *Ministerio dell' Educazione Nazionale* and obtainable at all the main sites (e.g., *Pompeii*), are far cheaper to buy than paying for the services of a guide.

Tourist literature can be obtained from the *Italian Government Tourist Office, 630 5th Avenue, New York, N.Y. 10019* and from the *Ente Provinciale per il Turismo* at each provincial capital; also plans and guide books of every town from the appropriate *Azienda Autonoma di Soggiorno*.

Accom-modation The A.I.G. (Italian Youth Hostels Association) has about 60 hostels, spread over nearly all parts of the country. They are still too far apart for walkers, however, so that the use of some means of transport is often unavoidable.

In the lowland areas it is usually possible to sleep out in the open from April to October; a down-bag is useful but not essential.

Mountain-eering In the *Courmayeur, Aosta, Mont Blanc* area conditions are similar to those of Switzerland. Mountaineering of all grades is possible and plans are best made in consultation with climbing clubs.

The *Dolomites*, close to the Austrian border, are a magnificent mountaineering area with many mountain huts. The rock is always good, and there are many routes world-famous for their length and severity.

In the *Apennines* the best climbing areas are in the wild massifs of the *Abruzzi* (*Gran Sasso* and *Maiella*) east of Rome.

Winter-sports take place in all three districts and all are equipped with mountain huts. The *Club Alpino Italiano* (C.A.I.) has 200 local branches in Italy. It publishes guides to the Italian mountains and organises assistance and aid of various kinds. It maintains about 600 huts in the finest mountain areas. Charge for bunk bed is about 500 *lire* per night. Further information from *C.A.I., Via Ugo Foscolo, 3, Milan*.

Touring Routes

In the following tours the chief cities have been linked in two circular routes:

(i) From the French frontier along the peninsula to *Naples* and back, via *Turin — Milan — Bologna — Florence — Perugia — Rome* returning via *Rome—Leghorn—La Spezia—Genoa*.

(ii) Across the N. Italian plain from *Milan* to *Venice* and back, via *Brescia—Verona—Padua* returning via *Mantua* and *Cremona*.

In addition there are two Alpine areas which can be described as regions rather than routes:

(a) The *Pennine Alps, Aosta Valley, Mont Blanc* (on the French frontier).

(b) *Upper Adige, Trentino, Dolomites* (on the Austrian frontier).

R.1. The Peninsula: Turin to Rome and Naples, returning via Genoa (1,430 miles)

The route leaves France by the *Mont Cenis* tunnel and enters *Piedmont*, a region of rugged mountain scenery, the country of the House of Savoy, the kings of which became the builders of modern Italy.

Bardonecchia, small mountain resort, *Susa*, old town, Roman arch, **Turin**, 69 miles, on R. *Po*, well-planned city, with net-work of fine avenues, arcaded shops, beautiful squares. Capital of Italy for a while in 19th century. Fiat, Lancia and Farina factories are here—and the Cinzano and Martini vermouth distilleries. Old Roman gateway; Castle, 17th century onwards; interesting churches in Baroque style, e.g., the *Superga* (in outskirts, at 2,200 ft. 6 miles from city centre). *Palazzo Cavour*, where the statesman lived and died. **(Y.H.)**

EXCURSIONS: (a) *Colli Torinesi*, hilly area giving good views of city. (b) *Piedmont Plain*, silk-producing area, mulberry trees, many attractive little towns with cobbled streets and painted churches. (c) *Torre Pellice*, 35 miles, headquarters of the Waldensians (*Valdesi*) the only considerable Protestant community in Italy, who took refuge in the high valleys near the French frontier; attractive and little-known mountain area; highest peak *Monte Viso*, 12,609 ft.

Route continues to *Vercelli*, through rice-growing district to *Novara*, 63 miles.

EXCURSIONS: (a) Lake of *Orta*, 25 miles, set amidst trees, (b) The Alpine valleys east of *Monte Rosa* mountain group (centre *Varallo*, 35 miles), (c) Lake *Maggiore* (40 miles long) with picturesque *Borromean* Islands. Chief resorts are *Stresa, Pallanza* and *Baveno*; many attractive villages, steamer services. North end of lake is in Switzerland (*Locarno*).

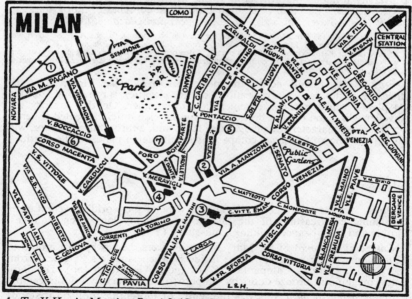

1. *To Y.H. via Martino Bassi* 2 (*San Siro*). 2. *La Scala Theatre*. 3. *Duomo* (*cathedral*). 4. *Post Office*.

ITALY

Milan, 30 miles, the most important commercial and industrial city in the country, cosmopolitan and independent; a vast city with great blocks of flats. Once the greatest of the Italian city states, it now has few ancient buildings. Immense Gothic cathedral (*Duomo*) third largest in the world; a mass of gleaming white marble; has 200 statues. View from roof includes the Alps. The *Piazza del Duomo* (cathedral square) is scene of big meetings. *Sforza Castle* (15th century); Scala Theatre, famous opera-house; *Brera* Picture Gallery, one of best collections in world; church of *Santa Maria delle Grazie* contains Leonardo da Vinci's "Last Supper"; *Galleria*, vast arcade of shops and restaurants; immense modern railway station; several interesting churches. **(Y.H.).**

EXCURSIONS: (a) Lake *Maggiore* (see *Novara* above), (b) *Pavia*, 24 miles, famous university, interesting churches; the *Certosa*, important monastery, now secularised and its land used for agricultural experiments; chapel has early Renaissance marble facade, (c) Monastery at *Chiaravalle* (on road to *Pavia*). (d) *Como*, 29 miles, (Y.H.) on beautiful Lake of *Como* (31½ miles long). Many steamer excursions on lake; chief resorts; *Cernobbio, Bellagio, Menaggio* (Y.H.). (Y.H. also at *Domaso* and *Lecco*.).

Continue through *Piacenza, Parma,* **(Y.H.),** 80 miles, *Reggio, Modena,* all towns of some interest. The railway runs near the *Via Emilia,* ancient road between the *Apennines* and the *Po* Plains, and near the great new motorway, "Autostrada del Sole", from *Milan* to *Reggio Calabria* via *Bologna, Florence, Rome* and *Naples.*

Bologna, 56 miles, important commercial centre, with many old buildings; University founded in 12th century, fine arcaded streets. Leaning Towers; Civic Museum, collection of Roman antiquities; churches of *San Francesco, San Petronio* (never finished), *San Domenico, San Giacomo.* **(Y.H.)**

EXCURSIONS: (a) *San Michele in Bosco* for view of city (tram), (b) the Adriatic coast, via *Faenza* (the home of Majolica porcelain—French *faïence*)—and *Rimini*, (Y.H.) to *San Marino* (about 90 miles); see R.2(i). (c) Fertile plains north of *Bologna*; rice is grown; you can walk along the dykes built to control the spring rise in river level; a typical little town is *Budrio*, 12 miles north-east.

From *Bologna* south across the mountains to *Florence.* This part of the *Apennines* is not particularly beautiful but the elevation is refreshing after the *Po* plains, which become extremely hot in summer. On this journey the traveller will come for the first time along the elaborately repeated S-bends which are so characteristic of *Apennine* Italy, and, approaching *Florence,* will note the softness of *Tuscany* compared with the harsh plains of the north.

Florence

On R. *Arno* and 67 miles from *Bologna.* One of the world's loveliest cities containing art treasures of the highest rank; many interesting churches, Gothic and Renaissance buildings, museums. **(Y.H.)**

Cathedral (*Duomo*) of St. Mary of the Flowers, begun by di Cambio in 1296, dome by Brunelleschi 1434; inside is Michelangelo's "Descent from the Cross". Giotto's Campanile, 267 ft. (good view from top). The Baptistry, magnificent bronze doors by Ghiberti; 13th century mosaics in ceiling.

Piazza della Signoria (this was the centre of Florentine life); on it stands the *Palazzo Vecchio,* now the city hall, open to the public. Statues include

Donatello's "Judith and Holofernes", Benvenuto Cellini's "Perseus with Head of Medusa", and copy of Michelangelo's "David" (original in *Accademia di Belle Arti*).

Churches of *Santa Maria Novella*, 13th century Tuscan-Gothic, frescoes by Ghirlandaio, *Strozzi Chapel*—frescoes by Orcagna; *San Lorenzo*, begun 1491 by Brunelleschi, never finished; *Santa Croce*, 13th century, fine frescoes by Gaddi and Giotto, tombs of famous Italians, including Michelangelo; *San Marco*, lovely cloisters, frescoes by Fra Angelico, Savonarola's cell.

The *Medici Mausoleum*, splendidly gloomy; very fine statues by Michelangelo in sacristy.

Palazzo Strozzi (15th century), has delightful lanterns, torch-holders, etc. *Palazzo Medici-Riccardi* (15th century) home of Lorenzo the Magnificent and the great Medici family; wall-painting of "Journey of the Three Kings";

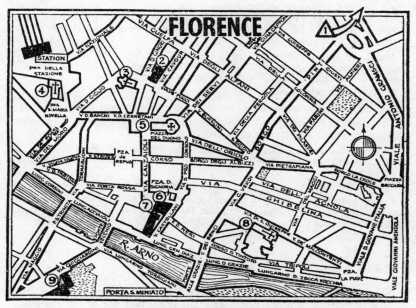

1. *To Y.H.* (*V. Augusto Righi*). 2. *Palazzi Medici-Riccardi*. 3. *S. Lorenzo Church*. 4. *S. Maria Novella Church*. 5. *Duomo* (*cathedral*). 6. *Palazzo Vecchio*. 7. *Uffizi Gallery*. 8. *S. Croce Church*. 9. *Pitti Gallery*.

Palazzo Pitti, begun 1450, first attempt to build artistic building with blocks of unhewn stone. Art gallery on first floor with paintings by Raphael, Titian and Tintoretto; cross *Ponte Vecchio* to *Uffizi Palace* where art gallery has one of finest collections in world—Botticelli's "Primavera" and "Birth of Venus", Michelangelo's "Holy Family" and many other masterpieces.

ITALY

Cross *Ponte di Ferro* and climb hill to *Piazzale Michelangelo* and up steps to *San Miniato* (11th-13th century). This view of Florence, set amidst hills, should not be missed.

EXCURSIONS; (a) *Fiesole*, 5 miles, medieval villas, Roman theatre. (b) *Pontassieve* (13 miles east) for *Sieve* Valley (north) and *Vallombrosa* (south) area rich in old monasteries, including *La Verna*, where St. Francis received the Stigmata. Lovely views, suitable walking district.

Continue south-east through *Arezzo*, 55 miles, (Y.H.), town of lovely squares. Church of *Santa Francesca*, frescoes. Route follows upper *Arno* valley, past the *Chianti* wine country to the *Tiber* valley. *San Sepolcro* and *Gubbio*, to the east, fine examples of medieval towns, are worth a visit. *Cortona*, hill city 800 ft. above railway; Lake *Trasimeno*, where great Roman Army was defeated by Hannibal in 217 B.C.

Perugia, 48 miles, (Y.H.), centre of *Umbria*, 1,000 ft. above valley, ancient city with fine Etruscan arch. *Palazzo dei Priori* (14th century); *Cambio* (exchange); Great Fountain; all in main square; many perfect medieval streets, particularly *Maestà della Volte* and *Viale Priori*. From church of *San Pietro*, view to Assisi.

Assisi, 18 miles, medieval town, home and work-place of St. Francis. *Basilica of San Francesco*, built over his tomb; story of the saint's life in 28 frescoes by Giotto; *Santa Chiara* at other end of town.

EXCURSIONS: (a) Convent of *San Damiano* (1 mile) 12th century. (b) The *Carcere*, 2 miles by the lanes past *Santa Chiara*, 1,000 ft. above town, amid woods. (c) Baroque *Santa Maria degli Angeli* housing *Porziuncola* chapel where St. Francis began his life's work.

The pastoral and agricultural countryside of *Umbria* is one of the loveliest parts of Italy and well repays exploration.

Foligno, 22 miles, (Y.H.), junction for lines to Adriatic coast (*Ancona*, 50 miles). *Spoleto*, 18 miles, medieval town amid hills; Phillipo Lippi's frescoes in cathedral.

EXCURSION: *Orvieto*, medieval buildings, cathedral with fine frescoes by Signorelli.

Route enters dry grassy *Campagna*; the ancient Roman road surface may be seen again and again alongside the modern road. *St. Peter's* dome rises in the distance when one is still 30 miles north of *Rome*. (97 miles).

Rome

On the R. *Tiber* and capital of modern Italy. The finest city in the world cannot be "done" in a few hours and it is important not to destroy enjoyment by attempting too much. Interest will be heightened by finding out something about the Roman Empire and the Roman Catholic Church before your visit.

Underground railway from main station to *Colosseum, St. Paul's* and Universal Exhibition grounds. Many bus services in city, cheap fares. (Y.H.).

The ancient city was built on the Seven Hills. The R. *Tiber* flows from north to south on western side. The *Vatican* is on west of river. Modern buildings, many of indifferent style, spread around the ancient city for miles.

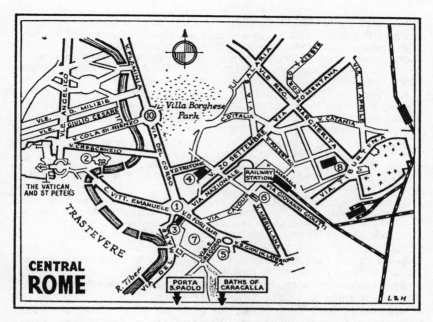

1. *Piazza Venezia.* 2. *Castel S. Angelo.* 3. *Capitoline Museum.* 4. *Quirinal Palace.* 5. *Colosseum.* 6. *S. Maria Maggiore Church.* 7. *The Forum.* 8. *University.* 9. *St. John Lateran.* 10. *Piazza del Popolo.*

Walk No. 1 Ancient Rome

From *Piazza Venezia* (city centre), 15th century *Palazzo Venezia*, huge Vittorio Emanuele monument (commemorates unity of Italy), Tomb of Unknown Soldier, to north-east Trajan's Column (2nd century). Along *Via dei Fori Imperiali* are remains of Imperial Forums, built when Roman Forum became too small. Take the steps from *Via del Mare* up to *Piazza del Campidoglio,* designed by Michelangelo (site of Capitol of Ancient Rome), Church of *Santa Maria in Aracoeli, Capitoline Museum,* magnificent Roman sculptures. Descend to *Via dei Fori* for entrance to **Roman Forum** area. Centre of ancient Roman life, now bewildering spectacle of neglected ruins; Arch of Septimus Severus (A.D. 203) temples and public buildings, Arch of Titus (A.D. 70). Leave Forum, cross to **Colosseum,** immense amphitheatre built A.D. 72-82, scene of gladiatorial combats and public spectacles. South of Forum is Palatine Hill, Roman ruins older than Forum. North-east of *Colosseum* in park, remains of Nero's palace. Along *Via San Gregorio,* through park of *Porta Capena,* to Baths of *Caracalla,* once most magnificent baths in Rome. Open-air opera in summer.

See also old city walls, particularly east of main station, and near *Lateran Gate.*

ITALY

Walk No. 2 Vatican and St. Peter's

Corso Vittorio Emanuele, cross river, *Via della Conciliazione*, to **Vatican City**, headquarters of the Roman Catholic Church, once capital of the old Papal States (most of central Italy) and now an independent city state. The Vatican Palace has been official residence of the Popes (Bishops of Rome) only since 1377, though they have lived in Rome since 498.

St. Peter's, the largest cathedral in the world, stands on the site of Nero's Circus, where St. Peter was executed in A.D. 66. The present magnificent Renaissance and Baroque church (partly designed by Bramante and Michelangelo) was built 1506-1626 over reputed tomb of St. Peter.

The *Piazza San Pietro*, over 250 yards across; colonnade by Bernini, 284 columns, 140 statues on balustrade; Egyptian obelisk from Nero's Circus. To right, Vatican Palace; official entrance by "Bronze Doors", Swiss guards in 17th century uniform; Pope uses only a few of the 1,400 rooms, rest occupied by museums.

Facade of basilica 124 yards wide, height of dome, 435 ft. View from roof and cupola. Brass marks in centre of floor indicate size of other cathedrals. Bernini's *Baldacchino* (canopy) over High Altar; mosaics; bronze statue of St. Peter, his foot kissed smooth by multitudes of pilgrims.

Gate to left of facade leads into Vatican City for exteriors of basilica and palace gardens. The City has its own printing and publishing works, wireless station and post office, and its own stamps and coins.

For Museums, leave *Piazza* on right, take *Via di Porta Angelica* and follow the walls to entrance.

Museum of Antiquities, remarkable collection of sculptures, etc. (note Laocoön and Apollo Belvedere); Vatican Library; *Borgia* Apartments (frescoes by Pintoricchio); *Stanze* (rooms) of Raphael—magnificent wall and ceiling paintings by Raphael; **Sistine Chapel** (where Popes are elected) celebrated paintings by Michelangelo on ceiling and altar wall; Picture Gallery (Pinacoteca), Italian paintings. It is advisable to follow the marked itinerary.

On Tiber, near Vatican, *Castel Sant'Angelo*, originally mausoleum of Hadrian (A.D. 136) later made into fortress, and connected to Vatican Palace by wall-top corridor.

Walk No. 3

From *Piazza Venezia* into *Via del Corso*, Baroque Palazzo *Doria*, turn left and continue to *Santa Maria sopra Minerva*, Gothic, built on site of Temple of Minerva; *Pantheon*, pagan Roman Temple, converted into church; work north-west to *Piazza della Colonna*, column of Marcus Aurelius (2nd century) elaborate carvings. Continue up *Corso*, then left for Mausoleum of Augustus; north to *Piazza del Popolo*, for gardens of *Pincio* and *Villa Borghese*. Return south by attractive *Piazza di Spagna*, *Quirinal* Palace, east to *Piazza del 'Esedra*, church of *Santa Maria degli Angeli* transformed from part of Baths of Diocletian. From station square, take *Via Cavour*, **Santa Maria Maggiore**, original magnificence is preserved; floor and columns of nave, also mosaics on arch and walls, date from 5th century. According to tradition, the Virgin appeared in a vision asking that the church be built where snow fell in morning; anniversary (August 5th) commemorated by shower of white flowers during Mass. Nearby, *Santa Pudenziana*, oldest church in Rome, founded A.D. 145, 4th century work oldest visible.

Walk No. 4

From *Piazza Venezia*, take *Via del Mare*—Theatre of Marcellus, along river, near *Ponte Palatino* note small classical temples and church of *Santa Maria in Cosmedin*, cross river to district of *Trastevere*, see churches of *Santa Cecilia* and *Santa Maria*, go up *Gianicolo* (Janiculum Hill), gardens, fine view, monuments to Garibaldi and his wife, and across river again near Vatican.

Other important churches: St. John Lateran, a mile south of station. The cathedral of Rome—various periods. Statues of the Apostles; canopy over high alter traditionally containing skulls of St. Peter and St. Paul; mosaic in apse; gold leaf roof decorated with arms of all the Popes; cloisters. The nearby Baptistry is 5th century.

The *Lateran* palace (museum) was once residence of the Pope. Opposite is building containing *Scala Santa*, said to be a staircase from Pilate's house; may only be ascended on the knees.

St. Paul's Without the Walls (*San Paolo fuori le Mura*) 1 mile south of *Porta San Paolo* (old city gate). Founded 323, badly damaged by fire 1823, rebuilt on original lines 1854; 5th century mosaics on triumphal arch escaped fire; interesting light from alabaster windows; fine cloisters (12th century).

There are over 200 churches in Rome; almost all have some interest; many are closed 12 noon-2 p.m., except the four "major basilicas" *St. Peter Vatican*, *Santa Maria Maggiore*, *St. John Lateran* and *St. Paul Without the Walls*.

Recommended: *San Lorenzo fuori le Mura* (east of station, beyond Città Universitaria) 6th and 13th century, cloisters 1241. *Sant'Agnese fuori le Mura* (1 mile north-east on *Via Nomentana*) 625 built over best preserved catacombs in Rome. *Santa Costanza* (nearby) unusual blue and white 4th century mosaics. *San Clemente* (near Colosseum) 12th century copy of 4th century church. *Santi Cosma and Damiano* (near Forum) 527. *San Pietro in Vincoli* (near *Via Cavour*) contains Michaelangelo's famous sculpture of Moses.

EXCURSIONS: (a) Appian Way (*Via Appia Antica*) for Catacombs of *San Callisto* originally burial places of early Christians, then their places of refuge during persecutions, Circus of *Maxentius*; ancient Roman tombs line the old road.
(b) *Tivoli* (20 miles east) *Hadrian's Villa*, extensive ruins of the emperor's favourite residence; *Villa d'Este*, fine Renaissance villa and gardens, superb ornamental fountains.
(c) *Ostia* (15 miles west) excavated city; good bathing at *Castel Fusano*.
(d) Volcanic *Alban Hills* (about 15 miles south-east), crater lakes of *Albano* and *Nemi*, attractive villages and towns.
(e) *Subiaco* (about 50 miles east), fine monasteries, founded by St. Benedict; beautiful scenery, pine trees.
(f) From *Avezzano*, 70 miles east, both the *Gran Sasso* mountain region (*Corno Grande*, 9,560 ft., highest peak of *Apennines*) and the *Abruzzi* National Park (wild mountain scenery, hills rise to 4,700 ft.) can be reached—cool and refreshing after Rome.

Leave Rome by *Porta Maggiore* and *Via Casilina*, across the *Campagna* and the *Latium* mountains. *Monte Cassino*, monastery founded 529, destroyed for 4th time in 1944, now rebuilt.

Caserta, with magnificent 19th century Royal Palace; has ornamental water 2 miles in length fed by aqueduct 30 miles long. Road continues through four-fold avenue of plane trees, then through vines (strung high, so that ploughing can continue underneath), reaching (150 miles from *Rome*) Naples.

ITALY

Naples

On picturesque bay with *Vesuvius* in distance, was originally a Greek city, then Roman for 7 centuries; a long time part of Spanish Empire. It is totally different from Rome and the cities of the north—a mixture of fine buildings, elegant quarters, and the squalid habitations of the larger number of its people. The great heat will discourage a lengthy stay in summer. *Naples* is a city of noise, motor-cars, buses, lorries and vociferous abandon—but its main quality is gaiety. (Y.H.).

Castel Nuovo, 13th-15th century; National Museum, paintings and ancient sculptures, particularly interesting for its collection of objects found at *Pompeii* and *Herculaneum*; Cathedral (14th century restored) with chapel of *San Januarius* in rich Baroque style. Gothic churches of *San Lorenzo Maggiore* and *San Domenico*; many Baroque churches—*San Paolo; Castell dell'Ovo*, on small island, for view; 17th century Royal Palace.

EXCURSIONS: (a) **Vesuvius** (10 miles), active volcano over 3,000 ft. high; can be ascended by rail, bus and chair-lift. Several important eruptions, e.g. A.D. 79 which buried *Herculaneum* under a sea of mud and *Pompeii* under a heap of ash; 1631, when 20,000 people were killed. A famous wine called "Lacrima Cristi" is grown on its slopes.

(b) **Pompeii** (15 miles). Vast excavated area, advisable to work out route beforehand; book and plan issued by *Ministero dell'Educazione*.

(c) **Herculaneum** (6 miles). A smaller city than *Pompeii*; the excavated portions are compact. See especially the Theatre.

(d) Circuit of *Sorrento* Peninsula, and *Salerno*. *Castellamare di Stabia* (20 miles), (Y.H. at *Agerola*, 11 miles), Sorrento (12 miles) (Y.H.), towns with fine sea views across Bay of Naples. From *Sorrento* by boat to Capri, holiday island of the millionaires, with its town perched 500 ft. up. Blue grotto. *Anacapri* is pretty village. *Amalfi* Coast Road—magnificent route along south side of peninsula, fine scenery of Gulf of *Salerno*. *Amalfi*, picturesque resort (Y.H. at *Praiano*); *Ravello*, magnificent Norman buildings; *Salerno* (Y.H.) in beautiful position on bay.

R.1(i). Naples to Sicily

The route proceeds inland from *Salerno* (Y.H.) through *Eboli* and *Auletta*, then south to *Lauria* (80 miles) through the limestone country and chestnut forests of *Basilicata*. On to *Castrovillari* (35 miles), an agreeable little town on sunlit uplands of *Calabria*—mountainous peninsula forming 'toe' of Italy and one of poorest regions, but has splendid forests and mountain flora—then due south to *Cosenza* (45 miles) via *Spezzano Albanese* (medicinal springs) and along wide gravel valley of the river Crati. *Tiriolo* (45 miles) has fine view of both Tyrrhenian and Ionian seas. Road turns westward via plateau of *Maida* —scene of British victory against Napoleonic Army in 1806—hence Maida Vale in London; *Pizzo Calabro* (Y.H.) on coast; *Vibo Valentia* (32 miles)— formerly military outpost of ancient Greece—has Norman castle affording magnificent view from battlements. After 30 miles to *Palmi* route takes coast road—steep, looped and zig-zagged to **Reggio Calabria** (30 miles) via Scilla (Y.H.)—the Scylla of Scylla and Charybdis of the Odyssey—through olive groves and luxuriant vegetation.

Sicily
Frequent steamers ply across narrows to *Messina*. Mountainous extension of Apennines and Atlas; highest at *Mount Etna*, 10,800 feet, largest active volcano in Europe. Cloudless skies, mild winters, but too hot and dry in mid-

summer; delightful in spring and autumn. Vines, almonds and lemons are grown, sulphur is mined near *Agrigento*, oil and asphalt exploited in south-east corner of island, sword-fish and tunny are netted. Remains of Greek and Roman buildings, Saracen mosques, Norman castles and Baroque churches abound. Simple and cheap hostel accommodation named 'Alberghi della Gioventu' and run by local tourist organisations is provided at *Catania, Agrigento, Syracuse, Trapani, Enna, Ragusa* and *Caltanissetta*. Messina—almost entirely destroyed by earthquake 1908 and aerial bombardment 1943; now rebuilt, broad streets parallel with sea; fine views from hills above town.

EXCURSION: *Lipari*, or *Aeolian*, Islands. By hydrofoil from *Messina*, or steamers from *Milazzo*. Seven islands, all volcanic; Stromboli remains active. Y.H. on *Lipari*.

Coast road westwards to *Castroreale* (Y.H.) (30 miles) and on to **Palermo** (125 miles) via *Cefalu*—backed by formidable cliff, 12th century cathedral, splendid mosaics. *Palermo* is rich in Baroque palaces and churches, luxuriant gardens. Massacre of Sicilian Vespers here Easter Day, 1282.

EXCURSION: Monte Pellegrino (8 miles) 2,000 feet headland affording magnificent panorama.

Road to *Trapani* (60 miles) goes inland past *Segesta* (fine ruins of Doric temple) through rolling, hilly terrain. Remote, little-known region N.E. of Trapani to Cape *St. Vito*, via *Erice*—medieval little town of Phoenician origin on isolated calcareous hill; incomparable views.

Marsala (20 miles) famed for golden wine. On to *Agrigento* (90 miles) visiting *Selinunte* en route—site of ruined Hellenic temples in romantic desolation. *Ragusa* is 65 miles further on in S.E. corner of island, delightful for lovers of Baroque, as is *Noto* (32 miles towards *Syracuse*).

Syracuse (24 miles). Ancient rival of Athens and Carthage: many classical ruins. *Catania* (33 miles). A thriving commercial city, built among the lava-flows which have repeatedly destroyed it.

EXCURSION: Etna. Lower slopes extremely fertile; scattered forest up to 6,000 feet. barren beyond. Snow-capped most of year; winter sports centre. Bus from *Catania* to *Rif. Sapienza*. CAI hut, or Observatory, for overnight accommodation.

Taormina (32 miles) balcony site above sea, with view of Etna. Greek, Roman and medieval monuments. Warm winter resort. *Messina* is 32 miles farther on.

Return R.1.   Naples to Genoa and San Remo

Take road to west through the "Phlegraean Fields" (*Campi Flegrei*) region of attractive volcanic hills, used as holiday resort by Ancient Romans; main centre *Pozzuoli*, with Roman amphitheatre; many other traces of Ancient Rome. Route follows coast, *Minturno*, Roman aqueduct and theatre; resorts of *Formia* and *Gaeta* (peninsula was fortress—huge castle). *Sperlonga* (Y.H.), 71 miles. Turn inland across the *Pontine Marshes*—intensively culti-vated in ancient times, then became malarial, now reclaimed, with model farms and villages. Near Rome imposing remains of Claudian aqueduct.

Enter Rome, 74 miles, by *Porta San Giovanni*, leave on north-west by *Piazza del Popolo* and make for *Bracciano*, Renaissance castle, large crater lake; return to coast at *Civitavecchia*.

Sardinia, Daily steamer from *Civitavecchia* to *Olbia* (7 hours). Mountainous, thinly populated, greater part uncultivated; much scented brushwood of eucalypt, myrtle, medlar and wild rose. Prehistoric monuments abound, especially "*Nuraghi*"—conical towers built of large blocks of unmortared stone. *Olbia* to *Sassari* (55 miles) across granite heights and volcanic hills,

ITALY

through cork woods. Y.H.s at *Porto Torres* and *Fertilia*. 65 miles south by third class coast road via *Bosa* (Y.H.) to *Oristano* (Y.H.). Cross-country to S.E., 65 miles is *Cagliari*—Pisan fortifications and port for crossing to Palermo. East coast route to *Olbia*, less frequented, more mountainous and spectacular than west-facing coast.

Route now mainly follows ancient *Via Aurelia* to French frontier. *Tarquinia*, medieval buildings, underground Etruscan tombs, Etruscan Museum; *Orbetello*. Etruscan walls; *Grosseto*, agricultural centre, 16th century ramparts; *Piombino*, iron industry, steamers to mountainous Isle of *Elba* (15 miles) where Napoleon was exiled, and escaped to France before Waterloo; inland to *Volterra*, considerable Etruscan remains, many medieval buildings; Leghorn (*Livorno*) modern port, 170 miles; good bathing along the coastline southwards.

Pisa, 12 miles, in 11th century was maritime republic like *Venice*: birthplace of Galileo. The architecture is mainly Romanesque. *Piazza del Duomo*, around which loveliest buildings are grouped. *Duomo* (cathedral) begun 1063, architect Buschetto; note delicate work in facade; leaning Tower, 1173, marble, view from top; list was caused by a land-slip. Baptistry, 1152, first expression of new sculpture in Italy. The pulpit in *Baptistry* by Nicola Pisano, and that in *Duomo* by Giovanni, his son, are very fine. Civic Museum, Gothic *Medici* Palace, *Santa Maria della Spina* (14th century), *Camposanto* (cemetery) with Gothic arcading and frescoes.

Inland to *Lucca* (Y.H.), 16th and 17th century walls (now with dry moats and charming gardens); fine Pisan Romanesque buildings, *Duomo* housing crucifix reputed to be miraculous, church of *San Michele*; some Gothic buildings.

Viareggio, large coastal resort; *Marina di Massa*, 30 miles, (Y.H.), good beach; *Carrara*, marble quarries; *Lerici*, 20 miles, (Y.H.), village on bay in which Shelley was drowned. **La Spezia,** big naval port on lovely gulf. Excursion to village of *Portovenere*.

North of *La Spezia* the *Riviera di Levante* stretches as far as *Genoa*. Towns such as *Levanto, Sestri Levante, Rapallo* and *Santa Margherita* are coastal resorts. *Portofino* on attractively hilly peninsula.

Genoa (Y.H.), largest port in Italy and rival to Marseilles. Birthplace of Christopher Columbus. Contrasts in streets between old houses and palaces and modern commercial buildings, due to former decay and modern revival of the city. Fine streets: *Balbi, Cairoli, Garibaldi, Piazza de Ferrari*. Very modern area (*Via 20 Settembre*) with Victory Square; old quarter, south of cathedral of *San Lorenzo* (12th-16th century). Several attractive churches. Excursion along the *Circonvallazione a Monte* for wide views of the city.

Between *Genoa* and the French frontier and coast is known as *Riviera di Ponente*. Between the cosmopolitan resorts are primitive peasant villages. The poor land encourages the teeming local population to seek a living in fishing, hence innumerable fishing villages.

Albissola Marina, 27 miles, good bathing. *Savona*, iron industry and port; *Finale Marina*, 18 miles, (Y.H.), another bathing resort. *Alassio*, less sea-side resort than a residential town, well laid out; *San Remo*, largest and most fashionable of Italian winter resorts; centre of early flower-trade; some picturesque old streets. Excursions to *Baiardo*, 3,000 ft. up in hills, magnificent panorama of *Riviera*.

Bordighera, resort, fine promenade; *Ventimiglia*, flower-trade and customs town. The actual frontier is at *Pont St. Louis* a few miles farther on.

R.2. Milan to Venice and return (410 miles)

Milan (see **R.1.** page 273), *Bergamo*, 36 miles, modern industrial town, with walled Venetian town at higher level. *Torre del Comune* (12th century tower), *Palazzo della Ragione*, *Colleoni* Chapel, *Santa Maria Maggiore*.

EXCURSIONS: Northwards to alpine valleys and Lake of *Iseo* (15 miles long).

Brescia, 33 miles, situated between Alps and plains, a town where Lombard and Venetian artistic ideas mixed. *Broletto*, 12th century government house with tower; *Rotondo*, 11th-12th century cathedral; *Loggia*, attractive Renaissance square; Roman museum; many Renaissance churches and palaces.

Desenzano, on south shore of Lake of *Garda* (32 miles long).

EXCURSIONS: By steamer or bus along lake, many attractive resorts and villages. Road on west side gives best views. (Y.H. at *Riva del Garda*).

Verona, 41 miles, on R. *Adige*; fine Roman remains: Arena, Forum, Theatre; cathedral, many churches; *San Zeno*, particularly interesting Romanesque style. Birthplace of Paolo Veronese.

EXCURSIONS: (a) Foothills of Alps, *Soave* wine-growing district. (b) *Montagnana*, particularly good town walls. (Y.H.)

Vicenza, 32 miles, north of *Berici* hills, renowned for architectural work of Andrea Palladio.

Padua, 20 miles, one of the old city states, then under Venetian rule for 400 years; university one of the most noted in Europe. Basilica of *Sant' Antonio*, astonishing mixture of Lombardy Gothic and Venetian Oriental (cupolas); Donatello's statue of Gattamelata; *Scrovegni* Chapel (1303), fine frescoes by Giotto. *Venice* 20 miles.

Venice

The barbarian invasion of the Dark Ages drove refugees to seek safety on islands in shallow lagoons; the city was founded in 811 and grew rapidly after 1000; kept independence as city republic until 1797; "Queen of the Adriatic" from 1400 onwards; eventually lost importance through discovery of America, and working of new routes to east.

Railway and road reach the 118 islands of the city by a 2-mile causeway, beyond which no motor traffic is allowed. You travel by boat, or by footpath crossing the canals by countless beautiful little bridges. The city is not too large to be explored on foot, and the narrow footways between tall buildings are shady. (Y.H.).

The *gondola* is the "taxi" of *Venice* but fares are expensive. On the canal steamers (*vaporetto*) the charge is about 50 lire per stage but it costs only 100 lire to go the length of the Grand Canal. There are also numerous motor-boat services (*motoscafi*).

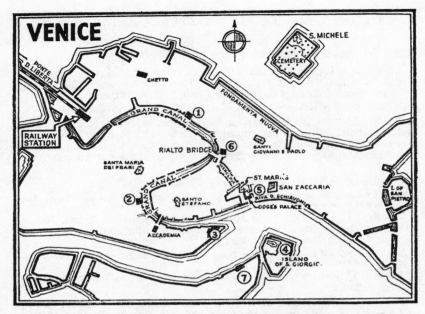

1. *Ca' d'Oro.* 2. *Palazzo Rezzonico.* 3. *S. Maria della Salute.* 4. *San Giorgio Church.* 5. *Bridge of Sighs.* 6. *Post Office.* 7. *Y.H. (Fondamente Zitelle* 86).

Tour No. 1 By Boat

From station by water-bus along **Grand Canal,** lined by fine palaces (the real frontages are on Canal, not inland) 2¼ miles to *St. Mark's. Ca' d'Oro,* "Golden House". (Gothic palace); 16th century **Ponte di Rialto,** bridge carrying shops; *Palazzo Rezzonico* (17th century); churches of *Santa Maria della Salute* on south bank, and *San Giorgio* on island opposite *St. Mark's:* land at *San Zaccaria.*

Tour No. 2 On foot from San Zaccaria landing stage to Rialto

Left along promenade, *Ponte dei Sospiri* (**Bridge of Sighs**) joining prison to *Palazzo Ducale* (**Doge's Palace**) finest non-church Gothic building, 14th-15th century, magnificent interior; paintings by great Venetian artists, including Tintoretto's "Paradise"—longest canvas painting in world. On quay, column with Lion of St. Mark. Opposite palace is *Libreria Vecchia,* by Sansovino (16th century), the *Logetta,* and *Campanile,* 300 ft., lift, good view.

Piazza San Marco, elegant square surrounded by buildings of many periods. **Church of St. Mark,** without parallel in western Europe. Founded 9th century as shrine for body of St. Mark; rebuilt 11th century, its mainly

Byzantine style reflects *Venice's* trade with the east. The four bronze horses (3rd century B.C.) brought to *Venice* in 1204 after conquest of Constantinople, together with other loot, adorn the church. Fine marble facings, and 12th-17th century interior and exterior mosaics.

Past clock tower (bronze figures strike the hours) into *Merceria*, attractive shopping street, *San Salvatore* (Renaissance interior). *Merceria* bears right then left (straight on for main post office) to *Rialto* Bridge, centre of busy district.

Interesting Gothic churches of *Santa Maria dei Frari, Santo Stefano, Santi Giovanni e Paolo* (with many tombs of Doges).

Ghetto (north-west of city), *Arsenale* (ancient naval arsenal of Republic, with fine walls), island of *San Pietro* for pretty gardens and quayside views.

EXCURSIONS: (a) *Murano* (steamer from *Fondamenta Nuova*), museum of ancient glassware and world-famous glass factories (b) *Torcello* (steamer as (a)) fine cathedral (c) Lido (steamer *Riva degli Schiavoni*) celebrated and sophisticated bathing resort, remarkable contrast to *Venice.*

Route continues across the last stretches of the *Po* Basin to *Rovigo. Po* and its tributaries here are all embanked; in spite of this, flooding often occurs. *Rovigo*, centre of the *Polesine*, tract of land which has been drained by good engineering work, thence through a region of lakes and marshes to **Ferrara**, 22 miles, (**Y.H.**); cathedral, Renaissance houses.

EXCURSION: to isolated abbey of *Pomposa* and lagoon of *Comacchio.*

R.2(i). Ferrara to San Marino. Southwards to Ravenna, 46 miles, (former capital of W. Roman Empire; Byzantine monuments and mosaics, also Dante's tomb). Thence to *Rimini* and *Riccione*, 33 miles, resorts with wide sandy beaches, and San Marino, an independent republic, perched on *Monte Titano*; one of the smallest states in world (38 sq. miles) and very old—6th century.

West to **Mantua**. The R. *Mincio* forms a string of lakes round the city. *Palazzo Ducale*, 13th-18th century, third in size only to *Vatican* and *Caserta*, frescoes, picture gallery; several other palaces built for Gonzaga family; church of *Sant' Andrea.*

Cremona, on R. *Po*; the *Torrazzo* (13th century) rises to 350 ft.; Lombard Gothic cathedral and 12th century baptistry; thence north-west to *Milan*, 50 miles, (**Y.H.**).

R.3. The Western (or Pennine) Alps

This region is contained roughly between two big international railway lines—the *Mont Cenis* route (via *Modane*) and the *Simplon* (via *Domodossola*). Much of the highest ground forms the frontier with France and Switzerland (*Mont Blanc, Matterhorn, Monte Rosa*); the *Gran Paradiso* group is all in Italy. Area offers everything from interesting valley walks to mountaineering of highest order; reached by train and bus from *Turin*; or by road from France and Switzerland.

Main valley, formed by *Dora Baltea,* tributary of the *Po*, is **Val d'Aosta.** French or a Franco-Italian dialect is spoken by many of the people, particularly in the west, and the French form of place names is frequently used.

ITALY

Aosta (80 miles from *Turin*), founded in 25 B.C. called *Augusta Praetoria*, after Caesar Augustus; interesting Roman and medieval buildings, surrounded by Roman walls.

EXCURSIONS: (a) **Great St. Bernard Pass** (8,170 ft.) 20 miles, route shows glaciers of *Grand Combin*; hospice; famous pass route to Switzerland (*Martigny*). (b) *Cogne*, centre of *Gran Paradiso* National Park. (c) *Valsavaranche* for ascent of *Gran Paridiso*, 13,324 ft. From *Pré St. Didier* Little St. Bernard Pass road (7,200 ft.) leads into France (*Bourg St. Maurice*). Good views. Short cuts for walkers. Excellent view of *Mont Blanc* from *Monte di Nono*, 2 hours' walk from main road.

Courmayeur (25 miles from *Aosta*), Italian counterpart of *Chamonix*—its background is the *Mont Blanc* range in its wildest and most rugged aspect. For serious climbers Italian Alpine Club Huts are plentiful; qualified guides in *Courmayeur*.

EXCURSIONS: (a) west: *Col de Chécroui* or *Val Veni*. (b) east: *Val Ferret* or *Mont de la Saxe*; all excellent for views of the high peaks. (c) for strong walkers; whole day, night at hut; rough steep track to *Rifugio Torino*, just below *Géant* Glacier. Expensive cable railway goes across French border to *Chamonix* with tremendous views; Mont Blanc road tunnel links *Entrèves* near *Courmayeur* with *Les Pélerins* near *Chamonix*.

R.4.   The Dolomites and Alto Adige

Contained between imaginary lines running north from *Brescia* and *Venice*. The mountains are of dolomitic limestone, coloured grey, yellow and even rose-red according to the light, sheer cliffs and towers frequently rise abruptly from meadows or forests, enabling the walker to get magnificent views without climbing. Y.Hs. are at *Campitello di Fassa*, *Feltre* and *Trento* and there are many Italian Alpine Clubs huts and simple hotels, as well as expensive resorts.

In the northern part of the area German is widely spoken, and towns and villages resemble Austria rather than Italy.

Approach via *Trento* or from *Innsbruck* over the *Brenner* Pass. Can be conveniently combined with visit to *Venice*. Many motor-coach services.

Trento, (Y.H.), on R. *Adige*, Italian-style chief town of *Trentino-Alto Adige*, which, like *Val d'Aosta*, now has partial independence.

EXCURSIONS: (a) *Lake Molveno*. (b) *Madonna di Campiglio*, centre for *Brenta* group and return via *Malè*. (c) *San Martino di Castrozza*—takes one in 63 miles to heart of mountains via *Cembra* valley and *Rolle* Pass (6,448 ft.).

Continue north through typical *Adige* country along Brenner route to **Bolzano**, more Austrian than Italian in appearance, good centre for Dolomites.

EXCURSIONS: (a) *Mendola* Pass, 4,462 ft. 15 miles (tram part way). (b) by "Dolomite Road" with magnificent views, including *Catinaccio* (*Rosengarten*) peaks, *Marmolada* (10,960 ft.), *Pordoi Pass* (7,356 ft.) to *Cortina d'Ampezzo* (67 miles), mountain resort, with road and rail connections to Lienz (c) Through the *Val Gardena* and *Ortisei* to *Sella* Pass (7,262 ft.). (d) Through *Merano* (well-known winter and summer resort) and *Venosta* valley for the *Ortler* group and *Stelvio* Pass into the *Engadine* (Switzerland).

Main route to Innsbruck continues up *Isarco* valley to Austrian frontier at *Brenner* Pass.

LUXEMBOURG

Geographical Outline

The Grand Duchy of Luxembourg, with an area of 998 square miles and no more than 50 miles from north to south and 35 from west to east, is one of the smallest states of Europe. But, for several reasons, it has an importance out of proportion to its size. Situated between Belgium, France and Germany, it lies on routes between the Rhine and the Paris basin and between the Belgian ports and central Europe. The basis of its prosperity is the large iron and steel industry. For touring, especially walking, its smallness and accessibility offer advantages and it has some very attractive and varied country with historical associations.

Land   The northern part, called *Oesling* or *E'slek*, is part of the *Ardennes* uplands (1,300-1,800 ft.) comprised chiefly of ancient slate formations into which rivers have cut steep-sided narrow valleys and spectacular winding defiles. The remaining two-thirds of the country, known as the *Bon Pays* (or *Gutland*) is some 400 ft. lower and is a continuation of the adjoining scarpland of *Lorraine*. Its resistant limestones and sandstones produce many striking landscape features, especially in the district known as the *Petite Suisse*. As in the *Oesling*, the *Bon Pays* is deeply cut by river valleys including the wine growing *Moselle*. Most of the streams drain towards the *Sûre* which itself joins the *Moselle* at *Wasserbillig*.

Climate   The prevailing winds are between south and west, producing a mild climate, west European rather than "continental". The lower valleys are humid in summer, but the hill country is cool and has less rainfall than the Belgian *Ardennes* by which it is sheltered.

Plants   One third of the country is wooded. In the *Ardennes* the valley slopes, thickly covered with oak and spruce forest, contrast with the plateau above, which is open and largely cultivated. For a few weeks about Whitsuntide, when the broom is in flower, this part of the country takes on a golden glow. In the *Bon Pays* magnificent beech woods cover the sandstone plateaux of the centre.

The People

Population   Of the population of 350,000 about two-thirds live either in the capital, *Luxembourg*, (70,000) or in the iron and steel districts. Racially the people are a product of the mingling of the early Celtic inhabitants (Belgae) with first Roman and later Germanic invaders.

LUXEMBOURG

Language

The people are tri-lingual. The mother tongue and everyday spoken language is Luxembourgian (*Letzeburgesch*), a Germanic West Frankish dialect, which is used by all classes of the community. The written languages, used everywhere, are German and French, which are both taught at school to all children. There is no language barrier as between one area and another as unfortunately occurs in some other countries. Instead, there is a tendency for the languages to serve different purposes, German predominating in everyday life (most newspapers are printed in it), whilst French is the language of the law courts and the council chamber. Such facility produces good linguists and English also is widely known.

Religion

Practically all the people are Roman Catholics. Since 1867 the country has been a bishopric centred on the cathedral of *Notre-Dame* in *Luxembourg City*.

History

Strategically part of the troubled borderland between France and Germany, the territory now known as Luxembourg has experienced many changes of fortune in accordance with the varying strengths of the great European powers. At the break-up of Charlemagne's empire in 843 it became part of the Middle Kingdom of *Lotharingia* whose name still survives in neighbouring *Lorraine*. But in 925 it became a fief of the kingdom of Germany. In 963 its immediate ruler, Siegfried, Count of Ardenne, built a stronghold on the site of the capital city, and this became known as "*Lucilinburhuc*" ("Little fortress"), from which the present name derives. His descendants increased their domains by marriages until, by 1354, these were four times the size of the state today. The prestige of the house of Luxembourg was such that, between 1308 and 1410, four of its members were elected emperors of the Holy Roman Empire.

A curious relic of these times survives in the most famous device in English heraldry. John the Blind, ruler of Luxembourg, died fighting for the French at the battle of *Crécy* (1346). His heroism so moved the Black Prince that he took from John's helmet the motto *Ich Dien* ("I serve") and the three feathers above it and adopted them as the device of the Prince of Wales.

Luxembourg's brilliant medieval period ended in 1443 with its purchase by Philip the Good of Burgundy, after which it formed part of the Netherlands and came in succession under Burgundy, the Spanish and Austrian Habsburgs and France and did not again achieve independence, as the modern Grand Duchy, until 1815. During these centuries, particularly in the wars of Louis XIV, the fortress was besieged a number of times and frequently changed hands. Its territory, also, was reduced in size.

In 1815 William I, King of the Netherlands, of the dynasty of Orange-Nassau-Vianden, became the first Grand-Duke. But Prussia was given the right to garrison the fortress. When, in 1830, Belgium became independent, there was a popular movement for union with it. The question was settled by the powers in the *Treaty of London* (1831), ratified 1839, when the western (Walloon) part was transferred to become the Belgian *Province of Luxembourg*. The independence of the remainder (now a linguistic unit) was guaranteed, but the fortress was left under Prussian control. Later Luxembourg was again involved in the rivalries of the great powers. But popular feeling turned against union with any other country and independence was realized in the second *Treaty of London* (1867), which guaranteed perpetual neutrality, settled the sovereignty as hereditary in the ruling house and required withdrawal of the Prussian garrison and the dismantling of the fortress. The Treaty has remained the basis of Luxembourg's existence as a state and though over-run by the Germans in both World Wars its independent political status has each time been restored.

Government The Grand-Duchy is a parliamentary democracy under a limited monarchy. Parliament consists of one house, the chamber of deputies, elected for five years, by men and women aged 21 and over, by proportional representation. The Cabinet, called the Council of Government, is headed by the President who is appointed by the Sovereign. An unusual additional body, with considerable influence, is the Council of State of not more than fifteen members appointed for life by the Sovereign.

Resources Agriculture, forestry and wine production give work to about a quarter of the population. The estates are generally small to medium sized and cultivated by their owners, rented farms being exceptional. Vine growing, for the production of both still and sparkling wines, is concentrated along the slopes of the *Moselle* valley bordering Germany. Whilst some of the forest is State owned and some in private hands, most of it is owned by the village communes and used to meet local requirements. There is a tendency for the oak of the *Ardennes* and the beech of the *Bon Pays* to lose ground to softwood plantations.

The chief industry is iron and steel production, based on the ore mines of the south-west, and yielding the highest per capita quota of any country in the world. 98% of the steel is exported. Lack of coal for the furnaces has long necessitated economic unions with another country; in the nineteenth century, within the German customs union; since 1921, with Belgium. Currently a member of the Benelux Union, the European Coal and Steel Community (administered from *Luxembourg City*) and the European Common Market, Luxembourg, because of this great industry, has an important place alongside larger nations on the continent.

Other industries include tanning, metal work, ceramics, brewing and cement.

Food and Drink The specialities include Ardennes ham, cooked cheese, trout and pike. The national drinks are white Moselle wine and beer. Coffee is much more frequently drunk than tea.

Culture

Architecture Apart from their often fine situation, the many medieval castles are interesting as buildings. The most imposing are *Vianden, Clervaux, Bourscheid, Beaufort, Hollenfels* (now a youth hostel) and *Bourglinster*. The city of *Luxembourg*, once an imposing fortress, particularly after being strengthened by Vauban, Louis XIV's famous military engineer, has preserved important works of military architecture.

LUXEMBOURG

At *Echternach*, which grew up around the abbey founded in 698 by St. Willibrord of Northumbria, are the considerable 18th century Baroque buildings of the present Benedictine Abbey, with an 8th century (Merovingian) crypt. The Town Hall, the famous *Dingstuhl*, was originaly built in the 14th century as a court of justice.

Other churches of interest are *Vianden* (13th century Gothic), *Luxembourg* cathedral (Renaissance), *Koerich* (Baroque), *Rindschleiden* (for its frescoes) and *Junglinster* (for its knights' tombs). Many churches newly built or re-built after the destruction of World War II have remarkable modern stained glass windows. Carved field crosses, mostly 18th century, are found all over the country.

Touring Information

Access — Luxembourg City is within 10½ hours' journey from London by rail and boat via Ostend and Brussels, the most direct route. Fares are £24·70 ordinary return, or £16·60 night return. By air in about 2 hours on daily flights; return excursion ticket, valid one month, £43·05.

Transport — There is a good railway system, largely electrified, but some local journeys are more easily made by bus. Train and bus fares are about 1·35 *fr.* per kilometre.

Money — The Luxembourg *franc* is tied to the same exchange value as the Belgian *franc*. It is divided into 100 *centimes*, but the smallest coin in general use is 25 *centimes*. Belgian money is accepted in Luxembourg, but not vice versa.

Maps — The whole country is covered by the Michelin map No. 8, scale 1:200,000 and the De Rouck map on a scale of 1:100,000, marking footpaths.

Walking — Luxembourg is one of Europe's finest pieces of hill country for moderate walking tours. The marked long-distance footpaths listed here-under give access to some idyllic forest and meadow country.

1. **Haute-Sûre Track**: Martelange—Ettelbruck.
2. **Attert Track**: Martelange—Redange—Useldange—Mersch.
3. **Our Track**: Ouren—Vianden—Diekirch.
4. **Seven Castles Track**: Gaichel (Eischen)—Mersch.
5. **North Track**: Wemperhardt—Kautenbach—Diekirch.
6. **Basse-Sûre Track**: Wasserbillig—Echternach.
7. **Moselle Track**: Wasserbillig—Stromberg (Schengen).
8. **Alzette Track**: Dommeldange (Luxembourg)—Mersch.
9. **Pre'tzerdall Track**: Boulaide—Pratze—Ettelbruck.
10. **Victor Hugo Track**: Vianden—Brandenbourg—Ettelbruck.
11. **Charles Mathieu Track**: Esch-sur Sûre—Wiltz—Vianden.
12. **Moellerdall Track**: Section Mersch—Larochette; and Beaufort—Echternach.
13. **Maurice Cosyn Track**: Diekirch—Beaufort.
14. **Mamer Track**: Mamer—Kopstal—Mersch.
15. **Wiltz Track**: Goebelsmuhle—Kautenbach—Wiltz.
16. **South Track**: Rodange—Rumelange.

Additional footpaths, marked with white triangles, link the youth hostels.

LUXEMBOURG

LUXEMBOURG

Scale |—————|—————| Miles
0   5   10

Tourist Footpaths ------
(Routes 1 to 16)
Youth Hostel
Footpaths ---

BELGIUM

Clervaux

Wiltz

Esch

Kautenbach

Vianden

GERMANY

Boulaide

Goebelsmuhle

Diekirch

Martelange

Ettelbruck

Beaufort

Echternach

Bettborn

Redange

Mersch

Wasserbillig

Hollenfels

Bourglinster

Grevenmacher

Mamer

LUXEMBOURG

Rodange

Remich

Schengen

Rumelange

FRANCE

287

LUXEMBOURG

Cycling	Although hilly in all its parts, Luxembourg is an ideal country for cycling as all roads are in good condition. Touring cyclists should avoid the few heavy traffic roads.

Canoeing and Boating — The *Moselle*, broad, calm and slow, with many disembarkation points and camping grounds along its banks, provides easy conditions. The 38 miles of the *Lower Sûre*, from *Ettelbruck* to *Wasserbillig*, present no serious difficulty; all the dams are provided with water-passes. It is swifter than the *Moselle*. Above *Ettelbruck* its practicability depends on the water level, and its sand banks and other obstructions require greater experience. The same can be said of the swift flowing *Our* and, with greater emphasis, of the *Wiltz*.

Touring Route

R.1. Arlon-Luxembourg-Moselle Valley-Mullerthal-Ardennes

Coming from *Arlon* (Belgium) enter Luxembourg by secondary road through *Septfontaines* (medieval church and castle) and *Ansembourg* (medieval and renaissance castles) to *Hollenfels* (Y.H. in medieval castle). Picturesque road to *Luxembourg* City (footpath; bus connection from *Kopstal*).

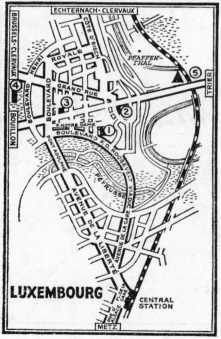

1. *Notre Dame Cathedral.*
2. *Grand Ducal Palace.*
3. *Post Office.*
4. *Radio Luxembourg.*
5. *Youth Hostel.*

Luxembourg City, capital of the Grand Duchy, is a town of 68,000 inhabitants, about equidistant from the borders of Belgium, France and Germany. Once one of the most important fortresses of Europe, the old town is situated on a steep-sided, rocky plateau and many picturesque ruined bastions and towers are still to be seen. The main part of the town is almost surrounded by a belt of parkland at the edge of the rocky slopes. The *Cathedral of Notre Dame* dates from 1618 and has an interesting Baroque portico. In the oldest part of the town amongst interesting, narrow streets, stands the Grand Ducal Palace, a building in 16th century Spanish style. Well worth seeing also is the view of the valley from the *Roc du Bouc.* Y.H.

East from *Luxembourg* to *Grevenmacher*, ancient and picturesque town on the *Moselle.* Y.H. among vineyards overlooking the valley. Continue along German border following *Moselle* and *Sûre* to *Echternach* (Y.H.) Footpath from *Grevenmacher* overlooking the valleys. Small old town with remarkable ancient buildings including town hall and abbey. Fine modern stained glass windows in choir of Basilica. Famous Whitsun "Dancing Procession" through streets in memory of St. Vitus.

From *Echternach* through the fine *Mullerthal*, sandstone rocks and beech woods, to *Beaufort* castle. By *Reisdorf* following R. *Our* to *Vianden*, perhaps the most picturesque place in the *Ardennes*. Pleasant old town with Gothic church and cloisters, dominated by impressive ruins of medieval castle. **(Y.H.)** North-west to *Clervaux* **(Y.H.)** medieval castle, Benedictine abbey. Then either to *Ettelbruck* **(Y.H.)** or *Wiltz*.

NETHERLANDS
Geographical Outline

The Kingdom of the Netherlands covers about 13,600 square miles, but this figure is increasing as more and more land is won from the sea. The name "Holland", generally used to describe the whole country, should properly be applied only to the provinces of North and South Holland, which form the north-west portion of the country.

Land More than one-fifth of the land is under sea-level and would be invaded by the sea if the country were not protected by dykes and dunes. The area between the dunes along the sea-shore and the higher land of the south and east was formerly lake and marshy swamp; but through much human effort the swamps, together with a large part of the *Zuiderzee* (now called *IJsselmeer*), have been converted into pasture and arable land known as *polders*. The pastures are split up by innumerable little ditches, very necessary in order to regulate the water level.

To safeguard the dunes, which are the natural defence against the North Sea, long-rooted grasses have been planted and dykes and piers have been built.

Climate The climate is quite temperate but with seasonal extremes of temperature due to the continental influence. The prevailing winds from the west are noticeable, as they pass unhindered over the flat country, tending to produce damp weather, but without excessive rainfall.

The coldest month is January, and July the hottest. A visit is well worth while at any time of the year, although spring and summer are the best touring seasons. April and the beginning of May are the best times for visiting the bulb fields.

Plants and Animals The undulating sand-hills are extremely beautiful; they are like mountain ranges compared with the level *polders* behind them. There is a large variety of vegetation on the dunes; near the shore are tangled masses of thorn and brambles, and farther inland fragrant birches and pines twisted by the storms into fantastic shapes. The ground is carpeted with wild flowers. Rabbits are evident, as well as hares, lizards, pheasants and many sea-birds.

Just behind the dunes, between *Alkmaar* and *Leiden*, is a strip of sandy ground, mixed with clay, where the famous bulbs are grown. Daffodils, tulips, hyacinths and gladioli in their season transform flat fields into wonderfully coloured carpets which must be seen to be believed.

Between the *Hague* and the *Hook* is *Westland*, the most important market-gardening area, where peaches, tomatoes, grapes and strawberries are grown under acres of glass.

In the province of *Drenthe* is a region of heather and moorland, whilst the provinces of *Friesland* and *Groningen* are predominantly given over to pasture.

Windmills and canals—a common sight in Holland.

The People

Population
With nearly 13 million people the country is one of the most densely populated in the world and the densest in Europe; the average is more than 900 persons per square mile.

Language
The language, Dutch, is a Germanic tongue. In towns and in youth hostels you should have no difficulty making yourself understood, as many people have a working knowledge of English and are only too eager to help.

Religion
About 41 per cent of the population is Protestant and another 40 per cent Roman Catholic; the remainder unclassified. Protestants, who are divided into many sects, are more numerous in the north. Roman Catholics are predominant in the provinces of *Limburg* and *North Brabant*.

History
The Dutch are the outstanding example of a nation forced to engage in unremitting struggle against the sea and in efforts to contain the great rivers which would otherwise flood the richest parts of their country. For a thousand years from Roman times the waters were victorious: the sea level tended to rise, the dune belt was pierced and towards the end of the period the Zuider Zee was formed.

These northern Netherlands were therefore much less developed than those of the south (see Belgium) when they came first under Burgundian and later under Habsburg rule in the middle ages. A change of fortune came with a new phase in which the sea level tended to fall slightly and with the introduction of windmills for pumping in the 15th century. The Dutch, schooled in self-reliance by the battle against nature, needed only this to turn to advantage their otherwise favourable situation for international trading. Wealth increased. The towns, particularly Amsterdam, prospered.

The ideas associated with the Reformation were naturally congenial to matter-of-fact merchants whose sources of wealth were independent of the church and of the feudal system represented by the Spanish overlordship of the Netherlands.

The rebellion, the famous Revolt of the Netherlands, which broke out against Philip II in 1555, reflected the new-felt strength of a people already forging the financial and commercial forms in which the trade of the modern world was to develop, and their impatience at a control which was both alien and rigidly traditional. It was successful only in the northern provinces. Here it found an apt leader in William of Orange and a new ally in the sea as a spring-board for assault. The east-west course of the Lower Rhine and Maas was also a decisive factor in determining that the two parts of the Netherlands should develop differently. The growth of Amsterdam at the expense of Antwerp, which remained tied to imperial Spain, symbolizes the new force affecting the balance of power. The revolt was only the beginning of an eighty years war. Not until 1648 was the independence of the young Republic acknowledged by its former master.

NETHERLANDS

Something of the spirit of this heroic age continued for another generation as shown in Dutch sea power, its rivalry with England in trade and empire building, and in scientific and artistic achievement. But, from the death of Rembrandt (1669), the sharp decline in artistic conviction may reflect a similar inadequacy of vision in the factions controlling the nation's policy, seen in the rivalries for the position of head of state (*stadtholder*) and in the long periods when the position was dispensed with. The House of Orange was alternately looked to for leadership and suspected as having dynastic ambitions. These, by a strange turn of fate, were satisfied when William III came to double the part of Stadtholder with the sovereignty of Great Britain (1688-1702) held jointly with his wife, Mary Stuart—a spectacular example of the swiftly changing relationships between the powers of western Europe which were to continue throughout the 18th century.

The end of the Republic came with an unhappy period of French domination during the Napoleonic wars. The modern Kingdom dates from 1815 when William I of Orange-Nassau proclaimed himself king. His rule was autocratic but his son, William II, was sympathetic to liberal ideas and the Netherlands were therefore more fortunate than other countries in 1848 in achieving a democratic constitution without a revolution.

In recent times Dutch influence has been exerted on the side of moderation in international affairs and the permanent Court of International Justice is situated at the Hague.

Government The Kingdom of the Netherlands is a parliamentary democracy under a limited monarchy. Parliament (the "States General") consists of two Houses. The Cabinet is not part of the Parliament, but any of its members may speak in either House. All citizens aged 23 or over have a vote and elections are based on proportional representation.

Resources The main occupations are connected with agriculture. Cereals, potatoes and sugar-beet, are grown on the higher lands of *Groningen, Friesland* and *Zeeland*, whilst on the damp lower ground of *Friesland* and the provinces of *North* and *South Holland* large numbers of cattle are reared, both for meat and dairy products. The bulb fields around *Haarlem* are a highly productive specialist industry supplying an international market.

Fishing is another important occupation and there are many fishing ports along the North Sea coast, notably *IJmuiden, Scheveningen* and *Vlaardingen*.

The importance of industry is increasing. There are coal mines in *Limburg*, recently discovered oil-fields and natural gas in *Drenthe*, shipyards in a number of towns, and a variety of industries producing consumer goods. Philips radio and electrical works, dominating the town of *Eindhoven*, is the biggest industry, employing more than 30,000 people.

Amsterdam and *Rotterdam* are great commercial cities. *Rotterdam*, one of the main transit centres for goods passing to and from Central Europe via the *Rhine*, is the largest port on the continent.

Food and Meals — Breakfast and lunch are similar, consisting of bread, thickly buttered, with cheese, sugar, chocolate, and perhaps slices of sausage and meat. The cheese is served in thin wafers, often with different kinds of bread and biscuits. Dinner, between six and seven, is the most substantial meal; vegetables and gravy are the usual dish. Fruit is abundant and good in season.

Among Dutch specialities are:

1. Smoked eels, called *paling*, which have the flavour of kippers.
2. Fresh salted herrings garnished with raw onions, eaten at stalls in the streets.
3. *Hutspot*, which is mashed potatoes, carrots and onions with meat.
4. *Boerenkool met worst*, curly cabbage with smoked sausage.
5. Pancakes, eaten with bacon or treacle.
6. *Rolpens*, fried smoked sausage.
7. Beefsteak and sauté potatoes.
8. *Rijsttafel*, consisting of rice and various kinds of Malay curry with a dozen or more different chutneys and garnishes.

Sport — Among the usual sports, in which there is a natural emphasis on those connected with water, special interest attaches to the traditional "Eleven Towns Race" in the province of *Friesland*, a one-day skating race over 125 miles, in which thousands of enthusiasts take part; it dates from the 17th century.

Culture

Architecture — There are a number of fine medieval castles and some notable Gothic and Renaissance churches. Many of these are mentioned at appropriate points in the itineraries. The main glory of the country, however, lies in its domestic architecture—the old houses which line the canals in *Amsterdam* and other cities, with their "stepped" gables and weathered façades.

Painting — An indication of Dutch influence in this field may be seen in the Dutch origin of such words as *landscape, easel, etch* and *sketch*.

In a period of 50 years from 1625 Dutch painters made a contribution to European art which, in several ways, was of the greatest significance. Catering for the plain tastes of a merchant class, their typical subjects were portraits, landscapes and domestic interiors. Realism was sought through precise observation and a technical competence which achieved complete mastery in recording the play of light. The many great names include Vermeer, Pieter de Hoogh, Frans Hals and Jan Steen. But all are transcended by Rembrandt for whom outward realism was only the starting point of a deeper study of men and nature.

Among the moderns, van Gogh (1853-90), has the same intense interest in the visible world and a great range of human sympathy expressed not in terms of light and shade but of strong colour in the full glare of the sun.

NETHERLANDS

Museums and Art Galleries
No one should miss the *Rijksmuseum* in *Amsterdam*, with its magnificent collection of paintings by Rembrandt and others, or the *Mauritshuis* in the *Hague*. Other fine galleries are the Frans Hals museum at *Haarlem* and the *Boymans-van Beuningen Museum, Rotterdam.*

Music
There are many good concerts, especially in *Amsterdam*, where the *Concertgebouw* Orchestra is world-famous. All the large towns have a concert hall as well as a theatre.

Science
Erasmus (1467-1536), did more than any other man to further the revival of learning associated with the Renaissance. The University of Leyden, (founded 1575) quickly achieved eminence and fame abroad in many branches of learning. Among its professors was van Groot (Grotius, 1583-1645), for long the great authority on international law.

Less known, perhaps, is the work of the draper's assistant, Leeuwenhoek (1632-1723) one of the true originals in the world of science—inventor of the microscope, and, throughout a long life, a prince of observers and recorder of unprecedented accuracy. His contemporary, Huygens (1629-95), improved the telescope, invented the pendulum clock and studied the properties of light. De Vries (1848-1935), the botanist, put forward the mutation theory of evolution.

Folklore
Folklore remains a part of Dutch life, often associated with the church. Easter Monday dance at *Ootmarsum* during which each house in the village is entered; over the whole of *Twente* bonfires are lighted; Island of *Terschelling*: Oppenried procession; *Limburg* and *Brabant*: carnival festivities (previous to Lent); *Zwolle*: St. Martin's Market; *Hindeloopen*: Whitsun wreaths; *Veluwe* region: folk dances.

National Costumes
National costumes can still be seen at the islands of *Zeeland; Marken* and *Volendam* (near *Amsterdam*); *Spakenburg* and *Bunschoten* (near *Amersfoort*); *Hindeloopen*; *Veluwe*; *Staphorts* (near *Zwolle* and *Meppel*).

Touring Information

Access
The best route from England is by boat from Harwich to the *Hook of Holland* (6¼ hours' crossing, return fare £17·00, or £20·90 from London). The night service, in particular, is very comfortable, with sleeping berths for all passengers. A weekly sailing operates from *Immingham* to *Amsterdam* from £11·50 single fare. Cyclists will find it more economical to travel via Dover-*Ostend*, cycling across Belgium to the Dutch frontier. Passengers from the north of England will find the steamer service from Hull to *Rotterdam* useful, but summer bookings must be made early.

Touring Areas
For touring purposes the Netherlands can be divided into eight main areas, as follows:

1. *Friesland:* a land of lakes, big farmhouses and pleasant pasture-land, with some interesting islands off the coast.

2. The Provinces of *North* and *South Holland:* flat country, polders, lakes, rivers, windmills, big towns.

3. The North Sea Coast: sandy beaches, dunes, fishermen's villages; the seaside resorts of *Scheveningen, Noordwijk* and *Zandvoort.*

4. *Betuwe:* orchards, big rivers.

5. *Veluwe:* woodland, heather.

6. The *IJsselmeer:* three polders reclaimed from the sea, with picturesque old towns on the original land.

7. *Limburg:* lovely hills, but partially industrialised.

8. The islands of *Zeeland.*

Transport
There is a close network of railways, wholly electrified, and most of the main towns are less than an hour's journey apart by rail.

A season-ticket valid for 8 days on all railway lines, also on buses *Amsterdam—The Hague* and on ferry *Enkhuisen—Staveren*, costs 52 *florins.*

There are frequent bus services between neighbouring large towns, but no long-distance services; cheap day tickets usually available. The bus terminus is nearly always near the railway station.

There is a comprehensive system of boat services and fares are as cheap as by land. A particularly worthwhile trip is the tour of the waterways of *Amsterdam* by motor-launch.

Money
The currency unit is the Guilder (*Gulden*), alternatively named *Florin*, abbreviated as Fl. or F., and divided into 100 cents. Notes are issued for 10 and 25 Guilders and in some higher denominations; metal coins are issued for 1, 5, 10, 25 cents, 1 and 2½ Guilder. A 5-cent copper coin is called a *stuiver*, a 10-cent nickel coin a *dubbeltje* and a 25-cent nickel coin a *kwartje.*

Restaurants
Eating out can be expensive, but there are lunch rooms and cafeterias in all large towns, where food is moderately priced. A meal costs about 5 *florins* or more; 15 per cent. service charge is included in bills in restaurants, so tipping is usually unnecessary. A popular and inexpensive restaurant is called *Rutecks.*

NETHERLANDS

Information Services

Every town and village of importance has its own information bureau, identifiable by the sign V.V.V.

Maps

The *Michelin* map No. 410, scale 1:400,000, and the *Geographia* road map, scale 1:500,000, are recommended; other good maps are those of the *Royal Netherlands Touring Club* (*A.N.W.B.*), obtainable only in the Netherlands.

Youth Hostels

There is an excellent network of over 50 youth hostels, mostly large (more than 100 beds) and all providing substantial but plain meals without meat. They are very crowded in July and August, and it is essential to book in advance.

Walking

The Netherlands does not claim to be a country for the walker, being for the most part flat and intensively cultivated. Some of the moorland areas in the east can, however, be covered pleasantly on foot. The Dutch themselves hold annually (usually in July) a 4-day long-distance walk from *Nijmegen*.

Cycling

It is ideal country for cycling. All Dutch people in fact, including the Royal Family, are cyclists. It is common to see whole families out cycling; young children are often strapped two to a cycle, one on the handlebars and the other behind the rider.

There are excellent cycle paths through woods and parks, along many interesting routes which are denied to the motorist and train rider. The surface of the roads is sometimes severe, and, if you have a lightweight machine, you would be well advised to leave it at home and hire a Dutch cycle (at about 5 *florins* per day, or 20 *florins* per week; deposit may be required; enquire at dealers and railway stations). The weight is not so important as the land is flat everywhere except in parts of *Limburg*, *Gelderland* and *Overijssel*.

Cycling westward is tiring at times, as the winds are unchecked by hills. If you intend to travel by cycle, boat and train, be sure to cycle with the prevailing west and south-west winds behind you as far as possible.

Cycles may not be left unattended in a town at the kerbside; they must be immobilised and placed in one of the many slots provided in the pavement, or leaned against the wall. It is advisable to make use of the many cycle parks (*Rijwielstallingen*) for a small charge.

Cyclists **must** use the cyclepaths indicated by a round blue sign on which a cycle is shown in white, but **have the option of doing so** when the sign is a black oblong with the word "rijwielpad" in white.

<table>
<tr><td>

Canoeing and Boating

</td><td>

Almost all the country can be traversed by canal, river or lake. The cruising office of the *Royal Netherlands Touring Club (A.N.W.B.), 5 Museumplein, Amsterdam,* has charts for sale. A small scale map, with the regulations of the waterways can be had from the *Netherlands National Tourist Office (A.N.V.V.)*.

</td></tr>
</table>

Amsterdam

The city gets its name from the dam which was laid across the mouth of the river *Amstel* in the 13th century, and the name *Dam* still exists in the square which forms the hub of the city, on which stands the Royal Palace and the New Church.

The centre of the city is built on islands formed by the intersection of two series of canals—one series forming concentric semi-circles and the other radiating outwards from the middle. The canals are bordered on either side by quiet quays, tree-lined and crossed by picturesque bridges. The old houses along the quays are full of architectural interest and complete a picture of great charm and character. This central area of canals and quays repays prolonged and leisurely exploration on foot.

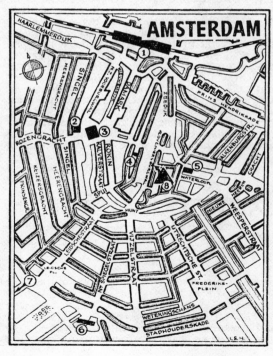

1. *Central Railway Station.*

2. *Post Office.*

3. *Royal Palace (on the Dam).*

4. *Town Hall (in Oudezijdsboorburgwal).*

5. *Rembrandt House (4-6 Jodenbreestraat).*

6. *Rijksmuseum (National Gallery)*

7. *Road to Schiphol Airport.*

8. *Youth Hostel (Kloveniersburgwal 97).*

NETHERLANDS

The two most attractive waterways are probably the *Oudezijdsvoorbrugwal*, running from north to south in the centre of the old city, and the *Reguliersgracht*, also running from north to south, but lying south of the *Amstel* river. Owing to the complicated layout of streets and canals it is almost essential to buy a good street plan, with index.

Amsterdam is the Dutch centre of art and science, with two universities. There are many museums, art galleries and other places of interest, a few of which are mentioned below.

The **National Museum** (*Rijksmuseum*), *42 Stadhouderskade*—one of the greatest art galleries in Europe, with a world-famous collection of masterpieces, including Rembrandt's "Night Watch". The Municipal Museum (*Stedelijk*), *13 Paulus Potterstraat*, has a good collection of modern art, including many paintings by Van Gogh. The Nautical Museum, *57 Corn Schuytstraat*. The Historical Museum, *4 Nieuwmarkt*. *Willet Holthuysen* Museum, *605 Heerengracht*, a 17th century residence with a splendid collection of furniture. The Tropical Museum, *2 Linnaeusstraat*.

The Royal Palace (1648); The oldest house—*1 Zeedijk*, an example of 15th century architecture, with a wooden façade and side walls of brick. *Leeuwenberg*, on the *Oudezijdsvoorburgwal*, one of the most magnificent houses, built about 1600. *Oude Kerk* (Old Church) on the *Oudekerksplein*. Consecrated in 1306, enlarged several times. The slender octagonal spire dates from 1564. *Nieuwe Kerk* (New Church) next to the Royal Palace; building begun in early 15th century; tombs of admirals, including the celebrated de Ruyter. Amsterdam University, *Oudemanhuispoort*. Asscher's diamond-cutting workshops, *127 Tolstraat*. Mint Tower, on the *Muntplein*, built 1620. Rembrandt's House, *4-6 Jodenbreestraat*, where the great Dutch painter lived from 1639-1658, is well worth a visit. Anne Frank House, *Prinsengracht 263*. Modern architecture can be seen at the Exchange in the *Damrak*. The Exchange, built in 1903, is important for its influence on subsequent 20th century Dutch architecture. *Kalverstraat*, the busiest shopping centre in the Netherlands.

Boat Tour of the Canals The most interesting excursion in *Amsterdam* is the *Rondvaart*, a motor-boat journey through the docks and canals of the city; the fare is 5 *florins* and the trip lasts about one hour and a quarter.

Transport Trams or buses are the best and cheapest means of transport within the city and the majority of the lines pass the Central Station and the *Dam*.

Ferries connect the opposite sides of the *IJ*, the central waterway to the north of the railway station; there is no charge for cyclists and pedestrians.

Useful Addresses V.V.V. (Tourist Information Office), is at *5 Rokin*; there is also an office on the *Stationsplein*. Central Police Station is at *117 Elandsgracht*, south-west of the city centre.

Touring Routes

Cycling is the most satisfactory means of seeing the Netherlands and the two routes described below are planned with this in mind. They can, however, be undertaken by train and bus.

R.1. Amsterdam to Amsterdam round the IJsselmeer (518 miles)

This route includes the whole country (except *Limberg*) and makes a very satisfactory 14-day cycling tour.

Leave *Amsterdam* by ferry from the *Ruyterkade* (adjoining Central Station) to the north part of the town and follow road to *Monnikendam* (9 miles). Here there is a ferry (45 mins.) to the former Island of *Marken* in the new *Markerwaard Polder*. Also buses (N.A.C.O.) from *Amsterdam* (leaving north of the "*IJ*") and from *Monnikendam*. **Marken** is famous for its picturesque wooden houses and the costume of its inhabitants which, although a tourist bait, is quite genuine. Y.H. at *Broek in Waterland*.

From *Marken* another ferry crosses in 30 mins. to **Volendam**, an interesting fishing village, where national costume is worn as everyday attire. *Marken* is Protestant and *Volendam* Catholic and, as with other isolated communities in Holland, the inhabitants rarely marry outside their own sect, so that individuality in manner and costume is still retained.

North of *Volendam* lies **Edam**, famous for its cheese. *Grote Kerk*, rebuilt in the 17th century, fine stained glass windows and an interesting collection of hour-glasses.

Bear west across *North Holland* to **Alkmaar**, world-famous for its cheese-market held every Friday morning. Colourful uniforms are worn (May to October) by the Guild of Cheese Porters. *Alkmaar* is, however, worth some attention on any day; ancient 16th century Weigh House overlooking the market; the church of St. Lawrence; the Town Hall; and many other fine buildings. The 170 ft. tower of the Weigh House, built in 1595-1599, contains a carillon of 35 bells, and mounted figures appear at the base of the tower and take part in a tournament every time the clock strikes the hour. Y.Hs. at *Schoorl* (6 mls.), *Bakkum* (8 mls.), and *Egmond-Binnen* (8 mls.)

East of *Alkmaar* on the *IJsselmeer*, lie *Hoorn, Enkhuizen* and *Medemblik*, three dreamy old towns which were once flourishing seaports; many handsome 17th century buildings. West Frisian Museum at *Hoorn* and *Zuiderzee* Museum at *Enkhuizen*. *Petten* is small bathing resort 12 miles north of *Alkmaar*. *Den Helder*, 13 miles further north, has boat service to *Texel*, (Y.H.).

NETHERLANDS

Den Oever, at N.E. tip of *North Holland* province, is starting point of **Great Dyke** (completed in 1932) which encloses the former *Zuiderzee.* The road (with cycle track) along the top of the dam is 18 miles long. Fine view from tower on dyke near *Den Oever.* At east end of the dyke the road forks; the main route continues right to *Bolsward,* but there is an interesting excursion to *Groningen.*

R.1(i) To *Groningen* **and the Frisian Islands.** At east end of Dyke, bear left for 6 miles to *Harlingen,* fair-sized port; boats from here in about 2 hours to *Vlieland* and *Terschelling,* two of the Frisian Islands (see below). *Franeker,* town hall (16th century) and church (15th century); Eise Eisinga Planetarium constructed in 18th century by a local wool comber is still a great curiosity. 18 miles farther, *Leeuwarden,* capital of *Friesland,* pleasant town of some 86,000 inhabitants. Frisian Museum. 18 miles north of *Leeuwarden* is village of *Holwerd,* whence boats to *Ameland,* third of Frisian Islands. All of these islands are admirable in summer for camping and bathing; miles of beach and sand-dunes. Y.Hs. on all the islands except *Vlieland.* Boat service to *Ameland* (regular) and *Schiermonnikoog* (dependent on tides).

Groningen, university town and capital of province of same name, can be approached direct from *Leeuwarden* or from *Holwerd* via *Dokkum.* It is a pleasant, well laid out town but, although over 900 years old, has only a few historic buildings left, such as the 15th century *Martinlkerk* and other old buildings near the *Grote Markt.* The market, held on Tuesdays Fridays and Saturdays is most interesting.

Continuing on main route, *Bolsward,* ancient town. Town Hall and Gothic Church, 1446, are architectural jewels. *Sneek* (7 miles) **(Y.H.)** among attractive lakes, good sailing and bathing; similarly at *Heeg* **(Y.H.** has own boats) south-west of *Sneek.* Leave main road at *Heerenveen* and turn north-east to fine woodlands of *Beetsterzwaag* and eastwards through *Donkerbroek* and *Appelscha,* turning south-westwards across moorland to *Steenwijk,* pleasant little town with medieval churches. Follow road beside the canal to **Giethoorn,** a remarkable and lovely village with no roads; the houses are connected by numerous wooden bridges spanning the many waterways. **Y.H.** at *Meppel,* 4 miles east. To *Vollenhove,* for visit to north-east *Polder,* or direct by *Gene-muiden,* noted for innumerable hay-stacks.

Kampen, interesting Hanseatic town on R. *IJssel,* entered by one of town's three fine old gateways. Old Town Hall (1350), the New Tower (*Nieuwe Toren*) 17th century; *Bovenkerk* (14th century). *Urk,* a former island, now part of north-east *Polder* is nearby and retains evidence of one-time isolation, including picturesque local costume.

Zwolle capital of *Overijssel* Province, surrounded by gardens and waterways, previously the ramparts and moats. The *Sassenpoort* (gateway) dating from 1408, is only part of ramparts still standing. *Grote Kerk,* 15th century, by *Grote Markt,* has fine organ. 15th century Town Hall; *Onze Lieve Vrouwekerk* (Church of Our Lady) with 230 ft. high 15th century tower known as the *Peperbus* (pepperbox); houses in *Diezerstraat:* many fine buildings in modern style. **Y.H.** at *Oldenbroek,* 8 miles south-westwards.

Elburg, town near *IJsselmeer* and *East Flevoland* polder; 16th century fortifications, fine gateway and 13th century church, small harbour. Return inland across a pleasant landscape of moorland and woods to *Epe* **(Y.H.).** Take *Apeldoorn* road to *Cannenburg* castle and on to 17th century castle *Het Loo,* in beautiful grounds just before *Apeldoorn.*

Apeldoorn (Y.H.), popular resort set in wooded countryside. *Berg en Bos* is square mile of natural woodland famed for its flower gardens and ponds; open-air swimming pool in beautiful setting adjoining this park.

South through wooded country to *Hoenderloo*, to **Hooge Veluwe National Park**, twenty square miles of unspoilt countryside between *Apeldoorn* and *Arnhem* where deer, moufflon and wild boar roam at liberty in their natural habitat. *Kröller-Müller Museum*, modern building in park, housing paintings, including many by Vincent van Gogh, costly furniture, fine sculpture and rare porcelain. **Y.H. at** *Doorwerth*.

Arnhem (Y.H.), on Lower Rhine, scene of desperate fighting after the air-borne landing of September 1944. The Airborne Cemetery and Monument are at *Oosterbeek* to the west. City Hall, 16th century Renaissance palace, known as *Duivelshuis* because of devilish figures carved on front; 16th century gateway by the *Grote Markt*; *Provinciehuis* near the *Rhine* bridge; Aquarium of the Moorland Reclamation Society, *Zijpendaalseweg*, a wonderful collection of Dutch fresh water and tropical fish. *Bronbeek* Museum: East Indian specimens, and live exhibition of silk worm cultivation.

EXCURSIONS: (i) North (No. 3 bus, 15 mins.) to **Open-Air Museum**, unique collection of Dutch houses and costumes, farmsteads, windmills, and old-time arts and crafts from every province. (ii) *Sonsbeek, Zijpendaal* and *Rozendaal* Parks.

Leave *Arnhem* by *Nijmegen* road, south through rolling *Betuwe* country-side, famous for its blossom-laden orchards in spring.

Nijmegen, frontier stronghold since Roman times; see the *Valkhof*, ruined castle with chapel built by Charlemagne; Renaissance Town Hall with Gobelin tapestries; 14th century Gothic *Grote Kerk*; 17th century Weigh House in Market Place. View into Germany from the heights of the town. **Y.H. at** *Ubbergen*.

Continue by *'s-Hertogenbosch* road, cross R. *Maas* to *Grave*. Fork left through *Uden* and *Veghel* to *St. Oedenrode*, scene of a guild festival, and straight on, across the *Eindhoven-'s-Hertogenbosch* main road to *Oirschot*. Branch left to *Hilvarenbeek* **(Y.H.)**, turning right again for *Tilburg*, industrial town, textile factories, but has palatial town hall.

On through wooded countryside of *Brabant* to **Breda**, from which Charles II returned to England at Restoration, 1660. *Begijnhof*, founded 1270 by Flemish sisters of mercy; Castle now occupied by Royal Netherlands Academy (Renaissance architecture); *Grote Kerk*, 13th century Gothic; admirable town planning in factory and residential districts on outskirts; lovely country-side all around. **Y.H. at** *Chaam*.

Road continues across flat heath and woodland via *Roosendaal* to *Bergen-op-Zoom*, **(Y.H.)** former flourishing seaport on the *Scheldt* estuary; Town Hall, 14th century Gothic *Grote Kerk*, from tower of which Antwerp can be seen; 16th century *Markiezenhof* and medieval gateways of *Gevangenpoort* and *Wouwpoort*. Religious procession on August 15.

NETHERLANDS

Southwards from *Bergen-op-Zoom* and into province of *Zeeland*, through sand-dunes for about 4 miles, then westwards to *Goes*, many local costumes can be seen at the Tuesday Market; 16th century church and part of 15th century Town Hall. Boat from *Katseveer*, north-west of *Goes*, to *Zierikzee* on *Duiveland* Island; 199 ft. tower of *Grote Kerk*, visible from far off, begun in 1454, never completed.

14 miles west of *Goes* is *Middleburg*, chief town of *Zeeland* in centre of interesting island of *Walcheren*, with ornate 15th century town hall, 12th century abbey and adjoining *Nieuwe Kerk* with 280 ft. tower affording wide views. Circuit of island by bus from *Middleburg* goes via *Veere*, where former trade with Scotland is shown by 16th century *Scotze Huizen*; pretty road westward to Netherlands most westerly town of *Westkapelle* and then along north shore of *Scheldt* estuary with views of ocean liners on their way to and from *Antwerp*; road then turns inland back to *Middleburg*. **Y.Hs.** at *Domburg* and *Vlissingen*.

Return to *Zierikzee* and on north-east to *Willemstad*, thence due north to *Rotterdam*.

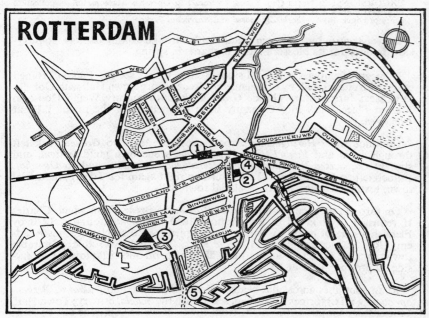

1. *Central Railway Station.* 2. *Post Office.* 3. *Youth Hostel* (*Rochussenstraat* 107/109.) 4. *Town Hall.* 5. *Maas Tunnel.*

NETHERLANDS

Rotterdam, (Y.H.) second city of Netherlands, largest port in Europe and second-largest in the world. From *Willemsplein* a most interesting cruise of 1½ hours round the docks. See the *Boymans Museum*, old masters, modern art and sculpture; the *Maas Tunnel* (3,525 ft. long) which links the two sections of the city; *Blijdorp Zoo*, *van Aerssenlaan* (most modern in world); *Delfshaven*, where the Pilgrim Fathers embarked for Plymouth and America. Zadkine statue commemorates war-time devastation of city, almost completely rebuilt in impressive style of contemporary Dutch architecture. "Euromast", 383 ft. look-out tower, with café-restaurant on top, constructed 1960.

Vlaardingen, old fishing port, lies 6 miles westwards, then 12 miles north to **Delft,** famed for its china, a delightful little town with tree-lined canals and handsome 17th century houses. *Nieuwe Kerk* (15th century), where the Dutch kings are buried; *Oude Kerk* (13th century); *Prinsenhof* (Prince's Court); Town Hall and *Oostpoort.*

Five miles from *Delft* is **The Hague** (*Den Haag* or *'s-Gravenhage*), the seat of government, a well-planned city with many fine buildings, parks and boulevards. By the *Hofvijver*, an oblong lake in the centre of the city, is the *Mauritshuis* Art Gallery, magnificent collection of paintings by old Dutch masters. Near the *Mauritshuis* is the *Binnenhof* (old palace of Counts of Holland), surrounding 13th century *Ridderzaal* (Knight's Hall). The *Gevangenpoort*, 16th century prison gate, open daily, is near large square known as *Buitenhof*, where is City Hall, and beyond it the 14th and 15th century Gothic *Grote Kerk* (good view from tower). Just north of *Grote Kerk*, in *Torenstraat*, is the *Torengarage*, a striking piece of modern architecture.

In the north of the town is the Peace Palace, with its beautiful gardens, founded by Carnegie and built 1907-13. All nations contributed large sums towards furnishing and equipping it. Municipal Museum, *41 Stadhouderslaan* (bus 1); Zeiss Planetarium, *39 Grote Marktstraat*; Mesdag Panorama, *65b Zeestraat*; Postal Museum, *82 Zeestraat*; *Bosch* Park; *Madurodam*, a miniature town, scale models, showing development through a thousand years. Y.H. at *Loosduinen*, 6½ miles S.W.

Ten miles north-east of *The Hague* is **Leiden,** university town with many lovely old houses, almshouses and public buildings, birthplace of Rembrandt, Jan Steen and other great Dutch painters. In town centre is the *Burcht* (castle); to south-east is 16th century *Hooglandsekerk*; to west across *New Rhine*, are the Fish and Eel Markets and 17th century Weigh House and Butter-market, and the Gothic *Pieterskerk*. Across the *Rapenburger* lies the University, housed in a 15th century convent. Y.Hs. at *De Kaag* (4 miles) and *Noordwijkerhout* (8 miles).

Take the road north-west through *Voorhout* to *Lisse* and **Keukenhof,** a former country house, whose grounds are given over to displays of Dutch bulbs, best seen in April or early May. Flower processions between *Sassenheim*, *Lisse* and *Hillegom* usually take place in second half of April, always on a Saturday.

Continue through *Vogelenzang* to **Haarlem.** A visit to *Haarlem* is worthwhile if only to see the Frans Hals Museum containing a number of fine portrait groups by Hals. 16th century *Grote Kerk*. (Y.H.)

NETHERLANDS

A straight road leads back to *Amsterdam*, 12 miles to the east, but the road via *Bloemendaal* to *Spaarndam* and thence to *Halfweg* is preferable. At *Spaarndam* is small monument inspired by symbolic story of the little boy, Hans Brinker, who held his finger in the dyke and saved the whole district from destruction by flood.

R.2. Amsterdam—Aachen via Eindhoven (140 miles)

This route crosses the central Netherlands from north to south and includes the hill-country of *Limburg* province.

Leave *Amsterdam* by road skirting *IJsselmeer* in south-east direction. *Muiden*, small port; "*Muiderslot*" (castle), on coast of former *Zuider Zee* near *Weesp*, is ancient stronghold with many historical associations; *Bussum*, town on edge of the *Gooi*, a pleasantly-wooded region. Hilversum, an elegant town, with parks and gardens and notable for attractive modern architecture; see Dudok's Town Hall; *Loosdrecht* lakes are nearby. *Hilversum* is the Dutch broadcasting centre.

Continue south-east passing Royal Palace at *Soestdijk* to *Soest* (Y.H.) and to **Amersfoort** (Y.H.). *Koppelpoort* (14th century) across river *Eem* is one of fine gateways; 15th century tower of Our Lady and ancient houses, "*Muurhuizen*", within former town wall. Thence across wooded heathland to *Utrecht*, an old town with two canals cut deeply below the houses. Cathedral Tower (14th century, nearly 370 ft. high) and remaining portions of Gothic cathedral (the nave having been destroyed by a hurricane); Central Municipal Museum (history and art), Gold and Silver Museum and Old Dutch Clocks Museums. Y.H. at *Bunnik*, 3 miles.

South of *Utrecht* road crosses flat plain between rivers *Lek* and *Waal* (twin branches of the *Rhine*) and *Maas*, to *'s-Hertogenbosch (Bois-le-Duc)*, pleasant town with magnificent Gothic cathedral and 17th century town hall. Y.H. at *Vught*, 3 miles S.

Twenty miles farther south lies *Eindhoven*, dominated by huge Philips electrical works and D.A.F. motor-car factory.

South-east, through attractive woods and heather country (Y.H. at *Beegden*) into province of *Limburg* to *Sittard* (Y.H.). Southern *Limburg* is an area for lovers of wilder country, with ruined castles. Explore, in particular, valley of R. *Geul,* leading to *Valkenburg*, popular tourist centre (grottoes). *Maastricht,* the provincial capital and old fortress town, has many fine churches including *St. Servatius*, the oldest in the Netherlands.

German frontier is reached at *Vaals* (Y.H.) and *Aachen (Aix-la-Chapelle)* is 2¼ miles beyond.

Many of the houses in Amsterdam date from the seventeenth century.

NORWAY
Geographical Outline

The Norwegian saying, "the sea unites but the land divides," reflects the nature of this country which stretches 1,100 miles from the North Cape, 320 miles north of the Arctic Circle, to the latitude of northern Scotland. It lies on the north-west edge of Europe and varies in breadth from 270 miles in the south to 4 miles near *Narvik*.

Land

Norwegian scenery may be imagined as a gigantic mass of rock, whose whole surface has been worked over by a small sharp tool. At a very early period the area N. and W. of a line from *Stavanger* to *Varanger*, was subjected to tremendous mountain-building movements which folded and buckled the Palaeozoic rocks into mountain ranges running north-east and south-west, and extending into the Scottish highlands. Then followed a long period when the mountains were gradually worn down by weathering and running water to a fraction of their original height. Except for a few peaks of more resistant rock, the land was reduced to a series of high plateaux. Partial subsidence of some ranges produced the line of skerries and islands which protect the coastal waters and fjords from storms.

During the comparatively recent Glacial Period, a thick ice sheet covered Scandinavia and a new surface was imposed on the basic pattern. Now the ice sheet has melted, revealing the characteristic marks of a glaciated region; steep sided valleys with U-shaped cross-section, bare rock surfaces often polished and scored with grooves, side valleys entering main valleys high above the main valley floor (hanging valleys) so that streams descend from them in waterfalls—a source of cheap electric power. Valleys often blocked by heaps of detritus which dam up the waters into long narrow lakes; area of these lakes greater than that of the cultivable land. The deepest glacier valleys becoming fjords, making a convenient means of reaching the interior of the country where land travel is often difficult. The depth of the fjords is approximately equal to the height of the surrounding mountains.

The coast-line has the astounding length of 21,000 miles.

Climate

In west Norway the climate is quite temperate, but tends to be moist. The country lies on the continental shelf, that part of Europe now submerged under shallow seas; the warm surface waters of the Atlantic favourably influence the temperature throughout the year and harbours as far north as *Hammerfest* are ice-free in winter. The long hours of daylight help to raise the average summer temperature. Norway lies in the track of prevailing south-west winds, bringing moisture at all

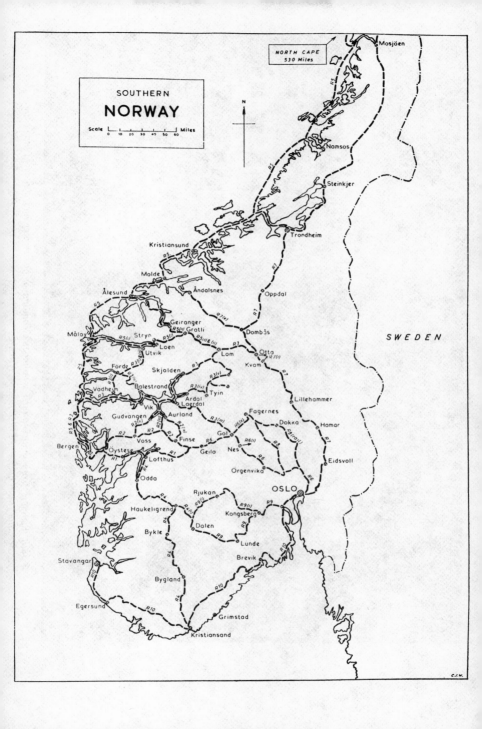

Youth hostelers from many countries come to Scandinavia in summer and winter. This is the picturesque youth hostel at Lillehammer, Norway.

seasons: rain in summer, snow in winter. Towards the eastern border the climate becomes drier and the annual range of temperature greater.

Plants and Animals The flora and fauna show somewhat the same variation vertically (from sea-level to mountain summit) and horizontally (from south to north). The plant sequence is forests of spruce and fir, containing some deciduous trees, with a gradual disappearance of the latter and replacement of spruce by pine; birch forests; thickets of willow and dwarf birch; open moors covered by a growth of mosses and lichens.

Flowering herbaceous plants belonging to continental Europe are found in the south-east; many berry-bearing plants occur in the forests; arctic perennials, together with heaths and saxifrages, are found on the highest mountains if there is sufficient soil, as well as in the north.

Similarly, arctic animals—polar hare, polar fox, wolverine, lemming and reindeer—are found in the north and also above the conifer line among the mountains. There are elk and roe deer in the forests of east Norway, red deer on the west coast. The bear, lynx and wolf, once numerous, are now rare, though the wolf is found from the *Røros* district northwards into *Finnmark*.

Many birds native to Norway are also known in Britain, while many that breed in Norway visit Britain as winter migrants. The moors shelter ptarmigan and capercaillie, and the coasts and islands of the north are the home of ducks and gulls valuable for their feathers or their eggs.

The People

Population One reason why Norway is an excellent hostelling country is that it has only about 3,500,000 inhabitants. Britain is twenty times more densely populated. *Oslo*, with about 500,000 inhabitants, is the largest city, followed by *Bergen* (120,000), *Trondheim* (118,000) and *Stavanger* (80,000).

Language Norway has two official languages which, though members of the same language family, differ in pronunciation, grammar and vocabulary.

Bokmål (formerly called *Riksmål*) derives from the Norwegianised Danish used by the educated classes. This is the language of *Wergeland, Ibsen, Bjørnson* and *Sigrid Undset*.

Nynorsk (formerly called *Landsmål*) builds directly on the village dialects. It developed rapidly as a medium for depicting country life, but was not so quickly accepted as the legal, artistic and social equal of *Bokmål*. It was used by *Vinje, Garborg* and *Duun*.

The long struggle between the supporters of *Bokmål* and *Nynorsk* has ended in a compromise. The local council decides which shall be the local

NORWAY

official language, used on road signs, public notices and in schools. About one-third of the children are educated in *Nynorsk*. A plan for gradually fusing the two into a single national language has been started but will take generations to complete. The latest spelling is wholly phonetic: "chauffeur" is *sjafør* and "all right" is *ålreit*. At present both are necessarily fluid in grammar and spelling.

However, guidebooks have an English key: in the towns and tourist centres most people speak English and a fair number of country people also speak it.

Religion About 96 per cent of the population are formally members of the Evangelical-Lutheran State Church. There are eight dioceses and about a thousand parishes, but many of these have to share a minister so that a clergyman's work in thinly populated areas may be very difficult.

In matters of belief, the Church preserves its independence. In 1942, for example, practically all the ministers resigned simultaneously rather than obey Nazi orders. The church enters into political life and there is a Christian People's Party in the *Storting*.

History During the Viking age Norway developed as a nation and colonial power under vigorous leaders. By 885 the country was united under one king, Harold Fairhair. Settlements were made in the Faroes, Orkneys, Shetlands, the Hebrides, Man, Ireland, northern Scotland, northern England and Iceland. Christianity was firmly established in the reign of Olaf Haroldson (1015-30), the St. Olaf of tradition. His brother, Harold Hardrada, aimed to conquer England but was killed at Stamford Bridge in 1066 a few weeks before the Norman invasion which was itself an offshoot of Viking expansion.

Norway itself developed a strong central government on the Norman model and, under Magnus IV (1263-80), reached the zenith of its medieval achievement as the first European country to have a national code of law.

Decline came with the increasing influence of Denmark, especially after the union of Kalmar in 1397 and with loss of trade to the Hansa monopolists. For four centuries control lay with Danish administrators; the Danish language became compulsory in churches and later in schools; links with the colonies were weakened and eventually broken.

Recovery began with the discovery of deposits of iron ore and the development of an export trade in timber. Norwegian merchants benefited when, in 1560, the Hansa monopoly was abolished. Under the absolutist regime of Christian IV (1588-1648), both countries had nominally equal status as twin kingdoms.

A movement for self-assertion began late in the 18th century. Its form and the nature of its demands are of interest as an example of emergent nationalism. It looked with pride to early Norwegian history and across the sea to English views of liberty and those of revolutionary France. It founded a society of sciences and letters, called for a national university and a national bank, found ways of circumventing the Danish mercantile system, encouraged the growth of a nation-wide economic community and (1810) founded a society to unite the country's liberal forces.

Matters came to a head in 1814 when, on the ceding of Norway to the king of Sweden, he claimed the crown by right of inheritance. The people's resistance was decisive and a national assembly, meeting at *Eidsvoll*, adopted a free constitution providing for a limited monarchy, a one-chamber parliament and for liberty of religion and of the press. On these terms the king was accepted and Norway was independent except for foreign policy and the king's right to appoint a governor. Both caused friction. The latter right was abolished in 1873. Subservience in foreign policy became ever more irksome. Sweden, with greater natural resources, could be comparatively self-contained: Norwegian prosperity depended on international connections for the growth of her great merchant marine and of distant enterprises such as Antarctic whaling.

The union with Sweden ended in 1905 and Haakon VII was elected king by popular vote. In 1956, King Haakon died and was succeeded by the Crown Prince, now King Olav V. Norway has become an outstanding example of a sparsely populated country, with difficult natural conditions, achieving a remarkably high standard of living.

Government The system of democratic government is similar to that in Britain. Executive power is nominally vested in the King, who governs through a cabinet (the *Statsråd*) chosen from the leaders of the majority in Parliament (the *Storting*). The *Storting* has, however, only one chamber, though for some purposes it divides into two houses, the *Odelsting* (112 members) and *Lagting* (38 members). Of its 150 members, elected for four years by a system of proportional representation, two-thirds must come from country districts.

Resources Norway is the world's largest producer of sulphur pyrites and is one of the few countries with molybdenum. Otherwise the mineral resources are somewhat meagre. But her fisheries are the largest in the world, forestry is important, and she leads Europe in the use of water-power.

Only about 3 per cent of the surface is cultivated, mainly in valley bottoms and around the fjords, and the Norwegian peasant farmer's life is a hard one. In mountain districts the cattle are taken up in summer to the high pastures by the women and children, who live in isolated *saeter* (mountain farms) while the men stay behind to look after the crops in the valleys.

Industry and agriculture now each support about 30 per cent of the population. Nearly a tenth is engaged in shipping, about 7 per cent in fishing and whaling, and commerce supports rather more, for Norway has the third largest merchant fleet in the world.

Customs Easter, Ascension, Whitsun and Christmas are all observed and other public holidays include New Year's Day, Labour Day, and Constitution Day (May 17). The main Christmas celebrations are held on Christmas Eve, though Christmas-tree parties go on for some time. The great national holiday, May 17, is marked in every town by decorations, flags and a children's procession. People celebrate Midsummer with bonfires and dancing. Private parties, family gatherings and especially weddings are always an excuse for great celebrations. A real country wedding lasts three days.

With their long tradition of country hospitality, Norwegians are excellent hosts, overflowing with friendliness and with a sound sense of humour. They enjoy explaining their country to foreigners. They are lovers of the open air and of many kinds of sport.

Travellers a century ago admired the scenery more than the people. Modern Norway, however, has a high standard of living; her authors, musicians, statesmen and explorers have won international fame. In their efforts to improve their country, Norwegians willingly spend public money on social services, new public buildings, theatre subsidies, university research, or temperance propaganda. Profits from the government football pools and the wine monopoly are used for some of these purposes.

Food and Drink Breakfast consists of coffee and *smørbrød* (literally: bread and butter) which is actually a half-sandwich. Several kinds of bread and six or more coverings may be available at breakfast. Many Norwegians, particularly in the towns, make no break for lunch but eat more *smørbrød*—a national "packed lunch"—at the office or the factory. Work can therefore end about 4 p.m. and the day's big meal, *middag*, follows at once. The final evening snack will be more *smørbrød*.

Norwegians get good fish and cook it well. Tinned fish, meat-paste and jam appear on *smørbrød*, as do various kinds of cheese including the special brown goat's-milk *gjetost*.

As a rule, coffee is strong and tea is weak. Milk, squash (*saft*) and a non-alcoholic beer (*Vørterøl*) are served everywhere but the sale of stronger beers can be prohibited by the local council.

Culture

Architecture The cold winters have always forced Norwegians to build substantial, warm houses. Timber is the traditional material, and the earliest houses were usually simple log cabins, with a fire in the centre. Each district developed a different style. From about 1600, stone flues, and later iron stoves, altered the plan of the rooms. Windows were introduced, and partitions divided the single room. The older houses with low walls and turf roofs often remained in use as barns. Such farms are still common.

Wood-carvings often decorated beams and doorposts in these houses. The best carvings, however, are found on the few remaining Viking Stave-churches, the finest old buildings in Norway.

Older town houses, and contemporary suburban houses, are also of wood, usually the "timber-frame" type of construction. Many pleasing modern designs can be found, but fires have ravaged so many towns that old buildings are rare.

The larger modern buildings are of reinforced concrete or brick. They follow general European trends, but are bold in character and show a care for detail worth further study. Churches are particularly noticeable, for many are rebuilt in post-war design, replacing those destroyed by the Nazis.

Painting and Sculpture
Little but decorative art was produced before the 19th century. Wood and stone carving, however, were very highly developed during the Viking and Danish periods, and decorative painting was also widespread.

The 20th century is dominated by *Edvard Munch* (1863-1944). Many of his best works are in the *Oslo* National Gallery and the frescoes in the University *Aula* are also his.

Frescoes decorate many of *Oslo's* modern buildings. See especially the City Hall. Many were painted by disciples of *Matisse*, such as *Revold, Per Krogh, Sørensen*.

Sculpture did not achieve national importance until *Vigeland* (1869-1943). His work dominates all Norwegian sculpture. Besides the *Frogner Park* plan, he produced many of the memorial statues in *Oslo*. The work of later sculptors can be seen on the restoration of *Trondheim* Cathedral and on the *Oslo Rådhus*.

Museums
There are many local historical museums, but, except in *Oslo* and *Bergen*, few general or scientific museums. *Bergen* however, has a fishery and an industrial art museum, while the University now controls the famous science museums.

Some of *Oslo's* fifteen museums will chiefly attract specialists, though others will interest everyone. There are three general historical museums; the City Museum in *Frogner Park*, and *Akerhus* fortress, by the harbour, cover *Oslo's* history, while there are Viking and medieval exhibits in the University's historical collections.

The theatres have their special museum and there is a ski museum at *Frognerseteren*. *Nansen's* "*Fram*", and the *Kon-tiki Raft* at *Bygdøy*, and *Amundsen's* home at *Svartskøg*, commemorate Norway's great explorers. Three Viking ships also have a special museum at *Bygdøy*.

In most counties there is an open-air folk-museum, and every hosteller ought to visit one. The most famous are at *Bygdøy*, near *Oslo*, and '*Old Bergen*' a bus trip away from Bergen city centre. The old Norwegian way of life can be studied not only in furniture, tools and clothes, but in houses and complete farms, reassembled in the museum, where guides wearing *bunad* (national costume) show visitors round.

Music
Of native instruments, the Hardanger fiddle (*Hardingfele*), which has four sympathetic drone strings, as well as the normal strings, had a strong influence on the melody and an even stronger one on the harmony of Norwegian music. The cultural revival of the 1840's was marked in music by the collection and publication of traditional ballads and dance airs.

NORWAY

Grieg is the greatest Norwegian composer. His songs, piano pieces and orchestral works are well known everywhere. His contemporary, *Svendsen* is Norway's greatest symphonic composer. Of modern composers only two are well known outside Norway—*Halvorsen*, a theatre composer, much of whose work is incidental music, and *Sinding* who is known for his symphonies and much excellent chamber music.

There are few orchestras and no special concert halls. Important concerts in *Oslo*, for example, are given in the University *Aula*.

National Dances   There is a living folk-dance tradition though many dances were only revived earlier this century. Two kinds are practised: song-dances (*folkeviseleik*) and music dances. In the song-dances old ballads and newer songs are given dramatic interpretation in ring-dances like those popular in medieval Norway. Such dances still flourish in the *Faroes*, where the steps were rediscovered.

The typical traditional music dances, the solo *Halling*, and couple-dances like the *Springar* and *Gangar* are extremely difficult, and give the man a chance to demonstrate his prowess. There are also easier couple-dances, set, and longways dances. They are danced to a fiddle, either the violin or the *Hardingfele*.

National Costume   Most parts of Norway preserve their special traditional dress or *bunad* and within each district there are many local variations, with costumes for everyday use and special occasions. Local patterns may derive from 17th century or even renaissance costume, but the different styles, graceful for women, gallant for men, have evolved in the home: the cloth is always hand-woven and home-dyed.

A girl's festival *bunad*, with its white blouse and apron, embroidered skirt and silver brooches, is a precious heirloom. Though everyday *bunad* is now rarely used, many girls, especially those from country homes, always wear the festival *bunad* on formal occasions or public holidays.

Literature   Norway shares with Iceland the pre-Christian *Eddaic* poems (8th-9th cent.) on historical and mythological themes, and the scaldic verse which spanned the transition (9th-10th cent.) from pagan to Christian themes. In prose, also, the early Icelandic sagas, including the *Heimskringla*, a history of the kings of Norway, are Norwegian in inspiration.

In the 19th century, following the attainment of independence, Norway again produced writers of international significance. *Wergeland* (1808-45) is the poet of freedom, both in political ideas and in his claim for stylistic freedom for the poet. *Björnson* (1832-1910) was a powerful advocate of emancipation of the European peoples through democracy and education, and a great representative Norwegian. His contemporary, *Ibsen*, (1828-1906), probes individual personality as well as social problems. He is the dramatist of self-realization. In his psychological analysis, and technically as a master of stagecraft, his influence on the theatre has been profound.

Among more recent writers *Sigrid Undset* should be mentioned as her novels (which have secured her a Nobel Prize) are available in translation.

The Theatre The theatre is a town institution and even today Norway has only a few, many of them dependent on public funds. All have permanent companies, and often produce, in translation, foreign works.

The "National Theatre" in the centre of *Oslo*, which produces *Bokmål* plays, is Norway's biggest playhouse, and has a reputation for fine, sincere acting. "*Det Norske Teatret*", the *Nynorsk* theatre nearby, was established to show that *Nynorsk* could rival *Bokmål* in this field also. Both are now subsidised.

In *Bergen*, the home of the first nationalist theatre, where *Ibsen* worked in the 1850's, "*Den Nationale Scene*" sets a high standard and has a wide repertoire.

Touring Information

Hostellers are Welcome In Norway the traveller of modest means, with a rucksack or bicycle is always welcome and the motorist has no pride of place.

Access The route from England is by boat from Newcastle to *Bergen* (*Bergen Line*) or *Oslo* (*Fred Olsen Line*). Minimum single fares are £20·00 to *Bergen* and £22·00 to *Oslo*. During the main summer months there are five sailings weekly to *Bergen* (crossing takes 19 hours) and three sailings a fortnight to *Oslo* (38 hours) *Fred Olsen Line* also run a summer service from Harwich to *Kristiansand*: minimum single fare £20·00. Norway can also be reached via Denmark or Sweden. Excursion return fares by air are comparable to sea fares; London-*Stavanger* is £56·80 (3 hours' flying time) and London-*Oslo* £69·00.

Transport The main land routes start from *Oslo*, *Bergen* and *Stavanger*. Buses serve most of the major routes in summer. If not too crowded they will carry bicycles and luggage.

The mountainous nature of the country made railway building extremely expensive and most lines keep to the valleys or coast except the celebrated *Oslo-Bergen* railway (see **R.2** and **R.6**) which climbs over the mountains between east and west. Main line trains are comfortable. Second class is the standard form of travel. Long distance trains, except a few Diesel expresses, make 10-minute halts at certain stations, allowing passengers time to obtain coffee at the buffets.

Boats are the oldest and still the best means of transport in coastal districts, and the best way of seeing much of Norway's finest scenery. They are also vital links in the country's economic life, and on a boat journey one learns a great deal about Norwegian life. In many villages the arrival of the boat,

NORWAY

with post, cargo and passengers, is an important event. The boats run in calm, sheltered channels inside the islands on almost all routes. Fares are low by comparison with buses and trains.

Timetables A most useful book for planning a tour is *"Norway – Time Tables and Fares"*, published by the Norway Travel Association and distributed to travel agents; a timetable of trains, boats, buses and ferries operating a regular service in Norway. Such information is particularly important in a country of big distances where transport services are infrequent and the traveller may run the risk of missing the only bus or ferry connection of the morning or afternoon.

Money The unit of currency is the *krone*, which is divided into 100 *Øre*. There are also 1 *krone* coins, and notes of 5, 10, 50 and 100 *kroner*.

Prices Most items of food are rather expensive, but the quality, particularly when served in restaurants, is good. Clothing and other manufactured articles are also expensive and there are no bargain souvenirs to be had.

Clothing It is prudent to travel with the minimum of luggage. Although ordinary clothing is sufficient for the summer, in the mountains colder temperatures must be expected and a sweater, wind-proof jacket, thick stockings and scarf should be included.

Vibram-soled boots are necessary for walking in the mountains; waterproofs and sou'wester are often worn. Towards the end of the season an extra sweater for the evenings is advisable.

Girls are advised to wear slacks, or shorts for cycling, and nowhere is there any objection to this.

Slacks and long-sleeved shirts should be worn in the evenings as a protection against gnats (*mygg* in Norwegian). These insects are troublesome on summer evenings all over Norway and are a menace in the north and in *Finnmark*, particularly during July.

Restaurants There are restaurants in most villages, but not, as a rule, on the open road. If a Youth Hostel does not supply meals, the warden can often recommend a good cheap restaurant. Reasonably priced food is often indicated by *Nynorsk* names like *Kaffi* and *Stova*. *Restaurant* will be more expensive, and *Turist* very expensive. Service is often slow, and a lunch bar is the best place for a quick meal in the towns.

Fish is cheap and always excellently cooked, but fishcakes (*fiskekaker*) are not to everyone's taste; sausages are plentiful and good. *Varme pølser* (hot sausages) are often sold in the streets.

Restaurants always supply tea, coffee, milk and squash, and unless they are *avhold* (temperance) cafés, beer as well.

Maps The Norwegian Ordnance Survey (*Norges Geografiske Oppmåling*) publish sheets covering the *Bergen-Hardanger* area on a scale of 1:100,000, the *Jotunheimen* mountains on a scale of 1:50,000 and the *Jostedalsbreen* and *Hardangervidda*. An excellent series of general maps on a scale of 1:325,000/1:400,000 covering all Norway on five sheets is published by Cappelen. A useful general map on a scale of 1:1,000,000, depicting all Norway and showing roads, railways steamer and ferry routes as well as youth hostels, is published by the Norwegian Y.H.A.

Norwegian maps are confusing because the same place may appear under different names on different maps and an unimportant place (from the point of view of communications) may appear in larger type than a more important place, particularly in the fjord country.

Place Names Many natural features can be recognised on the map with the aid of a slight knowledge of the meaning of Norwegian place forms. Here is a list of some important words, with the *Nynorsk* forms in brackets.

botn	bottom (of valley)	*nes*	headland
bre	glacier	*nord*	north
by	town	*seter (støl, stul)*	mountain farm
bygd	village	*sjø*	sea, lake
dal	valley	*steinbrott*	quarry
elv (Å)	river	*sund*	sound, channel
fjell	mountain	*syd (sør)*	south
fjellstue	mountain hut	*tind*	peak
fodsti	footpath	*tjern (tjørn)*	tarn
foss	waterfall	*ur*	scree, boulders
gate	street	*vatn, vann*	lake (small)
gård (gard)	farm	*vest*	West
hei	moor, heath	*vidd (a)*	mountain plateau
hytte	hut (cottage-size)	*vik (våg)*	inlet, creek
jøkul	glacier	*øst (aust)*	east
leirplass	camping site	*øy*	island

Tourist Huts The mountainous plateaux in the centre of Norway offer walkers and mountaineers unrivalled opportunities. The Norwegian Y.H.A. caters primarily for tourists using the roads, but there are some hostels in the mountains which serve as starting points. Mountain tourist huts, equipped not unlike hostels, fill the gaps. Some are privately run but many are owned by the Norwegian Mountain Association or by local district touring clubs.

The Association has also marked out the routes between the huts with cairns and supplies sketch maps of each district, which give the number of hours needed for each route. These schedules make no allowance for loitering.

NORWAY

The membership fee, 25 *kr.*, can be paid in London to the Norwegian State Railways, 21 Cockspur Street, London, SW1. Detailed information can be obtained there or at the *Oslo* office: *Den Norske Turistforening, Stortingsgate* 28 III.

The main areas served by the district clubs are *Jotunheimen* with *Jostedalsbreen*, the *Hardangervidda*, *Rondane* and *Trollheimen*.

Mountain-eering Although over fifty years have passed since British mountaineering expeditions discovered that Norway was a mountaineers' paradise, there are still unclimbed peaks and many unclimbed walls and ridges.

Among the great *Jotunheim* mountains the best climbing, for novices and experts, is found in the *Horungen* group, capped by the *Store Skagastølstind*.

North-west lie the *Sunnmøre Alps*, around the *Hjørundfjord*. *Øye*, on the *Norangsfjord* (an arm of the *Hjørundfjord*) is the best climbing centre.

In *Romsdal* there cannot be many unclimbed routes, but the mountains are fascinating, have taken on fantastic shapes and given fanciful names. *Åndalsnes* is the best centre.

In the *Nordmøre* mountains, east of *Kristiansund*, there are still opportunities for pioneers. The west wall of *Kalken* (*Hårstadnebba*) includes a 6,000 ft. chimney which has never been climbed. New routes might also be found on the *Trolla* ridge.

Much pioneer work remains to be done in north Norway. In the *Lofotens*, for example, there must be hundreds of peaks, some still unclimbed. Climbers have to take tents, but the climate is ideal for camping, and supplies are obtainable everywhere. Some islands can be reached only by rowing boat, but the main ports, *Svolvaer* and *Stamsund*, are served by the regular coastal steamers, the trip from *Trondheim* taking 36 hours.

Climbing in the *Lyngenfjord* area may involve real arctic exploration, for some places appear only as white spaces even on the ordnance maps. This district, too, is best approached by boat. From *Trondheim* to *Tromsø* takes about two and a half days, and a bus runs daily to *Lyngseidet*.

Ski-ing Skis were invented in Norway (in the *Telemark*) and all Norwegians learn to ski at an early age. Foreign visitors are increasingly making their first acquaintance with skis in Norway, where snow conditions are usually excellent from Christmas until late March and tuition and the hire of skis can be inexpensively arranged. Winter daylight is short but Norwegian hostels provide comfortable and pleasant facilities in the evenings.

Cycling Except in the cities and for a few miles outside them, all roads in Norway have loose surfaces. They are kept in good order, but are very muddy during the spring thaw, and often dusty in summer. Mountain roads are liable to be snowbound from November until late May, but roads at lower levels are open all year.

The steepness of the hills gave road engineers many problems, but tunnels, spirals and zig-zags have lessened the gradients, although a low gear is essential. Norwegian drivers are usually considerate about dipping their headlamps, but less careful about signalling, and give little elbow-room.

Traffic keeps to the right, and vehicles approaching from that side have right of way. Cyclists must signal all turns, and carry a white front light, white patch and rear reflector after dark. The strict rules about reporting accidents and against driving under the influence of drink apply to cyclists.

Norwegians regret that it is now necessary to carry a cycle-lock.

Canoeing and Sailing The Norwegian coast, with its thousands of islands and bays, is an ideal place for canoeing and sailing, both of which are popular sports. There are clubs everywhere along the coast from *Trondheim* to the Swedish frontier. There is, however, no large-scale hiring of boats.

The coast is well charted and buoyed, but local knowledge, easily obtained on the spot, is helpful and sometimes essential. There are practically no irksome restrictions on camping, bathing, etc., anywhere along the coast.

Inland canoeing is less practicable. There are many beautiful lakes, but, at places, the rivers are too rapid for navigation.

Practical Hints A tour in Norway needs planning. Distances are vast and walkers in particular will need to study the bus, train and ferry timetables. For cyclists it may often mean hard work to average more than fifty miles a day and the distance between the hostels is often greater than that. The Norwegian Y.H.A. officially discourages hitch-hiking.

Most offices are open until about 4 p.m. and in the summer shops, too, close early. After *middag*, however, it is usual to take a rest, or walk out-of-doors. Cinemas run non-continuous programmes and the doors are closed when the programme begins, even to ticket-holders. Smoking is not allowed in cinemas or theatres.

The Norwegian postal system is efficient. Parcels can be sent in advance to the hostels but they are not delivered. An "accompanying letter" (*Følgebrev*) is delivered, authorising the addressee to collect the parcel at the post office.

An eiderdown quilt is usually the only covering on a Norwegian bed; it is wise to anchor it with a blanket. All doors in Norway have draught-preventing raised thresholds.

A particular conversational phrase which requires explanation is "*vaer så god*" (literally, "be so good") often pronounced *vesgoot*. It has innumerable meanings, of which the following are the most important:
"Can I help you?" (used by shop assistants).
"Fares please." (on a bus).
"Here you are, please." (used when handing anything to anyone at a meal or elsewhere).

NORWAY

Touring Routes

These routes are intended for the guidance of hostellers travelling in the main summer season of mid-June to early September; outside this period many bus and steamer services cease to operate, or operate only on certain days of the week, and many youth hostels are closed.

Most of the routes are based on *Bergen*, the most popular approach to Norway from the West.

The Western Fjords

For many people, the western fjords, running deep into the heart of the country, typify Norwegian scenery, with their towering rock walls, snow capped peaks and magnificent waterfalls.

The great fjords all follow a similar plan. At the mouth the channel winds through a group of islands before entering the fjord itself; the sides at first slope gently but soon become steeper until they tower over a narrow inlet which penetrates the heart of Norway's mountain massif.

Local boats and ferries run within the fjords, while faster boats connect the important villages with the ports at the mouth, or direct with *Bergen*, the capital of the fjord country. Hostellers arriving at *Bergen* can thus sail up any fjord and then take the road that climbs into the mountains and over to the valleys beyond. In the reverse direction, the head of any fjord can be reached from *Oslo*, and thence to *Bergen* by boat.

Of the many fjords along the west coast, the most important are *Boknfjord* and *Hardangerfjord* south of *Bergen*, and farther north, *Sognefjord*, *Nordfjord* and *Storfjord*, the last leading to *Geirangerfjord*.

Bergen

Bergen, Norway's second city, is an important port, industrial and fishing centre. Founded in 1070, it was in the 12th century the capital of Norway and from the 14th to the 16th a trading port controlled by Hanseatic merchants. All these phases of its history have left their mark and, in spite of fires, the last in 1916, *Bergen* has more old buildings than any other town. There are, for example, the 12th century Church of St. Mary (*Mariakirken*), the 13th century *Håkonshall*, damaged during the war, the Hanseatic Museum and the old Quay (*Bryggen*). The 13th century cathedral is less interesting. Adjoining the *Bryggen* is the market place and open-air fish market. Funicular railway station is nearby, and trip to top of *Fløyen* (1,050 ft.) affords magnificent views of city and coast. The theatre, *Den Nationale Scene*, is centre for annual *Bergen* International Music Festival. The town has its picture gallery (*Billedgalleri*), and there is also the *Rasmus Meyer* collection of paintings (some by *Edvard Munch*) and furniture.

Due south of the city at *Fjøsanger* stands the *Fantoft* stave-church; not far away, at *Hop*, is *Trollhaugen*, *Grieg's* home, and the little hut where he composed, with his furniture and belongings. At *Fana*, further south, is a 12th century church, and nearby at *Lyse*, some 15 miles south of *Bergen*, are the ruins of Norway's earliest Cistercian monastery (12th century). On the nearby islands, especially at *Askøy* and *Godøysund*, are good bathing beaches which can be reached by motorboat.

Bergen Y.Hs are at *Ravneberget*, near lower station of *Ulriken* cable lift and at *Fløyen*. Both afford fine views of the city, fjords and mountains.

The office of the West Norway District of the Norwegian Youth Hostels Association is at Strandgaten 4.

R.1. Bergen to Geilo via the Hardangerfjord (156 miles)

This route is recommended for the hosteller who lacks time to travel farther afield. It gives a glimpse of fjords and of wild semi-mountain country, and if completed by a homeward trip on the *Oslo-Bergen* railway from *Geilo* to *Bergen* (see **R.2**) glaciers and mountains will be included as well. The through journey by bus and boat requires a minimum of one night's stop en route—but both walker and cyclist can well spend a week on the trip.

From *Bergen*, opposite the railway station, bus leaves for *Norheimsund* (2½ hrs.). Winding road, within sight of fjords most of way, through *Sam-*

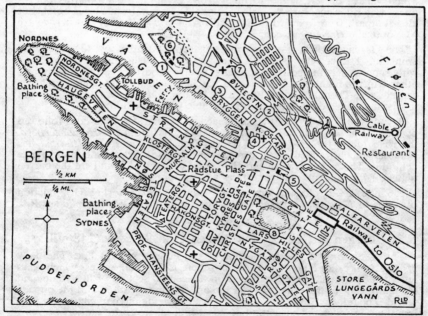

1. *Newcastle boats dock here.* 2. *Funicular railway station (for Fløyen).* 3. *Hanseatic museum.* 4. *Fish Market.* 5. *Post Office.* 6. *Håkonshall.* 7. *Church of St. Mary.* 8. *R. Meyer's collection.*

nanger and up on to the *Kvamskogen* plateau. From *Kvamskogen* (**Y.H.**) easy climb to summit of *Tveitakvitingen* (4,200 ft., magnificent view over *Hardanger*); good walking country. Road descends steeply, with many tunnels and fine views, to *Norheimsund* on *Hardangerfjord.*

The *Hardangerfjord* is more than 100 miles long and flanked by mountains rising to 5,000 ft. at some points, but because of its greater width it lacks the grandiose canyon-like appearance of some of the more northerly fjords. It is seen at its best in May, when the fruit trees are in bloom. Local costume is still worn on special occasions, and *Hardanger* embroidery is famous.

At *Norheimsund* a steamer connects with the bus, travelling up the fjord to *Lofthus* in 2 hrs., glimpses of *Folgefonn* glacier to south.

R.1 (i) **Norheimsund to Kvanndal** by bus (alternative to main route) via *Øystese* (**Y.H.**, good beach), *Fyksesund* suspension bridge and hydro-electric station at *Alvik.* From *Kvanndal*, ferry to *Kinsarvik* on main road *Lofthus-Geilo.*

Lofthus is tourist centre for western part of *Hardangervidda* and for impressive *Sørfjord* (see **R.4**). Buses leave *Lofthus* (change at *Kinsarvik*) for *Geilo,* 5 hr. journey. At *Eidfjord* road leaves *fjord* and begins steep ascent onto *Hardangervidda* (rise of over 4,000 ft. in about 30 miles) by way of wild *Måbø* valley; on left, some 10 miles from *Eidfjord,* the *Vøringfoss* one of finest waterfalls in Norway, 530 ft. high; best view from *Fossli* hotel, but also footpath from road to foot of fall. At *Dyranut* Pass (4,070 ft.) we are well onto the *Hardangervidda.*

The **Hardangervidda** is a high plateau, some 60 miles by 40, practically uninhabited, intersected by many lakes and tarns; it is a mixture of bare rock with snow lying on the higher points, coarse moorland with bilberry and other fruiting plants, and occasional patches of lush grass. Reindeer herds can be seen. There are no youth hostels on the *vidda,* but a number of small tourist huts, linked by paths. It is admirable walking country.

Beyond the *Dyranut* pass the road reaches the small *Skiftesjø* lake, followed by a series of larger lakes. At *Haugastøl,* 43 miles from the *Hardangerfjord,* the road meets the *Bergen-Oslo* railway (see **R.2**); on Lake *Ustevann* lies *Ustaoset,* much-frequented ski-centre, with the *Halingskarv* mountain range behind it. This is the head of the *Hallingdal* valley, and from here the barren plateau landscape gives place to trees and meadows.

156 miles **Geilo,** pleasant summer and winter-sports resort (**Y.H.**), junction of roads to *Numedal* and *Hallingdal.* For route from *Oslo* to *Geilo* see **R.6.**

R.2. Bergen to Geilo by the Bergen-Oslo Railway (148 miles)

This is the most attractive portion of the famous railway line. The daily expresses take 4 or 5 hours to *Geilo,* but there is a special express which takes less than 3½ hours. There is no road on the central section of this route, and for many villages the train provides the only communication with the outside world. The railway, completed in 1909, is an amazing piece of engineering, no less than 45 miles out of a total of 305 being taken up by tunnels or snow shelters. Although it does not reach altitudes of Alpine mountain railways its operation is no less difficult, owing to rigorous winter conditions. Electric traction from *Bergen* to *Voss.*

From *Bergen* line crosses peninsula, then skirts *Sørfjord*, not to be confused with a branch of *Hardangerfjord* bearing the same name, and *Bolstadfjord*; fine views of the water, but many tunnels.

63 miles, **Voss**, rail junction; oldest house in Norway (*Finneloftet*, built 1250), 13th century church; Y.H. at *Skulestadmo*, 2 miles north of town.

R.2 (i) Voss to Granvin (Hardangerfjord), 17 miles, 50 mins. journey. Electric railway, pleasant but unexciting countryside, mostly forested. From *Granvin* buses connect to *Norheimsund* and other points on *Hardangerfjord*

R.2 (ii) Voss to Gudvangen (for Sognefjord), 30 miles. Bus (6 services daily) in 1 hour 50 mins., shortest and cheapest route from *Bergen* to the inner *Sognefjord.* Following road No. 60 past *Skulestadmo* to *Lønehorgi*, a mountain 4,671 ft. high, worth climbing. Beyond *Upheimsvann* (Lake) we enter upper *Nærøy* valley, in watershed of *Sogn. Stalheim*, tourist centre, finely situated. Descend to *Gudvangen* at head of *Nærøyfjord*, narrow and rocky walled, probably second only to *Geiranger Fjord* (see **R.5 (ii)**) for grandeur. Ferry to *Kaupanger* for *Jotunheimen* (see **R.3**) or by bus to *Vangsnes* (Y.H.) and then ferry to *Balestrand* (Y.H.) for *Nordfjord* (see **R.5 (i)**).

Voss is only 150 ft. above sea level, but from this point the railway rises steadily, following attractive *Raundal* valley, which grows increasingly wild, the river becoming a torrent. *Mjølfjell*, 84 miles from *Bergen*, has large Y.H., 4 miles up valley; well-known ski-centre; mountain walks to *Ulvik* (upper *Hardangerfjord*, 6 hours). Pass through *Gravehalsen* tunnel, over 3 miles long, to *Myrdal*, at head of *Flåm* valley.

R.2 (iii) Myrdal to Flåm by electric railway (12 miles, 53 mins. journey). The *Flåmsbane*, said to be the most expensive railway in world to construct, has gradient of 1 in 18, many loops and tunnels, fine views, including numerous waterfalls; train stops at certain viewpoints for benefit of tourists. *Flåm* lies on beautiful **Aurlandsfjord** (branch of *Sognefjord*): ferries via *Aurland* to *Kaupanger* and other places on *Sognefjord*.

Train continues to ascend, affording fine view of *Flåm* valley on left just beyond *Myrdal* station. Enters barren treeless region adjoining *Hardanger Jøkul* where many timber snowsheds screen railway line. Shortly before *Finse*, railway reaches highest point of 4,268 ft. *Finse*, 118 miles from *Bergen* and highest railway station in north Europe, has fine view over lake to *Hardanger* glacier; Scott of the Antarctic and his party trained here—monument by lake side. Good centre for high mountain and glacier tours.

R.2 (iv) Finse to Aurland on foot, 5 to 7 days; magnificent wild country with many lakes; overnight stops at tourist huts *Geiteryggen, Steinbergdalen* and *Steine.* Y.H. at *Østerbø*; bus *Steine-Aurland.*

Railway continues between *Hardanger* glacier and *Hallingskarvet* range (peaks 6,300 ft.), through tundra country, all above tree line. At *Haugastøl* railway joins road from *Hardangerfjord* and follows it to **Geilo** (see **R.1**).

R.3. Bergen to Otta, via Sognefjord and Jotunheimen Mountains

This route combines some of the finest fjord country with the grandest mountains; a rather expensive journey, but most rewarding. Take cargo steamer service on over-night voyage, *Bergen-Sogndal*, for three-quarter length of *Sognefjord*, calling at all small ports en route; thence by bus *Sogndal-Krossbu* (for *Jotunheimen*). Quicker route by express boat from *Bergen* to *Leikanger* in 5 hrs., connecting bus to *Sogndal* (Y.H.), then continue by bus *Sogndal* to *Krossbu* in 4 hours. Quickest route is via *Voss* and *Gudvangen* (see **R.2 (ii)**)) to *Kaupanger* and *Sogndal* thence by bus to *Krossbu*, as above; a night must be spent at *Sogndal*, but breaks of journeys recommended also at other places en route, e.g. *Voss, Gudvangen.*

NORWAY

Sognefjord, Norway's longest fjord, stretches some 125 miles inland to the foot of the *Jotunheimen* mountains; at some points it reaches depths of more than 4,000 ft. and at many points the surrounding rocky slopes rise sheer to 2,000 ft. above the fjord. The offshoots, *Aurlandsfjord* and *Fjaerlandsfjord*, are narrower and grander than the main fjord, but are not entered by the express boats.

From *Bergen,* boat threads maze of islands, reaching entrance to *Sognefjord* after about 2½ hours (express boat) or 5½ hours (slow boat). Fjord here is 2 to 3 miles wide.

R.3(i) **Lavik to Stryn (Nordfjord),** 120 miles. Bus connects with boat from *Bergen*, 5 hours. Fine road, winding, but reaching no substantial heights, via *Førde* (Y.H.) (centre of area known as *Sunnfjord*—no actual fjord of this name) and *Jølster* Lake (Y.H. at *Vassenden*); fine views south eastward to *Jøstedal* Glacier. Cross *Utvikfjell* (2,100 ft., fine views) (Y.H. at *Byrkjelo*) and descend to *Utvik*, on southern arm of *Nordfjord*; continue along fjord by series of tourist resorts —*Olden* and *Loen*, each with attractive small lakes behind (*Oldenvatn* and *Loenvatn*) to *Stryn* (Y.H.) at head of fjord (see R.5 (i)).

Høyanger (on small *Hoyangsfjord*) is modern industrial town, with large hydro-electric works. At *Vik*, on south shore (express boats do not call) is fine 12th century stave church. *Balestrand*, at entrance to *Fjærlandsfjord* is tourist centre of *Sogn*, pleasantly situated among orchards (Y.H.).

R.3 (ii) **Balestrand to Stryn (Nordfjord),** 30 miles. 6 hours journey, including hour's break at *Vassenden*. This is a longer but more exciting route than R.3 (i). After leaving fjord, road rapidly reaches 2,300 ft. level, before descending to series of lakes in *Viksdal* (Y.H. at *Eldalsosen*). At *Moskog* this route joins R.3 (i) for rest of way to *Stryn*.

At *Hermansverk* a short cut can be taken to the *Jotunheimen* by taking a bus journey to *Sogndal* (Y.H.) and thence to *Krossbu*. Fjord boat continues to the "imaginary" port of *Solsnes*—a point in mid-fjord at which passengers are transferred to ferries for *Gudvangen* (see R.2 (ii)) and *Flåm* (see R.2 (iii)). On to *Lærdal* (also called *Lærdalsøyra*) (Y.H.), a village surrounded by high mountains and out of reach of sun during more than six months of year; dry climate, like the rest of innermost *Sogn*.

R.3 (iii) **Lærdal to Gol,** 77 miles. A good route for cyclists wishing to return to *Bergen* by R.1 or R.2. Also bus service in 3 hours. Road climbs narrow valley of *Lærdal* river (many rapids; famous for salmon fishing) to *Borgund* with one of finest stave churches in Norway, 12th century; decorated doors and roof-hole lighting. At *Borlaug* (Y.H.) branch road across *Fillefjell* Mts. to Lake *Tyin* (southern approach to *Jotunheimen*). Route follows road No. 52 up to Lake *Eldrevatn* (3,800 ft.) on *Hemsedal* mountain plateau, down into valley of rapid-flowing *Heimsil* river, past *Hemsedal* to *Gol*, on *Oslo-Bergen* railway. (See R.6) Thence to Bergen by R.1 or R.2.

From *Lærdal,* express steamers turn into *Årdalsfjord*, passing *Fodnes*, remains of enormous landslide to north-east, and on other side of fjord the mountain *Bodlenakkjen* (3,100 ft.), to reach *Årdalstangen*, village at head of fjord.

R.3 (iv) **Årdal to Tyin (Jotunheimen),** 32 miles. 1½ hours by bus. A fine approach to *Jotunheimen* mountains from the south. Spectacular climb from *Øvre Årdal* (hydro-electric works and aluminium factory) on brilliant green Lake *Årdal*, up valley of *Ardøla* (Tya) River by road with 43 sharp bends, reaching height of 3,400 ft. above sea level in 7 miles. Lake *Tyin*, 3,500 ft. above sea level, is second largest of *Jotunheimen* lakes with fine views of peaks to north-east. Bus, twice daily *Tyin* hotel to *Eidsbugaren* on Lake *Bygdin* and boat connection to *Bygdin*; fine boat trip, 1¾ hours. (Y.H. at *Valdresflya*, about 6 miles N. of *Bygdin*.)

Express boats terminate at *Årdalstangen*, but there is a bus service to *Skjolden* from *Sogndal* (2½ hours) up the west side of the *Lusterfjord*, gentler than most of *Sogn*, with several bays and small ports (Y.H. at *Gaupne*). On precipitous east side lies *Urnes*, with oldest stave church in Norway; animal carvings. Northern end of fjord is warm, dry and fertile; even tobacco can be grown.

Skjolden (**Y.H.**), extreme inland point of *Sognefjord* complex. Buses leave for *Jotunheimen* and *Otta*. Road blocked by snow October to May or longer. Leaving *Skjolden*, road climbs stiffly near *Opptun*, offering magnificent views over *Fortun* valley below. *Turtagrø*, tourist station (2,900 ft.) is at approach to mountain area.

EXCURSION: to *Fannaråki* (6,780 ft., highest inhabited point in Norway, meteorological station); ascent in 4 hours, descent 3; marked path.

10 miles beyond *Turtagrø* is one of highest road passes in Norway (4,690 ft.) near the old *Sognefjell* pass. *Krossbu* (22 miles from *Skjolden*, 60 miles by road from *Sogndal*) is good centre for western *Jotunheimen*.

The poet *Vinje* christened Norway's highest mountains, which are also highest in northern Europe, "**Jotunheimen**" or home of the giants. Over 40 peaks reaching 7,000 ft.; the highest, *Galdhøpiggen*, is 8,094 ft. No youth hostels in mountains, but good network of Tourist Huts with clear connecting paths which can safely be followed. Ascent of most peaks, however, involves crossing of glaciers, and it is foolhardy to attempt this except with party, owing to many crevasses. *Galdhøpiggen* can be climbed (from *Spiterstulen*) without crossing glacier.

Galdesand (between *Elveseter* and *Roisheim*) is probably best northern approach to high *Jotunheimen*.

R.3 (v) Jotunheimen Walking Tour. Among many possible tours in this area this one occupies 8 days; moderately strenuous. Nights are spent in tourist huts at places named. 1st Day: *Galdesand* to *Juvass* Hut (3½ hours). 2nd Day: Climb *Galdhøpiggen* and return to *Juvass* Hut. 3rd Day: Walk to *Spiterstulen* (3½ hours). 4th Day. Walk to *Glitterheim* Hut via *Skautflya* (5 hours). 5th Day: Walk to *Gjendesheim* (7 hours). 6th Day: rest day at *Gjendesheim*, on Lake *Gjende*. 7th Day: Follow *Peer Gynt's* Route along rock ridge of *Besseggen* (5,500 ft.) to *Memurubu*. Midday boat to *Gjendebu* (40 mins sail). 8th Day: Walk via *Eidsbugaren* to *Tyinholmen* (6 hours). Bus to *Tyin* Hotel whence connecting bus to *Lærdal* (Y.H.). (See R.3 (iii)).

Lom, 50 miles by road from *Skjolden*; in valley of River *Otta*; junction of road to *Nordfjord*. Continue down valley to **Otta**, in upper *Gudbrandsdal*, on *Oslo-Trondheim* railway (90 miles from *Skjolden*, 128 miles from *Sogndal*.) See **R.7 (i)**.

R.4. Bergen-Kristiansand, via Setesdal (328 miles)

A long tour, for the cyclist wishing to avoid the more crowded central fjord area. Can also be undertaken by bus and ferry in minimum of 3 days. It includes the remarkable *Setesdal* Valley, and at *Kristiansand* gives access to direct boat to England.

First stage, *Bergen* to *Odda*, may be made by bus and ferry, following **R.1** to *Lofthus*, thence by bus alongside *Sørfjord*; minimum journey time *Bergen-Odda* 8 hours.

Odda (**Y.H.**) is industrial town at head of long, narrow arm of *Hardangerfjord* known as *Sørfjord* and renowned for fruit blossom. West of fjord lies *Folgefonn* glacier, third largest in Norway (108 sq. miles).

EXCURSION: From *Tyssedal*, 3½ miles north of *Odda*, road leads up to huge *Skjeggeda* dam and power station; many waterfalls; boat trips on lake at top (*Ringedalsvatn*).

NORWAY

Continue by series of fine waterfalls to *Seljestad,* then steep climb of 3,000 ft. in 6 miles (fine backward views towards *Folgefonn* glacier) and descend to *Røldal.* Road now crosses *Haukeliseter,* southern extension of *Hardangervidda;* wild country, traditional meeting point of routes between east and west Norway. *Dyrskar* Pass (3,725 ft.) has snow all year, but is accessible for vehicles June-October. *Haukeligrend,* 65 miles from *Odda.*

R.4 (i) Haukeligrend to Dalen (for Telemark), 40 miles. Direct approach to *Telemark* (see **R.9)** from *Bergen,* and attractive route to *Oslo.* **Y.H.** at *Dalen,* where boats leave for journey on *Bandak* canel (see **R.9).**

At *Bjåen* road begins steep descent in **Setesdal** valley, one of most interesting parts of Norway. Upper part of valley was cut off from rest of country until road built 1938; many traditions preserved, national costume worn, folk-dancing popular. On west side of valley many extensive plateaux with small lakes providing good fishing.

Bykle **(Y.H.)** is typical village of area, many ancient houses, church decorated with traditional rose-paintings. *Valle,* 19 miles south, was formerly principal place of upper *Setesdal.* Mountain paths lead east and west; fine 18th century wooden church with carved altar. *Bygland,* on *Byglandsfjord,* has ancient tumuli.

Lower *Setesdal* is less interesting, and cyclists can shorten journey by taking train from *Byglandsfjord* **(Y.H.)** to **Kristiansand,** 45 miles **(Y.H.).**

From *Kristiansand* journey may be continued to *Stavanger* or *Oslo* by **R.10,** or direct boat taken for Harwich or Newcastle.

R.5. Bergen-Kirkenes by the North Cape (1,088 miles)

Voyage takes 5½ days by *Hurtigrute* steamers, serving 40 ports; stopovers may be made. Boats carry two classes and fares are inexpensive.

Måløy, reached on first morning after leaving *Bergen,* is junction for *Nordfjord.*

R.5 (i) Maloy to Loen (Nordfjord) by boat to *Sandane,* thence by bus. Approach to *Nordfjord* would not be by *Hurtigrute* but by smaller fjord steamer leaving *Bergen* daily, although some boats do not go as far as *Sandane.*

Nordfjord is typical Norwegian fjord, long and narrow with several arms; less accessible than *Hardanger* or *Sogn,* whilst not as magnificent as *Geiranger* (see R.5 (ii)), but it has Y.Hs. at tourist centres of *Stryn* and *Byrkjelo.* From *Stryn* bus conncetions to *Lom,* change at *Grotli,* or to *Geiranger* (via *Hellesylt* (Y.H.)).

Beyond *Måløy* boat enters complex of islands and inlets known as *Sunnmøre* and *Storfjord.* Boat calls at *Ålesund,* important herring-fishery port and commercial centre; good museum of *Sunnmøre* history. **Y.H.**

R. 5 (ii) Ålesund to Geiranger by the Storfjord. No regular boat service whole length of fjord but connecting bus and ferries. Bus *Ålesund-Magerholm,* ferry to *Sykkylven,* bus (by pleasant *Velledal* valley, rising to nearly 1,750 ft., fine views) via *Stranda* and *Hellesylt,* then by boat up *Geirangerfjord.*

Geirangerfjord is probably most remarkable of all Norwegian fjords; 9 miles long, barely 500 yards wide, bounded by cliffs almost a mile high, down which pour such famous waterfalls as *Brudesløret* (The Bridal Veil) and *De Syv Søstre* (The Seven Sisters). From *Geiranger* bus climbs to *Grotli* and *Lom* (for *Jotunheimen,* see R. 3 (v)).

Further ports of call are *Molde* **(Y.H.)** (for *Åndalsnes* and *Romsdal,* see **R.7 (ii)),** *Kristiansund* **(Y.H.),** a trawler port (not to be confused with *Kristiansand* in south Norway) and *Trondheim* **(Y.H.)**—see **R.7.**

326

On third morning after leaving *Bergen*, boat crosses Arctic Circle and enters the "Land of the Midnight Sun" (see **R.11**). After calling at various ports in the *Lofoten* Islands, at *Hammerfest*, **(Y.H.)** most northerly town in world, boat rounds North Cape, a 1,000 ft. cliff which can be approached by road from *Honningsvåg* **(Y.H.)**, and recahes *Kirkenes*, close to Soviet frontier, mineral port, terminus of route.

The Eastern Valleys

Five great valleys, *Østerdal, Gudbrandsdal, Valdres, Hallingdal* and *Numedal* run north and west from *Oslo* fjord. Their rivers are broader and quieter than the fierce streams of the western fjord country. Their sides are steep, but not vertical, and are often thickly wooded, while on the upper slopes are many *saeters*. The valley floors are broad, perhaps contain a lake, and big agricultural villages have developed. Each valley has its individual way of life, its traditional architecture, and its own beauty.

The valley roads climb gradually but steadily until they leave the shelter of the forests and emerge on to high, open moors. From *Gudbrandsdal* roads connect with all the north coast ports, while the road through *Østerdal* provides an alternative route to *Trondheim*. The *Valdres* roads lead to *Jotunheimen* and *Sognefjord*, and the *Hallingdal* and *Numedal* roads to *Hardangerfjord*. Mountain roads link the upper valleys together.

R.6.   Oslo to Geilo by the Hallingdal (157 miles by road)

This is the route of the *Oslo-Bergen* railway and of the main road. Rail journey in 4 to 5 hours.

Railway skirts edge of *Nordmarka*, an area of woods and lakes popular with Oslo inhabitants for ski tours, and at *Jevnaker* touches *Randsfjord*, Norway's fourth largest lake; in fact an inland lake, not a fjord. Beyond *Ørgenvika* is the beautiful Lake *Kørderen*, at foot of *Hallingdal*, a valley bounded by forest-clad mountains. Note typical high chimneys of houses.

At *Nes*, near *Nesbyen* **(Y.H.)**, is *Hallingdal* museum, with many folk-lore treasures.

R.6 (i) From Nes to Vassfaret. Paths lead into vast forest area of *Vassfaret*, where bears are still to be found.

At *Gol* valley bends sharply westward; junction for **R.3 (iii)** to *Lærdal* on *Sognefjord*.

R.6 (ii) Gol to Fagernes (Y.H.), 33 miles. Attractive road from *Hallingdal* to *Valdres* via *Sanderstølen* plateau (2,800 ft., but open all year). Bus twice daily. Also express bus through to *Lillehammer*.

Railway climbs steeply into upper *Hallingdal*, which widens considerably. *Torpo* has fine stave church, 12th century, with carved doorway. **Geilo, (Y.H.)** just below tree line.

For continuation of route to *Bergen* by rail see **R.2**; by road and ferry see **R.1**.

NORWAY

R.7. Oslo to Trondheim by the Gudbrandsdal (346 miles)

Of several alternative routes to *Trondheim* this is probably the most attractive. Train in approximately 8 hours. Rail and road follow Lake *Mjøsa*, Norway's largest lake (over 60 miles long). From *Eidsvoll* (Y.H.) to *Lillehammer* journey may be made by paddle-steamer (6 hours).

Hamar (Y.H.) is ancient town, over 900 years old; ruins of 12th century cathedral outside town to north. *Lillehammer* (Y.H.) is well-known tourist centre, particularly for winter sports, as snow lies later than in west Norway. Just outside town lies *Maihaugen* open-air folk museum, one of most interesting sights in Norway. Collection of over 100 types of buildings from past centuries, completely reconstructed and containing period furniture; amongst other exhibits are complete medieval farm from *Gudbrandsdal* and a stave church.

The **Gudbrandsdal** valley proper begins at *Lillehammer*. Generally narrow, with steep rocky sides. Many farms and farm villages; rough-hewn timber farmhouses often arranged in form of square. Woodcarving and weaving are typical crafts. Y.H. at *Sjoa*.

Ringebu has stave church dating from 1250. *Kvam*, 175 miles from *Oslo*.

R.7 (i) Kvam to Rondane Mountains. The *Rondane* is an attractive mountain area with dry climate, well provided with tourist huts and clearly-marked paths. A number of peaks exceed 6,000 ft. and are above snow line. *Rondane* can also be approached from *Otta* or *Sel*.

Otta is junction for routes to *Jotunheimen* (R.3.) and *Nordfjord* (R.5 (i)). Beyond *Sel* valley rises steeply, grows narrower, and scenery becomes wilder. *Dombås* (2,170 ft., Y.H.) is junction for road and railway to *Åndalsnes*.

R.7 (ii) Dombås to Åndalsnes via Romsdal, 67 miles. Day train 2½ hours journey. Rail and road follow upper *Gudbrandsdal. Lesjaskog* (Y.H.) is good centre for little-known walking country to north centred on *Aursjø* hut. *Romsdal* (valley of River *Rauma*), thickly wooded. *Åndalsnes*, small port, was scene of British landing in 1940. Y.H. at *Setnes*.

EXCURSIONS: into *Romsdal* mountains by fine *Trollstigs* road between peaks of *Trolltindene* (5,900 ft.) and fantastically shaped peaks named *Dronningen* ("Queen"), *Bispen* ("Bishop"), etc. Excellent climbing.

From *Dombås* railway climbs steeply onto *Dovrefjell*, a high mountain plateau, reaching highest station at *Hjerkinn* (3,356 ft.), then descending to *Trondheim*.

Trondheim (Y.H.), Norway's third largest town, founded in A.D. 997 was Viking capital; modern city retains many memorials of its past. Gothic cathedral begun in 1090 as the shrine of *St. Olav*; archbishops' palace is almost as old. The governor's residence, *"Stifts-gården"*, built in 1774-6, is the largest wooden building in Norway.

The town is a bishop's see, the home of Norway's Technical University, chief port of northern Norway and the gateway to the north. Trondheim fjord is very wide, bounded by rolling hills, with fields and woodland.

Sør-Trøndelag county provides excellent walking and ski-ing. There is a *Trondelag* folk museum at *Sverresborg* in *Trondheim*.

For continuation northwards from *Trondheim* to north Norway by land see **R.11**; by sea—**R.5**.

R.8. Oslo to Fagernes by Valdres (120 miles)

Railway, via *Dokka*, in 4½ hours. Bus, via Lake *Sperillen*, twice daily, 5 hours. *Valdres* valley can be approached by two routes. The eastern route, via *Randsfjord* Lake and *Dokka*, gives varied scenery—farming country, woods and moorland. Near Lake *Tonsvatn* the road reaches almost 2,500 ft. The western route follows Lake *Sperillen* and the *Begnadal* valley (Y.H. at *Hønefoss*) skirting the edge of *Vassfaret* forest (see R.6 (i)).

Routes join in at *Bjørgo* to enter **Valdres**, one of most beautiful valleys in Norway; thought to have been inhabited for at least 4,000 years. *Fagernes* (Y.H.), the only town is picturesquely situated on *Strandefjord* Lake, 1,180 ft. above sea level. It has a museum of local history and culture. Bus connections to *Gol* in *Hallingdal* (see R.6 (ii)), also to *Lærdal* (*Sognefjord*) and to southern *Jotunheimen* massif (*Tyin*, *Bygdin*).

The Telemark

Telemark is an inland area of unspoilt mountains and lakes, lying south-west of *Oslo*. Although not well known to English travellers, it is a fascinating region. The people still preserve many of their native crafts, as well as their own costumes and dialects. It is the original home of ski-ing; ski-jumpers from *Morgedal* were first to introduce the sport into *Oslo* in 1870-80.

R.9. Oslo to Dalen by rail and canal

An attractive, and leisurely approach to the *Telemark*, and a possible stage on the route to *Bergen* is the boat service on the *Bandak* canal which links various lakes between *Skien* on the south coast and *Dalen*, a voyage of 10 hours.

Some of this route can be covered by train from *Oslo* on the *Stavanger* line (**R.10**) as far as *Lunde* (3 hours). Thence by canal boat for 5½ hours' journey on meandering waterways, among mountains and forests, past *Kviteseid* (13th century church) to *Dalen* (Y.H.), small village at head of *Bandak* lake. For continuation to *Bergen* see R.4 (i).

R.9 (i) Dalen to Rjukan, 58 miles. This route crosses wild country at northern edge of *Telemark*, where it adjoins the *Hardanger* Plateau. Buses twice daily, 3 hours. *Rauland* (35 miles, slightly off road) is good example of *Telemark* village architecture and crafts. Cross *Møsvatn* Pass (3,280 ft.) and pass *Møsvatn* dam, a barrage containing the waters which provide power for the hydro-electric works at *Rjukan*. Road descends, with many bends, from the wild country above into a deep narrow valley which bustles with industrial activity. Here is the *Norsk Hydro* company's hydro-electric plant, built underground, with adjoining chemical factories, etc. *Rjukan* has a Y.H. and a cable railway which climbs 1,630 ft. to *Gvepseborg*. It is also starting point for ascent of *Gausta* (6.000 ft.), highest peak in *Telemark*. Return to *Oslo* by direct route via *Kongsberg* (Y.H.); bus and rail in 5 hours.

The South Coast

The west coast of the *Oslo* fjord, and all the south coast from *Tønsberg* to *Stavanger* is a popular holiday area for the people of *Oslo*, and is quite unlike the rest of the country. There are no deep fjords; the tree-clad hills are not so high or steep; there are many bathing beaches and holiday resorts, sheltered by islands and skerries and ideal for picnics.

NORWAY

R.10. Stavanger to Oslo (406 miles)

Stavanger (Y.H.), a port of call for steamers from Newcastle, is Norway's fourth largest town, and besides being a port and fishing centre, is the home of the canning industry. It is an old town with narrow streets and the danger of fire is still present. The cathedral, begun in Romanesque style by English monks (A.D. 1130) and with a Gothic choir dating from A.D. 1280 has some fine stained glass and a Baroque carved pulpit. The town has a museum and art gallery. The tourist bureau is in the old fireguard's tower—*Valbergstårnet* —from which there are good views. No other roads lead from *Stavanger* except that to the south, but there are regular ferries to *Haugesùnd* (**Y.H.**) and the *Ryfylke* fjords.

South of *Stavanger* lies the flat, often marshy, plain of *Jæren*, containing the most fertile soil in Norway; it is so warm that sheep can feed out of doors in winter. It is renowned for its bird life, especially in the migration season. There has been much forest-planting recently. *Jæren* is one of the few parts of the coast not protected by islands from the westerly gales.

Passing *Flekkefjord* (**Y.H.**) and on to **Kristiansand** (**Y.H.**) an important port, with street layout planned by Christian IV in 1641. Junction for *Setesdal* valley (see **R.4**). Do not confuse with *Kristiansund*, near *Trondheim*.

Lillesand is attractive little town with many old timber houses. *Grimstad* was early home of *Ibsen*; Ibsen museum in *Østergate* is oldest house of town (1750). There follows a series of ports, many connected with whaling industry. *Larvik* has ferry to *Fredrikshavn* (north Denmark) and road or rail connections to *Skien*, for *Bandak* canal (see **R.9**). Then entrance to *Oslofjord*, broad and beautiful approach to capital, dotted with summer resorts. *Horten* (**Y.H.**) has interesting naval museum and *Drammen* (**Y.H.**) an open-air museum known as *Marienlyst*. *Oslo* is 20 miles farther on.

Oslo

Oslo, which has been the capital for centuries, is Norway's only large city, and the chief home of Norwegian learning and culture. Though it is growing rapidly the main built-up area is small, and the city retains much of the atmosphere of a small town.

Oslo was founded in 1050, but after a disastrous fire (1642), Christian IV had it rebuilt on its present site behind *Akershus* fortress. He re-christened it *Christiania*, the old name being restored in 1925. The only old buildings besides *Akershus*, now a museum, are the 11th century *Gamle Akers* Church and *Gamlebyen* Church (1298), both now restored. *Oslo's* Cathedral, *Vår Frelsers Kirke* (Church of Our Saviour), built in 1699, has been restored twice.

Oslo's modern buildings are more striking. Visitors arriving by boat see first the new *Rådhus* (**Town Hall**) with its two broad towers and its big clock. The main sight of the town hall, and one of the most interesting in the whole city, is the series of mural paintings and sculptures, by Norway's leading modern artists, showing scenes from her history.

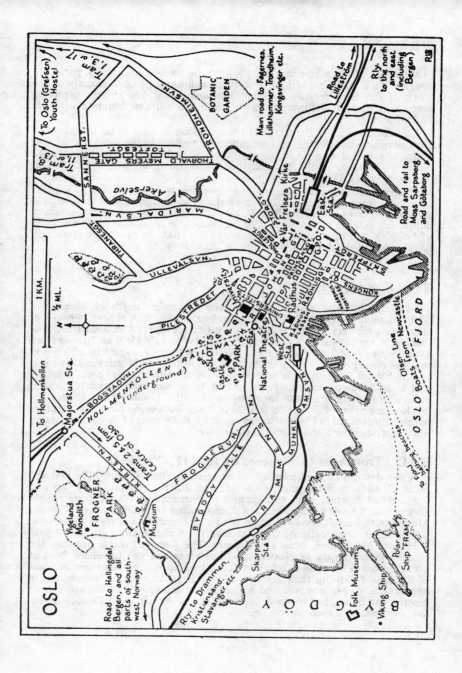

NORWAY

Modern *Oslo* is a spacious city, with wide streets, and many parks. In **Frogner Park** there is a unique sculpture exhibition, devoted entirely to the work of the 20th century sculptor *Vigeland*: some 150 statues depicting every type of human figure, from babyhood to old age, bursting with life and emotions.

Karl Johans Gate is the heart of *Oslo*, and on or near it lie the *Storting*, the University, the theatres and art galleries, the *Rådhus*, the Royal Palace and many of the best shops and hotels. Shops named *Heimen* and *Den Norske Husflids Forening*, exhibit and sell traditional handmade pottery, cloth and pewter work. (Y.H.).

Places outside the town are served by bus, and **Bygdøy** can also be reached by ferries from the quays in front of the *Rådhus* during the summer. On *Bygdøy* you can see the Kontiki raft, Nansen's ship *Fram*, a fine folk-museum containing 100 old houses and other buildings assembled from different parts of Norway, and three Viking ships, more than 1,000 years old, painstakingly re-assembled from fragments dug out of coastal mud.

The Far North

Northern Norway proper begins some 200 miles north of *Trondheim*. The climate is unexpectedly mild and, in the summer, with almost 24 hours of sunshine each day, there is little suggestion of the "Arctic Circle". The "**midnight sun**" is visible at *Bodø* from June 1st to July 13th, at *Tromsø* from May 18th to July 25th. North Cape from May 12th to August 1st. *Hammerfest*, the most northerly town in the world, is nearer the North Pole than it is to London yet the country is neither desolate nor barren. Bare rocks, glaciers and snow-covered mountains are indeed there but every patch of soil is cultivated and has its small farm, while the little *Lofoten* ports shelter the world's largest cod-fishing fleet and have many fish-curing factories. Summer temperature inland in **Finnmark** may reach 85°F. Swarms of mosquitoes make life unpleasant for a short time in early July.

R.11.   Trondheim to Kirkenes by road (1,200 miles)

A five-day rail and bus journey; more expensive than sea trip. The first 450 miles (*Trondheim-Bodø*) can be covered by rail; the remainder by bus and ferry. Road is open May to September approximately; sometimes rough, always with a loose surface, but is well-engineered and makes use of 6 ferries. Many youth hostels serve the main road and branches and there are several hotels and tourist stations. Good centres for walking and cycling, all with Y.Hs, are *Mo i Rana*, *Bodø* and *Tromso*. The *Finnmarksvidda* provides the best walking country in Norway and hostellers can use travellers' huts at hostel prices. The *vidda* is inhabited only by Lapps—the last nomadic race of Europe—following their reindeer herds. They differ from Norwegians in appearance, dress, language and way of life. *Kautokeino* and *Karasjok*, their centres, can be reached by road, or by two-day river trip from *Tana* to *Karasjok*; interesting, though expensive.

Youth hostelers from eleven countries, including the United States, are building the world's first mountain trail for bicycles in Norway.

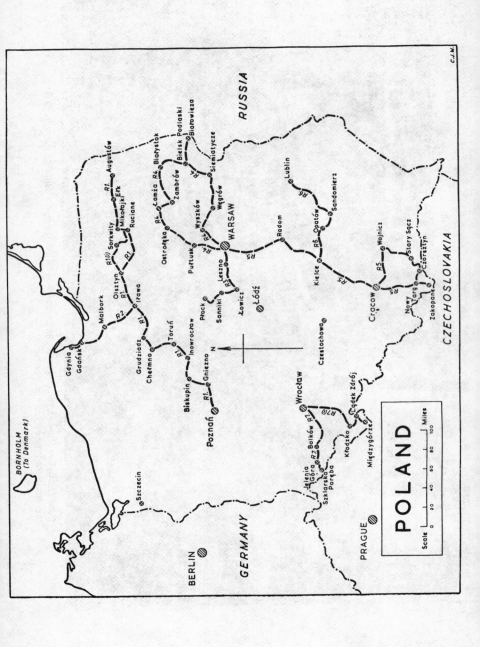

POLAND

Geographical Outline

Poland (121,000 sq. miles) has a frontier with East Germany along the *Oder* and its tributary the *Neisse;* with Czechoslovakia in the *Sudeten* and *Carpathian* mountains; and with the U.S.S.R. from the bay of *Danzig* through *Brest* to the *Carpathians*. It has a coastline in the *Baltic* of about 300 miles.

Land
Most of the country is a lowland, being part of the North European plain, here crossed by the rivers *Oder*, *Vistula* and *Bug*. The plain is diversified in the north by the morainic hills and lake basins left by the Scandinavian glaciers and forming attractive scenery in the *Pomeranian* and *Mazurian* lake districts.

South of the lowland are regions of ancient rocks: the *Lublin* plateau, the *Świętokrzykie* hills and the *Silesian* coalfield.

South again is the mountain frontier comprising the *Sudeten* mountains of ancient rocks and, divided from them by the *Moravian Gate*, the newer and higher *Carpathians* (of alpine age), mostly folded mountains, but containing the *High Tatra*, a small spectacular area of crystalline rocks with many peaks, of which *Rysy* (8,197 ft.) is the highest summit in Poland.

Climate
Despite Poland's easterly position in Europe it is reached by warm moisture-bearing winds from the Atlantic which alternate with very cold dry winds from the east. Spring comes at the end of March. Rainfall is moderate: from 18 inches in the central lowlands to 52 inches in the *Carpathians*.

Plants and Animals
The flora of the northern and central parts is typical of the Baltic region; in the *Carpathians* it is alpine. One fifth of the country is covered with forests. Pines predominate on sandy soil in the lowlands. Mixed forests are typical of the mountainous regions, in which the main conifers are spruce, fir and larch.

Chamois, marmot and alpine hare are found in the *Tatra*. The Białowieża forest (500 sq. miles) is the largest surviving area of primeval forest and shelters bear, beaver, wild boar, elk, lynx, deer and bison.

The People

Population
About 45 per cent of the 29½ million people live in towns, the six largest being: *Warsaw* (1,095,000), *Łódź* (698,000), *Cracow* (463,000), *Wroclaw* (*Breslau*) (415,000), *Poznań* (395,000), and *Gdańsk* (*Danzig*) (266,000).

POLAND

Language

Polish is one of the four Western Slavonic tongues, the others being Czech, Slovak and Wendish. It makes use of the Latin script.

Religion

About 95 per cent of the people are Roman Catholic, differentiating them from the predominantly Protestant or Orthodox faiths of neighbouring countries. Religion is a vital force and loyalty to the Church is one aspect of Poland's strong and heroic nationalism.

The once considerable Jewish community was the special target of Nazi terrorism and is now a remnant of some 45,000. Protestants number 280,000; Orthodox 100,000.

History

The Polish Slav tribes were first welded into a nation in the 10th century by princes of the Piast dynasty. The eventful, stirring and often tragic history of the country emphasizes its transitional position between western and eastern Europe. Unlike their Slav cousins the Russians they were Christianized (966) not from Constantinople but from Rome. On the other hand, all attempts to make them subservient, with other countries of the west, to the Holy Roman Emperor were successfully resisted. In Church and State the Poles remained independent. They took no part in the crusades and accepted large numbers of Jews fleeing from them. In time the Jews became an essential middle class of traders in a system where trade was forbidden to the masses and where the upper classes were too proud to engage in it.

Medieval Poland emerged as a strong state. After the union with Lithuania (then a forceful power) through the marriage of Jadwiga and Jagiello (1386) it was able to challenge and defeat the Teutonic Knights at the battle of *Grunwald* (*Tannenberg*) (1410). This led to the recovery, under Casimir IV in 1466, of the lost territory of Pomerania.

From this period dates the Seym (Parliament) which gave the numerous class of small gentry a voice in affairs—an example of representative government then unique in mainland Europe. Less satisfactory was the introduction of an elective system of kingship which put the real power into the hands of the great nobles. One result was the gradual decline of the peasantry into a state of serfdom.

In the 17th century the country was weakened by war with Sweden and by a long struggle with Islam. But at a crisis of history Poland saved Christian Europe when, at the request of the Pope, its army carried out its famous march under the warrior king Jan Sobieski and relieved Vienna from the Turks (1683).

But other powers were rising, and the position of Poland on its great plain was to prove, not for the last time, indefensible against concerted attack. Austria, Prussia and Russia decided to divide the country between them and there followed the three Partitions of 1772, 1793 and 1795.

The unexpected result and its sequels are a triumph of national spirit in face of adversity. Poland disappeared as a state, but Polish nationalism was born. Its leader was Tadeusz Kościuszko. Its strength was the will of the people. This was recognised by the Congress of Vienna at the end of the Napoleonic Wars (1815) by the creation of a small Kingdom of Poland (the so-called Congress Kingdom) with *Warsaw* as its capital and the Czar of Russia as its sovereign. A small Republic of Cracow was formed and put under the joint control of the Partition powers. Otherwise the Congress confirmed the Partitions. But the Kingdom was annexed by Russia 1831 and the Republic shared the same fate at the hands of Austria in 1848. Not until 1918 did Poland revive as an independent state through the work of Paderewski and Pilsudski.

The story of Poland since that date is of the greatest significance for an understanding of European affairs. In the Second World War the country was again partitioned. The sufferings of its people were unexampled; their spirit as heroic as ever. At the end, by the Potsdam Agreement, Poland was born again with new frontiers, losing territory in the east, gaining it in the west. The complex course of events, then and since, is of such importance that any visitor would do well to be familiar with it in some detail.

Government The Seym is a one-chamber parliament of 459 deputies for which elections are held every four years. Party systems exist but lack the essential features necessary to provide a choice between alternative governments.

The executive is a Council of Ministers.

In place of a president there is a Council of State of 15 members.

Resources Poland is a great agricultural country and nearly half of its people are engaged on the land. Post-war collectivised farming was soon abandoned and most land is privately farmed. Rye is the chief crop.

Coal, of which there are huge reserves in *Silesia*, is the chief mineral resource. Iron occurs in the central uplands; oil in the *Carpathians*.

In contrast to farming, industry is nationalised. There are important iron and steel, engineering, chemical and textile industries employing about a fifth of the working population.

Folk Costumes These are still worn in many parts of the country (and not for the benefit of tourists). Notably they can be seen among the Gural people of the *High Tatra*, and in the *Łowicz*, *Kielce* and *Kurpie* regions.

Culture

Architecture Indigenous styles are to be seen chiefly in rural areas, notably in wooden churches such as that at *Dębno* and in village houses.

In larger buildings, the Church, the ruling classes and the municipalities modelled their tastes on western fashions, all the main styles being successively adopted. Foreign architects, especially Italians, were frequently employed. In one case, *Zamość*, in the province of Lublin, a complete new town of the Renaissance period was built to the plans of the Italian architect Morandi.

POLAND

Painting and Sculpture
The outstanding sculptor working in Poland in medieval times was the German Wit Stwosz (Veit Stoss) (1447-1533). His masterpiece is the great altar of *St. Mary's Cracow*.
The long and still living tradition of folk art includes painting and sculpture, such as the remarkable beehive figures of *Silesia*, the flower paintings of *Zalipie* and the painted glass of *Podhale*.
The national school of painting which developed in the 19th century was dominated by Jan Matejko (1838-93). His theme, Polish history, was treated in a succession of noble works which give him an important place in European art.

Music
Nowhere is the heightened sensibility of the Slav more perfectly expressed than in the works of Chopin (1810-49) which embody the creativeness, idealism and sense of tragedy of the Polish spirit. Working sometimes from traditional material—such as the *mazurka*, a Polish peasant dance, or the *polonaise*, a court dance of the aristocracy—his own genius produced a new world of poetry and sound.

Literature
Poland has a vigorous and perceptive literature. The works of many of its poets and novelists (including all those mentioned here) have been translated into English.
Its poetry begins in the Renaissance (Poland's Golden Age of cultural activity) with the works of Jan Kochanowski (1530-84). In later times of national disaster poets writing in exile were leaders in the fight against oppression. Adam Miekiewicz (1798-1855), Poland's greatest poet, is also a national hero. Slowacki (1809-49) and Krasiński (1812-59) were other major poets of the period. In the most recent post-war times the publication (1955) of Adam Wazyk's *Poem for Adults*—with its castigation of "textbooks without windows" and other aridities—was a turning point towards revival.
Sienkiewicz (1846-1916) has great fame abroad, largely because of his "*Quo Vadis?*" but several of his novels of Polish life and history are available in translation, as also are: *The Peasants*, by Reymont (1867-1925) (Nobel Prizewinner, 1924); *Tales of the Tatras*, by Przerwa-Tetmajer (1865-1940); novels by Eliza Orzeszkowa (1842-1910) (the George Eliot of Poland). Żeromski (1864-1925), Zofia Kossak-Szczucka, Maria Kuncewiczowa and the dramas of Wyspiański. Though born a Pole, Joseph Conrad belongs more properly to English literature.

Science
The towering figure is Copernicus (1473-1543), not only the founder of modern astronomy but the prime mover in the revolution of thought which marks the transition from medieval to modern times.
Maria Sklodowska, the discoverer of radium, is best known to the world under her married name of Curie.

Poland is one of the less-traveled European countries.

POLAND

Touring Information

Access
London to *Warsaw:* (i) by *rail* via Hook of Holland and Berlin, in 31 hours, single £28·15, return £54·25 (ii) by *air* direct flight, tourist return, £76·75. London to *Katowice* (for *Tatra*), rail via Hook of Holland and Berlin in 34 hours, single, £29·85, return £56·65. London to *Gdynia*, monthly sailings by direct boat service in 3 days.

Transport
There is a good network of railways; frequent long distance coach services between large towns; local bus services in all parts of the country. Railway fares become cheaper per kilometre with increase of distance. Supplement payable on express trains. Bus fares are higher than train fares.

Money
The currency unit is the *zloty*, divided into 100 *groszy*. Difficulties in changing travellers' cheques are sometimes experienced in small towns; even in *Warsaw* and *Cracow* it may involve a lengthy procedure.

Public Holidays
1st January; 6th January; Easter Monday; 1st May; Ascension Day; Corpus Christi; 22nd July; 1st November; Christmas Day; 26th December.

Maps
Państwowe Przedsiebiorstwo Wydawnitcw Kartagraficznych, Warsaw, publish a general map 1:1,500,000, one sheet; also regional tourist maps on various scales, e.g. *Warsaw Region*; *Cracow Region*; *Karkonosze*; *Tatra*.

Accomodation
Poland is a founder member of the *International Youth Hostel Federation* and has about 250 hostels. They are mostly in schools and open only during the summer. In addition there are about 200 primitive hostels or refuges listed in the Polish youth hostel handbook.

The *Polish Touring and Country Lovers Society* (*P.T.T.K.*), *Marszalkowska 124, Warsaw*, has over 200 houses providing hostel-type accommodation.

An application to a Polish Consulate for a tourist visa must be accompanied by proof of reservation of accommodation.

Buying own food
Meals are provided at only a few hostels. Food is quite expensive; tea should be brought as it is prohibitively expensive even at tourist rates of exchange.

Camping
The Pomeranian and Mazurian lake districts are particularly attractive for camping.

Walking
The best known areas are the *Sudeten Mountains* and the *Tatra*. In the *Sudetens* way-marking has been extensively carried out. The remoter parts of the *Carpathians* provide an off-the-beaten-track challenge for experienced walkers.

Climbing	The best mountaineering is in the *High Tatra* (centre *Zakopane*). No significant glaciers. Chiefly rock climbing. Several P.T.T.K. huts.

Ski-ing	There is good ski-ing to be had in the *Carpathians* and in the *Sudetens*. Instruction is available at the main centres.

Zakopane has two cable railways. Season usually end of December to end of March.

Cycling	The best way of seeing much of the country. Road surfaces reasonably good; motor traffic light.

Canoeing and Sailing	The *Mazurian Lakes*, interlinked by rivers and canals, provide ideal conditions. There are many centres for water sports. P.T.T.K. (see *Accommodation* above) will provide equipment and arrange tours.

National Parks	Poland has a notable record of nature conservation and several of the national parks named in the touring routes will be of particular interest to naturalists.

Warsaw

Warsaw (*Warszawa*) (Y.H.), on R. *Vistula*, city rebuilt after almost total destruction in 1944. *Stare Miasto*, the Old Town, with famous merchant houses (*Market Square, Freta Street, Kamienne Schodki Street*); new cathedral; tomb of Unknown Warrior in *Saxon Gardens* was not destroyed; Jewish memorial in *ghetto*; famous statues replaced include Chopin's in *Lazienki Park*; Adam Mickiewicz's; the *Sigismund Column* in *Castle Square*. Chopin relics in building of *Frederic Chopin Society, Tamka Street. Lazienki Palace. Palace of Culture and Science*, a gift of the U.S.S.R. Several museums.

EXCURSIONS: (a) *Kampinoska Forest*, west of city, a proposed National Park; (b) *Żelazowa Wola*, birthplace of Chopin. (See R.3); (c) *Czersk*, 25 miles S. 13th century castle above *Vistula*.

Touring Routes

R.1. Poznań—Toruń—Ilawa—Augustów (360 miles)

Poznań (Y.H.), former capital of Great Poland; market square with Renaissance town hall and fine houses (rebuilt); cloth hall; reconstructed Gothic and Baroque cathedral, with tomb of Boleslaw I, first king of Poland; *City Museum* in town hall; *National Museum* (and art gallery); *Museum of Musical Instruments*; *Raczyński Library*; zoological and botanical gardens; palm house in *Kasprzak Park*. Cemeteries of Polish, Russian and British war graves.

EXCURSION: Wielkopolski National Park, 10 miles S., 17 sq. miles of lakes and forest; nature reserve with pre-historic remains. Rogalin Palace., 3 miles SE beyond Park, Baroque and Rococo; art collections; park with famous oaks. Kórnik (Y.H.), 8 miles; Palace with gardens, art collections and library.

POLAND

Gniezno, 30 miles, (Y.H.), small historic and industrial town in region of low hills and lakes; first kings of Poland crowned here; cathedral with famous 12th century bronze door and rich interior; many ancient churches, including 10th century Romanesque church and *St. John's Church* with 14th century frescoes.

Biskupin, 13 miles, reconstructed Iron Age Slav lake settlement. *Żnin,* 6 miles, (Y.H.). *Inowroclaw,* 25 miles (Y.H.), industrial town and spa. *Toruń,* 19 miles, (Y.H.), town on R. *Vistula,* birthplace of Copernicus; castle (1260), medieval churches, town hall, etc. *Pomerania Museum.*

Chelmno, 25 miles known as 'little Cracow'; associations with Teutonic Knights; city wall; Renaissance town hall; old churches and houses. *Grudziądz,* 17 miles, (Y.H.). *Ilawa,* 45 miles, and *Ostróda,* 20 miles, centres for **Western Mazurian Lakes** (canoeing, sailing, camping.)

EXCURSION: steamer from *Ostróda* by lake and canal to *Elbląg,* 40 miles, (Y.H.). *Frombork* (18 miles from *Elbląg*), *Copernicus Museum.*

Olsztyn, 22 miles, (Y.H.), starting point for tours of **Great Mazurian Lakes;** ancient city on R. *Łyna. St. Jacob's Cathedral;* castle (museum) with statue of Copernicus in courtyard. *Szczytno,* 27 miles, (Y.H.), museum. *Ruciane,* 25 miles, resort on *Nidy Lake.*

R.1. (i) Canoe route to Ruciane. Rail *Olsztyn* to *Sorkwitv,* 37 miles. Thence 60 miles by canoe down R. *Krutynia* and through many lakes to *Beldany Lake* and *Ruciane.*

Steamer from *Ruciane* to *Mikolajki,* 10 miles, (Y.H.).

EXCURSIONS: (a) Luknajno Lake, heronry and swannery reserve; (b) *Śniardwy Lake,* the "*Mazurian Sea*", largest lake in Poland.

Steamer to *Giżycko,* 18 miles, (Y.H.), centre for boating on *Kirajno Lake,* one of separately named parts of *Mamry Lake.*

EXCURSION: Cormorant reserve on island in *Dobskie Lake.*

Elk, 32 miles, (Y.H.); **Augustów,** 25 miles, (Y.H.), centre for canoeing and boating on rivers and lakes. (*Augustów* to *Warsaw,* 9 hours by rail).

R.2. Ilawa—Malbork—Gdańsk—Gdynia (80 miles)

Ilawa (R.1), (rail connections *Warsaw, Poznań, Gdynia*).

Malbork, 38 miles, small town with fine castle, once headquarters of Teutonic Knights; ancient market place with gabled houses and vaulted passages.

Gdańsk (*Danzig*), 28 miles, (Y.Hs.), port with eventful history from Hansa times; historic houses in Old Town fully restored; 16th century town hall; Gothic churches of St. Catherine, St. Mary and St. Nicholas. *Oliva* (suburb) has 12th century abbey and church with famous 18th century organ.

EXCURSION: *Kashubian Hills,* immediately W. of city; well wooded morainic hills with many lakes, NE end of *Pomeranian Lake District. Kartuzy, Kashubian Museum* and Carthusian Monastery. Y.H. at *Chmielno* and *Ostrzyce.*

Sopot, 7 miles, (Y.H.), seaside resort.

Gdynia, 5 miles, (Y.H.), chief port of Poland; was fishing village until 1920; remarkable creation on site with few natural advantages.

EXCURSION: *Slowiński National Park,* 120 sq. miles, includes some 45 miles of coast and lakes *Lebsko* and *Gardno;* great variety of birds. (Y.H. *Slupsk.*)

R.3. Warsaw—Lowicz—Plock (100 miles)

From *Leszno*, 20 miles W. of *Warsaw*, road skirts *Kampinoska Forest*, (a proposed national park). *Żelazowa Wola* (**Y.H.** *Chodaków*), 13 miles, village; small mansion in park was birthplace of Chopin, whose piano can be seen.

Łowicz, 23 miles, market town for rich countryside; collegiate church (1433), castle, carpet factory. Town and region are famous for living tradition of folk costumes and folk art (decoration of houses, paper cuts, weaving). Corpus Christi procession. (**Y.H.** in town and at *Zduny* and *Sobota*). *Sanniki*, 18 miles.

Płock, 24 miles, (**Y.H.**), town picturesquely situated on R. *Vistula*; 12th century cathedral. Return to *Warsaw* by river boat (summer service), 65 miles.

R.4. Warsaw through Kurpie region to Bialowieza Forest, returning through Podlasie region (400 miles)

Pułtusk, 36 miles, visit pottery workshop established 1450. *Ostrołęka*, 38 miles, (**Y.H.**). *Łomża*, 23 miles, (**Y.H.**); folk museum. *Zambrów*, 15 miles.

Bialystok, 42 miles, (**Y.H.**), provincial capital and industrial centre (textiles); *Branicki Palace*.

Białowieża, 65 miles, (**Y.H.**), one of the largest forests in central Europe (500 sq. miles, mixed forest and marsh); bear, bison, elk, wild boar, wild ponies, etc., in primeval conditions. Includes **Białowieża National Park** of 18 sq. miles. Museum of natural history.

Bielsk Podlaski, 32 miles, and *Siemiatycze*, 36 miles, are two centres of Podlasie folk weaving. *Wegrów*, 40 miles, famous for double-warp rugs. *Wyszków*, 30 miles. *Warsaw*, 35 miles.

R.5. Warsaw—Cracow—Zakopane—Krościenko—Cracow (375 miles)

Kielce, 95 miles (**Y.H.**), provincial capital in *Świętokrzykie* (*St. Cross*) *Mountains*: highest point, *Lysica*, (2,004 ft.) in **Świętokrzykie National Park,** (21 sq. miles); walking area; several **Y.H.** Museum in *Kielce*.

EXCURSION: Częstochowa, by rail, 65 miles, town with large monastery on hill, *Jasna Góra*, famous in Polish history; chief place of religious pilgrimage.

Cracow (*Kraków*), 75 miles, (**Y.H.**), handsome, historic city on *Vistula*; capital of Poland 1138 to 1609; University 1364; 13th century market square; *Marjacki* (*St. Mary's*) *Church* with famous altar piece by Wit Stowsz (Veit Stoss); *Sukiennice* (cloth hall); interesting streets; several museums; house of Matejko, the painter. On *Wawel Hill* above city is fine group of cathedral, castle and palace. Cathedral has tombs of national heroes. Castle has 8th century *chapel of St. Felix and St. Adauct*; Renaissance courtyard; *Jagiellon Library*; national art collection.

EXCURSION: Ojców National Park, 12 miles N. in *Prądnik Valley*: limestone rocks and caves; many species of trees and rare flora.

POLAND

Nowy Targ, 43 miles (Y.H.).

Zakopane, 12 miles, (2,800 ft.) (Y.H.), chief centre for **Polish Tatra (Tatry) Mountains.** *Tatra Museum.*

EXCURSIONS: (a) Kościeliska valley and caves; (b) Kasprowy Wierch (6,400 ft.), cable rail from *Kuznice*; (c) High Tatra walking tour, 7 days, to Morskie Oko Lake (Sea Eye) under Rysy (8,197 ft.). Accommodation at P.T.T.K. huts.

Return *Nowy Targ,* 12 miles, and turn E. to *Czorsztyn,* 15 miles, for 5½ miles passage by raft-canoe of **Dunajec** gorge in *Pieniny* mountains (**Pieniny National Park**). Land at *Szczawnica. Krościenko,* 4 miles, Pieniny Museum. Continue by road down *Dunajec* valley. *Stary Sącz,* 28 miles (Y.H.). At *Wojnicz,* 30 miles, turn W. to *Dębno,* 5 miles, ancient wooden village church. *Cracow* 50 miles.

R.6. Kielce—Sandomierz—Lublin (123 miles)

Kielce (R.5), E. to *Lagow,* 21 miles. *Opatow,* 15 miles (Y.H.), town with Romanesque church; medieval town gate.

Sandomierz, 18 miles, (Y.H.) picturesque small city in *Vistula* valley, much fought over (Mongols, 13th century, Sweden 17th century, and in two World Wars). Cross river at *Annopol,* 24 miles.

Lublin, 45 miles, (Y.H.), industrial city; historic Old Town rebuilt.

EXCURSIONS: (a) Zamość, 50 miles, (Y.H.) Renaissance planned town, founded (1580) by Polish chancellor Jan Zamoyski; (b) *Pulawy,* 30 miles, and Kazimierz, 7 miles, Renaissance city of *Vistula; Naleczów,* 12 miles.

R.7. Karkonosze Mountains. Wroclaw to Szklarska Poręba (52 miles)

Wroclaw (*Breslau*) on R. *Oder,* (Y.Hs.). Badly damaged in war, but town hall and other ancient buildings well restored. *Silesian Museum.*

Bolków, 40 miles, (Y.H.). *Jelenia Góra,* 20 miles, (Y.H.), centre for tours in **Karkonosze Range (Riesen Gebirge).**

EXCURSIONS: Snieżka (*Schneekoppe*) (5,253 ft.) highest summit; 4 hours from *Karpacz.*

Szklarska Poręba, 12 miles, (Y.H.); walking and winter sports centre for western part of range.

R.7 (i) Zlote and Bystrzyckie Hills. *Wroclaw to Klodzko,* 60 miles, (Y.H.) town with many picturesque buildings. *Lądek Zdrój,* (Y.H.), walking and winter sports centre. *Miedzygórze,* Y.H.) under *Snieżnik* (4,665 ft.)

PORTUGAL
Geographical Outline

Land

Portugal occupies less than one-sixth of the *Iberian Peninsula*, but includes most of its western seaboard. Its length from north to south is about 360 miles, and it varies in breadth from about 140 miles in the north to about 70 miles in the south.

Physically the country can be roughly divided into the region north of the *Tagus*—mainly hilly or mountainous, with a narrow coastal plain—and that south of the river, which is much flatter, although with some hilly districts.

Across the mountainous country the principal rivers cut deep valleys from east to west: the *Minho* (on the northern frontier), the *Douro*, the *Mondego* and the *Tagus*. All but the *Mondego* rise in Spain. They are difficult to navigate and are, therefore, not important for communication. The mountains are not high by alpine standards. The highest are in the *Serra da Estrêla* at 6,500 feet, but most are not much above 4,500 feet. They are, however, often bare and rugged in character and form rough and impressive scenery.

A remarkable and pleasing feature of Portugal is that, although a small country, the scenery is diverse due both to its physical features and to the uses to which the land has been put, and the appearance of the country often varies considerably within small distances.

South of the *Tagus*, especially, this diversity owes much to human influence, and wide stretches of bleak heathland are interspersed with areas of the cork oak and olive, and of extensive wheat growing. In the extreme south are the coastlands of the *Algarve* which have much of the character of *Andalusia* and of the neighbouring coasts of Africa.

Climate

Portugal has an equable climate, influenced by the Atlantic. It does not experience extremes of heat or cold—particularly near the coast—and this makes it suitable for touring at any time of year.

Rainfall is heaviest in the northern coastal areas and in the mountains. It is least in the extreme south.

In summer *Oporto* (in the north) is generally cooler than *Lisbon*, but in these coastal areas the heat is tempered by the on-shore breezes. In the extreme south (the *Algarve*) and towards the interior of the country, and also in valleys sheltered by the mountains from cooling breezes, the heat of summer is greater.

Winters in the coastal areas are mild, but coastal fogs, caused by cold Atlantic currents, are common.

Plants and Animals

The vegetation is a mixture of the temperate and the subtropical. Pines and deciduous trees familiar in Northern Europe frequently exist side by side with cacti, tree-ferns, palms and aloes from Africa and elsewhere—a characteristic well seen in the *Sintra* hills near *Lisbon*.

PORTUGAL

North of *Lisbon* pinewoods are common along the coastal plain, and forests of oak and chestnut cover the lower slopes of the mountains above the cultivated valleys. Lime, elm and poplar are also common.

Cork oaks are widely distributed, but particularly important in the *Alentejo* (south of the *Tagus*). They will be seen with the bark stripped from the trunks, to provide the cork which is of great importance in Portugal. The olive is also common and so too the locust tree with its curious edible seed pods. The *Algarve* is rich in fruit trees, especially almond and fig.

Three crops in particular produce a countryside unfamiliar in Northern Europe: maize is important in the north, grape vines as far south as the *Tagus*, and rice is grown in the valleys of several rivers.

Oxen are used for ploughing and as draught animals. Donkeys and mules are the usual beasts of burden. Wolves are found in the wilder areas, notably the *Serra da Estrêla*, and wild boars are preserved in certain districts.

The People

Population
Of the population of about 9 million people, a very high proportion live in the rural areas. The visitor will find that there is often a surprisingly large number of people to be seen in the countryside, particularly in the north where there is serious over-population. This density of settlement often belies the nature of the soils which are not on the whole particularly fertile.

The only large cities are *Lisbon* (pop. 817,000) and *Oporto* (pop. 305,000). Otherwise no town exceeds 50,000.

Ethnically the Portuguese are predominantly of Mediterranean type, but in the course of the country's long and complex history of invasion and exploration there has been intermingling with stocks from outside Iberia—Romans, Visigoths, Moors, Jews and Negroes. The present-day characteristics are generally of a short, dark and sturdy people, but in the north there are some traces of the fairer Germanic peoples.

Language
Portuguese is one of the three surviving Latin-derived languages of the Iberian Peninsula, the others being Castilian (Spanish) and Catalan. Resulting from this common origin it has some likeness to Castilian, particularly in written form, but it is a distinct language. Galician, the dialect of north-west Spain, is directly linked to Portuguese, but has decayed under the influence of Castilian.

A visitor with a knowledge of Spanish, or even French, might find it comparatively easy to get a grasp of written Portuguese, but the spoken language presents more difficulties.

Religion
The overwhelming majority of the people are Roman Catholic. The Church plays a considerable part in the life of the country.

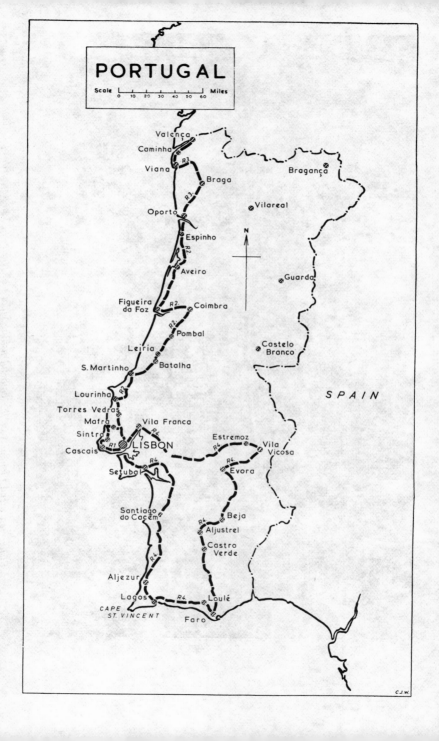

PORTUGAL

Scale   Miles
0   10   20   30   40   50   60

Valença
Caminha
Viana   R3
Braga   Bragança
R3
Oporto   Vilareal
Espinho
R2   N
Aveiro
Guarda
Figueira   R2   Coimbra
da Foz
R2
Pombal
Leiria   Castelo
S. Martinho   Batalha   Branco
Lourinha   R2
Torres Vedras   SPAIN
Mafra   Vila Franca
Sintra   R4   Estremoz
Cascais   R1   LISBON   R4   Vila
                    Vicosa
Setubal   R4   Evora
R4
Santiago
do Cacém   R4   Beja
Aljustrel
Castro
Verde
R4
Aljezur
Lagos   R4   Loulé
CAPE
ST. VINCENT   Faro

C.J.W.

Fishermen mend their nets in the colorful fishing village of Nazare, 70 miles north of Lisbon, Portugal.

History Portugal has no separate history until the 12th century; before that time its history was that of the whole Peninsula. Phoenicians and Greeks traded with the Iberian peoples and later the Carthaginians established an Empire here. This fell to the Romans at the end of the 3rd century B.C., although for more than a century the tribes of the Atlantic seaboard held out against them. In 27 B.C., the emperor Augustus created the province of *Lusitania*, which included most of the area of modern Portugal, and this lasted until the series of invasions which brought about the collapse of the Roman Empire. Of these invaders the most important were the Visigoths. They incorporated *Lusitania* in an unstable kingdom which survived until it fell an easy prey to the Moslems in the early 8th century A.D.

The name Portugal was first applied to the district around the modern *Oporto* and was derived from the Roman name for the city—*Portus Cale*. The birth of Portugal dates from 1125 when this district established its independence of the Christian kingdom of *Léon*. In the next 125 years the remainder of her frontiers were carved from land under Moorish (Moslem) control, but more than a century passed before Portugal decisively defeated the territorial designs of the neighbouring kingdom of *Castile*. This was achieved by John of Aviz at the battle of *Aljubarrota* (1385) which ushered in Portugal's great age of exploration and expansion.

By the end of the 15th century Portuguese explorer-traders, such as Bartholomew Diaz and Vasco da Gama, inspired by the work of Prince Henry the Navigator, had discovered the *Azores* and *Madeira*, explored the coasts of Africa, and established themselves in India, the East Indies and China. In 1500 they landed in Brazil.

In the first half of the 16th century Portugal was at the height of her power, but the efforts of so great an expansion had overtaxed the small country's strength and in 1581 she was conquered by Spain. Independence was regained sixty years later, but, although she was still to exploit the wealth of Brazil, she never fully recovered her strength and went slowly into decline. Her ascendancy in the East passed first to the Dutch, later to the British.

The country was occupied by the French during the Napoleonic Wars (until they were expelled by Wellington) and the royal family fled to Brazil. A few years later Brazil seceded from her union with Portugal.

The constitutional struggle of the 19th century culminated in the assassination of the king (Carlos) in 1908 and the establishment of a republic two years later. The new democracy was at first extremely unstable, but the appointment of Dr Salazar as finance minister in 1928, and prime minister in 1932, brought a more lasting political peace, disrupted by a popular uprising in 1974 and the setting-up of a less authoritarian regime, soon ousted by military and communist ascendancy.

Government The President and the Government (which is appointed by the President) have very wide powers. Portugal is not in any real sense of the word a Parliamentary democracy. The political structure is not a popular topic of conversation.

PORTUGAL

Resources Although Portugal is a predominantly agricultural country it has become much more industrial in the last few years; between 1962 and 1972 exports of manufactured goods have almost trebled, with particular emphasis on machinery. Grapes, olive oil, wheat, maize and potatoes are among the principal products of the soil.

Portugal is the world's largest producer of cork. The famous Port wine is very much a wine for export; other wines, more to the taste of the Portuguese, are produced for home consumption. The pine forests give rise to a considerable industry in timber, resins and turpentine. Another industry is the canning and export of sardines, caught by the coastal fishing communities.

Customs and Dress There are considerable regional variations in customs and dress, as yet largely unaffected by the modern tendency throughout Europe for standardization in dress and the preservation of local costume mainly for the tourist trade. Picturesque costumes may be seen at their best at the *romarias* or pilgrimages which combine religion with secular festivities. Dancing and singing play a prominent part in the life of the people. The traditional songs are of a slower rhythm than those of Spain. In *Lisbon* this is typified by the *fado*, popular in many cafes and restaurants. The climax of the harvesting (e.g. treading the grapes, stripping the maize cobs) is often made an occasion for gay festivals.

Food and Drink The staple diet is of fish, particularly cod, vegetables and fruit. Meat is rarely eaten by the ordinary people, in whose diet, rice, maize bread and beans play an important part. Cooking is usually done in olive oil.

Sport Bull fighting, usually conducted without the bulls being killed, is a popular sport; so, too, is football.

Culture

Architecture With one or two exceptions—such as the Roman temple of Diana at *Evora* and the Byzantine style church of *Sao Frutuoso* at *Braga*—the existing notable buildings date from times later than the creation of the kingdom of Portugal.

The familiar labels of the successive architectural styles, from Romanesque through to Baroque and later, can be attached to the great buildings, but in the Portuguese setting they often contain distinctive elements which set them a little apart.

Thus the Romanesque, found mainly in the north (which was earlier conquered from the Moors) is often a rather forbidding style, as for instance in the fortress-like cathedrals of *Braga* and *Coimbra*.

The Gothic comes, therefore, as a rather greater contrast to the Romanesque than do the same two styles in, for example, England. Its two finest achievements are both monastery churches—at *Batalha* and *Alcobaça*.

The Gothic passed into the Manueline, a style exclusively Portuguese, containing much Moorish influence and coinciding with the country's great age of discovery and conquest. Two famous examples exist close to each other in the *Belem* district of *Lisbon*—the church of *S. Jeronimos* and the tower of *Belem*.

Renaissance architecture was established in the 16th century, e.g. the cathedral of *Leiria*; and later the Baroque style—of which the monastery at *Mafra* is probably the most extravagant example—became predominant. In connection with these and later styles mention must be made of the unique Portuguese *azulejos*, glazed tiles used for interior and exterior decoration. Introduced by the Moors, *azulejos* were developed by the Portuguese and for centuries they have been used to add colourful decoration to buildings, both religious and secular. Although still produced, and in evidence everywhere, modern trends in building are curtailing their use.

Literature Portugal has a long and imposing literary history but its works are not generally accessible to those with no knowledge of the language.

An outstanding exception, however, are the poems of Camões (Camõens) (1524-80) who has a universal appeal as one of the greatest figures of the Renaissance. Both in the circumstances of his life and in his great epic *Os Lusíadas* ("The Portuguese"), which has been translated into English several times, he epitomises one of the supreme European achievements, the voyages of discovery and the linking up of the West with the Orient.

Touring Information

Access London to *Lisbon*: (i) by *rail*, via Dieppe and Paris, in 2 days, £35·25 single; (ii) by *air*, direct flight in about 2½ hours, tourist return £84·10; (iii) by *sea*, ferries from Southampton to *Lisbon*, 3 sailings every 2 weeks, from £50·00 single; ships going to the Caribbean and South America also accept passengers to *Lisbon*, but the voyage costs not less than £110·00 return.

Transport Portuguese trains have two classes, and run on broad-gauge track as in Spain. A supplementary charge is payable on some expresses, marked *Rapide* in timetables. Bus travel is cheap in Portugal, but services are rather infrequent.

Money The *escudo* is divided into 100 *centavos*. Copper coins are used for 10 and 20 *centavos*; nickel coins for 50 *centavos* and 1 *escudo*; silver coins for 2½, 5, 10 and 20 *escudos*; notes are issued for 20, 50, 100, 500 and 1,000 *escudos*.

349

PORTUGAL

Clothing
Although the climate is one of the best in Europe, and it is warm and sunny most of the year, there can often be a cool breeze in the evenings, and a waterproof is essential as rain can be heavy, particularly in the mountains.

Restaurants and Meals
Food is plentiful and wholesome; cooking is appreciated as an art and is often excellent. Sea foods, such as *caldeirada* (fisherman's stew), *porco a Alentejana* (pork stewed with clams) and *bacalhau*, the national dish of codfish, served in various forms are popular, as well as sweets and delicacies rich in eggs and sugar, such as *ovos moles de Aveiro* or *trouxas d'ovos das Caldas*.

Map
Michelin No. 37, scale 1:500,000, depicts all the country.

Accommodation
The idea of youth hostelling is as yet unfamiliar in Portugal; there are about a dozen youth hostels (*Pousadas de Juventude*), but few with accommodation for girls.

Other simple, clean and cheap accommodation is readily available in all parts of the country. The government regulates the prices charged and grades the standard. This information is obtainable in a free booklet from the Portuguese Tourist Offices and visitors are strongly recommended to obtain a copy. It will prove accurate, reliable and invaluable for finding accommodation.

Cycling
Portugal is a comparatively small country, and cycling is a convenient way of seeing it. Secondary roads are best used; although surfaces may be indifferent, motor traffic is not likely to be a nuisance. Cycles are carried cheaply on buses and trains and less rewarding areas should be crossed quickly this way.

Lisbon

Lisbon lies along the north bank of the *Tagus* where the *Mar de Palha* (the wide part of the estuary) becomes a narrow channel before entering the sea. Its history dates from Roman times, possibly before. For 500 years a Moorish city, it later became capital of the newly formed kingdom of Portugal, reaching its greatest prosperity with the age of Portuguese exploration and conquest overseas.

Much of it is built on hills, where streets are often narrow, steep and tortuous. Between the hills and along the *Tagus* run spacious avenues, the main links between different parts of the city.

Lisbon was almost entirely destroyed by earthquake in 1755. Much of the present plan of the city centre dates from the reconstruction (by the Marquis of Pombal) following the catastrophe. There are very few complete buildings older than this and therefore relatively little dating from the period of Portugal's greatest prosperity—the 15th and 16th centuries. Nevertheless, *Lisbon* is a beautiful and historical city.

Its four districts are, from east to west:

(*a*) The *Alfama* (old town), site of Roman and Moorish Lisbon: a hilly quarter of narrow streets, retaining much of their medieval appearance, dominated by Moorish *castle of São Jorge* (many later additions). Other interesting buildings: the *old cathedral* (*Sé Patriarcal*), with Gothic façade and choir, but rest of later date; church of *São Vincente de Fora* (Renaissance); church of *Madre de Deus*, containing museum of azulejos in cloisters.

(*b*) The *Cicade Baixa* (lower town), centre of modern *Lisbon* planned after 1755 by Marquis of Pombal. The **Rossio** (the fine spacious *Dom Pedro IV Square*) is the hub of Lisbon life. National Theatre on N. side. The Rossio railway station at the N.W. corner is a 19th century copy of the Manueline style. Northward runs fine spacious *Avenida da Liberdade*. To S. parallel streets of good proportion lead to *Praça do Commercio*, sometimes known as *Black Horse Square*, flanked on three sides by arcaded buildings, on fourth by *Tagus*. Ferry to *Cacilhas* from near S.E. corner.

(*c*) The *Bairro Alto* and (*d*) *Alcantara* districts contain buildings of great interest, in particular the ruins of the *Carmo* church, destroyed in the earthquake, the *Estrella* church with white marble dome and twin towers visible for miles around, finely decorated church of *S. Roque*, and *Aqueduct of Aguas Livres* (18th century), still in use.

At **Belém,** the western suburb, are the two most important Manueline buildings: the **monastery of Jerónimos,** full of beautiful detail, and the lovely **tower of Belém** standing out into the river.

The visitor should not fail to see two of Lisbon's finest aspects: the many parks and gardens of exotic plants and trees, and the splendid view of the city from *Cacilhas* on the south bank of the *Tagus*.

Touring Routes

M indicates males only.

As described, these routes are intended for cycling, but travellers by train and bus can use them with only minor modifications.

R.1. Lisbon to Lisbon via Mafra, Sintra and Cascais (86 miles)

Leave *Lisbon* by N.8 (due north) and follow the road through *Loures*. After 20 miles turn left along N.116 for *Mafra*; small town dominated by vast Baroque monastery and palace started in 1713 by King John V; church with famous carillons.

7 miles west is fishing village, *Ericeira*, famous for lobsters. To north are wild deserted beaches.

South along N.247 across plain towards *Sintra Hills*. At *Sintra* the royal palace in the upper village is a curious mixture of Moorish, Gothic and later

PORTUGAL

styles. Crags above village covered by ruins of a Moorish castle. On nearby hill-top is the "fairy castle" of *Pena* (19th century). The rugged volcanic *Sintra Hills*, with lush, sub-tropical vegetation, continue westward to the sea.

Continue W. to *Cabo da Roca*, western-most point of Europe; fine cliff scenery. Then, still on N.247, round coast to *Cascais*, fishing village and seaside resort for *Lisbon*. Nearby is *Estoril*, fashionable winter resort; famous casino.

On coast road N.6. from *Estoril* back to *Lisbon* is Y.H. on shore of *Tagus* estuary at *Catalazete* near *Oeiras*.

R.2. Lisbon to Oporto (285 miles)

This route covers many places of interest and beauty along the narrow coastal plain from *Lisbon* to *Oporto*. It combines many sites of historic and artistic interest with fine beaches and coastal scenery, and pleasant and varied countryside.

Leave *Lisbon* by N.8 (due north) and follow road through *Loures* to *Torres Vedras* (40 miles), centre of wine producing region and a town with strong associations with Wellington in the Peninsular War; he was made Marquis of Torres Vedras by the Portuguese.

North-westwards, via *Lourinha* and *Areia Branca* (Y.H.) to *Peniche*; interesting fishing town; 17th century ramparts on edge of headland of impressive cliffs. Opposite lies island of *Berlenga*, worth a boat trip from *Peniche*.

15 miles inland (on N.114) is *Obidos*; small town on hill, surrounded by medieval walls and dominated by castle. Follow N.8 north through *Caldas da Rainha*–spa town, with fine Manueline church—and after 7 miles turn off to *S. Martinho do Porto* (Y.H.); peaceful fishing village in wide bay, with sandy beaches, connected with sea by narrow exit through cliffs; much less frequented by tourists than *Nazaré*, 7 miles north, a fishing village in two parts, one on the cliffs, one on the shore, connected by funicular. It has no harbour; the boats are launched from the beach into the Atlantic breakers. The fishermen wear distinctive clothes of rough wool tartan; their womenfolk wear dresses underlaid with many layers of petticoats.

8 miles inland is small town of *Alcobaça*, famous for the Cistercian monastery of Santa Maria founded by Afonso Henriques, the first king of Portugal, to commemorate the capture of *Santarém* from the Moors. The Gothic church with later additions is the largest in the country and contains the tombs of King Pedro I and his mistress, Inez de Castro.

13 miles NE along N.1 is the equally famous church of the monastery of Our Lady of Victory at *Batalha*, celebrating the victory of *Aljubarrota* (1385) over the Castilians. The victor, King João I, lies buried here in the Founder's Chapel with his Queen, Philippa of Lancaster (daughter of John of Gaunt) and their sons, of whom the most celebrated was Prince Henry the Navigator. A beautiful and impressive church, with some English influence in its design, and later pure Portuguese influence in the Manueline additions.

The next town along N.1 is *Leiria*, dominated by a medieval castle; ruins of Romanesque church of S. Pedro below castle; 16th century Renaissance cathedral. (14 miles west, through forest of *Leiria* is **Y.H.(M)** at *S. Pedro de Muel*, on the coast).

From *Leiria* continue on N.1 via *Pombal*—medieval castle of the Templars— and *Condeixa*—nearby Roman excavations at *Conimbriga*—to *Coimbra*.

Coimbra is the third city of Portugal and one of the oldest University cities in Europe. The University is in the upper town, high above the *Mondego*, and here there are buildings from the Romanesque to the modern. The old cathedral is Romanesque: the new cathedral is an 18th century building. The Machado de Castro Museum is in a former episcopal palace. In the lower town is the Monastery of Santa Cruz, founded by Afonso Henriques but rebuilt in the 16th century. In the Praça do Comercio is the church of S. Tiago, rebuilt in 18th century but retaining its Romanesque doorways.

Leave *Coimbra* by N.111, following north bank of the *Mondego* through several historically interesting villages to *Figueira da Foz*, a modern and popular seaside resort with fine sandy beaches.

North on N.109 through pinewoods and farmlands of *Beira Litoral* with its distinctive windmills and water-wheels. *Aveiro*, a fishing town on edge of land-locked lagoon; canals lined with houses with 16th and 17th century façades. Several interesting churches of same period. The lagoon can be seen by a trip along the road to the coast at *Barra*, or better still by boat from the town. Salt drying in shallow beds around lagoon.

From *Aveiro* N.109 north to *Ovar* and along coast to *Espinho*, a seaside resort; 10 miles farther is *Vila Nova de Gaia* on the south bank of the *Douro*, facing *Oporto*. Here are the great port wine "lodges" where the wine is prepared and blended for shipment. A visit to one of the lodges is well worth while and easily arranged.

Oporto is reached by crossing the gorge of the *Douro*; both road and railway bridges are bold 19th century works. Second city of Portugal; a busy commercial centre with long connections with England; many historic buildings; modern university. Church of *Cedofeita*, Romanesque with 17th century restorations. Church and convent of *Santa Clara*, Gothic and Renaissance with splendid gilding in interior. Cathedral Romanesque with considerable 18th century restorations. **Y.H.(M)** at *Matozinhos*.

R.3. Oporto to Valença (Spanish Frontier) (98 miles).

This route covers the far north of Portugal to the *Minho* province on the Spanish frontier.

Leave *Oporto* by N.14 via *Vila Nova de Famalicao* to **Braga**: an important town in Roman times—*Bracara Augusta*. Held by the Moors until 1040. Cathedral, Romanesque with Gothic and later additions; archbishop is primate of Portugal. Many fine 17th and 18th century buildings.

EXCURSIONS: a few miles E. and S.E. are two hill-top pilgrimage churches—*Bom Jesus do Monte* (18th century) and *Sameiro*; fine views towards mountains on Spanish frontier. Further E. from *Bom Jesus* is ancient Iberian hill fort at *Briteiros*. The wild granitic *Serra do Gerez* is best explored from *Caldas do Gerez*, 28 miles E.

Leave *Braga* by N.201. Two miles out in a suburb is the Byzantine church of *S. Frutuoso*, a unique pre-Moorish relic.

PORTUGAL

19 miles from *Braga* is *Ponte de Lima*: pleasant little town where road crosses river *Lima* by bridge built in 1360 on Roman foundations. From here follow N.202 on north bank of *Lima* down its lovely valley to *Viana do Castelo*; attractive seaport with Manueline and Renaissance architecture, interesting churches. Funicular to *Monte de Santa Luzia*, gives splendid views of the coast, the town and the *Lima* valley.

Leave *Viana* by N.13 which hugs coast as far as mouth of *Minho*. *Caminha*: attractive small town; main square with 15th century battlemented buildings, 16th century church and fountain.

Continue along delightful *Minho* valley, the frontier between Spain and Portugal, to *Valença*, a village with 17th century ramparts and Romanesque church. *Vigo* in Spain is 20 miles farther.

R.4.   Lisbon—Evora—Faro—Lagos—Lisbon (512 miles)

This route covers southern Portugal, first the *Alentejo*, then the *Algarve* in the far south. Moorish influence lasted longer, and population is sparser than in the north. The *Algarve* can be very hot in summer.

Leave *Lisbon* by N.10 (or by modern motorway), to *Vila Franca de Xira*: bull breeding centre; arena with frequent bull fights during summer season. Cross R. *Tagus* by modern toll bridge and across flat monotonous sparsely inhabited country for 28 miles; then turn left at cross-roads on to N.4 to *Vendas Novas*. Soon the *Alentejo* is entered and the scenery changes, with rolling country and many cork-oak trees. *Montemor-o-Novo*, small town dominated by castle. 15 miles further is *Arraiolos*, noted since Middle Ages for woollen carpets; more castle ruins. Continue on N.4 to **Estremôz**, picturesque hill town, surrounded by fortifications (17th century). Castle has original 13th century keep, with splendid views of surrounding countryside. Town Hall (once a convent) late 17th century, in the *Rossio*. Also *Misericordia* chapel and hospital Palacio Tocha (17th century) and Gothic church of the convent of *S. Francisco*.

Continue on N.4 to *Borba*, a town notable for extensive use of marble in its construction, then take N.255 to *Vila Viçosa*, famous for the 16th century marble palace of Dukes of Bragança, situated in a great square, together with a church and convent.

South-westwards on N.254 to **Évora**, one of most interesting towns in Portugal; dates back to Roman times; 2nd century Roman *temple of Diana* still stands; towns also retains most of its medieval walls. See the cathedral, battlement chapel of *S. Bras*, church of *S. Francisco* (Moorish-Gothic), the buildings of *Praça do Giraldo* and numerous fine houses and squares, mainly of 16th, 17th and 18th centuries.

51 miles south, across hilly country along N.18 lies *Beja*, also a town of Roman origin. Convent of *Conceiçao* (Gothic-Moorish façade); 13th century keep of castle. Roman arch of *Porta de Évora*.

Continue on N.18 to *Ervidel* (13 miles) and join N.2 to *Aljustrel*, a mining town. From here to *Castro Verde* road runs across flat wheat-growing plain.

From *Almodovar* ascent of *Serra do Malhão* begins, and after *Ameixial* the descent into the *Algarve*, with fine views down into the plain. Olive, almond, fig, mulberry and other fruit trees are to be seen mile after mile on the road to *Faro*—an ancient town, but most of its historic buildings destroyed by earthquakes.

EXCURSION: *Olhão*, 6 miles E., fishing port with canning industry, by lagoon separated from sea by long sand-bar; town of white cubic houses.

Leave *Faro* by N.125 to *S. João da Venda*, fork right (N.125.4) to *Loulé* in centre of some of loveliest *Algarve* countryside. 13th century church; town famous for number and variety of Moorish-style chimneys that adorn the houses. West along N.270 to rejoin N.125. *Alcantarilha*, picturesque village. 12 miles W. is fishing port of *Portimão*. Nearby ıs *Praia da Rocha*, excellent bathing, fine beaches and cliffs. Continue on N.125 to *Lagos* (Y.H.). Seaside resort and fishing port with many old houses; in the *Praça da Republica* is the Customs House where, at one time, slave markets were held. Remarkable cliff formations at *Ponta da Piedade*, 1 mile S.

EXCURSIONS (a) to Cape St. Vincent, 20 miles W along N.125. Wild barren plateau, ending in lofty cliffs around the cape. At *Ponta de Sagres* are the remains of Prince Henry the Navigator's fortress where he established his maritime school and planned the explorations which established Portugal's empire, now restored as Y.H. See particularly the stone compass dial in the courtyard. (b) to the *Serra de Monchique*, 26 miles N. via *Portimão* (N.125) and N.124 and N.266 to *Monchique*. The *Serra* form a range of beautiful hills commanding fine views, particularly from the peak of *Foia* (2,958 ft.) above village of *Monchique*.

Leave *Lagos* by N.120, which crosses *Serra de Espinhaço de Cão* to *Aljezur* and on to *Santiago do Cacém* at southern end of range of low hills notable for their windmills. 10 miles W. lies fishing village of *Sines*: harbour protected by rocky headland; birthplace of Vasco da Gama.

Continue on N.120 from *Santiago do Cacém*, first over hills, then across rice growing plain of river *Sado* (new bridge completed in 1966 is for motor vehicles only) to *Alcácer do Sal*. Here take N.5 for 20 miles and at village of *Marateca* take N.10 for *Setubal*, from which it is 24 miles to *Tagus* estuary at *Cacilhas* where ferry can be taken across to *Lisbon*.

EXCURSION: a pleasant diversion from *Setubal* is to *Sesimbra*, 16 miles W. along *Serra da Arrábida* (leave Lisbon road at *Vila Nogueira de Azeitão* and take N.379 to *Sesimbra*). Interesting fishing port set in a coast of splendid cliffs, with lovely views from the Serra.

SCOTLAND

Geographical Outline

Scotland is a country in its own right, differing from England and Wales in history, tradition, institutions and culture.

Land Scotland has an area of 30,405 sq. miles. Its mainland extends 274 miles from the *Mull of Galloway* in the south-west to *Cape Wrath* in the north. To the north lie the *Orkney* and *Shetland* island groups, the latter on the same latitude as Labrador and the southern tip of Greenland. Off the west coast lie the *Hebrides* and other islands. Some 114 islands are inhabited.

The mainland has four regions: the *Southern Uplands, Central Lowlands, Highlands* and *North-East Coastal Plain*—a layout mainly determined by the nature of the rocks out of which erosion has fashioned the scenery of today. The rocks of the *Central Lowlands* (Old Red Sandstone and Carboniferous) have proved less resistant than the older formations of the *Southern Uplands* and *Highlands* on either side and from which they are marked off by geological faults.

Another major fault, dividing the Highlands into two, has smashed the hard rocks along its course so completely that erosion of their debris has been easy and has produced the *Great Glen (Glen More)* from *Inverness* to *Fort William*. The scale of faulting has been such that the rocks on one side of the glen have travelled horizontally 65 miles past their opposite numbers on the other.

The Highlands have 543 summits over 3,000 ft. in height. They are the worn stumps of a range many million of years older than the Alps and were originally of comparable altitude. The glorious landscape of the *North-West Highlands* is the front of this ancient range.

Contemporary with the upheaval of the Alps, volcanoes were active, notably along the line of the present islands of *Arran, Mull, Rum* and *Skye*. The basaltic island of *Staffa*, including the famous *Fingal's Cave*, cut by the sea in columnar basalt, is part of a lava flow from *Mull*. A fine example of an extinct volcano is *Arthur's Seat* in *Edinburgh*.

Drowning of the western coast is seen not only in the numerous islands but also in the deep indentations of the sea lochs.

More recently the Ice Age contributed to the detailed shaping of the landscape, as in the corries and lake basins of the *Highlands* and, more particularly, the crag and tail sculpturing of the site of *Edinburgh* and the "parallel roads" of *Glen Roy*. In *Edinburgh* it is easy to see how the bottom currents of an eastward flowing glacier or ice-sheet were deflected by the resistant basalt of the *Castle Rock*, so that they gouged out the hollows of *Princes Street Gardens* and the *Grass Market*. In between they left a sheltered "tail"

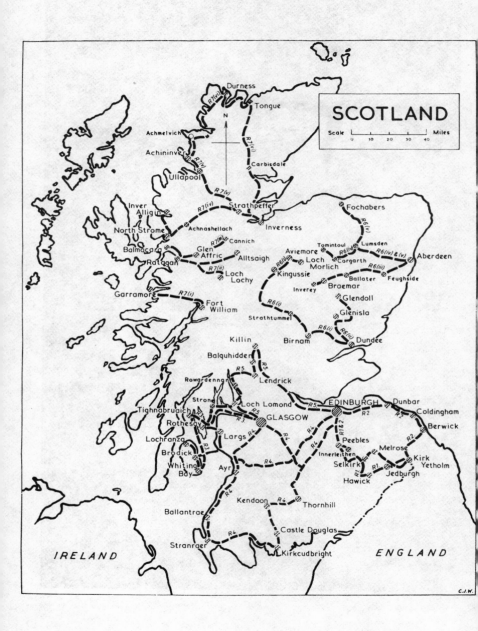

SCOTLAND

Scale ⊢——————————⊣ Miles
0   10   20   30   40

Durness
Tongue
R7(vii)
Achmelvich
Achininver
R7(vi)
Ullapool
R7(v)
Carbisdale
R7(iv)
Strathpeffer
Inver Alligin
Inverness
Fochabers
R6(v)
North Strome
Achnashellach
Balmacara
Glen Affric
Cannich
R7(iii)
Lumsden
Tomintoul
Ratagan
Alltsaigh
Aviemore
R6(ii)
Corgarth
R6(iv) & (v)
Aberdeen
R7(ii)
Loch Morlich
Loch Lochy
Kingussie
Ballater
Feughside
R6(iii)
Garramore
R7(i)
Fort William
Inverey
Braemar
Glendoll
Glenisla
Strathtummel
R6(i)
Glenisla
Killin
Birnam
R6(ii)
Dundee
Balquhidden
R5
R5
Rowardennan
Lendrick
Strone
Loch Lomond
R5
EDINBURGH
Dunbar
Tighnabruaich
R5
GLASGOW
Coldingham
Rothesay
R3
Largs
R4
R2
Berwick
Lochranza
R3
Peebles
R2
Brodick
Innerleithen
Melrose
Whiting Bay
Ayr
R4
Selkirk
Kirk Yetholm
R1
Jedburgh
Hawick
Kendoon
R4
Thornhill
Ballantrae
Castle Douglas
Stranraer
R4
Kirkcudbright

IRELAND

ENGLAND

C.J.W.

A mountain stream at Glencoe, Argyllshire, Scotland.

destined in after time to carry the *Royal Mile*. In *Glen Roy* the so-called "parallel roads" represent three terraces of former lakes which were temporarily dammed by glaciers at different levels.

Climate

The weather varies almost from hour to hour. Atlantic depressions particularly affect the north and bring high winds to the *Orkney* and *Shetland* islands. There is considerable difference in climate between east and west. Winters in the *Outer Hebrides* are mild, while in the north-east there may be heavy snow. Annual rainfall ranges from about 150 inches in the north-west to less than 26 inches in the *Lothians* and around the *Moray Firth*. Spring is generally the driest season. June is the finest month, especially along the western seaboard. July and August are warmer but wetter. September and October often provide good weather for the late holidaymaker. Long daylight is a feature of the northern summer.

Plants and Animals

The original extensive forests of Scots Pine which were the natural vegetation of most land below about 1,250 ft. were gradually destroyed through the expansion of cultivation, the need to drive out wolves and the use of timber for smelting, charcoal and shipbuilding. Remnants of the primeval forest remain in the Highlands, the best examples being the *Black Wood* of *Rannoch* in *Perthshire*, *Rothiemurchus Forest* in *Speyside* and the *Glen Affric* area.

On higher ground heather moorland is dominant on the poorer soils, but there are extensive areas of grass where conditions are more favourable.

A large number of Arctic-Alpine plants are widespread in the Highlands above the moorland. During June and July the rock ledges are festooned with flowers. Several species found at these high altitudes are relics of the Arctic flora which existed in Britain during the Ice Age. A flora with many of the same species is still found in Northern Canada, Greenland, Spitzbergen and Novaya Zemlya.

Red deer range over the Highlands and the Royal stags with their 12-pointed antlers make a splendid sight. Roe deer are found in the lower woodland. A herd of reindeer was introduced a few years ago to a reserve in *Speyside*. The wild cat, the most savage of British animals, is still common in the north, while the pine marten, once almost extinct, has found shelter in the increasing State forests.

The golden eagle with a wing span of up to eight feet is sometimes seen. The osprey, or white-tailed sea eagle, is again nesting in *Speyside*.

The People

Population

Scotland has rather more than five million inhabitants; three-quarters live in the industrial belt of the *Central Lowlands*. The shifting of population to the towns, common to so many countries, has been experienced in acute form and only about half-a-million now remain in rural areas. There has been great emigration, principally to Canada, the U.S.A. and New Zealand. Depopulation has been most serious in the *Highlands* and *Islands*; north of *Perth* there are now vast areas with only scattered houses.

SCOTLAND

There are four cities: *Glasgow* (1,050,000), *Edinburgh*, the capital, (476,000), *Aberdeen* (187,000) and *Dundee* (185,000).

The Scot is an amalgam of many races. Scots, Picts, Britons, Angles, Norsemen and Danes have all contributed something to the character of the people. Small groups of Flemish traders settled on the east coast and in more recent times the Irish have found in the industrial belt opportunities denied them in their native land.

The Highlanders, isolated by geography and language from the rest of the country, have retained longest their individual temperament, mode of life and culture.

Language The Scots tongue is more than a dialect of English. It has its own dialects, differing in pronunciation and vocabulary. In the common speech of the country people some words can be traced to the "Auld Alliance" over many centuries between Scotland and France or to the earlier Viking influence. In the old Norse colonies of *Orkney* and *Shetland*, especially, many Nòrse words survive. Many Scots who speak good English still seek out old Scots words or phrases to describe something graphically or to emphasise a point.

Gaelic is still spoken by some 90,000 people in the north and west, but all but a few are bi-lingual. The careful speech of many Highlanders is due to their thinking in an idiom completely different from English. Place names, including many in the southern counties, show the one time wide distribution of Gaelic.

Religion The Church of Scotland is presbyterian in organisation, i.e. its ministers are all of equal rank and are chosen by the congregation. Each parish is administered by a kirk session of elders. Among other presbyterian churches the most influential is the Free Church, which is strongest in the west and north-west Highlands, where strict Sabbatarian principles are maintained.

The Roman Catholic Church with some 780,000 members is strong in the industrial west where there are many people of Irish extraction In the Highlands and Islands there are Catholic communities, e.g. *Morar*, which remained unaffected by the Reformation.

The Scottish Episcopal Church is part of the Anglican communion.

History The Picts of the north baulked Rome in its aim to conquer the whole island of Britannia. Even the hold on the *Lowlands* was abandoned. The legions drew back from the *Antonine Wall* at the narrow neck between the *Firths of Forth* and *Clyde*. *Hadrian's Wall*, from the *Tyne* to the *Solway* became (A.D. 211) the northern frontier of the Empire.

Other invaders were perhaps better fitted to penetrate. By the 5th century the Scots, a Celtic people from Ireland, had established themselves in *Argyll*; the British (Welsh) held *Strathclyde* in the south-west; and Anglian people occupied *Lothian* in the south-east. The introduction (563) of Christianity from Ireland by St. Columba (following St. Ninian and St. Kentigern) ensured the dominance of Irish influences for 500 years. A united kingdom of *Alban* (of Picts and Scots, and later to be known as Scotland) was formed (843) under Kenneth Macalpine of *Dunstaffnage.* Meanwhile Norsemen had settled in the *Western Isles* and in *Orkney* and *Shetland* and by 875 they began to occupy the northern mainland. The kingdom annexed *Lothian* (1016); *Strathclyde* was united with it by dynastic succession in 1034.

English cultural influences become strong when Malcolm III married an English princess—the St. Margaret of Scottish history. Under David I (1124-53) a modified Norman feudal system was established. The Norsemen were pushed out of *Sutherland* and *Caithness* (1196), but English claims to overlordship of Scotland were the most pressing problem and led to the beginning (1200) of the "Auld Alliance" of Scotland and France. The defeat of Haakon of Norway by Alexander III at *Largs* (1263) ended the Norse supremacy in the *Western Isles.* (*Orkney* and *Shetland,* however, remained Norse until 1469 when they were acquired as a pledge for a marriage dowry). But on Alexander's death (1286) the whole kingdom passed to Margaret, the Maid of Norway. Her death on the voyage to Scotland left the throne open to many rival claimants. The English king, Edward I, acting as arbitrator, awarded it to John Balliol but insisted on his own supreme overlordship. The subsequent rebellion led by William Wallace, the seizing of the throne by Robert Bruce and his victory against the English army at *Bannockburn* (1314) are among the most stirring chapters of Scottish history.

The crowning of Bruce's grandson, Robert, the High Steward, as Robert II (1371) marks the beginning of the House of Stewart (Stuart), so fateful in the later story of England and Scotland. An important link with the Tudors, ruling in England, was the marriage (1503) of James IV to Margaret, daughter of Henry VII. But the alliance with France continued and provoked disastrous war with England.

Around the powerful figure of John Knox the Reformation gathered strength from 1559. Along with the Protestantism of Elizabethan England it was fatal to the spirited but tragic Mary, Queen of Scots. Her French connections, Catholic upbringing and capacity for intrigue were so dangerous to the new Protestant state as to lead to her execution in 1587. It was her son, James VI, who became James I of England at the Union of the Crowns (1603).

Stewart relations with Scotland on religious questions were no happier than with England. Most of the country had become Presbyterian and was resentful of Charles I's attempts at reaction. It therefore took the side of Cromwell in the English Civil War. For a time, during Cromwell's Protectorate, the two Parliaments were united at *Westminster.* After the Restoration of the Stewarts (1660) religious issues again clouded the relations between the kings and the Scottish people. Yet the loyalty of the *Highlands* to the Stewart House was seen in the revolt which was crushed at *Killiecrankie* (1689). It persisted after the Union of the Parliaments (1707). The rebellion (1715) in support of James Stewart, the Old Pretender, was followed by the more stirring and romantic rising (1745) around his son Charles Edward (Bonnie Prince Charlie), the Young Pretender, who met final defeat at *Culloden.*

SCOTLAND

The long-term result was the pacification of the *Highlands*, where the clans gave up their habit of raiding the industrious *Lowlands* and turned instead to arable cultivation wherever possible. But much of this work was undone by the Highland Clearances (1840) when thousands of inland crofters were either moved to the coast or forced to emigrate to make way first for sheep farms, later for deer preserves.

In other parts of the country the Industrial and Agrarian Revolutions took place at the same time as in England and with similar results.

Government Details of new legislation concerned solely with Scotland are considered at *Westminster* by the Scottish Grand Committee to which all Scottish members belong. Administration of many departments of government is carried out from *Edinburgh* under the Secretary of State for Scotland. The many and ancient differences between Scots and English law also necessitate separate Law Officers.

Resources Heavy industry has been the mainstay for more than a hundred years. There are shipyards on the *Clyde* and great new developments continue in the iron and steel industry which grew up on the *Lowland* coalfields. As the coal measures of the west become worked out new seams are opened in *Fife* and the *Lothians*. Other industries include jute (*Dundee*), granite (*Aberdeen*), chemicals (*Grangemouth*), thread (*Paisley*) and woollens (for which the *Border* towns have an international reputation). *Edinburgh* is primarily an administrative centre but has printing and associated industries and brewing.

Much of the abundant water of the *Highlands* has been harnessed for power. More than fifty hydro-electric stations have been built during the past twenty years.

More than two-thirds of the land is mountain, moorland or treeless deer forest. Of some 19 million acres, 10 million are rough grazing. Grass is the most important crop and the main produce is livestock: in the south-west, the world-famous Ayrshire dairy cattle and the hardy black Galloway; in the north-east, the Aberdeen-Angus and the Shorthorn. Sheep—the Blackface, Cheviot and Border Leicester—are plentiful. Intensive use is made of arable: along the east coast and around the *Moray Firth* is some of the best farmed land in the world. Most of the wheat is grown in the counties of *Fife*, *Angus*, *Perth* and the *Lothians*. Seed potatoes are an important export. Poultry keeping is on the increase. Eggs are the main produce of *Orkney*.

The type of agriculture carried on in the *Highlands* is known as crofting. There are some 20,000 crofts consisting usually of small areas of arable combined with common (i.e. shared) hill grazing. Crofts are to an increasing extent worked in combination with some other occupation such as fishing or catering for tourists.

Forestry has progressed rapidly in recent times. Of some 600,000 acres 500,000 have been planted by the *Forestry Commission* since 1919. Trees are now being planted in peaty soil formerly regarded as useless.

Sea fisheries are of greater relative importance than in England. Some 30 towns and 260 villages have for generations been dependent on fishing but there is now a trend towards centralisation. Most of the white fish catch is landed by trawlers based at *Aberdeen* and *Granton*. Scottish trawlers do not usually go so far as English trawlers and they cater more for the "quality" market. The value of the herring landed is over £2 million, but in the past 30 years this fish has been elusive and the markets of the Continent have largely disappeared.

Customs The Scots calendar retains survivals of Celtic and Norse festivals, Yule, the New Year, is still celebrated with Scandinavian fire rites such as the Burning of the Clavie at *Burghead* in *Moray*, the Fireballs ceremony at *Stonehaven*, Burning the Old Year Out at *Biggar* and the spectacular Up-Helly-a' at *Lerwick* in which a Viking galley is sacrificed to the flames.

Other customs include "first footing" in the "wee sma oors" of the New Year; handball games at *Jedburgh* and other Border towns at Candlemas (St. Bride's Day; 1st February); face washing in dew on *Arthur's Seat*, Edinburgh and crowning of a Beltane Queen at *Peebles* on Beltane (1st May). (Many of the Border Common ridings, although now spread over a period, are believed to have their origins in Beltane ceremonies); fairs at *Kirkwall, St. Andrews* and some other towns and the procession of the Burry Man (the spirit of vegetation) at *South Queensferry* at Lammas (1st August), traditionally a herd's festival. Hallowe'en (31st October), the season of the earth's decay, when our forefathers remembered their dead, is still a time when children (the guizers) dress up, blacken their faces and carry lanterns made of hollowed turnips. Bonfires lit at dusk show the Celtic origin of the night's festivities; the highlight of the children's parties—"dookin" for apples in a tub of water—is believed to have a Druidic origin.

Food and Drink Scots cookery is not sophisticated. But prime Scotch beef, salmon, grouse, venison and Scotch broth are worthy of any menu. The treament of fish has received most attention. These include the pale Finnan haddock, the coffee-coloured Arbroath smokie, the copper and gold Loch Fyne kipper and that delicate luxury smoked salmon. Oatmeal porridge with cream still competes with packaged breakfast cereals. There is of course the haggis, "chieftain o' the pudding race", which has a brief moment of glory at Burns suppers on 25th January.

Scots bakers are outstanding and there is a great variety of sweetcakes. Shortbread is world famous. Oatcakes with jam or cheese are excellent. In Scotland *pancakes* are English drop scones; *crumpets* are pancakes; *cookies* are buns. Buttery baps are well known in *Aberdeen* where the best are made. Among many other local pastries are *Forfar* bridies.

Skirlie, oatmeal fried with onions, is a tasty addition to a grill or fry. Athol brose, sometimes served as a sweet, is a potent mixture of whisky, cream and oatmeal, the proportions a well-guarded secret. Marmalade had its origin in *Dundee*.

SCOTLAND

Dress The kilt—the garb of the Gael—has increased in popularity with the open-air movement and the post-war revival of Scottish country dancing. In the Highlands, however, its wearing is regarded as the mark of the landlords. Despite bemedalled girl dancers at Highland Games it is a masculine garment. Traditional women's dress is worn by dancers at some Highland Games. On festive occasions another form is worn by the East Coast fisherwomen.

Sport The Highland Games—sports meetings which draw great numbers of visitors—originated in the gatherings of clansmen around their chiefs. The contests include tossing the caber (a tree trunk), putting the shot, throwing the hammer, wrestling, hill races, piping and Highland dancing. The principal gatherings are at *Braemar* and *Aboyne* in *Deeside*, *Lonach* in *Donside*, the Northern meeting in *Inverness* and the *Oban* and *Cowal* Games.

Golf had its origin in Scotland and there are few places without a course. Curling is another game which has spread from Scotland to many countries; indoor ice rinks have increased its popularity. Shinty—a vigorous form of hockey, with a dash of lacrosse—is a distinctly Scottish game which still has many enthusiasts in the *Highlands*. Bowling differs from the crown game played in much of England: the bias is built into the bowls and the greens are flat.

Association football is popular and rugby also has a large following. Seven-a-side tournaments—a variant introduced by rugby clubs in the *Borders*—provide fast-moving exciting games.

Culture

Architecture The broch, a circular defence tower with walls up to 16 feet thick, is found only in Scotland and is probably attributable to the Picts. The best example is at *Mousa* in *Shetland*. There are others in *Skye* and in *Glenelg*.

The oldest church is *St. Margaret's* chapel in *Edinburgh Castle*. The Romanesque is represented by *St. Regulus* in *St. Andrews*, *St. Magnus Cathedral* in *Kirkwall*, *Dunfermline Abbey*, the ruined abbeys of *Jedburgh* and *Kelso* and restored churches at *Iona*, *Dalmeny* and *Leuchars*. Gothic examples are *Glasgow Cathedral* and the ruins of *Arbroath*, *Dryburgh* and *Holyrood* abbeys and *Elgin Cathedral*. Decorated Gothic: *Sweetheart Abbey* near *Dumfries*, *Melrose Abbey* and *Dunblane Cathedral*. Notable examples of late Gothic are *St. Michael's, Linlithgow* and *St. Machar's Cathedral, Aberdeen*. This late period produced work of distinctively national character such as the open crown spires of *St. Giles', Edinburgh* and *King's College, Aberdeen*.

Castles show less outside influence than churches. Examples of domestic burgh architecture are preserved in most towns, but *Culross* near *North Queensferry* has the greatest number.

The era of the great architects and large mansions of the late 17th and 18th centuries is well represented. *Edinburgh University* was designed by Robert Adam, the architect of the classic revival. *Edinburgh's New Town* was built in the late 18th and early 19th centuries. *Glasgow School of Art* (1894) by Charles Rennie Mackintosh had a wide influence on the growth of the modern idiom on the Continent.

Music

The *Lowlands* have songs associated with Burns and the Jacobites and more modern songs inspired by Gaelic airs; *Hebridean* and *Highland* working songs, rowing songs and lullabies have great beauty. There has recently been a revival of country dance tunes, *reels, strathspeys* and other traditional forms. Bagpipe music— a developed form of folk music—reaches its most advanced level in the intricate *pibroch*.

Literature

The poems of Robert Burns—catching the very lilt and tone of Lowland Scots—have a unique place; he is popularly cherished and annually remembered in Burns' Night celebrations.

Scots writers have made notably spirited contributions to writing in standard English. They include James Thomson, the poet of *"The Seasons"*, Boswell, the biographer of Dr. Johnson, Thomas Carlyle and, among novelists, Smollett, Scott, R. L. Stevenson and John Buchan.

Science

Adam Smith's *"Wealth of Nations"* makes him the founder of political economy. Hugh Miller's *"Old Red Sandstone"* is a charming classic of writing on geology. The Scottish genius for practical application of knowledge is particularly well illustrated in the fields of transport and medicine. Telford, the engineer of canals and roads; Symington, the pioneer of steam navigation; and the inventors of the steam engine (James Watt), the bicycle (Kirkpatrick MacMillan) hard road surfaces (Macadam) and the pneumatic tyre (J. B. Dunlop)—all were Scots, as also were Simpson, the first user of chloroform as an anaesthetic; Lister, the pioneer of antiseptic surgery; and Fleming, the discoverer of penicillin.

Museums

In addition to the large collections in *Edinburgh* and *Glasgow*, (see Touring Routes), others of special interest include the *Albert Institute, Dundee* (whaling), *Dudhope Museum, Dundee* (archaeological and technological), *Aberdeen Art Gallery Museum* (wild life, natural resources and history of the north-east), *Marischal College Museum, Aberdeen* (prehistoric), *Inverness Museum* (Highland relics), *West Highland Museum, Fort William* (tartans, Jacobite treasures and weapons), folk museums at *Glamis* and *Kingussie*, Hugh Miller's cottage at *Cromarty*, Burns' cottage, *Ayr* and David Livingstone's birthplace at *Blantyre*. There are many local museums in the *Borders*.

SCOTLAND

Touring Information

Hostelling has long been accepted as part of the everyday life of Scotland and youth hostellers will find themselves welcome.

Transport   Trains provide the fastest means of long distance travel; bus services in the more populous areas are good. In remote districts services are maintained by small operators often on a one-bus-a-day basis. Steamer services on the Clyde are operated by a subsidiary of British Rail; the western mainland and the islands are served by David MacBrayne's steamships.

There are no train, bus or ferry services in the *Western Highlands* and *Islands* on Sundays.

Money   Scottish banks issue their own pound notes and although these are legal tender in England it may save some argument if they are exchanged for Bank of England notes before returning south.

Clothing   Ordinary English out of doors kit with the addition of a heavy sweater (or better two thin ones), or wind-proof jacket is all that is required by the ordinary traveller. Midge cream is recommended for summer use. Clegs (horse flies) are persistent attackers in bracken and heather.

Restaurants   Cheap if you find the right place. It is worth seeking local guidance for it is possible to get a meal for about 40p while the more pretentious places will charge 70p to £1 for the same food. High tea is the great Scottish meal and usually consists of fish or an egg dish, tea, scones and cakes. Good value almost everywhere. Mutton pies are traditional fare.

Fish and chips is now a national institution. A northern variation is chips and an oatmeal pudding which sometimes appears on the bill of fare as a "mealie jimmy". It is quite customary to carry away these delicacies wrapped in the daily newspaper.

Maps and Guide Books   For walkers, the *Ordnance Survey* maps, scale 1 inch to 1 mile, 78 sheets at 50p each. Particularly useful for cyclists are *Bartholomew's* ½ inch to 1 mile series, 24 sheets at 30p each. The *Ordnance Survey* ¼ inch to 1 mile series are useful general maps. *S.Y.H.A.* map of Scotland, 12 miles to 1 inch, showing hostels, 10p.

SCOTLAND

Regional guides include those published by (a) *Her Majesty's Stationery Office* for the *Forestry Commission*: *National Forest Park Guides* to *Argyll*, 35p, *Forests of N. East Scotland*, 25p, *Glen More (Cairngorms)*, 45p, *Queen Elizabeth (Ben Lomond, Loch Ard and the Trossachs)*, 60p; (b) *the S.Y.H.A.*: *Arran*; *Garth and Glen Lyon*: each 8p, *Glencoe and Glen Nevis*; *Edinburgh and the Borders*; *Skye*; each 10p, *Loch Lomond and the Trossachs*, 10p.

Climber's Guides, detailing rock climbing routes in the main areas are published by the *Scottish Mountaineering Club*.

Accommodation — There are about 90 youth hostels, providing good coverage for every touring area. Meals are only provided at a few hostels. Periods during which advance booking is advised are stated separately for each hostel in the *S.Y.H.A.* handbook.

For other accommodation see same section in Touring Information, England and Wales.

Camping — The same as for England and Wales.

Walking — The country provides an inexhaustible variety of experience for the walker, particularly for the tough and strenuous; but tours of all grades are possible.

Mountaineering — Most of the mountains rise either directly from the sea or from low-lying glens and so gain the full advantage of their comparatively moderate height. This fact, and the possibility of experiencing very severe (even sub-Arctic) conditions on their upper parts, makes proper preparation essential.

Of the vast tracts of uninhabited mountain country the finest is the *Cairngorm* area. The *Cuillins (Glenbrittle* Y.H.) and *Glencoe* (Y.H.) provide innumerable rock climbs of all grades of difficulty. In the north a number of fascinating peaks—among them *Liathach, Beinn Eighe, An Teallach* and *Stac Polly*—give good climbing and ridge walking. *Ben Nevis*, Scotland's highest mountain (4,406 ft.) can be easily reached by the path from *Glen Nevis* (Y.H.), but its great northern precipices offer superb rock climbing. In the *Loch Lomond* area the *Arrochar* peaks, near *Ardgartan* (Y.H.), offer enjoyable excursions and a training ground in rock climbing for the longer climbs further north. There is excellent rock climbing in the *Isle of Arran*.

Ski-ing — In good conditions ski-ing can be as good as at the best resorts in Norway and Central Europe. But weather conditions change quickly. The most stable snow conditions are in the *Cairngorms* (Y.Hs. at *Loch Morlich, Aviemore* and *Kingussie*) where the best time is in March and April. There is snow in January and February, and even in December, but bad weather then often makes ski-ing difficult.

SCOTLAND

In January and February, the *Southern Grampians* are most frequented as their weather is less severe than in the *Cairngorms* and the hostels at *Glen Clova* (*Glendoll*), *Glenisla*, *Garth* and *Killin* are nearer for week-end skiers. In the west, there is a reliable snow field on *Meall a'Bhuiridh* in *Glencoe* (with ski and chair lift) a few miles from *Glencoe* (Y.H.). *S.Y.H.A.* runs courses in ski-ing (and hires skis) at *Glenisla* and *Loch Morlich* (Y.H.).

Cycling Even on small by-roads surfaces are generally good, and such roads should particularly be taken in the south, where there is much traffic on main roads. They are, in any case, much more picturesque. In the north, main roads are crowded only in July and August. Distances between hostels in the north-west are just right for easy cycling.

A low gear is an advantage for some of the steep hills, particularly in the north, and also to counter strong winds on exposed moorland routes.

Canoeing The finest canoeing is among the many fjords, inlets and islands of the West coast, but experience is required because of tides and currents. The best area is round the *Firth of Clyde*. The whole of the coast has been canoed. The extreme north, however, is very stormy and should be visited only after long apprenticeship in calmer waters.

The principal rivers are the *Spey*, *Tay* and *Tweed*, but care requires to be exercised not to interfere with fishing interests. The fastest is the *Spey*. The *Tay*, near *Stanley* (just north of *Perth*) affords a magnificent stretch of white water which is used for the Scottish Slalom Championships. The *Tweed* is suitable, usually, only in spring and autumn as it is generally too low in summer. The finest resort for the average canoeist is *Loch Lomond* with its many bays and islands. For a first visit a *S.Y.H.A.* canoe course based at *Rowardennan* Y.H. is recommended. Visitors intending to undertake canoe trips in Scotland are advised to write to the Secretary of the *Scottish Canoe Association*, 1 Ashburn Gardens, Gourock.

Sailing As with canoeing, the west coast and the *Clyde Estuary* are the finest areas although there is a great deal of sailing on the *Firth of Forth* and *Firth of Tay*. *S.Y.H.A.* Sailing Courses are held at *Oban* and at *Tighnabruaich* on the *Kyles of Bute*. Dinghy sailing is popular; at most seaside resorts there are weekly races in which visitors can generally take part.

Fishing Brown trout, sea trout and salmon abound in the lochs, rivers and streams. Much of the fishing is privately owned and strictly preserved, but a large part is controlled by local angling associations who, for a modest charge, will issue permits to individual anglers to fish by the day, week or month. They are non profit-making concerns; fees received go towards re-stocking and to improvement of the fishing generally.

Many private owners of trout fishings will give permission for a day's fishing now and again to any angler who asks for it. Some never refuse, believing that the presence of anglers on the water acts as a deterrent to poachers who take fish other than by means of rod and line. Most of the salmon fishing is necessarily strictly preserved, but some good sport can be obtained on payment of very reasonable fees.

Pony Trekking This is popular in summer. The *Borders*, the *Angus Glens*, *Deeside* and *Speyside* are the main centres but in many other areas ponies—usually Icelandic, Exmoor or the sturdy Highland "garron"—are available for those who want to get away from the beaten tracks. There are hostel courses in the *Borders* at *Snoot* (Y.H.) and *Melrose* (Y.H.) and, in the Highlands, at *Ballater* (Y.H.).

Edinburgh

Edinburgh occupies one of the finest sites of any city in the world. Its "New Town" (1767) is a famous example of 18th century town planning. Best starting point is the **Castle**; view of city from ramparts; Regalia of Scotland; from half-moon battery is fired city's time signal, the one o'clock gun. **Scottish National War Memorial** crowns highest part of rock. Oldest part of *Castle* is 11th century *St. Margaret's Chapel*.

Between *Castle* and **Palace of Holyroodhouse** (chief royal residence in Scotland) stretches the *"Royal Mile"* which, with the closes and wynds on either side, was *Old Edinburgh*. *Outlook Tower* and *Camera Obscura* (view of *Princes Street, Forth* and hills beyond). **Greyfriars Churchyard** where the National Covenant was signed in 1638, and **National Library of Scotland** (see exhibition rooms) are both in *George IV Bridge*. **Royal Scottish Museum** in *Chambers Street*.

Separated from *Old Edinburgh* by *Princes Street Gardens* is the **New Town** with spacious streets and handsome squares. In *West Princes Street Gardens* is famous *Floral Clock* and *Scots-American War Memorial*. **Scott Monument** in *East Princes Street Gardens* may be climbed. Between the two gardens is the *Mound*; at foot is **Royal Scottish Academy**, behind which is **National Gallery**.

At E. end of **Princes Street** (one of most beautiful streets in the world) is **Calton Hill**, more remarkable for view from it than for its monuments.

National Portrait Gallery and (in the same building) **Museum of Antiquities** are in *Queen Street*. **Royal Botanical Gardens**, N. of *New Town*, finely laid out.

International Festival of Music and Drama, 3 weeks annually, late August and early September.

EXCURSIONS: (a) Linlithgow Palace, birthplace of Mary, Queen of Scots; (b) Forth Bridge and new road bridge at *Queensferry;* Dunfermline Abbey, burial place of King Robert Bruce; (c) Culross, a whole 17th century village of great architectural interest. Y.Hs. Eglinton Crescent and Bruntsfield Crescent.

Touring Routes
The Borders

A close-knit region, in the valleys of which are many towns rich in history. Excellent touring country for the cyclists. The intervening hills provide fine walking.

R.1. Walking Tour: Peebles—Kirk Yetholm—Peebles (110 miles)

Peebles, on R. *Tweed*. Bus, 6 miles, to *Innerleithen* where tour begins. Cross river to *Traquair* and by hill path over *Minchmuir* (1,856 ft.) to *Broadmeadows* (Y.H.), 8 miles, above *Yarrow Water*.

Selkirk, 5 miles, town on hill above *Ettrick Water*; statues of Sir Walter Scott and Mungo Park; *Abbotsford*, 5 miles, Scott's home, containing many relics; *Melrose*, 4 miles, small town with famous abbey ruins (Cistercian, 1136) (Y.H.).

EXCURSION: *Eildon Hills* (1,385 ft.) and ruins of Dryburgh Abbey, finely situated by *Tweed*: return by *Old Melrose and Newstead* (Roman fort, *Trimontium*).

Bus to *Jedfoot*. Walk to *Jedfoot Station*, then by Roman road SE over *Shibden Hill* to *Hounam*, 10 miles; path to *Bowmont Water* and *Kirk Yetholm* (Y.H.), 6 miles, northern terminus of *Pennine Way*.

Morebattle, *Oxnam* and *Mossburnfoot* to *Ferniehirst Castle*, 15 miles, (Y.H.).

Main road to **Jedburgh**, 2 miles; ruins of **Abbey** (12th century); *Queen Mary's House* in *Queen Street*, relics of Mary Queen of Scots. Bus up *Teviotdale* to **Hawick**, chief town of Roxburghshire. Walk, 6 miles, *Snoot* (Y.H.).

By *Ale Water* and *Wollrig* to *Ettrick Water*, and by *Bowhill* to *Broadmeadows* (Y.H.), 14 miles.

Bus up *Yarrow Water* to *Douglas Farm* (near *Gordon Arms Hotel*). Walk by *Stake Law* (1,784 ft.) and *Glen Sax* to *Peebles*, 11 miles, and by river path 3 miles, to *Barns*.

R.2. Cycling Tour: Edinburgh—Melrose—Berwick—Dunbar—Edinburgh (190 miles) (*For details see R.1*)

Edinburgh (Y.H.) to *Peebles* (visit *Neidpath Castle*), *Barns* 26 miles.

Innerleithen Traquair, *Gordon Arms* and down *Yarrow Water* to *Broadmeadows* (Y.H.), 30 miles.

Selkirk, *Abbotsford*, *Melrose Abbey* 12 miles.

Newstead (Roman fort, *Trimontium*), *St. Boswells*, *Dryburgh Abbey* and *Wallace Monument*, **Jedburgh**, *Ferniehirst Castle* (Y.H.), 17 miles.

Jedburgh, *Eckford* to *Kirk Yetholm*, 19 miles.

Cornhill, *Flodden Field* (site of battle, 1513); *Norham Castle*; **Berwick**; *Eyemouth*, fishing village; *Coldingham*, 36 miles, (Y.H.) (Bathing; coastal scenery: *St. Abb's Head*; *Coldingham Priory*).

Dunbar, 17 miles, and through fertile *East Lothian* countryside and *Haddington*, (county town, many interesting buildings, statue of John Knox). *Edinburgh*, 31 miles, (Y.H.).

The Clyde Coast and Isle of Arran

There are several holiday resorts along the southern shores. The islands of *Arran* and *Bute* are within easy reach, the former with a compact group of peaks for the hill walker. The sea lochs of the northern shores are well worth exploring.

R.3. Glasgow — Tighnabruaich — Arran — Strone — Loch Lomond (175 miles)

Glasgow, (Y.H.); largest city and chief seaport; famous ship-building yards; many industries. Gothic *Cathedral of St. Mungo* with fine 12th century crypt. *Art Gallery and Museum* (in *Kelvingrove Park*), chief European schools of painting well represented; *Pollok House*, 3 miles S., also has good art collections.

Steamer, from *Bridge Wharf*, down **Firth of Clyde** and through **Kyles of Bute** to *Tighnabruaich* (Y.H.).

Steamer (occasional direct service) to *Whiting Bay* **(Y.H.), Isle of Arran.**
EXCURSIONS (a) *Kildonan Castle*, 4 miles, and fine coast from *Bennan Head* to *Dippin Head;* (b) *Holy Island* and *Cave of St. Molies* (Runic inscriptions); (c) *Glen Ashdale* and hills behind hostel.

Lamlash, 5 miles; path over *Clauchland Hills* to *Brodick*, 5 miles, (Y.H.).
EXCURSIONS: (a) Goatfell (2,866 ft.); (b) ridge walk, *Ben Nuis, Ben Tarsuinn, Beinn a Chliab hain:* (c) ridge walk, *Goatfell, Cir Mhor, Beinn a Chliabhain:* (d) walk by *Glen Rosa* and *Glen Sannox* to *Corrie:* return by coast.

Continue, walk or bus, to *Lochranza*, 14½ miles, (Y.H.).
EXCURSION: *Catacol Bay, Lennymore Church* and *Coire an Lochain.*

Return to *Brodick;* steamer to *Ardrossan* or *Fairlie;* bus to *Largs;* steamer to *Rothesay* and *Dunoon.*
EXCURSION: *Benmore Forest* and *Puck's Glen* (arboretum) in *Strath Eachaig.*

Blairmore, 2 miles; steamer to *Craigendoran.* Train to *Balloch.* Walk, 2 miles, **Loch Lomond (Y.H.).**
EXCURSIONS: (a) steamer trips on *Loch Lomond*; (b) *Gareloch.*

The South-West

The magic of Robbie Burns draws people towards *Ayrshire,* but *Galloway* the *Stewartry* (*Kirkcudbrightshire*) and *Dumfriesshire* are being discovered by tourists. The coastal scenery varies from magnificent rocky headlands to great stretches of sand. Inland lies some of the finest scenery of the south.

R.4 Glasgow (or Edinburgh) to Kirkcudbright, Stranraer and Ayr (280 miles)

At *Abington* (43 miles from *Glasgow*, 40 miles from *Edinburgh*), in upper *Clydesdale*, B.797 S.W. up *Glengonnar Burn* to *Leadhills* and *Wanlockhead*, 8½ miles, (1,380 ft.) (Y.H.), highest village in Scotland; centre for walks.
EXCURSIONS: (a) *Lowther Hills* and *Enterkin Pass:* (b) *Wanlock Water:* (c) by *Willowgrain Hill* to *Sanquhar*, 10 miles, town famous in Presbyterian history.

B.797 to *Mennock*, 8 miles. Up *Nithsdale* to *Thornhill*, 10 miles, across *Nith* to *Penpont*, 2 miles. (*Keir*, 1½ miles S.E., birthplace of Kirkpatrick Mac-Millan, inventor of bicycle (1839); tablet in *Courthill Smithy*). *Maxwelton*, 3 miles, birthplace of "Annie Laurie". *Moniaive; High Bridge of Ken; Kendoon* (Y.H.), 17 miles.
EXCURSIONS: (a) *Lochinvar*, home of Scott's *"Young Lochinvar":* (b) ridge walks on *Rhinns of Kells* (2,668 ft.); (c) *Cairnsmore of Carsphairn* (2,612 ft.).

Castle Douglas, 20 miles (*Carlingwark Loch* and *Threave Castle*). *Kirk-cudbright*, 10 miles, handsome small town on *Dee* estuary.

SCOTLAND

Cardoness Castle, 1 mile, (view from tower). Along beautiful coast road to *Dirk Hatteraick's Cave;* ruins of *Barholm Castle* and *Carsluith Castle. Creetown,* 11 miles. *Newton Stewart,* 6 miles, finely situated market town of cattle raising district of *Galloway.* **Y.H.** at *Minnigaff. Glenluce Abbey,* 15 miles. *Stranraer,* 10 miles, for ferry to Larne, Northern Ireland.

EXCURSIONS: (a) *Mull of Galloway,* via *Kirkmadrine* church, sub-tropical garden of *Logan House* and sea-fish pond at *Port Logan;* (b) **Loch Trool** and *Glen Trool National Forest Park* (camping site at *Caldons*); (c) *Whithorn,* site of first Christian church in Scotland, built by St. Ninian, 397; museum has well-known early lettered stones and crosses.

N. by *Loch Ryan, Glen App, Ballantrae,* valley of R. *Stinchar* to *Pinwherry,* returning to coast at **Girvan,** 35 miles, fishing port and resort. Motor boat to **Ailsa Craig,** 10 miles, precipitous granite rock islet (1,114 ft.), bird sanctuary, breeding place of solan goose.

Kirkoswald: the country of "Tam o' Shanter"; *Culzean Castle,* 18th century building in Gothic style by Robert Adam; fine interior; gardens; *Auld Brig o' Doon, Alloway Kirk, Burns Monument, Burns' Cottage and museum. Ayr.* 22 miles. **(Y.H.).**

EXCURSIONS: (a) *Brown Carrick* (912 ft.), 6 miles S.W., very extensive view; (b) *Crossrague Abbey* (Cluniac, 13th century, fine ruins), 12 miles S.

Tarbolton, 8 miles, (*Burns' Bachelors' Club*); *Mossgiel,* where Burns farmed; *Burns Memorial and Museum*: *Mauchline,* 5 miles, *cottage of "Poosie Nansie".*

From *Mauchline* either NW. by *Symington* and *Dundonald* (castle) and N. by ancient burgh of *Kilmaurs* to *Glasgow,* 36 miles, **(Y.H.);** or by *Sorn, Muirkirk, Carstairs* and *Carnwath* to *Edinburgh,* 62 miles, **(Y.H.).**

Loch Lomond, Trossachs and Central Highlands

This, the best known and most readily accessible part of the Highlands, has much beautiful scenery, hills for climbers and walkers, and many lochs.

R.5. Balloch to Killin and either Edinburgh (130 miles) or Fort William (165 miles)

Balloch (bus from *Waterloo Street Station, Glasgow*). *Loch Lomond* **(Y.H.)** Walk, 2 miles to steamer (June to mid-September) or bus to *Balmaha.* Walk, 7 miles, *Rowardennan* **(Y.H.)** (or steamer all way).

EXCURSIONS: (a) **Ben Lomond** (3,192 ft.) by track in 3 hours. (b) Path along banks of *Loch Lomond* through *Craig Rostan* to *Inversnaid.*

Steamer *Inversnaid*; walk, 4 miles, *Stronachlachar* on *Loch Katrine*: steamer to *Trossachs Pier*; walk, 4 miles, through woods and along shore of *Loch Achray* to *Brig o' Turk* **(Y.H.)** and *Lendrick* on *Loch Vennachar.*

EXCURSIONS: the many walks and climbs include (a) **Ben A'an** (1,750 ft.), best viewpoint, 1½ hours from *Trossachs Hotel*; (b) **Ben Venue** (2,393 ft.).

Continue by road N. from *Brig o' Turk* to *Achnahard* and by track up *Gleann nam Meann* to top of pass; descend to ford (boggy ground) and cross to cart track to *Bailemore*; road to *Balquhidder,* 12 miles.

EXCURSIONS: (a) several walks along shores of **Loch Voil** (associations with Rob Roy, who is buried in churchyard); (b) hill walks on *Braes of Balquhidder*: (c) ascents: **Stobinian** (3,921 ft.); **Ben More** (3,845 ft.), very extensive view.

SCOTLAND

Path over *Kirkton Pass* through forestry plantation and down to *Ledchary*, 6 miles, in *Glen Dochart*; road to *Killin Junction*, 2 miles; train to *Killin* (Y.H.), at head of *Loch Tay*.

EXCURSIONS: (a) *Stronachlachan* (1,708 ft.), 1 hour, view of Loch and *Ben Lawers*: (b) *Finlarig Castle* and *Falls of Lochay*, 4 miles; (c) Ben Lawers (3,984 ft.); (d) walks on S. side of *Loch Tay*: (e) *Glen Ogle*.

Train to **Stirling**, 40 miles, (Y.H.) historic burgh; *Castle*: *Argyll's Lodging* (17th century) and other old houses; *Wallace Monument. Dunblane*, 6 miles. Beautiful Gothic *cathedral*. Site of *Battle of Bannockburn* (1314) 2 miles S. of *Stirling. Edinburgh*, 36 miles. (Y.H.).

Alternatively continue to **Western Highlands.**

Crianlarich, 14 miles, (Y.H.), many splendid hill walks. *Tyndrum*, 5 miles; *Dalmally*, 12 miles. By foot of *Loch Awe* and *Falls of Cruachan*, 7 miles. *Pass of Brander*, under *Ben Cruachan* (3,689 ft.). *Taynuilt*, 6 miles; road follows *Loch Etive* to **Oban**, 12 miles, (Y.H.) route centre for *Western Highlands* and *Islands*, finely situated on *Sound of Kerrara*.

EXCURSIONS: by steamer (a) *Staffa*, uninhabited island, famous basaltic formations, **Fingal's Cave** and other caves; and Iona, St Columba's island: *St. Oran's Chapel* (Romanesque) and historic *Cemetery*, ancient crosses; **Cathedral** (16th century); **Abbey**, rebuilt by Iona Community; (b) *Tobermory* (Y.H.), Island of Mull. Many other excursions by land and sea.

Ballachulish, 34 miles by rail, 37 by road. Glencoe (Y.H.), 2½ miles. Centre for experienced walkers and climbers.

EXCURSIONS: (a) Site of Massacre (1692), *Bridge of Coe, Clachaig*: (b) **Five Valleys walk:** morning bus 5½ miles up Glen; footpath S. along *Allt Lairig Eilde* to *Dalness*: down *Glen Etive* to school ¾ mile S. of *Invercharnan*: follow *Allt nan Gaoirean* and cross to *Caol Creran*: from *Corbhainn* W. below *Meall an Aodainn* to bridle road from *Glen Creran* and along it to *East Laroch* and *Glencoe*, 19 miles; (c) Bidean nam Bian (3,766 ft.); (d) **Aonach Eagach,** formidable ridge route, needing a head for heights; take local advice.

Ballachulish Ferry; *Onich*, and by shores of *Loch Linnhe* to **Fort William,** 15 miles. *Glen Nevis* (Y.H.) 3 miles. (See R.7). For walkers, fine route in good weather by *Gleann Seileach, Beinn na Gucaig* (2,017 ft.), splendid view, and N.E. to old military road to *Fort William*, 10 miles.

EXCURSIONS: **Ben Nevis** (4,406 ft.), highest mountain in British Isles; many other walks and climbs.

The Eastern Grampians

North-east of *Glen Garry* is the most extensive continuous upland region dominated in the north by the *Cairngorms* and in the east by the *Braes of Angus*. Among its famous rivers are the *Dee*, the *Don*, and the *Spey*. Its hills, though closely preserved for deer forest and grouse, have become a great mountain playground for walking, ski-ing and pony trekking. Separated from the *Cairngorms* by *Strath Spey* are the little-known *Monadhliath Mountains*, a haunt of the eagle, drained by the *Findhorn*, one of the most beautiful of Scottish rivers.

The route is divided into five sections, each penetrating the hills by different valleys.

371

SCOTLAND

R.6(1). Perth or Dundee to Birnam, Kingussie, Aviemore and Loch Morlich (100 or 116 miles)

Perth (Y.H.) or Dundee (Y.H.), to *Birnam* 14 or 30 miles;
EXCURSION: Dunkeld, old town and ruined cathedral, finely situated on *R. Tay.*

Leave *Strath Tay* at *Ballinluig,* 9 miles, and by *R. Tummel* to **Pitlochry,** 5 miles (see fish ladder for passage of salmon). W. at *Bridge of Garry.* Strath-*tummel* (Y.H.), 7 miles. Boating and fishing; good walking centre.
EXCURSIONS: (a) *Queen's View* and road S. side of *Loch Tummel;* (b) *Ben Vrackie* (2,757 ft.), easy route by path from *Moulin.*

Pass of Killiecrankie to *Blair Atholl,* 8 miles. Road and rail follow lonely *Glen Garry* to cross *Pass of Drumochter* (1,484 ft.) to *Dalwhinnie,* 24 miles. **Kingussie,** 14 miles, (Y.H.), on *R. Spey; Highland Museum;* many walks. **Aviemore,** 12 miles, (Y.H.).
EXCURSIONS: (a) *Loch an Eilean* and *Wolf of Badenoch's Castle;* (b) *Loch Einich (Eunach)*: Braeriach (4,248 ft.) from *Glen Einich* (not in stalking season): (c) *Dulnain Valley* in Mona-dhliath Mts.

Loch Morlich, 7 miles, (Y.H.).
EXCURSIONS: Ascents include Cairn Gorm (4,084 ft.) and Ben Macdhui (4,296 ft.).

R.6(2). Dundee to Glenisla and Glendoll (38 miles)

Dundee (Y.H.); *Alyth,* 17 miles; *Glenisla* (Y.H.), 9 miles.
EXCURSIONS: (a) *Mount Blair:* (b) *Canlochan Glen Glas* and *Maol* (3,502 ft.), source of *R. Isla.*

Glendoll (Y.H.), 12 miles by hill route (or from *Kirriemuir,* 19 miles, by *Glen Clova*); walking and climbing centre.

R.6(3). The Dee. Aberdeen to Ballater, Braemar and Inverey (64 miles)

Aberdeen (Y.H.), port and third city; "the granite city". *Old Aberdeen, King's College, Cathedral of St. Machar; Bridge of Balgownie* (14th century); *Harbour* and *Fish Market; Art Gallery and Museum; Brig o' Dee; Rubislaw Granite Quarry.*

A.943 on S. bank of *R. Dee* to *Brig o' Feugh* and *Feughside,* 20 miles
EXCURSIONS: (a) *Kerloch* (1,747 ft.) and *Glen Dye;* (b) *Forest of Birse:* (c) *Crathes Castle.*

Continue up *Dee* valley; *Banchory; Aboyne* (Highland Gathering, 1st week September). **Ballater,** 11 miles, (Y.H.).
EXCURSIONS: (a) *Craigendarroch, Pass of Ballater, Bridge of Gairn* and riverside track to *Ballater;* (b) *Pananich, Cambus o' May, Vat Burn, Loch Kinord:* (c) *Glen Gairn* and *Morven* (2,862 ft.): (d) *Glen Muich* and *Mount Keen* (3,077 ft.).

Crathie Church, 7 miles, closely associated with the Royal Family. **Balmoral Castle,** 1 mile, residence of the Queen. *Invercauld Bridge,* 6 miles. **Braemar,** 3 miles, (Y.H.) (Braemar Games, early September).
EXCURSIONS: (a) *Creag Choinnich* (1,764 ft.); (b) *Morrone* (2,819 ft.) view; (c) **Lochnagar** (3,786 ft.); (d) *Ben Avon* (3,843 ft.); (e) *Ben a Bhuird* (3,924 ft.).

Inverey, 4½ miles (Y.H.), at S. end of **Larig Ghru** route.
EXCURSIONS: (a) *Glen Ey* and *Colonel's Bed:* (b) *Glen Lui* and Ben Macdhui (4,296 ft.); (c) *Loch Etchachan* and Loch Avon; (d) *Pools of Dee* (source) and Braeriach (4,248 ft.) or Cairn Toul (4,241 ft.).

R.6(4). The Don. Aberdeen to Corgarff and Tomintoul (63 miles)

Aberdeen. By valley of R. *Don. Alford*, 26 miles; *Kildrummy Castle*, 10 miles; *Glenbuchat Castle*, 5 miles; *Strathdon*, 7 miles; *Corgarff* (Y.H.) 9 miles.
EXCURSION: *Sources of Don, Inchrory* and *Ben Avon* (3,843 ft.).
Continue by old military road (the *Lecht*) to *Tomintoul*, 11 miles, (Y.H.), centre for walks in *Strath Avon*.

R.6(5). Lower Spey and Lower Findhorn. Alford to Fochabers (33 miles)

1 mile N. of *Kildrummy* turn N. from *Don* valley. *Huntly*, 14 miles, town and castle; *Keith*, 11 miles; *Fochabers*, 8 miles, on R. *Spey*.
EXCURSIONS: (a) Elgin, ancient royal burgh, ruined cathedral; (b) *Forres*, 20 miles, for beautiful lower Findhorn Valley, *Findhorn Estuary* and *Culbin Sands.*

Hill routes between hostels, linking the above sections are: *Inverey* (R.6(3)) to (a) *Kingussie* (R.6(1)) by *Glen Feshie*; (b) *Aviemore* (R.6(1)) by *Larig Ghru*; (c) *Loch Morlich* (R.6(1)) by *Larig Ghru* or by *Shelter Stone* and *Glen Derry*; *Glenisla* (R.6(2)) to *Braemar* (R.6(3)) by *Monega Pass*; *Glendoll* (R.6(2)) to (a) *Braemar* by *Tolmount*; (b) *Ballater* by *Capel Mounth*; *Corgarff* (R.6(4)) to *Ballater* by *Loch Builg* or *Glen Finzie*.

The Northern Highlands

North and west of the *Great Glen* lies the finest scenery in Scotland. The mountains of *Ross-shire* and *Sutherland* are of great interest to the geologist as well as the climber. The *Cuillin Hills* of *Skye* are the most difficult and savage range in the British Isles—a challenge and an attraction to the climber. Associations with the Young Pretender, Bonnie Prince Charlie, abound in the country between *Inverness* and *Skye*.

Communication, except by water, is difficult. The route is divided into six sections, each based on a different approach from the *Great Glen* to various parts of the region.

R.7(1). Fort William to Mallaig (43 miles)

Fort William, *Glen Nevis* (Y.H.). Ferry to *Camusnagaul* for road on S. bank of *Loch Eil. Glenfinan*, 18 miles, on *Loch Shiel*: Prince Charlie's Monument. *Lochailort*, 7 miles; *Arosaig*, 10 miles; *Garramore* (Y.H.) 3 miles; fine coast scenery, views to islands; bathing.
EXCURSIONS: (a) Coastal walks; (b) Loch Morar (deepest loch, 1,080 ft.). Boat from *Mallaig* to (c) Loch Nevis; (d) Loch Hourn.

Mallaig, 5 miles; rail terminus; steamers to **Western Isles** and points on coast; ferry to *Armadale* on Isle of Skye.

Broadford (Y.H.), 8 miles from *Kyleakin* (ferry from *Kyle of Lochalsh*), or 15 miles from *Armadale* (ferry from *Mallaig*). Centre of a crofting area.
EXCURSIONS: (a) Elgol (bus) via *Torrin* for motor-boat across Loch Scavaig to Loch Coruisk; (b) path (experienced walkers only) to *Loch Coruisk* by the *bad step* from *Strathaird House.*

Road follows N.E. coast: *Sligachan*, 18 miles, climbing centre. Road (bus) via *Drynoch*, or walk (9 miles) over *Bealach-a-Mhaim* to **Glen Brittle** (Y.H.), climbing centre.

EXCURSIONS: (a) *Rudh 'an Dunain*; (b) Cuillin Hills (only for experienced climbers).

From *Sligachan*, *Dunvegan*, 24 miles, *Castle Skeabost*, 17 miles. *Uig*, 11 miles (Y.H.).

EXCURSIONS: *Kilbride* (Prince Charlie's landing place), *Kilmuir* (grave of Flora MacDonald) and *Duntulm Castle*.

Road over the *Quiraing*, fantastic rock scenery; *Staffin*, 9 miles.

EXCURSIONS: (a) boat, *Kilt Rock* and outlet of *Loch Mealt;* (b) The Storr (2,360 ft.) and **Old Man of Storr** (pinnacle).

Portree, chief settlement. Steamers to mainland: *Kyle of Lochalsh* or *Mallaig*.

R.7(2). Loch Lochy to Kyle of Lochalsh (57 miles)

Loch Lochy (Y.H.); fishing.

EXCURSIONS: (a) *Glen Roy* and its *"parallel roads"*; (b) *Loch Arkaig*; (c) *Spean Bridge* and *Commando War Memorial*.

Invergarry, 3 miles N.E. West by *Glen Garry* (large hydro-electric scheme) and new road to *Glen Loyne* and *Glen Moriston*, 9 miles (or from *Alltsaigh* (Y.H.) on *Loch Ness*, by *Invermoriston* to junction with this road, 18 miles). West by *Glen Clunie* and *Glen Shiel* to *Shiel Bridge* and *Ratagan* (Y.H.), 21 miles, on *Loch Duich*.

EXCURSIONS: (a) **Falls of Glomach** (370 ft.) highest in British Isles; (b) *Loch Duich* and *Eilean Donan Castle; (c) Glen Lichd* and *Sgurr Fhuaran (Ouran)* (3,505 ft.), one of *"Five Sisters of Kintail"*.

Mam Ratagan Pass (1,116 ft.) to *Glenelg*, 9 miles.

EXCURSIONS: (a) two Iron Age *brochs* at *Corrary* in *Gleann Beag;* (b) *Arnisdale* on Loch Hourn.

From *Glenelg*, steamer to *Skye* or continue on mainland. *Kyle* (Y.H.) end of railway from *Inverness*; ferry to *Kyleakin, Skye*; steamers to **Outer Hebrides**, (from *Ratagan* 23 miles by *Shiel Bridge* and *Dornie*, or 17 miles by *Totaig* and *Dornie Ferry*).

R.7(3). Inverness to Kyle of Lochalsh via Glen Affric (89 miles)
(Walking route only)

Inverness (Y.H.); capital of the Highlands; view from terrace by *Castle*; *Highland Museum*; Islands in R. *Ness*.

Beauly, 13 miles; bus along *Strath Glass* to *Cannich*, 17 miles, (Y.H.) walking centre. *Glen Affric* (Y.H.), 21 miles, at head of *Glen Affric*.

EXCURSIONS: Ascents include (a) *Ben Attow* (3,383 ft.); (b) *Mam Soul* (3,862 ft.).

Path by *Glen Fionn* and *Glen Lichd* to *Ratagan* (Y.H.), 14 miles, to join **R.7(2)**.

R.7(4). Inverness, Strathpeffer, Strome Ferry, Inveralligin (92 miles)

Route follows railway as far as *Strome Ferry.*

Inverness to *Beauly,* 13 miles; *Strathpeffer,* 10 miles, (Y.H.), walking centre; *Garve,* 9 miles. *Achnasheen,* 16 miles, (view); fork left for *Glen Carron; Achnashellach,* 9 miles, walking and climbing centre. *Lochcarron,* 12 miles, fishing village. *Strome Ferry,* 4 miles. Road to *Kyle of Lochalsh* and Y.H., 7 miles.

Achintraid (Y.H.), 5 miles N. by paths 9 miles by road via *Lochcarron.*

EXCURSION: *Bealach-nam-Bo* road and the mountains of *Applecross.*

Shieldaig, 10 miles, fishing village; ferry across *Loch Torridon* to *Inveralligin,* or 7 miles eastwards to Y.H. at *Torridon.*

EXCURSIONS: (a) *Diabaig,* fishing village, and coast; Y.H. at *Craig* (b) *Beinn Alligin* (3,232 ft.) (c) climbs (not in stalking season) of splendid peaks. Liathach (3,456 ft.) and Beinn Eighe (3,309 ft.).

R.7(5). Inverness, Ullapool, Achininver, Achmelvich (128 miles)

Garve, 32 miles. Road up *Strath Garve,* 15 miles and down *Dirrie More* to *Falls of Measach* 6 miles. Road forking left, A.832, leads to *Dundonnell,* 13 miles, on *Little Loch Broom* under impressive ridge and precipices of *An Teallach* (3,483 ft.).

Ullapool, 12 miles, (Y.H.), fishing town on *Loch Broom.*

Achininver (Y.H.) 27 miles (14 miles, walkers), centre for climbing **An Stac (Stack Polly),** (2,009 ft.) and fantastic sandstone peaks of *Coigach* district.

From *Ullapool* N. by *Drumrunie Lodge,* 10 miles, turn N.W. by *Loch Lurgain* through wild scenery to *Lochinver,* 21 miles; *Achmelvich* (Y.H.) 4 miles.

EXCURSIONS: (a) along coast to *Cnoc Poll* (352 ft. view); ascents of (b) Suilven (2,399 ft.) (c) *Canisp* (2,779 ft.) and Ben More Assynt (3,273 ft.).

R.7(6). Inverness, Carbisdale, Tongue, Durness, Achmelvich (204 miles)

Ardgay (bus from *Inverness,* 60 miles); *Carbisdale Castle* (Y.H.), 4 miles. *Invershin Ferry; Lairg,* 7 miles, on *Loch Shin.* Fork right up *Strath Tirry; Altnaharra,* 21 miles. Continue N. by *Loch Loyal. Tongue,* 16 miles, (Y.H.); fishing.

Continue round head of *Kyle of Tongue* to, 9 miles, road W. to foot of *Loch Hope,* 6 miles. Round head of *Loch Eriboll* and N. coast to *Durness,* 21 miles, (Y.H.): bathing.

EXCURSIONS: (a) *Smoo Cave;* (b) Cape Wrath.

Road S.W. to *Rhiconich,* 15 miles, at head of *Loch Inchard* and across primeval landscape to *Laxford Bridge,* 4½ miles; *Scourie,* 7 miles. By coast with many small islands to *Kylesku Ferry,* 12 miles. Road S. over pass (818 ft.) between *Quinag* (2,653 ft.) and *Glasven* (2,541 ft.) to *Skiag Bridge,* 7 miles, on *Loch Assynt. Lochinver,* 11 miles; *Achmelvich* (Y.H.), 4 miles.

SPAIN

Geographical Outline

Land   Spain (190,700 sq. miles), occupying most of the *Iberian Peninsula*, has been called a "kaleidoscope of landscapes", its various regions being as distinct as if they were different countries.

Its central feature is the *Meseta*, the plateau of *Castile*, *León* and *Estremadura*, crossed by mountain ranges including the *Sierra de Guadarrama* and the *Sierra de Gredos* which roughly divide it into a higher northern and a lower southern section.

South of *Madrid*, the rivers *Tagus* (*Tajo*) and *Guadiana* thread westwards across the plateau, their valleys separated by the *Montes de Toledo*. In its upper part the *Guadiana* crosses the desolate tableland of *La Mancha*.

The plateau stands isolated and distinct. The *Ebro*, the longest river, occupies the depression between it and the *Pyrenees*. The *Douro* (*Duero*) and its tributaries separate it from the *Cantabrian* mountains of the north, which back the narrow coastal plain running from *Finisterre* in *Galicia* through *Asturias* and *Old Castile* to the *Basque* provinces.

In the south the plateau ends abruptly in the *Sierra Morena* above the broad basin of the river *Guadalquivir*, the heart of *Andalusia*, beyond which rise the highlands of *Granada*. Here, behind the Mediterranean coast, rises the beautiful snow-capped *Sierra Nevada*, culminating in the *Pico de Mulhacen* (11,420 ft.), the highest point in Spain.

In *Murcia* and *Valencia* the important coastal lowlands are isolated from the rest of the country by complex groups of *sierras*. In *Catalonia* the coast, cutting across the grain of the country, has stretches of spectacular scenery, as in the granite cliffs of the *Costa Brava*.

From *Catalonia* the *Pyrenees* and their foothills run through *Aragon* and *Navarre* to the *Basque* country, forming a continuous mountain barrier between the Peninsula and the rest of Europe.

The *Balearic* and *Canary Islands* are politically part of Spain; the former are Mediterranean, but the latter, lying in the Atlantic nearer to Africa than Europe, are volcanic and almost tropical.

Climate   Climate varies on a more or less regional basis. The northern coast has frequent rain and mist even in summer. On the central plateau, the wettest season is in March and April, but rainfall is low generally; its temperature extremes of winter and summer can be very wide, 10°F to 95°F. In the Mediterranean provinces temperatures are usually a little lower in summer, but humidity makes the climate more trying, especially in *Valencia*; frost seldom occurs. In *Andalusia* there is no real winter except on very high ground.

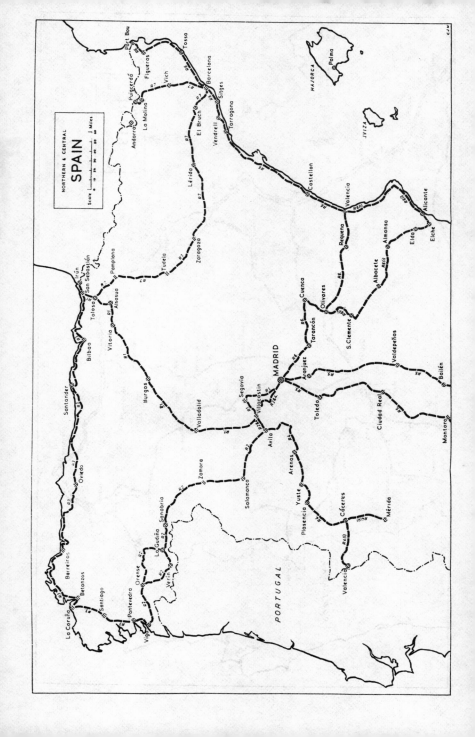

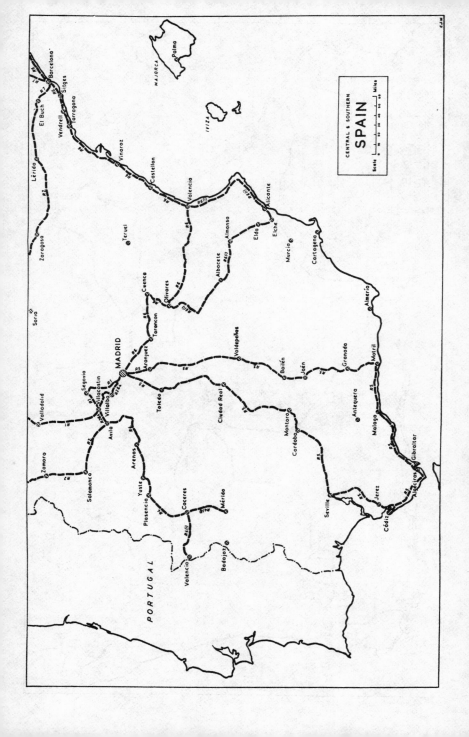

CENTRAL & SOUTHERN
SPAIN

Scale
0 10 20 30 40 50 60 Miles

MAJORCA
Palma

IVIZA

PORTUGAL

Barcelona
Sitges
El Buch
Vendrell
Tarragona
Lérida
Zaragoza
Soria
Vinaroz
Castellon
Teruel
Valencia
Almonsa
Albacete
Eldo
Elche
Alicante
Murcia
Cartagena
Cuenca
Olivares
Tarancon
Aranjuez
Valdepeñas
Almería
MADRID
Segovia
Alcozatin
Villalba
Toledo
Ciudad Real
Bailén
Jaén
Granada
Motril
Valladolid
Avila
Montoro
Antequera
Arenas
Córdoba
Málaga
Zamora
Solamonca
Yuste
Plasencia
Cáceres
Mérida
Seville
Jerez
Gibraltar
Algeciras
Cádiz
Valencia
Badajoz

Plants and Animals
In the wetter parts the plants of meadow, heath and woodland are those of western and central Europe. The arid parts either support evergreens such as ilex and a scrub (*matorral*) similar to the *garrigue* of southern France, or are lacking in soils and vegetation. But Spain is rich in species because of its wide range from plants similar to those of highland Britain, found in the hill areas of the north, to the cacti and sub-tropical flowers of the Andalusian coast.

The olive flourishes on lower ground in the southern half of the country and along the NE coast and the *Ebro* valley. In *Estremadura* it is joined by the cork oak. On the other hand the beech is confined to the northern half of the country, especially the mountains.

In contrast to many other parts of Europe small birds are not common in great numbers. Vultures, eagles, and hawks frequent the mountains. The dunes and marshes south-west of *Seville* now form a magnificent nature reserve.

Wolves from the *Pyrenees* and *Cantabrian* mountains spread south in winter to the mountains just north of Madrid. There are still a few Spanish ibex in the *Pyrenees*, and bears in the *Pyrenees* and *Asturias*. The animal life of the extreme south has obvious links with Africa, such as the 'Barbary apes' of *Gibraltar*.

The People

Population
Total is about 31 million. The six largest cities are *Madrid* (nearly 3 million), *Barcelona* (1,900,000), *Valencia* (590,000), *Seville* (430,000), *Malaga* (310,000), *Saragossa* (320,000).

Physically the basis of the population is a fusion of Celtic and Iberian peoples, conditioned by 600 years of Roman rule, after a short period during which the eastern seaboard was under first Greek and then Carthaginian influence. Visigothic penetration in the 6th century was ended by the Mohammedan conquest. The 700 years of Moorish rule in *Andalusia* have left a considerable legacy of racial and cultural influences.

Language
Castilian, a form of Spanish native to the capital, is now the official language of the whole country. It is derived from Latin but includes many words of Arabic origin. Catalan, spoken in the north-east and Balearic Islands, is distinct and is more like Provençal; the Galician dialect has a closer affinity to Portuguese. The Basques, who live near the Bay of Biscay, have a completely different language of unknown origin.

Religion
The great majority of Spaniards are Roman Catholics. The practice of other faiths is actively discouraged by the State.

History
The cave paintings at *Altamira* and other sites are a vivid link with a hunting culture of perhaps 12,000 years ago. Celtic cromlechs and Iberian remains, including the bust of the Lady of Elche (*Prado Museum*), relate to peoples native to the peninsula at the time of the Phoenician traders and the early historic settlements by

377

SPAIN

Greeks and Carthaginians. Such settlements were at first confined to the coast, but later extended inland for the sake of the silver mining and to secure recruits for the Carthaginian army of Hannibal.

As a result of the Punic wars between Carthage and Rome, Spain fell under Roman rule (206 B.C.), control being gradually extended to the whole peninsula. Only the extreme north-west, where Celtic traditions (though not the language) still linger, felt little of this influence.

At the collapse of the Western Empire Spain came under the control of the Visigoths, a Germanic people, who made their capital at *Toledo*. But the conquerors soon adopted both the language and the religion of the inhabitants. The Arab invasion (711), under Tarak, overthrew their kingdom, although a remnant of the nobles continued resistance in the *Cantabrian* mountains for 300 years.

Until 756 the Arab Emirs were dependent on the Caliphate at Damascus, but in that year an independent Emirate was established. In 912 it was constituted a Caliphate. During this period Moslem Spain, with its capital at *Cordova*, earned a reputation for science, arts and luxury without equal in the Western world.

In the 10th century the Christians of the north-west began a revival that in the course of the next three centuries gradually reduced the area of Moslem rule. Corruption and schisms contributed to the decline of Moorish Spain. In 1212 Alfonso VIII defeated the Moors at *Navas de Tolosa*, and soon their dominion was restricted to the kingdom of Granada, where philosophy continued to flourish. It finally fell in 1492.

During the period of the re-conquest Christian Spain consisted of a number of independent kingdoms and only with the marriage of Isabella of Castile and Ferdinand of Aragon (1479) did the basis of the modern State rise. In their zeal to maintain a strong central power the rulers threw out the Jews and later the Moors and tolerated the Inquisition in a drive for unity of state and faith.

Shortly after the unification the Spanish king Charles I (who had already inherited the Netherlands) became Emperor (as Charles V) of the Holy Roman Empire (1520). Together with the discoveries in America this accident of fate converted Spain almost overnight into the major world power. Brilliant leadership under Charles, who abdicated in 1556 to the monastery of *Yuste*, was followed by the less flexible rule of Philip II whose solemn palace at *El Escorial* contains the tombs of all subsequent kings. His policy of war against Protestantism, continued overseas expansion, and a naval attack on England, overstretched the economy and resources of the country. From his death in 1598 Spain sank gradually into powerless decadence.

The 18th century saw a brief attempt under the Bourbon Charles III to revitalise and centralise Spain, but his ideas found little favour and in a few years the Napoleonic Wars, here as elsewhere, were interrupting the course of history. Ties with the colonies were severed and Spanish life was split into a liberal and a clerical party whose vendetta for power dominated the unstable parliaments and frequent dictatorships of the 19th century.

In recent times the dictatorship of 1923-29 led to the abdication of the king, the brief rule of a left-wing republic and the bitter aftermath of civil war, 1936-39.

Government

The present government is based on a nationalist party formed by fusion of traditionalist and fascist parties during the civil war. The *Cortes* (parliament) consists of members elected by the municipal authorities (themselves elected on a limited franchise); members appointed by the government trade unions (membership of which is compulsory for employers and employees); members holding certain high offices including the President of the Supreme Court and the heads of universities; mayors of provincial capitals; representatives of the professions and members appointed by the chief of state.

Controversial discussion of the political structure is best avoided by the visitor.

Resources

Spain is a predominantly agricultural country and over 5 million people are employed on the land. Wheat is the chief grain crop; the vine is cultivated in all districts; the olive in the south and east and notably in the huge plantations around *Jaén*; figs and cork in *Estremadura*; dates in *Murcia*, especially around *Elche*; oranges (the main export) around *Seville* and in *Valencia* and *Castellon;* lemons in *Murcia*; onions in *Valencia*. The sherry of *Jerez* is perhaps the most distinctive export.

A special feature, providing some of the richest crops, is the huerta (irrigated) cultivation, highly developed in the south-east, notably the rice fields of *Valencia.*

The best cattle land is in the wet north and north-west. Sheep and goats are important in the more arid areas and transhumance (seasonal migration of flocks) is practised over great distances.

Forest products include eucalyptus and resin in addition to cork. There is a State afforestation programme.

Coastal fishing is chiefly for sardines, tunny and cod.

Mineral resources are rich and varied. They include iron (*Bilbao*), coal (*Asturias*), copper (*Riotinto*), mercury (*Almadén*) and lead (*Sierra Morena*). Some 300,000 workers are employed. A uranium plant was established in 1960.

Heavy industry is largely concentrated in *Catalonia* which is also noted for its textiles. The *Basque* provinces, with much dispersed industry, are the other chief manufacturing areas. In both regions, and generally throughout Spain, industry relies on hydro-electric power; drought can therefore seriously restrict production. There is little coal; charcoal remains an important domestic fuel.

Customs and Dress

Each region has its own. As holidays are still holy days, pilgrimages' and Saints' days are the centre of most festivities; Holy Week is celebrated with great ceremony.

In many places a night watchman closes the outer street doors at 10.30 p.m. It is very unusual for women to walk alone at night; if they do so they must expect comments from passing men. Cinemas start their last showing at 11 p.m.

In *Galicia* women wear the *manteo*, a bell-shaped skirt, and a shoulder cape. Men frequently wear a brown cloth hat with high crown and a rush cape.

SPAIN

Handicrafts include lace making, basketry and jet ornaments. The local dance is the *muneira*, danced to the bagpipes. Pilgrimages centre on *Santiago de Compostela*, the chief shrine of Spain. (*Santiago* is the Spanish for St. James).

In the *Basque* country men wear a traditional red beret on festive occasions. Basque bands consist of pipes and drums. There is a tradition of impromptu singing in a style reminiscent of the Middle Ages.

In *Catalonia* the traditional headgear is the *barretina*, a long fisherman's cap, coloured to match the sash. Footgear is the rope-soled boot. The local dance, the *sardana*, is danced by a whole village in concentric rings to the music of a *cobla*. *Montserrat* with its black Virgin is the chief object of pilgrimage; this monastery up in the hills has a world famous boys' choir.

In *Valencia* and the *Levant* silks and linen are common for women's dresses. Men working in the fields wear white trousers and, instead of a jacket, the blanket which serves as a basket and rug combined. The great festival of the year is *Las Fallas* on St. Joseph's Eve when each district constructs a satirical tableau of *papier maché* which is burnt amid a deluge of fireworks.

Andalusia shows the greatest Moorish influence in style of dress, as in much else; in *Granada* a traditional type of weaving with cubic designs, and boxes decorated with inlaid mosaics derive from the Muslim past. All the towns celebrate Holy Week with magnificent processions, each district competing for the most splendid figure of the Virgin. The original penitents' clothes, with pointed hooded headdresses, have become very ornate and represent the various guilds of the town. At various dates in spring and summer the *ferias* (fairs) are held, *Seville's* being the most famous. The *flamenca* dances are better seen at country festivals than at the commercialised *Sacromonte* at *Granada*.

In *Madrid* at Christmas the old *Plaza Mayor* is filled with Christmas trees, clay models for the cribs, and tambourines of all sizes. On New Year's Eve thousands crowd into the *Puerto del Sol* to eat a grape for each of the strokes of midnight.

Food and Drink

Regional specialities include: in *Galicia*, a maize cake, *borona*, baked in cabbage leaves; fish dishes, dairy products and Ribeiro wine; *Asturias*, cider and Rioja wines; in *Andalusia*, cold soups, called *gazpacho*; salads, fish dishes and sweets such as *yemas de San Leandro*; sherry, manzanilla. In *Catalonia*, *pasta* is the main element in the food of the people, with a fair proportion of meat; in *Valencia*, *paella*, a rice dish, and a very unusual drink, *horchata*, made from crushed sweetened nuts; on the central plateau, stews, bread dipped in garlic, breadcrumbs and milk. *Madrid* is famous for its bars, with every type of fish and marine product.

Sport

The national sports are bullfighting and football, in which Spain has won many honours in recent years. In the *Basque* country the chief sports are the annual log cutting competitions and sailing regattas. *Pelota*, the national game of the Basques, has spread all over Spain. *Seville* shares the honours with *Madrid* as a centre of the art of bullfighting.

Culture

Architecture Extensive Roman remains can be seen at *Mérida* (theatre and amphitheatre), *Itálica* and *Tarragona* as well as the great aqueduct at *Segovia*.

Certain Visigothic churches have the horseshoe arches which later became a characteristic feature of Moorish architecture. The great Mosque at *Cordova* was built during the early centuries of Moorish occupation. Examples of their later buildings are the *Giralda Tower* and *Alcázar* at *Seville* and the splendid *Alhambra* of *Granada*. Christian refugees to the north founded many churches in a hybrid style, Mozarabic. Pure Romanesque is often a foreign import in Spain, as with the pilgrims' churches along the route to *Santiago de Compestela*.

Of Gothic, introduced by the Cistercians, there are many examples of several periods: early, including the cathedrals of *Burgos, Toledo* and *León;* middle, including the cathedrals of *Barcelona, Gerona* and *Pamplona;* late, including the cathedrals of *Segovia, Seville* and the new cathedral of *Salamanca*.

Many lesser buildings illustrate the native Mudéjar style, the work of Moorish craftsmen.

Most of the castles for which Spain is famous are 15th century.

Renaissance motifs entered Spain as decorative features in a style called Plateresque, especially well displayed at *Salamanca*.

The Baroque style reached its most extreme in the fantastic excesses of ornamentation practised by the Churriguera family in the early 18th century. The best examples of this elaborate manner are in the cathedrals of *Santiago, Salamanca* and *Valladolid*.

The 19th and 20th centuries have brought few innovations to Spanish architecture, but the work of the Catalan Gaudé must be mentioned; his church of the *Sagrada Familia* in *Barcelona* attracts much attention.

Painting The world famous museum of the *Prado* in *Madrid* houses the greatest collection of Spain's masterpieces, though many outstanding individual items are found in the numerous palaces and churches with royal associations.

El Greco, the Cretan, using elongated features and striking colours, is almost modern in his effects. Velasquez, the Court painter of the 17th century, is strictly objective. Murillo captures in his laughing boys the carefree moments of ordinary people. Goya's searing realism brought home for the first time the horrors of war and the delusions of terror and the madhouse. Spain, too, is the homeland of Picasso, though his life's work has been done beyond the Pyrenees.

Music The popularity of folk music in the dances and festivities of the various regions has already been briefly indicated. Its tradition is perhaps stronger and truer in Spain than in any other European country and it pervades even the modern idioms of radio and cinema. Pilar Lopez and Antonio have made this music famous all over the world, and on the classical plane its motifs have been woven into the work of Albeniz, Granados and Manuel de Falla.

Tossa De Mar, Spain.

Literature   The golden age of Spanish literature coincided with England's Elizabethan age. Lope de Vega, Calderon and Alarcon produced between them some thousands of full length plays. Cervantes' masterpiece, *Don Quixote*, gave birth to the European novel. A long history of lyrical poetry stands behind the passionate verse of Garcia Lorca, and a succession of historians, from Bartolme de las Casas to Pindal have chronicled Spain's unique contribution to the heritage of the West.

Touring Information

Access   (i) By *rail:* there is a break of gauge between France and Spain and in each direction it is necessary to change after crossing the frontier. London to *Barcelona* via Dieppe-Paris, 27½ hours, £29·05 single; London to *Madrid* via Dieppe-Paris, 35 hours, £30·75 single. (ii) by *air:* London to *Barcelona* direct, night tourist, from £59·80 mid-week to £69·60 summer weekends; London to *Madrid* direct, night tourist £74·00 mid-week £81·40 weekends. Also direct flights in summer to *Malaga, Valencia* and *Bilbao*. (iii) by *sea:* car ferry from Southampton to *Bilbao*, three sailings every two weeks, 37 hour voyage, passenger fare from £21·00 single.

Supplements are payable for travel on many of the fastest trains, such as the 'Talgo' with specially articulated rolling-stock. Travellers intending to use Spanish railways extensively can buy 'kilometric tickets', consisting of books of coupons which are exchanged at booking offices for ordinary tickets; they offer a saving of about 80% if all the coupons are used—only obtainable in Spain.

Money   The *peseta* is divided into 100 centimos. There are coins of 10 and 50 centimos and of 1, 2.50, 5, 25, and 50 pesetas; and notes of 1, 5, 25, 50, 100, 500 and 1,000 pesetas.

Seasons for Touring   The central plateau is often arid and desolate and always dusty and hot in summer. This, and the long distances between towns and villages, make it advisable to cross these stretches by rail.

The south is best visited in spring or early autumn. In the east, the *Costa Brava* has become so popular that in mid-season it is difficult to get accommodation even in camping sites.

Clothing   As the climate ranges from delightfully mild in the north to sub-tropical in the south one should dress accordingly.

In towns, or when travelling by public transport, and in the evenings everywhere, women should wear a skirt or dress; and men slacks and long-sleeved shirt. In religious buildings women should cover the head; both sexes should cover the arms. Shorts, jeans, etc., are acceptable on beaches, for mountain walking, or for cycling in the country or through towns. The most

SPAIN

popular tourist beaches of Spain are now as international as any others, but elsewhere bikinis are likely to attract unfavourable comment.

Restaurants and Meals

Lunch is served between 2 and 3 p.m.; dinner from 9 p.m.

Food is excellent and abundant; the tastiness and delicacy of the different regional dishes is remarkable. The standard national dish is *cocido*, a stew made of boiled chickpeas, with meat, vegetables, dumplings, etc.; many local variants have their own names.

The range of tinned foods in shops is narrower than in many countries, and in the more remote villages it may be possible to obtain only such basic foods as bread and dried cod (*bacalao*). Fresh fruit in season is easily found, fresh milk is not.

Maps

Michelin No. 990, scale 1:1,000,000, is an adequate road map of Spain and Portugal. Large scale maps can be obtained only in the major cities; they are not of good quality. Climbing guide books, in Spanish, complete with simple maps, describe the mountain areas of the north-east.

Accommodation

The Spanish Y.H.A. (*Red Espanola de Albergues Juveniles*) has hostels in about 50 localities; most of them accommodate men, some of them are for girls only and only a few take both sexes. Many hostels are open in summer only.

Except in popular resorts, hotels are much cheaper in Spain than in the rest of Europe. Prices are fixed by the Government, and clearly displayed in each room.

Camping

Camping on public land is permitted; on private land with consent of owner. It is forbidden: within 1 km of towns; within 50 metres of a main road; within 150 metres of waters supplying reservoirs; in immediate vicinity of buildings of historic or artistic interest; in places prohibited by local authorities; in regions reserved for shooting or fishing, or in forestry areas without permission from the *Servicio Forestal*. Water supplies are sometimes difficult and it is advisable to carry sterilising tablets. It should be remembered that open country affords little protection against weather or intruders and camping should not be attempted except at recognised sites.

Ski-ing

Season usually December to March. Resorts at *La Molina*, *Nuria* and *Salardú* in the *Pyrenees*. Ski-ing can also be enjoyed in the *Sierra Guadarrama* within 40 miles of *Madrid*, and in the *Sierra Nevada* near *Granada*.

| **Cycling** | Cycle fares from the French Ports depend on total weight of cycle and equipment, as well as distance, but a free allowance of 30 kilos is usually given. |

Cycling is becoming more popular for touring, particularly in the northern provinces and on the east coast to *Barcelona*. Further south, and on the central plateau, the unrelieved heat and hard dusty going on unsurfaced roads are a great deterrent. It is prudent to carry an emergency supply of food and drink if going far off the main roads. Gradients and poor road surfaces make low gearing essential: a bottom gear of 30 is by no means too low. Start with new tyres and tubes: there are cycle shops in the large towns but British and American parts are not stocked.

| **Practical Hints** | Permission should be obtained for photographing interiors of museums, churches, etc., and close-ups of bull fights; also before photographing individuals. It is forbidden to photograph airfields, military zones and certain areas in the |

Pyrenees.

Milk should be boiled. Tap water is safe enough in the higher mountain areas and in the cities but elsewhere there is an occasional danger of typhoid, especially in summer.

Shops are closed every afternoon, but open again in the evening. All shops and places of business, except restaurants, are closed on *fiesta* days (which are numerous).

Touring Routes

M indicates males only: F females only; CS camping site.

R.1. Irún to Madrid (350 miles)

Irún, frontier town; **Y.H.** at *Fuenterrabia*, 2 miles northwards. Road N.1 to **San Sebastián** (**Y.H.**), 12 miles, capital of Basque province of *Guipúzcoa* and centre for Basque games and folklore festivals; favourite summer resort for Spaniards; *La Concha* beach has strict rules on bathing dress. Many agreeable excursions to coast and hill country are possible. CS at *Igueldo*, 5 miles.

Continue on N.1. Beyond *Tolosa* road climbs to pass of *Echegárate* (2,100 ft.) and enters countryside less watered by Atlantic rains. *Alsasua*, 45 miles **Y.H.**

Vitoria, 28 miles, capital of *Alava* province and still in Basque area. **Y.H.**

Road crosses R. *Ebro* at *Miranda de Ebro*, 21 miles **Y.H.**

SPAIN

Burgos, 50 miles; magnificent 13th century Gothic cathedral with fine western façade and twin spires; other interesting churches; *Castillo* where Edward I of England was married, fine view of city; in *Casa del Cordón* Columbus was received by Ferdinand and Isabella on his return from America. Two great monasteries on outskirts: one, *Las Huelgas*, contains many fine royal tombs and a good museum. During Civil War (1936–39) *Burgos* was administrative capital of Nationalist Spain. Y.H. in city, CS 2½ miles S.E. at *Fuentes Blancas*. N.1 continues due south to *Madrid*, 153 miles, but has little of interest either in towns or change of scenery.

Palencia, 52 miles, SW just off through road N.620; cathedral, Y.H.(M). **Valladolid,** 30 miles; Cervantes museum and many 16th century sculptured façades.

N.403 to *Villacastin,* 65 miles; N.110 to **Segovia,** 23 miles; fine Roman aqueduct, 16th century Gothic cathedral, castle, city walls, many fine old houses. CS. Minor road to *San Ildefonso de La Granja,* 8 miles, summer palace of kings of Spain with wonderful tapestries, some in designs by Goya; huge formal gardens where on special occasions magnificent fountains play.

Continue through wooded hill country up long pass to *Puerto de Navacerrada* (6,102 ft.) 11 miles; winter sport area with teleski and rack railway from valley. Excellent area for hill walking and rock climbing. Most Spanish mountaineering clubs have huts in the pass.

Road descends through similar country to village of *Villalba,* 13 miles. N.VI to *Madrid,* 25 miles, passing *La Voz de Madrid* radio station and *Casa del Campo,* permanent exhibition site for agriculture and regional crafts, entering *Madrid* near the University city.

Madrid (Y.Hs.) was made the capital in 1561 by Philip II. *Puerta del Sol,* city centre; all distances in Spain measured from here and clock fixes the standard time; focal point of Madrid's underground railway (*Metropolitano*). Old part of city lies immediately south, around and beyond *Plaza Mayor,* built in 1619 as market, bull ring and meeting place; through narrow arches narrow streets lead off down the hill; especially interesting is the *Cava Baja* with small factories for rope and implements and old coaching inns now largely converted to restaurants, of which the most famous, *Las Cuevas,* was once hide-out of famous bandit, Luis Candelas. Former Royal Palace on W. edge of town includes *Armería Real,* world's finest collection of arms and armour.

Fashionable part of city is around *Plaza de España* with its skyscraper, *Avenida José Antonio* and *Calle de Alcalá.* Latter street bisects very broad road running north and south through city at *Square of Cibeles* and chief post office. Southern part, *Paseo del Prado* passes in front of **Prado Art Gallery:** one of finest collections in Europe, unequalled for Velasquez, Goya and El Greco. Behind Gallery is main park, the very charming *Retiro,* with boating lake.

The two big bull rings stage fights every Sunday and on special *fiestas.* A worthwhile visit on Sunday mornings is to the *Rastro,* second-hand market, south from *Plaza Mayor.*

R.2. Madrid to Vigo (410 miles)

Leave *Madrid* by N.VI, bearing left at 10 miles, on to new road through *Galapagar* to **El Escorial**, 18 miles; huge fortress-like monastery in commanding position, built by Philip II with later additions; fine period rooms; El Greco paintings; pantheon has tombs of kings. **Y.H.**

At *Guadarrama* village, 7 miles, turn left to visit Valley of the Fallen where huge cross and a church hewn out of rock commemorate the dead of the Civil War. Return to *Guadarrama*. Road N.VI climbs very steep and long pass, which motorists can avoid by using tunnel, and descends to *San Rafael.* At *Villacastin*, 23 miles, turn S.W. on N.501 to **Avila**, 18 miles; (3,600 ft.) fine example of medieval walled city, built of red granite; cathedral; Romanesque churches; birthplace of St. Theresa, joint Patron Saint of Spain. *Peñaranda de Bracomonte*, 35 miles, a rather decrepit little town. **Y.H.**

Salamanca, 27 miles, one of oldest university towns in Europe; spacious arcaded *Plaza Mayor*; fine university buildings; especially famous Plateresque gateways; two cathedrals; many 15th and 16th century houses.

N.630 to *Zamora*, 40 miles, and for a further 13 miles, turning left on N.525 to cross hilly, remote area of *León* province to *Puebla de Sanabria*, 55 miles. **Y.H.(M)** by *Lago de Sanabria*, beautiful lake 10 miles N. of village.

N.525 continues through mountains to *La Gudiña*, 37 miles. Here either go N. on C.533 to join main road at *Freijido*, 33 arduous miles, or W. and N. via *Verín* to *Orense*, 69 miles (62 from *Freijido*), with famous bridge. **Y.H.** Thence to *Vigo*, 66 miles, some of them close to the Portuguese border in the inaccessible gorge of *Miño*.

Vigo, busy port close to beautiful coastal scenery; large fishing industry; beaches a few miles from town. **Y.H.**

R.3. Vigo to Irún (632 miles)

Vigo **(R.2)**. N.550 past airport to *Pontevedra*, 20 miles; picturesque town. **Y.H.**

Santiago de Compostela, 35 miles: the object of massive pilgrimages in the Middle Ages; cathedral with 12th century interior and sculpture, Churrigueresque front. **CS.**

Corunna (*La Coruña*), 40 miles, naval base on Atlantic coast; countryside akin to Scotland; likelihood of frequent rain. *Betanzos*, 15 miles, fork left and at *Jubia*, 23 miles, right on C.641 for 3½ miles, where fork left on C.642, following north coast to *Barreiros*, 82 miles. *Luarca*, 50 miles, has **Y.H.**

Oviedo, 60 miles, mining and industrial centre; cathedral, fine museum, **Y.H.** *Arriondas*, 41 miles; best approach to *Picos de Europa*, wild and beautiful mountain range, with *Covadonga* National Park. **Y.H.** at *Llanes.*

Santander, 90 miles; busy port, international university.
EXCURSION: Caves of Altamira, with famous pre-historic drawings.

Bilbao, 68 miles, industrial and mining port. Good minor roads to *Bermeo* and *Guernica*, 30 miles: scene of infamous bombing raid by Germans in Civil War, subject of one of Picasso's most famous paintings, *Amorebieta*, 8 miles, **Y.H.(F)**. *San Sebastián* **(R.1)**, 56 miles.

SPAIN

R.4. Madrid to Badajoz (329 miles)

Madrid to *Avila* (See R.2). In *Avila* take C.502 to *Venta del Obispo*, 30 miles, on eastern part of the wild *Sierra de Gredos*. Road over *Puerto del Pico* (4,485 ft.) to *Arenas de San Pedro*, 21 miles, and by C.501 to monastery of *Yuste*, 48 miles, where Emperor Charles V retired after abdication. *Plasencia*, 27 miles. N.630 to *Cáceres*, 53 miles, picturesque provincial capital. Y.H.(F).

R.4(i) Cáceres to Valencia de Alcántara. N.521 through sparsely populated olive and charcoal producing country to Portuguese frontier beyond *Valencia de Alcántara*, 55 miles. Lisbon via Santarem 165 miles along *Tagus valley*, or Y.H. at *Alburquerque* 20 miles S.E. of *Valencia de Alcántara* on C.530 to *Badajoz*.

Mérida, 45 miles, some of richest Roman remains outside Italy: aqueduct, theatre, amphitheatre, numerous arches.

Badajoz, 38 miles, provincial capital, has endured many sieges, Peninsular War and Civil War. Y.H.

R.5. Madrid—Granada—Malaga—Seville—Cordova—Madrid (855 miles)

The main road to the south, N.IV, which crosses the flat tableland of *La Mancha*, has little of interest except for the palace and gardens at *Aranjuez*, 33 miles. The wine growing district is reached at *Valdepeñas*, 95 miles; road then crosses *Sierra Morena* through a rocky defile to *Bailén*, 60 miles. CS at *Santa Elena*, 25 miles N. and another, 5 miles N.

N.323 to *Jaén*, 25 miles, centre of ranch country and area of large estates, olive plantations and orchards. Town has renaissance cathedral. Road crosses *Sierra de Lucena* to *Granada*, 62 miles.

Granada was last outpost of Moorish rule in Spain, and in the *Alhambra* palace a great variety of splendid Arabesque detail is preserved; delightful garden of adjoining *Generalife* should be visited. Fine Renaissance tombs in *Capilla Real* of cathedral. Gipsy caves on *Sacromonte*, now commercialised. Y.H. 2 CS near town.

EXCURSION: *Sierra Nevada*, light railway to 4,600 ft., road to 10,725 ft. Many fine walks but little accommodation.

Road continues S. to *Motril*, 46 miles, on Mediterranean coast. An area of great contrasts of climate; cane and palm plantations only a few miles from mountain snows.

N.340 to *Málaga*, 68 miles, (Y.H.), is winding road through fine coastal scenery. CS at old Moorish town of *Almuñécar*.

Coast road west from *Málaga* is *Costa del Sol*, much spoilt by unsightly tourist development. Many CS and beaches always easily accessible from it. *Marbella*, 37 miles, Y.H. Inland is *Sierra de Ronda*, attractive mountain area.

Algeciras, 50 miles, overlooks bay of *Gibraltar* (which can be approached from *San Roque*, 9 miles N.). Ferries to Tangiers and Ceuta in Morocco which can be seen clearly from headland of *Tarifa*, 15 miles S. CS.

Cádiz, 63 miles, major port of Spanish Empire in earlier times, now a naval base; Spain's biggest prison here. *Jerez de la Frontera*, 32 miles, town which gave its name to sherry; white walls, patios and numberless bodegas for trying the local product. **Y.H.** *Alcázar*, charming Mudéjar palace, 14th century but much restored. In this district, which for 200 years was border with last Moorish kingdom, many towns are known as *de la Frontera*.

Seville, 60 miles, was a centre of Moorish culture. *Cathedral*, largest Gothic church in the world, retains in its structure the tower, *La Giralda*, of former mosque; rich interior; tomb of Columbus; many art treasures. *Seville's* celebrations during Holy Week and its *Feria* during first week of April are unique and world-famous.

EXCURSION: *Itálica*, 5 miles N.W., Roman amphitheatre.

N.IV to *Carmona*, 20 miles; Roman cemetery. **Cordova** (*Córdoba*), 65 miles, was Moorish capital; *Mosque*, although partly rebuilt as a cathedral, remains the finest example of muslim art in western Europe. Old town is a maze of alleys with many picturesque patios. **CS.**

Shortest route onward is by N.IV rejoining outward route at *Bailén*, 65 miles. Tougher but more interesting is to turn N. at *Montoro*, 28 miles by N.420 to *Ciudad Real*, 90 miles, **Y.H.**, and N.401 to *Toledo*, 73 miles; desolate highland areas with poor roads, seldom visited.

Toledo is entered by very old bridge over gorge of R. *Tagus* which almost surrounds the city, once capital of Castile but now almost entirely given over to tourist trade. Splendid Gothic *cathedral* is best visited in afternoon when chapels are open, especially Capilla Mayor containing huge *Transparente*, remarkable example of Spanish Baroque. Maze of winding alleys is packed with medieval and renaissance buildings, including El Greco's house and museum of his works. **Y.H.**

Madrid 45 miles.

R.6. Madrid—Valencia—Barcelona—Costa Brava (620 miles)

N. III from *Atocha* railway station to *Tarancón*, 53 miles. N.400 to **Cuenca,** 53 miles, medieval walled town with houses overhanging cliffs above R. *Júcar*;
EXCURSION: *Ciudad Encantada*, 26 miles N; extraordinary rock formations.

From *Cuenca* turn S. on N.420 to *La Almarcha*, 39 miles, so rejoining N. III. *Cuestas de Contreras*, 60 miles, impressive scenery where R. *Cabriel* breaches central plateau. Descend to coastal plain through orange grove district to *Valencia*, 63 miles.

R.6(i) Alternative route La Almarcha to Valencia. N.III to *Honrubia*, 8 miles; S.W. to *San Clemente* to join N.301 for *Albacete*, 70 miles, provincial capital with steel, especially cutlery, industries. N.430 to *Almansa*, 45 miles. N.330 via *Villena* to *Elda* 36 miles. Fork right 5½ miles beyond, through *Novelda* to *Elche*, 12 miles, town of white cube-shaped houses in largest date palm grove in Europe (reputedly 300,000 trees). Outside town are many Iberian, Phoenician and Visigothic remains, and here was found the famous *Dama de Elche*, a very early sculpture now in the *Prado*.
N.340 to *Alicante*, 15 miles, busy port (steamers for *Mallorca* and N. Africa); modern town on bay; old town on hill. Coastal road, N.332; much fine scenery, but locally spoiled by overgrown resorts such as *Benidorm* and *Denia*. *Valencia*, 115 miles.

Valencia, provincial capital and port and centre of rich agricultural area (irrigated) producing citrus fruits, rice and wheat. Connections by sea to *Mallorca*. Few important buildings, but an important art gallery. Spectacular fiestas in mid-March (San José), Holy Week, May and late July. **Y.H.** at *Vall de Uxó*, 20 miles.

Castellón, 15 miles, Y.H.; also **Y.H.(F)** at *Nules,* 12 miles S.W. *Sagunto,* 14 miles; Roman theatre. *Tortosa,* 78 miles, granite built, walled town on R. *Ebro* lies some way from main road. Much damaged in Civil War, but Gothic cathedral still worth seeing for its fine carvings.

Tarragona, 53 miles, splendidly grouped, ancient city with extensive Roman remains surrounded by cyclopean walls, probably pre-Roman. Romanesque-Gothic cathedral. **Y.H.(M).**

At *Vendrell,* 18 miles, take coast road, C.246, via *Sitges* to *Barcelona,* 40 miles.

Barcelona, second city, chief port and industrial centre of Spain; capital of Catalonia; bustling, noisy and colourful; many fine buildings, Romanesque, Gothic, Renaissance and Baroque; Gothic cathedral in old town and other lovely buildings nearby, including 16th century palace—*Archivo de la Corona de Aragon*—and 14th century chapel of *Santa Agueda.* Unfinished church of the Holy Family (*Sagrada Familia*), begun 1882, by Gaudé (blocks of whose flats can also be seen), is a unique example of eccentric art. Permanent exhibition of regional crafts (examples can be purchased) at *Pueblo Español* on outskirts. *Mount Tibidabo* (funicular), fine panorama of city and coast. **Y.H.(M).**

N.E. by N.II along coast to *Arenys de Mar,* 25 miles, **Y.H.** Where N.II turns inland, keep to coast, through *Lloret* and *Tossa,* popular seaside resorts.

La Escala, 27 miles, small fishing port near which is *Ampurias* with remains of early Greek settlement, *Emporion,* and Roman town (excavated); museum. Road leaves coast to rejoin N.II at *Figueras,* 15 miles. Between *Palamós* and *Figueras* a number of attractive villages and bays can be reached on roads at right angles to through route. CS numerous.

EXCURSION: Gerona, 25 miles, finely situated medieval town, dominated by Gothic cathedral with widest nave in world and beautiful Romanesque cloisters. Churches of *San Feliú* and *San Pedro de Galligans.* Y.H.

Figueras to frontier by N.II to *Col de Perthus,* 15 miles, or by C.252 to *Port Bou,* 23 miles. The latter road is more eventful.

R.7. Puigcerdá—Barcelona—Saragossa—Irun (496 miles)

From frontier, *Puigcerdá,* mountainous road N.152. Turning to *La Molina,* 8 miles; fine winter sports resort. Cross pass to *Ribas,* 23 miles.

EXCURSION: *Nuria,* (6,000 ft.), rack railway.

Barcelona, NW by local road over hill to *San Cugat,* 11 miles, village with Benedictine abbey and church (12th century cloisters). *Tarrasa,* 10 miles, town with three very fine Romanesque churches. W. to *Esparraguera,* 11 miles.

Montserrat, 14 miles, famous monastery and place of pilgrimage, grandly situated on terrace of curious mountain; famous boys' choir. Continue W. over mountain to reach N.II, 7 miles; *Lérida,* 67 miles, provincial capital.Y.H.

R.7(i) Lérida to Andorra. C.1313 up *Segre* valley to Seo de Urgel (2,275 ft.), 85 miles. Enter Andorra, 6 miles beyond.

R.7(ii) Lérida to France over Pyrenees. *Lérida,* C.147 to *Pobla de Segur,* 70 miles, *Esterri,* 36 miles. Over *Bonaigua* pass (6,798 ft.) to *Salardú,* 23 miles, Y.H.(M) in *Valle de Arán,* less inaccessible than most parts of Spanish Pyrenees. On down valley to *Viella* 6 miles; and N.230 to border and *Cierp,* 26 miles.

Saragossa (*Zaragoza*), 89 miles, former capital of *Aragon;* industrial and commercial city; two cathedrals: *La Seo,* 12th-17th century; *Nuestra Señora del Pilar,* 17th century, huge building with many domes; Gothic alabaster altar. Y.H.

R.7(iii) Huesca and Pyrenees. *Huesca,* 45 miles, provincial capital. *Sabiñánigo,* 33 miles, turning for Ordesa National Park 28 miles, magnificent scenery. *Jaca,* 10 miles. *Canfranc,* 14 miles. *Somport,* 6 miles, historic frontier pass at 5,381 ft.

N.232 along *Ebro* valley to *Tudela,* 50 miles, notable church and bridge. 4 miles N. near N.121 are remains of very considerable Roman town.

Pamplona, 60 miles, capital of former kingdom of *Navarre;* citadel built by Philip II; Gothic cathedral. Y.H. Many by-roads lead up interesting Pyrenean valleys.

Tolosa, 41 miles. *Tolosa to Irún,* 23 miles (see **R.1**).

The Balearic Islands

These islands lie well out into the Mediterranean, and cannot conveniently be described in any of the touring routes to Spain, but their interest to visitors to that country merits a mention here. There are no youth hostels and few camping sites.

Majorca (*Mallorca*) is the largest island of the group. **Palma,** its capital, is served by steamers from *Barcelona* six nights a week and from *Valencia* and *Alicante* three nights each. The city is dominated by its Gothic cathedral, and many other old buildings merit attention. Tourist purchases have helped to keep local craft industries alive. There are good beaches nearby.

Tour of Majorca (188 miles). W. to *Paguera,* then inland to *Andraitx,* 19 miles. From here a splendid road threads its way through the mountains high above the island's long north-west coast. *Valldemosa,* 27 miles, 14th century monastery, associations with Chopin. *Sóller,* 13 miles. Constantly winding road comes down to *Pollensa,* 33 miles. *Puerto de Pollensa,* 4 miles. *Cape of Formentor,* 13 miles N.E. marks end of this ragged coast. S.E. to *Alcudia,* 5 miles, and *Artá,* 24 miles; splendid sea-shore caves 6 miles S.E. Then south to *Cuevas del Drach,* 14 miles, for more impressive stalactite caves. The circuit is completed by continuing S.W. to *Santany,* 19 miles, and N.W. to *Palma,* 33 miles, but as this southern corner of the island is uninteresting visitors may prefer to return directly to *Palma* via *Manacor,* 39 miles, from *Cuevas del Drach.*

The other islands are much smaller. **Minorca,** the most easterly, is rocky without being mountainous, and has many prehistoric remains. There are three steamers a week from *Barcelona* to *Mahon,* and weekly services from *Palma.* **Ibiza,** the most westerly, also has unusual antiquities. There are steamers weekly from *Barcelona, Alicante* and *Valencia.*

SWEDEN

Geographical Outline

Land

From the southern tip of *Skåne* to the borders of Norway and Finland in the north, Sweden extends for nearly 1,000 miles, whilst from the Skagerrak to the Baltic its greatest width is about 300 miles. Sweden's northernmost point, 200 miles beyond the Arctic Circle, is the same latitude as the northern coastline of Canada, while the city of *Malmö* is almost as far south as Newcastle upon Tyne. The country's total area is about twice that of Great Britain.

The geographical isolation of Sweden has played no small part in her history; water surrounds her on three sides, and the northern Baltic is icebound in winter. In the north-east, the river *Torne* forms the border with Finland, and the frontier with Norway is a formidable mountain barrier.

From these mountains the land slopes steeply to the west to give Norway her rugged grandeur, but more gently to the east, so that apart from the mountains close to the border, Sweden's northern landscape is typified by undulating forests cut by large rivers running in a north-west—south-east direction. The southern part is a plain, relieved only in the centre by hilly country.

The Swedes divide their country into three parts: *Norrland*, the north; *Svealand*, the district around the great lakes, centre of the ancient kingdom of *Svea Rike*, hence *Sverige* the modern Swedish name for the country and *Götaland*, the southern plain, once the home of the Goths.

Climate

Sheltered from the west by the mountain frontier with Norway, Sweden, except in the south, is less affected by Atlantic than by continental conditions to which it is open on the east. It has, therefore, a comparatively dry climate.

Spring is the driest and probably the most exhilarating season. In the short space of a month or so the sunshine gains in intensity and soon brings about the thaw of the river and lake ice and the budding of trees and wild flowers. In the north, the change is so sudden that full summer follows in a matter of weeks. Easter is the best season for winter sports.

Summer is short; June, July and August in the south; even shorter in the north. The sunlight, however, is intense and the hours of sunshine exceed those of Italy and Spain, though temperatures are lower. The midnight sun can be seen beyond the Arctic Circle for many weeks, and even in the south

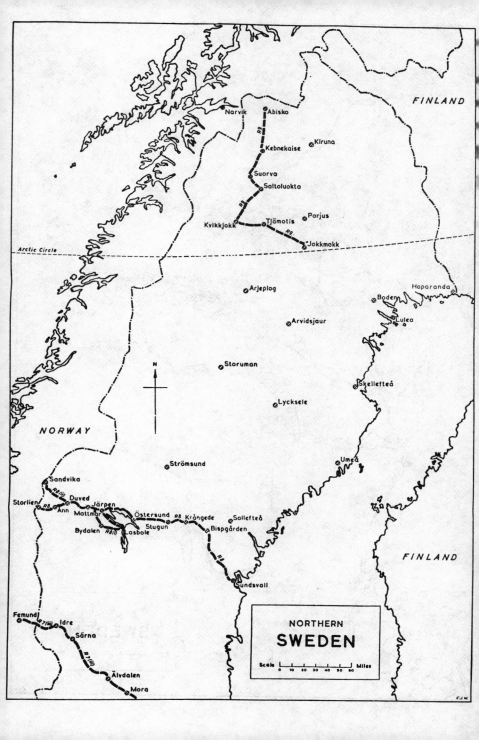

NORTHERN
SWEDEN

Scale
0 10 20 30 40 50 Miles

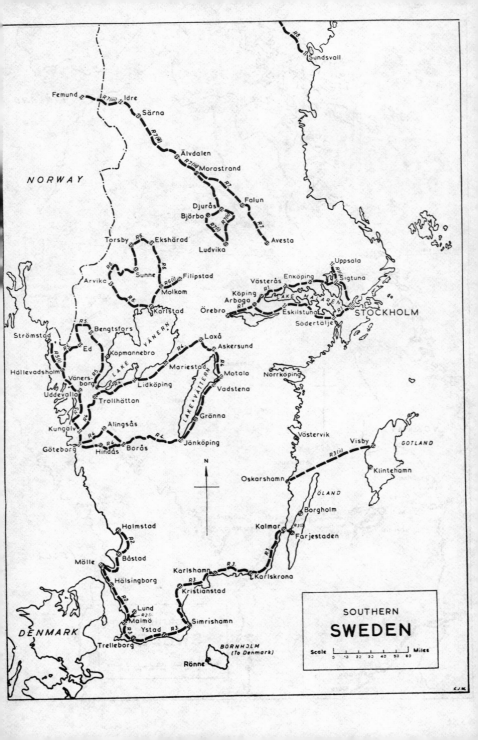

SOUTHERN
SWEDEN

Scale 0 10 20 30 40 50 60 Miles

summer nights resemble a twilight. Most summer rain—what there is of it—falls quickly, and sometimes heavily, usually following thunder, out of blue skies decked with billowy clouds.

Autumn, the wettest season, has superb colourings both in sky and landscapes, especially in the north. The south-west has a tendency to damper weather, with coastal mists.

Winter days are short; so short in fact in the north that artificial light must be used almost continuously in the home. Nevertheless the weather is often crisp, with brilliant sunshine and clear nights, giving fine opportunities for ski-ing and sleigh-riding. Again, the south-west has a tendency to damper, mistier weather.

Plants and Animals Forests cover more than half of the total area. Many are of the graceful silver birch, interspersed with rowan, alder and aspen, but the greater part is of sombre conifer, spruce and pine, and also juniper. In the far north-west, however, stunted birch and willow are best able to withstand the hard conditions. In the south, the deciduous trees which we know so well give a softer face to the landscape, and beech thrives particularly well in the chalk soils. This region therefore more nearly resembles our own woodlands, and the bird-life there is much the same. In central and south Sweden there are marshes where waders abound, and some islands around the south and east coasts are kept as bird sanctuaries. The far north is the most interesting area for a study of plant and animal life. The wild flowers and shrubs are magnificent in spring; since all follow one another in quick succession, there is a range of colours hardly to be rivalled elsewhere; Arctic flowers such as are found in the Alps, flowers of the woods and meadows, ling and alpine rhododendron. Then, in far greater profusion than we know, come the edible cloudberry (*hjortron*) and whortleberry (*lingon*). The latter is found all over Sweden in the woods, and forms a distinctive item in the cuisine.

The north, however, is not alone in having a show of colour; the island of *Gotland* has a magnificent display of roses in the capital, *Visby*, during the summer, and orchids and lilies in many varieties appear in the meadows in early June.

Members of the eagle and allied families nest among the crags of the north-west and blackcock is the most common gamebird. Even the cuckoo can be heard over the Arctic Circle. The reindeer is now only to be seen in the semi-tame herds kept by the Lapps, but deer and also elk are now relatively common since laws and heavy fees were introduced to limit hunting to a few days of the year. The lynx is found sometimes even in the central forests, but the wolf and bear have now been pushed well up into the mountain

SWEDEN

regions. Game-fish abound in the rivers and lakes; on the open parts of the big lakes, fishing is free; elsewhere licences can usually be obtained very cheaply. Crayfish are a delicacy much sought after in the autumn.

The People

Population — Sweden has a large area, but owing to the barren nature of most of *Norrland* her population is small—nearly 8 millions —and the majority of these live in the Southern tip and the cities of central Sweden. *Stockholm*, the capital, has a population of about 1 million but only two others, *Göteborg* and *Malmö*, have over 250,000 while all the rest, except *Norrköping* and *Hälsingborg*, have less than 100,000.

In the far north there are some 8,500 nomadic Lapps. Other elements include 35,000 Finnish-speaking farmers, fishermen and lumberjacks settled along the Finnish border, and 100,000 refugees mostly from Baltic countries.

Language — The three Scandinavian languages are very similar to each other and bear a general resemblance to the other languages of the Germanic family (English, German and Dutch). Swedish is a pleasant sounding language, many of the hard sounds of English and German being softened; this however, makes it a difficult language to understand until the ear has grown accustomed to its rising and falling lilt. It is said that Swedish intonation comes easier to Welshmen than to other folk.

Very many Swedes speak at least some English, but it is helpful to have some idea of the pronunciation of place-names, as even a Swede who speaks good English may find it difficult to understand the foreigner who cannot pronounce the name of the place he wants to get to. It is difficult for English-speaking people to acquire a really good Swedish pronunciation, but easy to get near enough for understanding.

The vowel sounds are similar to English, and can be long or short. The *o* in words like *god* (good), *bror* (brother) is long, like the English "oo" in "school". The modified vowels *ä* and *ö* are pronounced like the "e" in "bet" and the "u" in "fur" respectively. The vowel *å* is similar to the Scottish "o"; a Scotsman saying "boat" and a Swede saying *båt* will sound just the same. Consonants are as in English with three exceptions: *j* and *g* are softened before certain vowels to a "y" sound; *k*, while retaining the hard sound in words like *kaka* (biscuit) is softened to "sch" in words like *skina* (shine), *kyrka* (church). "W" is not used in Swedish except in foreign words and some family names, when it is pronounced like the English "v".

There are a number of French loan-words which look a little odd in Swedish, e.g. *adjö* (adieu).

A few place-names, indicating pronunciation, may help in pronouncing others; *Göteborg*, "Yuh-t-boy"; *Gällivare*, "Yell-i-var-e"; *Västerås*, "Vester-ohs"; *Norrköping*, "Nor-chuh-ping".

Religion
The State Church, to which the majority of the population nominally belongs, is Lutheran, and about 17% of the population can be reckoned regular churchgoers. *Uppsala*, is the seat of the Archbishop. There is freedom of worship for other denominations.

History
In the 9th and 10th centuries the Swedish Vikings raided eastwards for the slaves and furs which they traded to the Arabs via the Russian waterways. This ceased in the next century with the adoption of Christianity and the Swedes turned their energies more to colonizing their own territory. The early kings were often challenged by a strong aristocracy, even after a feudal system was established in the 13th century. But the Union of *Kalmar* (1397), by which Eric of Pomerania was crowned king of the three Scandinavian countries, strengthened royal power. Denmark was for long the dominant partner, but by the 15th century the balance of power was shifting. The peasants, already represented in the Riksdag, reacted against Denmark and, in 1523, placed the forceful Gustavus Vasa on the throne. In his reign of 37 years many changes were made which deeply influenced Sweden's role in European history. The Lutheran Reformation was accepted, the power of the church curtailed by confiscation of its lands, central government was further strengthened, and the monarchy, which had been elective, was declared hereditary. Agriculture and mining were developed. Commerce was greatly encouraged by freeing it from the control of the merchants of *Lübeck* and other Hansa towns.

Swedish influence as a European power was at its height in the century following the accession (1611) of Gustavus II Adolphus, the warrior king and strategist who, until his death in 1632 was the outstanding figure on the Protestant side in the Thirty Years' War (1618-48). By systematically seizing the southern and eastern shores of the Baltic he secured Swedish domination of the sea, reinforced (1658) under Charles X by the taking from Denmark of the provinces of *Scania, Halland, Blekinge* and *Bohuslän*. Sweden's hold on them was confirmed by the victory at *Lund* in 1676. But her fortunes changed in the Nordic war (1700-21) when many of the powers were ranged against her. Unwisely challenging Russia she was defeated at *Poltava* (1709) and her invasion of Norway (1718) proved abortive. As a result of the war she was forced to give up her Baltic empire with the exception of part of Finland.

A period of party strife between groups called the "Caps" and "Hats" (somewhat akin to Whigs and Tories in England) was ended by the strong rule of a reforming king, Gustavus III (1772-92), a patron of learning under whom the arts and sciences flourished. But his home and foreign policy made the nobles his enemies and led to his assassination. In the Napoleonic wars Sweden followed no consistent policy. The main outcome for her was final loss of Finland to Russia.

SWEDEN

A constitutional monarchy with ultimate power in the hands of the Riksdag was provided for in 1809 and next year the Swedes chose as their crown prince the French Marshall Bernadotte. Becoming king as Charles XIV John (1818-44) he demonstrated the possibility and advantages of neutrality, a policy consistently followed by subsequent governments. The 1850s were a period of industrial revolution (notably in the iron, timber and wood-pulp industries), of social reform and a new feeling of kinship with Denmark. Two-chamber government was established in 1866 and proportional representation, for both chambers, was adopted in 1909. Modern Sweden has enjoyed progressive governments and a firm attachment to the arts of peace.

Government The King has executive authority, but in practice this devolves on the Cabinet, led by the Prime Minister, which must have constant parliamentary support. The *Riksdag* (Parliament) consists of two Houses. Members of the Upper House are chosen by the popularly elected provincial assemblies and city-councils, and serve eight years. A general election, using proportional representation, elects the members of the more influential Lower Chamber every four years. The Social Democrats form the government but the other parties together exceed them in number. These are the Conservatives, Centre Party and Liberals, all about equal, and a few Communists.

Resources Agriculture supports about one fifth of the population, though de-population of rural areas is now an urgent and serious problem. Extensive research and mechanisation ensure a high yield and in normal years Sweden is virtually self-supporting in the principal foodstuffs. Only ten per cent. of Sweden's total area is arable and two thirds of this is in the south mainly in the form of large farms in *Skåne*, *Västergötland* and *Östergötland* and smaller ones in *Svealand*. In the north, farms occur in small patches along the river banks, and the farmers have to depend on fishing and logging to make ends meet.

Things to notice on the farms are; in the south, the tethered cattle, and in the north, the drying racks for hay; and in *Dalarna* province the raised larders (*härbre*) in the farmyards. The red colouring, Falun red, used everywhere except in the far north for preserving the wooden buildings, is an iron oxide by-product first produced in the copper mine at *Falu*, whence the name.

Both salt and fresh water fishing are of importance. On the northern rivers, the *karsinapata*, a type of salmon-trap is often set up across the rapids, and off the *Bohuslän* coast, the *sjöbodar*, the long-eaved fishing huts are built out on piles into the sea.

Forest products, now mainly in the form of pulps, paper, wallboard, matches, prefabricated buildings, chemicals and wood alcohol constitute about 40 per cent of Sweden's export trade. Most of the large sawmills and factories are on the north-west shores of the Baltic, on *Lake Vänern* and at the mouths of the rivers down which the logs are floated in the Spring.

Though the number of workers is comparatively small, mining is very important. Owing to the almost entire lack of coal, Sweden is unable to smelt all the iron ore she mines. She therefore smelts the high-grade ores of the central minefields mainly with charcoal, and exports the lower grades from the *Norrland* fields through *Narvik* in Norway. Other metals, chiefly copper, lead and aluminium, are processed in the *Boliden* district in the north-east.

Many Swedish inventions or developments, such as turbines, separators, ball-bearings and refrigerators, are in use throughout the world and engineering products are a major export.

Craft industries of glassware and woodwork centred in *Småland* province and a varied domestic industry in *Dalarna* province, are important in the industrial scheme.

Customs

Along with her conventions, Sweden has preserved a charming folklore. Most of the festivals are connected with the seasons, and are celebrated in song and dance, sometimes together with feasting.

Valborgsmässoafton, the eve of the first of May, is the occasion when students make a special greeting to Spring with bonfires and singing.

Midsummer's Eve (*midsommarafton*), celebrated in town and country all over Sweden. In the country districts, and especially in *Dalarna* province, the national costumes and dances are seen at their best during this celebration.

St. Lucia Day (December 13th) originally a pagan exorcising of the dark spirits of Winter, but now a festival day marking the opening of the Christmas season.

Foresters and fishermen in various communities have their own special festivals, but a nation-wide custom is the holding of crayfish suppers by lantern light, often outdoors towards the end of summer.

Food and Drink

A Scandinavian speciality is *smörgås*, which may be described as an open sandwich. The famous *Smörgåsbord* is an elaborate assortment of cold dishes, which may seem alarming at first, but you should take a plate and fork and start at the bread and butter end. There is a choice of crispbread called *knäckebröd* of various degrees of hardness, white bread (*franskbröd*), a dark sweet-tasting bread and possibly "thin bread" in irregular segments which looks rather like grey cardboard. The rest of the table is made up of dishes of pickled herring, sliced sausage, shrimps, salad components, cheese, smoked salmon and other fish. It is quite usual to come back again a second or third time before tackling the main dishes which are similar to those in any other country. The sweet course, not usually served with midday lunch, is generally a light fruit mixture. Various kinds of junket are also popular.

Milk is very commonly drunk with meals. The alternative seems to be beer (confusingly called *öl*) usually *Pilsner* or similar. There is a variety of soft drinks of superior quality. Anything ending in -*saft* is some kind of fruit juice. *Pommac* is somewhat like the German or Swiss *Apfelsöft*. *Solo* and *Loranga* are orange juice.

SWEDEN

Culture

<table>
<tr><td>Architecture</td><td>A visitor will not go far before noting the preponderance of modern buildings even in the smallest of country towns.</td></tr>
</table>

Architecture A visitor will not go far before noting the preponderance of modern buildings even in the smallest of country towns. This applies as much to the far north as to the south, though for different reasons. The development of the northern towns came about so recently that due regard could be paid to modern conditions. Farther south, however, replacement has often been necessary following the effects of fire on the older buildings, the majority of which were of timber.

The isolation of Sweden meant that Christianity arrived late, and consequently she is not so rich in architectural relics as countries closer to Rome. There is, however, much to see which reflects the cultural development of the country from the Stone Age burial grounds to the medieval churches, Renaissance palaces and modern social architecture.

Under the Vasa dynasty (1520-1654) castles were built on royal initiative at strategic points such as *Kalmar, Mariefred (Gripsholm), Uppsala* and *Vadstena*; and, notably in *Skåne*, others were built by the nobility. Many remain as monuments of a period when Swedish architecture was much subject to influences from abroad.

The first decades of the 20th century were characterized by a romantic national movement which attained its highest expression in the Town Hall of Stockholm (1923). New incentives were given by the Stockholm Exhibition (1930), where Functionalism was the dominant theme. Buildings of this character had, however, appeared earlier than this, the first being the Art Gallery in Stockholm (1916).

A new shopping area, claimed to be the largest in Europe, has been built in the city-centre. Space has been gained by building at different levels, including a new street, *Sergelgatan*, solely for pedestrians, and a system of roof gardens linked by bridges forms an elevated park. High office blocks create a distinctive skyline, and a new rail terminus has been built.

Art Artists working in Sweden in the 17th and 18th centuries were mostly foreigners summoned into the country. But, among native painters, Roslin (in Paris) and Martin (in London) had an international reputation. Towards the end of the 19th century Zorn (1860-1920), recorder of peasant life, was sought after as a portraitist both in Europe and America. Prince Eugen (d. 1947) represents the school of sentimental painting dominant in Sweden at the turn of the century.

Sculpture is dominated by Milles (1875-1955), considered one of the great sculptors of the 20th century. His work is well known abroad, especially in the U.S.A.

Sweden makes a notable contribution to the arts in industrial design: furniture, glass, china and many other every-day objects are almost always superbly designed.

Museums and Art Galleries Most large towns have at least one museum, which houses also sculpture and paintings, and the smaller towns often have a museum of some kind. In the country there are often parks called *gammalgård*, in which typical buildings of the district have been carefully preserved, completely equipped with furniture. *Skansen* Open Air Museum in *Stockholm* is an example on the national scale, since almost every province is represented.

Literature It is only in translation that Swedish writers have been able to reach the public of other countries. Swedenborg (1688-1772) is known to the world for the many mystical and theological works of his later life. Strindberg (1849-1912), poet and dramatist, innovator, and master of many styles, has been specially influential through his naturalistic novels and plays. Of modern writers in the Strindberg tradition works by Lagerkvist (Nobel prizewinner 1951) and Moberg are available in other languages including English. In a different vein, the historical novels of Selma Lagerlöf (1858-1940), the first woman to receive a Nobel Prize for Literature, include the classic *Gösta Berlings Saga*, a story of Varmland, and should be read for their vivid pictures of Swedish life and character.

Theatres The five largest towns—*Stockholm, Göteborg, Malmö, Norrköping, Hälsingborg* and also *Gävle*—have concert halls and theatres but, like the cinemas, these have few, if any, performances in summer. Concerts are, however, held on summer evenings in *Stockholm* in the National Museum (Art Gallery), in *Skansen* Open Air Museum, in *Kungsträdgården*, and under the piazza of the City Hall. *Stockholm* Festival of Music, Drama and Ballet is held annually in early June. Operas, performed at other times in the Royal Opera House, are given in summer at the *Drottningholm Court Theatre*.

Science Sweden shared in the Age of Enlightenment in the 18th century and produced a remarkable group of scientists of whom perhaps the best known are Celsius, in physics, and von Linné (Linnaeus) in botany. Sedenborg, too, wrote widely in mathematics, mineralogy and physiology before he became a mystic.

Her natural scientists in the 19th century include Retzius and Berzelius in the 20th century, de Geer, the geologist, and Svedberg, the physicist.

Touring Information

Sweden is such a large country and contains so many different types of landscape that you cannot hope to see it all on foot, or even on a bicycle. Distances are so great that the most you can do is to explore one of the many areas.

First in importance comes the lake and canal district of central Sweden. This is undulating country, alternating between open farmland and woods, with frequent glimpses between clearings across the lakes. Many of its modern industrial towns have historical associations from the days when they were trading centres.

Bohuslän and *Dalsland* lie to the west of the central lakes. The rocky coast of *Bohuslän* with its many fishing villages and bathing resorts contrasts with the wooded hilly district of *Dalsland* dotted with small farms and lakes.

Värmland is a province of lakes, fertile valleys and wooded ridges. The atmosphere of the old *bruk* and manor houses of this district gave Selma Lagerlöf the inspiration for the novels she wrote portraying the life of the people. Modern cellulose factories in forest settings now dot the landscape.

Bergslagen is the name of the central (mining) district included in the provinces of *Värmland*, *Västmanland* and *Dalarna*. The latter is one of the most popular provinces for touring since here, especially around *Lake Siljan* can be seen many of the customs and colourful local costumes in idyllic surroundings: woods, lakes and meadows, small white stone churches, and mellowed wooden farmhouses, some containing unique wall hangings *dalmålningar*).

Skåne, district of fertile plains, Sweden's richest agricultural country, has castles and manor houses surrounded by parks and gardens, and, along the coasts, sandy bathing beaches; *Blekinge* is an area of cultivated valleys between beech-wooded hills; then there are the unique islands of *Öland* and *Gotland*. *Jämtland* is an area for mountain walking and winter sports. *Ångermanland* and *Medelpad* are provinces of forests, lakes, mountains, large rivers and forest industries.

In the far north lies a vast area of pine forests, giving way to treeless lake-dotted mountains, the land of the Lapps. This is splendid country for mountain walking, climbing, fishing and ski-ing, and is best reached by train from *Stockholm* to *Kiruna* by the main route, returning by the inland route through *Östersund*.

The best approach from Britain is by steamer to *Gothenburg*. There are sailings three times a week from *Tilbury* and the minimum single fare is £20·50, but in summer the cheaper accommodation becomes fully booked a long time ahead.

Other routes are from *Immingham* to *Gothenburg* by the Tor Line, thrice weekly, from £19·00 or, for those wishing to combine Sweden and Denmark, via *Harwich* or *Newcastle* to *Esbjerg*. The many routes between Sweden and Denmark include frequent services from *Copenhagen* to *Malmö* and from *Elsinore* to *Hälsingborg*, the shortest route.

Transport Rail fares are comparatively cheap for long distances, according to the zone tariff system. A second class ticket *Göteborg—Stockholm* (456 km) costs 101 *kr.*, return 167 *kr.*, whereas *Göteborg—Abisko* (1,914 km) costs only 198 *kr.*, return 327 *kr.* Return tickets are valid two months. Seat reservation, which is compulsory on certain express trains, costs 4 *kr.*, and 2nd class sleepers cost 25 *kr.* Good restaurant and coffee service on long distance trains.

There are special holiday tickets (*Semesterbiljett*) for long distances, cheap circular tour tickets and cheaper fares for parties.

In *Norrland* efficient bus services (*Post diligensen*) run by the Post Office connect north-south railway lines with coast and remote inland districts.

Steamers to *Visby* (*Gotland*) sail from *Vastervik, Oskarshamn, Sodertälje* and *Stockholm.*

There is no charge on river ferries and these run according to demand, Many small boats run out to islands off the coasts and on all bigger lakes, except Lake *Vänern*, and are part of the normal communications on most lakes in Lapland.

Timetables The national timetable, *Sveriges Kommunikationer*, with international sign language, includes rail, some lake-boat and most bus services.
Trafikleder i Lappland is a special bus and boat timetable for the *Kebnekaise, Sjöfall* and *Sitasjaure* areas issued free by *Svenska Turistföreningen.*

Money The Swedish crown (*krona*—abbreviated as *kr.*) is divided into 100 *ore.*

Clothing Fairly light clothing can be worn in summer, but spring nights can be sharp with frost, especially farther north. Be prepared for sudden bursts of thundery rain and take an anti-midge protection in summer.

Restaurants Most towns have inexpensive restaurants (*Konsum* or *mjölkbar*) which serve good quality food. A midday or evening meal can be had for about 8 *kr.* The smallest communities can be relied upon to have a *konditori* which serves coffee and pastries.

Maps The largest series is *Topografiska kartan över Sverige*; the far north is at a scale of 1:100,000 and the rest of the country at 1:50,000. There are also 16 special maps of the mountain areas (*Svenska fjällkartan*) scales 1:100,000 and 1:200,000, which would be suitable for walking holidays there. Cyclists should use the new *Turist kartan*, 10 very large sheets at 1:300,000. For a general-purpose road map, there is the *G.L.A. Bilistens vägkarta* in two sheets, north and south; the overall scale is 1:1,000,000, but the far north is shown only at 1:2,000,000.

SWEDEN

Walking Tours — Swedish hostels are too far apart for hostel-to-hostel walking tours, and it is necessary to use bus or train to cover the longer stretches. The best walking country served by youth hostels is to be found in *Värmland*, to the north of Lake *Vänern* (see **R.6**), and round Lake *Siljan* in *Dalarna* (see **R.7**). Undoubtedly, however, the finest walking is to be had in the mountain areas of the north.

Mountaineering and Fell-Walking — The Swedish highlands span about 550 miles through *Lapland* (see **R.9**), *Jämtland* (see **R.8**) and *Härjedalen* to *Dalarna* (see **R.7**). The highest (nearly 7,000 ft.) and most rugged mountains, with glaciers in some parts, occur in north-west *Lapland* and will attract mountaineers. But they and the other mountain areas are particularly suitable for long fell-walking tours. Best season in *Lapland*, mid-July to early Sept.

Almost uninhabited, the highlands have a wild spaciousness hardly to be found elsewhere in Europe. Careful planning and some experience is essential before attempting a long tour, which should not in any case be undertaken alone. Conditions are quite different from those found in the Alps, notably the remoteness from habitation and so it may be necessary to carry provisions for several days.

The Swedish Touring Club (STF) has marked tracks, provided bridges, rowing boats, motor boats on lakes and accommodation as follows:

(a) STF mountain stations; beds, meals, and usually a store and self-cooking facilities; make reservations and reckon 35 *kr*. per day full board: in *Lapland* at *Abisko*; *Kebnekaise, Ritsemjåkk, Saltoluokta, Kvikkjokk, Vietas* and *Kittelfjäll*; *Jämtland* at *Blåhammaren, Sylarna* and *Storulvån* and in *Dalarna* at *Grövelsjön*.

(b) STF mountain huts; no staff, no meals and no advance booking: about 70 huts on the cairned trails between tourist stations, equipped with bedding, cooking utensils and, in most cases, firewood. Key at nearest tourist station or at *STF* offices in *Stockholm, Göteborg, Hälsingborg* and *Malmö*.

(c) STF shelters (unlocked); Lapp style conical huts, unfloored with turf-covered sides.

Overnight fees for STF members: huts 10 *kr*., shelters 4 *kr*. (Non-members 13 *kr*. and 7 *kr*. respectively). STF membership costs 30 *kr*. a year; family members and those under 20 years, 10 *kr*. Pamphlet available from STF, Stureplan 2, 103 80 *Stockholm*, 7.

Leave huts and shelters as you would wish to find them: wood supply inside; windows, doors and outbuildings secured. Carelessness could be fatal as an open window could mean a snow-filled hut. Similarly at unmanned boat crossings leave a boat at each side. This means rowing three times.

Ski-ing — All the above mountain regions are excellent for ski-ing. In *Lapland* the best months are March and April, but in the far north it may still be possible to the end of May.

Cycling — Trunk roads and many country main roads, especially in the south, have permanent surfaces suitable for cycling; other roads may be roughly surfaced. Apart from the north-west, Sweden is not difficult terrain for cyclists and winds are comparatively light. Most towns have cycle shops where running repairs can be carried out but spares for English and American bicycles are almost impossible to obtain.

Canoeing and Boating — Canoeing is possible for long stretches on many canals, rivers and lakes, along the shores of which convenient camping sites can easily be found. At some tourist hotels, canoes are loaned out by the STF (*Grövelsjön* in *Dalarna* and *Tärnaby*, in Lapland). Suggested routes are through the *Göteborg—Hindås—Alingsås* lake district, the *Dalslands Canal*, *Mälaren* and surrounding lakes and rivers, *Grövelsjön* and surrounding lakes and down *Torne* river from *Tornetrask* to *Jukkasjärvi*.

Sailing is popular around the coast, especially from *Stockholm* and *Göteborg*. Most boats are privately owned, so that hiring out is not so usual. There are, however, sight-seeing trips on the waterways of these ports.

Stockholm

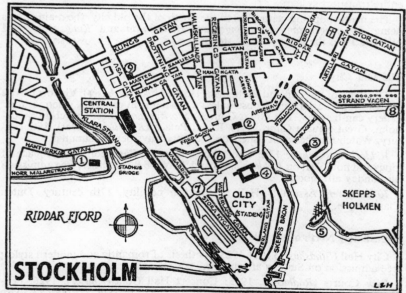

1. *Town Hall.* 2. *Opera.* 3. *National Museum.* 4. *Royal Palace.* 5. *Youth Hostel Ship "Af Chapman."* 6. *Riksdag (Parliament House).* 7. *Riddarhuset.* 8. *Road to Skansen.* 9. *Post Office.*

SWEDEN

Stockholm, beautifully situated on its islands, comprises the Old City, the "Stone City" and the suburbs and satellite towns of recent growth.

A useful plan of the city and its communications is *"Sparvägskartan"* which costs 1 *kr.* and can be bought on buses.

Its centre is the island known as the city between the bridges, or the old city (*gamla staden*). In direct contrast to the historical buildings found here are the modern flats lining the waterfront and the concrete and steel bridges which span the waterways.

Boats arriving from the west, i.e., from Lake *Mälaren*, tie up close by Central Station at *Norr-Mälarstrand* and *Klara Strand*, while sea-going steamers arrive at *Skeppsbron* on the east side a mile from the railway station.

The focal point of roads from the north is *Norra Bantorget*, just north of the station, and from the south, the clover leaf crossing known as *Slussen*, ¼ mile south of the station.

Most of the public-service vehicles are electric; a standard fare of 1 *kr.* is charged, valid for buses and underground (*Tunnelbanan*), and the ticket can be used for a further journey in the same zone within an hour of issue. Excess is charged for journeys into other zones and double fare after midnight. During summer tourist tickets can be bought, for unlimited journeys on the city's entire transport system.

The main shopping-centre lies to the north of the old city, the main streets being *Regeringsgatan, Drottninggatan, Hamngatan* and *Kungsgatan,* and NK and PUB the most popular stores.

The Old City

The Bank of Sweden and Parliament House (*Riksdagshuset*). Visitors can be shown round Parliament House unless a session is in progress, when visitors' gallery can be used. The Great Church (*Storkyrkan*) oldest church in Stockholm. Great Square (*Stortorget*). Royal Palace (*Kungliga Slottet*); 18th century. Watch for the smelt fishers on the waterways here in summer.

Riddarholmskyrkan: 13th cent. abbey, Swedish Pantheon, burial place of kings and notables; on *Riddarholm* island, S.W. of *Riddarhuset*; free admission on Sunday afternoons.

Riddarhuset: Assembly Hall of Swedish nobility, 17th century, Dutch Classic style.

Immediately North of the Old City

City Hall (*Stadshuset*) 1911-1923, synthesis of romantic and modern styles; free admission on Sunday afternoons.

Law Courts (*Rådhuset*), 1915; Concert Hall (*Konserthuset*), 1926, neo-classical; faces the lively flower and produce market (*Hötorget*), with *"Orpheus"* fountain by Milles. *Kungliga Teatern* (Opera and Ballet) season August-May. Royal Dramatic Theatre, season Sept.–mid-June. *National Museum*; painting and sculpture, and concerts on summer evenings.

To the North, but farther from City centre

Stadium built for Olympic Games in 1912; football and athletic events on Sunday afternoons. College of Technology (*Tekniska Högskolan*) with fountain "*Monument of Industry*", by Milles, at front. Gustavus III Pavilion 1790 in Haga Park with exquisite period furnishings. Natural History Museum (*Naturhistorika Riksmuseum*), including botanical garden; Train from *Engelbrekts Pl.* or *Östra* Station to *Freskati*. *Millesgåden*, with Milles' works on terraces overlooking city.

East of Old City (Skeppsholmen and beyond)

Nordic Museum (*Nordiska Museet*) and Royal Armoury (*Kgl. Livrustkammaren*) historical collections. *Skansen*, open air cultural museum, theatre, zoological gardens, music and dancing. *Waldemarsudde*, art collection. National Historical Museum (*Stat. Historiska Museum*); fine collection of religious art and archaeology. Other museums farther east are the Maritime museum (*Stat. Sjöhistoriska*), the Ethnographic museum, the Technical museum (with unique Atomarium) and the Museum of Modern Art on *Skeppsholmen*.

Outside City to the East

Stockholm Archipelago for superb bathing and boating. Popular resort of *Saltsjöbaden* (swimming, yachting, boating) 30 mins. by rail from *Saltsjöbaden* Station at *Slussen* or by steamer from *Nybroplan* in 1½ hrs.

South of Old City

Co-op Head Office and *Katarina* lift for fine view; Civic Centre (*Medborgar huset*); Forest Cemetery and Crematorium (*Skogskyrkogården, Enskede*) Gunnar Asplund's last work; Handicraft Institute (*Stat. Handverksinstitut*); fine view from building over city. Southern Hospital (*Södersjukhuset*), one of Sweden's finest modern hospitals. Ericsson's telephone factory; an example of industrial architecture.

Outside City to the West

Drottningholm Castle; 7½ miles by steamer from *Klara Strand* in 40 mins. 17th century, French baroque, museums; theatre is 18th century and preserved in original form. Open in summer when performances of operas are staged.

Gripsholm Castle, Mariefred. Sailings to *Mariefred* from *Klara Strand* in summer in 3½ hrs. or by train from Central Station, 1½ hrs. Mainly 16th century; portrait collection one of the finest in Europe.

There are many indoor and outdoor swimming baths and it is also possible to bathe during the summer in the maze of creeks to be found at some distance from the city.

Many camping sites are open during the summer and details of them can be had from the Stockholm Tourist Association, Gustav Adolfs Torg, 20.

Vällingby is a modern suburb of interest to architects and can be reached by underground from the centre of Stockholm in about 30 minutes. Modern apartment buildings of different kinds, low ones as well as small "skyscrapers", surround an attractive shopping centre with a restaurant and underground station.

SWEDEN

Touring Routes

R.1. Stockholm—Örebro—Stockholm, round Lake Mälaren (250 miles)

This district is the cradle of the Swedish nation and abounds in historical monuments and associations. It contains a large number of fine castles and country houses. Lake *Mälaren* is dotted with innumerable islands, many of them extremely beautiful. Steamer service in summer from *Stockholm* (*Klara Strand*) to some places mentioned in this route; a pleasant means of exploring lake, although route is based on road travel.

From *Stockholm* take road E.4 through north-western suburb of *Ulriksdal* with palace built by Charles X (17th century) to (23 miles) **Sigtuna, (Y.H.)** one of oldest and most picturesque towns in Sweden. Nearest railway station *Märsta* is 3 miles eastwards. Town founded 11th century; ruins of four large churches testify to its former importance. *Sigtunastiftelsen* is well-known college for ecclesiastical studies and adult education.

EXCURSION: *Skokloster* Castle, with collection of trophies from 30 Years' War, is one of finest in Sweden. Boat trips in season.

R.1(i) Sigtuna to Uppsala, 20 miles. (Y.H.) Do not omit this detour unless very short of time. From *Sigtuna* continue north to join main road from *Stockholm* at *Alsike*. Uppsala is older of the two ancient universities and seat of Archbishop of Sweden. Many associations with great botanist Linnaeus. Cathedral is beautiful gothic building. Castle (16th century) mainly occupied by County Council, but great hall open to visitors—here Queen Christina abdicated in 1654. University library ("*Carolina Rediviva*") contains valuable collection of books and manuscripts, greatest treasure being Codex Argentius, translation of Bible into ancient Gothic by Arian Bishop Ulfilas (5th century) so-called from silver colour of its lettering.

EXCURSION: *Gamla Uppsala*, 2½ miles, bus or train, is site of capital of pre-Christian kingdom of *Svea* (hence modern name for *Sweden—Svea-rike*, meaning kingdom of the *Svear*). Little church said to stand on site of Temple of Odin. Great mounds are burial places of ancient chieftains. On one of these royal council was held and assembled tribes addressed by their kings.

From *Sigtuna* take secondary road via *Erikssund* to join main highway (E.18) at *Övergran*, then through *Enköping*, old market town with monastery ruins (Y.H.), crossing county boundary from *Uppland* into *Västmanland* just before reaching (26 miles) *Västerås*.

Västeras (Y.H.) manufacturing town and county capital pleasantly situated on bay of lake. Tower of A.S.E.A. factory with its cupola said by local people to be frequently mistaken for cathedral. Latter is building in mixed romanesque style built of weathered red brick. *Djäkneberg* is pleasant open-space affording good view over town and lake; names and dates cut on rocks and stones are work of local eccentric.

EXCURSION: 10 miles S.W. to *Tidö* castle (1620): stands in fine park on peninsula in lake.

Main road (E.18) leads via *Kolbäck* and *Munktorp* to *Köping* (22 miles), with small open-air museum and Y.H.

Continue from *Köping* to (10 miles), *Arboga* small town with many interesting 15th century buildings (Y.H.). Here Sweden's first parliament was held in 1435 under Engelbrekt, whose statue, 1935, commemorates 500th anniversary. Beyond *Arboga* main road crosses county boundary into small province of *Närke* and continues along Lake *Hjälmar* to mouth of *Svartån* (Black

406

River) and (45 miles) *Örebro* (Y.H.) important in Swedish history from its foundation in 14th century to 1810 when Bernadotte was here elected crown prince.

Returning, take roads on south of Lake *Hjälmar* to (25 miles) **Eskilstuna,** (Y.H.) home of Swedish steel industry. Before days of safety razors and electric shavers *Eskilstuna* razors were world famous. Town takes its name from English missionary St. Eskil (11th century) martyred by pagans and buried here. Fine public park and *Södermanland's* county open-air museum; two ancient smithies are preserved as museums. Continue eastwards on road E.3 to (20 miles) *Strängnäs*, delightful cathedral town on lake-side.

Mariefred (Y.H.), for *Gripsholm Castle*, is 12 miles farther on.

Boat services to bathing beaches on islands of *Segerön* and *Granliden*. Through picturesque wooded country to *Södertälje* (Y.H.). Here is another open-air museum. 15 mile motor way from here to suburbs of *Stockholm*.

R.2. Skåne and Halland. Malmö to Halmstad (104 miles)

This part of Sweden was for a long time under Danish rule, and it is said that inhabitants are still more happy-go-lucky than their fellow Swedes. Certainly the traveller crossing from Denmark will be struck by Danish look of the town and the countryside of fertile plains.

Malmö third largest town in Sweden and ancient capital of *Skåne*. Many fine old buildings; St. Peter's Church, 1319, *Malmöhus* castle, 16th century and modern architecture; City Theatre, 1944, *Friluftstaden* Garden Suburb. Ferry service to *Copenhagen*.

R.6(i) Malmö to Lund, 11 miles. *Lund* is ancient town, well worth visit. Founded by *Knut* (Canute) the Great, King of Denmark, Norway and England. University founded 1666. Romanesque cathedral has astronomical clock and is one of oldest and most interesting churches in Sweden. Restaurant in University club house is open to public.

Landskrona (25 miles) has well-preserved 17th century castle and moat. (Y.H.)

EXCURSION: by steamer, 35 mins. to Island of *Ven*, to see observatory built by Danish astronomer Tycho Brahe (16th century).

Hälsingborg, (Y.H.) fine modern town built round older nucleus. Wide view from castle tower (*Kärnan*) 186 steps. Maritime museum at *Råå* to S. of town, bathing beach at *Pålsjöbaden* nearby. Ferries to *Helsingör* in Denmark and *Travemunde* in Germany.

Continue N. to *Kulla-Gunnarstorp* (4 miles), with enormous 19th century mansion standing near old castle (1570), park open part of each morning in summer. *Viken* (2 miles) is popular sea-side resort; *Höganäs* (4 miles) has only coal mine in Sweden.

Mölle (Y.H.) is pleasant resort on *Kullen* peninsula, below *Högkull* hill (615 ft.) with high cliffs and some interesting caves; area is nature reserve, and entrance fee charged. Powerful light-house on point of peninsula.

Continue along coast via *Angelholm* (Y.H.) through *Hallandsås* hills by attractive *Sinarp* valley to *Båstad*, fashionable resort with international tennis and golf tournaments, fine gardens.

SWEDEN

Turn E. on road No. 115 via *Ö. Karup.* 2½ miles E. at *Hasslöfs* church, take road south to *Lugnarohögen* for fine ship-form burial mound dating from bronze age. North to *Laholm,* on River *Lagan,* picturesque little town; ruins of medieval fortress, moat now salmon nursery. Excellent bathing at *Mellby-strand,* 4 miles W.

Tour ends at *Halmstad,* port with remains of old fortifications; sculpture by Milles "Europa and the Bull" on fountain in *Stora Torg.* From *Halmstad* to *Göteborg* by coast road, 90 miles, but less interesting than coast farther south.

R.3. The extreme South. Malmö to Kalmar (255 miles) Öland & Gotland

Route follows coast of provinces of *Skåne, Blekinge* and *Småland.* Road E.6 *Trelleborg* (20 miles) (**Y.H.**) is port for ferry to *Sassnitz* (East Germany); continue on road No. 10 past several fishing villages and small resorts to *Ystad,* (**Y.H.**), one of best-preserved old towns in country; many half-timbered houses in Danish style. E. of old town is modern resort, *Ystads Saltsjöbaden.* District contains many castles and manor-houses. Steamer service to *Rönne* on Danish island of *Bornholm.*

20 miles E.N.E. from *Ystad* is magnificent 16th century castle of *Glimminge-hus,* well-preserved, four-storey keep. Coast reached again (7 miles) at *Simrishamn,* old seaport; steamer service to *Bornholm. Kivik* (10 miles), fishing village and bathing resort; **Y.H.** at *Haväng,* near *Ravlundabro*—take track near shore from *Vitemölla,* 2 miles.

Beyond *Degeberga* is well-preserved castle of *Vittskövle* (16th century). *Kristianstad* is garrison town; two of ancient city gates preserved on new sites. Trinity (*Trefaldighets*) church is good example of 17th century architecture. At *Sölvesborg* (18 miles) road No. 15 enters province of **Blekinge,** formerly Danish possession often called "Garden of Sweden" owing to its well-tilled valleys. Road circles *Pukaviks* bay to (19 miles) *Karlshamn,* port and industrial town; (**Y.H.**) boat excursions to *Blekinge* archipelago.

Kullåkra, 10 miles E. of *Karlshamn* by rail, is station for *Tjärö* Island (**Y.H.**) reached by road to *Järnavik,* 2 miles, then motor boat. Bicycles can be left in waiting room at *Järnavik.* 11 miles farther is *Ronneby,* (**Y.H.**) with picturesque wooden houses around church.

Karlskrona (16 miles), Sweden's principal naval base, built on islands; founded by Charles XI in 1679; planned in Baroque style, with fine streets and buildings. *Blekinge* Museum in *Västra Prinsgatan.* Y.H. at *Kristianopel,* 15 miles along coast.

At *Brömsebro* (5 miles) leave *Blekinge* for *Småland;* name means small lands, derived from former division into many small estates; soil is poor but the province has won fame for its glass and furniture industries.

Kalmar historic town. Fine example of 17th century planning. Baroque cathedral; town hall; merchant houses; city wall and gates. Massive castle, partly 12th century, partly renaissance. Fine interior. Swedish American Day celebrated in courtyard 2nd Sun. Aug.

EXCURSION: 26 miles W.N.W. to *Orrefors* (Y.H.), known throughout world for its artistic glassware.

R.3(i) Kalmar to Isle of Öland. Boat *Kalmar* to *Färjestaden*, every hour; also from *Oskarshamn* (**Y.H.**) (50 miles N.) steamer twice daily to *Byxelkrok*, north *Öland*.

Apart from narrow coastal strip, island consists of long chalk ridge, infertile but with interesting flora and bird life. Archeological remains and windmills abound. Bus service on circular route links *Borgholm* (capital and only town) (**Y.H.**) and *Färjestaden* with most parts of island. 3 more Y.Hs on island.

R.3(ii) To Island of Gotland. Steamers daily from *Oskarshamn* to Visby. Also from *Öland* to *Klintehamn* on *Gotland*. Can also be reached from *Stockholm*. *Gotland* "Isle of the Goths" lies 50 miles from Swedish coast; sunny climate, with southerly type of flora in lowlands and pine and heather on uplands. *Visby*, capital and only town is former *Hansa* city which in 12th and 13th century was fabulously wealthy. Most of churches now roofless, but merchants' houses still stand along narrow streets, giving vivid impression of Middle Ages; city wall, still almost complete, is over 2 miles in length (recommended walk). Y.H. 3 more Y.Hs on island. Bus services connect most places.

Whole island is rich in prehistoric remains, interesting churches, old manor houses; many bathing beaches. Island of *Stora Karlsö*, off W. coast and by motor boat from *Klintehamn*, is bird sanctuary.

R.4. Göteborg and The Great Lakes. Göteborg—Jönköping— Göteborg (361 miles)

Göteborg (**Y.H.**) was founded 1619 when south of Sweden and all Norway was under Danish rule; it was well placed for trade with the New World and the Far East. Dutch merchants and town-planners helped in its development and the signs of their influence remain in the buildings and canals in parts of the city. *Göteborg* has always tended to look west; connections with English and Scots families remain in surnames.

The principal sights are *Götaplatsen* (*Göta* Square), with Milles sculpture "Poseidon", Art Museum, Concert Hall (one of finest in Europe), and Municipal Theatre. Botanical Gardens and *Trädgårdföreningen*, a terrace restaurant with music and dancing in beautiful garden surroundings. *Gustav Adolfs Torg*, main square at centre of busy street *Östra Hamngatan*. *Liseberg* amusement park is a smaller edition of the famous *Tivoli* in Copenhagen with gardens, music, restaurants and entertainments.

From *Göteborg* follow course of canalised *Göta* River for 12 miles to charming ancient little town of *Kungälv* (**Y.H.**). On opposite side of river is 14th century fortress of *Bohus*. Take road on east side of river to *Alvängen* (12 miles) and on to *Trollhättan* (25 miles) (**Y.H.**) industrial town and tourist centre. Here are locks which raise canal to level of lake *Vänern*. Hydro-electric station at *Trollhätten* Falls, one of largest in Europe, can be visited by arrangement. Many walks and viewpoints in neighbourhood.

EXCURSION: 9 miles to *Vänersborg* (**Y.H.**), lake and canal port at entry into Lake *Vänern* (Sweden's largest lake). Journey from *Göteborg* to *Vänersborg* can be made by *Göta* Canal steamer (about 8 hours).

Turn E. via *Grästorp* to *Lidköping* (50 miles) small industrial town on bay. Returning to main route follow lakeside road to *Kinnekulle*, peculiarly terraced rocky hill, 1,000 ft. with wide views. Look-out tower on *Högkulle* (ascend from either *Råbäck* or *Gassäter*). Several ancient castles in neighbourhood. Along lakeside to *Mariestad* (**Y.H.**) (34 miles from *Lidköping*) pleasant lakeside town, 17th century cathedral. Continue on E.3 via *Hassle* to *Laxå* (28 miles) small industrial town with interesting wooden church and museum,

SWEDEN

on main railway line *Stockholm-Göteborg*, and most northerly point on this route. *Örebro* on route **R.1** is 40 miles N.E. Turn south on road No. 205 via *Röfors* and past two small lakes to *Askersund* **(Y.H.)** at end of Lake *Vättern* (26 miles); follow road No. 50, one of most beautiful lakeside roads in Sweden to *Motala* (38 miles) industrial town and port for *Göta* canal; 13th century cathedral; tomb of von Platen, engineer of canal, in lakeside park. Bathing beach at *Varamobaden*. *Vadstena* **(Y.H.)** lies 10 miles south, is port of call for canal steamers; Renaissance castle (1545); abbey established by St. Brigitte, founder of Brigittine religious order. Near *Väversunda* (10 miles) is Lake *Tåkern*, haunt of many birds. W. of road is *Omberg* (760 ft.), wooded hill rising sheer from lake, famous for its bird-life and plants. Y.H. at S. end of hill just before reaching *Alvastra*, 4 miles. Nearby are abbey ruins and prehistoric lake-dwelling site. At *Rök* (8 miles) is famous rune stone. Just to south is *Hästholmen*, lake port with steamer to *Hjo* **(Y.H.)** on opposite bank. *Ödeshög* **Y.H.** is 5 miles south of *Hästholmen*. *Gränna* **(Y.H.)**, 20 miles, is charming village in district famous for its orchards. Here is a 300 years old pear-tree preserved as ancient monument. *Andree Museum* contains relics of ill-fated attempt to reach North Pole by balloon (1897).

EXCURSION: to island of *Visingsö* by steamer or motor boat in about half an hour; many ancient barrows and earthworks; medieval churches; rich vegetation.

Jönköping (Y.H.) is 25 miles farther along E.4 at south end of lake; new museum at *Fiskartorget*; 17th century Town Hall; open-air museum in park; modern match industry (with museum). Turn west on road No. 40 for 35 miles to *Ulricehamn* **(Y.H.)** health resort with sanatoria on Lake *Åsunden*. Continue to *Borås* (20 miles) textile manufacturing town **(Y.H.)**. From here two routes to *Göteborg*: 52 miles via *Alingsås* **(Y.H.)** and *Näs*, on Lake *Sävelången*, famous for school of arts and crafts, or 45 miles via *Hindås*, noted winter sports centre.

R.5 Bohuslän and Dalsland. Göteborg—Hällevadsholm— Vänersborg—Göteborg (248 miles)

From *Göteborg* take road No. 160 on W. bank of *Göta* River to (12 miles) *Kungälv* **(Y.H.)**. Fork north-west on E.6 12 miles to *Jorlanda* **Y.H.** and 5 miles on to *Spekeröd*; to north is magnificent coastal scenery: *Stenungsund* (3 miles) has good bathing beach. Y.H. at *Ödsmål* in 18th century parsonage. *Uddevalla* (22 miles) **(Y.H.)** in valley between tall cliffs. Nearby are gravel-beds with biggest mass of fossil shells in world. Motor-boat services and tours to nearby islands. *Hällevadsholm* lies 25 miles to north.

R.5(i) Hällevadsholm to Strömstad 28 miles. *Tanumshede* (15 miles) is centre of district abounding in tumuli, rock carvings, rune-stones and many others prehistoric remains. Leaving main road at *Skee*, descend to *Strömstad*. (Y.H.).

EXCURSION: to *Koster* Islands, by motor boat (*Sydkoster* is of interest to botanists), and by road to *Blomsholm*, with remarkable standing stones in ship form dating from iron-age.

Main route continues past beautiful *Bullaren* lakes via *Mon* to *Ed* **(Y.H.)**, charming tourist centre at end of *Stora Le* lake. *Pipekulle* is worth climbing for view. Take lakeside road to (20 miles) *Nössemark*, then ferry across lake to *Sund* and continue 20 miles to *Bengtsfors* **(Y.H.)**. Good views from hills where marked footpaths are shown on local maps. *Köpmannebro* (30 miles) on Lake *Vänern* may be reached either by road or by **Dalsland Canal**, pleasant

SWEDEN

and little used waterway, composed of lakes and canals, ideal for canoeists; steamer services from *Bengstfors* in 6 hrs. Canal aqueduct and bridges at *Håverud*.

From *Köpmannebro* turn south on lakeside road to *Vänersborg* (Y.H.) Bathing and motor-boat excursions. Return to *Göteborg* on route R.4 via *Trollhättan*. (Y.H.)

R.6. Värmland. Karlstad—Arvika—Torsby—Karlstad (330 miles)

Train from *Oslo* (150 miles) or *Göteborg* 155 miles (change at *Kil*) to *Karlstad* (Y.H.) ancient county capital on north shore of Lake *Vänern*; open-air museums; Cathedral (1730), (restored 1916); town is excellent centre for excursions into varied countryside.

Take road west for 28 miles to *Värmskog* (Y.H.). Turn north to *Arvika* (25 miles) and via *Åmotfors* Y.H. and series of delightful small lakes—*Racken, Gunnern,* and *Rottnen* for 55 miles to *Sunne,* (Y.H.), attractive small resort on isthmus between middle and upper *Fryken* lakes. These three lakes and surrounding countryside (*Fryksdalen*) form background to Selma Lagerlöf's novel *Gösta Berlings Saga.*

EXCURSIONS: (a) To *Mårbacka* farm house home of Selma Lagerlöf (8 miles). (b) Lake steamer to *Fryksta* (on southern lake) (Y.H.).

Turn N. along magnificent upper lake (steamer service) to (32 miles) *Torsby* (Y.H.). Here and at *Gräsmark* farther south, on Lake *Rottnen,* are hills worth climbing for views—e.g., *Tossebergsklätten* (1,120 ft.). On to *Ekshärad* (25 miles) by road No. 234, then south on road No. 62; fine views from *Ekesberget.* Continue south along river *Klarälven* into an old mining district, via Y.Hs at *Hagfors* and *Ransäter,* to *Sunnemo* (25 miles) on road No. 204, wooden church (1653); and to (20 miles) *Molkom.*

R.6(i) Molkom to Filipstad 28 miles. Pleasant little town, centre of *Bergslagen,* an area in which mining has been carried out for six hundred years or more. Mausoleum of John Ericsson, the inventor.

Main route returns via *Kil* to *Karlstad* (45 miles).

R.7. Dalarna. Ludvika—Falun—Avesta (173 miles)

Dalarna is one of the most picturesque districts in Sweden. In some places old costumes still worn on festivals, and traditional songs and dances still performed. *Dalarna* (name means the dales) derived from two great valleys. The eastern *Dalälv,* flows into Lake *Siljan,* one of most beautiful lakes in Sweden. This route is practicable for walkers, with some assistance from lake steamers; twice weekly from *Leksand* to *Tällberg, Rättvik* and *Mora.*

From *Filipstad* (see R.6(i)); or from *Stockholm,* 4 hrs. by rail) to **Ludvika,** industrial town on Lake *Väsman* from where there is choice of two routes to *Djurås.*

R.7(i) Ludvika to Djurås via Björbo 53 miles. Skirting pleasant Lake *Väsman,* then through good hill country to *Björbo* (fine bridge over western *Dalälv*) and *Floda,* typical *Dalarna* village. Walkers can take hill path from *Skallberget,* 10 miles S. of *Björbo. Djurås* lies at junction of eastern and western *Dalälv* valleys. *Tjärnboberg* (1,240 ft.) can be climbed from *Sifferbo.* Look-out point on *Djurmoklack* (1,196 ft.).

R.7(ii) Ludvika to Djurås via Borlänge, 38 miles. Main road via *Rämshyttan* on Lake *Rämen* and forested hill country to Borlänge, main town of *Dalarna,* with iron works. Interesting open-air museum (Y.H.). Thence by *Dalälv* valley to *Djurås.*

411

SWEDEN

From *Djurås* through delightful village of *Gagnef* to *Leksand* (Y.H.) on Lake *Siljan*; midsummer festival here, open-air play, maypole dance, long-boats rowed across lake. Good views over lake from several nearby hills. District is famed for rural handicrafts. Bridge from *Gesunda* to *Sollerön* island (church with good view from tower). Fine view from *Gesundaberget* (1,500 ft.). *Mora* is goal of annual ski-contest *"Vasaloppet"* run from *Sälen*, 53 miles away, to commemorate message sent by ski-runners to Gustav Vasa in 1521 to tell that *Dalarna* supported him. Statue of Vasa by Zorn and Zorn museum. Y.H. at *Orsa* 7 miles to north.

R.7(iii) Mora to Femund (Norway) via Österdalälven, 76 miles. An approach to Eastern Norway, through wild and little-frequented country. Rail to *Älvdalen* (26 miles), then by buses, changing at *Särna* (Y.H.) and *Idre*. From *Femund* connections by boat and bus to *Röros*.

Road No. 70 on north side of lake, 18 miles to *Vikarbyn* but longer by footpath over *Fåsås* hill.

EXCURSION: 3 miles N. to attractive mountain village of *Röjeråsen*, famous for view over lake, etc. Look-out tower.

Rättvik (4 miles) is tourist centre; notable white church with unique mural paintings; open-air museum *(Gammelgård)*. Y.H. at *Boda*, 12 miles N.

South-east on road No. 80, via *Bjursås* to *Falun* (Y.H.) (30 miles), famous for its copper-mine worked since 13th century under same company; museum at mine buildings and the old mine town.

Skirt Lake *Runn* to *Vika* on road No. 266 and enter picturesque **Säterdal**, deep and fertile, with many old villages. *Säter*, once a provincial capital, has fine old houses. Good view from *Bipsberg* (1,020 ft.). *Hedemora* has fine church and houses of 18th century and earlier and an old theatre. Tour ends at *Avesta* (steel works) whence train to *Stockholm* in 1½ hrs.

R.8. Jämtland. Sundsvall to Storlien (235 miles)

This region rivals *Dalarna* for varied charm and surpasses it in the height of its mountains, which rise to 5,000 ft. near the Norwegian frontier. Excellent walking country. Walkers should make *Östersund* starting point for their tours, but cyclists or bus travellers should start from *Sundsvall*. (Train *Stockholm-Sundsvall* in 7 hours.)

Sundsvall (Y.H.) is busy timber export centre; factory on offshore island of *Alnö* is largest wood-pulp plant in Sweden. From tower on rocky height (*Norra Stadsberget*) extensive view over Gulf of *Bothnia*.

Route follows road and *Indal* River (*Indalsälven*) used for logging; numerous power-stations. *Bispgården* (58 miles), fine view of valley. 5 miles farther lie the *Döda Fallet* ("Falls of Death"), formed by sudden change in course of river in 18th century. *Ragunda* has 13th century church. At point where river leaves Lake *Gesunden* rapids have been harnessed to feed one of largest underground hydro-electric stations in Sweden. Follow pleasant north shore of lake to *Stugun*, at foot of *Stuguberget* (1,234 ft.); rare orchids in nearby forests, protected by law. At *Näverede* leave river valley and cut across plateau to *Östersund*, beautifully situated on arm of Lake *Storsjön*, county capital, tourist centre and only sizeable town in *Jämtland*; founded 1786; second highest town in Sweden (1,200 ft.); new church on hill above station, is fine example of modern architecture (1940). *Jamtli* open-air museum (one of best in Sweden) has many old buildings re-assembled from various parts of province. Y.H.

EXCURSIONS: (a) Round *Frösön* by steamer. (b) Over briuge to island of *Frösön* and climb *Östberget* (1,536 ft.) magnificent view over lake and surrounding mountains; *Frösön* church, and near it open-air theatre where Peterson-Berger's opera *"Arnljot"* is performed every year in July.

Storsjön Lake, not to be confused with another and smaller Lake *Storsjön* lying to S.W. in province of *Härjedalen*, lies nearly 1,000 ft. above sea level, amongst fertile country, with fine mountain background; road round lake is one of most beautiful in Sweden. Take this road, or railway, along E. and N. side of lake via *Mattmar* to *Järpen*.

R.8(i) Östersund to Järpen on foot. Walkers should start their tour at *Östersund* (train from *Stockholm* in 9 hrs.) Train to *Mattmar*, then bus to *Hallen* (Tourist hotel), then footpath inland to tourist hotel at *Bydalen* in beautiful *Storån* valley; excellent centre for mountain tours (e.g., ascent of *Drommen* (3,740 ft.) fine view, 2½ hrs. climb). From *Bydalen* strike north over summit of *Västerfjället* (3,800 ft., 2 hrs.) and continue in 3½ hrs. to *Sällsjö* (Tourist hotel) for visit to fine waterfall *Storbofallet;* thence by footpath or road to *Mörsil* (5 miles) and rail or bus on to *Järpen*.

Slagsån is 3 miles west of *Järpen* on road E.75 and marks the beginning of series of tourist resorts such as *Hålland* and *Undersåker*, in *Undersåker* valley; many excursions into mountains. *Åre* on lake of same name, is one of finest tourist centres in *Jämtland*, both summer and winter.

EXCURSION: Ascent of *Åreskutan* (4,658 ft.) one of highest peaks in *Jämtland*, via *Östra Platån* and *Mörvikshummeln* (funicular and ski-lift or on foot). Whole trip on foot takes 6 hrs. return. Unrivalled view from summit.

From *Duved*, 5 miles beyond *Åre*, *Mulfjället* can be climbed in 4 hrs. (3,384 ft.). At *Duved* road and railway separate.

R.8(ii) Duved to Sandvika, 29 miles. This was once main road to Norway (for *Trondheim*); wild but beautiful country. Bus as far as *Tännforsen* (magnificent waterfalls, 85 ft. drop). Tourist station at *Sadvika*, on Norwegian side of frontier.

Railway and road E.75 bear S.W. to Lake *Ånn*, over 1,700 ft. Y.H. at *Ånn*. *Enafors* is approach to one of finest mountain regions in Scandinavia, comparable to Norwegian *Jotunheimen*, well equipped with tourist huts, tourist hotels and marked footpaths. Northern group is called *Snasahögarna* (highest peak *Storsnasen*, 4,799 ft., one day's ascent); farther south are *Sylarna*, *Helagsfjället* and other groups.

Railway continues from *Enafors*, climbing to highest rail point in Sweden (1,970 ft.) and passes *Storlien*, popular winter sports centre, to cross Norwegian frontier.

R.9. The Far North—Lapland and the "King's Way"

This is one of the most fascinating but inaccessible parts of Sweden. Formerly inhabited only by Lapps, now a popular tourist area for Swedes but distance puts it beyond reach of most English travellers. It is a region of vast mountain masses, solitary lakes, with sparse vegetation surprisingly beautiful in the season of summer flowers. Swarms of midges make June and July unpleasant; best months are late May, August and early September.

SWEDEN

Best approach point is probably *Jokkmokk* or *Porjus* reached either by train from *Östersund* in 14 hrs., or from *Stockholm* by rail to *Boden* in 17 hrs., thence by bus in 4 hrs. Travellers coming via Norway can approach by rail from *Narvik* to *Abisko* in about 2 hrs., taking route in reverse direction.

Jokkmokk, just north of Arctic Circle, is important Lapp church and market centre, with a Lapp high school for adult education. Y.H. Typical Lapp summer encampment with reindeer enclosure is about 7 miles S.

From *Jokkmokk* combined bus and boat service via *Tjåmotis* in about 7 hrs. to *Kvikkjokk*—magnificent approach up beautiful Lake *Saggat*, ringed with mountains rising to 4,000 ft. STF mountain station.

Kvikkjokk, oldest tourist resort in Lapland, lies on the **Kungsleden** a through footpath of about 220 miles, waymarked by STF and provided with tourist huts, tourist stations or farmhouse accommodation at day's walking distances. Numerous lake crossings are necessary, and in some cases boats must be ordered in advance by telephoning from previous tourist hut. Routes between mountain stations refer to actual days of travel and one day in every three must be considered for resting or bad weather.

From *Kvikkjokk*, 52 miles, 5 days' walking through forest, across watershed and moorland to *Saltoluokta*, finely situated on Lake *Langas*. (STF mountain station). Boat in 3 hrs. (not every day) to *Suorva*, then on foot for 32 miles, 3-4 days, skirting eastern edge of *Stora Sjöfallets* National Park, to *Kebnekaise* STF mountain station, for *Kebnekaise* mountain group (highest peak 6,966 ft., highest mountain in Sweden); popular mountaineering centre. Final section of journey, *Kebnekaise* to *Abisko*, 54 miles, 4 days' walking largely above level of vegetation; huts on route are locked, and keys must be taken from *Kebnekaise*.

Abisko, at N. end of *Abisko* National Park (flowers and wild life preserved in 20 square mile area of upland valley), is very popular tourist centre on Lake *Torneträsk*; STF mountain station; motor boats on lake; midnight sun visible June 12th to July 4th. Rail across frontier to *Narvik* in 2 hrs.

SWITZERLAND

Geographical Outline

Land
Switzerland, a mountain country set in the heart of Europe and totally cut off from the sea, occupies an area of nearly 16,000 sq. miles, at least half of which is accounted for by the Alps. A further sixth is covered by the Jura mountains. The Foreland between the two ranges is a broad region of low hills and lakes and is the most important economically.

The Swiss Alps are the highest and grandest portion of the Alpine chain. From the neighbourhood of the St. Gotthard pass two main ranges extend to the west, the *Bernese Alps* (sometimes loosely described as the *Bernese Oberland*, which correctly describes only their northern slopes) and the *Pennine Alps*, highest peak *Monte Rosa*, 15,217 ft. A further two ranges extend to the east, the *Glarus* and the *Grisons Alps*, whose main peaks are somewhat lower.

The *Jura* range stretches along the Swiss-French frontier for some 200 miles, rising abruptly from the central plateau. Its highest ridges, about 6,000 ft., are to the west of *Lake Geneva*.

Climate
The range of climate for such a small country is immense, being influenced by height, the western rain-bearing winds and the shelter of the mountains. The *Valais* and the *Engadine* are amongst the driest regions, while the *Lugano* region enjoys a mild winter and abundant sunshine. The *Föhn*, a warm south wind from Italy, influences the central mountain area, while the *Bise*, a bitter north wind from Central Europe, often blows across the Foreland in winter. The permanent snowline occurs at 9,000 to 10,000 ft.

Plants and Animals
Mixed forests occur up to about 4,500 ft., followed by coniferous forests and meadows (the true "alps" used for summer grazing) up to about 7,000 ft. Juniper and rhododendron then give place to the Alpine flora, including gentians, saxifrages and edelweiss, and to bare rocks before the snowline is reached. On south-facing slopes cereals can be grown as high as 6,000 ft. The warm trench of the *Valais* is famous for its wines, apricots and peaches, and around the lakes of *Canton Ticino* the vegetation has Mediterranean features.

Among the wild animals are the Alpine partridge, mountain hare, chamois and marmot, whose shrill whistle is often heard near the snowline. Laws exist for protecting wild life and many regions are reserved areas and parks.

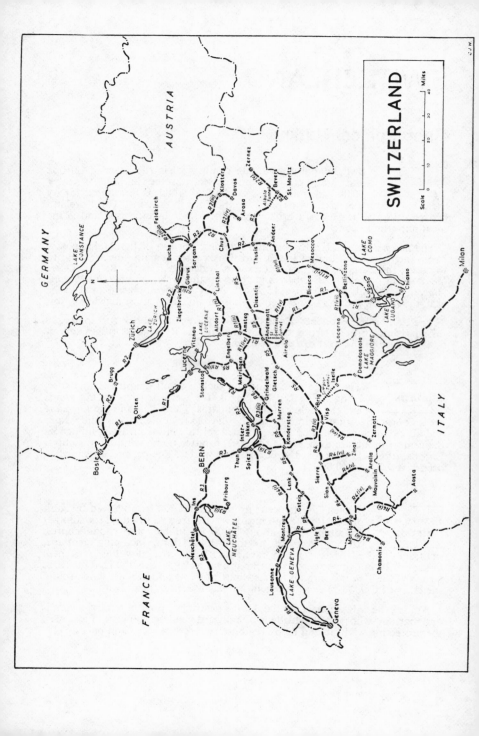

The People

Population Most of the 6 million people live in the *Foreland*—chief cities *Zürich* (651,000), *Basel* (345,000), *Geneva* (285,000), *Berne* (163,000). The foot of the *Jura* and the shores of the larger lakes—*Constance, Geneva, Lucerne* and *Lugano*—are closely settled, but the Alpine districts are sparsely inhabited.

Language German is the language of over 70 per cent of the people; when writing (or speaking to foreigners) there is little to distinguish their German from that of Bavaria, but in conversation amongst themselves, they use a dialect ("*Schwyzerdütsch*"), virtually a separate language, varying considerably from canton to canton.

French is the language west of a line drawn from *Delle*, on the French border, to the *Matterhorn*. It is spoken by about 20 per cent of the population. Italian is spoken in the southernmost canton, *Ticino* and there is a small group (about 40,000 people) in the *Engadine* and *Upper Rhine Valley* who speak *Romansch*, an ancient language of Roman origin.

For many of the more responsible jobs, in office and factory, and in the civil service, it is necessary to speak at least two of the national languages.

To the German-speaking Swiss their country is known as *die Schweiz*, to the French-speaking it is *la Suisse*, to the Italian-speaking *Svizzera*.

Religion Almost three-fifths are Calvinist Protestants, their church being organized by cantons, with no federal control. The others are chiefly Roman Catholic (in *Fribourg, Lucerne, Ticino* and *Valais*). Liberty of conscience is guaranteed by the constitution.

History From the four language groups, history has forged a Swiss nation united and independent, proud of its traditional liberty and democracy.

On August 1, 1291, the leaders of *Uri, Schwyz* and *Unterwalden* met together in the *Rütli* Meadow, taking a solem oath of Perpetual Alliance "One for All and All for One"; they demanded, and obtained, certain concessions from their Habsburg overlords, eventually becoming independent. This event is regarded as the foundation of the Swiss Confederation and is commemorated on the National Day each year. Other cantons gradually joined the Alliance and some areas, such as *Ticino*, were added by conquest. Swiss pikemen on many occasions repelled larger armies, forcing other countries to recognise the nation's internal unity. But the nature of the Confederation, each canton retaining self-government, prevented Switzerland from becoming a European power, and the country was further divided by the Reformation led by Zwingli in *Zürich* (1521-31) and by Calvin in the then independent republic of *Geneva*. Napoleon and his allies overran Switzerland but in 1815 the country was freed and assumed its present form. Since 1815, the Swiss have maintained a strict neutrality in all wars, and this fact has contributed to their prosperity and high standard of living. It has also made their country the headquarters for many international organisations, including the International Postal Union and the Red Cross.

SWITZERLAND

Government The Confederation consists of 22 cantons, each with its own government and administration. The Federal Government is responsible for defence, foreign affairs and the transport and postal systems. The canton constitutions are similar to each other and to the Federal constitution, except that in the three small cantons of *Glarus, Appenzell* and *Unterwalden* the ancient custom of the *Landsgemeinde* is still in existence; all adult males meet together once a year in an open-air "parliament" to discuss policy and administration for the ensuing year, and to elect their Council.

Resources The main source of wealth is the tourist trade, based upon the unrivalled scenic beauties of the Alps, but agriculture and industry play an important role. Small-scale farming is carried out with meticulous care, and every square foot of cultivable land is put to good use. Cattle are kept in all regions and the higher altitudes are grazed whenever the season permits, while hay is harvested from most precarious slopes from late spring up to late summer.

The mountain grazing period is from June to October. The flocks and herds are taken up the mountain as soon as the receding snow permits, allowing only a few days for the preparation of the summer huts. The life is arduous, and in many cases only the men accompany the animals; they descend gradually as the high grasslands, or "alps" (from which the mountains derive their name), are grazed. The milk during this period is made into cheese.

But the Foreland is the most important region both for agriculture and industry. The latter is not confined to the towns but is dispersed widely to take advantage of the abundant hydro-electric power. This has enabled Switzerland to become a highly industrialized country, despite the necessity of importing most of its raw materials. The main enterprises are precision engineering, watch and clock making and textile manufacture. Banking and insurance also add considerably to the wealth of the country. Wine is grown on the warm slopes overlooking the western lakes and the dairy industry is renowned for cheeses and chocolate.

Customs The people are law-abiding, of great integrity and extremely industrious. It is their hard work and business sense which have created a prosperous state out of a small mountainous country. They are also very thrifty; almost everybody is privately insured against sickness or accident, and there is no national health service, although there is now an unemployment, disability and old-age pension scheme. The Swiss cherish their old traditions and national costumes and processions. Most of the festivals take place in the mountain regions in the spring, and are concerned with the departure of the snow and preparation for the summer on the alps. In the canton of *Appenzell* the cows wear wreaths as well as their customary bells, and the men accompanying wagons of furniture for the summer stay in the mountain pastures wear their best traditional costumes. In the *Valais* similar processions take place, and the cows are allowed to fight until the strongest establishes herself as Queen of the herd. She is given the largest bell, and her "subjects" obey and follow her for the rest of the season.

The *Basle* carnival, on the first Monday in Lent, is an occasion for processions of grotesque figures, masked dances and abandoned jollity. At *Zürich* about the middle of April a procession takes place wherein an effigy of winter is burned to the accompaniment of the church bells. In *Lugano*, situated on the southern slopes in the vine district, a vintage procession with dancing and singing is held on the last Sunday of September and, in *Neuchâtel*, the first weekend of October. Lesser vintage festivals are held in the regions of *Locarno, Lake Geneva* and the *lower Valais*.

The most interesting religious festival is that of Corpus Christi in the *Lötschental*, see **R.3. (ii)**.

August 1 (National Day) is celebrated in the country districts with processions in local costume, dancing, fireworks and bonfires lit on the surrounding heights. In the large towns more sophisticated amusements are added and processions usually include carnival floats.

Food

Breakfast is continental, with excellent coffee, rolls and butter. The main meal is at midday when practically everything closes down for two hours; a light supper is taken in the evening. Meat is expensive and is not usually eaten more than two or three times a week, being replaced by cheese, eggs or sausages. Mutton is little used; rabbit (from domesticated animals) and kid are expensive, and so is fish.

Various cantons and regions have their own culinary specialities. In the Alpine regions there is "hard food" such as cheese, dried meat, fruitbread, etc., while in the lakeside regions there are various fish specialities. From the farmhouses of the plateau comes the *Berner Platte*—smoked sausage, bacon, ham, sometimes boiled beef, pickled cabbage and potatoes or green beans; but the national dish of German-speaking districts is *Rösti*—potatoes boiled, diced, fried and then baked. French-speaking districts favour the *fondue*—pieces of bread dipped into communal pot of melted cheese; and in the south are Italian dishes such as risotto, spaghetti and minestra.

Culture

Architecture

Good examples of both Gothic and Renaissance architecture are to be found in the main towns, particularly in *Berne*, which has retained its charming old-world character. In *Zürich, Geneva* and other places a remarkable harmony has been achieved between old and new.

Perhaps the most typically Swiss popular art is to be seen in the domestic buildings of the countryside. In the *Emmental* district the large timber-built farmhouses are particularly fine, with their wide-spread roofs, balconies and verandas. The traditional "chalet" of the posters is chiefly found in the *Oberland*. The chalet of the *Valais* is more roughly built, usually quite black, and the houses are crowded together on the hillsides, separated only by narrow cobbled lanes or alleyways. Close by are the barns and granaries of similar construction, supported 3 or 4 ft. above the ground by a pillar at each corner, with a stone disc about 3 ft. in diameter to prevent mice and rats from gaining access. In the south-east, the houses are solidly constructed of stone, while in the Italian-speaking regions they resemble those of north Italy, with shallow-pitched roofs and tiled floors.

SWITZERLAND

Painting　　Conrad Witz, (early 15th century) has a place among European painters as perhaps the first to include realistic (and still identifiable) representations of landscapes in his pictures. Hodler (1853-1918) treated landscapes in a forcefully simple yet naturalistic style. The strange art of Klee (1879-1940) owes nothing to either of these compatriots but stems from his theory that each work should grow according to its own laws.

Local Costumes　　There are a great variety of local costumes, most of them now only worn for festivals and processions, but they are likely to be seen on Sundays in the *Valais, Appenzell* and in villages of central Switzerland which are off the beaten track.

Literature　　The attraction of its lakes (and, later, its mountains), its political liberty and convenience as a refuge for exiles, have led writers from many countries to visit or settle in Switzerland; they include Voltaire, Mme. de Staël, Gibbon, Byron, Shelley and Samuel Butler. But its native contributions to civilization have been distinctive in several fields.

Pestalozzi (1746-1827) by his writings and practice was the founder of modern ideas of primary education. Rousseau (1712–78) was one of the makers of the new age in Europe, achieving masterpieces in autobiography and political and educational theory. Gottfried Keller (1819–90) was famous as a lyric poet and his *Leute von Seldwyla* and *Züricher Novelleu* are leading examples of 19th century German short stories. Burckhardt (1818–97) is well-known for his history of Renaissance art. Karl Barth (1886–1966) was one of the leading contemporary Protestant theologians.

Science　　H. B. de Saussure (1740-99), inspirer of the first ascent (1786) of Mont Blanc, was the chief pioneer in the study of alpine botany, geology, meteorology and mineralogy. The professors Auguste Piccard (1884-1962) and his twin brother J. F. Piccard (1884-1963) pioneered the exploration of the upper atmosphere by daring balloon flights. Auguste also began investigation of the ocean depths by descents in a steel sphere, and this work has been continued by his son Jacques (b. 1922). Jung (1875-1961) ranks second only to Freud in the study of the processes of the psyche.

Touring Information

General

For generations past Switzerland has been the holiday-maker's paradise. The scenery is superb, the hotel industry is highly developed, communications are good, and everything is clean, punctual and well ordered.

For the youth hosteller, this perfection of organisation has its disadvantages. There are so many foreign tourists in the main holiday regions that real contact with the local people becomes difficult. At every point in these regions, even on the mountain peaks, there are signposts, restaurants, and other attributes of civilisation, restricting opportunity for adventure or solitude. But the answer, as in many other countries, is to avoid the main holiday centres and make for the lesser known areas, such as the upper *Rhône* Valley and the *Jura*.

Touring Areas

The most popular mountain areas are the *Bernese Oberland* (approached via *Interlaken*), the *Engadine* (*St. Moritz*) and the Alps of southern *Valais* (*Zermatt*). Lower-lying but no less popular are the Lake of *Lucerne* and the sunny vine-clad valleys of the *Ticino*. Less well-known areas are the *Jura* mountains (approached via *Basel* or *Geneva*) and the *Grisons* south of *Chur*, both well provided with youth hostels.

Seasons

The winter sports season starts before Christmas in the Alpine regions, slackens off in January owing to short days and intense cold, and reaches its climax in mid-February when hours of sunshine are longer and weather conditions more stable. Spring, the season of Alpine flowers, comes to the mountains in late May. Mid-July to mid-August is the most popular period in the Alps generally, especially during the first week in August when the main resorts are usually packed. Accommodation is easier to find in June, early July and September, all suitable months for walkers and cyclists. The season in southern *Ticino* is Easter to June, or autumn; in July and August it is likely to be uncomfortably hot.

The great summer attraction is climbing, and every variety is offered from the easiest grade to the most difficult.

Access

Through trains from French channel ports, *Boulogne* and *Calais*; quickest connection leaves London mid-afternoon in summer, arriving *Basel* (*Bâle*) early next day. 2nd class return fare London–*Basel* is £40·70. Via *Dieppe* and *Paris* is a little cheaper, but this route involves longer journey and inconvenient change of stations in Paris. You can purchase through tickets from London entitling you to enter Switzerland at one frontier station (e.g. *Basel*) and leave at another (e.g. *Delle*—see **R.3**) on homeward journey, with option of travelling via *Paris*.

On *Basel* station you can have a hot bath, breakfast, change money and buy provisions. Good connections reach all parts of the country during the day.

Tourist return flight fare from London to *Berne* is £68·20.

SWITZERLAND

Transport   A network of excellent roads and railways climbs or penetrates the mountains in breathtaking feats of engineering. Among the principal passes are the *Simplon, St. Gotthard, Great St. Bernard, Susten* and *Furka*; these are open to traffic from mid-June to end of October approximately. Railway tunnels under the *Simplon* and *St. Gotthard* carry cars in a shuttle service, and a new toll road goes under the *Great St. Bernard* pass.

Virtually all Swiss railways are electrified, and three-quarters of the mileage is state owned. Light railways ascend many of the peaks, such as that of the *Jungfrau*, which climbs nearly to the summit (11,342 ft.). These and the narrow-gauge railways are usually privately owned and tariffs are often higher than on the Federal system, but the private companies issue many excursion tickets.

Rail travel costs on average 50 *centimes* per kilometre second class single on the Federal Railways, with progressive reductions for journeys of more than 150 kilometers and about 25 per cent reduction for a return ticket. Railway tickets can be used for corresponding steamer journeys on many of the lakes.

Swiss Holiday Ticket—These tickets for return, circular or single transit rail journeys from a frontier station or airport, have the special advantage that they include 5 vouchers allowing the holder to travel at half fare on excursions by rail, boat or certain buses. The cost of the ticket is a flat rate of 30 *francs* (second class) plus about half the fare for the distance travelled, which makes it cheaper than an ordinary ticket for return or round journeys of more than 300 km., even if the vouchers are not used. It is valid one month, but can be extended for additional periods of ten days at a cost of 8 *francs*.

Swiss Holiday Pass—A new type of ticket introduced in 1972 allowing transport by rail (main line and private) post buses, mountain railways and cable systems and lake steamers. There are passes available for 8 days, 15 days or one month commencing at 100 *francs* second class 8 day to 275 *francs* 1st class one month—only obtainable outside Switzerland.

Regional Holiday Season Ticket—These tickets cost varying amounts (reduced by 25% for holders of the Swiss Holiday Ticket) according to the size of the ten regions for which they are available. They are valid 15 days, on any 5 of which holders travel free anywhere within the region; on other days half fare is allowed on any number of journeys.

"Sunday" Ticket—Many of the private lines offer especially cheap travel for week-end excursions; particulars are displayed in the companies' offices and stations.

The Postal Services provide excellent motor coach facilities at about the same price as rail travel, and run trips over all the high passes in summer. Tickets for these journeys are bought from the post office where the bus is to be boarded, well in advance if possible, though a few hours is often sufficient. The half-fare vouchers supplied with Swiss Holiday Tickets may be used. Bus services rarely duplicate rail routes but start from terminal points of railways to reach otherwise inaccessible areas.

Timetables The official timetable, *Amtliches Kursbuch/Indicateur Officiel*, is a most useful guide to all transport services. Explanations are given in German, French or Italian in accordance with language spoken in area concerned and there is an introduction in English. A table of fares per distance by ordinary railway routes is given in the green pages; and fares on private lines are also given listed according to their table numbers in the timetable section of the book. Motor-bus services are listed in the yellow pages and single fares are quoted.

Money The Swiss *franc* is divided into 100 *centimes* or *Rappen*. There are silver coins for 5, 2 and 1 *franc* and 50 *cts.*, nickel and copper coins for smaller values down to 1 *ct.*, and notes for 10, 20, 50, 100, 500 and 1,000 *francs*.
There are no currency restrictions and at exchange offices (*Bureaux de Change* or *Geldwechsel*) you can buy and sell most foreign currency. Banks are open all day, but close two hours for lunch.

Clothing For mountain regions take ordinary summer clothing with warm garments for evenings when the temperature often drops rapidly, a mackintosh whatever the season, and boots for walking on mountain paths. It is preferable to dress fairly conventionally in the towns, especially when sightseeing.

Restaurants and Meals Restaurants are good but expensive, although à la carte dishes are generous and there is a choice of inexpensive local wines. The cheapest set lunch or supper of two courses costs about 5 *francs* except at temperance restaurants (*Gemeinde-stube/Restaurants sans alcool*) which are cheaper.

Public Holidays Federal holidays, when banks, shops and offices are closed, are January 1, Good Friday, Ascension Day, December 25, Easter Monday, Whit Monday, August 1. The first four have Sunday transport services. Many of the cantons observe additional public holidays, notably Corpus Christi and August 15 in the Catholic cantons.

Maps The Swiss produce some of the finest maps in the world, all the country is mapped on the *Landeskarte Carte Nationale* series on a scale of 1:50,000, ideal for walkers; there are also series at 1:100,000 and 1:25,000 . For cyclists the *Michelin* series of four maps, on a scale of 1:200,000, is the most satisfactory.

Accommodation *Swiss Youth Hostels are closed to visitors who have passed their 25th birthday.* This restriction indicates the importance of the tourist trade in Switzerland; the youth hostels can only escape the various tourist taxes by limiting their services to "youth" in the narrowest sense.

SWITZERLAND

For the "over-25's" there are, however, many simple hotels and boarding houses (*pensions*). Try the small villages on southern shore of *Lake Lucerne*, in the southern *Valais* from *Val de Bagnes* to *Val d'Anniviers*, Canton *Glarus* and the *Ticino*, except lakeside resorts; avoid well-known resorts and, as far as possible, period July 15 to August 20.

Alpine Huts ———————— The Swiss Alpine Club (*Schweizer Alpen Club/Club Alpin Suisse*) maintains many climbers' huts. Membership entitles ———————— to reduced hut charges (*5fr.* as against *9fr.* for non-members) and priority at busy seasons. Membership is limited to men, minimum age 18 years. For information write to the *Swiss Alpine Club, Section Zermatt, CH-3920 Zermatt, Switzerland.*

Camping ———————— All the best sites are listed by the *Fédération Suisse des Clubs de Camping, Lucerne,* in a free booklet, complete with map, ———————— obtainable by writing to the *Swiss National Tourist Office, 608 Fifth Avenue, New York, N.Y. 10020.*

Cycling ———————— In spite of the hilly nature of the country, many Swiss ride bicycles, and there are cycle shops in towns, and most ———————— large villages on the plateau or in main valleys. Main road surfaces are good and there are some cycle tracks. After a severe winter metalled surfaces on such passes as the *St. Bernard* and *St. Gotthard* are badly damaged by frost and snow. The best combination of scenery and not too strenuous riding is around the central lakes. Avoid the hot dusty trench of the *Rhône Valley,* unless you intend to make steep ascents into the lateral valleys.

Practical Hints ———————— Access to mountains is free and unhindered, but you should not camp or wander about on grass which is being grown for the hay crop.
———————— The whole of Switzerland is linked by an automatic telephone system, the exchange will tell you the nearest doctor or chemist on duty after normal closing hours.

Voltage is now almost universally 220 A.C. Electrical appliances of British or American manufacture require adapters to fix them to the sockets, which are of a different type.

Cigarettes, including Virginia, are cheap; so are watches, but they are subject to heavy customs duty.

Touring Routes

R.1. Basel to Chiasso via Lucerne and St. Gotthard Pass (200 miles)

This is the main north-south route, both for railway and road, giving access to the Lake of *Lucerne*, the Italian-speaking canton of *Ticino* and the lakes of northern Italy. Fast trains from *Basel* to *Lucerne* (60 miles) in 70 mins; to *Lugano* (185 miles) in about 4 hours. Main road No. 2.

Basel, second largest city; near frontier with France and Germany, Rhine port, international rail junction, commercial and industrial centre. Founded by the Romans, it was in 15th century one of most important cities of Europe; University dates from 1460; joined Confederation in 1501. Red sandstone Minster on hill in old town, founded 11th century, rebuilt in Gothic style after an earthquake; behind Minster, Rhine Terrace, for view; *Marktplatz*, with 16th century *Rathaus* (City Hall); *Spalentor* (14th century gate); *Spalenbrunnen*, fountain with peasants dancing to bagpipes; 18th century houses, especially in *Rittergasse*; paintings by Holbein in Museum of Fine Arts. Y.H. in *Elisabethenstrasse*.

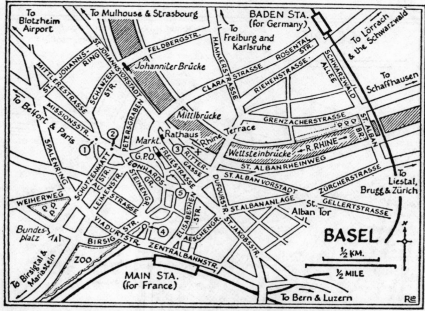

1. *Spalentor.* 2. *Spalenbrunnen.* 3. *Minster* 4. *Birsigtal Rly. Station.* 5. *Barfüsser Platz.*

SWITZERLAND

EXCURSIONS: (a) By Rhine steamer from the *Schifflände* (summer only, not every day) in 1½ hrs. to walled town of *Rheinfelden*; (b) By valley of *Birs* River to *Delémont* (25 miles) Y.H., good approach to Northern *Jura* mountains; fast train in 30 mins. (c) By *Birsig* Valley light railway to *Flüh* (30 mins.) thence 1 mile to *Mariastein*, picturesque church.

From *Basel* road and rail pass through agricultural countryside, famed for its cherry orchards, into hills of *Jura*, 5-mile tunnel, descent to *Olten* on R. *Aare*, small industrial town with old buildings, covered wooden bridge. Across fertile plateau to *Sursee*, old walled town, late Gothic town hall and Baroque church. Along *Sempacher* lake *Rigi* and *Pilatus* come into view.

Lucerne, (Y.H.), on R. *Reuss* where it quits lake, popular tourist resort; *Kapell-Brücke*, roofed wooden bridge crossing *Reuss* diagonally (1333), 112 paintings (16th century) in roof—lives of St. Maurice and St. Leger, deeds of local heroes; *Spreuer-Brücke*, smaller covered bridge, paintings of "Dance of Death"; 13th century ramparts with 9 towers (*Musegg Türme*); Lion Monument, to memory of Swiss Guards who died defending Louis XVI and Marie-Antoinette; old quarter round *Kornmarkt*, with 16th century Old Town Hall; Glacier Garden, potholes formed by glacier which once extended from *Gotthard* to cover site of *Lurcerne*; *Hofkirche*, 16th-17th century cathedral. Town crowded every year for International Musical Festival, mid-August.

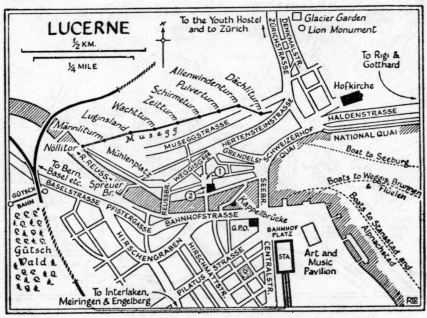

1. *Kornmarkt.*   2. *Old Town Hall.*

426

EXCURSION: Pilatus, long ridge S.W., to with impressive rocky outline: several peaks—highest (*Tomlishorn*) 6,995 ft. Tradition that final resting place of Pilate's body was in small tarn on mountain and storm clouds are caused by his unquiet spirit. (*Pilatus* has highest rainfall in the country.) *Lucerne* municipal bus from station to *Hergiswil*, thence on foot via *Brunni* hotel, on marked track, 4¼ hrs.; magnificent view. *Pilatus* may also be reached by steamer to *Alpnachstad* (1½ hrs.) then by world's steepest rack railway (3 miles, 30 mins.); alternatively by trolley bus to *Kriens* then by two cable railways, via *Fräkmuntegg*, in total 39 mins., but it must be noted that the *Pilatus* mountain railways are expensive.

R.1(i) **Lucerne to Engelberg** (25 miles). Train in 1 hr., passes through farming country to *Stans*. 5 hrs. climb or mountain railway to *Stanserhorn* 6,270 ft.; fine view over several arms of Lake *Lucerne*; up valley of R. *Aare*, narrow and steep at first, then widening to Engelberg (3,300 ft.), summer and winter resort surrounded by mountains (snow covered *Titlis*, 10,625 ft.). Famous Benedictine abbey, founded 1120, ruled whole valley until end of 18th century. Y.H.

EXCURSION: (among many others) via *Trübsee* Lake to 7,267 ft. *Jochpass*, 4½ hrs. on foot or by funicular to *Gerschnialp*, thence cable railway to *Trübsee* and chair lift to *Jochpass*; total journey 30 mins. *Jochpass* provides good walker's approach to Bernese Oberland via *Meiringen* (see R.6.)

Road and railway keep to north side of lake (rail tickets can be used on steamer on payment of difference in fare, if any).

Lake Lucerne (*Vierwaldstättersee*—Lake of the Four Forest Cantons—*Uri, Schwyz, Unterwalden* and *Lucerne*) is the cradle of the Swiss Confederation and scene of the exploits of William Tell. The area is influenced by the warm south wind (*Föhn*) which shortens winter and gives mild summer climate; when blowing strongly it causes fierce storms on lake. Population is Catholic; Swiss Guard in Rome is mainly recruited here.

The scenery grows wilder eastwards, and much of the south shore consists of steep cliffs.

On the 3 hour steamer trip from *Lucerne* to *Flüelen* the route begins via *Weggis, Vitznau* and *Gersau*; pleasant resorts on north shore, with sheltered southerly aspect. Between two latter is large lakeside Y.H. of *Rotschuo*.

EXCURSION: From each of above resorts, footpaths 2-3½ hrs. to ridge of Rigi, famous mountain with several peaks—highest, *Rigi-Kulm*, 5,742 ft. Also rack railway from *Vitznau* to *Rigi-Kulm* in 35 mins. Magnificent view from summit, extending 100 miles. Excellent walks among alpine meadows and forest, e.g. *Rigi-Kaltbad-Scheidegg-Gäettrli Pass-Gersau*, 4 hrs.

South of *Vitznau* two rocky points known as the *Nasen* (noses) jut out, reducing width of lake to barely half a mile. *Gersau* was for over 400 years the world's smallest independent republic.

Lake again narrows at *Brunnen*, small town at mouth of fertile *Muota* valley, where *St. Gotthard* railway line rejoins road and lake.

EXCURSION: Tram from *Brunnen* landing stage in 20 mins. to *Schwyz*, chief town of canton which gave name to Switzerland; interesting old churches and houses; striking modern Federal Archives building containing original document of Alliance of 1291.

South of *Brunnen* arm of lake is known as *Urnersee*; steep banks, strange rock formations, waterfalls. On leaving *Brunnen* steamer crosses lake to the *Rütli*, a steeply sloping meadow famous in Swiss history (see page 7) 15 mins. walk from landing stage. Close to landing stage is natural rock monument, 80 ft. high called *Schillerstein* or *Mythenstein* with inscription dedicated to Friedrich Schiller, German author of play *Wilhelm Tell*.

SWITZERLAND

On E. side of lake is finely engineered road from *Brunnen* to *Flüelen*, with good views. Below road is rocky ledge known as *Tellsplatte*, where during *Föhn* storm, Tell leapt from boat in which Gessler was carrying him to prison; Tell's Chapel with frescoes of events in his life.

At *Flüelen*, port at S. end of lake, rejoin railway for *St. Gotthard*. 2 miles *Altdorf* (station half mile from town), typical little central Swiss town, capital of canton of *Uri*, traditional scene of Tell's shooting apple from his son's head. Schiller's play performed at weekends in summer by local cast.

R.1(ii) Altdorf to Linthal via the Klausen Pass, 30 miles (post bus in 3 hrs.). One of finest pass roads in country, reaching 6,400 ft., with impressive views of *Clariden* and *Tödi* mountains, passing *Bürglen* (Y.H.), supposed birthplace and place of death of Tell; old chapel with pictures of Tell story. Route can be pleasantly covered on foot, following old pass road which deviates from motor road. *Linthal*, railhead in canton *Glarus* (see R.2(i)).

St. Gotthard railway and road ascend *Reuss* valley past *Erstfeld* (railway works) to *Amsteg*.

R.1(iii) Amsteg to Maderan Valley. Bus to *Bristen*, 3 miles. Wild and beautiful valley, fine pine woods and many waterfalls. Road to *Bristen* (Y.H.) thence mule track to S.A.C. hotel, 4,377 ft., only habitation near head of valley, continue to *Hüfi* Hut at edge of glacier. Return via *Stäfel Alp* high level path and *Golzern Alp*, small village and pretty lake, bathing. Several S.A.C. huts, climbs and glacier passes for the experienced.

Road crosses *Reuss* at *Pfaffensprung* (Priest's Leap) waterfall. Railway enters first spiral tunnel, passes *Wassen*, doubles on its tracks and passes village twice more (2 spiral tunnels).

R.1(iv) Wassen to Meiringen by the Susten Pass, 33 miles (post bus in 2¼ hrs.), superbly engineered road with tunnels and viaducts. Up wild valley of *Meienreuss* into barren glacier country; through a tunnel, over 6,000 ft. above sea level, under *Susten* Pass, from Canton *Uri* into Canton *Bern*; on left is the *Steingletscher* (Stone Glacier), magnificent panorama; meals at *Steingletscher* hotel. Descent by the *Gadmen* valley into meadows and orchards, to *Meiringen* and Bernese Oberland.

At *Göschenen* (Y.H.) railway enters St. Gotthard Tunnel, 9⅓ miles long, 12 to 15 minutes transit, opened 1882. In *Göschenen* cemetery is monument to Louis Favre, its builder, and the 277 workmen who were killed in its construction.

From *Göschenen* road climbs the *Schöllenen* Gorge, between high rocky walls, old and new Devil's Bridges, over R. *Reuss*, near splendid 100 ft. cascade; memorial to Russian troops who forced pass in 1799. There is also a rack railway from *Göschenen* to *Andermatt* in 15 mins. Sit on left-hand side for best views.

Andermatt (4,760 ft.) small resort in green bowl among hills, noticeably cooler than *Lucerne* area. Key position at junction of *St. Gotthard*, *Furka* and *Oberalp* Passes (see R.5), fortified, garrison, tiny airfield. Easy walks.

Road turns S.W. to *Hospental*, (Y.H.), then S. more steeply (grass-grown bridle track for walkers); wild scenery. From *Rodont* Bridge, 1 mile W. to attractive *Lago di Lucendro*. Several little lakes, top of pass 6,935 ft., named after *St. Gotthard*, chosen as its patron in 13th century. The railway line is now 3,000 ft. below. Old hospice on S. side, where snowdrifts in winter often reach 40 ft.

SWITZERLAND

The *St. Gotthard* pass marks the northern boundary of the Italian-speaking canton of **Ticino** (*Tessin*). It is not only a language frontier but also the limit of southern Europe. The *Ticino*, wrested from *Milan* between 1402 and 1512, made an independent canton 300 years later, is a land of sharp contrasts. Bleak precipices and rocky slopes rise from oak and chestnut forests, from valleys where maize, tobacco and vines are grown. The rivers are almost all swift-flowing streams, often with gorges. In summer, long hours of brilliant sunshine are the rule, but rain, though of short duration, can be torrential while it lasts. In the north are the usual alpine plants, pines and larches; near the lakes grow almonds, peaches, cypresses and palm trees; wild cyclamen can be found in autumn. The *Ticino* is the most important wine-producing area of Switzerland and the vines are draped on granite posts or wooden frames, often they are used to form a cool arbour in front of the Italian-style houses. Many villages are picturesquely sited, with a campanile rising above clustered roofs. The best time to visit the south is Easter to end of June, or in October when the chestnuts in their autumn colouring are a magnificent sight.

The road from the *St. Gotthard* goes down by many zigzags, then crosses R. *Ticino* into rocky *Val Tremola* (Valley of Trembling); short cuts by bridle-path. *Airolo*, first small town of Italian appearance, where railway emerges from tunnel, good centre for exploring granite *Gotthard* massif and for ski-ing.

EXCURSIONS: (a) West to *Val Bedretto* (upper valley of R. *Ticino*) for mountain walking and climbing. On foot *Airolo* to *Bedretto* village in 2 hrs., or by post bus in 35 mins. Above *Bedretto* is *Pizzo Rotondo*, highest peak of *St. Gotthard* group (10,500 ft.). (b) On foot via *Madrano* and *Altanca* to Lake *Ritom* and *Piora* Valley.

Rail and road enter *Val Leventina* (name given to this section of valley of *Ticino* river, from Lepontians, early inhabitants), and descend through picturesque gorges. Two spiral tunnels near fine ravine of *Dazio Grande*. *Faido*, small resort, 16th century wooden houses. Route bordered by steep cliffs, many waterfalls, *Biaschine* ravine (two more spiral tunnels), *Giornico*, in pretty position, surrounded by chestnut trees, vineyards, at foot of mountains rising 6,000 ft. above valley, fine 12th century Lombard-Gothic church.

Valley widens, southern vegetation—maize, figs, walnuts; *Biasca*, junction with *Val Blenio*.

R.1(v) Biasca to Disentis via Lukmanier Pass, 38 miles. Beautiful *Blenio* valley (River *Brenno*), rising at northern end to *Lukmanier* (*Lucomagno*) Pass, 6,295 ft., giving access to Romansch-speaking upper Rhine valley (see R.5) by steep descent with 11 tunnels. Light railway *Biasca* to *Acquarossa*, thence post bus in 2¾ hrs. to *Disentis/Muster*.

Continue down flat valley of *Ticino*, here called *Riviera*, to **Bellinzona**, capital of *Ticino*, important strategic town, key to passes; three castles built by Duke of Milan, taken 1508 by Swiss; good view from *Castello Corbaro*: several old churches, old houses.

R.1(vi) Bellinzona to Thusis via San Bernardino Pass, 68 miles. Light railway to *Mesocco*, then post bus; total journey 3½ hrs. Following *Valle Mesolcina*, enter canton of *Grisons*, still Italian-speaking; *Mesocco*, small resort, 12th century church; landscape becomes more alpine, *San Bernardino* (5,300 ft.), good centre for easy mountain excursions in beautiful surroundings; San Bernardino Pass (6,770 ft.), with little *Lago Moësola*, fine views; descent to valley of *Hinterrhein*, centre for climbs in *Rheinwald* group, view of *Zapport* Glacier. Continue through forests, gorges and meadows, to *Andeer*, then through the *Via Mala* (Evil Road), a wild gorge with walls of 2,000 ft., to *Thusis* (Y.H.) (see R.2).

SWITZERLAND

R.1(vii) Bellinzona to Locarno and Lake Maggiore, 12 miles; rail in 30 mins. Across broad plain of *Magadino* to *Locarno* on R. *Maggia* and *Lake Maggiore;* old streets, interesting churches, bathing, lakeside walks; lake steamers—regular service to *Brissago*, special excursions to *Stresa (Italy)*.

EXCURSIONS: (a) *Madonna del Sasso*, monastery and pilgrimage church, good viewpoint. On foot in 30 mins. (by the *Via Crucis*) or by funicular railway in 6 mins. (b) Northwards into *Val Maggia*, broad valley between precipices, waterfalls; 17 miles, *Bignasco*, good centre for walks, junction of two valleys. Light railway from *Locarno* in 55 mins. (c) Up the *Centovalli*, gentle valley with luxuriant vegetation; light railway over Italian frontier to *Domodossola*, whence connection to *Simplon* (see R.4).

Main route continues alongside the *Monte Ceneri;* rail through tunnel. **Lugano**, largest town in canton, tourist resort, between *Monte San Salvatore* and *Monte Bre* on shore of beautiful and irregularly shaped Lake *Lugano*; mild southern climate, boating and swimming. Visit old part of town, streets with wide arcades, cobbled roadways with stone tracks for the cartwheels; churches of *San Lorenzo* and *Santa Maria degli Angioli:* Civic Museum with old Ticinese furniture. Two **Y.Hs.** in district.

EXCURSIONS: (a) By funicular to *Monte San Salvatore* (3,000 ft., 10 mins.) or to *Monte Bre* (3,060 ft., bus from *Piazza Giardino* to *Cassarate*, then funicular; total time 40 mins.). Both have fine views, but often obscured by heat haze in summer. (b) By boat east to *Gandria*, picturesque but tourist-conscious fishing village (20-30 mins.) or south to *Morcote*, lovely position, 13th century church (1 hr.).

Road and rail continue south along shore. Cross lake by causeway of *Melide* (see Swiss miniature town), foundations built on natural rock bar, along E. of lake to *Capolago*, for rack railway up *Monte Generoso* (5,580 ft., 1 hr.) and magnificent views over Alps. Return trip by steamer from *Lugano* is inexpensive. Through hilly but fertile district to *Chiasso* (frontier with Italy). *Como* is 4, *Milan* 32 miles farther.

R.2. Basel—Zürich—St. Moritz (217 miles)

This route crosses the northern plateau from west to east. For the first hundred miles or so there is little scenery of note; it is prosperous, well-tilled farm land, alternating with tidy towns and villages; easy but unexciting going for cyclists (who may conveniently break the journey at *Brugg-Altenburg* (Y.H.). Only the eastern part of the route is among high mountains.

Express trains from *Basel* to *Zurich* in 1¼ hrs., to *Chur (Coire)* in 3½ hrs. to *St. Moritz* in 6 hrs.

Basel (see **R.1**) road and rail follow R. *Rhine* (frontier with Germany) *Rheinfelden* combines modern spa with ancient town; well known for its beer. Route ascends fruit-growing area of *Frick* Valley, descends to quaint old town of *Brugg* on R. *Aare*; attractive **Y.H.** in old castle of *Altenburg*; *Baden*, spa on R. *Limmat* (Y.H.).

Zürich between wooded hills at foot of 24-mile long Lake *Zürich*, on Rivers *Limmat* and *Sihl*; largest city in Switzerland, commercial, industrial and university centre; fine modern buildings as well as old quarters; was a

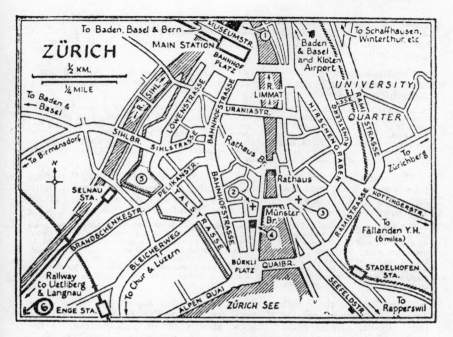

1. *Landesmuseum* (*National Museum*). *Fraumünster*. 3. *Grossmünster*. 4. *Post Office*. 5. *Botanic Garden*. 6. *Youth Hostel* (*Mutschellenstrasse*).

settlement 2,000 or 3,000 B.C. A German "Free City", it joined Switzerland in 1351, and was a centre of the Reformation under Zwingli. Federal Polytechnic is famed throughout Europe. *Gross-Münster* (cathedral) founded by Charlemagne, present building 11th/15th century; *Fraumünster* (13th century, restored); old streets near R. *Limmat*; National Museum (*Landesmuseum*) showing history and development of Switzerland (furniture and architecture, including complete rooms, local costumes); 3 miles long lake promenade. Main shopping thoroughfare is *Bahnhofstrasse*. (Y.H.)

EXCURSIONS: Pleasant walks with good views on *Zürichberg* (east) and *Uetliberg* (southwest); lake steamers; bathing and boating; Y.H. at *Fällanden* on Lake *Greifensee*, 6 miles east of *Zürich*.

From *Zürich* follow Road No. 4 through the *Sihl* valley (pleasant wooded country) or by electric train from *Selnau* station (on west of *Zürich* city centre) to *Uetliberg* (2,863 ft.; 25 mins.) then excellent ridge walk via *Albis* peaks in 5 hrs, to *Sihlbrugg*, rejoining Road No. 4. From *Sihlbrugg*, choice of by-roads to *Einsiedeln* small country town (2,900 ft.) most important Catholic pilgrimage centre of Switzerland; Benedictine monastery founded 984, burnt down several times; present buildings dating from 18th century include splendid Baroque church, containing shrine of miraculous "Black Virgin"—main pilgrimage September 14.

From *Einsiedeln* return to Lake of *Zürich* and follow Road No. 3 or main railway, across level tract of land reclaimed from R. *Linth*, to *Ziegelbrücke*, junction for *Glarus*.

R.2(i) Ziegelbrucke to Glarus, 7 miles. *Glarus* (also called *Glaris*) at foot of *Glärnisch* mountain and in *Linth* valley is capital of canton of same name, cut off to south by high peaks and glaciers of *Tödi* (11,886 ft.) and *Clariden* groups. Little known to foreign tourists; many fine walks and climbs. Holds *Landsgemeinde* (open-air "parliament") first Sunday in May. Chief resorts *Elm, Braunwald* (Y.H.), *Linthal* (17 miles); *Klöntal* lake surrounded by cliffs and forests; 400 year old game sanctuary near *Kärpfstock* mountain, many chamois. For route to *Altdorf* (Lake *Lucerne*) via *Klausen* Pass see R.1(ii).

The route becomes picturesque; *Weesen*, small resort on *Walensee*, lake 9 miles long, between chestnut woods and pasture terraces on south and steep cliffs of *Churfirsten* mountains on north. Y.H. at *Filzbach* above southern shore. South-east to *Sargans*, junction for *Buchs* and Austria.

R.2(ii) Sargans to Feldkirch (Austria) via Liechtenstein, 21 miles. Beyond *Buchs* rail and road cross *Rhine* and enter principality of Liechtenstein. This tiny independent state of about 60 sq. miles and 12,000 inhabitants is governed by a prince, with elected parliament of 15 members. Army abolished in 1866. Customs, monetary and postal union with Switzerland, but issues its own stamps; Roman Catholic and German-speaking. Mainly mountainous, with fruit-growing industry in valleys. Good walks in *Triesenberg* and *Samina* Valley districts. Capital, *Vaduz*, can be reached by bus in 10 mins, from railway station of *Schaan*; royal castle from 10th century, much restored.

From *Sargans* route follows Rhine south; *Bad Ragaz*, spa using water brought 4 miles by conduit through gorge from *Pfäfers*. Scenery becomes more alpine, several ruined castles; shortly before *Landquart* enter the canton of the *Grisons*.

The largest and most sparsely populated Swiss canton, the **Grisons** is named after the grey clothing worn at a meeting in 1424 at which the "grey league" was established to secure the independence of the region. This canton, although long allied with the Swiss, did not become a member of the Confederation until 1803. One third is barren rock or ice; many valleys are over 5,000 ft. high. Important trade route in olden times, it formed the Roman province of *Rhaetia*, a name still in use today. The people are said to be descendants of an ancient Italian tribe and in Upper Rhine and Inn valleys speak *Romansch*, derived from Latin, though most speak German as well. Three southern valleys use Italian; German is official language of about half the population. Officially Protestant, but nearly half the people are Catholics. The narrow-gauge privately owned Rhaetian or South-eastern Railway affords some of the most spectacular rail travel in Switzerland. Many old castles and fortresses along the river valleys.

R.2(iii) Landquart to Davos, 43 miles by the Rhaetian railway, through picturesque *Prätigau* Valley, several small villages, gorges, ruined castles; *Klosters*, resort, walking, ski-ing, climbing. Railway mounts through forests, then descends to Davos, fashionable ski and mountain resort in wide valley above 5,000 ft. level; exceptionally sunny, particularly in winter; many sanatoria. Several mountain railways, including 2½ mile *Parsenn* funicular to *Weissfluhjoch* where Swiss Federal Institute for Snow and Avalanche Research is situated, continued by cable railway to summit of *Weissfluh* (9,344 ft.); fine ski-runs. Y.H.s at *Wolfgang*, north of *Davos*, and at *Davos-Stafelalp*, south of *Davos*.

Route follows Rhine to **Chur** capital of canton; (**Y.H.**); narrow streets, 11th/12th century cathedral, bishop's palace. Terminus of 3 railways; Federal, Rhaetian and *Oberalp* line to *Brigue* (see **R.5**).

R.2(iv) Chur to Arosa, 22 miles. Impressively constructed railway line with many tunnels and bridges, including *Langwies* viaduct; meadows, forests and gorges. *Arosa*, 6,000 ft. is summer and winter resort. **Y.H.** Many walks and climbs. Chair-lift to *Hörnli* (8,190 ft., 15 mins.) and aerial cableway to *Weisshorn*.

EXCURSION: On foot via *Urdenfürkli* pass in 6 hrs. to *Lenzerheide-Valbella*, **Y.H.** attractive mountain valley.

Between *Chur* and *St. Moritz* it is worthwhile taking a slow train (*omnibus*), affording time to enjoy the scenery and fewer passengers trying to look out of the same window.

Reichenau, where *Vorderrhein* and *Hinterrhein* unite to form R. *Rhine*, route turns south through *Domleschg* Valley, gentle slopes dotted with castles (many ruined), villages and churches. *Thusis*, at junction of three valleys (2,370 ft.), small resort. *Hohen-Rhätien* castle for viewpoint; *Ehrenfels* Castle now *Sils im Domleschg* **Y.H.** (For route to *Bellinzona* and *Ticino* via *San Bernardino* Pass see **R.1 (vi)**.)

At *Thusis* (**Y.H.**) most picturesque part of journey begins; rail by narrow *Schyn* Gorges, road through *Pass Mall* protected by stone galleries from rock falls. Near village of *Solis*, invisible almost 1,000 ft. above route, road crosses R. *Albula* by bridge 250 ft. high, railway bridge 290 ft. *Tiefencastel*, on postbus route to *Chur* via *Lenzerheide* (see **R.2 (iv)**) and to *St. Moritz* (see below) via impressive *Julier Pass*. Valley widens, wooded country, distant peaks of 10,000 ft. *Filisur* (3,500 ft.) village with typical local houses, impressive view of viaduct; line follows walls of narrow rocky valley, rising 1,000 ft. in 5½ miles, many tunnels and loops. *Bergün/Bravuogn* (4,475 ft.) pretty village, in sheltered position, 12th century church, walking and ski-ing. 7½ miles of track, impressive tunnels, loops and bridges, to cover 3½ miles of distance and rise 1,360 ft. to 3½-mile long *Albula* tunnel, reaching *Inn* Valley at *Bever*. The road goes over the pass (7,595 ft.) and reaches valley at *La Punt* farther north.

The **Engadine** (Valley of the *Inn*, *En* in Romansch) streches nearly 60 miles from *Maloja* in west to *Tirol* frontier in east. Protected from west winds, the rainfall is low; owing to high altitude, sunshine is strong and nights cold; long winter with excellent snow for ski-ing. Tree-line is at 7,000 ft., about 1,000 ft. higher than in rest of country. Larches are common; alpine flowers fine in June. The houses are sturdily built of stone, white-washed, often with scroll-like decorations; the interiors are lined with pine-panelling and the small square windows frequently have decorative wrought-iron grilles. The Upper *Engadine* valley is at the same altitude as the *Rigi* summit.

German, Romansch and Italian versions of place names are used, to the confusion of the visitor. Usually the official form in the Engadine is *Romansch* though the German may be more commonly seen on maps, e.g. *Sils* (Rom.: *Segl*), *Bergün* (Rom.: *Bravuogn*). Some Romansch words occurring in place names are *Piz*=peak, *vadret*=glacier, *fuorcla*=pass, *lej*=lake, *munt*=mountain, *ova*=stream.

SWITZERLAND

R.2(v) Bever to Zernez (for Swiss National Park), 21 miles. Rail and road down valley of *Inn*; *Zuoz*, has some fine old houses, small resort; 5 miles below *Zuoz*, road crosses *Punt Ota* (high bridge) boundary between Upper and Lower *Engadine*; valley descends to *Zernez*, (Y.H.) best approach to Swiss National Park, nature reserve since 1909, 50 sq. miles, with about 100 peaks rising to 10,000 ft., some most impressive scenery. Several cabins provide overnight accommodation and simple fare. Only the marked paths may be used and no plants or animals harmed. Fine show of flowers particularly in June, many chamois, ibex, golden eagles, marmots foxes and other alpine animals and birds. But this is in no sense a zoo; the animals are completely wild, so do not expect to see them all; field-glasses are useful.

Main route continues to *Samedan*, chief village of Upper *Engadine* (5,604 ft.) quieter alternative to *St. Moritz*. **St. Moritz** (rail terminus) (5,990 ft.) spa, fashionable winter and summer resort, with enormous hotels, in beautiful position on small lake. Cheap temperance restaurant near station. Y.H. in *St. Moritz-Bad* (south of *St. Moritz*). Many walks, climbs and tours. Europabus motor coaches in summer to *Milan, Lugano, Landeck/Tirol, Munich, Bolzano* and *Garmisch-Partenkirchen*.

EXCURSION: Cable railway in two stages to *Corviglia*, then chair-lift to *Piz Nair* (10,040 ft.), total journey time 21 mins.

R.3. French Frontier—Berne—Lucerne (158 miles)

This is an attractive route, crossing the *Jura* mountains and the Bernese Oberland. Express trains from *Paris* to *Berne* cross Swiss frontier at *Delle* (via *Belfort*) or at *les Verrières* (via *Dijon*). No through trains from Channel ports by these routes in summer (all go to *Basel*). Route described here is from *les Verrières*, but if travelling via *Delle* you can join route at *Berne*.

Fast trains from *les Verrières* to *Berne* in 1½ hrs., and to *Interlaken* in 3 hrs.; from *Interlaken* to *Lucerne* in 2 hrs.

From *les Verrières* rail and road cut through *Jura* mountains by wooded *Val de Travers*, emerging at *Neuchâtel*.

Neuchâtel, capital of French-speaking Protestant district, several centuries ruled by a count, ally of Swiss, made canton 1815. Lake 24 miles long had many prehistoric settlements. Town is educational centre, with university, said to be best French accent in Switzerland. Abbey church and castle, fine patrician houses; museum in Hotel Peyron. (Y.H.)

EXCURSIONS: (a) Ridge walk of *Chasseral*. Tram 7 to *La Coudre*, then funicular to *Chaumont* (3,870 ft.) or on foot from *Neuchâtel* in 1½ hrs. From *Chaumont* fine ridge walk in 4 hrs. to *Chasseral* (5,300 ft.) view to Alps in clear weather. (b) By rail in 25 mins. 18 miles to *Bienne* (*Biel*), (Y.H.) bilingual town on lake of same name; centre of watchmaking industry; visits to watch factories can be arranged. (c) by steamer, on certain days only, by canal through to the *Lake of Morat*, or *Murtensee* (Y.H. at *Faoug* at southern end of lake). *Morat* (*Murten*), scene of victory of Swiss over Charles the Bold in 1476, is unspoilt medieval town, with walls, gates, arcaded shops.

10 miles beyond *Neuchâtel* is **Ins**, road and railway junction for **Fribourg**.

R.3(i) Ins to Fribourg, 26 miles; rail in 1 hr. capital of canton, on R. *Sarine* (Ger.: *Saarne*) which forms language boundary from here southwards. Old city on rocky hill in bend of river, many attractive old houses, 14th/15th century cathedral with famous organ and recitals. Catholic educational centre, university. Local costumes may be seen at Wednesday and Saturday markets. Corpus Christi procession worth seeing.

Route enters German-speaking Switzerland, crosses central plateau to *Berne*.

Berne, in wooded, hilly country, with view of distant Alps; chief city of wide ranging canton. Joined Confederation in 1353 and quickly became most powerful canton. *Aargau* and *Vaud* have since been formed out of parts of its possessions. Seat of Federal Government and administration. Headquarters of Universal Postal Union. Principal sights of the city are the Minster, 15/16th century; *Bundeshaus* (Federal Parliament); Historical Museum; *Zeitglockenturm*, originally city gate, clock with puppets, performance starts 8 mins. before each hour, best at midday; *Käfigturm* (Prison Tower); Baroque *Erlacher Hof* in *Junkerngasse*. View-points: Parliament Terrace, Minster Terrace, and *Schänzli*. Bear pit near *Nydegg* Bridge; bears have been kept since 1513—they figure in arms of *Berne*. Many attractive old streets with arcades and fountains, especially *Kramgasse*, often gay with geraniums in window boxes. Swimming pool near zoo. Y.H. in *Weihergasse*.

EXCURSION: By road or rail to *Langnau* (Y.H.), 23 miles. Centre of **Emmental**, sub-alpine region with characteristic fine wooden farmhouses; most cheese sold as Gruyére is made here.

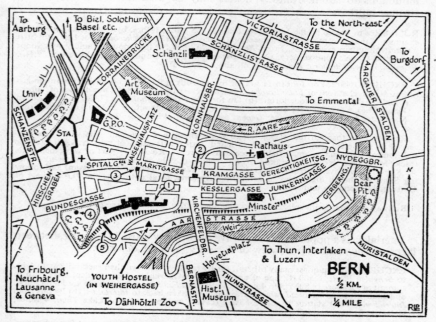

1. *Bundeshaus* (Federal Parliament). 2. *Zeitglockenturm*. 3. *Käfigturm*.
4. *Universal Postal Union Monument*. 5. *Funicular*.

SWITZERLAND

South-east to *Thun* on river, near Lake *Thun* (14 miles long) 12th/15th century castle, arcaded streets, covered bridge.

Thun is the gateway to the **Bernese Oberland,** one of the most famous holiday areas in the world, on the northern slopes of the Bernese Alps. This range, although not the highest in Switzerland (the *Matterhorn* and *Monte Rosa* are higher than the 14,026 ft. of the *Finsteraarhorn,* highest peak of the Bernese Alps), is unique in the grandeur of its sharply towering peaks, its glaciers, waterfalls and charming alpine meadows. The sub-alpine portions are characterised by neat villages whose wooden chalets have wide eaves, verandas and window-boxes. Its great scenic beauties have given rise to a highly-developed tourist industry, and the resorts and youth hostels are crowded during the summer season and again in the winter sports season.

Steamer to *Interlaken* along 14 mile Lake *Thun* calls at *Oberhofen* on north shore **(Y.H.);** *Spiez,* attractive town among orchards with medieval castle containing collection of Bernese furniture and handicrafts, junction for railway to *Montreux,* **(R.4(i));** and *Faulensee* on south shore **(Y.H.).** Complete journey *Thun-Interlaken* takes 2 hrs.; grand views from lake of high mountains to south. Railway tickets may be used for the corresponding steamer journey.

R.3(ii) Spiez to Brigue by the Lötschberg Railway, 63 miles, 1¼ hrs. by fast train. Yet another example of magnificent railway engineering (opened in 1913). *Reichenbach,* for beautiful little *Kiental;* mountain excursions. From *Kandergrund* (2,825 ft.) line mounts rapidly with loops and spiral tunnels, fine scenery, to *Kandersteg* (3,875 ft.) mountain and ski resort **(Y.H.).** *Blümlisalphorn, Balmhorn, Doldenhorn,* all about 12,000 ft.

EXCURSIONS: (a) on foot in 1¼ hrs. or by chair-lift in 9 mins. to beautiful mountain-girt *Oeschinensee,* at foot of *Blümlisalphorn.* Nature reserve on south side; fine display of "alpenrosen"—a kind of rhododendron. (b) On foot over the *Gemmi* pass (7,620 ft.) to *Leuk* in *Valais* **(R.4),** 6 hrs. Fine zig-zag mountain path, safe throughout; or by aerial cableway from *Kandersteg* to *Stock,* thence over *Gemmi* pass to *Leuk* (4 hrs.).

Railway runs through tunnel 9 miles to *Goppenstein* in *Lötschental.* The valley has preserved its unspoiled nature, completely isolated until construction of railway. Characteristic old houses, black barns, small richly decorated churches. Road only part of way, then mule track. Main peak is lovely pyramid of *Bietschhorn* (nearly 13,000 ft.), very difficult climb. At *Kippel,* impressive procession at Corpus Christi (2nd Thursday after Whitsun) and following Sunday—church dignitaries in colourful vestments, local costumes, the "Grenadiers of God" in 17th century uniform.

Railway descends, with splendid views of *Rhône* valley, to *Brigue* (see R.4).

Interlaken is a popular and expensive resort, very warm in summer, between lakes of *Thun* and *Brienz;* view of *Jungfrau.* **Y.H.** at *Böningen.*

EXCURSIONS (amongst many others): (a) By rail to *Wilderswil* then rack railway in 1 hr. to *Schynige Platte,* 6,500 ft., one of finest views on Oberland; alpine garden. Easy path to summit of *Faulhorn* (8,803 ft.) in 4 hrs. Descent from *Faulhorn* may be made via *First* (2 hrs.) and chair-lift to *Grindelwald,* whence train may be taken back to *Interlaken.* (b) By bus from *Interlaken* (West) station to *Beatushöhlen* (caves) on north side of Lake *Thun,* 4 miles; stalactite formations; admission charge.

R.3(iii) Interlaken to Grindelwald and Lauterbrunnen. This route visits the most famous mountain resorts of the Bernese Oberland, and can easily be done by railway (rack-and-pinion in steeper parts) either in sections or as a complete circuit, as described here.

From *Interlaken* (Ost) station, rail and road pass *Zweilütschinen* and enter valley of *Schwarze Lütschine;* beyond *Burglauenen* valley widens; 12 miles to Grindelwald, a popular resort at 3,420 ft. (Y.H.).

EXCURSIONS: (a) On foot via the *Kleine Scheidegg* (6,770 ft.) in 6-8 hrs. to *Lauterbrunnen.* (b) On foot to the *Grindelwald* glaciers; should not be missed; easy footpaths. (c) Ascent of *Faulhorn* (8,803 ft.) by moderately easy marked track in 5½ hrs., or by chair-lift to *First* in 4 sections (total 30 mins.) then on foot in 2 hrs. (d) By *Grosse Scheidegg* (6,434 ft.) to *Meiringen* —see R.6.

From *Grindelwald* the *Wengernalp* rack railway (accompanied by footpath but no road) climbs over 3,300 ft. to the Kleine Scheidegg pass (6,770 ft.), 5¼ miles in 36 mins.

EXCURSION: *Kleine Scheidegg* is starting point of famous Jungfrau Railway, highest in Europe and a spectacular feat of engineering. It climbs 4,500 ft. in less than 6 miles, mostly by rack system. Fare is dear, but is much less expensive for holders of Swiss holiday tickets (see page 11). Railway runs first along crest of *Scheidegg, Eigergletscher* station (7,620 ft.) with views of *Eiger, Mönch* and *Jungfrau* glaciers. Rest of track ascends in remarkable tunnel cut through the *Rotstock* and the *Mönch* but viewpoints are arranged at stations (hewn out of rock) of *Eigerwand* (9,405 ft.) magnificent view over mountains, glaciers and plains to Vosges and Black Forest; *Eismeer* station (10,370 ft.), *Joch* station (11,340 ft.) where view is even more magnificent, walks on glacier, ski-ing throughout year. Hotel, skating rink, tourist house with dormitories. Tunnels lead to view-points and to observatory and meteorological research institute.

From *Kleine Scheidegg* railway descends via *Wengen* (4,200 ft.), winter and summer resort, linked to outer world only by railway—no road to *Lauterbrunnen. Lauterbrunnen* is resort hemmed in by precipices and many waterfalls, of which best are *Staubbach, Trümmelbach* and upper *Schmadribach;* falls are fed by glaciers on *Jungfrau* and other mountains.

EXCURSION: On foot in 2½ hrs. or by narrow-gauge railway in two stages in 30 mins. to *Mürren,* very fashionable winter-sports resort at 5,400 ft. with wonderful view of *Eiger* (the Ogre), *Mönch* (the Monk), *Jungfrau* (the Virgin) and other peaks. Y.H. at *Gimmelwald. Schilthorn* (9,754 ft.) is a fairly easy climb on a marked track; descent also to *Kiental.* From *Lauterbrunnen* to *Interlaken,* 7½ miles, down valley of *Weisse Lutschine.*

From *Interlaken* to *Brienz* journey may be made by road, rail or steamer (rail tickets interchangeable for steamer). Scenery more mountainous than around *Thun* and the lake is over 800 ft. deep. Steamer in 80 mins. *Brienz,* attractive large village, centre of wood-carving industry with special technical school. (Y.H.).

EXCURSION: By rack railway (steam operated) in 35 mins. to the *Rothorn* (7,714 ft.), with very fine views. Good mountain path in 4 hrs. to *Brünig* pass on road to Lake *Lucerne.*

Direct road proceeds from *Brienz* to *Brünig* pass, but detour via *Meiringen* is recommended. *Meiringen* (Y.H.) is chief village of *Hasli* Valley, small mountain centre at junction of seven valleys, including *Grimsel, Susten* (see R.1 (iv)), *Brünig, Grosse Scheidegg* and *Jochpass* (see R.6).

EXCURSIONS: *Meiringen* is starting point for fine "3-Pass Tour" by postal motor coach: *Grimsel, Furka* and *Susten* (the first two both over 7,000 ft.). Round trip in 9 hrs. (including lunch break).

Route turns north. Road and narrow-gauge rack railway rise steeply with many good views to *Brünig* Pass (3,396 ft.), then down between rocky walls and dense pine woods to several small resorts, including *Sachseln,* with tomb and shrine of Switzerland's most recent saint, Nicholas von der Flüe, hermit and hero of 15th century; along *Sarnersee,* below *Pilatus* to *Lucerne* (see R.1).

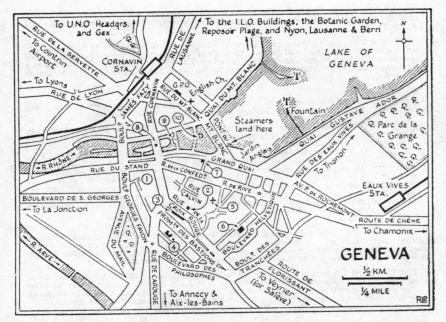

1. *Grand Theatre*. 2. *Hôtel de Ville*. 3. *Reformation Monument*. 4. *University*.
5. *Cathédrale de Saint Pierre*. 6. *Museum of Art and History*. 7. *Tour Molard*.
8. *Tour de l'Ile*. 9. *Pont de la Machine*. 10. *Ile Rousseau*.

R.4. Geneva to Brigue (128 miles)

This route traverses the French-speaking cantons of *Geneva, Vaud* and *Valais*, a sunny, fertile region with many fashionable resorts and access to numerous mountain valleys. From *Lausanne* onward the route is that of the Direct-Orient express (*Paris* to the Balkans). *Geneva* is not easily reached from England by train as a change of stations at Paris is necessary, but there are frequent flights from London.

Fast train from *Geneva* to *Brigue* in 3 hrs. Main Road No. 1 to *Lausanne*, thence No. 9.

Geneva, on R. *Rhone* and *Arve*, at south-west tip of Lake Geneva; banking and commercial city, intellectual centre of French-speaking Switzerland, with university, watch and jewellery manufacture. The "Rome of Protestantism" was the headquarters of Calvin and his followers in the 16th century. Headquarters of International Red Cross, World Health Organisation, International Labour Office, a section of the United Nations, and many religious and welfare organisations. **(Y.H.)**

Renaissance *Hôtel de Ville* (Town Hall) with ramp instead of steps. Imposing Reformation Monument in University Gardens, including statues John Knox and Oliver Cromwell, with carved extracts from speeches in various languages; *Tour de l'Ile* and *Tour Molard*, gateways; hydro-electric works (*Forces Motrices*) and electricity station (*Pont de la Machine*) on R. *Rhône*; Museum of Art and History. From *Quai du Mont Blanc*, Mont Blanc, over 40 miles away, may be seen in clear weather. Fine promenades and parks; 400 ft. fountain at end of jetty. Best shopping street is *rue de la Confédération*, continued under names of *rue du Marché* and *rue de la Croix d'Or* to south of lake. Walk along *Route de Lausanne* to *Reposoir*, pleasant bathing beach.

EXCURSIONS: Geneva is almost entirely surrounded by French territory, and for longer excursions a passport is necessary. (a) On foot to the *Jonction* (south-west corner of city), where blue *Rhône* meets grey *Arve*. (b) Tram to *Veyrier* (20 mins.) and cross frontier to France, cable railway or rough footpath onto the *Salève*, limestone ridge of about 4,000 ft. with magnificent views over Lake and Alps. (c) By Lake steamer to Swiss or French resorts— e.g. to *Nyon* in 1¼ hrs.

From *Geneva*, road and rail routes run north along lake, but much of shore is private property. *Coppet*, chateau of Mme. de Staël; *Nyon*, old houses, 16th century castle.

EXCURSION: By narrow-gauge railway in 45 mins., 12 miles to *St. Cergue* (3,400 ft.) small centre for *Jura* mountains. (Y.H.). Chair-lift from *Archette* (15 mins. from *St. Cergue*) to *La Barillette* (4,700 ft.); magnificent views over Lake of *Geneva* and Alps. From *St. Cergue* ascent of *La Dôle* (5,540 ft.) on foot in 2¼ hrs.; descent may be made to *Les Rousses* in France (Y.H.).

Lausanne, junction for *Berne*, also Paris via *Vallorbe*, in a steep situation on slopes of *Mont Jorat*, cleft by gorges formed by R. *Flon* and *Louve*, above its port of *Ouchy*. University; seat of Supreme Federal Court of Justice; capital of canton of *Vaud*. Fine 12th/13th century Gothic cathedral, approached by covered stairway; *St. Maire* castle, 15th century, housing canton government offices; picturesque cobbled streets (Y.H.).

EXCURSIONS: (a) By road or rail (21 mls., rail in 40 mins.) to *Croy-Romainmôtier*, on line to *Vallorbe*. *Romainmôtier* is old town with one of finest churches in Switzerland. (b) steamer to *Thonon* (France) in 70 mins. for access to *Savoy* Alps.

Shores of lake grow steeper, many vineyards, attractive hill villages, views of Savoy mountains. *Vevey*, 12th century church, restored. The *Dents du Midi* are seen to south. From here onwards lake is sheltered from the *bise* and for several miles shores form continuous resort. *La Tour de Peilz*, headquarters of Nestlés. *Clarens, Montreux, Territet* (Y.H.), fashionable resorts.

EXCURSIONS: By mountain railways to heights behind the towns such as *les Pléiades*, *Rochers de Naye*, *Caux* and *Les Avants* (famous for wild narcissi late May to early June); all with splendid views across lake to Alps.

R.4(i) Montreux to Spiez (85 miles). Picturesque route by narrow-gauge railway from *Montreux* to *Zweisimmen*, (Y.H.) then by standard-gauge line to *Spiez*. Total journey 3 hrs. Railway climbs from *Montreux*, many loops and fine views over lake, to *Les Avants* (3,200 ft.) and enters sub-Alpine western (French-speaking) extremity of Bernese Oberland. Railway keeps at or above 3,000 ft. level most of way, passing *Château-d'Oex* (smart resort; Y.H.), *Saanen* where French language gives way to German), *Gstaad* (noted for winter sports); thence down *Simmental* valley to reach Lake *Thun* near *Spiez* (see R.3). Journey *Montreux-Spiez-Interlaken* can also be made by Europabus service in 4 hrs.

SWITZERLAND

Castle of Chillon, fine 12th/13th century fortress picturesquely situated on rock in lake. Long used as a state prison, and one internee, Bonivard, was subject of famous poem by Byron; Shelley, Dickens and others have cut their names on the walls of his cell.

At *Villeneuve,* route leaves lake, and enters upper valley of R. *Rhône* between mountain groups of *Diablerets* to east and *Dents du Midi* to west. Beyond *Bex* enter canton *Valais.*

Canton **Valais** is the 90-mile trench of the upper *Rhône,* straight except for a right-angled bend at *Martigny,* and its tributary valleys. The people work immensely hard to gain a living against so many adversities—poor soil, extremes of climate, rock-falls, avalanches, flood and drought—that the canton is sometimes called the "haunted Valais". Devout Catholics, the main colour in their lives is provided by the festivals of the Church and the local ceremonies, such as blessing of the fields and animals. Reputed to be partly of Saracen origin, they keep their old traditions and customs, and the distinctive costume of the women is black or of dark colour, with straw bonnet perched above coiled plaits; still worn in some places on Sundays. Some communities have two villages; they live near the *Rhône* during the winter and migrate in spring to the mountains, with schoolteacher and priest. Water is brought to the lower slopes by a centuries-old system of ditches and conduits known as *bisses.* French, including several dialects, is spoken in the west, German in the east.

To the north, foothills of the central mountains form sunny terraces with resorts and sanatoria; to south rise the *Pennine Alps.* These great snow-covered mountains lie at the head of long, wild valleys and also form high spurs which isolate the valleys from each other. Light railways, or postal motor coaches, make connections with the main line, which follows a long straight course near the *Rhône,* through vineyards, orchards and maize fields. In summer the contrast between the baking heat here and the crisp climate of the valley heads is very striking.

St. Maurice has oldest monastery in the Alps, founded 4th century, some work dating from 10th century. Valuable treasure may be seen.

Martigny, where valley turns N.E. Fine covered bridge over R. *Dranse.* **(Y.H.).**

R.4(ii) Martigny to Aosta (Italy) via the Great St. Bernard Pass, 50 miles. Coach in 3 hrs. In winter the coaches use the *Great St. Bernard Tunnel,* opened March 1964, 4 miles long, for motor vehicles only (toll). *Orsières* is picturesque village at nearly 3,000 ft. (Y.H. at *Champex*) *Great St. Bernard Pass,* 8,111 ft., between *Grand Combin* (14,160 ft.) and *Mont Blanc* ranges. Hospice founded in 11th century, accommodates travellers in distress; monastery, chapel and library, post office; famous dogs trained to rescue travellers. Italian frontier. Finely-engineered road down *St. Bernard Valley* (largely French-speaking) to *Aosta.*

R.4(iii) Martigny to Chamonix, 23 miles. Road and rail by impressive gorges of R. *Trient* across frontier into France and skirting massif of *Mont Blanc,* with superb views. *Martigny* to *Châtelard* by rack railway in 1 hr. or by postal bus in 1½ hrs. Railway continues to *Vallorcine* (France) whence connection by French National Railways to *Chamonix* (Y.H.).

R.4(iv) Martigny to Mauvoisin (Val de Bagnes), 21 miles. One of wildest of southern valleys; waterfalls, glaciers and snowclad peaks; unusual alpine flora. Rail *Martigny* to *Chable* in 45 mins. (Y.H. 2 miles south, at *Bruson*) then bus past *Fionnay* (summer resort) to *Mauvoisin* (1 hr.), centre for mountain and glacier tours.

Continuing up *Rhône* Valley, *Sion,* chief town of Valais, bishopric since 6th century, old quarters between *Tourbillon* hill, ruined castle, and *Valère* hill, fortress and 13th century church. Cathedral, 15th century, 10th century tower. (Y.H.)

R.4(v) Sion to Arolla (25 miles). Motor bus into lovely *Hérens* valley via *Evolène* and *Les Haudères* (Y.H.), quiet summer resorts, then to *Arolla* (6,440 ft.) in 2 hours, small mountaineering centre amid larches and Arolla pines, surrounded by snowy peaks and glaciers.

Continue alongside *Rhône* past vineyards and orchards to small town of *Sierre,* interesting museums. *Sierre* is overlooked by tripartite health and winter sports resort of *Montana-Vermala-Crans:* many sanatoria.

R.4(vi) Sierre to Zinal (17 miles) by *Val d'Anniviers,* perhaps most beautiful of tributary valleys of Upper *Rhône.* Bus 1½ hrs. via *Vissoie* to *Zinal,* 5,505 ft., small mountain centre amid peaks and glaciers of *Dent Blanche, Gabelhorn* and *Weisshorn.*

Beyond *Sierre* German-speaking territory is entered. *Leuk,* interesting old town, 15th century church, castle, from which *Gemmi* Pass route leads to *Kandersteg* (see **R.3 (ii)**). To north of road, *Lötschberg* line to *Berne* may be seen climbing above *Rhône* valley. *Visp,* village with medieval houses and old church. (Y.H.)

R.4(vii) Visp to Zermatt, 22 miles. Narrow-gauge railway in 1½ hrs. Road goes only as far as *St. Nicklaus.* Railway climbs by gorges and tunnels to *Stalden.*

EXCURSION: 12 miles (bus in 70 mins.) up beautiful *Saas* valley to *Saas-Fee* (5,900 ft.), climbing and walking centre, surrounded by high peaks, notably *Mischabel* group; easy ascent of *Mellig* (8,813 ft.) in 2 hrs., or chair-lift (to *Plattjen*) part of way.

Continue up *Nicolaital,* narrow picturesque valley, with restricted views, several small villages. *Matterhorn* not seen until shortly before *Zermatt* (5,300 ft.), climbing, tourist and winter sports centre, overshadowed by *Matterhorn* (14,980 ft.). Alpine Museum, containing relics of accident to Whymper's party, first to ascend *Matterhorn,* 1865. Y.H.

EXCURSIONS: (a) Via *Riffelalp* and *Riffelsee* to rocky ridge of *Gornergrat* (10,290 ft.). Rack railway in 50 mins. Magnificent views across glaciers to *Monte Rosa* group (15,200 ft.) and *Matterhorn.* Return by *Obere Kelle, Grünsee* (Green Tarn), warm enough for bathing, and foot of *Findelen* Glacier. (b) *Schwarzsee* and *Hörnli* Hut (9,494 ft.) at foot of *Matterhorn;* chairlift in 2 sections. (c) *Schönbiel* Hut, views of sheer north face of *Matterhorn* and *Dent d'Hérens.*

Road and rail continue to **Brigue,** junction for *Lötschberg* railway to Bernese Oberland (**R.3 (ii)**), *Furka-Oberalp* railway to *Andermatt* and *Chur* (**R.5**). *Brigue* has 17th century *Stockalper* castle, with gilded "onion" domes, old houses, steep narrow streets.

EXCURSION: Bus in 35 mins. to *Blatten,* 5 miles, then on foot in 2 hrs. or by cable railway in 8 mins. to *Belalp,* 7,010 ft., for splendid view of *Aletsch* glacier, largest in Europe, stretching 16 miles from *Jungfraujoch* and edged by 11,000 ft. peaks.

Brigue is at entrance to **Simplon tunnel,** 12¼ miles, longest in world, leading to *Domodossola* in Italy; frontier for rail tariff purposes is at *Iselle,* at southern entrance to tunnel. A road crosses the *Simplon* pass (6,590 ft.) with hospice kept by the St. Bernard monks. *Brigue-Domodossola* bus in 3½ hrs.

R.5. Brigue to Chur via Andermatt (138 miles)

Road and narrow-gauge railway. Fast train in about 5 hrs. Also bus on central portion *Gletsch-Andermatt* (20 miles, 1½ hrs.) with better views than train (via *Furka* pass, 7,992 ft.).

SWITZERLAND

This route forms an alternative link between western and eastern Switzerland; slower and more expensive than via *Zürich*, but with finer scenery; open early June to mid October.

Road and rail ascend *Rhône* valley, flanked by mountain peaks; *Fiesch*, small resort. **(Y.H.)**

EXCURSIONS: (a) Up remote *Binn* valley, noted for rare minerals and flowers. (b) *Eggishorn* (9,626 ft.). 4 hrs. steep walk, magnificent prospect of *Aletsch* glacier and surrounding peaks.

Orchards and vineyards are left behind, valley now known as *Goms*, alpine meadows and forests, number of small villages suitable for walking centres, seldom visited by foreign tourists. At *Gletsch*, fine view of imposing 1,600 ft. ice-fall of *Rhône* Glacier, hanging high above valley. Bus from *Gletsch* to *Andermatt* passes edge of glacier, and crosses desolate *Furka* pass. Rail descends lonely valley (road may be seen at higher level) to *Hospental* at foot of St. Gotthard road **(Y.H.)** and *Andermatt* (see **R.1**).

Beyond *Andermatt* route rises again, with views of *St. Gotthard* mountains in loops and spirals to bare, stony *Oberalp* Pass (6,733 ft.) with small lake, and descends into the *Grisons*. *Tschamut* (5,405 ft.) small climbing and walking centre, from which Lake *Toma*, source of R. *Vorderrhein*, may be visited. *Sedrun*, climbing and ski-ing centre; *Disentis/Mustèr*, junction of Oberalp and Rhaetian railways (but many through trains), small spa and market town, in broad green valley below 9,000 ft. peaks; Benedictine abbey, originally founded 7th century. Mountain excursions in the *Medel* group and along the *Lukmanier* Pass route.

The valley is now known as the *Bündner Oberland*; here, as in the Engadine, Romansch is spoken; many unspoilt villages in excellent walking country; *Ilanz*, with old houses, churches and gateways; **Y.H.** at *Miraniga*, near *Meierhof*.

EXCURSIONS: (a) On foot to *Piz Mundaun* (6,780 ft.), by marked path, for fine view (b) By road (7½ miles, bus in 40 mins.) to *Flims*, pleasant small resort with woods and lakes; thence chair-lift, 2¼ miles long (2 sections) in 20 mins. to *Alp Naraus*, nearly 7,000 ft.; thence aerial cableway to *Fil de Cassons*.

From *Ilanz* the line runs 10 miles through extraordinary limestone gorges to *Reichenau*, junction of *Vorderrhein* and *Hinterrhein*, and down *Rhine* to *Chur*. **(Y.H.)** (For *Thusis* and *Engadine*, see **R.2**.)

R.6. Lake Geneva to Lake Lucerne by Oberland Pass Route (14 days' walk)

A route for keen walkers experienced in fell or mountain walking; rough mountain paths and low temperatures on alpine passes make boots and adequate outdoor clothing essential. Passes marked (*) ought never to be attempted in unsettled weather.

By train or road from *Montreux* **(Y.H.)** along the eastern edge of the lake, then skirting the flood plain of the *Rhône* to *Aigle*, a little town in pleasant surroundings.

One hour railway journey up the *Ormonts* valley to *Les Aviolats*; thence on foot in few minutes to Y.H. at *Vers l'Eglise*. From here an easy path follows the river for two miles up to *Les Diablerets*, winter sports resort almost surrounded by lofty mountains. Uphill road for 3 miles in 2 hours to *Col du Pillon* (5,086 ft.) affording view of magnificent *Creux-de-Champ*, streaming with ice. Thence to *Gsteig*, a downhill walk of 5 miles between snowy peaks; alternatively, a bus goes from *Les Diablerets* to *Gsteig* in 45 minutes. A footpath of 4 miles goes across the *Krinnen* pass (5,446 ft.) to *Lauenen* (choice of easy ascents to surrounding peaks). From here the *Truttlisberg* pass (6,699 ft.) strikes eastwards for 8 miles (6 hours) to *Lenk*; mountaineering centre with sulphur springs. On to *Adelboden* (Y.H.) via the *Hahnenmoos* pass (6,400 ft.) an easy walk in about 5 hours.

EXCURSION: *Engstligen Falls* 1½ hours by footpath and on to the *Engstligenalp* (6,470 ft.) in further hour.

From *Adelboden* to *Kandersteg* via the *Bonderchrinde* pass (7,830 ft.) is an 8 mile walk (6 hours). Take the chair lift from *Kandersteg* to *Oeschinen* (see R.3 (ii)) and follow the path for 8 hours across the *Hohtürli* pass to the hotel at *Griesalp*. Track and footpath up the valley on to the *Sefinenfurgge* pass (8,583 ft.), a way between the topmost crags and affording view of *Jungfrau* to the east, *Blümlisalp* to the south west; descend to *Gimmelwald* (Y.H.) (10 miles in 8 hours). Follow the high level path for 2 miles along the side of the *Lauterbrunnen* valley to *Mürren*, set on a mountain terrace.

EXCURSION: Chair lift (longest in Europe) up to the *Schilthorn* (9,742 ft.).

From *Mürren* to *Grütsch Alp*, an easy walk in 1 hour, the track lies beside the railway but affords splendid views of the crests of the *Silberhorn, Jungfrau, Mönch* and *Eiger*. Descend by the rack railway (¾ mile) to *Lauterbrunnen*, thence by footpath up the valley side eastward for 1½ miles to *Wengen*. Track for 3 miles up on to the *Wengern Alp* and sight of deep ravine of *Trummelbach*; on for 1½ miles to *Kleine Scheidegg* (6,772 ft.).

EXCURSION: Walk for 45 minutes to snout of *Eiger* glacier (ice caves).

On for 6 miles on the *Kleine Scheidegg* pass to *Grindelwald* (Y.H.) (see R.3 (iii)). By road and bridle path for 3 hours beneath the rock walls of the *Wetterhorn* to the *Grosse Scheidegg*, a col at 6,434 ft. in the shadow of the *Wetterhorn*. Path descends via *Schwarzwald Alp* to *Rosenlaui*, tiny summer resort, and on to *Meiringen* (Y.H.) by easy paths between meadows (4 hours from top of the pass).

EXCURSION: *Reichenbach Waterfalls*; by tramway and funicular to *Upper Reichenbach Fall*. Here Sherlock Holmes made his seemingly final exit.

Road and path from *Meiringen* to *Innertkirchen*, via the *Aar* gorge (3 miles; small toll) thence easy track up the *Gental* valley to the *Engstlen Alp* (11 miles). From *Engstlen Alp* to *Jochpass* (7,267 ft.) is a walk of 1½ hours; varied scenery and near views of glaciers of *Titlis*. Descend in 3 hours via *Trübsee* and *Gerschnialp* to *Engelberg* (Y.H.) (see R.1. (i)).

From *Engelberg* the road ascends the *Aa* valley, passing the *Tätschbach* waterfalls, then by track to the top of the *Surenen* pass (7,563 ft.) in 4½ hours; fine retrospect of *Titlis*. Descend in 4 hours to *Altdorf* near end of southern arm of Lake Lucerne (see R.1).

YUGOSLAVIA

Geographical Outline

Land — Yugoslavia lies south-easterly from the Alps, extends into south-east Europe and is as much Balkan as central European; bordered by Austria and Hungary to the north, Italy to the north-west, Albania and Greece to the south and Rumania and Bulgaria to the east.

Most of the country is mountainous; the *Julian Alps* lie to the north, the *Dinaric Alps* extend along the Dalmatian coast and comprise great areas of mountain country in the centre and south. Mountain limestone, dry and barren *karstland,* makes precipitous walls behind the narrow strip of the Adriatic coastline, more gentle to the north-east where the R. *Sava* flows across the country through *Zagreb* and to *Belgrade* to join the *Danube.*

Narrow valleys lie parallel to the coast, making access difficult, but the R. *Neretva* has cut through the western edge of the mountain mass and made a through route from the coast to the interior. The deeply indented Adriatic coastline has a shore-length of 1,300 miles, with hundreds of islands lying between *Rijeka* and *Dubrovnik,* all rather barren with poor limestone soil, but the rocky Dalmatian coast is majestically beautiful and has many resorts, flourishing on tourism. This coastal area divides unequally into four regions; to the north is Istria, the peninsular between Trieste and *Rijeka* with a rocky indented coast and pebbly beaches. Then comes the Croatian coast between *Rijeka* and *Zadar,* where the barren mountain limestone makes steep rock faces, sheltering the coast resorts from the *bora,* the harsh winter wind. From *Zadar* south-eastwards to *Cavtat* is the Dalmatian coast proper and, here again, the coastal strip is backed by the mountain limestone barrier; steep-sided inlets, bays and many islands make this the most beautiful sea-coast of Europe. To the south the Montenegran littoral stretches to the Albanian frontier, nearly 100 miles of remote and mountainous coast with sandy beaches and the spectacular fjord of *Boka Kotorska.*

Yugoslavia is comprised of six republics and they are best described separately to give a better idea of the composition of the country.

Slovenia is closest to the West; bordered to the north by the *Julian* and *Karawanken Alps,* by Austria and Italy and, at various times, ruled by these two countries. The republic is almost entirely mountainous; *Ljubljana* the capital is on the international railway route. The people of Slovenia are Slavs, but they use the Latin alphabet and are European in outlook.

Croatia comprises almost all the coastal region of Yugoslavia, from Istria southwards to *Herceg Novi,* beyond *Dubrovnik,* and inland to the Hungarian frontier. The *Plitvice Lakes National Park* lies equidistant between *Zagreb* and *Zadar*; the international railway line of the Orient Express runs through Croatia, so does the *Zagreb/Belgrade* motor-way. Croatians use the Latin alphabet and, like the Slovenes, are Western in outlook, history and tradition.

444

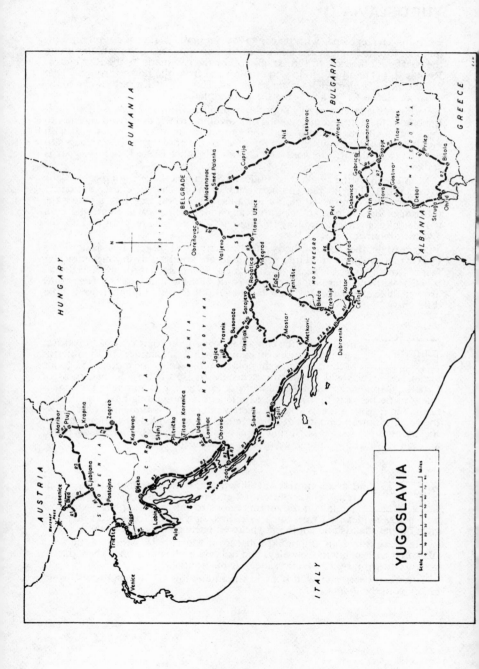

YUGOSLAVIA

YUGOSLAVIA

Bosnia-Herzegovina, with its capital at *Sarajevo*, is almost entirely mountainous; forested mountains inland but the barren limestone mountains along the coast cut off access to the sea, except for the gap made by the R. *Neretva*. Routes **R.4 (1)** and **R.4** follow the main road from the north through *Banja Luka*, *Jajce*, *Sarajevo* and *Mostar* to the sea. The people are Serbs and Croats, speaking Serbo-Croat and using the Latin aphabet.

Serbia is the largest of the Yugoslav republics, with *Belgrade* as its capital; it includes the autonomous regions of Vojvodina to the north and Kosmet to the south. Although land-locked and mountainous, often forested but with great tracts of mountain pasture, the relief of the country falls northwards to the plains of the R. *Danube*. The Cyrillic alphabet is used, Serbo-Croat is spoken.

Montenegro is the smallest republic, its Slav name *Crna Gora* means Black Mountain. It lies at the southern end of Yugoslavia's coast; extremely mountainous country, adjoining Albania. Its remoteness has resisted the tourism of the Dalmatian coast, but its capital, *Titograd*, is connected by a wonderfully engineered railway to *Belgrade*. The people are Serbs and use the Cyrillic alphabet.

Macedonia, the most southerly and most remote of the republics is bordered by Albania, Bulgaria and Greece; mountainous and harshly dry in summer. A fast motorway from *Belgrade* to Athens via *Skopje* goes through Macedonia, together with the international railway route of the Orient Express. The people are very like the Serbs but their language and Cyrillic alphabet are a little different.

Climate   In Slovenia the climate is part Alpine, part central European; most favourable in summer until September. In the interior of the country – shut off from the sea by the mountains – wide variations in seasonal temperatures occur. In Bosnia and Serbia, most of Croatia, Montenegro and Macedonia it is very hot in summer; autumn is likely to be best for touring. The Montenegran mountains have the highest rainfall in Europe and remarkably severe winters. The Dalmatian coast enjoys the Mediterranean climate but mild winters can be spoiled by the icy wind off the mountains, the *bora*. Spring comes early on the Mediterranean coast, autumn is warm and sunny, even beyond October.

Plants and Animals   Large variations in climate and terrain are matched by a wide range of vegetation; from coniferous forests in the north and the inland mountain regions to sub-tropical plants – mimosa and bougainvillea and trees such as palms, figs, citrus fruits – on favoured sites on the islands and southern, sheltered parts of the coast.

Vines are grown in Dalmatia, tobacco in Macedonia. Much of the *karst* plateau is barren, but in the valleys and hollows in the limestone, where there is water, vines and other Mediterranean fruits flourish.

There are bears and wild boar in the mountains of Slovenia and Bosnia, chamois in the *Julian Alps*.

The People

Population Official estimates, recently published, show a population of about 20 million. Nearly 8 million of this figure are in Serbia, another 8 million are almost equally shared between Bosnia and Croatia; almost 2 million live in Slovenia, 1½ million in Macedonia and ½ million in Montenegro. In addition to the five nationalities of Yugoslavia (Serbs, Croats, Slovenes, Macedonians and Montenegrins) there are minority groups of Turks, Rumanians, Albanians, Hungarians, Slovaks and Gypsies.

Language The three official languages of Serbo-Croat, Slovenian and Macedonian closely resemble one another. Serbo-Croat, the first language of Yugoslavia is written in the Latin alphabet in Croatia, but in Serbia and Montenegro the Cyrillic alphabet is used. The Latin alphabet is used for Slovenian and a form of Cyrillic for Macedonian, although both these are near enough to Serbo-Croat to understand with a Serbo-Croat phrase book.

Most notices in tourist resorts are in the Latin alphabet and, even in Serbia and Macedonia, Cyrillic is supplemented by a Latin alphabet translation.

English is widely understood in towns and tourist resorts, so is French and German. Italian is spoken in Dalmatia.

Religion Most Yugoslavs belong to the Orthodox faith, fewer are Roman Catholic; the remainder are Muslim. Roman Catholics predominate in Slovenia and Croatia, the Orthodox faith is followed in Serbia and Montenegro, while Bosnia and Macedonia are largely Muslim.

Church and state are quite separate; there is no religious teaching in schools and no public holidays at Christmas and Easter. Yugoslavia is, however, rich in religious monuments, as described in the touring routes that follow. Visitors to mosques should enquire whether non-Muslims can be admitted; shoes should be taken off before entering.

History The name Yugoslavia means "the country of the South Slavs". The Slavs came here in the 5th century A.D. from what is now Poland and by the 7th century they had become predominate throughout the Balkan peninsula. Before this all the country south of the R. *Danube* had been part of the Roman Empire and the inhabitants Celts and Illyrians. The Western part of this territory – what is now Slovenia, Croatia and Bosnia – was ruled from Rome, was Latin speaking and used the Latin alphabet; the Eastern part – Serbia, Montenegro and Macedonia – was under the rule of Constantinople and the language was Greek. This division, marked by the east/west line of the *Danube* and *Sava* rivers and an imaginary north/south line through *Sarajevo* and *Dubrovnik*, was the fundamental boundary between the Eastern and Western civilisations in Europe. Even before this there had been Greek settlements on the coast and there are remaining traces of Stone Age settlements.

Slovenia originally belonged to the western Slavs (not the south Slavs), or Slovenes. In the 7th and 8th century it was part of an independent principality named Carantania which included what is now southern Austria

YUGOSLAVIA

(Carinthia). In the 9th century Carantania became a German province and most of Slovenia remained German or Austrian for more than a thousand years, excepting a break early in the 19th century when Napoleon set up the Illyrian provinces, briefly uniting Slovenia with Croatia and Dalmatia.

Croatia, coming under Frankish rule, became independent under King Tomislav in the 10th century. Later Croatian kings extended their rule to the Dalmatian coastal towns which had previously been ruled by Constantinople, but in 1102 the Croatian crown passed to the heir to the Hungarian throne and Croatia became part of the Hungarian kingdom. Istria, at various times under the authority of Franks, Germans and the Byzantine empire came to be dominated by Venice.

Serbia became independent of the Byzantine empire in the 12th century under Stevan Nemanja, an enterprising ruler who resisted invasion by Hungarians and Bulgarians, gained the territory of Albania, Macedonia and northern parts of Greece, established the Serbian church and promoted arts and commerce. In 1345 the Serbian King Duzan proclaimed himself Tsar of the Serbs and Greeks but his empire was short-lived and by the end of the century, marked by Serbian defeat at the historically significant battle of *Kosovo* on 28th June 1389, Serbia was entirely overrun by the Turks and remained under Muslim rule for nearly five hundred years.

Bosnia was under the authority of Hungary for much of its history; it gained independence in the 13th century under King Tvrtko who ruled Bosnia, Serbia, Croatia and Dalmatia but after his death the Hungarians again seized power, only to be overrun by the Turks in 1463. Bosnia embraced Islam with little difficulty, inasmuch as the Bosnian church was out of favour and persecuted by the Orthodox church; many Bosnian noblemen accepted Turkish rank but one of them, Stevan Vuksic, set up an independent dukedom in southern Bosnia and assumed the title of Herceg; this province is called Hercegovina and thus named after him.

Macedonia, up to the end of the 10th century was under Byzantine or Bulgarian rule, but since then has been part of the history of Serbia except for the long period of Turkish dominance from 1371 to 1912.

Montenegro was in the 9th and 10th centuries the independent kingdom of Zeta but became part of the medieval Serbian empire. In the late 14th century the Turks assumed nominal rule but constant conflict ensued between the Montenegrins and the Turks and the country was never conquered. By the mid-19th century Montenegro was recognised as an independent principality, becoming a kingdom in 1910 and so remained until the First World War.

Most of the country had come under Turkish rule by the end of the 19th century; Dalmatia, apart from *Dubrovnik*, belonged to Venice for three hundred years up to the end of the 18th century when it passed to the Habsburgs, who already had Slovenia and Croatia.

Napoleon's armies took Dalmatia, Slovenia and Croatia in 1809 and set them up as a province named Illyria, with *Llubljana* as capital; this, however, lasted only four years and then the Habsburgs resumed their authority.

By this time Serbia had gained a large measure of independence from their Turkish rulers and, with Montenegro, came to the assistance of Bosnia in bringing about a successful insurrection against the Turks in the 1870s. The

Congress of Berlin in 1878, however, declared that Bosnia should be administered by the Habsburgs who, in 1908, arbitrarily seized complete power. Bosnia opposed such Austrian authority; nationalism flourished, encouraged by Serbia and the fact that the Turks had been driven out in the Balkan wars of 1912–13.

On 28th June 1914, the anniversary of the Serbian defeat at *Kosovo*, the Austrian Archduke Franz Ferdinand was assassinated in *Sarajevo* by a young Bosnian nationalist; the spark that touched off the holocaust of the First World War.

King Peter, a Serbian, became sovereign of the kingdom of Serbs, Croats and Slovenes, set up soon after the end of the First World War; his son Alexander succeeded him in 1921 and, in 1929, the kingdom changed its name to Yugoslavia, but Istria and the ports of *Rijeka* and *Zadar* remained Italian. Alexander was assassinated in Marseilles in 1934, his young son Peter succeeded him under a Regency but, early in 1941, Yugoslavia was invaded by Germany and King Peter and the Government escaped to London.

Slav resistance to Nazi occupation was established in guerilla armies of partisans; one of their leaders was Josip Broz, a Croat who became known as Marshal Tito. He was backed by the Allies, fought the Germans throughout the occupation and, by the end of the war, his communist partisans had command of all the country. As early as November 1943 Tito had declared Yugoslavia to be a Federal Socialist Republic and, in the elections of 1945 he secured a great majority to confirm his leadership; thus he has remained.

Government Yugoslavia is a Federal Socialist Republic of six countries – Serbia, Croatia, Slovenia, Bosnia-Herzegovina, Macedonia and Montenegro – each enjoying a large measure of internal self-government. The autonomous provinces of Vojvodina and Kosmet are associated with Serbia. The central government in *Belgrade* deals with foreign affairs and defence, but each republic administers its own affairs within the authority of the federal constitution.

Resources Yugoslavia's economy is based almost equally upon agriculture and industry. Maize, rye, potatoes, suger beet, plums and apples are main crops; some are exported, together with tobacco and wines. Copper, lead, zinc and bauxite are exported; manufactured exports comprise textiles, footwear, ships, vehicles and machines of almost every description. Tourism is significant in the economy of the country, the government promotes and subsidises the industry and each republic has its own tourist offices.

Food and Drink A variety of regional dishes and different ways of cooking make for interest. Meat dishes are highly flavoured, usually grilled. *Cevapcici*, small grilled fingers of minced meat and served with raw chopped onions, are popular. So too is *Raznjici*, made of cubes of pork grilled on a skewer and similar to kebab. *Cevapcici* and *Raznjici* can make a cheap meal, for they can often be bought to take away. Pastry dishes named *burek*, with meat, cheese or vegetable fillings are often cheap; yoghourt, called *kisolo mljeko*, is served with them. Pancakes are almost a national dish; they are usually served with very sweet fillings. Turkish coffee

YUGOSLAVIA

is the national beverage, served thick and strong in very small cups. Mineral waters are excellent and in great variety. Wine is cheap, mostly light; *Reisling* and *Sylvaner* are everywhere popular. Plum brandy named *Slivovica* is Yugoslavia's best known drink, it comes in a range of quality, always strong and potent.

Sport   Sailing, fishing and hunting are popular sports. Sheltered waters along the coast afford excellent sailing and boats may be hired by the day in the seaside resorts. Sea fishing is free and there is no close season; fresh-water fishermen enjoy a splendid choice of fish but fishing permits must be obtained. Football is most popular throughout the country and Yugoslav teams match those of other countries in international events. Winter sports facilities are best in Slovenia but many mountain resorts in Bosnia and Croatia are also equipped to international standards.

Culture

Art and Architecture   A few relics of Stone and Iron Ages remain and traces of Greek occupation can be seen in Macedonia and on the Adriatic coast.

Roman architecture is evident, some as early as the 3rd century B.C., although most of it belongs to the 1st and 2nd centuries A.D. contemporary with the empire-building campaigns of Tiberius and Trajan; the ampitheatre at *Pula* and Diocletian's palace at *Split* are leading examples. Byzantium retained remnants of Roman power against the Slav invasions of the 5th century and the basilica at *Poreč* with its magnificent mosiacs belongs to this era.

The 9th century Slav churches of St. Donat at *Zadar*, St. Barbara at *Trogir* and St. Cross at *Nin* all show Roman and Byzantine influence. St. Sophia at *Ohrid*, an 11th century church, is a perfect example of Byzantine architecture.

Architecture in medieval times is shown at its best in the monastic buildings of Serbia and Macedonia, a composite style of Roman and Byzantine with stone and brick external decoration and Byzantine frescoes adorning vault and wall. Serbian mural painting achieved its best in the 14th century but it declined with the coming of the Renaissance and the Turkish invasion.

Romanesque art and architecture flourished on the Adriatic coast in many churches and in the cathedrals at *Rab* and *Trogir*. *Zadar* became artistically important for its gold and silver work – now treasured in churches there. Enigmatically ornamented stone tombs belonging to the Bogomils, a heretical religious sect, made their appearance at this time; many thousand such memorials, decorated with geometric symbols or figures of soldiers, dancers or huntsmen, remain scattered or grouped in remote cemeteries in Bosnia, Dalmatia and Montenegro.

Gothic architecture is restricted to Slovenia and Croatia where Gothic churches are everywhere evident, many of them decorated with endearingly naive frescoes. The cathedral at *Sibenik* is a beautiful example of Gothic architecture overtaken by the Renaissance.

Minarets everywhere give point to Turkish influence in architecture from the 15th century onwards; the mosques at *Sarajevo, Banja Luka* and *Tetova* are particularly fine, the bridges at *Mostar* and *Visegrad* stand as elegant examples of Turkish architectural skill.

Renaissance architecture, often Venetian, is evident along the Adriatic coast. *Dubrovnik* is particularly rich in styles of architecture; Gothic, Renaissance, Roman and Venetian Baroque churches, palaces and monasteries all contained within the city walls.

Sculpture by Ivan Meštrović (1883–1962) is best known. His work in unmistakably heroic style, is seen at the *Mount Avala* war memorial near *Belgrade* and in churches throughout the country. Paintings by Paja Jovanovic (1859–1957), popular in Western Europe at the turn of the century, are on show in the National Museum in *Belgrade*.

Literature Yugoslav literature in poem and ballad form, epic tales of Slav defiance of Turk, translated and published by Vuk Karadzic in the mid-19th century, remain popular. Ivo Andrić, a Bosnian (b. 1892), won the Nobel prize for literature in 1961. His famous book "The Bridge on the Drina", the story of life in *Višegrad* from the 16th century up to the First World War, has been translated into English.

Folklore Traditional dress is to be seen on special occasions and on market days in the country. Eastern modes of dress are worn in those parts of the country which have been subject to Byzantine and Turkish influence; the fez is evident.

Folk dancing and singing are everywhere popular. The Serbian national dance, the *kolo*, is the most common – danced in a group, hands linked – often accompanied by wind instruments.

Costume and dance are part of the way of life; many old wedding customs of dancing and feasting remain and festivals of folk dancing and singing are popular throughout the country.

Touring Information

Access From London: (i) *rail* (a) Tauern Express (afternoon departure), daily through service throughout year to *Jesenice* (frontier), 26 hours; *Ljubljana*, 27 hours; *Zagreb*, 30 hours; *Split*, 40 hours; (b) Rijeka Express (morning departure) summer only, daily through service via *Ljubljana* to *Rijeka*, 30 hours; *rail* via Calais and Paris; (c) Direct-Orient and Simplon Expresses, through service to *Ljubljana* (33 hours), *Zagreb* (36 hours) and *Belgrade* (41 hours). Return rail fares range from £62·70 to *Jesenice* to £72·95 to *Skopje*; (ii) by *air*; tourist returns, valid 1 month, London–Belgrade £94·00, London–Dubrovnik £91·20.

Transport The main railway route through Yugoslavia passes inland via *Zagreb*, *Vrpolje* (junction for *Sarajevo* and *Dubrovnik*), *Belgrade*, *Niš* and *Skopje*. There is no railway along the coast, and connections to *Dubrovnik* from the interior are slow.

YUGOSLAVIA

Transport to many of the more remote places is provided by local buses, and there are special direct summer services between main centres and holiday resorts. Tickets are bought before boarding buses; they can usually be had a day in advance from the bus station or local tourist office.

The Adriatic coast can be pleasantly seen by using steamers of the *Jadranska Line*, linking *Rijeka, Split, Dubrovnik* and places between. Local services call at several small ports, including many on islands, whereas the more expensive express steamers, some of them making extended voyages between *Venice* or *Trieste* and *Piraeus*, make fewer calls.

Money

The unit of currency is the *dinar*, divided into 100 *paras*.

Visas

A visa is no longer needed by citizens of most countries visiting Yugoslavia for holiday purposes, or making transit through the country.

Accommodation

The *Yugoslav Youth Hostels Association* has about thirty hostels; a few are tented and only open in summer, but others are mostly open throughout the year. Many are situated on the coast, some others in less frequented places in the interior and there are large hostels in *Belgrade, Dubrovnik, Sarajevo, Skopje* and *Zagreb*.

Mountain huts of varying standards of amenities are maintained by Alpine Clubs in all the country's high mountains, notably those of Slovenia, Croatia and Bosnia. They are normally open to all so far as space allows. Prices, seasonal closing periods and other particulars should be checked with the local tourist office before setting out on a mountain tour.

Private houses will often put tourists up for 20 dinars a night and full board may be had for about 50 dinars. In tourist resorts letting is arranged through the local touring office, to whom also payment is made. Rooms are divided into categories according to facilities. To book a room in advance write to the *Turistički biro*, at the place where you wish to stay.

Members arriving in Yugoslavia without having booked accommodation are recommended to enquire at the local tourist office.

Camping

There are many tourist camping grounds throughout the country, where those bringing their own tents may make use of the facilities for about 10 dinars daily per person, the charge varying according to standard of equipment provided. Camping is also possible in certain open spaces on obtaining permission from the municipal or forest authority concerned. No special document is required. A survey of camping sites, revised annually, can be obtained from the *Yugoslav State Tourist Office*.

**Information
Services**

Yugoslav State Tourist Office, 630 5th Avenue, New York, N.Y. 10019, and the *Yugoslav Information Center, 488 Madison Avenue, New York, N.Y. 10022* can supply general information about the country, and addresses of local tourist associations.

Holidays

National holidays are 1st and 2nd January, 1st and 2nd May, 4th July, 29th and 30th November. Republic holidays are 7th July in Serbia, 13th July in Montenegro, 22nd July in Slovenia, 27th July in Bosnia and Croatia, 2nd August and 11th October in Macedonia.

Clothing

The climate on the coast is generally similar to that of Italy, and light clothing is required. In the mountains it can be very cold, especially early and late in the day, necessitating ample reserves of warm clothing; when exploring isolated areas a down sleeping bag is advisable as accommodation may not always be easy to find.

Maps

Large scale maps of Yugoslavia are not generally available, except these of the *Julian Alps* and *Kamnik Alps* in *Freytag & Berndt's* 1:100,000 series. Other maps are *Freytag & Berndt's,* scale 1:600,000, two sheets, *"West Yugoslavia"* and *"East Yugoslavia".* *Kummerly & Frey* publish a quite detailed road map, scale 1:1,000,000 on one sheet.

Walking

The *Julian Alps* and *Kamnik Alps* of Slovenia provide excellent walking of all degrees of strenuousness in magnificent country and are not too uncomfortably hot in summer. For walking tours in other parts the height of summer in best avoided. Subject to this, suitable areas of exceptional interest include the *Plitvice Lakes National Park,* the *Mount Tara National Park,* the mountains south-west of *Sarajevo,* and the neighbourhood of *Lakes Ohrid* and *Prespa* in Macedonia.

**Mountain-
eering**

Triglav (9,400 ft.), the highest peak in Yugoslavia, is in the *Julian Alps*—a continuation at a somewhat lower level of the *Karawanken* range just north of the border. It is regarded by mountaineers as the foremost challenge in the country. The *Julian Alps* and the *Kamnik Alps* are well provided with huts, with a warden in charge. Meals can be obtained at many of the huts and need not be booked in advance.

The mountains in the centre and south of the country—in Croatia, Bosnia, Montenegro and Macedonia—often separate small communities with their own local traditions and customs. The mountains themselves are very wild and, since good walking maps are practically unobtainable, it is essential to be well equipped with both information and supplies.

YUGOSLAVIA

Cycling

Road surfaces in Slovenia and the north are mostly good and those roads linking the cities and resorts throughout the country are first class, but cyclists can expect rough going on unmetalled roads on less frequented routes. Cycles must be in first-class order, with all attachments fixed strongly enough to withstand vibration. A variable gear is essential. Spares for British machines are unobtainable.

Canoeing and Rafting

The spectacular gorges of the River *Drina* in Bosnia can be navigated by log-raft from *Foča* to *Višegrad* (see **R.4**), and on the River *Tara* from *Durdeviča Tara* to *Foča*. Approach is by rail from *Sarajevo* via *Ustiprača* to *Foča*, where rafts may be hired, through the *Foča Tourist Association*.

Touring Routes

R.1. Jesenice—Ljubljana—Pula—Rijeka (270 miles)

Walkers or cyclists can enter from Austria by *Wurzner Pass* (3,400 ft.) across *Karawanken Alps* from which it is an hour's walk down to *Podkoren*, the first town in Yugoslavia. Nearby village of *Kranjska Gora* is suitable starting point for walking and climbing tours in Julian Alps. First stop for international express trains is *Jesenice*, from which return to *Kranjska Gora* can be made by local train. Paths in *Julian Alps* are well marked, but hut tours involve a good deal of scrambling, with use of pitons and fixed wire ropes.

Jesenice, frontier station and factory town. **Bled**, 7 miles; popular tourist resort in idyllic setting; boating and swimming in warm waters of lake **(Y.H.)**; walk to *Vintgar Gorge* and *Falls*. *Bohinj Bistrica* village, 13 miles, near **Lake Bohinj**; remote and quiet **(Y.H.)**; walks to *Savica Falls*; *Valley of the Seven Lakes*: climbs include *Triglav* (9,400 ft). Return to *Bled*. *Radovljica*, 5 miles; medieval town with fine view of Alps.

Ljubljana, 26 miles; capital of Slovenia; university town; baroque architecture in attractive Old Town; *Cathedral of St. Nicholas* and *Golovatz Castle*: *National Museum and Art Gallery*: *Modern Gallery*.

Postojna, 35 miles; magnificent caves, largest in Europe; miniature railway takes visitors 3 km. into the caves; enormous dimensions, perfect acoustics; symphony concerts here during season. Route then skirts Italian territory, keeping to limestone uplands enjoying fine views over *Trieste*, then descending steeply to sea level.

Koper, 35 miles; 15th century Cathedral; palaces. *Piran*, 10 miles, one of many picturesque bathing and fishing resorts on coast of **Istria**. At *Buje* leave main road for coast road. *Poreč*, 32 miles, village; *Basilica of Euphrasius* with famous mosaics in style of *Ravenna*.

Across eroded limestone to *Pula*, 35 miles; port, with remarkably well-preserved Roman amphitheatre, 2nd century A.D., and *Temple of Augustus* Summer season of opera and films in amphitheatre. **(Y.H.)**

Through popular resorts on E. Coast of Istria to **Rijeka,** 65 miles, chief port of Yugoslavia.

EXCURSIONS: (a) islands of Krk (with walled town of same name; cathedral and castle) and Cres; (b) *Senj*, 45 miles, on gulf, once hide-out of Uskok pirates; *Učka*, mountain with fine view over bay and islands, accessible by road.

R.2. Ljubljana—Maribor—Zagreb—Plitvice Lakes—Zadar (385 miles)

Ljubljana. *Kamnik*, 14 miles; castles of *Mari Grad* and *Stari Grad*. Road over **Kamnik** Alps by *Stahovica* and *Crnilec Pass* (2,931 ft.) to *Gornji Grad*, 17 miles, mountain resort. Through gorge to *Mozirje*, 12 miles. *Celje*, 18 miles; town of Roman foundation; medieval and Renaissance buildings. Mountain road to *Slovenska Bistrica*, 25 miles, famous for its wines.

Maribor, on R. *Drava*, 13 miles chief city of Slovenian Styria; in country-side of apple orchards; many Renaissance and Baroque buildings showing Austrian influence; museum in Castle. *Ptuj*, 16 miles; wine making town on Roman site; *Temple of Mithras*, Wine Museum. S.W. to *Ptujska Gora*, 8 miles; 15th century church with fine wood carvings. At *Rogatec* enter Croatia. *Krapina*, 31 miles from *Ptuj*.

Zagreb, 39 miles, capital of Croatia and second city of Yugoslavia; rich cultural centre; opera, theatres, concerts; several museums and galleries; parks. (Y.H.)

EXCURSIONS: (a) Mt. Sljeme (3,395 ft.) 5 miles N. (b) Zelanjac Gorge near *Klanjec* in *Sutla Valley*, 32 miles; (c) *Samobor*, 15 miles, picturesque village.

Karlovac, 35 miles S.W., fortified town. S. up *Korana* valley; *Slunj*, 32 miles; castle. **Plitvice Lakes National Park**, 27 miles; series of sixteen beautiful lakes linked by waterfalls. Through forest country via *Titova Korenica*, 13 miles; (Y.H.) at *Bihac*; *Udbina*, 20 miles; *Ploča*, 10 miles; and across *Velebit Mountains* at 3,427 ft., to coast road at *Jasenice*, 35 miles.

Zadar, 20 miles (Y.H.) (see R.3).

R.3. Rijeka—Zadar—Split—Dubrovnik (405 miles)

Rijeka (see R.1). Steamer to **Zadar** (or 141 miles by coast road, with many beaches); ancient town on peninsula; *Roman Forum* and many other Roman remains; associations with 4th Crusade (1204); held by Venetians for most of 600 years, then by Habsburgs; Venetian walls and fortifications, narrow alleys; *Church of S. Donat*, 9th century, now a museum. (Y.H.)

EXCURSIONS: (a) Nin, 12 miles, village near ruined Roman town. *Anona Civitas*: capital of Croatia in 9th century; 9th century *Church of S. Croce* and ruined *Church of S. Ambrogio*; (b) cruising by fishing boats among the many islands.

Šibenik, by steamer (or road, 45 miles); busy port on extraordinary island-studded inlet; town built steeply on hillside, dominated by *Castle of St. Anne* (view); famous Gothic and Renaissance cathedral, built of local stone, in-cluding its remarkable wide roof. (Y.H.)

EXCURSIONS: (a) *Skradin* (boat or bus) for Krka Falls; (b) island of Zlarin, known for corals and sponges; local costumes; bathing.

Trogir, 36 miles, on small peninsula; originally Greek settlement (3rd century B.C.); now largely Venetian in appearance; Romanesque and Gothic cathedral with rich carvings; *Kamerlengo Castle*; *Church of St. Barbara* (9th century) and many other interesting buildings.

Road along Riviera of the Seven Castles; fortified villages among olive groves and vineyards.

Split (*Spalato*), 17 miles; name means "in the palace" and the city has grown in the vast 10-acre **Palace of Diocletian** (c. A.D. 304); Venetian and other buildings among the Roman columns; circular Cathedral, designed as Emperor's mausoleum; general view of Palace from cathedral tower; narrow Venetian streets; important archaeological and ethnographic museums; medieval churches. Direct journey by road to *Dubrovnik* is 145 miles.

EXCURSIONS: **Meštrović Museum** on route to *Solin*, near which are ruins of Salona, Roman capital of Dalmatia; museum. Medieval fortress of *Klis* in hills above.

Steamer to **Hvar**, ancient Greek *Pharos*, island noted for mild climate, subtropical vegetation, flowers and fruit. Steamer to **Korčula**, home of Marco Polo, on well-wooded island of same name. Steamer to *Dubrovnik*.

Dubrovnik, formerly *Ragusa*, with long tradition as independent republic trading by land and sea all over Europe. Splendid walls and towers entirely contain old town; walk around ramparts takes about half an hour and affords views across city, notably from *Minčeta Tower*; main street built after earthquake (1667); palazzi in narrow streets; *Cathedral of S. Biagio* with many treasures; *Rector's Palace*; *Franciscan Monastery*; Summer Festival; national costumes often worn. Busy resort, best visited out-of-season; mild winters. **(Y.H.)**

EXCURSIONS: (a) *Mt. Sergius* (1,350 ft.) with Napoleonic fort; on foot by winding path from *Minčeta Tower* (about 1 hour) for panoramic view. (b) *Lokrum*, island where Richard Coeur de Lion was shipwrecked; (c) *Trsteno*, tropical botanical garden and *Falls of R. Ombla*: (d) Trebinje, 15 miles, small market town in Herzegovina with Turkish buildings and oriental atmosphere (see R.4).

R.4. Dubrovnik—Mostar—Sarajevo—Foča—Dubrovnik (387 miles)

Follow coast road N.W. to *Metković*, 56 miles, by hairpin bends up valley of R. *Neretva*.

Mostar, 31 miles, chief town of Herzegovina, named from its famous Turkish bridge (1566) over *Neretva;* gaunt surroundings of *karst* cliffs; many mosques, including 16th century *Karadjoz Bey's*.

Continue up spectacular *Neretva* valley; *Jablanica*, 30 miles; road follows barrage lake to *Konjic*, 15 miles, and across *Mt. Ivan* to *Sarajevo*, 38 miles.

Sarajevo, capital of Bosnia-Herzegovina. Constrasts between oriental town of Turkish period, 19th century town of Austro-Hungarian administration and modern industrial and residential town. Among many mosques, particularly fine are the *Gazi-Husref-Bey Mosque* (16th century) and the *Medresa Seminary* near the famous souks. View from *Mt. Trebević* (cable-car); rich National Museum; Museum relating to assassination here of Archduke Franz Ferdinand, which sparked off the 1914–1918 war. **(Y.H.)**

R.4(i) **Sarajevo to Jajce.** *Kiseljak*, 23 miles; spa. *Busovača*, 16 miles. Travnik, 18 miles, the "green city", in beautiful countryside, once residence of Turkish Governor of Bosnia; Suleiman Mosque; *Mosque of Konak:* tomb of Pashas and Turkish cemetery. Through wooded mountain country, road reaching 3,041 ft., and descending to *Donji Vakuf*, 23 miles; market town on R. *Vrbas*.

Jajce, 22 miles, historic town in delightful natural setting where R. *Pliva* falls 100 ft. to join *Vrbas*. Reputed burial place of St. Luke. Declaration of Republic made here in 1943. Fortress; Franciscan church; wooden Turkish watermills.

Road E. climbing to 4,534 ft. Fork right at *Podromanija*, 29 miles; *Rogatica*, 20 miles; *Goražde*, 23 miles, on R. *Drina*; fishing centre. At *Foča*, 21 miles, begins the two-day passage of the **Drina Gorges** by log-raft to *Višegrad* through spectacular canyons. *Foča* is fishing centre; fine *Aladža Mosque;* town and district were scene of much fighting in Second World War. *Tjentište,* 19 miles; War Memorial, focus of national patriotism. Road climbs *Sutjeska* valley and descends to *Gacko,* 26 miles. *Bileća,* 30 miles; where R. *Trebišnjica* disappears underground. *Trebinje,* 17 miles; *Mosque of Osman Pasha; Bey's House.* Westward by steeply engineered road, 19 miles, to *Dubrovnik.*

R.5. Sarajevo—Višegrad—Mount Tara—Belgrade—(228 miles)

Sarajevo (see **R.4**). East by twisting mountain roads to *Podromanija,* 29 miles, *Rogatica,* 20 miles and *Višegrad,* 25 miles; 16th century bridge of eleven arches over R. *Drina,* finest Turkish bridge in Yugoslavia.

At *Kremna,* 25 miles, by-road leads into **Mt. Tara National Park;** densely forested, with rich flora and fauna. *Titova Užice,* 44 miles; finely situated industrial town. **(Y.H.)**

Road north to *Karan,* 13 miles; fine Serbian Orthodox church with 14th century frescoes. By winding road through *Kosjerić* and *Bukovi* to *Valjevo,* 36 miles, famous for plums and other fruit. Road enters plain of R. *Sava. Obrenovac,* 30 miles. *Belgrade,* 20 miles.

Belgrade, capital of Serbia and of the Federal Republic, in historically fateful position on *Pannonian Plain* at confluence of *Sava* and *Danube.* Citadel of *Kalemegdan:* Meštrović statue, the *Pobednik* (Victor); Orthodox Cathedral; National Museum; Fresco Art Gallery (copies of medieval frescoes in the monasteries). **(Y.H.)**

EXCURSIONS: (a) **Mt. Avala** (1,702 ft.), 12 miles, with monument to Unknown Warrior by Meštrović; view over *Belgrade:* (b) **The Iron Gates of the Danube:** steamer down river through *Djerdap Gorges (Iron Gates)*—one of the grandest natural features of Europe; night at *Kladovo,* returning upstream next day; (c) *Smederevo,* 30 miles, huge 15th century fortress on *Danube:* (d) **Fruška Gora,** wooded hills about 45 miles N.W., with several Orthodox monasteries built as refuge from Turks.

R.6. Dubrovnik—Cetinje—Skopje (331 miles)

Road S. along coast, *Cavtat,* 9 miles; agreeable little resort. *Gruda,* 11 miles. *Hercegnovi,* 11 miles, built in tiers overlooking *Boka Kotorska,* extraordinary fjord-like inlet; lush, sub-tropical vegetation; Spanish, Turkish and Venetian fortresses.

EXCURSIONS: (a) *Savina Monastery* with valuable library; (b) *Mt. Radostak* (4,700 ft.), view over the *Boka.*

Road skirts around *Boka Kotorska,* passing through *Zelenika* **(Y.H.)** and ancient, historic ports of *Risan* **(Y.H.)** and *Perast* to *Kotor,* 30 miles, at its head (also steamer from *Hercegnovi*); town famed (with *Perast*) for its seamanship; spectacular setting at foot of *Mt. Lovćen* (5,770 ft.); Romanesque cathedral: Maritime Museum.

Steep zig-zag road climbing to nearly 4,000 ft. up *Mt. Lovćen* with magnificent views over the *Boka.* Road continues across arid *karst* to **Cetinje,** 26 miles, former capital of Montenegro; museums. **Titograd,** 30 miles, rebuilt town and new capital, on ancient site.

R6(i) South Montenegrin Littoral. At *Budva,* 26 miles from *Kotor,* road begins to hug a coast more indented than Dalmatia, and without islands; good beaches. *Budva,* steamer from *Hercegnovi,* or by road from *Kotor,* 8th century church with 17th century Venetian paintings. *Bar,* 28 miles, near ruins of older town; railway inland to *Titograd.* *Ulcinj,* 18 miles, once a haunt of pirates.

YUGOSLAVIA

R.6(ii) Durmitor Mountains. From *Titograd* via *Nikšić*, 35 miles; mountain road to *Šavnik*, 28 miles and *Žabljak* (4,500 ft.), 25 miles; base for walks and climbs in mountains reaching 8,000 ft.

Mountain road to *Andrijevica*, 62 miles. From *Murino*, 11 miles, road climbs to *Čakor Pass* (6,067 ft.) on Serbian border, descending to Peć, 38 miles, centre of Metohija district (part of Kosmet, an autonomous area of Serbia, with an Albanian minority); town of oriental character. Residence of Patriarchs of Serbian Orthodox Church, with many treasures. (Y.H.)

At *Dečani*, 10 miles S., detour 2 miles N.W. through mountain scenery to 14th century Romanesque-Byzantine monastery of *Visoki-Dečani*, fine building with particularly interesting frescoes.

Djakovica, 13 miles; town noted for gold and silver filigree work. *Prizren*, 23 miles; similarly noted, picturesque town under fortress of *Kaljaja*; medieval frescoes in *Church of Our Lady of Ljeviska*, 14th century; *Mosque of Sinan Pasha*.

Road E. over **Šar Planina** mountains. *Gabrica*, 35 miles. *Kačanik*, 6 miles. S. through gorge between *Black Mountains* of *Skopje* and *Šar Planina* mountains near peak of *Ljuboten* 8,189 ft. At *Cučer*, 13 miles, detour 1 mile E. to *Church of Sveti Nikita*: medieval frescoes.

Skopje, 10 miles; on R. *Vardar*; capital of Macedonia; scene of disastrous earthquake, July 1963. *Emperor Dušan Bridge* (14th century); *Dhaut Pasha's Hammam* (Turkish bath); *Mosque of Mustapha Pasha*; *Mosque of Isa Beg*; *Kuršumli Han* caravanserai; *Kale* fortress; *Orthodox Church of St. Spas* with fine wood carving and paintings. (Y.H.)

EXCURSIONS: (a) *Mt. Vodno*, view of *Skopje* and *Vardar* valley; (b) *Nerezi*, 3 miles; church with famous 12th century frescoes, important in art history; (c) through *Treska* gorges to Monasteries of *Matka* and *Sveti Andrija* (St. Andrew); frescoes.

R.7. Skopje—Bitola—Lake Ohrid—Tetovo—Skopje (288 miles)

Skopje (see **R.6**). *Titov Veles*, 33 miles; town finely situated on both sides of gorge of *Vardar*, with many mosques, but crowned by modern Serbian Orthodox Church; junction of two routes into Greece. *Gradsko*, 16 miles, where Roman *Via Egnatia* joins historic route through *Vardar* gap. *Stobi*, 3 miles S., excavated Greek and Roman town; impressive remains.

By *Via Egnatia* across mountains to *Prilep*, 36 miles; modern market town, tobacco growing centre. *Vissovi*, 13 miles, necropolis of 1500 B.C. *Bitola*, 10 miles (near ancient *Heraclea*); Church of St. Dimitri (wood carvings); many mosques. Mountain road W. reaching 3,875 ft., to *Resen*, 21 miles, and another pass, 3,872 ft., to *Ohrid*, 24 miles.

Ohrid, ancient and delightful town beautifully sited on *Lake Ohrid*; enjoys exceptionally mild climate although altitude of 2,300 ft., crystal clear waters, famous for trout, pebble beaches, important in history of Orthodox Church; Cyrillic script invented here. Many churches and monasteries with remarkable frescoes, notably *St. Sophia*, in town, where Turks white-washed walls to obliterate paintings and thus preserved them, *St. Clement* higher up and *St. Jovan Kaneo* on castle hill with fine prospect of lake. At S. end of lake, reached by boat, or 19 miles by road, is *Monastery of St. Naum* (10th century) in lovely situation with sandy beach. (Y.H.)

Young people in Yugoslavia look and dress as fashionably as their Western counterparts.

YUGOSLAVIA

Lake-side road N.W. to *Struga*, 10 miles. *Velešta*, 6 miles; Albanian type village. Road skirts Albanian frontier. *Debar*, 27 miles. At *Boletin*, 15 miles, in *Radika* valley, track on right to *Monastery of St. Jovan Bigorski* impressively sited building, with famous Filipovski wood carvings. Return to *Boletin;* continue up *Radika* gorge between high mountains (*Korab*, 9,070 ft.). *Lake Mavrovo*, 12 miles. Road climbs to 4,462 ft., and descends to *Gostivar*, 15 miles. *Tetovo*, 16 miles, at foot of *Šar Planina* mountains, for mountaineering and winter sports; famous *Coloured Mosque*. *Skopje*, 27 miles.

R.8. Skopje—Niš—Belgrade (294 miles)

Skopje (see R.6). *Kumanovo*, 20 miles. (7 miles W. among mountains is remote *Matejić Monastery*). Near *Strezovce*, 11 miles, enter Serbia. At *Bujanovac*, 12 miles, join valley of R. *Morava*. Vranje, 10 miles, town of district noted for flax and tobacco; Turkish bridge, Turkish baths, Derenka fountain; two residences of pashas. *Vladicin Han*, 15 miles, small Turkish town. Road passes through *Grdelica Gorge* for 19 miles to *Grdelica. Leskovac*, 11 miles, industrial town; two museums; traditional Balkan houses.

Niš, 28 miles, rail and road centre at confluence of *Nišava* and *Morava*; birthplace of Constantine, first Christian Roman Emperor; a place much fought over throughout history; fortress originally Byzantine, now of Turkish appearance, seventeen sides and five bastions; notorious *Čele Kula* (*Tower of Skulls*) (1809), barbaric memorial of Ottoman rule; rebuilt *Monastery of Panteleimon*; *Archaeological Museum*.

Continue down fertile, populous valley of *Morava. Aleksinac*, 21 miles; *Cuprija*, 36 miles, a bridge town.

EXCURSION: Valley and gorge of R. Ravanica, many caves and water-sinks in limestone; Ravanica monastery of 1381, 7 miles.

Direct road to *Belgrade* is busy motorway, or route can be taken westwards across hills via *Kragujevac* (Y.H.) and *Topola*. An alternative route goes 15 miles northwards to remarkable fortified **Manasija Monastery** (15th century), with moat and eleven towers; beautiful (though damaged) frescoes. Road N.W. down fertile *Resava* valley. *Svilajnac*, 15 miles. Turn W. across motorway to *Rača*, 10 miles; unusual 18th century wooden church; *Topola*, 21 miles.

Mladenovac, 15 miles; *Mt. Avala* (see R.5), 23 miles; Belgrade, (see R.5), 12 miles.

INDEX

Abbreviations used: Is = Island(s), L = Lake, Mon = Monastery, P = Peninsula, R = River, V = Valley.

For names beginning Bad, Col, La, Le, Les, Mont, etc., see under place name, e.g. Bad Aussee = Aussee, Bad.